# Introduction to Quality Growth

Koki Hirota
Editor

# Introduction to Quality Growth

## Concept, Theoretical Background, Policy and Measurement

Springer

*Editor*
Koki Hirota
Tokyo, Japan

ISBN 978-981-95-6219-0 ISBN 978-981-95-6220-6 (eBook)
https://doi.org/10.1007/978-981-95-6220-6

Translation from the Japanese language edition: "Shitsu no takai seicho gairon Daiichi bunsatsu Riron hen & Shitsu no takai seicho gairon Daini bunsatsu Jireibunseki hen" by Koki Hirota, © The JICA Ogata Sadako Research Institute for Peace and Development 2025. Published by The JICA Ogata Sadako Research Institute for Peace and Development. All Rights Reserved.

The original submitted manuscript has been translated into English. The translation was done using artificial intelligence. A subsequent revision was performed by the author(s) to further refine the work and to ensure that the translation is appropriate concerning content and scientific correctness. It may, however, read stylistically different from a conventional translation.

This work was supported by the JICA Ogata Sadako Research Institute for Peace and Development.

Originally published by The JICA Ogata Sadako Research Institute for Peace and Development, 2025



This Springer imprint is published by the registered company Springer Nature Singapore Pte Ltd.
The registered company address is: 152 Beach Road, #21-01/04 Gateway East, Singapore 189721, Singapore

# Foreword

"Quality growth" represents a forward-looking paradigm of development—one that transcends the conventional focus on the expansion of production and income to embrace the vital, human-centric dimensions of inclusiveness, sustainability, and resilience. It is a vision of growth that not only seeks to raise national production and income but also aspires to confront the pressing issues that shape people's daily lives, such as inequality, employment, environmental degradation, natural disasters, and economic crises. Equally important, it calls for strengthening institutions and governance so that such challenges can be addressed with effectiveness and fairness.

The concept of quality growth has been the subject of active discussion both in Japan and abroad. Its formal articulation emerged on the global stage through international fora, notably the Asia-Pacific Economic Cooperation (APEC) Leaders' Meeting in 2010, and its ethos has since been embedded within the United Nations (UN) Sustainable Development Goals (SDGs), adopted in 2015. Japan's Development Cooperation Charter (DCC), which sets forth its policy on development cooperation, designated quality growth as a strategic priority in 2015—a commitment reaffirmed in the revised Charter of 2023. In alignment with this policy, the Japan International Cooperation Agency (JICA) has embraced quality growth, alongside human security, as a central mission in its cooperation with developing countries.

Today, the world—Japan included—faces an increasingly intricate and interlinked set of challenges: the existential threat of climate change, the far-reaching impacts of pandemics, and the geopolitical and economic upheavals arising from wars and violent conflicts. These risks have intensified threats to human security, even as enduring problems such as poverty, inequality, unemployment, and environmental destruction remain unresolved. Against this backdrop, the importance of the quality growth ideal—rooted in inclusiveness, sustainability, and resilience—has never been more evident.

As a development approach, quality growth raises profound and practical questions: What precisely do inclusiveness, sustainability, and resilience entail, and how do they intersect with more traditional notions of growth? By what means can we measure quality growth? And above all, how can it be achieved in concrete terms?

This volume seeks to address these questions by offering a comprehensive examination of the concept from the perspective of economic theory, as well as from ongoing efforts to measure its progress. It further considers the trajectories of Indonesia, Vietnam, Peru, Costa Rica, and Madagascar as case studies, assessing their development through the lens of quality growth.

The book is the product of the "Study on Quality Growth" project undertaken by the Ogata Sadako Research Institute for Peace and Development of JICA. We were privileged to entrust Dr. Koki Hirota—one of the foremost authorities in the field—with the task of writing and editing the volume. He was joined by JICA staff members and other specialists with deep expertise in the economies of the case study countries. Given the multifaceted nature of the quality growth concept, we also benefited from background papers, research materials, and insights contributed by a diverse range of scholars, practitioners, institutions, and partner organizations both in Japan and overseas. To all of them, we extend our deepest appreciation.

This work is complemented by a companion volume, *SDGs, Transformation, and Quality Growth: Insights from International Cooperation* by Dr. Akio Hosono, which explores strategies for achieving quality growth by drawing upon Japan's rich experience in development cooperation. Anchored in the concept of socio-economic "transformation"—a notion closely aligned with quality growth—these two volumes together present concrete strategies for policymakers and practitioners in development agencies worldwide. The case studies span a wide spectrum of development fields, including industry, infrastructure, agriculture, and urban development, across countries in Asia, Africa, and Latin America. We hope that reading both works will offer readers a deeper and more integrated understanding of the pathways toward quality growth.

It is our earnest hope that this series will serve as both an intellectual stimulus and a practical guide—advancing the global discourse on quality growth and inspiring concrete steps toward its realization in countries around the world, including Japan.

September 2025

Yoichi Mine
Executive Director
JICA Ogata Sadako Research Institute
for Peace and Development
Tokyo, Japan

# Preface and Acknowledgments

This book presents a new approach to growth amid international efforts toward sustainable development, without taking the stance of degrowth that has gained attention recently. In the 21st century, the world faces a complex array of challenges that are more diverse than before. Inequalities in many developed countries are exacerbating national fragmentation, while shocks such as disasters, infectious diseases, and economic crises are having an ever greater impact. Abnormal weather events caused by climate change have become a daily occurrence around the world. Against this backdrop, the Asia-Pacific Economic Cooperation (APEC), a regional economic forum, together with Japan, proposed a new approach to growth in the early 2010s, in which countries' responses to these challenges should be included as elements of growth. This approach is consistent with the SDGs. Moreover, although it is not directly referred to by APEC and Japan, it has also led to recent international discussions on reviewing and creating indicators for measuring prosperity. However, "quality growth" does not negate traditional economic growth but rather asserts that economic growth remains indispensable for achieving prosperity and eradicating poverty. This book seeks to elucidate the approach of quality growth from an economics perspective.

To discuss this new path for growth, it is necessary to clarify the underlying theory, propose specific policies to achieve it, and visualize the results. Measuring the results is important because, as long as prosperity is assessed using traditional gross domestic product (GDP) indicators, the goal of increasing GDP will inevitably continue to be the central policy objective. Ultimately, this book aims to clarify three pillars of the concept of quality growth: its theoretical background, policies for realization, and indicators for measuring results, through which a comprehensive discussion of the quality growth approach will be conducted.

The central part of this book focuses on the theoretical background, with inequality, resilience, and climate change interrelated in complex ways with growth. Each of these relationships has been explored in depth in numerous studies, and while my review is at the level of an economics textbook, a unique feature of this book is that it brings them all together. To date, policy responses to inequality and disaster prevention have generally been pursued separately from growth strategies. While it might seem obvious to consider these factors holistically, in reality, this approach has proven extremely difficult. Furthermore, although prosperity has been determined based on GDP, factors other than income are also essential for improving wellbeing.

Here, drawing on recent research, I argue that the quality growth approach takes these aspects into account. In short, not only income but also other factors related to wellbeing, which are not measured by the market—including inequality and resilience—are part of what constitutes growth. Next, regarding policy, country case studies present reviews of policies that have actually been implemented, which leads to discussions not only on policies specifically related to each element of quality growth, but also on overarching policy frameworks for achieving it as a whole. Finally, in exploring possible indicators, I introduce international discussions on revising GDP and developing new indicators, before proposing a new index for measuring quality growth based on these past considerations.

This book adds value to the existing literature on growth, particularly for developing countries. First, although there has been much discussion of individual themes such as inequality, climate change, disasters, and economic crises, this book brings them together and discusses their interrelationships—a feature rarely found in other works. Second, regarding policy, a strong point is that it examines actual policies implemented through case studies of several countries and affirms their results. These studies were conducted by experts with direct knowledge of the countries examined, many of whom were actively involved in development activities in the field. This makes the discussions of the theoretical background and the proposals for overarching policy frameworks more realistic and allows readers to understand how each country's development is assessed from the perspective of quality growth. Third, the book provides a comprehensive review of new indicators that have emerged since the 1990s. The proposed new index presented here is based on previous research, and, furthermore, I show specific figures for several countries as examples.

This book is divided into Part I, which covers the concept, and Part II, which presents the case studies. In Part I, Chaps. 1 and 2 clarify the background and definition of the quality growth concept, while Chaps. 3 to 6 review the theoretical background of the relationship between inclusiveness, resilience, sustainability, and growth, and provide policies for each subject. Chapter 7 focuses on infrastructure as an example of a policy for achieving quality growth, while Chap. 8 addresses issues related to indicators. Chapter 9 summarizes Part I, providing a comprehensive overview of the discussion and the proposed overarching policy framework, as well as presenting some ideas on how quality growth can be measured. The Appendix to Chap. 9 provides examples of indexation for sample countries. Part II presents case studies that illustrate how growth, inclusiveness, sustainability, and resilience have evolved in Indonesia, Vietnam, Peru, Costa Rica, and Madagascar. I believe that a deeper understanding of the arguments in this book can be obtained through these case studies, while referring back to the foundations established in Part I.

This book is the final compilation of the research project launched in 2016 by the JICA Ogata Sadako Research Institute for Peace and Development. Thanks to the cooperation of many people, we were finally able to publish this book. I would like to express my sincere gratitude to everyone who has supported this research project. We would particularly like to express our deepest appreciation to Dr. Naohiro Kitano, who suggested focusing on this theme as a research project, and to Ms. Rinko Jogo, Ms. Etsuko Masuko, Ms. Sachiko Mitsumori, Mr. Fumiaki Ishizuka, Ms. Yoonjung Kim, Ms. Yukari Saito, and Ms. Kae Yoshino, who managed the research project for many years. This was a long-term research project, and without their continuous support, this book would not have been completed.

We also received valuable comments from many experts on the draft. In particular, Dr. Akio Hosono, Senior Research Advisor at the JICA Ogata Research Institute, provided us with invaluable advice not only through his comments on the draft but also on the conceptualization of quality growth itself. This book covers a wide range of topics, and we received valuable comments from Dr. Mikio Ishiwata, Mr. Ichiro Sato, and Ms. Akiko Oda of JICA, as well as many experts from the JICA Ogata Research Institute and relevant departments of JICA. Thanks to their input, the content of this book has been greatly enriched. Despite the cooperation of so many experts, there are still areas that need improvement, and there may be inaccuracies or errors in the analysis. We would appreciate any comments and other contributions from readers in order to further improve the content and usefulness of this book, as well as to advance the concept of quality growth. We hope that the book will reach a wide audience and achieve more inclusive and desirable growth that enhances the lives of as many people as possible while reducing poverty around the world.

Tokyo, Japan Koki Hirota

# Contents

# Editors and Contributors

## About the Editors

**Koki Hirota** earned his B.A. in Economics from the University of Tokyo and holds a Ph.D. in Economics from Saitama University in Japan. His professional career spans several prominent roles in international development finance and policy, including Chief Economist, Director General of Operation and Strategy Department, and Director General of Southeast Asia and Pacific Department at the Japan International Cooperation Agency (JICA), and Chief Representative in Jakarta for Japan Bank for International Cooperation and in Hanoi for the Overseas Economic Cooperation Fund. In academia, he was a Professor at the Graduate School of Humanities and Social Sciences at Saitama University and a Visiting Fellow at the JICA Ogata Sadako Research Institute for Peace and Development. His recent publications include *Challenges in Fiscal and Monetary Policies in Mongolia* (co-edited, Springer, 2023) and *Addressing Social Infrastructure Needs in Asia: Towards a Pandemic Resilient Society* (co-edited, JICA, August 2025).

## Contributors

**Masayuki Eguchi** Tokyo, Japan

**Yasuo Fujita** Tokyo, Japan

**Koki Hirota** Tokyo, Japan

**Keiko Kubota** Department of Economics, Tohoku Gakuin University, Sendai, Miyagi, Japan

**Stace Nicholson** USA Office, Japan International Cooperation Agency, Washington, DC, USA

**Keiichiro Yuasa** Governance and Peacebuilding Department, Japan International Cooperation Agency, Tokyo, Japan

# Abbreviations

| | |
|---|---|
| 5Ps | People, Planet, Prosperity, Peace, and Partnership |
| ADB | Asian Development Bank |
| AFC | Asian Financial Crisis |
| AI | Artificial Intelligence |
| APEC | Asia-Pacific Economic Cooperation |
| APO | Asian Productivity Organization |
| ARA | Assessing Reserve Adequacy |
| ASEAN | Association of Southeast Asian Nations |
| BLI | Better Life Index |
| CAR | Capital Adequacy Ratio |
| CBA | Cost-Benefit Analysis |
| CCT | Conditional Cash Transfer |
| CINDE | Costarican Coalition of Development Initiatives |
| CNC | Critical Natural Capital |
| $CO_2$ | Carbon Dioxide |
| COMEX | Costa Rican Ministry of Foreign Trade |
| COP | Conference of the Parties |
| COVID-19 | Coronavirus Disease 2019 |
| CPIA | Country Policy and Institutional Assessment |
| DCC | Development Cooperation Charter (Japan) |
| DICE | Dynamic Integrated Climate-Economy |
| EITI | Extractive Industries Transparency Initiative |
| EKC | Environmental Kuznets Curve |
| EPA | Economic Planning Agency (Japan) |
| ESCO | Energy Service Company |
| EU | European Union |
| FDI | Foreign Direct Investment |
| FONCODES | National Fund for Compensation and Social Development (Peru) |
| FRTL | Fiscal Responsibility and Transparency Law (Peru) |
| G7 | Group of Seven |
| G20 | Group of Twenty |
| GCI | Global Competitiveness Index |

| | |
|---|---|
| GDP | Gross Domestic Product |
| GFC | Global Financial Crisis |
| GFCF | Gross Fixed Capital Formation |
| GHG | Greenhouse Gas |
| GIH | Global Infrastructure Hub |
| GNH | Gross National Happiness |
| GNI | Gross National Income |
| GNP | Gross National Product |
| GPI | Genuine Progress Indicator |
| GRIPS | National Graduate Institute for Policy Studies (Japan) |
| Gt | Gigatons |
| GVCs | Global Value Chains |
| HCI | Human Capital Index |
| HDI | Human Development Index |
| IAM | Integrated Assessment Models |
| ICOR | Incremental Capital-Output Ratio |
| ICT | Information and Communication Technology |
| IDI | Inclusive Development Index |
| IHDI | Inequality-Adjusted Human Development Index |
| IIP | International Investment Position |
| IMF | International Monetary Fund |
| INEC | National Institute of Statistics and Census (Costa Rica) |
| INEI | National Institute of Statistics and Informatics (Peru) |
| IPCC | Intergovernmental Panel on Climate Change |
| ISEW | Index of Sustainable Economic Welfare |
| ISI | Import Substitution Industrialization |
| JBIC | Japan Bank for International Cooperation |
| JETRO | Japan External Trade Organization |
| JICA | Japan International Cooperation Agency |
| LDR | Loan-to-Deposit Ratio |
| MDB | Multilateral Development Bank |
| MDGs | Millenium Development Goals |
| MEDD | Ministry of Environment and Sustainable Development (Madagascar) |
| MEF | Ministry of Economy and Finance (Peru) |
| MGI | McKinsey Global Institute |
| MIGA | Multilateral Investment Guarantee Agency |
| MOFA | Ministry of Foreign Affairs (Japan) |
| MPI | Ministry of Planning and Investment (Vietnam) |
| NiCT | National Institute of Information and Communications Technology (Japan) |
| NIE | New Institutional Economics |
| NPL | Non-performing loan |
| ODA | Official Development Assistance |
| OECD | Organisation for Economic Co-operation and Development |

| | |
|---|---|
| PC | Personal Computer |
| PIMA | Public Investment Management Assessment |
| PISA | Programme for International Student Assessment |
| PPP | Public-Private Partnership |
| PPP | Purchasing Power Parity |
| PROCOMER | Foreign Trade Corporation of Costa Rica |
| PROPYME | Program for Strengthening the Innovation and Technological Development of SMEs (Costa Rica) |
| QII | Quality Infrastructure Investment |
| R&D | Research and Development |
| Rp | Indonesian Rupiah |
| SDGs | Sustainable Development Goals |
| SDSN | UN Sustainable Development Solutions Network |
| SEEA | Satellite System for Integrated Environmental and Economic Accounting |
| SEEA-CF | SEEA Central Framework |
| SMEs | Small and Medium Enterprises |
| SNA | System of National Accounts |
| $SO_2$ | Sulfur Dioxide |
| SOE | State-Owned Enterprise |
| SUV | Sports Utility Vehicle |
| SWFI | Sovereign Wealth Fund Institute |
| TFP | Total Factor Productivity |
| UAE | United Arab Emirates |
| UK | United Kingdom of Great Britain and Northern Ireland |
| UN | United Nations |
| UNCTAD | United Nations Conference on Trade and Development |
| UNDP | United Nations Development Programme |
| UNECE | United Nations Economic Commission for Europe |
| UNESCO | United Nations Educational, Scientific and Cultural Organization |
| US | United States of America |
| USD | United States Dollar |
| USSR | Union of Soviet Socialist Republics |
| VEPR | Vietnam Institute for Economic and Policy Research |
| WDI | World Development Indicators |
| WEF | World Economic Forum |
| WEO | World Economic Outlook |
| WGI | Worldwide Governance Indicators |
| WITS | World Integrated Trade Solution |
| WTA | Willingness to Accept |
| WTO | World Trade Organization |
| WTP | Willingness to Pay |

# Part I

# Conceptual Approach

# Introduction

# 1

Koki Hirota

## 1.1 Overview

The purpose of this book is to define and explore what constitutes quality growth. Quality growth is a specifically defined type of growth, and in this book, I will discuss this concept by introducing relevant theories and illustrating it through country experiences as case studies. While these ideas will be discussed in substantial detail in the following chapters, quality growth refers to growth that does not increase inequality, is resilient to various external shocks, and maximizes people's long-term wellbeing. At present, the only countries or official institutions that use the term "quality growth" in their official documents are Japan and the Asia-Pacific Economic Cooperation (APEC), a regional economic forum. Although the definitions employed differ slightly, to all intents and purposes, the overarching aims remain almost identical.

In the Development Cooperation Charter (DCC), approved by Cabinet decision in 2015, the Japanese government identified quality growth—the concept set out in this document—as a priority issue for Japan's development cooperation. This recognition of quality growth as an ongoing priority was demonstrated in the revision of the charter in 2023. The Japan International Cooperation Agency (JICA) subsequently incorporated the goal of achieving quality growth into its organizational mission. However, this does not mean that quality growth is only applicable to developing countries, or even to the field of development cooperation. It is a paradigm for desirable economic growth that should be universally pursued. This is evident from the fact that APEC, which is not an aid organization, also advocates quality growth as the type of growth it is striving for. I believe that the most innovative aspect of quality growth is that the approach aligns with and promotes

K. Hirota (✉)
Tokyo, Japan



K. Hirota (ed.), *Introduction to Quality Growth*,
https://doi.org/10.1007/978-981-95-6220-6_1

the realization of the current international direction, which emphasizes the Sustainable Development Goals (SDGs) and wellbeing by incorporating factors other than income that contribute to our prosperity as part of growth. In this first chapter, I will touch on this point briefly, introduce the issues to be discussed, and explain the structure of this book.

As quality growth is still a component of growth, it is undoubtedly better for economies to grow at a faster pace so that the nation can become wealthier as a whole. In addition, it is considered ideal when growth benefits all groups within society (inclusiveness), and the society remains safe and secure against external shocks. Furthermore, it is desirable for growth to be sustained for as long as possible without interruption. However, in reality, it is extremely difficult to achieve all of these things at the same time, with every country in the world currently grappling with at least some problems. Today's economic growth and the indicators used to measure it do not fully account for inclusiveness, resilience and sustainability. For instance, the United States (US) faces growing inequality as a significant social problem, while China's greenhouse gas (GHG) emissions have become the world largest, posing a threat to the global environment. For all countries, achieving long-lasting high growth, inclusiveness, resilience, and sustainability should be key priorities. However, in reality, we see weaknesses and imbalances among these factors. The causes of this might be rooted in the lack of a common understanding of what brings people prosperity and happiness, a methodology for achieving a good balance between these and integrated measurement.

In order for us to live happily, it is necessary to pay due attention to inclusiveness, resilience and sustainability while also increasing the rate of growth. Widening inequalities reduce the utility of the country as a whole. This is not only because the marginal utility of income growth is greater for low-income groups but also because people's happiness is largely felt through comparison with others. If excessive GHG emissions continue, the wellbeing of future generations will be sacrificed. This leads us to some important questions that are central concerns of this book: Is it possible to achieve a certain level of economic growth without causing these negative aspects? If there is a trade-off between growth rate and inclusiveness or sustainability, what choices should we make? For example, some may believe that having less inequality is good for economic growth. However, if this were the case, then all countries should have expanded their efforts to reduce inequality. In reality, however, there are many countries where inequality is worsening. This implies that either redressing inequality stimulates growth or that governments are not aware of this relationship—or perhaps it is because, even if they are aware of this, it is difficult to improve inequality for various practical reasons.

There has been little discussion about the extent to which the overall situation has improved, or people have become happier, by integrating high growth rates with inclusiveness, resilience and sustainability. Even if each of these is pursued individually, the results may not lead to overall optimization. To achieve such optimization, it is necessary to consider inclusiveness, resilience, and sustainability as part of growth, while at the same time developing a common understanding on how the interrelationships between them have been established in the first place. This brings some foundational questions: What is meant by inclusive growth? How can it be achieved? The same questions can also be asked of resilient growth and sustainable growth. In addition, it is necessary to clarify the linkages of these factors with the mechanisms by which economic growth itself occurs. The policy choices that will bring about optimum results for all must be considered on this basis, which should be measured to confirm the achievement. In this book, to discuss quality growth, I first review what inclusive growth, resilient growth, and sustainable growth are, and confirm the relationship of economic growth with inclusiveness, resilience, and sustainability. Based on this, I will consider how we should consider to integrate these and measure the overall performance.

There is also the question of why the Japanese government and APEC are putting forward the concept of quality growth at this point in time. The view that it is not just the size of growth that matters but also the way in which it occurs has long existed. Inequality has been an important theme in economics since the days of Adam Smith and Karl Marx, and it remains so today. While the issue of the sustainability of the global environment—particularly in regard to global warming—is not just a recent concern, there is a growing awareness that these events affect us negatively, extending beyond gross domestic product (GDP). Domestic inequality in developed countries has continued to widen over the past few decades, resulting in a significant impact on political choices, immigration, and trade policies. Natural disasters and economic crises, once they occur, have an impact that is now incomparable to what occurred in the past. The concept of quality growth is now being proposed in the context of major changes in global society.

Growth that benefits all groups in a society by taking inequality into consideration is called inclusive growth. The domestic inequalities that have been expanding in many developed countries since the 1980s are now a global concern. There has also been an active debate about how globalization, artificial intelligence (AI), and automation negatively impact the incomes of the middle class, causing inequality to widen. Information and communication technology (ICT), which is driving growth, involves almost no marginal costs, so wealth is becoming more concentrated among the super-wealthy class. Financial crises and other external economic shocks have become regular occurrences, so the resilience of economies to external shocks is becoming increasingly important. Economic shocks include not only those that affect the world or the region as a whole—such as the Asian Financial Crisis (AFC) of the late 1990s and the Global Financial Crisis (GFC) of 2007—but also those crises that plunge some types of countries into economic collapse. Such countries include Venezuela, Nigeria, and Mongolia, which were affected by the sharp drop in world resource prices in the mid-2010s. Global crises, such as the Coronavirus disease 2019 (COVID-19) pandemic and Russia's invasion of Ukraine, are ongoing or even worsening. In addition to damage from economic shocks, the destruction caused by natural disasters has increased. The Great East Japan Earthquake of 2011 caused significant damage by historical standards. Since then, major natural disasters have continued to occur around the world. Global concern about natural disasters, as well as economic shocks, has been increasing in recent years.

Concerns about the sustainability of growth are becoming increasingly serious. The term “sustainable growth” is generally used in discussions about the environment and climate change. Since the Paris Agreement was established in 2015, it is now widely recognized that climate change is an urgent issue that must be addressed through international cooperation. However, there are still deep-rooted differences of opinion between developed countries and emerging and developing countries regarding the respective responsibilities and approaches that should be taken. Underlying this is the fear of a slowdown in growth due to the promotion of measures to combat climate change, stemming from the belief that growth and sustainability exist in a trade-off relationship.

In addition, the sustainability of growth is not merely a matter of the environment and climate change. The so-called middle-income trap, in which the growth of many emerging countries reaches a plateau at the middle-income stage, has been observed. New global phenomena are also apparent, such as the shift toward a service-oriented economy related to the growth of ICT and AI. It also includes the onset of premature deindustrialization in developing countries, where the share of the industrial sector in GDP reaches its peak before it is fully developed and begins to decline earlier than it did in the case of developed countries today. In other words, there is a need for new perspectives that reorganize growth pathways and strategies. The term “quality growth” could be considered as the approach to growth in the twenty-first century, in the sense that it addresses global issues and other changes currently underway.

The reason why Japan is trying to present this approach of growth is that the government’s policies are shifting to focus more on the elements of quality growth. Since the collapse of the bubble economy in the 1990s, there have been a number of growth strategies implemented to try to pull Japan out of its long-term economic stagnation. However, looking at the messages from recent administrations, while continued growth remains at the heart of economic policy, a broader approach is being taken. In concrete terms, there have been many catchphrases demonstrating the elements of quality growth, such as “dynamic engagement of all one hundred million citizens,” “work style reform,” “the 100-year life era concept,” “promotion of active roles of women,” “enhancement of disaster resilience,” “productivity revolution and Society 5.0,” and so on. While I will discuss these areas in more detail in the following chapters, the policies Japan is currently pursuing are an attempt to make quality growth a reality. Although measuring all these in an integrated way is a challenge that must be addressed, recent government initiatives suggest Japan is shifting in a direction where growth, inclusiveness, resilience, and sustainability are viewed in an integrated way. The government announced a basic plan for wellbeing in 2021 and a grand design for a new capitalism based on a virtuous cycle of growth and distribution in 2022.

It is important to note that the concept of quality growth emanates from the field of development cooperation. Specifically, Japan believes that an emphasis on both growth and inclusiveness, resilience, and sustainability is essential for developing countries today, based on the experiences of its development cooperation in Asia and other regions. Over the years, Asian countries have dynamically transformed their economies through the development of the manufacturing industry and the improvement of agricultural productivity. Japan has supported the development of institutions that have made this transformation possible. Among these efforts are Japan's unique industrial policies and policy-based institutional finance, about which international opinion remains divided. Of course, many of the lessons of the past do not apply automatically, and the situation will differ from country to country.

In addition, looking at these recent developments, developing countries appear to be taking different growth paths from developed countries. An example of this can be seen in the new trends of premature deindustrialization noted above. In response to these new challenges, the most important point is to foster the ability to generate growth endogenously and to promote societal transformation. This is something that is universal and common to all eras. This represents a different kind of sustainability than that of sustaining growth in the face of climate change. In other words, it is a discussion about how to create the conditions that will allow growth to continue endogenously into the future and promote societal transformation. The reason why the concept of quality growth emerged from the context of development cooperation is that it was recognized from the discussion to prepare the revised DCC that it is crucially important for developing countries to place importance on growth, inclusiveness, resilience and sustainability comprehensively. Such an integrated approach is made possible by mainstreaming these elements of quality growth into various policies, maximizing the welfare of society as a whole.

The reason why I refer to quality growth as a new approach is that it does not make economic growth—as expressed by GDP—the sole objective of a country's growth policy, nor does it advocate degrowth as an antithesis to it. This way of thinking is consistent with the international debate on the SDGs and Beyond GDP (indicators that go beyond GDP). Thus, the approach of quality growth presented in this book also provides a theoretical background for discussing the SDGs. With the addition of many economic goals drawn from the Millenium Development Goals (MDGs), the SDGs have greatly expanded the scope of their connection with business, and there is now a much greater momentum in Japan to tackle them as a whole society than there was with the MDGs.

Since the SDGs had their origins in previous international development goals and climate change discussions, they naturally stress inclusiveness and sustainability. The SDGs explicitly use the terms inclusiveness, sustainability (expressed in two distinct ways as "sustained growth" and "sustainable growth"), and resilience. Therefore, delving into the concept of quality growth will also contribute to establishing a methodology for achieving the SDGs. Regarding Beyond GDP, the international argument that the purpose of economic policy is to increase people's wellbeing—and that this is not expressed solely by increases in income—has become particularly active in recent years. There has been extensive discussion about improving GDP system and developing new indicators that go beyond GDP, and in fact, many new indicator ideas have been put forward. As I will discuss in more detail in Chap. 8, the issues raised in these international discussions have essentially taken the same direction as those of quality growth.

The quality growth approach is only effective when the three elements of theory, policy, and indicators are all in place. The purpose of this book is to provide a discussion of these elements. It is therefore organized as follows: Part I, this chapter, provides an overview of the concept, including policies and indicators. Chapter 2 discusses the definition of quality growth. Chapters 3 through 6 introduce the literature on growth and inclusiveness, resilience, and sustainability, analyzing them from a variety of perspectives. I then discuss policies that will increase inclusiveness, resilience, and sustainability. Chapter 7 takes infrastructure as an example of a sectoral approach to achieving quality growth. It clarifies that "quality infrastructure investment (QII)" essentially aims at the same goal as quality growth. Chapter 8 addresses the issue of indicators in relation to how quality growth is measured. Chapter 9 provides the conclusions. It first confirms the relationship between quality growth and the SDGs, before summarizing the relationships between growth, inclusiveness, resilience, and sustainability. It then proposes a means by which quality growth can be measured and an overarching policy framework for achieving this goal. In the Appendix, there is also a preliminary proposal for developing new indicators. The empirical part of this book, from Chaps. 10 to 14, reviews the economic growth trajectories and policy developments in five countries from the perspective of quality growth: Indonesia, Vietnam, Peru, Costa Rica, and Madagascar. By comparing the perspective of quality growth with actual national development, it may be possible to clarify the application of this approach to the real world and identify some areas that need further consideration.

## 1.2 Relationship Between Economic Growth and Poverty Reduction

The remainder of this chapter will provide an overview of the trajectory of economic growth and inequality to date, setting the stage for the discussion of quality growth beginning with the next chapter. Note that the term "growth" here specifically refers to changes in the size of GDP and does not account for factors beyond income. First, I will affirm the relationship between growth and poverty reduction and discuss how medium- to long-term growth trends differ depending on the era and characteristics of each country. Then, I will provide an overview of the trends in income inequality, which vary greatly between countries; indeed, no clear commonality in these changes can be identified.

Poverty reduction is one of the biggest policy issues not only for developing countries but also for developed countries. This is why the SDGs clearly state that eradicating poverty is the greatest global challenge and begin with poverty reduction as Goal 1. The goal of economic development is to ensure that as many people as possible can achieve prosperity and that the poor can escape poverty. We know that the affluence people perceive is dependent not only on income but also on other factors, such as health, living conditions, and safety. It is also affected by the size of various stocks, such as assets and the natural environment. However, despite these limitations, income can still be said to broadly represent the degree of prosperity of countries and people.

Economic growth, as expressed in income, is essential for poverty reduction. Analyzing data from 1950 through 1999, Dollar and Kraay (2001) demonstrated that the income of the poor is higher in countries with greater per-capita incomes, and that a positive correlation exists between economic growth rates and the growth of the income of the poor. When this relationship is extended to the period from 2000 to 2015, the former still shows a strong positive correlation (Fig. 1.1). However, the relationship in the latter case is less clear (Fig. 1.2), with considerable variation on the vertical axis (growth rate of income of the poor). In other words, even if average income growth rates rise, this does not necessarily lead to a corresponding growth in the income of the poor. Overall, while there is generally a positive correlation between the growth of income of the poor and the growth of average incomes, it should be noted that many countries have a below-average rate of income growth, that is, the income growth rate of the poor remains below the average growth rate of income.

In any case, if rapid growth continues overall, income levels will improve and poverty reduction will make significant progress. For example, in China, the average annual real GDP growth rate was 9.5% between 1990 and 2017. During that period, China made great strides in poverty reduction, and the poverty rate declined dramatically, from 61% in 1990 to 4% in 2015. This suggests that the higher the overall growth rate, the faster the income of the poor will grow. Behind this lies the "trickle-down theory," which is a widely known theory in development economics. According to this theory, if the economy grows, the benefits of that growth should

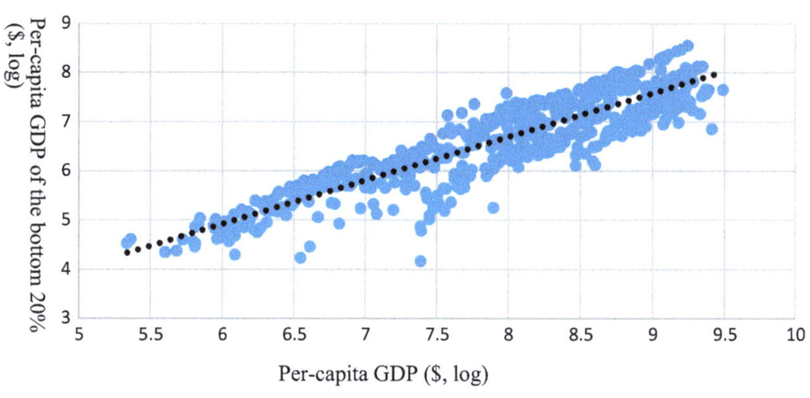


**Fig. 1.1** Correlation between per-capita income and the income of the poor (real, 2010 prices) (*Source* Author's calculation based on World Bank Open Data)

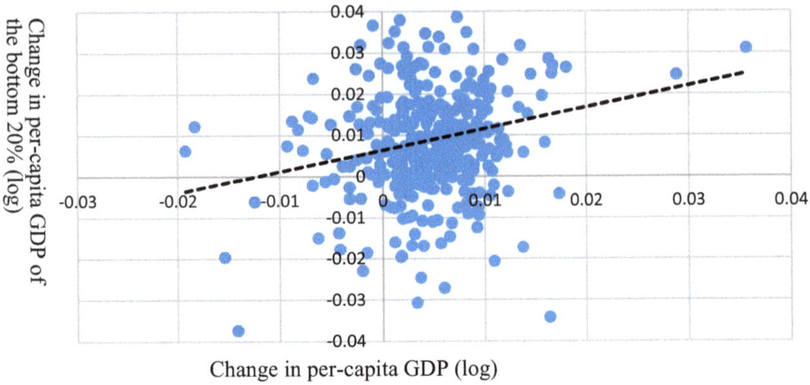


**Fig. 1.2** Correlation between growth in per-capita income and the income of the poor (real, 2010 prices) (*Source* Author's calculation based on World Bank Open Data)

"trickle down" to the poor. This led to the belief that poverty problems would eventually disappear as the economy grew.

However, there are two points to note regarding the overall idea that growth reduces poverty. The first is that it is not easy to achieve and sustain high growth over the long term. Although emerging economies as a whole have shown high growth rates since the start of the twenty-first century, many have not yet begun catching up with developed countries. Growth rates vary widely between countries, and it is not uncommon for countries to enter periods of stagnation after continuous growth for a certain period of time. This raises the question of what the driving force behind high growth is and how it can be sustained. There are various aspects to this debate, but they can be summarized into two main concerns: the growth engine and the expense or sacrifice of future generations. The former is related to the theory of growth—an important concern in economics. The distribution of the fruits of growth is another concern of economics, where it is now generally accepted that trickle-down effects do not necessarily work in the real world. In fact, many developed countries are experiencing a widening gap between rich and poor, with an increasing number of people not benefiting from growth while poverty has become a major social issue. The latter is specifically related to global warming today.

Today, no one would base policy on simplistic trickle-down theory alone. Reducing inequality is, indeed, one of the major components of poverty reduction. If income inequality increases while growth remains constant, poverty will actually worsen. Mathematically, calculating both the growth rate and changes in inequality can help confirm the impact of inequality on poverty reduction; however, the reality is more complex. This is because changes in inequality can lead to differences in the subsequent level of economic growth itself. Conversely, the way that economic growth proceeds also affects the level of inequality. This relationship is complex, and there are various ways of looking at it; as will be discussed later in this book, there is still no clear consensus. As mentioned above, because of its importance in achieving poverty reduction, the phrase "inclusive and sustainable" is often used by development cooperation organizations whose ultimate goal is poverty reduction.

## 1.3 The Trajectory of Economic Growth

The global economy has grown exponentially since the Industrial Revolution. Coupled with explosive growth in the population, global GDP expanded by 18.6 times in just one century. This is equivalent to an average annual growth rate of 3% (or 1.6% growth in GDP per capita). Over the long history of humankind, the phenomenon of economic growth has mostly occurred during the last century or two. However, my perspective in this analysis is a little narrower, focusing instead on a country-by-country basis. The time frame is limited to a span of a few decades that I will treat as the long term, and I will look at how economic growth was sustained within that time. This book focuses on the period after World War II, and in particular, the 1960s onwards, when many developing countries gained independence.

### 1.3.1 Differences in Growth Rates by Income Level

#### 1.3.1.1 Developed Countries and Developing Countries

Looking at changes in GDP growth rates per capita by income level from the 1960s until the outbreak of the COVID-19 pandemic, low-income countries as a whole—but typified by sub-Saharan Africa—followed a pattern similar to the global average during the 1960s and early 1970s. However, from the 1980s onwards, there were some trends that differed according to income group. In the 1980s and 1990s, growth in low-income countries stagnated significantly. In contrast, the growth rate of developed countries exceeded the global average during this period. As we entered the twenty-first century, this situation changed completely. The rapid growth of emerging countries began, and the growth of low- and middle-income country groups became particularly high. In contrast, the growth of developed countries was lower than in any previous period, and growth in developed countries fell below 2%. In summary, the path of world economic growth in the twenty-first century shows a trend towards global economic convergence. Developed countries' share is shrinking due to the rapid growth of emerging countries, especially China.

While developed countries' share of the world economy has declined by 15.3% on a purchasing power parity (PPP) basis, China's share has grown by 10.8% over the same period, and such emerging countries as India and Brazil also experiencing growth. As Baldwin (2016) states, globalization is characterized by the ability of firms to break down their production processes into smaller steps (unbundling) using ICT and the supply chain. By doing this, firms in developed countries have shifted many of their production processes to countries with lower wages. However, only a few countries have taken advantage of this opportunity to attract foreign firms and accelerate their growth. Therefore, while the global economy seems to be converging in terms of income groups, it should be noted that only a few countries in the lower middle-income group are catching up to the developed countries, which grew rapidly in the past, while other countries have not. Where does this difference come from? To answer this question, it is necessary to understand the mechanisms of growth.

### 1.3.2 Differences in Growth Rates Due to Country's Characteristics

Determining the trends in countries' growth rates by grouping countries with certain characteristics is useful for examining the factors supporting growth. Here, I will look at the characteristics of (1) countries that are highly dependent on natural resources, (2) geographically isolated countries, such as small island and landlocked countries, (3) conflict-affected countries, and (4) countries in transition.[1] Following this, I also review growth rates by region.

Natural resources are important in discussions on the sustainability of growth. The group of so-called vulnerable countries includes many that are geographically isolated, such as island states and landlocked countries. These countries face major constraints in sustaining growth, and many are vulnerable to natural disasters. Conflict-affected countries are another vulnerable group of countries that generally have significant governance issues. Countries in transition are those countries that shifted to market economies after the fall of Communist regimes in the early 1990s. These countries' growth trajectories provide some valuable insights into growth sustainability. There are significant differences in growth trends between regions, as well as commonalities in their historical backgrounds related to institutions and growth sustainability.

[1] The classification of countries by group follows the definitions of international organizations and growth rates up to the outbreak of COVID-19, with values calculated based on the classifications before its onset.

a) High-income, middle-income, and low-income countries are based on the World Development Indicators (WDI) of the World Bank.
b) Developed countries are based on the World Economic Outlook (WEO) Database of IMF, and developing countries are based on the Development Assistance Committee of OECD.
c) Resource-dependent countries are based on the UNCTAD (2016) and UN (2018).
d) Small island developing states and landlocked countries are based on UN (2018).
e) Countries affected by conflict are based on UNESCO (2011) as well as countries where major conflicts have occurred since then.
f) Countries in transition are based on the UN (2018).

#### 1.3.2.1 Resource-Dependent Countries

The United Nations (UN) defines a resource-dependent developing country as one in which the proportion of resources in exports exceeds 60%, and I examined the growth trajectory of these countries. The growth rate of resource-dependent countries was far lower than the world average in the early 1960s, the 1980s, and since 2015. In the other periods, the increases and decreases were similar to the global average, and the difference in growth was not significant until the beginning of the twenty-first century, except for a period in the 1990s. Since 2000, their growth has exceeded the global average in many years. This is because the rapid growth of emerging economies, including China, has driven a global increase in production activities and increased demand for resources.

Being blessed with natural resources definitely helps growth. Therefore, when any country discovers that it has reserves of resources, it will actively try to develop them. However, as will be seen in more detail in Chap. 5, the relationship between resources and growth has some complications. In discussions about development in the 1960s, it was thought that the terms of trade for primary commodities would deteriorate over the long term compared with those of industrial products, so it would be essential for a country's long-term growth to extricate itself from an export structure that relied on primary commodities. There are also issues that are often discussed, such as how being rich in resources can slow down development in sectors other than the resource sector, and that resource rents can make governance difficult. This is the so-called "resource curse" theory. According to historical trends, the growth rate of resource-dependent countries has at times exceeded the global average and at other times fallen below it, so it is hard to say whether there is a simple and unique relationship.

Next, I divided the types of resources into fuel resources (oil, natural gas, coal), mineral resources, and other commodities (agricultural products, etc.) and examined the trends for each, with around 30 countries in each group. I found that there were differences in growth patterns depending on the resources on which the country depended. Countries that are dependent on "other commodities," centered on agricultural products, grow at almost the same rate as the global average. The growth of fuel-dependent countries generally matches global economic trends, but the fluctuations are greater than the global average. The growth performance of mineral-dependent countries lies between those of the fuel-dependent and other commodity-dependent countries. Therefore, my examination of the relationship between natural resources and growth will be fuel resources first, followed by mineral resources. Overall, over the past 20 years, resource-dependent countries have grown faster than the global average. It can be said that growth driven by natural resources has led to sustained and rapid growth over a considerable period of time. The theory of the "resource curse" attempts to explain why having resources can be a constraint on growth. While those involved in the development business tend to focus on only the negative aspects of resources when discussing this, the relationship with growth is not that simple. Looking at past trends, having resources can increase the growth rate overall, but at the same time, it would seem that special attention is needed in economic management.

#### 1.3.2.2 Small Island Developing States and Landlocked Countries

According to the UN classification in 2018, Small Island Developing States consist of 38 countries, as well as 19 non-UN members or Associate members of the Regional Commissions. Characteristics common to small island developing states are their small populations, with half having fewer than 200,000 people. They are also heavily reliant on specific sectors such as tourism and commodity exports, and many are vulnerable to disasters (IMF 2015). There are also 44 landlocked countries, of which 32 are countries classified as landlocked developing countries under the UN definition. Their transportation problems are more serious, as their transport costs are reportedly more than double those of coastal countries.[2] Other commonalities of landlocked countries include high natural resource dependence and many are among the poorest nations in the world, with most located in sub-Saharan Africa and Central Asia.

The real GDP growth per capita for these island states has been about the same as the world average. These countries have extremely small economies, and due to geographical constraints, it is difficult for them to be self-sufficient in their daily necessities, so their trading systems are inevitably open to the outside world. This openness also makes them susceptible to external risks. As a result, their growth rates are also "dependent" on the global growth rate, and thus, they have been unable to catch up to developed countries. Although being open to the outside world facilitates easy access to the technology transfer necessary for development, small island states are not attractive places for foreign investors due to their high transport costs, small populations and limited domestic markets. As a result, achieving the technology transfer necessary for accelerating growth is challenging.

The growth trajectory of the 32 landlocked developing countries is similar to that of mineral-resource-dependent countries, with little difference between the 15 resource-dependent and the 17 non-resource-dependent countries. In other words, natural resources do not seem to be contributing to these differences. This group includes not only resource-dependent countries but also countries affected by conflict and those undergoing regime change, and it is not always clear which of these factors has the greatest impact on growth patterns. Geographical constraints are certainly a major impediment to growth, but there are also countries such as Ethiopia, Rwanda, and Uganda that have enjoyed relatively long periods of high growth. Thus, geographical constraints, such as landlockedness alone, do not decisively affect growth patterns. In other words, if appropriate policies are implemented, there may be the possibility of achieving sustained growth. The relationship between geographical conditions, technology and other endowments and growth is discussed in Chap. 6.

[2] For instance, export costs per container average USD 3,142 for landlocked countries (as of 2014), more than double the USD 1,422 average for transit coastal countries (World Bank 2014).

#### 1.3.2.3 Conflict-Affected Countries

Conflicts, whether they occur between or within countries, can inflict serious damage on the lives and livelihoods of residents and have a major impact on people's economic activities. Not only do conflicts hinder investment, causing production to stagnate, but they also restrict daily life and consumption. Although there is no precise definition of a conflict-affected country, the classification is usually made using such metrics as the number of casualties, refugees, or internal displacements due to a conflict or the scale of forced migration. There were 35 countries worldwide that were referred to as conflict affected in the report by the United Nations Educational, Scientific and Cultural Organization (UNESCO) in 2011, but more countries have been experiencing major conflicts since then, such as Azerbaijan, Libya, South Sudan, Syria, and Ukraine.

The economic impact of conflicts varies with the scale and length of the conflict. As Collier (2007) points out, many conflicts have continued for years and civil wars, in particular, tend to last longer than conflicts between countries. Since conflicts happen at different times and under different conditions in each country, comparing their impacts based solely on when they occurred is almost meaningless. On the other hand, examining the relationship between conflict and growth in individual countries reveals that while growth rates rebound and rise sharply in the short term following the resolution of conflict, this does not necessarily mean that high growth rates will be sustained. Conflicts can have a long-term negative impact through the destruction of human and physical capital, and in order to overcome these and return to a path of sustained growth, it is essential to establish the basic conditions for growth. These factors will be discussed in detail in Chap. 6.

#### 1.3.2.4 Countries in Transition

The UN defines 17 countries as "economies in transition." These include Russia, former Yugoslav countries, and countries in Central Asia and the Caucasus, but exclude Eastern Europe and the three Baltic states. The general economic trend of these countries after 1991 shows a major economic slump in the first few years following their independence, followed by growth in excess of the world average until 2009. Since the global economic crisis, their growth has been about the same as the world average, and slightly below the average for middle-income countries. The trend of Eastern European countries, which are not included in this group here, is broadly similar to that of these countries in transition.

This pattern of growth is also similar to that of countries experiencing conflict. In other words, regime change brings about a temporary downturn followed by a period of recovery. Once this effect has worn off, the basic elements of economic growth will determine future trajectories. Since their human and physical capital was not directly destroyed during the regime change period, its negative impact is less severe than that of conflict-affected countries. However, the old regime was unable to continue, and there were many inefficiencies in their economic management, institutions, and governance. The fact that the growth rates of these countries have approached the global average growth rate since the GFC suggests that the recovery process associated with the regime transition has ended. For some countries where current growth rates are lower than the average for middle-income countries, lingering issues may stem from the negative legacy of the old regime's institutions and governance. Institutions and growth are also discussed further in Chap. 6.

#### 1.3.2.5 Growth Rates by Region

As has been widely observed, since the late 1970s, East Asia has consistently grown faster than any other region. The slump in oil prices and regime transitions have caused growth rates in the Middle East and Europe/Central Asia to decline significantly at certain times. Growth also stalled in sub-Saharan Africa and Latin America in the 1980s and 1990s due to sovereign debt problems. In recent years, continued high growth in India has bolstered South Asia, bringing its growth rate on par with that of East Asia.

The differences in regional growth rates suggest that there may be factors common to the regions that similarly influence their growth. When researchers analyze the factors underlying growth, a regional dummy is often included as an explanatory variable, based on the assumption that there are some common factors in each region. A considerable volume of research has been undertaken to determine what these factors are. For example, there was once a great focus on the colonial structure in Latin America and Africa. A well-known World Bank (1993) study attempted to uncover the secrets of high growth in East Asia. The study highlighted how policies supporting growth reflected the characteristics of the region. They are rooted in the social systems and culture of each country and are path-dependent, having evolved through history. While this book does cover the characteristics of regional histories and institutions in detail, the relationship between sustained growth, institutions and policies is reviewed in Chap. 6.

### 1.3.3 Preliminary Considerations on Sustained Growth

Before discussing sustainable and sustained growth—presented in Chaps. 5 and 6—I would like to touch on its meaning here. Generally speaking, sustained growth has been referred to as the phenomenon of economic growth continuing at a specific rate or above over a certain period of time. For example, Berg, Ostry, and Zettelmeyer (2012) set the threshold for sustained growth at 2% real GDP growth per capita, continuing for five or eight years or more. Using this definition, they attempt a quantitative analysis of the factors of sustained growth of 140 countries since the 1950s (introduced in Chap. 6). However, other discussions of sustained growth generally seem to have a longer-term span in mind. For example, developing countries need several decades to develop their industries and increase their GDP per capita to catch up with developed countries; therefore, it is better to look at decades rather than years. When discussing sustainable and sustained growth in this book, I will be considering a time frame of more than 10 years—and in some cases—many decades.

Is there a certain pattern to growth when viewed over the long term? Pritchett (2000) adopts this perspective in a study that sets out the following six patterns of change in developing countries' GDP per capita (on PPP basis) over the 1960–1992 period. The author finds that developing countries experienced unstable and volatile growth rates compared to the more stable growth of developed countries, typified by the following shapes and groupings:

A. Hill: A growth rate of at least 1.5% throughout the period (27 countries),
B. Steep hills: A growth rate of at least 3% throughout the period (11 countries),
C. Plateau: Growth of at least 1.5% until a turning point, and 1.5% or less after the turning point (16 countries),
D. Mountain: Growth of at least 1.5% until a turning point, after which growth is negative (33 countries),
E. Plain: Growth of 1.5% or less throughout the period (17 countries), and
F. Accelerations: Growth of 1.5% or less until a turning point, after which growth is above 1.5% (7 countries).

According to this classification, the A, B, and F groups have continued to grow at a certain level or above, while the remaining groups lack sustained growth. Pritchett (2000) states that growth regression analysis does not provide sufficient information on the causes of such differences, and in order to understand the factors behind growth, he proposed that it would be necessary to address the following three questions. First, what are the conditions that lead to an acceleration or a continuous decline in growth? Second, what happens to growth when major changes take place in trade, the macroeconomy, investment policy, or government? Finally, why do some countries absorb or overcome external shocks while others are overwhelmed by them? These three overarching questions are very close to the perspectives I will be discussing in this book. Regarding the first two issues, Pritchett (2000) argues that we need to take a close look at the forces driving growth and the basic conditions (economic policies and governance) that enable it. The third point is the discussion of resilience.

Using the same data sources as Pritchett (2000), I extend the analysis period and observe the subsequent situation in several countries. For the countries used as case studies in this book, Costa Rica continued to show a general hill-growth pattern. Indonesia, which used to show an acceleration pattern, experienced a slump due to the AFC and a period of stagnation but followed a broader recovery trajectory afterward. Peru has emerged from the mountain's downward trend and growth has continued. On the other hand, Madagascar has clearly deteriorated from its previous plain pattern. These changes show that while growth rates follow a particular pattern for a certain period of time, this is not necessarily ever-lasting. Sometimes, low growth reverses into a recovery; in other cases, it falls into a long-term downward trend. The mechanisms of growth that bring about such changes are discussed in Chaps. 5 and 6. Before advancing further, however, I would like to point out that the discussion of sustainable and sustained growth is of this nature.

## 1.4 Distribution of the Fruits of Growth

The current income inequality among countries is much greater than it was in the world before the twentieth century. Throughout the nineteenth century, most of the world's income inequality occurred within countries. Since the Industrial Revolution, the differences between countries have grown, and they have outstripped inequalities within countries after World War II, reaching a plateau in the 1960s. Bourguignon and Morrisson (2002), who illustrate this trend, provide estimates through 1992, and the World Bank (2016) extend these estimates from 1988 through 2013, showing the situation from the 1990s onward. According to this analysis, global inequality, as measured by the Gini coefficient, has been shrinking overall since the 1990s, and international inequality declined from comprising 80% of total inequality in 1988 to 65% in 2013. Of course, this is largely due to the growth of emerging countries.

Inequality within countries has unfolded differently in each country. In terms of the Gini coefficient, we see a large difference in its absolute numbers between developed countries and developing countries. Many of the countries with small inequalities are developed countries and former communist countries, while many countries in Latin America and Africa generally have large inequalities. Although inequality has grown in most member countries of the Organisation for Economic Co-operation and Development (OECD) since the 1980s, the situation in developing countries varies. Even in developing countries that traditionally had large inequalities, income growth among the poor often exceeds the income growth of the rich. For example, looking at changes in the Gini coefficient in representative emerging economies, Brazil and Mexico—with historically high levels of inequality—have consistently decreased their level of inequality since the 2000s. On the other hand, inequality in South Africa has worsened considerably since around 2000.

There are two key directions in the relationship between inequality and growth. One is how inequality changed as a result of growth—i.e., whether it reduces inequality or expands it. The other is how the scale of inequality affects the subsequent growth rate. The former issue concerns the economic activities that brought about growth also increased the income of some income groups in particular. Various factors are likely to be involved, such as changes in technology and industrial structure, as well as institutional factors. As the scale of inequality is directly linked to poverty reduction, it follows that, ideally, growth should narrow inequality. The more equal a society's income distribution is, the more poverty reduction will progress along with economic growth. Conversely, if inequality increases, the poverty reduction effect of economic growth will be reduced by the same amount. Table 1.1 shows an example of how rapid growth in inequality erases the effects of growth and may even cause poverty to increase. However, if growth widens the income gap while raising the overall growth rate of the economy, there may be debates about which is preferable for society as a whole. If this relationship were clearly understood, policymakers might then be able to choose an optimal

**Table 1.1** Impact of growth and changes in the Gini coefficient on poverty (model case)

| | Initial situation | After 10% economic growth | 10% growth +15% increase in inequality |
|---|---|---|---|
| Total national income | 50 | 55 | 55 |
| Income of the rich | 35 | 38.5 | 40.15 |
| Income of the poor | 15 | 16.5 | 14.85 |

*Note* Calculations of changes in income for the whole country, the rich, and the poor in the event of a 15% deterioration in the Gini coefficient from 0.20 to 0.23. *Source* Author's calculations

combination of high growth and changes in inequality. In reality, however, this is not possible.

The other direction concerns the question of whether a society with high inequality or low inequality is more likely to grow. The magnitude of inequality may have a direct impact on the subsequent level of growth. For example, there is a view that a society with higher inequality is likely to have higher savings rates (because the poor have to spend more on their basic needs and, therefore, cannot save), and that this will lead to higher growth as savings are invested. If this is true, then having less inequality is not necessarily good for growth. To confirm the actual trends related to the above, I plotted the relationship between inequality and growth in recent years in two figures. Figure 1.3 shows the correlation between the average growth rate of per-capita GDP between 1996 and 2015 on the horizontal axis and the change in the Gini coefficient from the 1996–2000 period to the 2010–2015 period on the vertical axis. Overall, many countries reduced inequality over this period (a decrease in the Gini coefficient is indicated as a negative value). However, there is no clear relationship between per capita average growth rates and inequality (the relationship is not statistically significant).

Next, in Fig. 1.4, we see how growth rates differ depending on the initial size of inequality. The horizontal axis shows the Gini coefficient for 1985 (if data for that year were not available, the earliest data available thereafter before 1990),

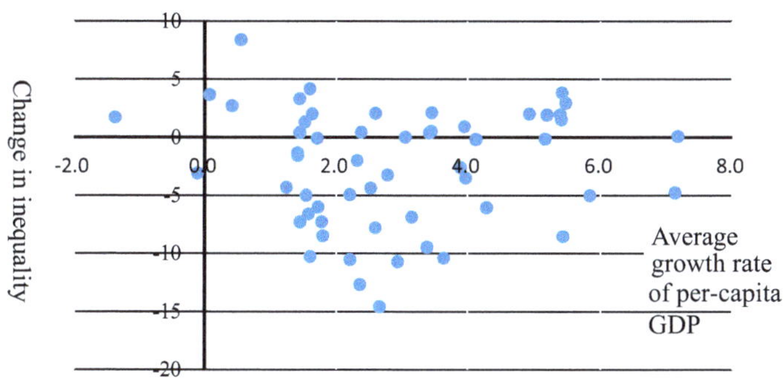


**Fig. 1.3** How inequality changes with growth (*Source* Author's calculation based on World Bank Open Data)

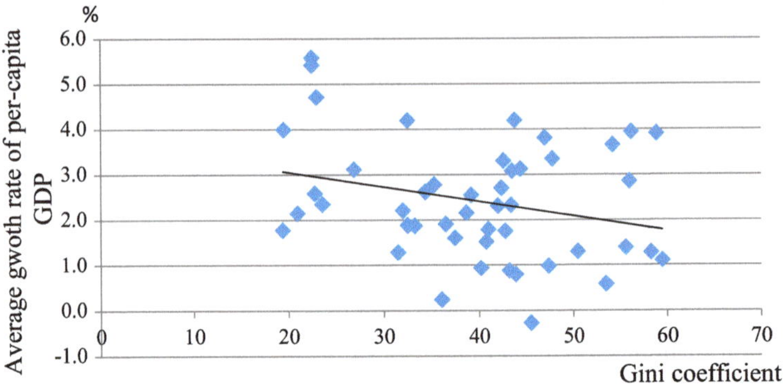


**Fig. 1.4** Difference in growth rates of per-capita GDP due to the scale of inequality (*Source* Author's calculation based on World Bank Open Data)

and the vertical axis is the average growth rate of per-capita GDP for the 1986–2015 period. From this figure, it can be seen that the lower the inequality, the more growth tended to exceed the average. Of course, it is not possible to discuss the relationship between inequality and growth based on this figure alone. More detailed empirical evidence and the underlying theory are necessary, and in fact, a number of studies have been conducted to date (introduced in Chap. 3). Following the discussion on the definition in the next chapter, my discussions of quality growth begin with inclusiveness from Chap. 3, where I will not only review underlying theories but also discuss the global phenomena, policies, and prescriptions with respect to inequality.

## References


Baldwin, Richard. 2016. *Great Conversion: Information Technology and the New Globalization.* Belknap Press.

Berg, Andrew, Jonathan D. Ostry, and Jeromin Zettelmeyer. 2012. "What Makes Growth Sustained?" *Journal of Development Economics* 98 (2): 149–166.

Bouruignon, François, and Christian Morrisson. 2002. "Inequality among World Citizens: 1820 –1992." *American Economic Review* 92 (4): 727–744.

Collier, Paul. 2007. *The Bottom Billion: Why the Poorest Countries Are Failing and What Can Be Done About It.* Oxford University Press.

Dollar, David, and Aart Kraay. 2001. "Growth Is Good for the Poor." World Bank Policy Research Paper No. 2587.

International Monetary Fund (IMF). 2015. *Macroeconomic Developments and Selected Issues in Small Developing States.* IMF.

Pritchett, Lant. 2000. "Understanding Patterns of Economic Growth: Searching for Hills among Plateaus, Mountains, and Plains." *World Bank Economic Review* 14 (2): 221–250.

United Nations (UN). 2018. *World Economic Situation Prospects 2018.* United Nations Publications.

United Nations Conference on Trade and Development (UNCTAD). 2016. *State of Commodity Dependence 2016.* United Nations.

United Nations Educational, Scientific and Cultural Organization (UNESCO). 2011. *EFA Global Monitoring Report 2011: The Hidden Crisis: Armed Conflict and Education*. UNESCO.
World Bank. 1993. *The East Asian Miracle: Economic Growth and Public Policy*. Oxford University Press.
World Bank. 2014. Improving Trade and Transport for Landlocked Developing Countries. World Bank-United Nations report in preparation for the 2nd United Nations Conference on Landlocked Developing Countries (LLDCs).
World Bank. 2016. *Taking on Inequality Poverty and Shared Prosperity 2016*.

**Koki Hirota** earned his B.A. in Economics from the University of Tokyo and holds a Ph.D. in Economics from Saitama University in Japan. His professional career spans several prominent roles in international development finance and policy, including Chief Economist, Director General of Operation and Strategy Department, and Director General of Southeast Asia and Pacific Department at the Japan International Cooperation Agency (JICA), and Chief Representative in Jakarta for Japan Bank for International Cooperation and in Hanoi for the Overseas Economic Cooperation Fund. In academia, he was a Professor at the Graduate School of Humanities and Social Sciences at Saitama University and a Visiting Fellow at the JICA Ogata Sadako Research Institute for Peace and Development. His recent publications include *Challenges in Fiscal and Monetary Policies in Mongolia* (co-edited, Springer, 2023) and *Addressing Social Infrastructure Needs in Asia: Towards a Pandemic Resilient Society* (co-edited, JICA, August 2025).

# 2 The Concept of Quality Growth

Koki Hirota

## 2.1 Quality of Growth and Quality Growth

### 2.1.1 Quality of Growth

In this chapter, I define quality growth and provide some background on its emergence as a concept. I then present the standpoint from which I will elucidate quality growth in the chapters that follow.

Research on the quality of growth has until now been limited, primarily because defining the term quality of growth has proved challenging. Even when definitions have been provided, subsequent research has spanned a broad spectrum of areas, so it can be difficult to pinpoint a singular focus. Themes that seem to be relevant to the quality of growth—such as inequality, climate change, disaster prevention, and economic crisis—have been discussed as independent topics and policies have been proposed for each. There has not yet been a systematic effort to integrate these topics and consider the overall picture of growth.

One of the seminal documents discussing the quality of growth is Thomas et al. (2000), prepared by a team from the World Bank Institute. The report is comprehensive, sharing many points with the description of quality growth advocated by the APEC and Japan. According to the Thomas et al. (2000), "development" is defined as improving the quality of people's lives. To achieve this end, the report calls for not only income, but also equal opportunities in education, healthcare and employment, environmental sustainability, global financial risk control, governance, and anti-corruption. It then draws the following three conclusions to improve the quality of growth: first, balanced accumulation of physical, human

K. Hirota (✉)
Tokyo, Japan



K. Hirota (ed.), *Introduction to Quality Growth*,
https://doi.org/10.1007/978-981-95-6220-6_2

and natural capital; second, consideration for distribution in the support of the development process; and third, institutional framework for good governance.

Thomas et al. (2000) also mentions the relationship between the quality and quantity of growth (i.e., growth rate). For example, if subsidies are provided for physical capital aimed at accelerating growth, investment in human capital will decrease by the same amount, and thus, the overall level of social welfare will decline. On the other hand, the stability of growth may be impaired, negatively impacting the poor. And if natural capital is excessively exploited, growth sustainability may be compromised. Therefore, countries that emphasize the quality of growth seek to better address the difficult trade-offs between quality and quantity of growth. Such balance and the potential trade-offs are closely relevant to the subject of this book. Thomas et al. (2000) states that the ideal form of growth is one in which these are appropriately balanced.

The backdrop against which the World Bank Institute prepared this report was probably the increased international debate on poverty reduction. The idea of a comprehensive framework for poverty reduction and the introduction of poverty reduction strategies for heavily indebted countries was adopted in 1999. Thomas et al. (2000) called for a comprehensive framework for the poor to accumulate assets and capabilities, which includes structural, societal and environmental aspects in the growth process. At that time, the World Bank was promoting a methodology called the Comprehensive Development Framework, which incorporated these ideas. With such efforts underway, it seemed natural that a report would be compiled that focused on aspects other than income and attempted to discuss economic growth in a comprehensive manner.

However, despite this initiative, the approach of discussing such quality of growth across a combination of various fields did not gain international traction. The discussion of Thomas et al. (2000) on balancing growth, quality and quantity—and the need for an appropriate balance between the two—remains valid today. Identifying the factors that comprise quality of growth, understanding the relationship between these factors, and examining how each relates to income growth can provide a starting point for understanding the kind of growth that will maximize people's welfare and wellbeing. In addition, it will also be necessary to measure income and other aspects of growth in an integrated way.

### 2.1.2 The Emergence of the Concept of Quality Growth

In 2010, APEC presented the concept of quality growth as a desirable form of growth for the first time. APEC was established in 1989 as a forum for regional economic cooperation, and each year, the leaders of the member countries gather to discuss their growth and development. At the summit meeting in Yokohama in November 2010, a growth strategy for the post-GFC era was agreed upon (APEC 2010b). In the leadup to this, at the APEC Growth Strategy High-Level Policy Round Table held in August, the statement "Toward Higher Quality Growth for APEC" was issued (APEC 2010a). This statement defined quality growth as growth incorporating the five attributes introduced in the next section. APEC has continued to promote the realization of quality growth in subsequent meetings. At the 2015 APEC Summit Meeting, the "APEC Strategy for Strengthening Quality Growth" was announced as an annex to the Leader's Declaration, and an action plan for quality growth was drawn up (APEC 2015a, 2015b). In 2020, an evaluation report on the progress of quality growth in the Asia-Pacific region was prepared (APEC 2020). Thus, there is a certain degree of shared understanding among APEC member countries regarding the kind of growth to pursue. However, this understanding is not widely known among the citizens of member countries beyond the APEC Forum, nor does it serve as the basis for policy in each country. Moreover, there is almost no discussion of quality growth in international forums outside of APEC.[1]

Of the individual countries, Japan has defined the quality growth that it should aim for in its national documents. In February 2015, the Japanese government revised its Official Development Assistance Charter after a 12-year interval. The new charter was renamed the Development Cooperation Charter, and its contents reflected the changes taking place in the international community and development cooperation over the past decade. Quality growth was identified as a form of growth that could achieve poverty eradication. The Japanese government's reference to quality growth may have been influenced by APEC, as quality growth was first mentioned at a summit in Yokohama. At the same time, the expression "quality" was being used as a keyword in the government discussion regarding development cooperation, such as quality infrastructure investment (QII). However, as stated in this charter, quality growth was recognized as a vital perspective for promoting development in developing countries in the changing international society of the twenty-first century. What is particularly noteworthy is that quality growth was recognized as a growth approach specifically for developing countries, emerging with the context of development cooperation. This is different from the APEC approach, which covers all countries in the Asia-Pacific region, including developed countries.

In the academic field, Joseph E. Stiglitz is probably the most prominent expert to discuss quality growth. Of Stiglitz's wide-ranging and extensive achievements, inequality and developing country development (including criticism of the Washington Consensus) are the areas attracting a particularly large number of contributions. In addition, he has long led international discussions on indicators that go beyond GDP to represent people's wellbeing. All of these themes are linked to quality growth. For example, in the recent joint publication The Quality of Growth in Africa, quality growth is defined as part of a comprehensive discussion of African growth (Kanbur, Noman, and Stiglitz 2019).

[1] Outside of APEC, there was a discussion of quality growth at the "Summer Davos 2011" of the World Economic Forum (WEF) in Dalian, which included elements of inclusiveness, sustainability and innovation.

### 2.1.3 Three Keywords that Indicate Changes in the Global Society

Why have APEC and Japan started to discuss a new approach to growth? In this regard, the MOFA (2014) report provides a useful reference. It summarizes the discussions of experts prior to the Japanese government's revision of the Official Development Assistance (ODA) Charter to the Development Cooperation Charter in 2015.[2] Referencing the basic recognition of the current international community, the report notes that "We see the increase of income levels in many developing countries, led by emerging countries that are achieving rapid growth." However, it then states that developing countries are also facing new development issues, which are becoming increasingly complex, and thus, their development "cannot be measured by a country's average income level alone." In response to the diversification, complexity and broadening of development issues, three key words—inclusiveness, sustainability, and resilience—are introduced here to describe changes in the international environment, providing a compass for development cooperation. Looking briefly at the meaning of each term, inclusiveness refers to the disparity within countries despite the rise in overall incomes and the existence of vulnerable countries that are left behind for various reasons. The issue of sustainability covers the deterioration of the global environment and the fact that growth cannot be sustained for some reason, such as the middle-income trap. The issue of resilience refers to increasingly severe disasters due to environmental and climate change, food crises, infectious diseases, and terrorism. The following is my brief supplement to each of these three.

Regarding inclusiveness, income inequality in developed countries has generally increased since the 1980s. Income inequality is not just an issue in developing countries but is one of the biggest issues in developed countries as well. The idea that inequality will automatically improve as a result of development (Kuznets' inverted U hypothesis, which I will discuss later) is no longer universally applicable. Various factors, such as changes in business (digitization, the development of AI and automation, the increase in non-regular employment, incentive systems for corporate executives, high salaries for ICT engineers, etc.), and labor shifts across the border due to globalization are widening this gap. These social changes are not just a problem for developed countries but are also the direction in which the modern economy as a whole is moving, so it is inevitable that they will spread to developing countries as well. In this case, every government needs to manage its economy within the social structural changes of inequality. In other words, it has become clear that the problem of income inequality within a country requires a universal policy response.

Regarding sustainability, MOFA (2014) states its goal "to materialize sustainable development in the three areas of economy, society and environment, based

[2] The expert committee consists of eight members and was established to advise the Ministry of Foreign Affairs on how to prepare the Development Cooperation Charter in the process of amending the ODA Charter.

on an awareness of the deterioration of the global environment and the limits of the earth." In other words, in modern society, it is recognized that global warming caused by climate change is hindering future growth, and needless to say, the situation is becoming more serious. Although the global community signed up to the Paris Agreement, which established international targets, at Conference of the Parties (COP) 21 in 2015, a critical concern is that the carbon budget (the amount of carbon dioxide $CO_2$ that can be emitted to keep global warming within acceptable limits) may be used up by 2030. Global warming is a fundamental issue that affects human life through irreversible effects on ecosystems, rising sea levels and more severe weather-related disasters.[3] At the same time, it affects future economies and undermines the growth of future generations.

Regarding resilience, MOFA (2014) states the importance of "building a resilient society against various threats that countries face, such as economic crises, disasters, climate change, and conflicts." In terms of the economy, as seen in the 2007–08 GFC, with globalization, the effects of a single country's economic crisis can spread around the world almost instantaneously. The magnitude of the shocks has also become more serious. Earthquakes that cause a great deal of damage and loss of life, such as the 2004 Indian Ocean earthquake and tsunami and the 2011 Great East Japan Earthquake, have become more frequent. The threat of terrorism has also become more serious, along with the rapid spread of the pandemic around the world. Russia's invasion of Ukraine has led to enormous loss of life and has become a major problem that involves the whole world. Overall, these external shocks are becoming more and more serious. Thus, as demonstrated in the above report, inclusiveness, sustainability, and resilience are key concepts aimed at addressing the most critical issues in the current international environment, while quality growth seeks to achieve growth that responds to these concerns. In modern society, it is not possible to formulate a growth strategy without taking these issues into consideration. This recognition basically applies to the case of APEC, as I will examine in the next section.

## 2.2 Definition and Point of Issues of Quality Growth

Drawing from the above background, the following section provides an overview of how the Japanese government, APEC, and academia define quality growth. It also presents my own perspective as a basis for further discussion.

[3] In many discussions on sustainability, one area of focus is climate change, as a critical factor that will undermine future growth. Climate change is also mentioned in discussions of resilience, where the shocks caused by climate change manifest in various ways, including more severe disasters, desertification, rising sea levels, impacts on agriculture and fisheries, and the spread of infectious diseases. In this book, the long-term impact of global warming on the sustainability of growth is analyzed as a sustainability issue, while the current risks to society are discussed as resilience issues.

### 2.2.1 Japanese Government View

The definition of quality growth by the Japanese government is set out in the Development Cooperation Charter 2015 (hereafter "DCC 2015" to distinguish it from the 2023 revision).[4] Section II (1) Priority Issues establishes that "... growth should not be merely quantitative in nature.... Rather, it should be 'quality growth.' Such growth is inclusive in that the fruits of growth are shared within society as a whole, leaving no one behind. It is sustainable over generations in terms of consideration for, among other aspects, harmony with the environment, sustained socioeconomic growth and addressing global warming. And it is resilient, able to withstand and recover from economic crises, natural disasters and other shocks." (see Box 2A for the full text of this section).

**BOX 2A DCC 2015 II. (1). A**

**A. "Quality growth" and poverty eradication through such growth**

The world's poor population is still large in number, and reducing poverty, especially eradicating absolute poverty, is the most fundamental development challenge. Especially as regards fragile states that have not been able to grasp the opportunities for development for different reasons and as regards people in vulnerable situations, it is important to provide both assistance from a humanitarian point of view and assistance designed to set the development process in motion and overcome vulnerability.

At the same time, in order to resolve the poverty issue in a sustainable manner, it is essential to achieve economic growth through human resources development, infrastructure development and establishment of regulations and institutions, as well as the growth of the private sector enabled by the aforementioned actions, which are aimed at self-reliant development of developing countries. However, such growth should not be merely quantitative in nature, given that some of the countries that have achieved a measure

[4] As this chapter looks at the background to the emergence of quality growth and its definition, I use the expert report for DCC 2015 as the main source of my analysis. The 2023 revision of the Development Cooperation Charter also clearly states that quality growth continues to be a priority policy. Specifically, the relevant section recognizes that quality growth aims to eradicate poverty and that quality growth is still defined as growth that combines inclusiveness, sustainability, and resilience, as in the previous Charter. The revised Charter takes into account changes in the world situation over the eight years since the previous Charter was formulated and expresses the recognition that, in Japan's cooperation efforts to eradicate poverty through quality growth, the strengthening of economic and social self-reliance and resilience, such as food and energy security, and digital and quality infrastructure, have become more important. These items were, in fact, mentioned in the DCC 2015 and are considered to be essential for achieving quality growth. I will explain these in detail in the following chapters, including Chaps. 4 (Resilience and Supply Chains), 6 (Digital Transformation), and 7 (Infrastructure).

of economic growth face challenges such as widening disparities, sustainability issues, inadequate social development, and political and economic instability. Rather,, it should be "quality growth." Such growth is inclusive in that the fruits of growth are shared within society as a whole leaving no one behind. It is sustainable over generations in terms of consideration to, among other aspects, harmony with the environment, sustained socioeconomic growth and addressing global warming. And it is resilient, able to withstand and recover from economic crises, natural disasters and other shocks. These are some of the challenges Japan has tackled in its postwar history. Japan will take advantage of its own experience, expertise and technology as well as lessons learned in order to provide assistance to realize "quality growth" and poverty eradication through such growth.

From this perspective, Japan will provide assistance necessary to secure the foundations and the driving force for economic growth. Its scope includes: the development of industrial infrastructure and industries through improvements in such areas as infrastructure, finance and trade and investment climate; sustainable cities; introduction of information and communications technology (ICT) and high technology; promotion of science technology and innovation; research and development; economic policy; vocational training and industrial human resources development; employment creation; and the promotion of agriculture, forestry and fisheries that includes the development of food value chains. At the same time, Japan will provide assistance necessary to promote people-centered development that supports basic human life, taking full account of the importance of human and social development. It encompasses health care, safe water and sanitation, food and nutrition, quality education for all, disparity reduction, empowerment of women, culture and sports that brings about spiritual affluence.

Before looking in more detail at each of the three components of inclusive, sustainable and resilient growth that make up quality growth in the following chapters, I would like to raise the following three points in relation to this definition of quality growth.

First, it is essential to note that "reducing poverty…is the most fundamental development challenge," and "it is essential to achieve economic growth" in working toward the solution. In other words, poverty reduction is impossible without economic growth. As mentioned in the previous chapter, this has been empirically demonstrated. The Japanese government has consistently argued that economic growth is necessary to eliminate absolute poverty. This point is emphasized here in the DCC 2015. In the discussion of quality growth, it is easy to get caught up in the words of inclusiveness, sustainability and resilience, and forget the original focus on growth, even though this definition clearly states that economic growth is essential for poverty reduction. The idea that economic growth is the starting point of poverty reduction is no different from saying that increased investment and employment—as well as improved technology and productivity—are the starting points of poverty reduction. From this viewpoint, the DCC 2015 refers to improvements in the investment environment, human resource development, innovation, and research, as well as the development necessary to "secure the foundation and driving force of economic growth." To promote this, economic policies and systems are also important. New industries are born when innovation occurs, and the economy and society are transformed. Industrial growth increases employment, with economic and social transformation promoted by human resources development. If this process continues, developing countries will be able to sustain economic growth.

The second point concerns the relationship between economic growth and the three key concepts: inclusiveness, sustainability, and resilience. Notably, the DCC 2015 states that "... growth should not be merely quantitative." This phrasing suggests that prioritizing inclusiveness, sustainability, and resilience might limit growth in production. In other words, if these three could be enhanced without reducing the growth rate, it would be fairly straightforward for policymakers to pursue growth, inclusiveness, sustainability, and resilience independently. There would be no need for such a debate on quality growth in the first place. This view is shared by Thomas et al. (2000), which emphasized the need for an appropriate balance between the quality and quantity of growth. The relationship between economic growth and the three key concepts is complex and subtle. In some cases, it is unclear whether the relationship represents a trade-off or is complementary. This ambiguity is one of my underlying concerns in this book, and thus, I will revisit it frequently in the following chapters.

Here are some introductory questions related to this. In terms of inclusiveness, opinions differ on the relationship between income inequality and economic growth. Some argue that greater inequality promotes growth, while others suggest that it depresses growth. In terms of sustainability, measures to curb GHG emissions—though absolutely necessary in the long term—will reduce productivity and depress economic growth in the short term because they increase the cost of production without increasing output. Regarding resilience, expenditure on preparing for external shocks increases the resilience of society; however, disaster prevention investment and securing fiscal space in case of emergency also sacrifice short-term production growth. When there is a trade-off between the three key concepts and growth, it is important to consider how much of each should be pursued and how to balance them with growth. Understanding this relationship for each is the starting point for unlocking the concept of quality growth.

Thirdly, the three key concepts do not work independently but rather influence each other. For example, climate change and natural disasters are closely related, and they both affect economic growth as external risks. Disasters, infectious diseases, terrorism and economic shocks are not only issues of resilience but also inclusiveness, as they disproportionately affect the poor. It is therefore essential to understand how each of these three concepts interact. Moreover, this interconnectedness highlights the need to measure overall improvements in people's welfare, especially in situations where these relationships are unclear.

### 2.2.2 APEC's View

APEC defines quality growth as growth consisting of five elements of balanced growth, inclusive growth, sustainable growth, innovative growth, and secure growth. An overview of each is provided in Table 2.1.

Of the five elements, inclusive, sustainable, and secure growth are fundamentally aligned with Japan's DCC 2015, with the main difference being that APEC has added balanced growth and innovative growth. Balanced growth is comprised of three components: growth across member states, growth within economies, and growth through infrastructure development. The first, the correction of imbalance between member countries, is a perspective that is unique to regional cooperation organizations. The second, domestic balance, is particularly relevant to this book. Domestic balance closely relates to macroeconomics, such as domestic structural adjustments aimed at promoting investment and employment. Examples include the development of competitive markets and financial systems, along with the expansion of domestic demand, which in turn promotes poverty reduction and inclusive growth. While domestic balance does not explicitly refer to the relationship between short-and long-term growth or trade-offs between inclusiveness/ sustainability and growth rates, the emphasis on balance may imply that growth and each of the three elements can be maximized. The balanced growth advocated by APEC provides a perspective that is particularly indispensable in the formulation and implementation of policies, aspects not covered in the DCC 2015. Innovative growth encompasses advancements in emerging fields such as the green economy, ICT, and biotechnology, as well as human resource development. These items are representative examples of driving factors that contribute to economic growth in this era. APEC's focus on innovation-related areas is easier to understand

**Table 2.1** Quality Growth as defined by APEC

| Element | Specific strategies |
|---|---|
| Balanced growth | Balanced growth within the region and within each country, infrastructure development |
| Inclusive growth | Employment creation and promotion of human resource development, promotion of small and medium enterprises, financial inclusion, strengthening of social welfare and resilience through safety nets etc., creation of new opportunities for women/the elderly/vulnerable groups, promotion of tourism |
| Sustainable growth | Energy security and efficiency and low-carbon policies, low-carbon energy development, promotion of environmental services, green job education and training and green industrial development, sustainable agriculture and natural resource development |
| Innovative growth | Building a smart society through ICT, digital prosperity, professional human resource development, dialogue and information sharing on innovation policies, intellectual property systems, cooperation on standards, life science innovation |
| Secure growth | Protecting economic systems, disaster preparedness and infectious disease, food security, combat corruption |

*Source* APEC (2010b), summarized by Author

as a growth strategy. By continuing these innovations, growth will be sustained over the long term.

### 2.2.3 Academia's Focus

As Kanbur, Noman, and Stiglitz (2019) state, concerns about the quality of growth include the following: "(1) the distribution of income gains from growth; (2) the translation of economic growth into non-income dimensions of wellbeing, such as employment, health, education, and security; (3) the structural transformation of the economy, so that the sources of growth and employment are diversified away from dependence on low-productivity primary commodities and informal activities toward modern manufacturing (including 'industrialized agriculture') and services; (4) management of the urbanization process so that it enhances the quality of life; and (5) environmental sustainability." Here, as with APEC and Japan, inclusiveness and sustainability (environment) are presented as elements of desirable growth, emphasizing that desirable growth can be achieved by economic transformation and realized through non-income wealth. Transformation is related to the mechanisms of growth, and the non-income dimension is related to the perspective that "growth should not be merely quantitative" in the DCC 2015. In that light, I can say that this definition is broadly consistent with that of APEC and Japan.

Based on the above discussion, the relationship between quality growth and modern society is summarized in Fig. 2.1,[5] which highlights the key features of quality growth: (1) aiming for high growth, (2) promoting socioeconomic transformation through innovation, institutions and human resource development as sources of growth, and (3) pursuing simultaneously improvement in inclusiveness, sustainability and resilience, even if the short-term effects of these factors on growth are uncertain.

### 2.2.4 Discussion Points of Quality Growth and Subsequent Chapters

I would like to conclude this chapter by highlighting some key considerations for discussing the various aspects of quality growth. First, the concepts of growth, inclusiveness, sustainability and resilience do not necessarily unfold in the same time frame. For example, poverty reduction is an urgent issue that requires immediate action. To that end, it is desirable to expand the economy in the short term

[5] As mentioned above, the sustainability of growth involves two different aspects: maintaining the natural environment, which is a prerequisite for economic activity, and fostering economic and social mechanisms that bring about innovation. The latter increases the growth rate and is related to production factors, which is why it is shown separately from sustainability in Fig. 2.1. This point will be discussed in detail in Chap. 6.

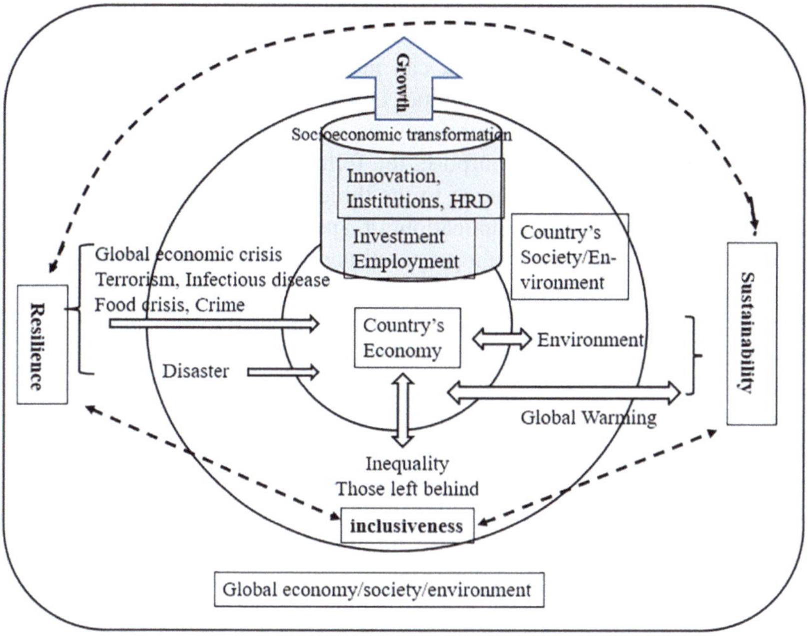


**Fig. 2.1** Relationship between contemporary socio-economic issues and quality growth (*Source* Author)

and increase overall social welfare. This is somewhat distinct from being growth-sustaining. For example, resource-rich countries can increase their incomes by exploiting their natural resources in the short run. However, this does not guarantee future prosperity. Sustained growth means a continuous transformation of the economy and society over some decades, and the key challenge for sustained growth is to build a foundation that will make this possible. In other words, it is a discussion that takes a long-term perspective.

Inclusiveness is a discussion that requires both a short-term and long-term perspective. Large inequalities reduce the overall welfare of the current generation and may have a negative impact on long-term growth in terms of human capital formation. For sustainability, $CO_2$ emissions remain in the atmosphere for a very long time, leading to negative impacts for future generations. Resilience, on the other hand, addresses uncertainty. Building resilience to external shocks often involves sacrificing an increase in short-term production to mitigate the effects of potential future shocks. Neither APEC nor the DCC 2015 necessarily take this difference in time frames into account. However, quality growth does seek to account for such differences. When searching for the optimal policy mix within limited resources, these differences in time frames make analysis more difficult and complex. I mentioned the importance of balance and the need to view all changes in an integrated way. However, it can be challenging to compare a specific change across different time frames, and confirming the results of long-term events can also be difficult. On the one hand, we can theoretically organize the relationship between growth and each of the three elements to better estimate the impact of policies—and develop indicators that can measure any changes in an integrated way. On the other hand, we can conduct empirical analysis and learn from past experiences. As times change, there may be situations where past examples no longer apply; however, for this purpose, the following chapters will introduce the relevant theory and evidence relating to the three elements and growth.

The second factor is the application of specific strategies and methodologies. Numerous policies have been proposed and implemented to address various national issues, including those related to growth, inclusiveness, sustainability, and resilience. Even so, significant room for improvement remains, alongside growing challenges—such as the middle-income trap, vulnerable countries being left behind and conflict-affected countries—for which effective solutions are still being sought. For each of these areas, improved policies will be required both now and in the future. Many current policies remain effective, and quality growth does not imply a completely new approach. However, quality growth policies require mainstreaming these three elements across sectors, maximizing wellbeing that includes factors other than income, and ensuring that growth opportunities for future generations are not compromised. A new policy framework is needed to achieve this, and it will be necessary to apply it to individual projects. In this book, I discuss infrastructure in Chap. 8 as a specific example of policy by sector, and propose an overarching policy framework in Chap. 9.

The third factor is related to the measurement of quality growth. In the following chapters, I use GDP to consider the relationship between factors such as growth and inclusiveness. This is because I first want to confirm how non-income aspects that cannot be measured in the market, such as inclusiveness, are related to growth measured by GDP. People's happiness and wellbeing are not determined by income alone and the issue of time frame differences mentioned above is also relevant to this measurement. I explore two issues: the scale of the current level of welfare and the sustainability of future growth. While there is a limit to what I can present in this book, I explore this point in detail in Chap. 9, where I present a draft version of the measurement proposal starting from GDP and integrating non-market elements.

The fourth consideration is whether quality growth is a theory of growth that only applies to developing countries, or whether it also includes developed countries. The APEC argument clearly includes developed countries. On the other hand, the arguments presented by the Japanese government and academia appear to be based on the premise of growth in developing countries (although it is not explicitly stated that this does not apply to developed countries). I believe that the concept of quality growth can be applied universally. The main reason for this is that growth, inclusiveness, sustainability and resilience are factors that are deeply involved in the welfare of people and the eradication of poverty in every country. In addition, as argued in Chap. 1, the quality growth concept provides an answer to the global concerns of developed countries, including the SDGs and the emphasis on well-being. This serves as a crucial guideline for developed countries to consider the nature of growth in countries that have achieved high-income levels. At the same time, it is also essential for emerging and developing countries to create their own long-term vision. Of course, the priorities will differ depending on the stage of development, the political and economic situation of the country, and differences in endowments. However, the principle of making growth, inclusion, sustainability, and resilience the main elements of improving welfare and eradicating poverty, and maximizing (and measuring) these, is something that can be applied to any country.

This chapter is based on Hirota (2016) with substantial additions.

## References


Asia-Pacific Economic Cooperation (APEC). 2010a. The APEC Growth Strategy High-Level Policy Round Table Toward Higher Quality Growth for APEC, Beppu, Japan, August 7–8, 2010. https://www5.cao.go.jp/keizai1/kokusai-keizai/apec/pdf/201008_en.pdf.

Asia-Pacific Economic Cooperation (APEC). 2010b. The APEC Leaders' Growth Strategy, Yokohama, Japan, November 14, 2010. http://www.apec.org/Meeting-Papers/Leaders-Declarations/2010/2010_aelm/growth-strategy.aspx.

Asia-Pacific Economic Cooperation (APEC). 2015a. Annex A: APEC Strategy for Strengthening Quality Growth. https://www.apec.org/meeting-papers/leaders-declarations/2015/2015_aelm/2015_annex-a.

Asia-Pacific Economic Cooperation (APEC). 2015b. Annex to the APEC Strategy for Strengthening Quality Growth. http://www.apec.org/~/media/Files/LeadersDeclarations/2015/SQG.pdf. Accessed August 30, 2023.

Asia-Pacific Economic Cooperation (APEC). Policy Support Unit. 2020. APEC Strategy for Strengthening Quality Growth: Final Assessment Report. APEC.

Hirota, Koki. 2016. "Shitsu no takai seichō to kaihatsu kyōryoku taikō" [Quality Growth and Development Cooperation Charter]. Literature Review No. 1, 1-11, JICA Ogata Sadako Research Institute for Peace and Development.

Kanbur, Ravi, Akbar Noman, and Joseph E. Stiglitz. 2019. "Introduction." in *The Quality of Growth in Africa*, eds. Kanbur, Ravi, Akbar Noman, and Joseph E. Stiglitz. Columbia University Press.

Ministry of Foreign Affairs, Japan (MOFA). 2014. "ODA taikō no minaoshi ni kansuru yūshikisha kondankai hōkokusho" [Report of the Advisory Panel on the Review of the ODA Charter, June 2014]. http://www.mofa.go.jp/mofaj/gaiko/oda/about/kaikaku/taikou_minaoshi/files/yusikisya_report.pdf.

Thomas, Vinod, Mansoor Dailami, Ashok Dhareshwar, Daniel Kaufman, Nalin Kishor, Ramón López, and Yan Wang. 2000. *The Quality of Growth*. Oxford University Press.


**Koki Hirota** earned his B.A. in Economics from the University of Tokyo and holds a Ph.D. in Economics from Saitama University in Japan. His professional career spans several prominent roles in international development finance and policy, including Chief Economist, Director General of Operation and Strategy Department, and Director General of Southeast Asia and Pacific Department at the Japan International Cooperation Agency (JICA), and Chief Representative in Jakarta for Japan Bank for International Cooperation and in Hanoi for the Overseas Economic Cooperation Fund. In academia, he was a Professor at the Graduate School of Humanities and Social Sciences at Saitama University and a Visiting Fellow at the JICA Ogata Sadako Research Institute for Peace and Development. His recent publications include *Challenges in Fiscal and*

*Monetary Policies in Mongolia* (co-edited, Springer, 2023) and *Addressing Social Infrastructure Needs in Asia: Towards a Pandemic Resilient Society* (co-edited, JICA, August 2025).

# Growth and Inclusiveness

# 3

Koki Hirota

## 3.1 Definition and Issues of Inclusive Growth

This chapter focuses on inclusiveness, one of the pillars of quality growth, and reviews the discussions surrounding the concept and its relationship with growth. It begins by defining inclusive growth and tracing the evolution of this concept. I argue that inclusiveness of growth addresses two key issues: structural inequality with regard to vulnerable people and income inequality generally seen in any society. Subsequently, I consider the relationship between economic growth and inequality, particularly for vulnerable groups in society who are most susceptible to structural disadvantages. Furthermore, I examine debates on the relationship between economic growth and income inequality and conclude with a review of policies aimed at improving inclusiveness.

### 3.1.1 From Pro-Poor Growth to Inclusive Growth

The term "inclusive growth" has been used frequently since the mid-2000s to refer to the type of growth that adequately considers the needs of the poor. Until that time, terms such as "pro-poor growth" and "broad-based growth" were used. Pro-poor growth focuses on increasing the share of growth benefits directed toward the poor (with greater emphasis on the results), while broad-based growth aims to ensure access to opportunities for broader segments of the population (with an emphasis on the process) (Klasen 2010). Both ideas are focused exclusively on the poor rather than on society as a whole. The notion of pro-poor growth lacks a

K. Hirota (✉)
Tokyo, Japan



K. Hirota (ed.), *Introduction to Quality Growth*,
https://doi.org/10.1007/978-981-95-6220-6_3

strict definition, with international organizations providing their own ideas in their literature or websites.

The term "inclusive growth" has evolved to encompass a wider range of concerns than pro-poor growth. The World Bank notes in its policy research working paper that while pro-poor growth focuses solely on the welfare of the poor, inclusive growth seeks to address opportunities for the majority of workers, the poor, and the middle class (Ianchovichina and Lundstrom 2009). The Asian Development Bank (ADB) provides a similar definition (Ali 2007).[1] While pro-poor growth centers solely on the poor, inclusive growth considers the welfare of the entire population. Accordingly, domestic income inequality, i.e., comparisons with the income levels of the wealthy, has naturally become a point of increased focus. The continued widening of inequality in developed nations since the 1980s may have contributed to this shift in focus. Another reason for the change in terminology—whereby inclusive growth has replaced pro-poor growth as the most commonly used term—relates to the differing areas of focus of the two terms: pro-poor growth is limited to the poor, while inclusive growth covers the whole of society. Additionally, there is an increased awareness of (1) the varying impacts of growth across regions and population groups (e.g., women and ethnic minorities) and (2) the importance of involving all people in the process of growth (Ranieri and Ramos 2013).

### 3.1.2 How Is Inclusive Growth Defined?

Inclusive growth is a perspective that focuses on poverty and inequality, but it also places importance on the issue of vulnerability. For example, the United Nations Development Programme (UNDP) defines inclusive growth as a process that has different impacts on various vulnerable groups, rather than merely focusing on income distribution (Ranieri and Ramos 2013). The definition of inclusive growth reflects an idealized form of growth—or the development of a norm—and, as such, it serves as a kind of policy argument. Because of this, many papers have been published by the international organizations tasked with preparing guidance on desirable policy directions. The following sections examine discussions in several documents published by the World Bank, ADB, UNDP, and the OECD.

The World Bank currently uses the term "shared prosperity" in relation to inclusiveness. However, as mentioned in the previous chapter, the World Bank has long advocated for inclusive development, a goal that has not fundamentally changed. The World Bank's approach to inclusive growth can be found on its website or

[1] Ali (2007) states that pro-poor growth refers to growth that benefits the poor more than other groups in its aim for growth, while inclusive growth is aimed at providing greater opportunities to the entire population by bolstering the safety net for the poor. Another example is the IMF working paper, stating that pro-poor growth is a form of growth that reduces poverty, and inclusive growth is a form of growth that does not exacerbate inequality (Balakrishnan et al. 2013).

elsewhere before the term "shared prosperity" became commonly used. One document that is still accessible is a paper by Ianchovichina and Lundstrom (2009). This was a background paper that helped to disseminate the idea of inclusive growth. It argues that inclusive growth refers to both the pace and the distribution of growth, with the former being particularly important. In other words, the paper argues that absolute growth was more important for poverty reduction than growth relative to different income groups, especially from a pro-poor perspective.

In justifying this, the paper refers to an empirical study that shows income growth accounts for 70% of short-term and 97% of long-term poverty reduction. Next, it states that in order for growth to be sustained over the long term, it is necessary to involve a wider range of fields and have the majority of workers participate. To this end, it stresses the importance of micro- and macro-economic policies to remove constraints, and in particular, it emphasizes the importance of improving productivity and developing human resources on the supply side as well as ensuring equal opportunities in employment on the demand side. In specific terms, it calls for improved market accessibility, a fair business environment, and other supportive measures. Furthermore, it states that no countries have achieved growth without economic transformation and that economic growth cannot be sustained over the long term without realizing structural reform. In the paper, inclusive growth is used to consider the question of how to involve vulnerable groups in this process. The following three characteristic points are addressed. First, it emphasizes the importance of high rates of growth. Citing empirical studies that demonstrate how income growth, resulting from economic growth, reduces poverty more effectively than changes in income distribution, it stresses that inclusive growth is a concept that is distinct from pro-poor growth. Second, it argues that job creation is more important than income redistribution from a long-term perspective. Third, regarding inequality, it states that while the relationship between economic growth and income inequality remains unclear, some policies—such as controlling inflation and improving education and infrastructure—have simultaneous effects in driving growth and reducing inequality. Notably, it does not explicitly mention vulnerable groups here.

Since 2016, the World Bank has published a flagship report every two years entitled *Poverty and Shared Prosperity*. Shared prosperity is a measure of inclusiveness—specifically, the difference between the growth rate of the bottom 40% of the income distribution and the overall growth rate. This is a relative perspective on poverty reduction. As shared prosperity is one of the goals set by the World Bank, alongside the eradication of absolute poverty, it seems that while the importance of eradicating absolute poverty through growth is still recognized, there is now a stronger awareness of the issue of inequality in recent years.

The ADB has positioned the promotion of inclusive growth as one of the three pillars of its long-term strategy for 2020 (ADB 2008). Its view on inclusive growth is similar to that of the World Bank. The strategy includes two main points: The first is that high growth expands economic opportunities, and the second is that greater accessibility to economic opportunities ensures members of society can participate in and benefit from economic growth. It emphasizes the importance of human resource development for disadvantaged people, especially through education, access to health care systems, and social security and argues women are the largest group unlikely to benefit from economic growth. It positions equal opportunities for women and their empowerment as fundamental requirements for inclusive growth. Meanwhile, the policy paper published prior to the announcement of its long-term strategy in 2008 noted that domestic inequality is widening in Asian regions. It called for the realization of pro-poor distribution to eradicate absolute poverty by 2020 (Ali 2007).

It also stated that income inequality is linked to unequal access to economic opportunities and that there are two types of inequality: positive inequality, which provides incentives, and negative inequality, which reduces productivity due to lack of equal opportunities. Two important aspects emerge from this perspective. First, inclusive growth appears to be strongly concerned with inequality. This might reflect a regional feature, as distributive considerations have become more important in Asia, where high growth rates are being achieved. Second, it emphasizes the roles of vulnerable people—particularly women—in growth and the extent to which they benefit from growth.

Regarding the UNDP, the International Policy Centre for Inclusive Growth (IPC-IG)—established by the UNDP in 2004 in cooperation with the Government of Brazil—defines inclusive growth as a form of growth that improves levels of poverty and inequality, encompasses all classes rather than focusing solely on the poor in the growth process and includes factors other than income (IPC-IG 2013). In the background paper to the IPC-IG publication, Ranieri and Ramos (2013) reviewed 15 previous studies on inclusive growth and summarized the elements of the definition found in each of them by classifying them into 14 keywords. Of these, reducing inequality was the most frequently mentioned, appearing in 11 studies, followed by poverty reduction (9 studies), economic growth (6 studies), productive employment (5 studies), capability and empowerment (5 studies), equal opportunities (3 studies), and social security (2 studies). The remaining keywords—gender equality, accessibility to infrastructure, targeted policies, sufficient provision of fundamental social services, good governance, removal of obstruction to investments, and benefits of growth—appeared in just one study each. The emphasis on including factors other than income is consistent with the perspective taken throughout this book.

The OECD has been actively publishing research on inequality in recent years, likely reflecting an awareness of the continued widening of inequality in most OECD countries. The OECD defines inclusive growth as a form of growth that improves living standards and shares increased prosperity more evenly across social groups, where inequalities other than income, such as education, health, and employment, are important factors, and where income and opportunity inequality undermine long-term growth (OECD 2014). In addition, the OECD (2014) comprehensively examines the status of inequality, welfare conditions, structural issues, and related policies and systems in OECD member countries. It also argues that aid can play an important role in promoting inclusive growth in vulnerable, developing countries. As the OECD's main focus is on its member countries, it naturally emphasizes inequality more than absolute poverty. The OECD (2014) notes that inequality in income and opportunities impairs long-term growth, as education, health, and employment opportunities are critical growth determinants. It also stresses that unemployment and low-quality jobs have a disproportionately negative effect on specific groups, such as women, immigrants, and young people.

Among other international organizations, the International Monetary Fund (IMF) has been actively publishing research on growth and inequality in the form of working papers and other documents in recent years, analyzing the relationship between inequality and growth, the relationship between economic policy and inequality, and other topics.

### 3.1.3 DCC 2015: Vulnerability and Inequality as Factors of Inclusive Growth

DCC 2015, as mentioned above, states that the eradication of poverty is the most fundamental development challenge, and then goes on to say

> Especially as regards fragile states that have not been able to grasp opportunities for development for different reasons and as regards people in vulnerable situations, it is important to provide both assistance from a humanitarian point of view and assistance designed to set the development process in motion and overcome vulnerability.

Following this, it argues that "… such growth should not be merely quantitative in nature, given that some of the countries that have achieved a measure of economic growth face challenges such as widening disparities, sustainability issues, and inadequate social development … it should be 'quality growth.' Such growth is inclusive in that the fruits of growth are shared within society as a whole, leaving no one left behind." The background report by the experts defines inclusiveness as "… no one is left behind and everyone can benefit from the fruits of development…", and "… as economic growth sometimes widens inequality and may not immediately lead to poverty reduction, sufficient consideration is necessary to ensure that growth is inclusive …" (MOFA 2014; underline added by Author). The above discussion shows that DCC 2015 recognizes that inclusiveness of growth includes two elements, vulnerability and inequality, with a strong relationship between the two—for example, the disabled are more likely to fall into poverty (World Bank 2006). However, it will be easier to understand inclusive growth if we examine and organize these two individually.

### 3.1.4 Prolonged Vulnerability in the Context of Inclusive Growth to Be a Matter of Structural Inequality

Vulnerability refers to the state of being fragile and easily broken and generally describes being susceptible to the negative impacts of external events. As an example, Joseph E. Stiglitz, in his special contribution to the 2014 UNDP Human Development Report (UNDP 2014, 84–85), defines vulnerability as follows: "At its basic level, vulnerability is defined as an exposure to a marked decrease in standard of living." There are various types of shocks involving external risks. Hoogeveen et al. (2005) provide examples such as natural disasters; health risks such as disease, disability, and infectious diseases; risks over the course of the lifecycle; social risks such as crime and terrorism; economic risks including unemployment, political risks, and environmental risks such as pollution. In this book, I address preparedness against such external risks as an issue of resilient growth.

At the same time, Stiglitz also notes that "It is of special concern when it is prolonged, and when standards of living fall below critical thresholds, to the point of deprivation." In other words, prolonged risk means that a situation of structural vulnerability has arisen. When a specific group of people are consistently in such a situation, they should be considered structurally vulnerable. These vulnerable groups are always at a disadvantage for one reason or another and are therefore unable to save money or make other preparations. In this way, structural vulnerabilities can be considered a problem of structural inequality. The report (UNDP 2014, 70) also argues that: "Structural vulnerabilities are often manifested through deep inequalities and widespread poverty…" Stiglitz notes that "One of the biggest contributors to vulnerability … is inequality." Hoogeveen et al. (2005) distinguish between the risk of falling into poverty due to external shocks and the challenges of vulnerable groups who are in a state of poverty over the long term, thus requiring special consideration. I suggest that, in a simplified way, the former is a matter of resilience, and the latter is a matter of inclusiveness, as it is caused and sustained by structural inequality.

The types of vulnerable groups vary depending on the history and culture of each country. UNDP (2014) explains that while vulnerability has traditionally been considered related to external shocks, it is also strongly linked to structural causes. It identifies the poor, informal, socially excluded workers, women, people with disabilities, migrants, minorities, children, the elderly, youth, whole communities and regions (if they face conflict/civil unrest) as vulnerable groups. In many countries, it is commonly observed that individuals with certain characteristics, such as women, people with disabilities, and ethnic minorities, are in structurally unequal situations compared to others. Hoogeveen et al. (2005) also state that vulnerable groups are distinguished from others by observable characteristics. They also list women, ethnic minorities, people with disabilities, orphans, internally displaced people, and the socially secluded as vulnerable groups. These groups are characterized by low income due to inequality, making them more susceptible to external shocks. Such inequalities are often rooted in the historical and cultural background of each society and remain embedded in social structures.

The problem of inequality needs to be examined from two perspectives. Firstly, as mentioned here, structural inequality that is attributable to historical and cultural backgrounds leads to income inequality. Secondly, even without these inequalities, income inequality is inevitable as a result of economic activity. These two aspects should be discussed separately. Considering the former, inequality is caused by the unequal treatment of a specific group due to social systems and conventions. While such discrimination should be eliminated morally and humanely, from a growth perspective, this form of discrimination is also not beneficial for society, as it leads to a loss of human resources over the long term. On the other hand, the latter aspect—the inevitability of income inequality—can generally occur in any market economy, even in environments where structural inequality does not exist. Provided that the efforts and talents of each individual make a difference in promoting economic affluence, income inequality can serve as an incentive for stimulating economic vitality.

It has been historically demonstrated that excessive egalitarianism undermines economic vitality, as shown by the failure of Communism. Moreover, classic economics has also noted the positive aspects of inequality on growth, arguing that, when there is a large gap in income, the overall savings of society increase. As such, income inequality has not universally been denied from a growth perspective. However, if inequality is fixed across generations in a society, it is unlikely that this social structure allows low-income people to freely develop their potential over the long term. In other words, restraining human resources development could have a negative impact on long-term growth. Recent theoretical discussions increasingly emphasize the aspects of inequality that undermine growth. These points will be examined in the latter half of this chapter.

### 3.1.5 Two Essential Issues of Inclusive Growth: Structural Inequality and Income Inequality

Referring to the review of literature by Ranieri and Ramos (2013), the issues of inclusive growth can be classified as shown in Table 3.1. In classification (1) in the table, employment and investment are production factors whose increase accelerates growth. Note that the explanation of quality growth in the DCC 2015 does not include these factors in its discussion of inclusiveness. This is an issue that concerns economic growth in general, and so it will be discussed in more detail in Chap. 6. Classification (2) refers to "inequality of opportunities," regardless of whether these inequalities arise from structural factors or poverty, these differences will cause inequality in the basic opportunities that individuals can obtain in their lives. Regarding (3), this is a problem of distribution and how best to make this adjusted. Income inequality can affect human capital formation in the medium to long term through inequality of opportunity, and in terms of the national economy, it is also directly related to growth through its impact on capital accumulation and demand.

In a society with structural inequality, people in a certain group are unable to realize their full potential abilities through various channels, which in turn impedes the accumulation of human capital. This causes low growth across society as a whole. In societies with substantial income inequality, the poor have limited resources to spend on education and health care, which similarly impedes human capital accumulation, also leading to low growth (Fig. 3.1).

**Table 3.1** Issues of inclusive growth and classification

| Classification | Issued related to inclusive growth |
|---|---|
| (1) Overall economic growth | Employment, investment, investment environment (e.g. infrastructure), absolute poverty |
| (2) Inequality of opportunity | Employment and educational opportunities, gender equality, empowerment, health care services, governance |
| (3) Income inequality | Relative poverty, income redistribution (e.g. social security, taxation) |

*Source* Author

**Fig. 3.1** Channels of inequality's impact on growth (*Source* Author)

Regarding the latter channel, it is important to keep the following two points in mind. First, even in a society where there are many impoverished people due to substantial income inequality, when education and job opportunities are provided on equal terms and mobility across income classes is ensured, income inequality may not necessarily lead to low accumulation of human capital, and thus low growth. However, we must see the reality that some degree of income inequality persists across generations,[2] and even in Japan, we see that parents' income levels make a difference in their children's university entrance rates. Considering a reality like this, it is hard to imagine that, in developing countries, equal opportunity is ensured regardless of income level. Accordingly, it would be necessary to improve income inequality to some extent while pursuing structural equality of opportunity. Second, the impact of income inequality on growth is not limited to the formation of human capital. Income inequality affects the mechanism of economic growth, such as investment and consumption, and it is therefore not only equality of opportunity that affects growth. As I will discuss in more detail in the

[2] For example, the World Bank (2006) argues that the persistence of income inequality over multiple generations can often be measured in terms of intergenerational wage elasticity, citing several research examples across from the US and Europe (e.g., 0.6 in the US, 0.2 in Canada and Finland, 0.57 in the UK). It also shows that, although similar studies are conducted only exceptionally in developing countries due to data limitations, these prevailing studies suggest that mobility is relatively low in developing countries.

following sections, a comprehensive examination of the mechanisms of inequality and growth is needed.

## 3.2 Structural Inequality and Economic Growth

### 3.2.1 Where Does Structural Inequality Come From?

Inequality within a country can be observed in various fields. The World Bank's (2006) *World Development Report* comprehensively addresses the issues of development and inequality, showing that inequality can manifest in multiple areas, such as healthcare, education, and income. These factors eventually interact with each other, perpetuating across generations through political, economic and socio-cultural mechanisms, thereby creating an "inequality trap." As an example of such an interaction, the report refers to Deaton (2003), which suggests that inequality in access to healthcare systems is not primarily caused by income inequality but is instead influenced by inequality in land ownership, women's agency, democratic rights, and other factors. Furthermore, it argues that children's academic results differ considerably depending on their family's wealth, place of residence and parents' educational levels. The report also highlights how unequal competitive environments resulting from inequality of opportunities affect the income individuals can earn through the acquisition of basic knowledge and the use of their abilities.[3] This makes equality of opportunities in education, and health, and employment important pillars of inclusive growth.

So how can equal opportunity be achieved? Currently, income inequalities can be attributed to two sources: structural inequalities rooted in historical, social, and cultural factors, and disparities arising from market economic activities independent of these structural inequalities. Below, I look at the relationship between economic growth rates and structural inequalities by examining their effects on typical vulnerable groups.

### 3.2.2 Gender Inequality and Economic Growth

There have been numerous significant studies on gender, including *The World Development Report* 2012 (World Bank 2012), which comprehensively addresses development and gender equality. The report begins with the statement, "Gender equality is a core development objective in its own right" (p. xx). Achieving gender equality is one of the MDGs, which included realizing gender equality in elementary and secondary education and employment and the number of female parliamentarians (as a proxy variable for agency). In 2015, gender equality was

[3] Following the above-mentioned analysis, World Bank (2006) provides policy proposals aimed at equalization of opportunities, on themes such as human capacity (education, healthcare), social protection, legal and land systems, infrastructure, and market and macroeconomic management.

reaffirmed in the objectives of the SDGs, which are more extensive than those in the MDGs. The SDGs include the targets of abolishing harmful practices, recognizing unpaid work, and encouraging women's participation in decision-making and leadership—all of which are related to structural inequality rooted in history and culture.

Regarding the relationship between gender and economic growth, previous studies conclude that progress in gender equality is positive for growth (e.g., Gonzales et al. 2015; World Bank 2012). These studies share two areas of common ground in their reasoning: (1) the increased entry of women into the labor market, and (2) increased spending on education within the household as a result of increased female incomes. However, there are also empirical analyses suggesting that the impact of gender equality differs depending on the country.[4] The female labor participation rate has been rising year by year. The global rate rose from 50.2 to 51.8% in the period from 1980 to 2008, while the gender income gap narrowed from 32 to 26% (World Bank 2012).[5] Despite these gains, gender inequality persists. Unpaid housework and certain jobs, such as nursing care and caregiving—almost exclusively done by women—and high female labor participation rates in informal sectors serve as barriers preventing women from entering the formal labor market. If gender inequality improves and more women are able to enter the labor market, opportunities for women to demonstrate their abilities will also increase.

In the light of growth theories, any increase in women's participation in the labor market would first increase employment and, second, improve productivity and promote innovation through the realization of women's abilities. Through these channels, gender equality should promote growth. In Japan, where the problems of a declining birth rate and the aging population are pronounced, the creation of a society in which all groups of citizens are dynamically engaged is being promoted. This might be considered the Japanese version of an inclusive growth strategy, and the focus on the active participation of women at the core of this strategy is also consistent with the perspective of quality growth.[6]

---

[4] For example, Amin et al. (2015) found that progress in gender equality was significantly positive for economic growth in poor countries, but not in relatively rich countries.

[5] The World Bank (2012) explains that the female labor participation rate has a U-shaped relationship with income growth in any country, and it has increased over time at all income levels. The reason for the former trend is that female labor participation decreases in low-income families as household income increases, but as they become more affluent, their educational levels rise; thus, they return to work due to postponing marriage and child-rearing leading to a decline in the birth rate. Regarding the latter trend since the 1980s, the rapid increase of women's labor participation rate in Central and South America, Middle East and North Africa, where this rate was particularly low, drove overall growth.

[6] Under the "Plan for Dynamic Engagement of All Citizens" (approved by the Cabinet Office, June 2, 2016), a policy to provide an environment where jobs and child-rearing can be balanced was put forth. For the period from leaving her job (after marriage/childbirth) until returning to work (as child-rearing becomes easier), the female labor participation rate falls. According to the Cabinet Office (2012) (which estimated 3.42 million for this potential job seeker), if these women returned to work, Japan's GDP would increase by about 1.5%.

Another issue is a difference in wages and productivity between men and women that the World Bank (2012) points out. Wage difference is attributable to differences in educational levels and access to economic resources, such as access to credit. It has been pointed out that gender differences in educational fields result in a difference in lifetime earnings. As for productivity difference, there is one study indicating that the estimated gender difference in agricultural harvests may be 20–30%. A narrowing of gender differences in productivity through increased female productivity means an increase in overall productivity, thus promoting growth. Gonzales et al. (2015) state that in low-income countries, improving women's health care and educational opportunities (particularly health) is important, while the impact of women's entry into the labor market is particularly significant in developed economies.

Regarding educational spending within the household, women tend to allocate a larger share of household spending toward education than men, so when women participate in economic activities and increase their income, it encourages their children to go to school (Aquirre et al. 2012). Increased educational spending leads to greater employment and productivity for children in the future and, thus, has a positive impact on economic growth in the same way as the above. The contribution to economic growth through changes in the allocation of household spending is specific to gender inequality, compared to other vulnerable groups.

This is how gender inequality affects economic growth. Aquirre et al. (2012) estimate that raising the female labor participation rate to the same level as men would boost GDP by 5% in the US, 9% in Japan, 12% in the United Arab Emirates (UAE), and 34% in Egypt. Gonzales et al. (2015) also estimate that a 0.1 improvement in the UN gender inequality index would lead to a 1% increase in GDP per capita.

### 3.2.3 Ethnic Minorities and Economic Growth

Ethnic minority groups are especially susceptible to structural inequality. World Bank (2006) gives the example of the Quechua in Ecuador, who were routinely exposed to violence, coercion, and racial discrimination. However, the political balance of power has changed, and indigenous people are now able to participate more fairly in social activities. There are many historical examples like this. Generally speaking, inequality between ethnic groups within a country leads to conflicts, brings about instability, and negatively affects growth. Even so, the conclusions of empirical studies on this relationship vary.

As a research approach, it is common to use growth regression analysis to find the potential impact of ethnic diversity on economic growth, and then consider the reasons for this.[7] In terms of regions, there have been many analyses of Africa due

[7] Growth regression analysis is often used to examine the determinants of economic growth. Barro (1997) analyzed the factors influencing economic growth, including the expansion of political

to its multiple ethnicities and stagnant growth. Research focusing on ethnic groups tends to concentrate on ethnic divisions, and quantitative analysis that clarifies how ethnic differences lead to inequalities in employment and educational opportunities and how this affects growth rates, appears to be a task for the future.

The conclusions of studies examining the relationship between ethnic minorities and economic growth are not uniform. According to the frequently cited study by Easterly and Levine (1997), low growth in Africa is attributable to low enrollment rates, political instability, underdeveloped financial systems, distorted exchange rates, and inadequate infrastructure. Ethnic diversity is related to all of these factors except political instability. The study explains that in countries polarized along ethnic lines, it is more difficult to reach a consensus about public policies and public goods due to active rent-seeking, which can result in adverse effects, as mentioned above. With regards to the relationship with political instability—generally considered to be a factor—they reference empirical studies that show ethnic diversity is unlikely to have any impact.[8] According to Easterly and Levine, 28% of the difference in growth rates between Africa and East Asia from 1960s to 1980s can be explained by ethnic diversity. Similar relationships have been identified in another study that extends the definitions of ethnicity (generally using language differences) to physical characteristics and religions (Alesina et al. 2003).

In contrast, Collier (1998) and Collier and Gunning (1999) argue that whether ethnic diversity has a negative impact on economic growth depends on the political system. Their empirical study shows that if a country is ethnically polarized, it leads to low growth due to the loss of social trust and increased transaction costs, but the magnitude of this impact varies considerably depending on the political system—in democratic countries, most adverse effects are offset.[9] Regarding the relationship between ethnic polarization and violent conflict, the study suggests the risk is highest in countries that are moderately polarized, as in these cases,

rights, as one of the variables that can affect the growth rate. The expansion of political rights is represented by the democracy index, which is hardly affected by ethnic diversity. Burnside and Dollar (1997) published a well-known paper on growth, aid, and institutions, which includes ethnic fractionalization as explanatory variables. Based on empirical results from previous studies, they show that ethnic factors are positively correlated with low growth rates.

[8] The study explained that although nine measures representing political instability, such as assassinations and antigovernment demonstrations, were analyzed, only one (constitutional changes) was found correlated with ethnic diversity. They suggested that, in some countries, ethnic conflicts can coexist with governments that have been successful in suppressing political opposition for many years.

[9] In Collier (2009), ethnic fragmentation (the extent of which is expressed by the number of languages used) is negatively correlated with growth, but when the cross term of ethnic fragmentation and democracy is added, ethnic fragmentation is no longer significantly related to growth, while this cross term itself is significant. In other words, whether or not ethnic division affects economic growth depends on the development of democratic institutions, and in countries with significant ethnic division, the lack of democracy has a significant negative impact on the economy. Bluedorn (2001) shows that the cross term between ethnic polarization and democracy is always positive, which indicates that democracy reduces the negative impact of ethnic polarization on economic growth.

negative economic growth is more likely. Collier (2009) argues that while ethnic diversity may reduce the productivity of public investment, it can simultaneously increase the productivity of private investment, which offsets this negative impact. In countries with high incomes, democracy promotes growth even when there are similarly diverse ethnic groups. In low-income countries, however, it tends not to work this way because there are fewer opportunities to make use of diversity and little space to do so. As a result, they are concerned that democracy reduces political violence only in high-income countries and may have the opposite effect in low-income countries.

In response to these empirical analyses, which suggest that ethnic diversity leads to low growth, Sachs and Warner (1997) conclude that the relationship between ethnic diversity and economic growth is unlikely to be statistically significant. They state that low growth rates in Africa can be mostly accounted for by macroeconomic policies (openness to international markets being the most important factor). Other factors, such as geographical features and climate, also play a role, but most of the growth factors can be explained by these macroeconomic variables, thereby eliminating the need for an "African dummy" variable in the equation. One key finding is that ethnic diversity was not significant in terms of growth rates in the regression analysis. The study also examined whether ethnic diversity has an effect on macroeconomic policies, finding a significant correlation between the openness of the economy and the quality of its institutions. However, when the "ex-colonial" variable was added to the equation, ethnic diversity was no longer statistically significant regarding such policies. The reason for adding "former colony" is that the closed nature of economies may be largely attributable to their colonial history. Accordingly, the study does not support the idea that ethnic diversity leads to low growth.

As such, when reviewing previous studies, it is difficult to say that a clear conclusion has been reached regarding whether ethnic diversity is negatively related to economic growth. Given that ethnic diversity alone does not have a clear effect on economic growth, how does structural inequality between ethnic groups affect economic growth? As previously mentioned, further analysis of this question may require micro-level country or case analysis. In theory, economic growth for a country is promoted over the long term if inequalities in education, healthcare and employment are improved. It should be noted that inequality of political power and income inequality often occur together. Easterly and Levine (1997) point out that ethnic diversity leads to rent-seeking and inefficient transaction costs, which means that public goods may not be provided adequately. It is not difficult to imagine that inequality in political power between ethnic groups may underlie such behavior. Alesina et al. (2012) argue that the problem is not ethnic polarization, but it is instead the income gap between ethnic groups that poses issues for economic development. They note a strong negative correlation between income inequality among different ethnic groups and GDP per capita.[10] While the reasons behind the occurrence of income gaps may be specific to ethnic issues, I can consider the impact of the resulting income inequality on economic growth to be a general theoretical issue of the relationship between the two. I will examine this point in Sect. 3.3.

### 3.2.4 Other Vulnerable Groups and Economic Growth

Although there is no definition of who is exposed to the risk of structural inequality, it is evident that there are many other groupings besides women and ethnic minorities. Hoogeveen et al. (2005) list various groups—such as orphans, the elderly, internally displaced people, landless laborers, people with disabilities, people engaging in specific jobs, sex workers, the socially secluded (e.g., HIV patients) and slum residents—as vulnerable groups. Regional inequalities in economic opportunities can also lead to income gaps. Since people have no choice about where they are born, it is appropriate to include regional inequalities within the broader category of structural inequality. The challenges for vulnerable groups, with the exception of regional inequality, are generally discussed from ethical and moral perspectives in terms of social policy and rarely considered in relation to growth rates. From a growth theory viewpoint, production could expand if the employment and productivity of these groups improved and could expand further if their access to education and health services also improved. For example, public support for employment can be justified if its overall economic effects exceed the cost of such policies.

Lastly, regional inequalities can be widely observed in both developed and developing countries. It should be noted that regional inequalities tend to appear in combination with other forms of inequality. The World Bank (2006) points out that, in most cases, the backdrop of regional inequality is related to long-standing inequalities of political power, not just the natural endowment or access to markets. Moreover, it argues that when historically marginalized ethnic, racial, or social groups are concentrated in specific regions, intergroup inequalities often manifest as regional inequalities. In many cases, ethnic minorities live in remote areas, which means inequality increases for both geographical reasons (poor access to markets) and inferior political power due to ethnicity. The World Bank (2006) cites fiscal incentives, public spending, improved labor mobility, and fair agency between groups as policy interventions that can change inter-regional relationships.

[10] Generally speaking, an ethnic group who are in the majority is thought to hold greater economic power, but there are also cases in which ethnic minority groups have greater economic power, as can be seen in communities of overseas Chinese in parts of Southeast Asia, for example.

## 3.3 Inequality and Economic Growth

The rate of increase in individual incomes as a result of a country's economic growth is not uniform, differing from person to person, so growth inevitably changes the situation of income inequality. Consequently, the revised level of income inequality may affect subsequent economic growth (see Chap. 1). These two factors repeat the cycle of growth → inequality → growth, with influencing each other. Combined, the sum of these factors determines the growth rate and inequality. The relationship between income inequality and economic growth has been the subject of a large volume of studies, and therefore, I am only able to introduce a small part of the literature. This section focuses on three questions: firstly, how does income inequality change with economic growth, as represented by the Kuznets' Inverted U-hypothesis? Secondly, how do income inequalities emerge and evolve? And thirdly, how is the impact of income inequality on economic growth? The first question concerns the causal relationship by which economic activities brought about growth and thereby increased the incomes of some groups in particular. More directly, this relates to changes in the economic structure and the relationship between institutions and inequality. The third question addresses whether income inequality influences economic growth as an explanatory variable, and is therefore completely different in nature from the first question. Discussions on the inclusiveness of growth tend to focus on the first perspective, but in order to consider quality growth, it is also essential to take into account the impact of inequality on growth. In other words, quality growth is a concept that takes both of these into account.

### 3.3.1 Changes in Income Inequality Resulting from Economic Growth

Kuznets' Inverted U-Curve hypothesis—commonly included in development economics textbooks—is the most well-known and widely cited theory concerning the relationship between growth and income inequality. The theory suggests that income inequality initially widens as the economy develops but begins to decrease beyond a certain threshold. Kuznets identified a clear trend that, when looking at changes in pretax income since the 1880s in the US, the United Kingdom (UK) and Germany, income inequality began to narrow in the 1920s after initially widening. He attributed this shift to the movement of workers from the agricultural sector, where income per capita was relatively low, to the non-agricultural sector, with higher incomes as these countries developed. This labor migration initially increases income, so the income gap between workers remaining in the agricultural sector and those in other sectors widens, but as the amount of surplus labor decreases and rates of return equalize across sectors, this gap later narrows.

Kuznets explains this mechanism with a model that uses differences in per capita income between two sectors, changes in labor share across two sectors, and the degree of income inequality within each sector as indicators.[11] Kuznets (1955) noted that data constraints limited the empirical evidence to only around 5%, with the remaining 95% comprising inference based on his optimist assessment that this is what the data ultimately would show. Nevertheless, his findings have had substantial impacts on subsequent research. Furthermore, this hypothesis also formed the basis of the trickle-down theory, whereby economic benefits are assumed to automatically spread throughout the economy if a country as a whole grows. The idea of trickle-down has long influenced development discussions and policies.

Whether Kuznets' Inverted U-Curve accurately reflects real-world economic development has yet to be determined. The theory raises two questions: why the pattern appears and whether development in developing countries has actually followed the inverse U-curve shape.

On the first point, Kuznets refers to labor migration across sectors. This argument was powerful, and in subsequent literature that cites Kuznets' Inverted U-Curve, cross-sectoral labor migration has been recognized as a factor that causes such change. However, this explanation has not always been supported by empirical evidence. Williamson (1991) focused on relative labor compensation as a potential cause of the inverted U-curve and showed that this pattern applies fairly well to actual conditions, according to cross-sectional data. Moreover, the degree of income inequality in developed countries after the First World War was no different from that in the most unequal economies among today's emerging countries, such as Brazil. Given this, and by reviewing the growth history of the US and UK, he attributes changes in income inequality to changes in wage structures, showing that in times of widening inequality, the following factors can be observed: (1) technological development in labor-intensive sectors and the resultant uneven rise in productivity between sectors, (2) delays in the deepening of labor skills, (3) increases in birth rates, and (4) increases in foreign immigrants. Such changes have kept the wages of unskilled laborers relatively low. On the other hand, in the phase of narrowing income inequality, he points out that there was labor-neutral or labor-intensive technological progress in the service and agricultural sectors and the decline of the population growth rate.[12]

[11] Kuznets (1955) makes two points about the dynamics behind the widening of inequality that occurs in the process of economic growth. The first concerns the role of savings. He states that, as in the real world, savings are held mostly by the wealthy, and income from these savings leads to widened inequality. Second, income distribution is more unequal in urban areas than in rural agricultural areas, which indicates that inequality accelerates as urban migration progresses. Based on this, he attempts to explain the change in inequality that results from economic growth using a labor migration model. As for developing countries, he cited the examples of India, Sri Lanka, and Puerto Rico and points out the possibility that inequality would continue to widen as their economies grow.

[12] Williamson (1991) argues that asset inequalities are another independent factor that can cause income inequality, but they are not decisive. This stands in contrast with Piketty (2013), who focuses on the role of assets in causing inequality. Regarding capital, which is another production factor, Williamson argues that the impact of capital on inequality is complex and varies depending on the country. As capital is complementary to skills and a substitute for non-skilled labor, an

With regard to the second point, some studies support the inverted U-curve hypothesis, while other empirical analyses do not. Referencing studies that support this hypothesis, Williamson (1991) argues that income inequality does indeed narrow as per capita income increases, especially at higher economic development stages.[13] Barro (2008) adds that the inverse U-curve has been confirmed through empirical analyses and that income inequality is estimated to change from widening to narrowing at a threshold income level of United States Dollar (USD) 3,050.[14] However, in recent years, income inequality has been increasing again after following the inverted U-curve pattern, at least in developed countries, so it has become clear that a simple inverted U-curve hypothesis does not apply to actual trends. For example, looking at the trends in US economic development and inequality, an inverted U-curve appears until about 1980, but inequality has clearly been widening since then (Lindert 1998; Cabinet Office 2007). Empirical studies on developing countries also demonstrate cases where the inverted U-curve does not apply. Bruno et al. (1996) found that studies from the 1970s supporting the inverted U-curve did not consider national differences, which led to misleading conclusions. They argued that analyses using panel data do not support the inverted U-curve hypothesis.[15] In their reputable textbook on development economics, Todaro and Smith (2003) argue that there is no clear relationship between growth and income distribution and point out that few development economists believe the inverted U-shape curve to be inevitable, citing examples of developing countries where the income growth of the poorest 40% of the population was higher than the growth of gross national product (GNP) per capita (Sri Lanka in the 1960s, Costa Rica, El Salvador, etc.). They note that since there are no clear trends of changes in the Gini coefficient in the development process in many developing countries, the degree of inequality is probably more of an unchanging part of the socioeconomic structure of each country.

Regarding changes in inequality after the 1980s, Milanovic (2016) argues that changes in inequality in developed countries since the 1980s should really be

increase in capital will widen income inequality. However, it also causes a decline in overall compensation in society as a whole, so it is unclear how overall income distribution will be affected, according to Williamson.

[13] Simultaneously, Williamson (1991) notes the difference between the estimated curve of inequality and its actual situation is greatest at the low- to middle-income stages. He states that this relationship is weak because the starting point of income inequality assigned to each developing country in history varies significantly. This implies that some developing countries may avoid a widening of inequality at the initial growth stage.

[14] This refers to the income level of the tipping point as calculated when the regional dummy is included as an explanatory variable. If the regional dummy is excluded, this would be USD 1,920 (2000 price). Both regressions show that there is a significant positive correlation with GDP per capita and a significant negative correlation to the square of GDP per capita.

[15] Bruno et al. (1996) examined the trend in economic growth and income inequality in 45 countries between 1947 and 1993 and found that only 7% of the variance in the Gini coefficient was due to time series effects, with the remaining 92% explained by differences between countries.

thought of as a "second wave," while accepting Kuznets' hypothesis as an explanation for historical changes up to the end of the 1970s. He states that the earlier phase of Kuznets' hypothesis—up until the early 1970s—can be attributed to labor migration from agriculture to manufacturing. In the second wave, however, changes in inequality can be attributed to labor migration from manufacturing to the service sector. Milanovic explains that the reason for this transformation is the technological change and the replacement of labor by capital. In the latter case, inequality has widened as the returns for capital owners have increased due to skill-oriented technological progress and globalization, with globalization a factor behind these changes in inequality.

Milanovic (2012) instead proposes an "Elephant Curve," which suggests that changes in inequality can be seen worldwide in the age of globalization (Fig. 3.2). Examining changes in real income globally from 1998 to 2008, income grew significantly for the super-rich, particularly in the US, and for an emerging global middle class, notably in Asia. Conversely, the income growth of the middle class in developed countries decreased significantly (the large dip in this figure). These changes are not an issue at the country level but rather reflect global dynamics. This suggests that in considering current inequality, it is necessary to account for not only the distribution within a single country but also the impact of globalization. Globalization has changed the landscape of global economic growth since the 1980s and has also influenced the nature of inequality.

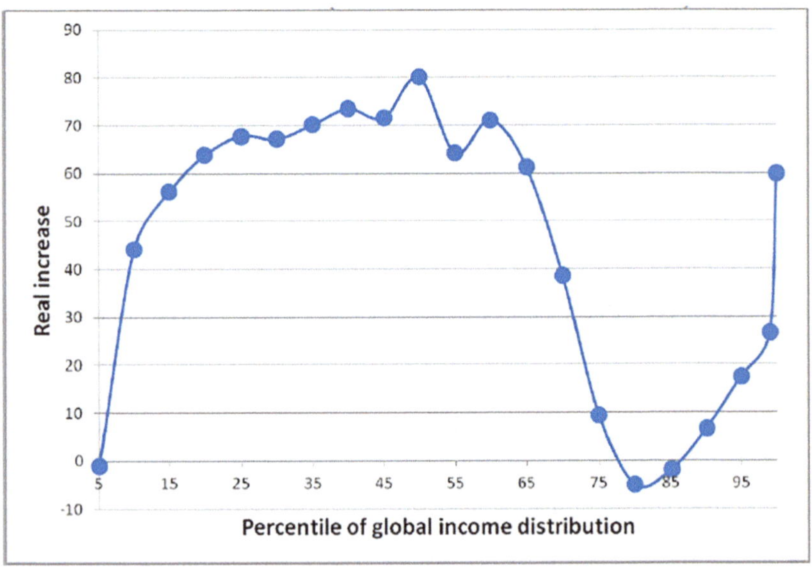


**Fig. 3.2** Relative growth in real income per capita on global income scale (*Source* Milanovic 2012)

### 3.3.2 Factors Causing Income Inequality in Modern Society

When discussing the question of how income inequality changes with economic growth and whether the Kuznets' Inverted U-Curve hypothesis holds true, the fundamental goal is to identify factors that cause income inequality. Even assuming there is no structural inequality, income inequality inevitably arises as a result of economic activities in a market economy. Theories have been developed to understand the structure of market economies, reflecting the historical background of each era—as typified by Ricardo and Marx. Piketty (2013) highlights assets as essential mechanisms of capitalism that drive inequality.[16] The fact that changes in inequality as a result of growth are not uniform, as mentioned above, suggests that economic and industrial structures, institutions and other social and environmental factors that drive growth—and in turn, influence, income distribution—vary greatly depending on country and era.

With the inconclusive discussion of Kuznets' Inverted U-Curve hypothesis, it seems likely that the debate on the cause of this change has entered a new stage, with the background of widening income inequality in OECD countries. Today, as the world is becoming increasingly globalized, the dynamics that amplify income inequality in developed countries may also work in a similar way in developing countries. It is important to identify these forces.

In Japan, there has been some debate about income inequality since the end of the 1990s. Tachibanaki (1998, 2006, 2016) argues that income inequality in Japan has been widening due to the following factors: the increased share of non-regular employment (doubling since around 1990); the increase in the number of divorces and single female-headed households; the increase in the number of elderly living alone; less-progressive taxation that benefits high-income earners; changes in wages setting methods (due to the weakened negotiating power of labor unions); the reform of wage structures toward performance-based pay systems; the increase in start-up business founders; and the reduced equality of opportunities in education and employment. Otake (2005) and the Cabinet Office (2007) argue that changes in the Gini coefficient have resulted from the aging of the population: the higher the age group, the wider the income inequality within the same age group. Therefore, if the population is aging under conditions in which income inequality remains unchanged in each of the age groups, the apparent inequality will widen. In addition, the Cabinet Office (2007) also points out that advancements in ICT and

[16] Focusing on asset stock more than income flow, Piketty (2013) argues that a basic principle of the empirical rule of capitalism is that the return on wealth (asset) ($r$) is always greater than growth rate ($g$), and that the narrowing of inequality for a certain period after World War II was a temporary effect of war and depression. While pretax return on capital has been consistent in a range between 4 and 5%, the growth rate is at most less than 4%, so those with capital can accumulate more wealth through investment. He argues that in the modern era, as only a small group of corporate owners are privileged to earn high incomes, wealth inequality is widening. Thus, inequality is structurally increasing in capitalist societies due to this mechanism.

progress in globalization have led to an increase in demand for skilled laborers, and the resultant rise in incomes has caused inequality to widen.

The US has the largest income inequality among developed countries. Stiglitz (2012) refers to several factors in the US that are characteristic of modern societies, such as rent-seeking by the financial industry, the reduction of progressivity of taxation, and the deterioration of wages for low-income workers resulting from globalization. And because the markets create inequality by their nature, he emphasized the important role of government in correcting market failures. He notes that there are differences between developed countries in after-tax incomes and in wealth and mobility among different income groups, which can be attributed to differences in government policy. Krueger (2012), the chair of the White House Council of Economic Advisers during the Obama administration, points to globalization, reduction of progressivity of taxation, an increase in high-income earners in the financial industry, and changes in technologies to require a higher level of skill (i.e., increasing the wages of skilled laborers) as factors to widen income inequality.

The relationship between income inequality, globalization, and technological advancement, such as ICT and AI, is a subject that has been most frequently discussed in recent years. Unskilled laborers in developed countries now face competition with unskilled workers in emerging economies due to the shift of manufacturing industries to emerging countries as a result of globalization. Baldwin (2016, 2019) argues that non-skilled laborers are susceptible to lower wages due to technological advancements, such as the development of AI, in addition to the impact of globalization. Stiglitz (2017) argues that globalization may benefit a country as a whole if it is managed appropriately, but this is not the case in the US, which makes it necessary for the government to strengthen its interventions by correcting the excessive development of financial products as well as improving corporate governance and social security systems.

Based on such discussions of Japan and the US, it seems that changes in income inequality accompanying economic growth are determined by a combination of three factors: (1) traditional factors, such as inter-sectoral labor mobility and the rate of return on capital; (2) characteristic changes in the modern economy, such as technological advancements in areas like ICT and AI, globalization, and changes in wage and employment structures; and (3) factors arising from social change, including aging populations and the increase in the number of single-person households. As structural factors, these elements are at least exacerbating inequality in developed countries, and some of these also affect inequality in developing countries. Income inequality in developing countries is less uniform than in developed countries, as some contributing factors may not necessarily apply, such as aging, or have more complex effects.

It is also important to consider why the absolute level of inequality differs so greatly between countries. Table 3.2 lists the countries with the lowest and highest Gini coefficients after tax. As can be clearly seen, absolute levels of income inequality are low in (former) Communist countries and some high-income countries in northern Europe. On the other hand, the countries with the highest income inequality are located in Africa and Latin America. The list provides evidence that income inequality is rooted in social structures and systems that stem from their historical background. As mentioned, Bruno et al. (1996) argue that differences in the Gini coefficient can be attributed to the characteristics of each country. In a simple analysis, I found that being located in Africa, Central and South America had a strongly positive correlation with the Gini coefficient, and the effect (coefficient) was large. For Asia, similar positive correlations are also observed, but the coefficient was small. In addition, a negative correlation is observed between the Gini coefficient and the history of countries that were once part of the Communist Bloc.[17]

Among studies of inequality in developing countries, dependency theory—influential in the 1960s and 1970s—focused on the relationship between social structures and inequality. According to dependency theory, the social structure of developing countries, both domestically and internationally, is dual, consisting of a modern sector (center) and a traditional sector (periphery). The periphery is economically dependent on the center, meaning that the former is inevitably exploited by the latter, and thus inequality is perpetuated in a structural manner. The theory assumes that the causes of underdevelopment do not lie in internal factors such as savings, investment and education, but rather in external relationships. The idea that the way to development was to end such a subordinate relationship became the theoretical basis for import substitution policies; however, this theory has lost support as import substitution policies ended in failure.

In contrast to dependency theory, which emphasizes external relationships, new institutional economics (NIE) argues that the institutional framework is the most decisive factor for long-term economic growth. This theory, first introduced in the 1930s by economist Ronald Coase, has its origins in analyses of transaction costs

[17] For 104 countries with available Gini coefficient data since 2010, strong correlations were observed between the Gini coefficient (independent variable) and a dummy indicating membership in the Communist Bloc, or location in Africa, Central America, South America, or Asia (explanatory variables), as shown below (Data from WDI).

| | (1) | (2) |
|---|---|---|
| Constant | 38.637*** (8.530) | 29.433*** (8.401) |
| Per capita GDP (log) | 0.148 (0.282) | 0.450 (1.156) |
| (Former) Communist regime | −7.481*** (−4.354) | −2.496** (−1.812) |
| Africa | | 10.147*** (6.449) |
| Central and South America | | 14.960*** (8.641) |
| Asia | | 3.075** (1.765) |
| $R^2$ (adjusted) | 0.142 | 0.536 |

Figures in parenthesized are t-values; *** 1% significance level, ** 5% significance level, * 10% significance level

**Table 3.2** Countries with lowest/highest Gini coefficients

| Rank | Country name | Gini coefficient | Rank | Country name | Gini coefficient |
|---|---|---|---|---|---|
| 1 | Slovenia | 25.4 | 133 | Zimbabwe | 50.3 |
| 2 | Belarus | 25.6 | 134 | Panama | 50.9 |
| 3 | UAE | 26.0 | 135 | St. Lucia | 51.2 |
| 4 | Czech | 26.2 | 136 | Angola | 53.3 |
| 5 | Slovakia | 26.2 | 137 | Botswana | 53.3 |
| 6 | Ukraine | 26.6 | 138 | Colombia | 53.5 |
| 7 | Moldova | 27.0 | 139 | Brazil | 53.9 |
| 8 | Iceland | 27.2 | 140 | Eswatini | 54.6 |
| 9 | Finland | 27.7 | 141 | Zambia | 57.1 |
| 10 | Belgium | 27.7 | 142 | Namibia | 59.1 |

*Note* Gini coefficient (after tax) is the figure among highest during years available since 2015
*Source* World Development Indicators (WDI). Accessed September 4, 2023

and corporate behavior, but when extended to the economy of a country, suggests that institutions—by providing low economic transaction costs and incentives for technological advancement—are essential to a country's economic growth. Therefore, the difference in institutions and social structures determines not only the initial level of inequality but also the extent of economic growth. A study by Acemoglu and Robinson (2012) has become well-known in recent literature on the relationship between institutions and economic growth. They argue that an inclusive political and economic system provides resources for sustainable growth, contrasting it with countries where political and economic institutions are predatory. The former countries contain systems that are centralized but where political power is not monopolized by specific individuals or societal groups, while the latter includes not only centralized systems, such as rule by emperor or one-party dictatorships. It may also include countries that have not yet established a centralized system. In the latter group, since more effort is focused on the monopolization of political power than on driving economic growth, it is argued that the creative destruction necessary for growth will never take place. On the other hand, in the former group, an inclusive political institution not only brings positive cyclical growth to an economy but also avoids the risk of reverting to a more exploitative system through the checks and balances provided by laws and the mass media.

I summarize the discussion so far in a flow chart (Fig. 3.3). Initial income inequality changes over time as the economy grows, but the degree of inequality varies depending on the political system and institutions, as described in Stiglitz (2012). Changed income inequality affects the extent of subsequent economic growth. I will discuss this final point in the next section.

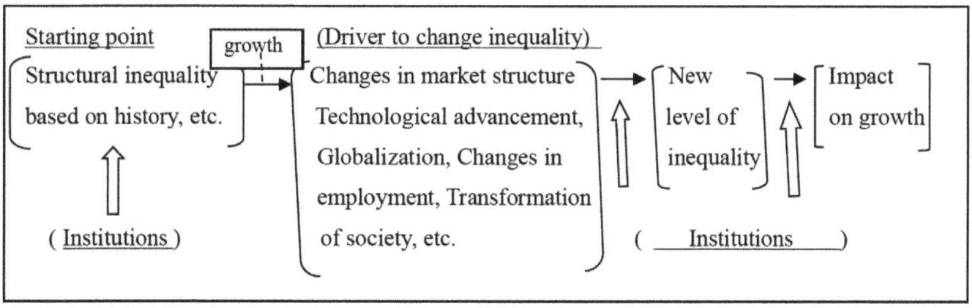


**Fig. 3.3** Changes in inequality and societal systems (*Source* Author)

### 3.3.3 The Impact of Income Inequality on Economic Growth

The next question concerns whether inequality affects growth rates, and if so, whether societies with greater or lesser inequality achieve higher growth. While there is still no definitive answer, most recent studies argue that high income inequality impairs growth. Figure 1.4 relates to this finding. The following section provides an overview of the debate surrounding the impact of income inequality on economic growth.

Classical economists in the UK believed that inequality and growth existed in a trade-off relationship. The basis of this argument is that the rich always have higher marginal savings than the poor. Accordingly, the greater the inequality, the greater the savings, and the more they are diverted to investment, thereby promoting growth. Over time, and especially after World War II, income equality increased in developed countries alongside rapid economic growth in developing countries. This view began to be questioned, including by economists at the World Bank. They argued that the potential of the poor to boost economic growth had been overlooked (Williamson 1991). By the late 1970s, debates about income inequality in developing countries had subsided, and the focus shifted to other issues such as macroeconomic stability, the problems of debt. According to Inaba (2016), while classical economic theories and Marxism could not separate production activities and income distribution, the development of financial systems and the spread of stock ownership made it possible for anyone to become a capitalist. Consequently, the relationship between production and distribution came to be separated in neoclassical theory, and interest in income distribution issues declined.

It was not until the 1990s that discussion of the relationship between the two became more active again. In the first half of the 1990s, many empirical studies on the potential impact of inequality on economic growth were conducted, some of which referred to the role of human capital.[18] At this time, the endogenous growth theory emerged, emphasizing the role of human capital as a key factor in sustained

[18] Williamson (1991) also states that human capital came to be recognized as an important element of economic growth in the twentieth century. More equal societies aim to improve labor

economic growth. There were two distinct lines of thought in the 1990s: one that income inequality promotes growth and another that income inequality impedes economic growth. More recently, Piketty (2013) focused on the role of physical capital, providing a new perspective that is distinct from many studies conducted over the past 20 years (Inaba 2016).

Regarding the argument that income inequality promotes economic growth, the basis of this view is that, as mentioned above, economic growth is brought about by investment, where investment is a function of savings, and the rich are able to save a higher proportion of their income than low-income earners, who spend most of their income on basic living expenses and have little left over to put into savings (a high consumption ratio). Thus, in societies with high income inequality, the overall savings of society as a whole increase as the proportion of the rich in society increases. Different saving rates by income seem to reflect reality and are used in economics. In addition, since inequality arises as a result of the success of business activities, it is often noted that inequality can create incentives for entrepreneurship and innovation, promoting growth.

Regarding the argument that income inequality impedes economic growth, the perspectives supporting the idea that income inequality impedes economic growth are centered on (1) investment in human capital, (2) demand creation, (3) fiscal policy, and (4) political and social stability. First, as previously mentioned, when inequality widens, poor households are unable to make sufficient investments in human capital, such as education and health services. In societies where the development of human resources lags and individuals are unable to make full use of their potential, long-term growth is impaired. This view is widely shared and referenced in the literature, including the World Bank (2016). Some of the arguments related to this perspective include the following: constraints on borrowing may prevent the poor from investing in education (Perotti 1996; Deininger and Squire 1998), widening inequality may lead to increased fertility, thereby reducing per capita educational investment (Perotti 1996)[19]; and inequality may be

---

skills through educational investment. In this case, the demand for skilled labor changes depending on whether economic growth is skilled-labor-intensive or non-skilled-labor-intensive, and this will affect changes in income inequality. He notes that, historically, the UK in the nineteenth century and Brazil today appear to support the scenario of widening inequality, while growth in East Asia seems to be a scenario of more equal societies, but more evidence is needed to support this observation.

[19] As for population decrease, based on the idea of production function, a decline in birth rates generally leads to decreased employment, so economic growth is reduced. However, as capital per capita increases due to the population decrease, real GDP growth per capita will temporarily accelerate. Therefore, whether the decrease in population can be offset depends on whether households increase their savings in response to this increase or not. In other words, while a decrease in population lowers growth, any decline in economic growth might be limited if investment in human capital is increased. Furthermore, according to endogenous growth theory, when the formation of human capital has an economic externality, it may also promote long-term growth (Hirata 2012). Myrskyalä et al. (2009) compared the birth rate and the level of social development between 1975 and 2005. The results suggest that, despite the conventional belief that birth rates would decline as

negatively correlated with enrollment rates and institutions—such as government effectiveness and corruption—ultimately hindering development (Easterly 2007).

Next, regarding the creation of demand, in light of the fact that long-term economic stagnation and widening inequality are occurring concurrently in developed countries, there is a view that increased inequality is causing a decline of domestic demand and hence impairing growth (e.g., Stiglitz 2012[20]; Krueger 2012). This is the flip side of the classical argument: the poor spend most of their income on daily necessities, so domestic demand decreases if inequality increases. According to Krueger (2012), the income share of the richest 1% in the US rose by 13.5 percentage points in the period from 1979 to 2007. Considering the difference in the marginal propensity to consume between the rich and the rest, it is estimated that USD 440 billion worth of consumption (equivalent to 5% of total consumption) is lost each year.

In addition, policies are determined by how median voters act, and their income deviates from the average if income inequality increases. In this case, median voters choose to increase taxes for capital accumulation and subsidies or to introduce regulation in order to redistribute income, and these fiscal policies will hinder capital accumulation and consequently impede growth (Persson and Tabellini 1994).[21] There is also the view that if income inequality widens, society and politics will become unstable. This will increase uncertainty in the contractual environment and reduce investment, and as a result, growth will decrease (Perotti 1996; Keefer and Knack 2000). Dabla-Norris et al. (2015) suggest that greater inequality, in addition to conflict, may damage growth by amplifying financial crises and balance of payment deficits.

Given the conflicting forces that may shape the impact of income inequality on growth rates, numerous empirical studies have examined these issues. Regarding the relationship between income inequality and growth rates throughout US history—often cited as evidence for the trade-off—Williamson (1991) suggests that closer analysis reveals that income inequality is unlikely to have promoted capital accumulation. Inequality in the US widened rapidly for 80 years from the 1820s onward, and during that period, both savings and capital accumulation increased concurrently. However, Williamson concludes that much of this increase can be attributed to factors other than income inequality.[22]

the economy developed, the 2005 data showed that the birth rate actually increased once a certain level of development was reached (0.86 in the Human Development Index [HDI]).

[20] In addition to this, Stiglitz (2012) points out that inequality reduces public investment spending, distorts the economy by rent-seeking, and demotivates laborers.

[21] This relationship is considered statistically insignificant in estimates by Perotti (1996) and Deininger and Squire (1998).

[22] Williamson (1991) examines the increase in the net savings rate, breaking it down into changes in demand for investment, changes in income distribution, changes in capital goods prices, and other factors. He analyzed several scenarios, but in all cases, the impact of income distribution did not exceed a quarter of the total. In the UK, although inequality widened sharply from the 1820s onwards, the investment rate did not begin to rise until the 1850s.

Regarding empirical studies conducted in the 1990s, while those researchers such as Persson and Tabellini (1994) argued that income inequality impedes growth, Li and Zou (1998) and Forbes (2000) found a positive correlation between income inequality and growth rates. Notably, while previous studies relied on cross-sectional data, these studies used panel data. Besides these conflicting findings, Deininger and Squire (1998) found that while income inequality has no significant relationship with growth rates when regional factors are controlled for, asset inequality has a significant negative correlation with growth rates. Furthermore, some researchers conclude that the relationship between income inequality and growth is not always consistent. Barro (2008) argues that the relationship between income inequality and growth can have opposing impacts depending on the level of per-capita income: income inequality can have a negative impact on growth in low-income countries while generating positive effects in high-income countries, with a threshold estimated at USD 11,900 (2000 figures).[23]

In recent years, numerous estimates have been presented by the OECD and IMF, arguing that income inequality has a negative correlation with growth. Cingano (2014) and OECD (2015) examine overall changes in inequality (from 1985 to 2005) and its cumulative impact on growth during the periods (from 1990 to 2010). Their results show that income inequality is negatively correlated with growth and that a one-point change in the Gini coefficient reduces the annual growth rate by about 0.15%. They report that the widening of income inequality between 1985 and 2005 lowered GDP growth in Mexico and New Zealand by more than 10% between 1990 and 2010 and the growth rate of the US, the UK, Sweden, Finland, and Norway by more than one fifth during that period (Cingano 2014).

From the viewpoint of quality growth, Berg and Ostry (2011) are noteworthy for highlighting that income inequality affects the length of periods of sustained high growth. According to their research, most developed countries and Asian countries have experienced sustained high growth episodes of more than 10 years, whereas the duration of sustained high growth in Central and South America and sub-Saharan Africa is about two-thirds that of Asia. In addition, the growth episodes in developed countries and Asian countries tend to end with a soft landing, whereas in Africa, they lead to a hard landing. Berg and Ostry also found that income inequality has the strongest positive correlation with the duration of high growth among all the explanatory variables. This effect is so substantial that each 10% narrowing of inequality leads to a 50% increase in the length of the growth episode. The main reasons stated behind this are policy choices of median voters and political instability, as mentioned above. They then go on to suggest policy proposals, such as targeted subsidies, labor policies, equality of opportunities, pro-poor policies, and progressive taxation. Ostry et al. (2014) confirm these results using new data sets, with the conclusion that income redistribution to adjust inequality does not

[23] In the study, growth regression was conducted using the Gini coefficient and the cross term between the Gini coefficient and per capita income as explanatory variables, and the correlation to growth was found significantly negative in low-income countries and statistically positive in high income countries.

affect growth unless it is extreme. Berg and Ostry (2011) suggest that growth sustainability and resilience would be strengthened in an inclusive economy, which should be worth noting from the perspective of quality growth.

The review in this section suggests that both the impact of growth on income inequality and that of income inequality on growth are not necessarily simple one-way relationships. Regarding the latter, inequality includes factors that can both positively and negatively affect growth, and the relative importance of these factors depends on the circumstances of each country. For example, in developing countries caught in the poverty trap, there are likely to be significant constraints on funds available for investment, so it is essential to raise the overall national savings rate. However, in developed countries such as Japan, stimulating demand is now crucial for revitalizing the economy. In this example, changes in inequality would contribute to growth in the opposite direction. There is also the issue of differing timeframes, which was not adequately assessed in previous studies. For example, while issues such as savings and demand are relatively short-term concerns, human capital development through education is clearly a long-term priority. From the perspective of quality growth, the latter view is essential to achieve the sustainability of growth. In conclusion, while maintaining a short-term policy balance to meet the circumstances of each country, it is necessary to promote comprehensive efforts to reduce inequality in the medium to long term.

## 3.4 Summary and Policies to Improve Inequality

I have seen that there are two main issues that inclusive growth seeks to address: structural inequality and income inequality. In order to address the former, policy measures are required to improve inequality of opportunity, particularly in education and healthcare, and to reform social structures that are attributed to institutional, cultural, and geographical factors. On the other hand, the basic policy response to adjust income inequality is the redistribution of income through taxation and subsidies. This is because income redistribution enables the poor to gain equal opportunities, including better access to education and healthcare.[24]

The SDGs include the reduction of inequality in Goal 10, which states "Reduce inequality within and among countries." I can see that it involves key policy

[24] In every country, governments adjust income inequality through redistribution. Therefore, when considering the impact of inequality on growth, the elements of income redistribution should also be considered. Berg et al. (2018) conducted an empirical analysis of the effects of inequality and redistribution, stating that no integrated study of the effects of inequality and redistribution on growth had previously been conducted. The conclusions are as follows: (1) growth increases and sustains when post-tax inequality is small; (2) redistribution does not affect growth unless it is extreme; and (3) inequality affects growth through human capital accumulation, life expectancy, and fertility channels. As for (2), while theory states that redistribution through tax rate hikes and subsidies may have a negative impact on growth by reducing economic efficiency, it may also have a positive impact on growth through benefits to the poor. The results of empirical estimation show that the correlation between redistribution and the duration of growth is weak.

measures aiming at improving equality of opportunities and income redistribution, both domestically and internationally (see Fig. 3.4). The Goal 10 Targets are presented in Appendix (see p. 67). It should be noted the targets listed in Goal 10 are limited to those related to institutions (e.g., eliminating discriminatory laws) and income redistribution (e.g., fiscal policies), whereas policies to improve inequality in various fields, such as education, health, and gender, are described in other goals. For example, "By 2030, eliminate gender disparities in education and ensure equal access to all levels of education and vocational training for the vulnerable, including…" (Target 4.5), "End all forms of discrimination against all women and girls everywhere" (Target 5.1), and "By 2030, provide access to safe, affordable, accessible and sustainable transport systems for all, improving road safety, notably by expanding public transport, with special attention to the needs of those in vulnerable situations, women, children, persons with disabilities and older persons" (Target 11.2). At first glance, we may understand that the SDGs mention inequality only in Goal 10, but, in fact, it is included in most of the goals in the SDGs. This is only natural, given that the SDGs are based on the principle of "no one left behind." The overall picture of policies related to inequality in the SDGs should be understood from the context of the structures described in this chapter.

Policies to improve inclusiveness have been implemented in various ways depending on the situation in each country; however, they generally involve reducing inequality of opportunity and implementing income redistribution. As for the fundamental policy menu, for example, the World Bank's Poverty and Shared Prosperity Report (2016), a biennial report on poverty reduction, lists the following policies as measures to improve both inequality in developing countries such as: (1) early childhood development and nutrition, (2) healthcare and education, (3) conditional cash transfers (CCT), (4) rural infrastructure, 5) taxation. These policies can be broadly categorized as follows: (1), (2), and (4) address inequality of opportunities, (5) focuses on income redistribution, while (3) targets both. Regarding early childhood development and nutrition (1), the lack of nutrition during

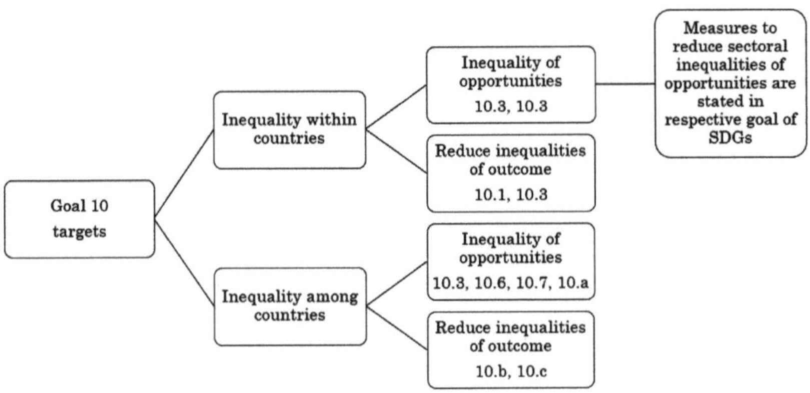


**Fig. 3.4** Structure of Goal 10 of the SDGs (*Source* Author)

infancy may lead to cognitive disorders that affect an infant's subsequent development, highlighting the need for government intervention to prevent such risks. Regarding CCT, these programs provide a cash subsidy to the poor to support income redistribution while also improving equal opportunities by requiring school attendance in elementary education for children and medical checks for children and mothers as conditions for receiving such cash payments. This scheme was started in Mexico in the 1990s after positive results were confirmed in a social experiment. However, it should be noted that these measures need to be consistent with broader macroeconomic policies.

In Brazil, for example, as a result of implementing this policy on a large scale, the number of poor people fell considerably, and domestic income inequality narrowed in the 2000s. For a country with a large gap in income like Brazil, this kind of policy mix for income redistribution and human resource development was essential in the long term. However, it is also important to balance these measures with other fiscal spending in the short term. In fact, once the global energy market boom ended in the mid-2010s, the country's fiscal situation deteriorated significantly, causing major turmoil. In addition, the human resource development achieved through conditional cash provision takes time to bear fruits in the form of economic growth. Balancing policies aimed at achieving inclusiveness with measures that promote economic growth is essential. With regard to point (4), rural roads and electrification have a substantial effect on inequality in rural infrastructure. These factors are closely related to improving market accessibility. Regarding taxation, the report mentions not only progressive taxation, but also the component of taxes and tax administration.

Lastly, I take a brief look at Japan's recent policy on inclusive growth. Japan has long focused on inclusiveness in its policies, such as establishing universal health insurance in 1961. Recently, inclusiveness has attracted renewed attention in policymaking as a way of responding to societal changes, such as widening inequality and increasing child poverty etc. Under the slogan of the "Ichioku-Sou-Katsuyaku" [Dynamic Engagement of All Citizens], a new policy to promote inclusiveness has been launched. The Cabinet Office approved "The Japan's Plan for Dynamic Engagement of All Citizens" in 2016, in which "a society participated by all citizens—whether they are women or men, the elderly or youth, people who have experienced a failure, people with disabilities and people fighting an illness can play active roles in their respective homes, workplaces and local communities or any other places"—is defined as "a society in which all citizens are dynamically engaged."[25] It is a characteristic of Japan that many measures in the plan are related to the declining birthrate and aging population; however, inequality clearly underpins many policy items, such as equal pay for equal work, childcare support, and the creation of an environment where all children can receive the education they want. What is distinctive about this plan is that it considers the cycle between

[25] Cabinet Decision on "The Japan's Plan for Dynamic Engagement of All Citizens," June 2, 2016, https://japan.kantei.go.jp/content/jpnplnde_en.pdf.

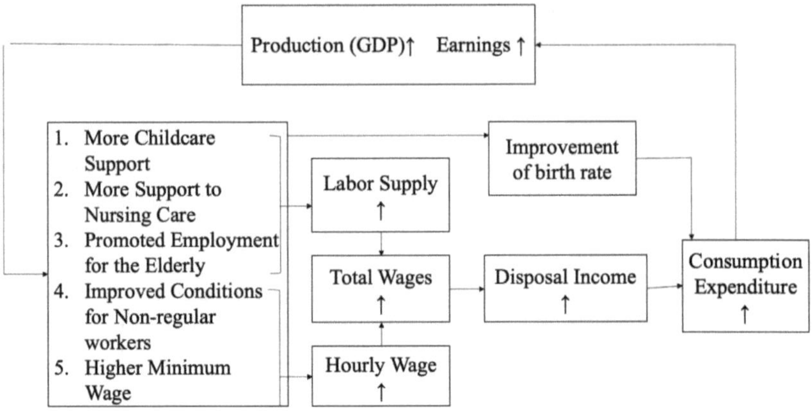


**Fig. 3.5** The positive feedback loop between growth and distribution with the goal of achieving a society that enables the dynamic engagement of all citizens (*Source* Cabinet Decision on "The Japan's Plan for Dynamic Engagement of All Citizens June 2, 2016" (p. 8) (Only the item names are shown here—their descriptions are omitted.)

growth and distribution, and it clearly states its policy stance that not only seeks to improve inequality but also achieve economic growth at the same time. The framework of the plan is shown in Fig. 3.5. This model clearly shows the feedback loop that, for example, income improvement for low- and middle-income earners will circulate back into increased production through increased consumer spending.

### 3.4.1 Closing Remarks of the Chapter

As described in the 2006 World Development Report (World Bank 2006), equity is a guiding principle for building social systems regardless of culture and religion. If a society ensures an equal opportunity for everyone to become prosperous in proportion to their efforts, the society becomes more vital and promotes economic growth. Equality of opportunities is a fundamental factor in achieving quality growth. If structural inequalities such as those found in gender and ethnic minorities are improved, individuals are able to make better use of their potential, and economic growth is accelerated as a result in the long run. However, in reality, there are many forms of inequality that continue across generations. In most countries, equality of opportunity is undermined when income inequality resulting from economic activity is too large.

The inclusiveness of growth, as advocated in the DCC 2015—which states that "the fruits of growth are shared within society as a whole, leaving no one behind"—must be considered in the light of both structural inequality and income inequality. The relationships that we have seen so far can be summarized in Fig. 3.6. I should consider these two issues in regard to policies on inequality and

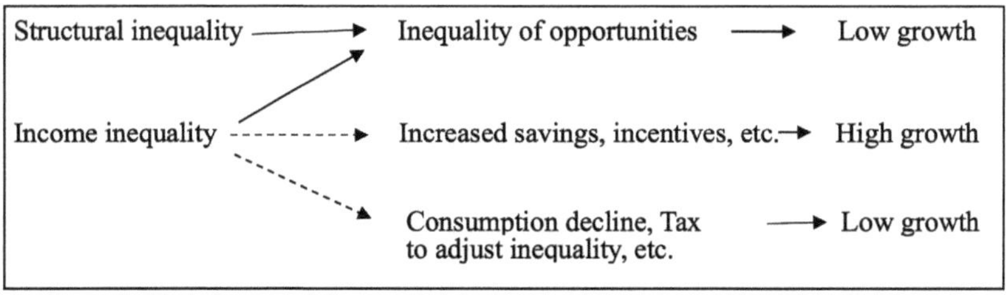


**Fig. 3.6** Structural inequality, income inequality, and inclusive growth (*Source* Author)

growth, while, needless to say, a safety net for the absolute poor and vulnerable groups is essential from the perspective of human security.

In summary, we need policies to ensure a transformation to bring about growth without widening inequality. When implementing human resource development, it is of the utmost importance to achieve equal opportunities. Simultaneously, it is crucial to cooperate with the private sector in human resource development, including the promotion of foreign direct investment (FDI) by improving the investment environment and building industries that can provide decent work in terms of the relationship between societal transformation and inequality. In other words, policies should be designed to ensure that improving human capital leads to social transformation and innovation. Such policies will also help achieve sustained growth in the long run. Consideration should also be given to the negative aspects that large inequality may bring to economic growth. While achieving equal opportunities is necessary over the long term, redistributing income while maintaining the vitality of the economy is necessary in the short term. Finally, I referred to a study showing that, in a society with less inequality, growth episodes are longer and soft landings occur at the end of growth episodes. This viewpoint may be an area that deserves further research, considering the complementarity between inclusiveness and sustainability as well as resilience.

This chapter is based on Hirota (2016) with a substantial revision and update.

## Appendix: Goal 10, SDGs

Goal 10. Reduce inequality within and among countries.

10.1 By 2030, progressively achieve and sustain income growth of the bottom 40% of the population at a rate higher than the national average

10.2 By 2030, empower and promote the social, economic and political inclusion of all, irrespective of age, sex, disability, race, ethnicity, origin, religion or economic or other status

10.3 Ensure equal opportunity and reduce inequalities of outcome, including by eliminating discriminatory laws, policies and practices and promoting appropriate legislation, policies and action in this regard

10.4 Adopt policies, especially fiscal, wage and social protection policies, and progressively achieve greater equality

10.5 Improve the regulation and monitoring of global financial markets and institutions and strengthen the implementation of such regulations

10.6 Ensure enhanced representation and voice for developing countries in decision-making in global international economic and financial institutions in order to deliver more effective, credible, accountable and legitimate institutions

10.7 Facilitate orderly, safe, regular and responsible migration and mobility of people, including through the implementation of planned and well-managed migration policies

10.a Implement the principle of special and differential treatment for developing countries, in particular least developed countries, in accordance with World Trade Organization agreements

10.b Encourage official development assistance and financial flows, including foreign direct investment, to States where the need is greatest, in particular least developed countries, African countries, small island developing States and landlocked developing countries, in accordance with their national plans and programmes

10.c By 2030, reduce to less than 3% the transaction costs of migrant remittances and eliminate remittance corridors with costs higher than 5%.

*Source* United Nations. "Resolution adopted by the General Assembly on 25 September 2015." A/RES/70/1. 21 October 2015

## References

Acemoglu, Daron, and James A. Robinson. 2012. *Why Nations Fail: The Origin of Power, Prosperity, and Poor*. Profile Books.

Alesina, Alberto, Arnaud Devleeshauwer, William Easterly, Sergio Kurlat, and Romain Wacziarg. 2003. "Fractionalization." *Journal of Economic Growth* 8: 155–194.

Alesina, Alberto, Stelios Michalopoulos, and Elias Papaioannou. 2012. "Ethnic Inequality." NBER Working Paper No. 18512, National Bureau of Economic Research. NBER.

Ali, Ifzal. 2007. "Pro-poor to Inclusive Growth: Asian Prescriptions." ERD Policy Brief Series No. 48. ADB.

Amin, Mohammad, Veselin Kuntchev, and Martin Schmidt. 2015. "Gender Inequality and Growth: The Case of Rich vs. Poor Countries." Policy Research Working Paper 7172. World Bank.

Aquirre, DeAnne, Leila Hoteit, Christine Rupp, and Karim Sabbagh. 2012. *Empowering the Third Billion Women and the World of Work in 2012*. Booze & Co.

Asian Development Bank (ADB). 2008. *Strategy 2020: The Long-Term Strategic Framework of the Asian Development Bank 2008–2020*. ADB.

Balakrishnan, Ravi, Chad Steinberg, and Murtaza Syed. 2013. "The Elusive Quest for Inclusive Growth: Growth, Poverty, and Inequality in Asia." IMF Working Paper WP/13/152. IMF.

Baldwin, Richard. 2016. *Great Convergence: Information Technology and the New Globalization.* Belknap Press.

Baldwin, Richard. 2019. *The Globotics Upheaval: Globalization, Robotics, and the Future of Work.* Oxford University Press.

Barro, Robert J. 1997. *Determinants of Economic Growth: A Cross-Country Empirical Study.* MIT Press.

Barro, Robert J. 2008. "Inequality and Growth Revisited." Working Paper Series on Regional Economic Integration No. 11. ADB.

Berg, Andrew G., and Jonathan D. Ostry. 2011. "Inequality and Unsustainable Growth: Two Sides of the Same Coin?" IMF Staff Discussion Note SDN/11/08. IMF.

Berg, Andrew, Jonathan D. Ostry, Charalambos G. Tsangarides, and Yorbol Yakhshilikov. 2018. "Redistribution, Inequality, and Growth: New Evidence." Journal of Economic Growth 23 (3–1): 259–305.

Bluedorn, John C. 2001. "Can Democracy Help?: Growth and Ethnic Divisions." *Economics Letters* 70 (1): 121–126.

Bruno, Michael, Marin Ravallion, and Lyn Squire. 1996. "Equity and Growth in Developing Countries." Policy Research Working Paper 1563. World Bank.

Burnside, Craig, and David Dollar. 1997. "Aid, Policies and Growth." World Bank Policy Research Working Paper 1777. World Bank.

Cabinet Office, Japan. 2007. "Heisei 19 nendo nenji keizai zaisei hōkoku" [2007 Annual Report on the Japanese Economy and Public Finance]. Cabinet Office.

Cabinet Office, Japan. 2012. *Danjyo kyōdō sankaku kaigi kihon mondai kankyō chōsa senmon chōsa kaigi hōkokusho saishū hōkoku- dai 1 bu jyosei ga katsuyaku dekiru keizai shakai no kōchiku ni mukete (Jyosei to keizai WG hōkoku)* [Final Report; Working Paper by Research Council on Issues and Effects of Joint Participation in Planning and Deciding Policies by Men and Women as Equal Partners: Part 1 "Society in which all women shine," women and economy working group report].

Cingano, Federico. 2014. "Trends in Income Inequality and its Impact on Economic Growth." OECD Social, Employment and Migration Working Papers No. 163. OECD.

Collier, Paul. 1998. "The Political Economy of Ethnicity." WPS/98–8, Centre for the Study of African Economics, Institute of Economics and Statistics. University of Oxford.

Collier, Paul. 2009. *Wars, Guns, and Votes: Democracy in Dangerous Places.* Harper Collins.

Collier, Paul, and Jan Willem Gunning. 1999. "Why Has Africa Grown Slowly?" *Journal of Economic Perspectives* 13 (3): 3–22.

Dabla-Norris, Era, Kalpana Kochhar, Nujin Suphaphiphat, Frantisek Ricka, and Evridiki Tsounta. 2015. "Causes and Consequences of Income Inequality: A Global Perspective." IMF Staff Discussion Note SDN/15/13. IMF.

Deaton, Angus. 2003."Health, Inequality and Economic Development." *Journal of Economic Literature* 41 (1):113–58.

Deininger, Klaus, and Lyn Squire. 1998. "New Ways of Looking at Old Issues: Inequality and Growth." *Journal of Development Economics* 57: 259–287.

Easterly, William. 2007. "Inequality Does Cause Underdevelopment: Insights from a New Instrument." *Journal of Development Economics* 84: 755–776.

Easterly, William, and Ross Levine. 1997. "Africa's Growth Tragedy: Policies and Ethnic Divisions." *The Quarterly Journal of Economics* 112(4): 1203–1250.

Forbes, Kristin J. 2000. "A Reassessment of the Relationship Between Inequality and Growth." *American Economic Review* 90 (4): 869–887.

Gonzales, Christian, Sonali Jain-Chandra, Kalpana Kochhar, Monique Newiak, and Tlek Zeinullayev. 2015. "Catalyst for Change: Empowering Women and Tackling Income Inequality." IMF Staff Discussion Note SDN/15/20. IMF.

Hirata, Wataru. 2012. "Jinkō seichō to keizai seichō: Keizai seichō riron karano lesson" [Population Growth and Economic Growth; Lessons from Economic Development Theories]. *Monetary and Economic Studies* 31 (2): 121–162. Bank of Japan Financial Research Institute.

Hirota. Koki. 2016. "'Shitsu no takai seichō' to hōsetsusei" [Quality Growth and Inclusiveness]. Literature Review 8: 1–32. JICA Ogata Research Institute.
Hoogeveen, Johannes, and Emil Tesliuc, Renos Cakis with Stefan Dercon. 2005. "A Guide to the Analysis of Risk, Vulnerability and Vulnerable Groups." World Bank. https://www.researchgate.net/publication/238528462_A_Guide_to_the_Analysis_of_Risk_Vulnerability_and_Vulnerable_Groups
Inaba, Shinichiro. 2016. *Fubyōdō tono tatakai: Rousseau kara Piketty made* [Inequality and the Struggle: from Rousseau to Piketty]. Bunshun Shinsho, Bungeishunju.
Ianchovichina, Elena, and Susanna Lundstrom. 2009. "Inclusive Growth Analysis: Framework and Application." Policy Research Working Paper 4851. World Bank.
International Policy Centre for Inclusive Growth (IPC-IG). 2013. "After All, What is Inclusive Growth." http://www.ipc-undp.org/pub/IPCOnePager188.pdf. Accessed September 3, 2023.
Keefer, Philip, and Stephen Knack. 2000. "Polarization, Politics and Property Rights-Links between Inequality and Growth." World Bank Policy Research Working Paper 2418. World Bank.
Klasen, Stephan. 2010. "Measuring and Monitoring Inclusive Growth: Multiple Definitions, Open Questions, and Some Constructive Proposals." ADB Sustainable Development Working Paper Series No. 12. ADB.
Krueger, Alan B. 2012. "The Rise and Consequences of Inequality in the United States." Remarks of the Chairman of Council of Economic Advisors, at the Center for American Progress in Washington, DC. January 12, 2012, https://obamawhitehouse.archives.gov/sites/default/files/krueger_cap_speech_final_remarks.pdf. Accessed Oct. 26, 2025.
Kuznets, Simon. 1955. "Economic Growth and Income Inequality." *American Economic Review* 45 (1): 1–28.
Li, Hongyi, and Heng-fu Zou. 1998. "Income Inequality Is not Harmful for Growth: Theory and Evidence." *Review of Development Economics* 2 (3): 318–334.
Lindert, Peter. H. 1998. "Three Centuries of Inequality in Britain and America." Working Paper #97–09. University of California.
Milanovic, Branko. 2012. "Global Income Inequality by the Numbers in History and Now: An Overview." Policy Research Working Paper 6259. World Bank.
Milanovic, Branko. 2016. *Global Inequality*. Havard University Press.
Ministry of Foreign Affairs (MOFA), Japan. 2014. *ODA Taikō minaoshi ni kansuru yūshikisha kondankai hōkokusho* [Report of the Advisory Panel on Revision of the ODA Charter], June 2014.
Myrskyalä, Mikko, Hans-Peter Kohler, and Francesco C. Billari. 2009. "Advances in Development Reverse Fertility Declines." *Nature* 460 (7256): 741–743.
Organization for Economic Co-operation and Development (OECD). 2014. *All On Board- Making Inclusive Growth Happen.* OECD Publishing.
Organization for Economic Co-operation and Development (OECD). 2015. *In It Together: Why Less Inequality Benefits All.* OECD Publishing.
Ostry, Jonathan D., Andrew Berg, and Charalambos G. Tsangarides. 2014. "Redistribution, Inequality, and Growth." IMF Staff Discussion Note SDN/14/02. IMF.
Otake, Fumio. 2005. *Nihon no fubyōdō* [Inequality in Japan]. Nikkei Publishing.
Perotti, Robert. 1996. "Growth, Income Distribution, and Democracy: What the Data Say." *Journal of Economic Growth* 1 (2): 445–483.
Persson, Torsten, and Guido Tabellini. 1994. "Is Inequality Harmful for Growth?" *American Economic Review* 84 (3): 600–621.
Piketty, Thomas. 2013. *Le Capital Au XXI$^{e}$ Siecle.* Éditions du Seuil.
Ranieri, Rafael, and Raquel Almeida Ramos. 2013. "Inclusive Growth: Building Up a Concept." Working Paper 104, International Policy Centre for Inclusive Growth. IPC-IC.
Sachs, Jeffrey D., and Andrew M. Warner. 1997. "Sources of Slow Growth in African Economies." *Journal of African Economies* 6 (3): 335–376.
Stiglitz, Joseph E. 2012. *The Price of Inequality.* W. W. Norton & Company.
Stiglitz, Joseph E. 2017. *Globalization and Its Discontents Revisited.* N.W. Norton.

Tachibanaki, Toshiaki. 1998. *Nihon no keizai kakusa: Shotoku to shisan kara kangaeru* [Economic Inequality in Japan- Examining from Income and Assets]. Iwanami Shoten.
Tachibanaki, Toshiaki. 2006. *Kakusa shakai: Nani ga mondai nanoka* [Society with Inequality: What are Problems?]. Iwanami Shinsho.
Tachibanaki, Toshiaki. 2016. *21 seiki Nihon no kakusa* [Disparity in 21st Century Japan]. Iwanami Shoten.
Todaro, Micheal P., and Stephen C. Smith. 2003. *Economic Development 8th Edition.* Pearson Education.
United Nations Development Programme (UNDP). 2014. *Human Development Report 2014.* UNDP.
Williamson, Jeffrey G. 1991. *Inequality, Poverty & History.* Blackwell Publishing.
World Bank. 2006. *World Development Report 2006: Equity and Development.* World Bank.
World Bank. 2012. *World Development Report 2012: Gender Equality and Development.* World Bank.
World Bank. 2016. *Poverty and Shared Prosperity 2016: Taking on Inequality.* World Bank.

**Koki Hirota** earned his B.A. in Economics from the University of Tokyo and holds a Ph.D. in Economics from Saitama University in Japan. His professional career spans several prominent roles in international development finance and policy, including Chief Economist, Director General of Operation and Strategy Department, and Director General of Southeast Asia and Pacific Department at the Japan International Cooperation Agency (JICA), and Chief Representative in Jakarta for Japan Bank for International Cooperation and in Hanoi for the Overseas Economic Cooperation Fund. In academia, he was a Professor at the Graduate School of Humanities and Social Sciences at Saitama University and a Visiting Fellow at the JICA Ogata Sadako Research Institute for Peace and Development. His recent publications include *Challenges in Fiscal and Monetary Policies in Mongolia* (co-edited, Springer, 2023) and *Addressing Social Infrastructure Needs in Asia: Towards a Pandemic Resilient Society* (co-edited, JICA, August 2025).

# Growth and Resilience

# 4

Koki Hirota and Keiichiro Yuasa

## 4.1 Definition of Resilience and Discussion About Resilient Growth

### 4.1.1 Definition and Conceptual Framework of Resilience

In this chapter, I review the concept of resilience and examine discussions of its relationship to growth. As noted in Chap. 2, the Development Cooperation Charter of Japan (DCC), published in 2015, defines "resilience" as being "able to withstand and recover from economic crises, natural disasters and other shocks."

APEC has identified "secure growth" as one of the elements of quality growth, encapsulating not only external shocks but also broader economic and social events. While APEC emphasizes the necessity of preparedness and the ability to respond to external shocks, it also includes issues related to the trade system, prevention of terrorism, anti-corruption, and transparency as elements of resilient growth. This reflects the importance of enabling businesses to conduct their economic activities with confidence in a stable and secure environment. This chapter discusses resilience from the perspective of DCC 2015, with a focus on responses to external shocks. Economic systems and governance relate not only to securing business activities but also to driving growth and transforming economies over the medium to long term. The contribution of these systems toward sustained growth is discussed in the next section.

K. Hirota (✉)
Tokyo, Japan

K. Yuasa
Governance and Peacebuilding Department, Japan International Cooperation Agency, Tokyo, Japan



K. Hirota (ed.), *Introduction to Quality Growth*,
https://doi.org/10.1007/978-981-95-6220-6_4

This chapter will focus specifically on natural disasters and economic crises, with a brief case study of COVID-19 as an event that posed a significant global concern. Climate change will be discussed as a sustainability issue in the next chapter, as addressing this problem will require a long-term response. However, as one of the most direct impacts of climate change is the increase in natural disasters, the discussion in this chapter will include some analysis of climate change. I start by defining resilience and considering the issues involved, then clarifying what distinguishes it from vulnerability. I then review natural disasters, infectious diseases, and economic crises in relation to growth before finally examining policies to enhance resilience.

The World Economic Forum (WEF) provides a comprehensive analysis of external risk and resilience. WEF (2013) introduces a definition of resilience that was originally used in engineering to mean the ability of "bouncing back faster after stress, enduring greater stresses, and being disturbed less by a given amount of stress." For global risk, as the object under consideration is a social system, the WEF proposes an additional definition: "maintaining system function in the event of disturbance." More specifically, resilience means the ability to (1) adapt to change, (2) withstand sudden shocks, and (3) recover to a desired equilibrium. Therefore, the WEF argues that recovery from economic crises and adaptation to environmental changes should be understood as issues of resilience.[1]

As resilience represents the ability to withstand and recover from external shocks, the following three steps are appropriate for a discussion of the concept. First, we need to consider external shocks and the kinds of external risks that can have a significant impact on a country's economy. Second, we should examine what makes countries susceptible to external shocks and which types of countries are particularly sensitive. As we will see later, this is a question of country-specific vulnerability. Finally, there is the question of what determines the ability to withstand and recover from external shocks. This last point constitutes the essence of resilience, which leads to the policy question of how resilience can be strengthened. To represent this relationship between external shocks, vulnerability, and economic resilience, Briguglio et al. (2008) propose a simple diagram, shown in Fig. 4.1. Each country has its own inherent vulnerabilities, and by cultivating resilience against these vulnerabilities, countries can mitigate the impact of external risks. Therefore, even if similar external shocks occur, the actual impact will differ between countries. This framework was proposed as a way to examine the indicators of small countries' vulnerability and economic resilience. However, the framework appears to be applicable more broadly to other aspects, including natural disasters.

It does not seem that vulnerability and resilience can always be clearly distinguished. However, by organizing both concepts in the following way, the difference

[1] Some papers refer to the resilience of the economic sector as economic resilience (e.g., Hallegatte 2014; Briguglio et al. 2008; Fujii et al. 2014). Since I mainly discuss the relationship between resilience and growth here, I use the term resilience in this chapter to refer primarily to its economic dimension.

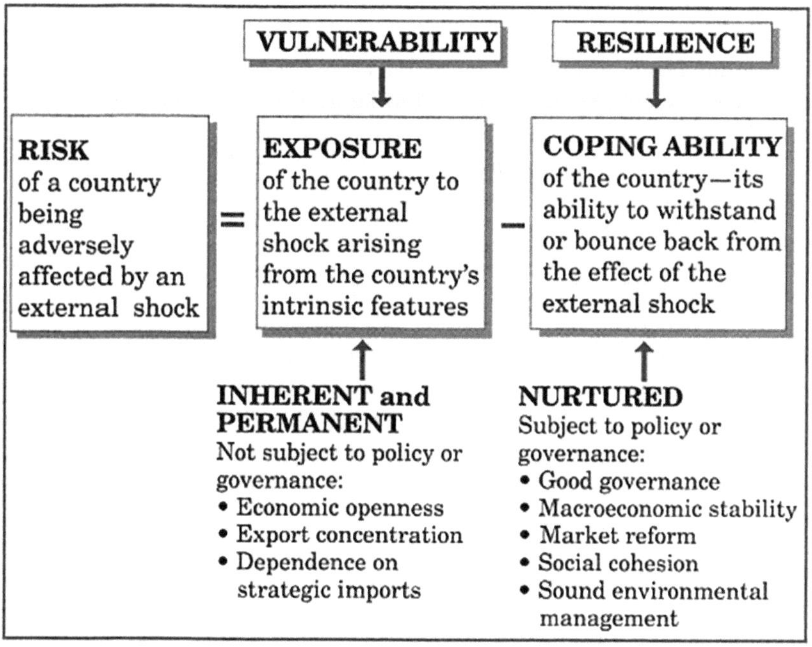


**Fig. 4.1** External shocks and risks, vulnerability, resilience (*Source* Briguglio 2004)

between the two becomes clearer. That is, vulnerability relates to the inherent characteristics of a country, regardless of governance and policies, while resilience is constructed through policies and governance that influence how a country responds to external shocks. For example, the degree of economic diversification determines whether a country is economically vulnerable to external shocks. So, the more diversified an economy becomes through policies, the more resilient it will be to external shocks. By making this distinction, the policies we should adopt in response to external shocks become clearer.[2] I start by introducing the first and second points—i.e., the meaning of external risk and vulnerability, and how these concepts are commonly viewed.

[2] Briguglio (2004) argues that resilience includes elements inherent to a country. In contrast, Guillaumont (2009) states that "Vulnerability can be perceived as the result of three components: (1) the size and frequency of the exogenous shocks…; (2) exposure to shocks; (3) the capacity to react to shocks, or resilience." Based on this, he argues that a distinction needs to be made between structural vulnerability, which is not related to policy, and vulnerability that is derived from policy. While the concepts in this book are based on those of Briguglio (2004), it should be noted that policies may pose the risk of exacerbating vulnerability, and that the exacerbation of vulnerability as a result of policy failure can amplify the impact of external shocks.

### 4.1.2 External Shocks and Growth

Regarding the first aspect of this discussion, the WEF characterizes external shocks based on the concept of risk. Kaplan and Mikes (2012), as cited in the WEF Global Risks 2013 report (WEF 2013), identify three categories of risks: (1) preventable risks (internal risks within organizations such as unlawful conduct by employees); (2) strategic risks accepted voluntarily for higher returns (such as a bank assuming credit risk when making a loan), and (3) external risks that arise outside an organization's management capabilities (such as natural and political disasters or macroeconomic shifts). Resilience relates to category (3). Various types of external risks fall under category (3), and the WEF identifies three key types based on expert opinion surveys: first, economic and environmental risks linked to climate change; second, risks related to the rapid expansion of digital technology; and third, risks associated with health catastrophes (WEF 2013).

The WEF (2020) shows that the likelihood of the occurrence of global risks is particularly high for (1) extreme weather events, (2) failure to respond to climate change, and (3) natural disasters, while in terms of the magnitude of impact, the top three risks are (1) failure to respond to climate change, (2) weapons of mass destruction, and (3) biodiversity loss. From their surveys, we can see that in the first half of the 2010s, the prevailing view was that economic shocks comprised the most likely risk. Economic-related events, such as income inequality, financial crises, and fiscal imbalances, ranked high in terms of both likelihood and impact. This perception seems to be a result of the Global Financial Crisis (GFC) that began in 2007. In contrast, by the latter half of the 2010s, environmental concerns, including climate change, were increasingly viewed as a top priority. While global economic conditions have settled somewhat and concern about an economic crisis or shocks has declined, this can be seen as a sign of increased awareness of climate change and the environment, as reflected in the adoption of the Paris Agreement and the SDGs.

Regarding risks and growth, Brunnermeier (2021) points out that if one only chooses to avoid risk, there will be no downturn due to risk, but the long-term growth rate itself will be lower. In contrast, accepting a certain degree of risk will lead to higher average growth in the long run, even if it fluctuates. Needless to say, some kinds of business activities, such as start-ups and research and development (R&D), are the foundation of growth, but also involve significant risk. If we follow the classification of risks set out by Kaplan and Mikes (2012) above, risk is unavoidable in achieving high economic growth. In addition, this relationship also applies to the third type of risk. For example, if a company builds its factories solidly, increases its inventories, and keeps its retained earnings to withstand any disaster or economic crisis, productivity under normal conditions will be severely impaired. The same is true for a country. Investing in disaster prevention to reduce the risk of a disaster of any size to zero is not an optimal allocation of resources.

In other words, pursuing only resilience will reduce the growth rate. Alternatively, if resilience is totally lacking, the damage caused by shocks will be far greater and any recovery will be slower. This tradeoff will be touched on again in the next section in the discussion of the relationship between disasters and growth. The choice to accept a certain degree of risk involves two issues: controlling the size of the economic downturn caused by the shock and recovering from the subsequent economic downturn. The former includes major shocks that sometimes occur at the global level, such as the GFC, which was beyond the control of a single country. The latter may involve not only a short-term recovery from the shock but also the need to address long-term and structural issues.

This is important in that if we can prevent a major downturn in the economy and enable a rapid recovery while assuming a certain degree of risk, the growth rate itself will have a greater chance of being high. When we discuss resilience, we usually focus only on the need to build a safe and secure society, and in terms of recovery, we aim to return to the previous state. However, society requires a certain degree of risk-taking to achieve not only sustained growth but also higher growth, provided that we can control fluctuations and achieve a rapid recovery from shocks—a point that does not seem to have been examined extensively in previous studies. In the section on resilience below—before continuing the discussion on resilience and growth—I examine the idea that resilience has a greater impact on the economy than is generally discussed.

### 4.1.3 Vulnerability

The second aspect, then, concerns the question of vulnerability and what determines whether a country is economically vulnerable to external risks. Briguglio (2004) states that economic vulnerability stems from the degree of an economy's openness (measured by the ratio of trade to GDP), the concentration of exports, and dependence on imports of strategic commodities. It is easy to understand how a high degree of economic openness makes an economy more susceptible to external shocks. It should be noted, however, that while a high degree of openness poses external risks, it also provides opportunities for growth. Moreover, a high level of exports increases a country's susceptibility to changes in international prices.[3] The same is true for countries with a high dependence on imports of strategic commodities. These three characteristics typically apply to small countries, such as island nations.

The OECD also discusses economic vulnerability (Röhn et al. 2015). Citing various previous studies, the OECD report uses domestic imbalances in the financial sector, non-financial sector, asset markets, public sector, and external sector to create an index of vulnerability to global changes in finance, trade, and market confidence. Vulnerability to economic crises is discussed in more detail in Sect. 4.3 of this chapter.

[3] Although the above discussion focuses on trade in goods, this also applies to services. One of the major effects of the COVID-19 pandemic was the decline in tourism revenue due to the restrictions on travel.

On the other hand, discussions of vulnerability to disasters often focus on geographical conditions, leading to both a technological perspective on infrastructure construction and a social perspective, such as community disaster management. The economic debate on disasters is broadly divided into those related to the government sector, especially in terms of public finance, and those related to business. Regarding the former, the key topic is advance investment in disaster prevention based on geographical conditions, together with expenditures on recovery after an event. For the latter, as the term BCP (business continuity plan) was coined around the 1970s, it has long been recognized that the occurrence of a disaster could significantly impede the continuity of a company's business.

Needless to say, it is essential to protect the lives of employees, maintain production, and preserve data. In terms of vulnerability, as supply chains become more global, the risks of a disaster that could threaten the continuity of production are increasing. These fears became a reality in 2011 with the Great East Japan Earthquake and floods in Thailand. Many companies with parts manufacturing plants in the Tohoku region were severely impacted by the earthquake and tsunami, disrupting their production. The organization of production bases for parts is one indicator of vulnerability. The response to such risks is to make production lines more earthquake-resistant, to incorporate options for alternative sources of procurement, and to reassess component inventories.

To date, efforts have been made to measure the degree of a country's vulnerability. For example, Guillaumont (2009) provides indicators for structural vulnerabilities. The components of structural vulnerability are shown in Fig. 4.2. Since the indices include not only economic structures but also such factors as geographical isolation and natural disasters, they incorporate a broad range of elements commonly perceived as vulnerabilities. If we break down vulnerability as shown in Fig. 4.2, it is evident why small countries, especially island states, are classified as highly vulnerable. That is, most of those countries have such factors as a small population, small markets, geographical isolation, a generally high concentration of commodity exports, and a high proportion of primary industries—all of which are relevant to the exposure index. Furthermore, with regard to shock indicators, they are susceptible to disasters and their agricultural production and exports are unstable. Thus, policies to increase resilience are particularly critical in these countries.

These discussions have since deepened, often linked with discussions concerning the allocation of concessional funding to developing countries, particularly small island developing states. Against this backdrop, several vulnerability indices were developed by international organizations and in 2024, the UN High Level Panel on the Development of a Multidimensional Vulnerability Index proposed a vulnerability index—based on structural vulnerability and lack of structural resilience, and comprising three dimension: economic, environmental and social—as a response to the UN General Assembly Resolution 75/215 of 2021. The concepts constituting this structural vulnerability are as follows: Exposure to fluctuations in international trade and financial flows, Exposure to fluctuations in export earnings, Exposure to fluctuations in strategic import prices, Exposure

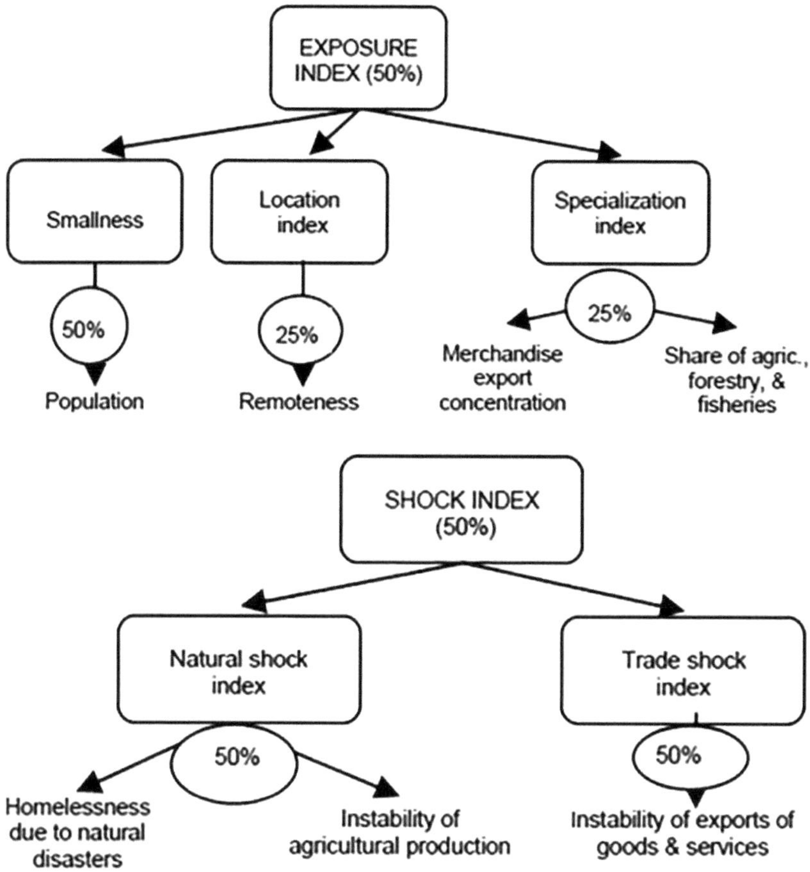


**Fig. 4.2** Structural vulnerability indicators (*Source* Guillaumont 2009, 204, Fig. 1)

to natural hazards, Exposure to extreme weather events, Exposure to ecosystem pressures, Exposure to global health shocks, Spillover effects of reginal violence, Exposure to entrance of international forced displacement of people (UN 2024).

### 4.1.4 Resilience

Finally, the third aspect is resilience. According to the WEF (2013), building resilience is necessary in order to be prepared for unforeseen risks where knowledge on how to respond is limited. It then presents countries' five subsystems (economic, environmental, governance, infrastructure, and social) as essential to nurturing resilience. This framework is comprehensive in that it includes both economic and environmental aspects. The framework also identifies three perspectives related to system resilience—robustness, redundancy, resourcefulness—and two related to system performance in the event of a crisis: response and recovery.

Robustness refers to the ability to absorb and withstand crises—specifically, the safety valves and firewalls built into a country's system to prevent the impact of shocks from spreading and the decision-making mechanisms for dealing with crises. Redundancy means the excess capacity and backup systems that enable continuity in the event of disturbances.[4] Resourcefulness means, for example, the size of social capital or human capital and, where possible, the ability to turn adverse effects into positive ones. The flexibility of the system is important, as is the extent to which it can be linked to innovation. Response refers to the ability to act quickly when facing a crisis, such as through information gathering and an inclusive response involving the private sector. Recovery refers to the ability to return to a normal state and can be defined as a government's ability to provide information and make policy decisions.

In recent discussions, the UN (2024) presents the lack of structural resilience as one of the two elements of a vulnerability index as mentioned earlier. The concepts constituting this are as follows: Low capacity to integrate with international markets, Lack of economies of scale, Low domestic economic capacity, Inadequacy of water supply, Lack of resilience of agricultural system, Lack of resilience to heat shocks, Demographic pressure, Ineffective social service provision, and Lack of gender equity. Here specific details are provided on what is particularly crucial for our society.

Most previous studies on resilience have focused on either economic crises or disasters. The Japanese government, for example, dealt with the economic impact of the global economic crisis and the Great East Japan Earthquake as separate topics in its white paper. Aizenman et al. (2019) discuss fiscal space in normal times and fiscal resilience when considering a fiscal response to economic fluctuations. Since fiscal stimulus is desirable in an economic crisis, fiscal space makes it possible. This relationship also applies to disaster recovery. The WEF (2013) discusses this in the context of redundancy.

What do economic crises, disasters, and pandemics have in common, and what are their differences? Briefly, natural disasters reduce physical stock and human capital, while pandemics affect only human capital. However, economic crises do not directly destroy capital but reduce capital utilization. Each has a different pathway of impact on the economy, which then spreads geographically and over time. Looking at a disaster, its primary effect is physically limited to a specific area, but it may have secondary effects on production as it spreads along the supply chain, which then impacts demand. When a major disaster occurs, a temporary increase in demand related to reconstruction can be expected due to increased

[4] Taking electricity as an example, a certain level of excess capacity for generating electricity above the current level of demand is constantly maintained. Otherwise, if a serious disaster or accident were to occur, the entire system would be at risk.

reconstruction by corporations and fiscal spending. However, from a medium- to longer-term perspective, because priority is placed on investment in reconstruction, it could lead to a decline in spending on education in both fiscal and household terms. This would not only affect demand for those expenditures but also have a negative impact on social capital formation over time.

I will discuss the relationship between resilience and growth in the following section, but before that, let us look at some commonly held views on this relationship. First of all, it is generally believed that greater resilience will contribute more to sustained growth. In other words, resilience is viewed as a factor that enables sustained growth. Discussions in the field of development almost always involve goals like "inclusive and sustainable development," while resilience is usually not included as part of such a mission statement. I consider this to be because resilience is regarded as a factor that enhances sustained growth. However, there are significant differences between resilience and sustainability. Therefore, it is quite appropriate to discuss them separately.

Sustained growth simply means a continuous increase in production factors or a continuous improvement in productivity. In this way, a country can increase the scale of its output. On the other hand, increasing resilience means improving preparedness for external shocks, even at the expense of short-term production. This is true in the case of natural disasters, pandemics, or even economic crises. For example, a company should build a sturdy factory that can withstand earthquakes or floods up to a certain magnitude or have a financial reserve or insurance policy in place in case a disaster strikes. The same applies to economic crises, where a certain amount of fiscal space is set aside for emergency fiscal mobilization in case a crisis causes a drop in demand. Put simply, if these measures are not taken, such resources would instead be used for production, so increasing resilience has the effect of lowering growth in the short run. From this point of view, it makes sense to distinguish between resilience and sustainability, discuss them separately, and examine how they interact.

At the end of this section, I summarize Table 4.1, outlining the different effects of economic crises, disasters, and pandemics in terms of vulnerability and resilience. The table can be considered with reference to the GFC, the Great East Japan Earthquake, and the COVID-19 pandemic. As can be seen, economic crises, disasters, and pandemics affect different areas of society and impact the economy through distinct pathways. Each of these three risks is linked to each of the three factors of production: productivity, capital, and labor. In this sense, they also represent external shocks when discussing resilience. Naturally, policies to increase resilience to each of these will also differ.

**Table 4.1** Vulnerability and resilience vis-a-vis different external risks

| Item | Economic crisis | Natural disaster | Pandemic |
|---|---|---|---|
| Direct impact | Economic system | Physical and human capital | Human capital |
| Spread of impact | Starts in one country and spreads globally | Mostly region-specific (but spreads globally through supply chains) | Starts in one country and spreads globally |
| Channel of economic impact | Demand shock and subsequent decline in utilization of capital | Primarily a supply shock (destruction of physical and human capital, production constraints) | Both supply shock (destruction of human capital, stagnant logistics) and demand shock (lower demand due to restrictions on mobility) |
| Vulnerability | Economic structure and fundamentals; Governance | Physical capital and supply chain resilience; Governance | Public health Governance |
| Response and recovery | Economic policies focusing on fiscal and monetary policy | Investments in disaster prevention; Post-disaster investment in recovery | Balance between healthcare policy (e.g., containment) and economic policy |

*Source* Author

## 4.2 Natural Disasters and Economic Growth

### 4.2.1 Trends in Damage Caused by Natural Disasters

Figure 4.3 shows the long-term trend in damage caused by natural disasters. Until the 1960s, when major disasters occurred, the number of deaths was extremely high. The deadliest year in this respect was 1931, when 3.7 million people died in the Yangtze-Huai River floods in China. The second-deadliest year was 1929 (three million deaths), when northern China was struck by famine due to a severe drought. The last time the death toll exceeded one million was in 1965, when India was hit by famine due to a drought. The key factor behind the decline in such extremely high death tolls since the 1970s is the reduction in death tolls resulting from drought and famine. As far as records show, there have been no famines with a death toll in excess of 100,000 since the Ethiopian famine in the early 1980s.

Drought-related deaths are the result of famine caused by the effects of natural phenomena on agriculture. Although the risk of famine has not been eliminated—as it still occurs at times in Africa—our ability to overcome famine has improved considerably due to advances in agricultural technology, increased household

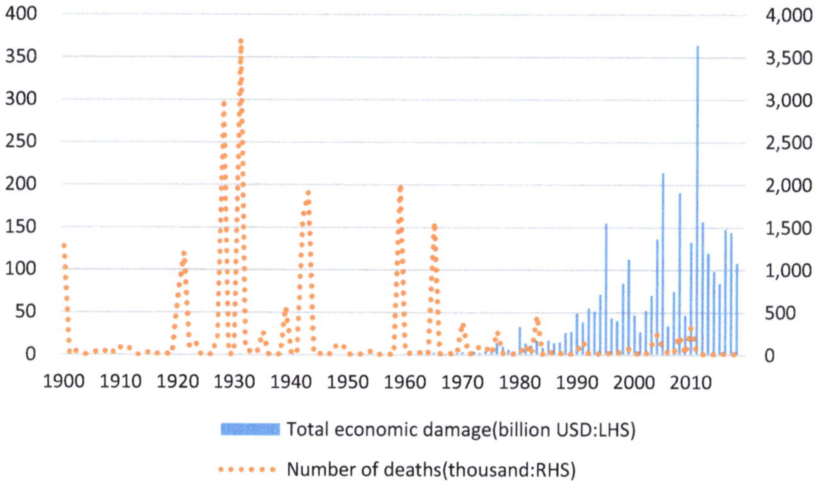


**Fig. 4.3** Trend in damage caused by natural disasters (*Source* Author's compilation from our world in data)

incomes, and better international cooperation. On the other hand, the number of deaths from other natural disasters that directly affect people has not been declining as much as it should: there have been years since 2000 with large death tolls from earthquakes and windstorms, while other large-scale natural disasters continue to cause major catastrophes. Alongside this, the economic damage caused by disasters has increased significantly since the 1980s. In contrast to the number of fatalities, the amount of damage has tended to increase. A breakdown of the damage shows that damage caused by extreme weather events is increasing, while floods are still causing a certain amount of damage every year. In particular, the amount of damage jumps when a severe earthquake occurs. This raises the question of how these trends relate to economic growth.

### 4.2.2 The Relationship Between Damage from Natural Disasters and Economic Growth

Growth has not necessarily reduced the human toll of disasters. It is true that as an economy grows and, for example, earthquake-resistant housing increases, the human suffering caused by earthquakes declines. In this respect, economic growth reduces human suffering from disasters. However, as an economy grows and urbanization leads to population growth in cities, the lowest-quality housing tends to be built in areas with the poorest living conditions. This increases the risk of damage in the event of a disaster. This is the tradeoff between urbanization as a result of economic growth and human suffering. In other words, economic growth can both increase and reduce the number of human casualties from a disaster. The

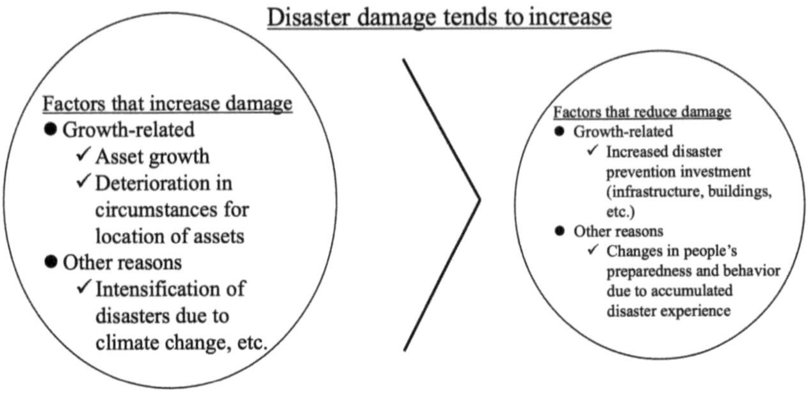


**Fig. 4.4** Changes in the scale of damage from disasters (*Source* Author)

people most likely to be affected are the poor, a situation that will persist until the economy develops further and slum areas become more habitable. Ishiwatari (2016) points out that one-third of the world's poor live in disaster-prone areas. Thus, the strengthening of resilience to disasters is important from the perspective of inclusiveness.

Similarly, for economic damage, as the economy grows, damage is mitigated by better infrastructure and housing. Yet this can also increase the value of the assets lost in the event of a disaster, as assets become more accumulated and concentrated. There is also the problem of deterioration of location. Ishiwatari (2016) states that "As population growth and urbanization progress with socioeconomic growth, populations tend to concentrate in hazardous areas, including overcrowded areas, low-lying areas, and hillsides, so assets that are vulnerable to disasters, such as low-quality housing and infrastructure facilities, are accumulated." As with human suffering, there are many cases where disasters have had a particularly large economic impact on the poor. The fact that economic damage from disasters is on a rising trend suggests that the factors that increase damage with growth far outweigh those that reduce damage associated with growth. This is illustrated in Fig. 4.4.

### 4.2.3 Impact of Natural Disasters on Economic Growth

The fact that damage from disasters has been increasing suggests that investment in disaster prevention has not kept pace with the rising risks. There are several possible reasons for this. First, investments to prevent increases in damage may not be commensurate with the benefits gained. Second, such investments may not be prioritized, since the occurrence of a disaster is uncertain. Third, the budget may be insufficient to invest in disaster prevention.

To understand how disasters affect the economy and growth, let us look at the mechanisms by which disasters affect the economy and growth. When a disaster occurs, production is affected by the destruction of capital. As production decreases, people's incomes decline as well. In addition, as resource allocation is prioritized toward capital spending, such as means of production and housing for reconstruction, consumption expenditures are likely to be negatively affected. Regarding disaster-related damage, Hallegatte (2014) states that prior studies often distinguish between direct losses due to the physical phenomena of disasters and indirect losses caused by the after-effects of a disaster, with the latter having a longer-lasting impact. He introduces additional perspectives on disaster impacts, such as asset losses and various types of production losses. The latter include business disruptions, production losses directly resulting from asset losses, supply chain disruptions, macroeconomic impacts such as reduced demand, prolonged adverse effects on investment, and increased production driven by reconstruction demand.

Disasters cause physical damage to the capital stock. Since growth is a concept based on flow, we need to consider how the destruction of capital—a stock—in a disaster affects production, or flow. Hallegatte (2014) explains the mechanism as follows: when capital is destroyed by a disaster, factories can no longer operate and roads cannot be used for logistics. The total value of the destroyed assets is equivalent to the value those assets would have produced in the future. A distinctive feature of disasters is that the lost capital is not destroyed in the order of least productive first. While disasters depress output through lost capital, the random destruction of capital further disrupts the desirable mix of capital, shifting the initial production curve downward.

Figure 4.5 illustrates this relationship. First, production shrinks due to the reduction of capital caused by disasters. If the damage is minor, the decline will only be marginal; capital is reduced from Ko to Ko-$\Delta$K, and consequently, output changes from A to B, alongside the existing production curve. However, if the damage is large, the production curve itself shifts downward, as described above, and production declines further to point C. In the case of an economic crisis, capital is not fully utilized. Theoretically, because the capital with the lowest productivity is the first to cease operating, such a shift in the production curve will not occur. By contrast, in the case of a disaster, this mechanism does not apply. As the loss of capital occurs randomly—including highly productive capital—the negative impact on productivity in the economy will be significantly greater.

Hallegatte (2014) further notes that positive externalities of lost capital (e.g., infrastructure) and the spillover effects must also be considered. At the same time, losses can be offset depending on the level of idle assets. He also emphasizes that the effect of economic stimulus during the reconstruction period depends on the economic situation at the time. For example, disasters do not always occur when economic stimulus is desirable; however, losses of this type can be recovered over time. Hallegatte (2014) explains that the total value of lost production is the difference between baseline production in the absence of disaster and actual

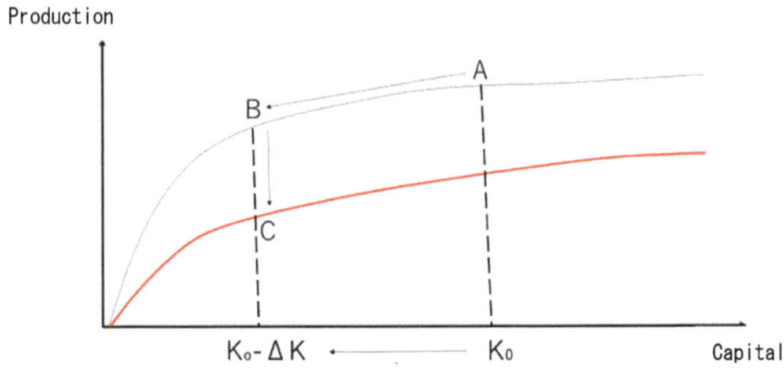


**Fig. 4.5** Effect of a disaster on production (*Source* Hallegatte 2014)

production, and that the larger the scale of the disaster, the longer the recovery period will be.

Hallegatte also argues that instead of simply returning to the pre-disaster state, disasters bring about a variety of changes. For example, a disaster may cause a previously existing production unit to disappear and, conversely, a new unit may emerge in its place. When a disaster destroys a factory's production lines, the factory often installs the latest equipment. This increases productivity, so the production is greater than before the disaster. It is possible that a disaster will hasten the renewal, even if not through a company's own strategy, and that this will result in accelerated capital after the reconstruction period. The same is true for social capital: if higher-standard roads are built after a disaster, this will reduce travel times, which in turn has a positive impact on business activity.

Thus, the possibility arises that disasters may ultimately have the effect of increasing productivity. It remains unclear whether these improvements would have happened had the disaster not occurred. In a sense, disasters force the renewal of capital, and while this is generally viewed as improving productivity, it would be difficult to argue that the timing of renewal—when induced by disaster—could ever be optimal.

### 4.2.4 Empirical Analyses of Natural Disasters and Growth

How, then, can empirical studies illustrate the relationship between disasters and growth? Many studies have been conducted, but conclusions have been varied and no clear consensus has emerged.[5] Sawada et al. (2011) examined the impact of disasters by distinguishing between natural disasters and man-made disasters, such as war and economic crises. Analyzing 189 countries between 1968 and 2001, they found that natural disasters have a larger negative short-term impact than man-made disasters. However, they also showed that natural disasters have a positive

[5] See, for example, studies by Cavallo and Noy (2011), Ishiwatari (2016), and Inui (2018).

impact on growth in the long run. Albala-Bertrand (1993) used a macroeconomic model to demonstrate the impact of disasters on output, finding that capital losses from disasters have very little impact on output. The study concluded that public support should be limited to assistance for disaster victims.

On the other hand, Skidmore and Toya (2002) found that disasters have a positive impact on growth. This is because disasters destroy capital stock, which does not directly affect GDP itself, while investment in reconstruction boosts GDP. They argued that climate-induced disasters also have a long-term positive impact on growth. Their contention is that while total factor productivity (TFP) is the largest driver of growth, disasters are positively correlated with both investment in human capital and TFP. This is because disaster-prone countries have a high risk of physical capital destruction, so investment is redirected to human capital in the long run.

Lastly, Sawada and Shimizutani (2008) found that in the Great Hanshin-Awaji (Kobe) Earthquake in 1995, the impact on consumption was lower for households that owned assets than for those that did not, since the former were able to borrow money. In other words, the poor are not only more likely to be materially affected by a disaster due to their poor living conditions, but they are also more likely to suffer greater negative economic impacts. This case illustrates how disaster is related to inclusiveness.

Conversely, two studies published by the World Bank found that disasters have a negative impact over the long term. Hochrainer (2009) examined the long-term effects of major disasters from 1960 to 2005 by comparing counterfactual scenarios—assuming no disaster occurred—with actual economic trends. Hochrainer found that disasters reduce GDP by an average of 2%, a median reduction of 4%, five years after they occur.[6] Raddatz (2009), also of the World Bank, estimated that climate-related disasters above a specific level reduce GDP per capita by 0.6%.

In addition, Hallegatte and Dumas (2009) argued that in developing countries, beyond their impact on productivity, disasters can create a poverty trap when they reduce income. This, in turn, reduces educational opportunities and investment and can hinder long-term development. This point is particularly important, as it suggests that disasters, if they leave "scars" on human capital formation, can constrain long-term growth. Similar outcomes can also be applied to economic crises and infectious diseases. Cavallo et al. (2013) show that disasters only affect growth if they result in political change over the long term, while they do not affect the economy over the short or long term unless they are extremely large-scale.

Thus far, there is no consensus on the impact of disasters on economic growth—a critical issue when considering disaster resilience. This uncertainty affects the way investment in disaster reduction is directed to enhance resilience. If economic growth is higher in disaster-prone countries, it could mean that growth is

---

[6] The World Bank's *Investing in Resilience* report, published in 2015 when the 3rd UN World Conference on Disaster Risk Reduction was held in Sendai, Japan, also states that disasters reduce growth by 2%.

more easily achieved when they limit disaster-related investment to the bare minimum—such as to save lives—and keep the disaster-prone conditions unaddressed. Although this assertion may seem counterintuitive, theoretically, it could be interpreted to mean that directing investment toward productive investment rather than toward disaster prevention will lead to higher growth. In other words, empirical findings that disaster-prone countries are more likely to have strong growth could indicate that the increased growth was a result of a resource allocation strategy that favors productive investment over disaster prevention measures.

Indeed, in many developing countries, this situation appears to be the case, at least to some extent. Investment in disaster prevention is deferred in favor of investments directly related to productivity, such as electricity and transportation. Ishiwatari (2019) finds that investment in disaster reduction is limited in low-income countries, which tend to start increasing their investment in disaster reduction only when the damage caused by disasters increases as a result of economic growth. Many prior studies have focused on how disasters affect investment decisions, such as the shift from physical to human capital, but how investment is allocated must also be considered between the objectives of production and disaster prevention. This seems to be a key point when considering resilient growth. However, as far as I am aware, no studies exploring this perspective have been conducted so far.

What we want to understand is not only how disasters affect growth but also how we should prepare for disasters with a known likelihood of occurring. From a macro perspective, the key question is how much should be allocated to investment in disaster prevention in the context of promoting growth. One of the main challenges in conducting such an analysis is the lack of reliable data on how much countries spend on disaster prevention. Not only are there no international statistics on the scale of government investment in disaster reduction, but even individual countries lack consistent data on the level of such investment. In one of the few studies to tackle this issue, Ishiwatari and Sasaki (2020) examined past flood control investments in nine major flood-prone countries in Asia and calculated the funding gap between the investment and future demand for disaster prevention through modeling. Determining the actual value of past investment in disaster prevention can support analysis of how the level of such investment impacts growth.

There has been no comprehensive analysis of how effective disaster prevention investments are in promoting growth and what level of allocation is desirable from a macro perspective. At this moment, one possible approach would be to take a micro-level approach: a cost–benefit analysis (CBA) of individual projects and programs. Flood control was the first area of CBA conducted in the US, and this kind of analysis is now frequently used for large projects everywhere. Ishiwatari (2016) presents several examples, including the case of flood control, where such investment in the US has an average cost–benefit ratio of 4, compared to 3.3 in Japan. By comparing CBA with other public investments, the economic rationale for the allocation of funds will be ensured.

However, CBA typically calculates benefits by focusing on the scope of individual projects, so it does not take into account the broad spillover effects or social transformation that may lead to growth over the long term. For example, the synergistic impact of concentrated investment and the stimulation of innovation can increase productivity, leading to long-term growth, but these aspects are not included in CBA. In recent years, some studies have been conducted on how infrastructure can have wider economic benefits. For example, ADB et al. (2018) suggest that the wider economic benefits of transportation can be analyzed through network analysis, general equilibrium modeling, and other methods. For now, it can be said that investments in resilience have the potential to produce growth effects beyond those indicated by CBA. Thus, a greater emphasis on resilience is likely to be desirable for long-term growth. Further study in this field is expected to contribute to unraveling the role of resilience in growth.

### 4.2.5 Policies to Increase Resilience to Disasters

The types of disasters that strike countries vary significantly, as does the degree of exposure each country faces. Consequently, policies for increasing resilience to disasters differ by country. Nevertheless, international guidelines exist in the form of the Sendai Framework for Disaster Risk Reduction. The SDGs, in their target 11.b of Goal 11 (Cities and Human Settlements), call on states to "...develop and implement, in line with the Sendai Framework for Disaster Risk Reduction 2015–2030, holistic disaster risk management at all levels."

This framework, adopted at the Third UN World Conference on Disaster Risk Reduction held in Sendai in 2015, sets the direction for countries to work together to reduce the risk of disasters and build resilience to disasters. This framework identifies the following four priority areas that require sectoral and cross-sectoral action by countries.

i. Understanding disaster risk
ii. Strengthening disaster risk governance to manage disaster risk
iii. Investing in disaster risk reduction for resilience and,
iv. Enhancing disaster preparedness for effective response and to "Build Back Better" in recovery, rehabilitation, and reconstruction.

Priority (i), understanding disaster risk, begins with the collection and analysis of relevant data and includes risk assessment and the use of technology such as geospatial information. Data collection and risk assessment seem to be essential, especially in helping to determine the extent to which resources should be allocated for the purpose of disaster risk reduction. In a broad sense, for the five subsystems (economy, environment, governance, infrastructure, and society) listed in WEF (2013) to assess resilience, the collection, analysis, and utilization of data could be extremely important not only for society and the environment but also for the economy. Priority (ii), governance, encompasses not only laws, regulations, and public policy, but also collaboration with communities. The participation of all stakeholders, including women's leadership, children, and people with disabilities, is also mentioned.

Priority (iii), investments in disaster reduction, states that investment by the public and private sectors in disaster reduction, including software, is essential. It is interesting to note that preventive investment is assumed to be more cost-effective than investing in post-disaster recovery and reconstruction. This may be based on the fact that ex-post evaluations of many projects indicated a high internal rate of return. Here, land use policies and building codes are also mentioned as a preventive action. One of the perspectives of resilience highlighted in WEF (2013) was redundancy. It is, for example, the question of how many years of flooding probability should be assumed for the design of dikes to control flooding. From the perspective of redundancy, this entails constructing higher and longer dikes in terms of flooding probability, but it also needs to be cost-effective. In this regard, it is hoped that more sophisticated CBA techniques and other quantitative methods will be refined to include a growth perspective as mentioned.

Priority (iv) includes strengthening preparedness, such as disaster forecasting and warnings, as well as better recovery and reconstruction, as part of an effective response. The latter involves making various improvements during post-disaster rehabilitation, reconstruction, and recovery, as well as building communities that are more resilient to future disasters. This appears to apply to all subsystems and incorporate robustness and responsiveness, using the terminology of WEF (2013), and is related to the argument that disasters have a positive effect on productivity. In the case of public infrastructure, governments can plan for a better reconstruction. In addition, in order to encourage firms to upgrade their production facilities, governments must provide entrepreneurs with a sense of safety that they will be protected from the next disaster of similar magnitude. This is a precondition for long-term growth. From this perspective, Priority (ii), which calls for the participation of all stakeholders, is extremely important.

The preceding sections have provided an overview of the relationship between natural disasters and growth. While the human toll from disasters has not necessarily decreased, the economic costs have continued to rise. Disasters cause economic damage through the destruction of capital and, at least in the short term, seem to have a negative impact on growth. While there is no consensus on the long-term effects, the impact of human capital formation can be a "scar" and undermine long-term growth. While international guidelines for disaster resilience have been put in place, in terms of stimulating growth, a common understanding has yet to be established regarding the appropriate level of domestic resources to allocate to investment in disaster prevention.

## 4.3 Infectious Diseases and Economic Growth

### 4.3.1 How Damage Caused by Infectious Diseases Affects Economic Growth

Infectious disease outbreaks endanger human lives and severely disrupt economic activity. Throughout history, humankind has experienced external shocks from the spread of infectious diseases, such as plagues in medieval Europe and the 1918 Spanish flu. As of September 2022, the death toll from the COVID-19 pandemic had claimed more than 6 million lives, with over 600 million people infected globally. Infectious diseases remain one of the greatest external risks facing global society.

The pathways through which infectious diseases affect the economy differ from those of disasters. Disasters affect production by destroying physical and human capital while also having negative impacts on consumption during recovery. Infectious diseases, on the other hand, do not destroy physical capital but affect human capital. On the supply side, the spread of infectious diseases negatively impacts production because human capital is reduced or not fully utilized. At the same time, disruptions to logistics can further constrain output. In the modern era, when one country is hit by a disease outbreak, negative effects can spread to the rest of the world via the global value chain, as the disease becomes a pandemic. The initial outbreak of COVID-19 occurred in China, but its impact spread around the world. Attempts at containment measures led to the sharp contraction of demand. This was because the service sector comprises the largest share of the economy in developed countries, with much of it based on the movement of people and the provision of face-to-face services.

COVID-19 and the subsequent containment measures had a significant short-term negative impact on economies worldwide—from both supply and demand perspectives. Agarwal and Gopinath (2021) once estimated that global economic GDP losses from the pandemic would amount to USD 5.3 trillion over five years if COVID-19 were to have a prolonged impact. Policy responses to COVID-19 in most countries centered around two pillars: health policy and economic policy. At least in the short term, there was a tradeoff between containment-based health policy and economic activity. Baldwin and di Mauro (2020) show that the stronger the containment measures to control the number of new cases, the greater the negative impact on the economy. Given that human lives were at stake, a strong health policy was vital in controlling the infection and ensuring that the healthcare system would not be overwhelmed. In parallel, a macroeconomic policy response was necessary to mitigate the impact on the economy. This recognition was deeply entrenched, having been highlighted by the World Bank (2020) and others. Many countries, including those in Europe, as well as Japan and the US, took unprecedented economic measures. Ultimately, the extent to which a society was affected by this tradeoff depended largely on the degree of resilience built up during normal times.

### 4.3.2 Responding to Infectious Diseases from a Resilience Framework

After the outbreak of COVID-19, Japan was able to keep the number of infections and deaths somewhat low compared to global trends. This occurred despite the country's proximity to China—the epicenter of the pandemic—and the high volume of human movement between the two countries. The Western media speculated on the reasons for Japan's initial success,[7] often pointing to the country's high overall hygiene standards and widespread awareness of hygiene practices. These were perceived as a strength in terms of Japan's inherent vulnerability profile. In contrast, the Japanese government's expert panel emphasized the effectiveness of the country's cluster-based countermeasures,[8] highlighting Japan's resilience through its policy response. This is depicted in Fig. 4.1, where the former concerns the vulnerability of the country as a whole, while the latter demonstrates the resilience.

Japan declared a state of emergency on April 5, 2020, in accordance with the Act on Special Measures Against Novel Influenza (the "Special Measures Act"). Following this declaration, prefectural governors were granted greater powers to invoke emergency measures for specific time periods and regions. Unlike in previous crises, it was almost unprecedented for local government leaders to take the lead in Japan. In general, local governments' responses were more timely and effective in implementing policies suited to local conditions than those at the national level. The existence of a system that allowed local government to have some decision-making authority suggests that the system already possessed a certain level of institutional robustness in responding to the crisis and limiting the spread of the infection.

The fact that the country was able to react quickly without a medical crisis was also deserving of praise. The five perspectives from WEF (2013) offer a useful framework for assessing this resilience across various dimensions. For example, constraints on the testing system were a major topic of discussion, or Japan lagged Europe, the US, and China in developing new drugs and a vaccine, which may be related to its "resourcefulness." Another serious problem was the slow passage of the budget, which was a prerequisite for implementing economic countermeasures. This is related to the "response" dimension among the five WEF resilience factors.

It is beyond the scope of this book to provide a detailed examination of COVID-19. Instead, I offer a summary of the discussion by Hirota (2020), presented in Box 4A, as a policy case study. It considers healthcare infrastructure facilities for COVID-19, particularly for mild or asymptomatic patients, from the standpoint of quality growth.

---

[7] See, for example, New York Times (March 26, 2020), BBC (April 20, 2020), Foreign Policy (May 14, 2020), and Financial Times (May 25, 2020).

[8] Expert Meeting on the Novel Coronavirus Disease Control, "Analysis of the Response to the Novel Coronavirus (COVID-19) and Recommendations" (May 29, 2020) https://www.mhlw.go.jp/content/10900000/000635389.pdf. Accessed July 9, 2020.

**Box 4A: [Policy Case Study] 'Redundancy' of healthcare facilities for COVID-19**

Hirota (2020) discusses healthcare infrastructure during the first half of 2020, when COVID-19 was still an unknown infectious disease and posed a major threat to society. While the context has since evolved, the risk of another epidemic of an unknown infectious disease remains, and society as a whole should continue to strengthen its resilience against such disease threats. One of the key challenges in early treatment was the wide variation in COVID-19 symptoms, ranging from critical, serious, mild, and asymptomatic cases, which made treatment and recuperation difficult to manage. Hirota (2020) discussed how societies should prepare appropriate treatment and recuperation facilities, including those with mild or asymptomatic infections.

When Japan declared a state of emergency in April 2020, there was a serious concern that the healthcare system would be overwhelmed due to a shortage of healthcare workers and hospital beds. According to the relevant Japanese statutes, COVID-19 patients should, in principle, be hospitalized in infectious disease beds at designated medical institutions for infectious diseases. Thus, at the beginning of the outbreak, even patients with mild infections and asymptomatic pathogen carriers were admitted. The relevant law also permitted the hospitalization of patients at other (non-designated) medical institutions in cases of emergency or other unavoidable circumstances.

As the crisis unfolded and the number of infections rose, those with such symptoms were widely hospitalized at non-designated facilities. When the situation deteriorated further, the policy was revised so that such patients were, in principle, instructed to recuperate at home. Tragically, some deaths occurred among the home care patients due to infections. Once the state of emergency was declared, local leaders negotiated with private-sector hotels to provide accommodation for mildly infected and asymptomatic patients. Globally, many developing countries did not reach the World Health Organization's standard minimum number of beds per population (3.5 beds per 1,000 people) in the first place. This raises an important question: How should countries prepare for the risk of infectious diseases, which may or may not occur, and how should they prepare for a shortage of hospital beds? Hirota (2020) examines this issue from the viewpoint of resilience, as described in this chapter.

A key characteristic of COVID-19 is that most infected individuals exhibit mild symptoms or are asymptomatic.[9] However, even for mildly infected individuals, early isolation is essential to reduce the spread of infection. Given these characteristics, the following considerations are important in increasing society's resilience in managing the isolation of infected people: (1) the effectiveness of isolation in preventing the infection's spread, (2) the number of beds required to secure capacity, (3) flexibility of scaling resources to increase or decrease the number of isolated patients, (4) the cost of implementing isolation measures, and (5) the financial burden of maintaining such facilities in normal times.

Regarding Japan's experiences during COVID-19, six options were available in terms of locations for treating individuals with mild or asymptomatic infections: newly built hospitals specializing in infectious diseases, vacant general hospital beds, temporarily constructed makeshift hospitals, private homes, hotels, and public facilities designed for other purposes. These are summarized in Table 4.2, assessed in terms of how effectively they align with the five WEF perspectives introduced earlier in this chapter. The more effective a facility is at controlling infection, the better. However, if the burden of maintaining the facility during normal times is excessive, this will put pressure on hospital management and the fiscal burden on society will eventually increase. A comprehensive, balanced approach is therefore necessary—one that enables a coordinated, society-wide response to infectious disease outbreaks. The difficulty here is that in many countries, hospitals and other healthcare facilities are privately managed, and in such cases, it is not possible for each hospital to have sufficient facilities that can scale up to manage the spread of infectious diseases. To analyze the costs for the study, a benchmark number of infected patients (more than

[9] Initially it was estimated that approximately 80% of those infected were mild or asymptomatic, while 14% were serious, and 6% were critical (Anderson et al. 2020).

**Table 4.2** Pros and cons of options to treat mild and asymptomatic cases of COVID-19 patients

| | Effectiveness of disease control | Sufficient number of beds | Flexibility to increase/ decrease capacity | Costs associated with isolation | Costs in normal times |
|---|---|---|---|---|---|
| New hospitals for infectious diseases | ◎ | X | X | ◎ | X |
| Utilization of vacant general hospital beds | △ (risk of nosocomial infection in hospital) | ○ | ○ (to respond quickly to some extent) | △ (large cost, adverse effect on management of hospitals) | ◎ |
| Makeshift hospital | ○ | △ | △ | △ (construction) | ◎ |
| Convalescence at home | X | ◎ | ◎ | ◎ | ◎ |
| Use of hotels | ○ | ◎ | ○ | △ (rented) | ◎ |
| Use of public facilities | ○ | ○ | ◎ | ○ | ◎ |

*Note* ◎ excellent, ○ good, △ fair, × very poor
*Source* Author

60,000 mildly infected and asymptomatic pathogen carriers at the peak of infection) was set.[10] Hirota (2020) introduced the actual cases of responses, estimated the assumed cost burden for some of these options, and discussed how the policy options that seem realistic should be considered while identifying the limitations and challenges involved.

The following section provides a brief summary of this approach. First, the option to build new hospitals for infectious disease or increase beds specified for infectious disease patients in general hospitals in advance of a crisis would require tremendous expense and seems not to be financially viable. Secondly, the use of vacant beds in general hospitals for treating all mildly infected or asymptomatic people in the event of an outbreak may have limitations because of the cost burden on individual hospitals, the impact on nosocomial infections, and the treatment of patients with other illnesses. Therefore, in reality, the use of vacant beds in general hospitals will have to be limited (e.g., for the treatment of serious patients). Thirdly, there have been examples of makeshift hospitals being assembled around the world. Most of these examples seem to treat patients with serious conditions such as pneumonia. Considering that the cost in normal times is avoidable and that a temporary hospital does not need to be fully functional for mildly infected patients, this would be one way to secure extra capacity of medical infrastructure.

Fourth, during COVID-19, home care was the most common place for mildly infected and asymptomatic people in virtually all countries. At least initially, there were significant concerns about home care due to a lack of knowledge of COVID-19, particularly as the fatality rate appeared

[10] According to the "Development of the Medical Provision System for Novel Coronavirus Infections with a View to the Future" (administrative communication dated June 19, 2020) by the Ministry of Health, Labour and Welfare's Headquarters for the Promotion of Countermeasures against Novel Coronavirus Disease Control, in the most severe urban scenario, the number of patients requiring medical care with mild symptoms and no symptoms was 62,844.

to be high. Home care as an extra capacity requires no additional costs, either in isolation or in peacetime, but may have serious consequences if an infected person experiences a rapid deterioration of symptoms and carries the risk of transmission to family members. Many developing countries—particularly lower-income ones—often have large families living together in small houses in poor conditions. Therefore, home treatment presents a much higher risk than in developed countries.

Fifth, in Japan, private hotels were used for the medical treatment of mildly infected and asymptomatic people (there are similar examples in other countries). In Japan, all medical costs for designated infectious diseases are publicly financed, so people treated there were not charged for their stay. However, in addition to the large fiscal cost burden, renting a hotel is inevitably inefficient, as renting an entire building creates unused rooms. Most of the hotels used were private-sector hotels, but public lodging facilities of the state or local government, for example, should be actively utilized as places to recuperate. This may be the option for developing countries where state-owned enterprises (SOEs) still manage hotels, by which such hotels can play a public role as infrastructure in case of emergencies.

In addition, it is possible to prepare contracts in advance for hotels that are constructed through public–private partnerships (PPPs) or financed by government-affiliated banks to serve as additional lodging facilities in cases of emergency. Furthermore, there are public facilities with lodging facilities (e.g., government training houses). If such public facilities were made available, the costs associated with the facilities would be reduced, with only minimal additional costs, such as utility upgrades.

In summary, it is essential to respond quickly to rising case numbers in the event of a disease outbreak and to ensure that the costs of maintaining the facilities—both in normal times and during crises—remain sustainable for the nation. From this perspective, the first option is to use existing public facilities that can be repurposed as treatment centers in the event of a pandemic. Multipurpose public facilities, which are more financially manageable due to budgetary constraints, can be beneficial for society as a whole. Even if sufficient capacity cannot be secured at the peak of a pandemic, prioritizing suitable accommodation allows the authorities time to prepare for subsequent measures. The second option is the use of hotels. While hotels can offer comfortable accommodation, they can also entail a large fiscal burden, and therefore, this option may not be feasible for some developing countries. However, this could certainly be a viable strategy in terms of exploring the role of the public sector in countries with state-run hotels.

A third option is the construction of makeshift healthcare facilities. Where suitable locations are available, tents and other temporary outdoor healthcare facilities are a viable option for developing countries. In disaster-prone countries, costs can be kept down by planning for the shared use of common facilities for temporary housing. For example, cots, toilets, and tents made of cardboard can be utilized for disaster purposes, and prefabricated facilities can be assembled—another example of multipurpose use. In cases where additional capacity is still required, convalescence at home remains a last resort, taking into account the patient's underlying health conditions.

## 4.4 Financial Crises in Developing Countries and the Transition to Economic Resilience

Financial crises are a significant risk in terms of their potential to bring steady economic growth to a halt and can have detrimental impacts on people's lives. Some of the best-known examples include: the Great Depression that began in 1929 following the New York stock market crash; the Latin American debt crisis and the subsequent recession of the 1980s, often referred to as the "lost decade;" the Asian Financial Crisis (AFC) of 1997–98, triggered by the collapse of the Thai baht, later spreading to South Korea and Indonesia; and the GFC of 2007–08, in which subprime mortgage problems in the US caused several financial institutions to fail, setting off a global recession.

Although the term "financial crisis" is often used to refer to a crisis in the banking system, such as a series of bank runs, Claessens and Kose (2013) identify four types of crises: currency crises, sudden stop crises (crises in capital balances or international payments balances), public debt crises, and banking crises.

Such crises are frequent occurrences. According to Laeven and Valencia (2012), between 1970 and 2011, there were 147 banking crises, 218 currency crises, and 66 public debt crises.[11] In addition, 30% of banking and currency crises and 70% of sovereign debt crises occurred in conjunction with one or both of the other types of crises.

On the other hand, Reinhart and Rogoff (2011) identify five types of crises: public external debt crises, public domestic debt crises, banking crises, currency crashes, and inflation spikes. Based on an analysis of the past 800 years, their study shows the surprising frequency of financial crises, and their likelihood of occurrence does not vary much between developed and developing countries. Also, different types of crises often occur simultaneously. They also highlighted the tendency of crises to spread across borders.

As shown in Fig. 4.6, many countries have experienced banking crises at regular intervals since the 1970s.[12] The 2008 GFC saw banking crises occur simultaneously in more than 20 countries worldwide. Although the US was the epicenter of the GFC, banking crises ensued throughout Europe and as far away as Mongolia and Nigeria. About half of the world's economies experienced negative growth and unemployment rose in many countries—even those that did not have a banking crisis.[13] With the increasing movement of people, goods, and money across national borders, national economies cannot remain insulated from large-scale crises occurring outside their borders. There are many more channels through which such impacts can be transmitted, including sharp declines in trade volumes, reversal of capital inflows, sharp stock selloffs and drops in stock prices, or major fluctuations in exchange rates.

---

[11] In the database of Laeven and Valencia (2012), a systemic banking crisis is defined as (1) significant signs of financial distress, such as bank runs, banking system losses, and bank liquidations, as well as (2) policy interventions vis-a-vis major banks to address sizable banking system losses. A currency crisis is defined as a currency's annual depreciation of 30% or more compared to the USD, while a public debt crisis is defined as a default or a deferral of debt repayment. Although the database does not include sudden stop crises, Claessens and Kose (2013) define these as a sudden decline in capital flows—specifically, a drop of at least two standard deviations below the sample mean compared to the prior year.

[12] According to the analysis by Laeven and Valencia (2012), banking crisis cycles are often linked to credit cycles. Of the 129 banking crises in their database, 45 of these were preceded by a credit boom.

[13] According to the WEO database, economic growth in 2009 was negative in 93 of the 192 countries for which data is available. Comparing unemployment rates between 2007 and 2010, the numbers show increased unemployment in 72 of the 112 countries for which data are available.

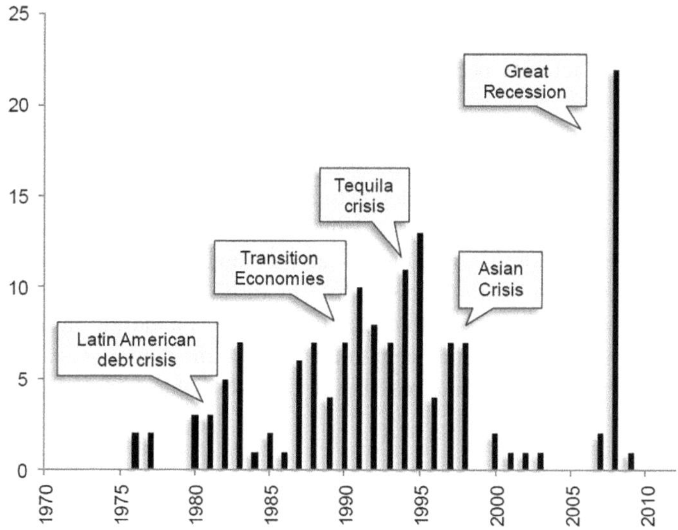


**Fig. 4.6** Number of banking crises (by initial year) (*Source* Laeven and Valencia 2012, 10)

The potential fragility of currencies, capital inflows, public debt, and banks—all of which depend on credit[14]—is a common cause of repeated financial crises. In the case of currency, for example, a 10,000 yen bill has value only if everyone believes it will continue to be exchangeable at this value. In Zimbabwe, a 100 trillion dollar bill was in circulation in 2009, but it was not even worth the price of a bus fare. Even for less extreme cases than this, if a currency's value plummets, causing inflation to soar, maintaining a stable exchange rate compared to other currencies becomes impossible.

Capital inflows, which usually take the form of loans and purchases of stocks and bonds by foreign investors and financial institutions, are also based on the expectation that the returns from these financial instruments in terms of price appreciation, dividends and yields are commensurate with the risk. If, for some reason, the market perceives that the risk/return equilibrium has been disrupted, and additional funding becomes difficult to obtain or an outflow of funds begins, it could cause share prices to decline or payments of interest and principal to be deferred.

For public debt, although the funds for repayment are generated through tax revenues or proceeds from the sales of government assets, the implicit assumption is usually that the repayment will be made by refinancing. In general, when

[14] The word "credit" has two meanings. The narrow definition is the provision of funds now on the condition that the money will be repaid in the future (e.g., a loan). The broad definition is trust in someone and the judgment that they are worthy of trust. Although it is an ambiguous term, I am using the term "credit" in this book because it represents the essence of finance.

government bonds, foreign bonds and loans mature, it is not expected that the repayment will be made from revenue from tax revenues and asset sales. In some cases, refinancing actually became difficult when confidence that public debt can be repaid collapses.

Banks are also inherently vulnerable, since their business model is based on lending funds at higher interest rates over the longer term from monies deposited on a short-term interest basis by depositors. Although regulations require banks to maintain a certain level of capital adequacy, if depositors become nervous and everyone tries to withdraw their money at the same time, they will be unable to do so because cash will run out. This, in turn, will spread to other banks, resulting in a panic. In addition, financial institutions, including investment banks and insurance companies, often have mutual cross-holdings of assets and liabilities. This increases the risk of a chain reaction in the event of a default or a collapse in asset prices.

### 4.4.1 Crisis Mechanism

There are three generations of economic theories on why crises occur. The factors in these theories often combine in an actual crisis.

The first-generation theory originated in the arguments of Krugman (1979), who pointed out the problems of such macroeconomic policies as excessive fiscal and monetary expansion. This theory holds that the gradual erosion of economic buffers due to weak fundamentals—such as a decline in foreign reserves caused by an overvalued currency and a sustained current account deficit—can at some point lead to the simultaneous occurrence of speculative attacks and capital withdrawals. This theory is often used to explain the debt crises that unfolded in some developing countries in the 1980s (Caves et al. 2007).

The second-generation theory is the notion of multiple equilibria, as demonstrated by Obstfeld (1994). If the fundamentals are neither sufficiently positive nor clearly negative, the likelihood of a crisis increases when other investors withdraw their capital. Therefore, the best strategy in this case is to withdraw one's own capital to contain any potential losses. Alternatively, if other investors continue investing, the best strategy is to remain invested and earn a return (Table 4.3). In other words, if investors behave as if there is a crisis, then that crisis becomes self-fulfilling. The crisis that beset European currencies in 1992–93 is seen as a case where this aspect of multiple equilibria outweighed a deterioration in fundamentals.

The third-generation theory focuses on balance sheet vulnerabilities and moral hazards. During the AFC of 1997–98, countries that were previously viewed as solid from a macroeconomic policy perspective experienced successive crises due to sharp increases in inflows of short-term external debt. For governments and companies in developing countries, the least expensive option is often to repeatedly raise funds with short-term maturities from developed countries that have ample funds. However, if the exchange rate depreciates, repayment costs may rise sharply,

**Table 4.3** Multiple equilibria structure (simplified depiction)

| | | Investor B | |
|---|---|---|---|
| | | Remains invested | Withdraws capital |
| Investor A | Remains invested | (1) Both A and B get a return<br>(Equilibrium. No crisis develops) | (2) A's risk of total loss increases<br>B's loss is limited<br>(Investor A changes mind and withdraws capital. Moves to (4)) |
| | Withdraws capital | (3) A's loss is limited<br>B's risk of total loss increases<br>(Investor B changes mind and withdraws capital. Moves to (4)) | (4) Both A and B incur some losses<br>(Equilibrium. Crisis occurs) |

Let us first consider investor A's options. When investor B remains invested, the options available to investor A are either (1) or (3); the rational choice is (1), since this is the profitable option. When investor B withdraws capital, the options available to investor A are either (2) or (4); the rational choice is (4), since losses will be reduced. The same is true when the positions are switched, so (1) and (4) are both stable equilibria

*Source* Author

and they will not be able to refinance at the same terms of interest rates, further increasing costs. Furthermore, a moral hazard situation can emerge when financial institutions operate under the assumption that they will be bailed out with public funds if they fail. This can lead to excessive borrowing and elevated risk-taking.

### 4.4.2 Vulnerability Factors and Policy Space

As Ghosh et al. (2009) point out, a crisis occurs when there is both an underlying vulnerability and a specific trigger. However, triggers can take many forms, including economic and political, as well as domestic and foreign factors. A recent example is the crisis in Mozambique, which defaulted on its foreign debt in 2017. The crisis was triggered primarily by the discovery of hidden debt liabilities at SOEs. Another example is that of Mongolia, which saw its net foreign reserves turn negative in 2015, after deducting the amount held by the People's Bank of China. This put the country in an extremely difficult position with massive external debt maturities totaling USD 2.7 billion (about 24% of 2017 GDP) in 2017–18. This was triggered by a combination of factors, including a decline in the price of copper and other key resources and lower capital inflows due to delays in decisions on mining development. In 2017, the IMF, JICA, and others arranged a financial assistance program for the country, and a default was avoided. As a special case, in 2012, Iran was subjected to sweeping financial sanctions from the West and other countries, including a freeze on central bank assets and a blocking of interbank transactions. This precipitated a serious crisis, including a sharp drop in the exchange rate.

Since triggers themselves are hard to predict, when discussing resilience to financial crises, it is important to consider how to address vulnerabilities while keeping an eye on the trigger risks.[15] From this perspective, it is worth noting that the Asian countries most affected by the 1997–98 crisis proved much more resilient in the 2007–2008 GFC. It is difficult to compare the impact on these countries of the AFC, which had its epicenter in the Asian region, with the impact of the GFC, which was a spillover of problems in advanced countries. However, Jeasakul et al. (2014) calculate that declines in capital outflows and exports from Asia during the GFC exceeded those during the AFC. This article also points out that the initial decrease in real GDP was more severe in Asia than in other regions, including those countries where the GFC originated.

However, the impact of the shock from the GFC on Asia was limited, and there were no events like plunging exchange rates or a wave of bankruptcies of financial institutions and corporations, as occurred during the AFC. The region's resilience was also demonstrated by the fact that by 2010, exports and capital inflows had recovered to above their pre-crisis levels.

Jeasakul et al. (2014) point out that after the AFC, Asian countries reduced their financial and external vulnerabilities through financial and structural reforms that strengthened regulations[16] and introduced oversight to prevent financial institutions from excessive leverage and widening exchange rate bands. A quantitative analysis examined real GDP losses during the GFC using the five factors that indicate financial and external vulnerability as shown in Table 4.4. The analysis shows that the factors with the greatest impact in terms of losses were growth of credit to GDP (the higher the pre-crisis growth, the larger the loss) for financial vulnerability, and external debt to GDP (the higher the pre-crisis level, the larger the loss) and foreign reserves to short-term external debt (the lower the ratio of foreign reserves to short-term external debt, the larger the loss) for external vulnerability.

Didier et al. (2011), who also research the resilience of emerging economies during the GFC, argue that increased fiscal space, stronger domestic balance sheets, and confidence in the ability to implement expansionary fiscal and monetary policies enabled countercyclical economic policy management to mitigate recession both before and during the crisis.

During a crisis, the key challenges faced by governments are likely to be lower revenues, difficulties in financing budget deficits, and the depletion of foreign reserves due to capital outflows. Under such pressure, policymakers have no other

[15] In some cases, the existence of a vulnerability may be related to the likelihood of a trigger, such as the relationship between economic conditions and political turmoil. If addressing vulnerabilities helps to lower the likelihood of a trigger being set off, then focusing on vulnerabilities is even more pertinent.

[16] Specifically, this refers to measures such as loan-to-value, debt-to-income, credit growth regulations, restrictions on currency and maturity mismatches, deposit reserve requirements, and risk weight adjustments, among others. Minsky (1992) states that there is instability in the capital economy: during a boom period, speculative financing increases and inflation risk rises. If the authorities try to keep this in check with a tighter monetary policy, debt deflation takes place, which effectively becomes a vicious cycle of selling caused by insufficient cash flow and falling asset prices.

**Table 4.4** Elements of financial and external vulnerability (subject to quantitative analysis)

| Financial | External |
|---|---|
| Change in credit to GDP | Gross external debt |
| Increase in bank NPLs to total loans | Net external debt |
| Credit to deposit ratio | Foreign reserves to short-term debt |
| Banking system's net foreign assets | Current account deficit |
| Increase in bank capital to total assets | Cumulative net non-direct investment inflow |

*Note* NPL = non-performing loan
*Source* Author based on Jeasakul et al. (2014)

option than to quickly cut spending, increase taxes, and raise interest rates, but this creates a procyclical situation that depresses the economy even more. In contrast, if the fiscal balance was in good shape before the crisis, with low public borrowing, and confidence in fiscal discipline remains high while the risk of default is considered to be low, a government can compensate for a drop in private-sector business activity by implementing a temporary fiscal stimulus that raises funds at reasonable interest rates and maturity terms.

In addition, in a financial crisis, policymakers who need to defend their currency often have to significantly tighten monetary policy, which can further weaken the domestic economy. However, if markets are confident in the central bank's ability and autonomy to manage monetary policy appropriately, the risk of speculative pressure on the currency will be limited. In this case, policymakers can avoid drastic interest rate hikes that risk driving the economy into a severe recession. In addition, if the financial sector is well-regulated and sufficiently sound, financial intermediaries will be able to function smoothly, and monetary policy will be more flexible and effective than would otherwise be the case. For example, Thailand's policy interest rate, which stood at 5.0% before the GFC in 2006, was successively lowered to 3.25% in 2007, 2.75% in 2008, and 1.25% in 2009.[17]

### 4.4.3 Balance Sheet Composition

The expansion of financial markets, including the development of bond and stock markets and an increase in the number and size of users of financial services, has been a key factor in improving balance sheets. The ability to raise funds with longer maturities in the country's own currency reduces exchange rate fluctuations and refinancing risks. Didier et al. (2011) further argue that before the

[17] However, as mentioned above, it is difficult to make direct comparisons between the AFC and the GFC. While the AFC was driven by rapid outflows of capital from some countries in Southeast and East Asia to the developed countries, during the GFC, unease spread throughout the developed economies. In addition, China's massive economic stimulus package of 4 trillion yuan supported external demand in neighboring emerging Asian economies.

**Table 4.5** Comparison of International Investment Positions in 2017 (Thailand: TH; Turkey: TR; Argentina: AR) (in USD billions)

| | TH | TR | AR | | TH | TR | AR |
|---|---|---|---|---|---|---|---|
| Assets | 456 | 228 | 334 | Liabilities | 489 | 684 | 313 |
| Direct investment | | | | Direct investment | | | |
| Capital | 68 | 34 | 41 | Capital | 212 | 167 | 53 |
| Loans | 49 | 9 | – | Borrowings | 17 | 14 | 24 |
| Portfolio investment | | | | Portfolio investment | | | |
| Equities | 27 | 0 | 38 | Equities | 125 | 52 | 24 |
| Bonds | 27 | 1 | 20 | Bonds | 41 | 125 | 129 |
| Financial derivatives | 2 | – | – | Financial derivatives | 3 | – | 3 |
| Other investments | 81 | 75 | 178 | Other investments | 91 | 325 | 80 |
| Foreign reserves | 203 | 108 | 55 | | | | |

*Source* Compiled by Author from *International Financial Statistics [IFS] Yearbook* 2018[18]

GFC, emerging economies had become less dependent on external financing due to improvements in their current account balances. In addition, the ratio of debt (bonds and loans) to external liabilities declined, with assets exceeding liabilities on a net basis after deducting external assets, while equities increased.

During a financial crisis, exchange rate depreciation can help to absorb shocks by making exports more competitive, but a high level of external debt will increase the burden in local currency terms. However, during the 2007–2008 GFC, exchange rate depreciation had a limited impact on emerging economies, and even had the positive effect of increasing external assets in terms of the local currencies. Moreover, external liabilities in the form of foreign investors' equity holdings decreased as share prices declined. However, Sahay et al. (2015) caution that excessive expansion of financial markets increases the costs of economic and financial volatility. They highlight the importance of proper regulatory supervision and the need to prevent excessive financial development.

Table 4.5 compares the 2017 external assets and liabilities (International Investment Position, or IIP) of Thailand, Turkey and Argentina. The IIP is an indicator published by the IMF that shows a country's breakdown of external financial assets and liabilities. Compared to Turkey and Argentina, Thailand's highly stable direct investment capital comprises a much larger share of its liabilities. Moreover, its foreign reserves exceed its liabilities of portfolio investments in bonds, which tend to become rapidly depleted in times of financial instability. Thailand was the epicenter of the 1997–98 crisis due to concentrated speculative attacks from the market, but it was not a target of speculation in 2018, even as emerging economies such as Turkey and Argentina experienced dramatic capital outflows.

[18] The IIP in Table 4.5 provides a concise and easily understandable description of the main components. For example, "Capital" under "Direct Investment" in principle means investments in

**Table 4.6** Foreign reserves and appropriate ARA levels in 2017 (in USD billions)

| | Thailand | Turkey | Argentina |
|---|---|---|---|
| Foreign reserves | 203 | 108 | 55 |
| Appropriate ARA level | 93–140 | 134–201 | 63–95 |

*Source* Author's calculation using ARA template

### 4.4.4 Foreign Reserves

Many studies have examined foreign reserves as an indicator of vulnerability to a crisis. Frankel and Saravelos (2010) conclude that in 50 of the 83 studies reviewed, foreign reserves as a percentage of GDP, M2, or short-term debt were statistically significant indicators, as was the 12-month change in foreign reserves.[19] Their study also concluded, based on correlation analysis, that the substantial accumulation of foreign reserves by many developing countries prior to 2008 played an important role in reducing their vulnerability to the GFC.

If a country has accumulated enough foreign reserves, it can temporarily intervene to control excessive exchange rate fluctuations, even when the exchange rate is under speculative pressure. Moreover, when a country is perceived as having the ability to manage this pressure, it also helps to reduce its vulnerability to speculative attacks. Three months' worth of imports and total short-term external debt are often used as indicators for measuring the adequacy of foreign reserves.

In recent years, the IMF has used the Assessing Reserve Adequacy (ARA) method to calculate and publish appropriate foreign reserves levels for developing countries based on the value of exports, broad money, short-term debt, and other liabilities, as well as differences in exchange rate regimes and the existence of capital controls. Using this method to compare the foreign reserves of the three aforementioned countries with their appropriate levels in 2017, the following table shows that while Thailand had ample foreign reserves, Turkey's and Argentina's reserves were below recommended levels (Table 4.6).

Foreign reserves are also a new factor to be considered in the framework of debt sustainability analysis for low-income countries, revised by the IMF and World Bank in 2017. Although this framework is mainly concerned with debt crises, it also puts forth the idea that the accumulation of a certain level of foreign reserves[20] can enhance the debt-carrying capacity of low-income countries.

investment targets where the percentage of voting rights held is at least 10%. At the same time, "Equities" under "Portfolio Investments" includes shares held for asset management purposes. Both of these are called equity.

[19] Jeasakul et al. (2014) and Didier et al. (2011) also mention the accumulation of foreign reserves as being a factor in resilience to financial crises.

[20] In the revised framework for assessing low-income countries' debt sustainability, debt-carrying capacity improves when, all other things being equal, foreign reserves increase to about 5.1 months of goods and services imports. However, accumulation of additional foreign reserves beyond this point has a slightly negative effect. While accumulating foreign reserves provides a buffer against a crisis, many analysts believe that this accumulation incurs the loss of opportunity in terms of

This section has provided an overview of financial crises and resilient growth. Financing is a powerful and indispensable part of economic growth. Still, financing is essentially driven by leverage, so it carries the risk of amplifying crises. Financial crises have been a recurring event throughout history. The indirect factors that contributed to past crises remain present today. These include increased fundraising from international financial markets by countries with relatively low income levels and the growing diversification of financial instruments and services through the evolution of financial technology. In order to achieve resilient growth, policy measures should be designed with the expectation that an external shock will eventually occur. Such measures include building foreign reserves and other buffers and using appropriate financial regulation and supervision to control the risks related to the financial sector and the external balance sheet.

## 4.5 Summary and Policies for Increasing Resilience

The following section summarizes this chapter and discusses policies on resilience to external shocks. Resilience is defined as the ability to withstand and recover from external shocks. Global external shocks take a variety of forms, including disasters, pandemics, and economic crises, and in general, external shocks from different sources are not often discussed collectively. Regardless of the differences in sources, there is a common expectation that the magnitude of the impact of external shocks on a society is determined by that country's inherent vulnerability and the resilience that can be fostered through policy. According to Briguglio (2004), a country's inherent vulnerability is not dependent on its policies or governance. Examples of this are the openness of an economy and the concentration of exports. However, some of these characteristics can also be shaped by policies over a longer period. Policies can influence the structural vulnerabilities discussed in the previous chapter: characteristics of a society, such as inequality, culture, and national consciousness, over the long run. Addressing these policies will help to enhance sustainability. Resilience refers to the ability of a country to respond to external shocks, relying on policies and governance that are shaped over the short- to medium-term span. On this basis, a model policy framework for promoting quality growth in the face of external shocks is presented in Fig. 4.7.

I introduced a framework for resilience that breaks it down into five perspectives. These perspectives can be further analyzed by the five WEF subsystems. These subdivisions allow us to consider policies that will increase resilience to different shocks in a larger and integrated framework. Different external shocks have different pathways for growth and require different measures for improving resilience. Disasters wreak direct destruction on physical and human capital. This affects production, and the affected households experience asset shocks, causing them to reduce consumption.

the potential to invest these funds elsewhere, as well as negative external ripple effects. Obstfeld (2011), Rodrik (2006), and others have explored these issues in detail.

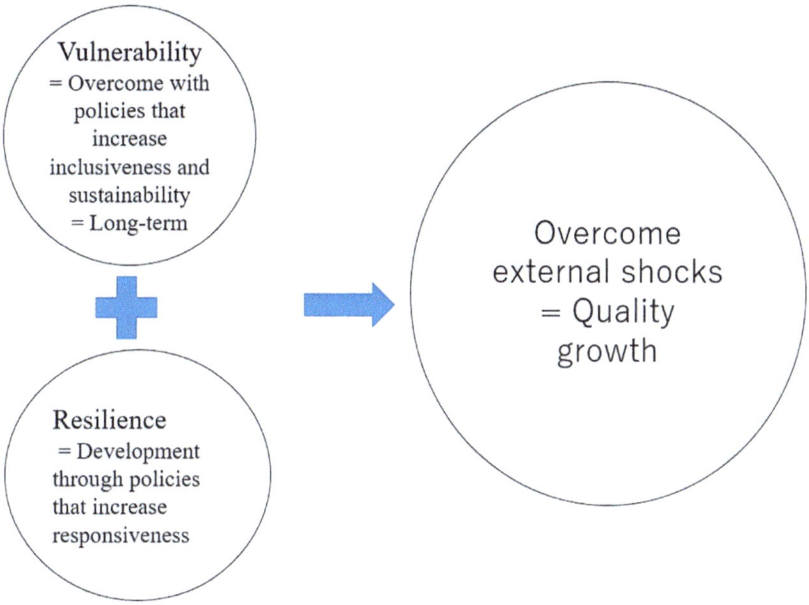


**Fig. 4.7** Overcoming external shocks to achieve quality growth (*Source* Author)

When a country enters the recovery phase after a disaster, GDP tends to grow as investments are made for reconstruction. While disasters cause losses to the economy in the short term, opinions differ as to their longer-term effects. This is because, as some argue, the capital destroyed by the disaster is rejuvenated during the recovery process, so it becomes more productive, or investment shifts to human capital, thus promoting long-term growth. This is the so-called "Build Back Better" approach. At the same time, the policy balance between how much investment should be allocated for disaster prevention and achieving high growth is an area for future study and discussion. The underlying premise is that accepting an appropriate level of risk—combined with resilience—will increase the base rate of growth itself.

Infectious diseases have a negative effect on production through their impact on human capital, and the effect on production through the global value chain is amplified. In addition, strong containment policies to control the spread of disease curb economic activity. We tend to think that developed countries are less affected by pandemics than developing countries because of their better nutrition and healthcare. However, the recent crisis has demonstrated that this is not necessarily the case. This is because restrictions on the movement of people have a particularly large impact on the service sector, which accounts for a large share of developed countries' economies. The economic impact of COVID-19 may not necessarily lead to a long-term decline in household spending compared to an economic shock, as it does not affect the assets of individuals.

However, restrictions on movement can have a larger negative impact in the short term, and if this causes a chain reaction of corporate bankruptcies and higher unemployment, the impact may be more protracted. Finally, the concept of "Build Back Better" is also applied to the case of infectious diseases. Countries and regions that were severely hit by SARS, such as Taiwan, studied their experience of the crisis and improved their own national systems. This is thought to have strengthened their resilience in the COVID-19 crisis.

Lastly, economic crises take different forms, such as currency, balance of payments, debt, and banking crises, but none of these destroy physical or human capital. Once a crisis breaks out, an economic downturn ensues, leading to high unemployment, falls in demand, and cuts in investment. Capital has not been destroyed, but its utilization becomes significantly lower. While economic crises clearly depress growth in the short term, it is not clear whether they lead to higher growth over the long term. Experiences vary from country to country. A review of the subsequent growth rates of countries that went through economic crises shows that growth is usually below or at best equal to the original growth rate. The US and Germany regained their previous growth rates following their respective crises in 2007 and 2008, but Iceland, Thailand, and Japan have yet to fully do so. Other countries, such as Mexico, are on a higher growth trajectory than before (Laeven and Valencia 2012).

Countries that have experienced an economic crisis often try to avoid a similar situation by reassessing their economic management. Therefore, after going through a crisis, they will be better prepared to respond to the next external shock. In other words, an economic crisis changes economic management. This is another form of "Build Back Better," but one based on economic management. Southeast Asian countries that experienced the AFC tightened their fiscal management after that crisis, significantly improved their fiscal balances, and built up foreign exchange reserves. These actions helped to reduce the impact of the GFC. Table 4.7 shows the differences in the Indonesian government's response to the AFC and the GFC, according to Muhammad Chatib Basri, former Minister of Finance, and Sjamsu Rahardja.

**Table 4.7** Indonesian government's policy response to two economic crises

| The 1998 crisis | The 2008 crisis |
|---|---|
| 1. Monetary policy: extremely strict. The Bank Indonesia increased interest rate levels to very high levels. Deposit account interest rates reached 60% in the peak crisis period. As regards liquidity, the government implemented a liquidity squeeze<br>2. Fiscal policy: to begin with there was a budget surplus, then this was reversed by permitting a large budget deficit<br>3. Banking health: Prudential banking regulations were extremely weak. NPLs reached 27%. LDR became more than 100%<br>4. Response towards banking: closure of 16 banks, which then led to rushes<br>5. Policies focused towards structural reform by carrying out economic liberalization, getting rid of monopolies, licensing<br>6. Exchange rate regime: managed floating. Economic players were not used to exchange rate risk changes and did not carry out hedging | 1. Monetary policy: Bank Indonesia's interest rate was reduced by 300 basis points from 9.5 to 6.5%. Liquidity was relaxed<br>2. Fiscal policy: the stimulus was implemented. The budget deficit enlarged, taxes reduced<br>3. Banking health: Prudential banking regulations were relatively tight. NPL less than 4%, LDR 77%, CAR around 17%<br>4. Response towards banking: deposit insurance increased from Rp 100 million to Rp 2 billion per account<br>5. Safeguarded relatively open trade regime<br>6. Exchange rate regime: flexible. Economic players start to become used to exchange rate risk changes |

*Note* LDR = loan-to-deposit ratio, CAR = capital adequacy ratio, Rp = Indonesia Rupiah
*Source* Basri and Rahardja (2010)

While a uniform policy is difficult, given the range of different external shocks, it is useful to categorize policy responses into (1) preparedness and readiness, (2) ability to withstand and mitigate the impact of shocks, and (3) recovery. I propose Table 4.8, showing representative policies for disasters, pandemics, and economic crises. Common factors include advance planning, prior investment or fiscal space to ensure readiness, rapid response to outbreaks, and better systems during recovery. In particular, the creation of institutions and systems is the key to all responses to external shocks and a stronger subsequent recovery, and this needs to be considered from a long-term perspective. Overcoming vulnerability is also important for sustainable growth. I will discuss institutions and sustainable growth in more detail in the next chapter.

**Table 4.8** Representative policies for external shocks

| | Disasters | Pandemics | Economic crises |
|---|---|---|---|
| Preparedness and readiness | Disaster prevention plans<br>Disaster prevention investments<br>Training and education<br>Risk assessment (hazard maps)<br>Governance | Infectious disease prevention<br>Prevention planning<br>Investment in healthcare | Securing fiscal space<br>Accumulation of foreign currency reserves<br>Appropriate financial regulation<br>Preparing a safety net |
| Withstanding to and mitigating shocks | Emergency response to an outbreak<br>Communication<br>Warnings and evacuation | Containment of outbreaks<br>Securing the healthcare system<br>Economic sustainability | Government intervention in a crisis (fiscal stimulus, monetary policy etc.) |
| Recovery | Use of insurance<br>Build Back Better: Reconstructing better housing and infrastructure, reconstructing better industry and livelihoods | Creating better systems<br>Economic stimulus packages | Policy intervention in markets<br>Creating a better economic system |

*Source* Author

## References


Agarwal, Ruchir, and Gita Gopinath. 2021. "Pandemic Economics." *Finance and Development.* December 2021, 10–12. IMF.

Aizenman, Joshua, Yothin Jinjarak, Hien Thi Kim Nguyen, and Donghyun Park. 2019. "Fiscal Space and Increasing Fiscal Resilience." ADB Economics Working Paper Series No. 582. Asian Development Bank.

Albala-Bertrand, J. M. 1993. "A Macroeconomic Model for Sudden Disaster Impacts." *World Development* 21 (9): 1417–1434.

Anderson, Roy M, Hans Heesterbeek, Don Klinkenberg, and T Deirdre Hollingsworth. 2020. "How Will Country-Based Mitigation Measures Influence the Course of the COVID-19 Epidemic?" *The Lancet* 395 (10228): 931–934.

Asian Development Bank (ADB), Department for International Development (UK), Japan International Cooperation Agency, and the World Bank. 2018. "The WEB of Transport Corridors in South Asia."

Baldwin, Richard, and Beatrice Weder di Mauro. 2020. "Introduction." in *Mitigating the COVID Economic Crisis: Act Fast and Do Whatever It Takes,* eds. Richard Baldwin and Beatrice Weder di Mauro, 1–24. CEPR Press VoxEU.

Basri, Chatib Muhammad, and Sjamsu Rahardja. 2010. "The Indonesian Economy amidst the Global Crisis- Good Policy and Good Luck." *ASEAN Economic Bulletin* 27 (1): 77–97.

Briguglio, Lino. 2004. " Economic Vulnerability and Resilience: Concept and Measurements (Part 2. 2)." In *Economic Vulnerability and Resilience of Small States*, eds. Lino Briguglio and Eliawony J. Kisanga. Formatek.

Briguglio, Lino, Gordon Cordina, Nadia Farrugia, and Stephanie Vella. 2008. "Economic Vulnerability and Resilience: Concepts and Measurements." Research Paper No. 2008/55, UNU-WIDER. United Nations University.

Brunnermeier, Markus K. 2021.*The Resilient Society*. Endeavor Literary Press.

Cavallo, Eduardo, and Ilan Noy. 2011. "Natural Disaster and the Economy: A Survey." *International Review of Environmental and Resource Economics* 5: 63–102.

Cavallo, Eduardo, Sebastian Galiani, Ilan Noy, and Juan Pantano. 2013. "Catastrophic Natural Disasters and Economic Growth." *The Review of Economics and Statistics* 95 (5): 1549–1561.

Caves, Richard E., Jeffrey A. Frankel, and Ronald W. Jones. 2007. *World Trade and Payments: An Introduction*. Pearson International Edition.

Claessens, Stijn, and M. Ayhan Kose. 2013. "Financial Crises: Explanations, Types, and Implications." IMF Working Paper.

Didier, Tatiana, Constantino Hevia, and Sergio L. Schmukler. 2011. "How Resilient and Countercyclical Were Emerging Economies During the Global Financial Crisis?" Policy Research Working Paper 5637. World Bank.

Frankel, Jeffrey A., and George Saravelos. 2010. "Are Leading Indicators of Financial Crises Useful for Assessing Country Vulnerability? Evidence from the 2008–09 Global Crisis." NBER Working Paper No. 16047. National Bureau of Economic Research.

Fujii, Satoshi, Koichi Kume, and Yohei Kobayashi. 2014. "Keizai rejiriansu no kōchiku to keizai seichō" [Economic Resilience and Growth]. RIETI Policy Discussion Paper Series 14-P-006. Research Institute of Economy, Trade and Industry.

Ghosh, Atish R., Jonathan D. Ostry, and Natalia Tamirisa. 2009. "Anticipating the Next Crisis: What Can Early Warning Systems Be Expected to Deliver?" *Finance & Development* 46 (3): 35–37.

Guillaumont, Patrick. 2009. "An Economic Vulnerability Index: Its Design and Use for International Development Policy." *Oxford Development Studies* 37 (3): 193–228.

Hallegatte, Stephane. 2014. "Economic Resilience: Definition and Measurement." Policy Research Working Paper 6852. World Bank.

Hallegatte, Stephane, and Patrice Dumas. 2009. "Can Natural Disasters Have Positive Consequences? Investigating the Role of Embodied Technical Change." *Ecological Economics* 68 (3): 777–786. ff10.1016/j.ecolecon.2008.06.011ff. ffhal-00719266f.

Hirota, Koki. 2020. "Shitsu no takai seichō no shiten kara kangaeru shingata korona uirusu ni taisuru kyōjinsei no arikata: Iryō infura tōshi ni taisuru ronkō" [Resilience to COVID-19 from the 'Quality Growth' Perspective: A Proposal of Medical Infrastructure Investment]. JICA Ogata Sadako Research Institute for Peace and Development.

Hochrainer, Stefan. 2009. "Assessing the Macroeconomic Impacts of Natural Disasters: Are There Any?" Policy Research Working Paper 4968. World Bank.

Inui, Tomohiko. 2018. "Shizen aaigai to keizai seichō" [Natural Disasters and Economic Growth]. *The Keizai Seminar*, February/March 2018: 22–25.

Ishiwatari, Mikio. 2016. "Saigai ni taisuru kyōjinsei ga shitsu no takai seichō ni kōken suruniwa: Bōsai enjyo ga chokumen suru kadai" [How Disaster Resilience Can Contribute to Quality Growth: Challenges Facing Disaster Risk Reduction Assistance]. JICA Research Institute Literature Review No. 3. JICA Ogata Sadako Research Institute for Peace and Development.

Ishiwatari, Mikio. 2019. "Investing in Disaster Risk Reduction: Scale and Effect of Investment in Flood Protection in Asia." United Nations for Disaster Risk Reduction.

Ishiwatari, Mikio, and Daisuke Sasaki. 2020. "Bridging the Gaps in Infrastructure Investment for Flood Protection in Asia." Working Paper No. 202. JICA Research Institute.

Jeasakul, Phakawa, Cheng Hoon Lim, and Erik Lundback. 2014. "Why Was Asia Resilient? Lessons from the Past and for the Future." IMF Working Paper.

Kaplan, Robert S., and Annette Mikes. 2012. "Managing Risks: A New Framework." *Harvard Business Review* 2012 (June): 48–60.

Krugman, Paul. 1979. "A Model of Balance of Payments Crises." *Journal of Money, Credit and Banking* 11: 311–325.

Laeven, Luc, and Fabian Valencia. 2012. "Systemic Banking Crises Database: An Update." IMF Working Paper.
Minsky, Hyman P. 1992. "The Financial Instability Hypothesis." Working Paper No. 74. Levy Economics Institute.
Obstfeld, Maurice. 1994. "The Logic of Currency Crises." NBER Working Paper Series.
Obstfeld, Maurice. 2011. "The International Monetary System: Living with Asymmetry." NBER Working Paper Series.
Raddatz, Claudio. 2009. "The Wrath of God- Macroeconomic Costs and Natural Disasters." Policy Research Working Paper 5039. World Bank.
Reinhart, Carmen M., and Kenneth S. Rogoff. 2011. *This Time is Different: Eight Centuries of Financial Folly*. Princeton University Press.
Rodrik, Dani. 2006. "The Social Cost of Foreign Exchange Reserves." NBER Working Paper Series.
Röhn, Oliver, Aida Caldera Sánchez, Mikkel Hermansen, and Morten Rasmussen. 2015. "Economic Resilience: A New Set of Vulnerability Indicators for OECD Countries." OECD Economics Department Working Papers, No. 1249. OECD Publishing.
Sahay, Ratna, Martin Čihák, Papa N'Diaye, Adolfo Barajas, Ran Bi, Diana Ayala, Yuan Gao, Annette Kyobe, Lam Nguyen, Christian Saborowski, Katsiaryna Svirydzenka, and Seyed Reza Yousefi. 2015. "Rethinking Financial Deepening: Stability and Growth in Emerging Markets." IMF Staff Discussion Note.
Sawada, Yasuyuki, Rima Bhattacharyay, and Tomoaki Kotera. 2011. "Aggregate Impacts of Natural and Man-Made Disaster: A Quantitative Comparison." RIETI Discussion Paper Series 11-E-023.
Sawada, Yasuyuki, and Satoshi Shimizutani. 2008. "How Do People Cope with Natural Disasters? Evidence from the Great Hanshin-Awaji (Kobe) Earthquake in 1995." *Journal of Money, Credit and Banking* 40 (2-3): 463–488.
Skidmore, Mark, and Hideyuki Toya. 2002. "Do Natural Disasters Promote Long-Run Growth?" *Economic Inquiry* 40 (4): 664–687.
United Nations (UN), President of the General Assembly's High Level Panel on the Development of a Multidimensional Vulneability Index. 2024. *High level panel on the development of a Multidimensional Vulnerability Index FINAL REPORT.*
World Bank. 2015. "Investing in Resilience." World Conference on Disaster Risk Reduction in Sendai. https://www.gfdrr.org/sites/default/files/publication/Investing-in-Resilience_1.pdf. Accessed June 19, 2025.
World Bank. 2020. "Protecting People and Economies: Integrated Policy Responses to Covid-19." World Bank.
World Economic Forum (WEF). 2013. *Global Risks 2013 Eighth Edition.* WEF.
World Economic Forum (WEF). 2020. *Global Risks 2020 15th Edition.* WEF.

**Koki Hirota** earned his B.A. in Economics from the University of Tokyo and holds a Ph.D. in Economics from Saitama University in Japan. His professional career spans several prominent roles in international development finance and policy, including Chief Economist, Director General of Operation and Strategy Department, and Director General of Southeast Asia and Pacific Department at the Japan International Cooperation Agency (JICA), and Chief Representative in Jakarta for Japan Bank for International Cooperation and in Hanoi for the Overseas Economic Cooperation Fund. In academia, he was a Professor at the Graduate School of Humanities and Social Sciences at Saitama University and a Visiting Fellow at the JICA Ogata Sadako Research Institute for Peace and Development. His recent publications include *Challenges in Fiscal and Monetary Policies in Mongolia* (co-edited, Springer, 2023) and *Addressing Social Infrastructure Needs in Asia: Towards a Pandemic Resilient Society* (co-edited, JICA, August 2025).

**Keiichiro Yuasa** is a Senior Director of Public Governance and Financial Management Team of Japan International Cooperation Agency (JICA). He leads the team to implement development cooperation in the areas of Public Administration, Financial Sector Development, Public Financial Management, Trade Facilitation and Customs Modernization. In his overseas assignments, he has been stationed at JICA Offices in Thailand and Sri Lanka where he had played important roles to plan and implement various development cooperation projects in the fields of governance, transportation, agriculture, etc. He occasionally delivers lectures on macroeconomics or credit risk analysis at the University of Tokyo or training courses organized by International Monetary Fund (IMF). He earned his B.A. in Economics from the University of Tokyo and holds a Master in Public Administration from Harvard University.

# Sustainable Growth: Respecting the Needs of Future Generations

# 5

Koki Hirota and Keiichiro Yuasa

## 5.1 Two Perspectives on Sustaining Growth

The third theme of quality growth—the sustainability of growth—will be discussed in this and the next chapter. The Development Cooperation Charter of Japan (DCC), adopted in 2015, aims for continued growth over the long term, stating that "growth… is 'sustainable' across generations, including consideration of harmony with the environment, sustainable economic and social growth and the perspective of combating global warming." In discussing the sustainability of growth, two different meanings are encapsulated: The first relates to the external environment surrounding our societies—climate change and natural resources—while the other concerns the economic and social mechanisms that allow the economy to continue to expand. While these are different topics of discussion, there are significant linkages between the two.

The term sustainability (or sustainable) came into frequent global use in 1987 when the World Commission on Environment and Development advocated the concept of "sustainable development" in its report to the UN General Assembly. In this report, "Our Common Future," sustainable development was defined as "development that meets the needs of the present without compromising the ability of future generations to meet their own needs." The Commission, as its name makes clear, proposes a path towards achieving both the en*vironment and development*. In Our Common Future, reference was made not only to traditional environmental issues such as factory pollution, but also to global warming, acid

K. Hirota (✉)
Tokyo, Japan

K. Yuasa
Governance and Peacebuilding Department, Japan International Cooperation Agency, Tokyo, Japan





K. Hirota (ed.), *Introduction to Quality Growth*,
https://doi.org/10.1007/978-981-95-6220-6_5

rain and the destruction of tropical forests. The section titled "Changing the quality of growth" in the report states that "Sustainable development involves more than growth. It requires a change in the content of growth, to make it less Material- and energy-intensive and more equitable in its impact." The expression "more than growth" is a perspective on quality growth that goes beyond simply aiming to increase incomes. By stating that the reduction in resources that accompanies growth should be taken into account, the Commission's objective is straightforward: sustainable development means achieving growth that does not come at the expense of future generations, i.e., quality growth. It is noted here that this does not mean that growth can be sustained only by balanced growth between the environment and the economy.

The discussions on sustainable development at the UN continue with the Earth Summit, convened every ten years since 1992, and then the SDGs, adopted in 2015. At the first Earth Summit in Rio de Janeiro, Brazil, held in 1992, the balance between economic development and environmental protection, along with the globally shared costs and benefits, was discussed. Agenda 21, adopted at that time, was a program of action for achieving sustainable development. Although many parts of the document relate to the environment and climate change, reference is made to elements necessary for continued growth, such as sound economic policies, poverty alleviation and human resource development, including health.

This discussion continued at the subsequent summits, held in 2002 and 2012, ultimately leading to the development of the SDGs. The SDGs include goals related to more than just environmental and climate change issues while also addressing human resources and economic development. In the SDGs, Goal 8 referred to growth in its name: Goal 8 will "promote sustained, inclusive and sustainable economic growth, full and productive employment and decent work for all." It is worth noting that the words "sustained" and "sustainable" are used with different intentions. There is a distinction between the goal that growth will continue for a specific period of time ("sustained") and the goal that future growth will not be impaired ("sustainable"). In Table 5.1, I distinguish between the concepts of sustained and sustainable in the targets for growth for Goal 8. There are many other goals in the SDGs related to "sustainable"—such as Goals 13 to 16—and "sustained," which includes the goals for human resources development. As noted at the beginning of this chapter, Japan's DCC is also conscious of the two aspects of "sustainable economic and social growth" and "sustainable growth across generations."

These two objectives appear to have become recognized within UN agencies. In its strategy paper, UNDP distinguishes between "sustaining economic growth" and "environmentally sustainable growth," and sets out actions for each of these two categories (UNDP 2017). Exports, private capital and economic crises are specifically mentioned in relation to the former, while natural capital—such as renewable resources—and environmental pollution are mentioned in the context of the latter. In discussing sustainable growth in this book, I also characterize and discuss these two separately (see Table 5.2). For growth to be sustainable, production and consumption must continue to expand over the medium to long

**Table 5.1** Targets in SDG Goal 8 related to growth

| Category | Target |
|---|---|
| Sustained | 8.1 Sustain per capita economic growth in accordance with national circumstances and, in particular, at least 7% gross domestic product growth per annum in the least developed countries<br>8.2 Achieve higher levels of economic productivity through diversification, technological upgrading and innovation, including through a focus on high-value added and labour-intensive sectors<br>8.3 Promote development-oriented policies that support productive activities, decent job creation, entrepreneurship, creativity and innovation, and encourage the formalization and growth of micro-, small- and medium-sized enterprises, including through access to financial services |
| Sustainable | 8.4 Improve progressively, through 2030, global resource efficiency in consumption and production and endeavour to decouple economic growth from environmental degradation, in accordance with the 10-Year Framework of Programmes on Sustainable Consumption and Production, with developed countries taking the lead |

*Note* Targets from 8.5 onwards relate to employment inclusiveness, etc.
*Source* Categorization by Author

term (sustained), following pathways that do not come at the expense of future generations over a long time span (sustainable).

In order to realize the former goal of "sustained" growth, the conditions for it need to be put in place, such as human development, technological advancement, and industrial upgrading and transformation. This is a subject of the economic development mechanism, which is directly related to growth theory in economics. On the other hand, the latter perspective—growth that is not at the expense of future generations—is an argument for pursuing a form of growth in which the global natural environment is not significantly altered by climate change, among other factors. Natural resources are another area covered by the latter concept, as any change in their stock is likely to be irreversible. It can be said that the management of natural resources is a subject of economic policy, but from the perspective of ensuring that growth is not disrupted by resource depletion, it should be included

**Table 5.2** Two issues of sustainability of growth

| Point in question | Type of growth sustainability | Areas discussed | Objective |
|---|---|---|---|
| Sustained | Growth that continues over a long period at a high rate | Technology, productivity, economic policy and institutions | Build mechanisms that enable economies to become more prosperous long term |
| Sustainable | Growth that does not pass the burden to future generations | Environment, climate change, natural resource management | Wise use of the Earth's natural environment and resources |

*Source* Author

in the latter category. Referring back to the APEC definition of quality growth, the former is expressed as "innovative growth," while the latter is expressed as "sustainable growth."

The discussion of climate change and growth should be considered separately from the economic growth mechanism, although they are related. The latter concerns the engines of growth—capital, labor, technology and productivity—with a focus on the institutions that support them, while the former is essentially a question of the negative externalities created by economic activity. Reducing the negative impacts of climate change will lead to additional costs in the short term. In other words, there is a tradeoff with short-term growth. Thus, it will be necessary to compare the current and future benefits and losses. Such consideration is also related to the limitations of the current definition of GDP, as the market mechanism on which GDP is premised has the fundamental problem that social costs, such as climate change, are not reflected in the cost of production. This chapter discusses the environment, climate change and the use of natural resources, followed by a review of growth engines, such as innovation, in the next chapter.

## 5.2 Sustainability of Growth and the Environment, Climate Change and Resources

All economic activity changes the environment, leading to impacts that may threaten our way of life. Pollution problems caused by manufacturing and mining have existed for a long time, but the problem has become more serious as the economy has expanded. Over time, governments have regulated production activities that are harmful to health, and as a result, technologies have been developed that are less likely to cause environmental degradation. However, as economic activity causes more or less change in the environment, it is still inevitable that there will be negative consequences on the environment.

Climate change is a particularly significant issue among these negative impacts. Although scientists were already aware of its growing impacts, the issue of climate change due to GHGs did not gain global attention until the late 1980s: the international conference on climate change in Villach was held in 1985, and the Intergovernmental Panel on Climate Change (IPCC) was established in 1988. Subsequently, at the Earth Summit in 1992, the United Nations Framework Convention on Climate Change was adopted for the first time. At this point, there was a major consensus on the need to stabilize the concentration of GHG emissions from economic activities in order to prevent global warming. Climate change and pollution are fundamentally the same in that economic activity alters the natural environment. However, GHGs do not cause direct harm to human health and well-being, and their emissions are not visible or confined to specific regions. There is also a wide range of estimates regarding the impact of GHGs on the environment, and it takes much longer for the environment to change than it does for ordinary pollution problems.

On the other hand, we know from experience that the environment does not unilaterally deteriorate with economic growth. As people become more affluent, they become more conscious of environmental issues and seek a better environment. In economics, the concept of negative externalities is used to discuss relationships in which the environment is worsened by economic activity. For example, when water or air pollution is caused by production activities, it has a negative impact on the health, life and utility of residents living nearby. Additional costs are required to avoid these impacts. When negative externalities occur, such as environmental degradation, it is necessary to ask producers to bear these costs. For this reason, governments directly regulate such production activities, or alternatively try to internalize these costs (social costs) through taxes or subsidies. As the economy advances, the response to environmental problems will also advance, halting the deterioration of the environment and even improving it. This can be seen in Japan, where pollution used to be a social problem during the rapid growth period, but nowadays, the air quality in metropolitan areas, for example, has greatly improved. The reasons for these changes should be self-evident: in the early stages of economic development, negative environmental impacts increase with growth, but then the environment improves as society becomes even more affluent. This relationship is known in academic terms as the Environmental Kuznets Curve (EKC).

### 5.2.1 How Does Economic Growth Change Environmental Pollution?

A commonly cited hypothesis in response to this question is that there is an inverse U-shaped relationship between environmental quality and economic development. The first researchers to examine this relationship were Grossman and Krueger (1991), who found such a relationship in their study on how Mexico's environment would be affected by the North American Free Trade Agreement (NAFTA). The study identified a relationship between three air pollutants and income levels between 19 and 42 countries and found that for sulfur dioxide ($SO_2$) and "dark matter," the relationship was that pollution increased with income at low per capita income levels, but began to decrease above a certain income level. The tipping point was found to be between 4,000 and 5,000 USD (1985 prices). On the other hand, for another air pollutant—suspended particles—a consistent downward trend was observed. The relationship between $SO_2$ and the economy is illustrated in Fig. 5.1. This inverted U-shaped relationship has become known as EKC, referencing the famous hypothesis between inequality and income.

Grossman and Krueger (1991) found three factors that cause growth to alter the environment in this way. The first is the scale effect, in which the expansion of economic activities through trade and investment increases pollutant emissions. The second is the composition effect, where trade liberalization has two opposing effects. On the one hand, it leads to specialization in industries with a comparative advantage through trade. For example, Mexico expands agriculture and labor-intensive traditional industries. Thus, these industries become more

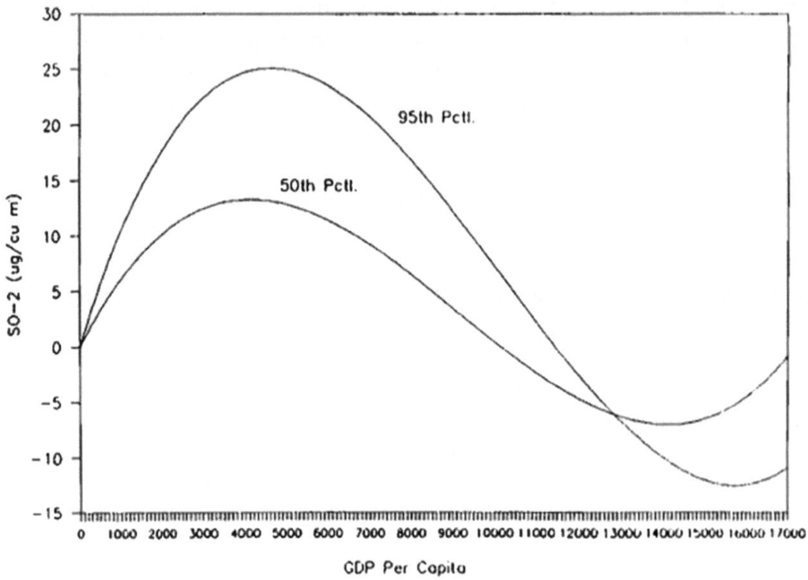


**Fig. 5.1** Environmental Kuznets Curve (*Source* Grossman and Krueger 1991)

active, resulting in a reduction in pollution. On the other hand, in terms of investment, investors may shift their investment to countries with lax environmental regulations, such as Mexico. The balance between these two opposing forces will ultimately determine the increase or decrease in pollutants. The third is the technique effect, where trade and investment transfer cleaner technology to developing countries, and increased incomes lead to greater environmental awareness among the population, thereby improving the environment. This perspective is often cited in many subsequent studies.

Shafik and Bandyopadhyay (1992) is another representative early study on EKC, analyzing changes in ten environment-related indicators for 149 countries, using three models as basic correlations, covering the period from 1960 to 1990.[1]

---

[1] Shafik and Bandyopadhyay (1992) proposed the following basic three equations for the relationship between income and environment:

(1) $E_1 = a_1 + a_2\log Y + a_3\text{time}$.
(2) $E_1 = a_1 + a_2\log Y + a_3\log Y^2 + a_4\text{time}$.
(3) $E_1 = a_1 + a_2\log Y + a_3\log Y^2 + a_4\log Y^3 + a_5\text{time}$.

(Y is income per capita on PPP basis).

How income growth changes pollution in the environment depends on which function fits best. An inverted U shape would be case (2) and the coefficients of the quadratic function are dominant. On the other hand, a cubic function suggests that the relationship between income and environmental change can be N-shaped. Of the ten environmental indicators covered by this study, the study

Their study was featured in the World Development Report 1992: "Development and the Environment." The empirical results showed five environmental quality indicators with a linear relationship: access to clean water and urban sanitation improved with income, while municipal waste, dissolved oxygen in rivers and $CO_2$ emissions worsened. On the other hand, an inverted U-shaped relationship is shown for suspended particulate matter and $SO_2$ (although the shape of the curve and the tipping point at which the increase turns into a decrease differ). They also found that deforestation was not significantly related to income, and that fecal coliforms in rivers were the only indicator that followed an N shape (cubic-shaped model). They revealed that the differences in change due to pollutants are significant by further expanding the scope of the study from Grossman and Kruger (1991). Another early study that is often mentioned is Panayotou (1993), who coined the term EKC for the inverted U-shaped relationship between environmental pollution and income.

As mentioned above, the EKC concept of how the environment changes as a result of economic growth is a relatively recent discussion. Nonetheless, a great deal of research has been conducted since the 1990s. The following is a summary of the major findings from studies focusing on EKC, including Dinda (2004), Uchiyama (2009), Bo (2011), Narita (2016) and Andrée et al. (2019).

- How per capita income growth changes the environmental quality depends on the type of pollutant.
- For air pollution that has a direct impact on people's health, an inverted U-shaped relationship appears to apply (e.g., $SO_2$ and nitrogen oxides).
- The relationship between $CO_2$ emissions and growth is inconclusive, such as an inverted U-shaped relationship, monotonically increasing, or an N-shaped relationship, depending on the study.
- For other types of pollutants, an inverted U-shaped relationship has not always been shown. Some studies show monotonically increasing pollution (e.g., urban waste) or suggest an N-shaped relationship (e.g., for water pollution), for example.
- Factors that cause growth to change the environmental quality include the increase of the economic scale, changes in the structure of the economy, technological progress, increased demand for a good environment, easier access to funds to invest in environmental protection measures as the economy develops and improved administrative functions and greater compliance with environmental regulations as a result of development.
- Criticisms of the EKC approach include the fact that technology develops globally, irrespective of the growth of individual countries, and that it is impossible to treat and analyze countries with different economic structures and environmental pollution pathways with a single framework. Moreover, while EKC is

states that for $CO_2$ emissions, the coefficients of the first-order term have extremely high explanatory power and thus appear to have a linear shape of increase, but the second- and third-order terms are also statistically significant.

a discussion of change in one country, it can also affect pollution in other countries through trade.

Suppose the impact of economic growth on the environment changes in the way depicted by the inverted U-shape relationship. In that case, environmental management strategies can be more focused and the environment will naturally improve with growth. By controlling current pollution so that it does not reach a level where future environmental recovery is impossible, future pollution will decrease, and society will be able to avoid passing on the burden to future generations. However, many developing and emerging countries are still on the upward part of the inverted U-shaped curve in terms of income levels. Therefore, even if the relationship holds, controlling pollution to avoid exceeding critical thresholds in each country remains a major challenge.

As for $CO_2$, it is not certain whether emissions will decrease with growth after a tipping point and $CO_2$ remains in the atmosphere for a long period of time. Moreover, even if an inverted U-shape relationship were to be established, $CO_2$ emissions would continue to increase in the foreseeable future in many developing countries, as they are still in the middle of an upward trend due to the industrialization process. For developed countries, even if their emissions begin to decrease after the tipping point of the inverted U-shape, such a change generally means a shift from manufacturing to services within a country, while production activities that used to generate emissions in the domestic manufacturing production process may have simply been transferred to other emerging countries from which industrial products are imported. It would be quite a challenge, therefore, to keep $CO_2$ emissions at a level that does not exceed a critical point beyond which damage becomes irreversible, even if there is an inverted U-shape relationship.

If the relationship between economic growth and $CO_2$ emissions is an inverted U-shape, then technology will evolve as incomes increase, and $CO_2$ emissions will continue to decline indefinitely. Indeed, technological progress has improved the efficiency of energy consumption required for production, with Nordhaus (2013) noting that the carbon intensity of economic activity in the US, i.e., $CO_2$ emissions per unit of production, has decreased at an average annual rate of 1.8% since 1930. On the other hand, he reports that overall $CO_2$ emissions have increased at an average rate of 3.4% per year over the last 80 years, meaning that net emissions increased at an average rate of 1.6% per year. It is estimated that global net emissions have increased by approximately 2.6% per year. If the effect of the increase due to scale is sufficiently large to offset technological improvements, then reducing emissions becomes very difficult. Achieving a pathway in which technology develops at a pace that ensures the rate of emission reductions always outpaces the rate of economic growth is considered very difficult. Thus, instead of relying solely on technological progress, policy interventions to curb $CO_2$ emissions are now being strongly pursued globally.

With regard to the composition effect, the fact that $CO_2$ emissions have decreased due to changes in industrial structure in developed countries does not mean a reduction on a global basis. The key concept in this case is consumption-based $CO_2$ emissions. In general, $CO_2$ emissions usually refer to the amount emitted by economic activities such as power generation, transport and manufacturing within a country (this is called production-based emissions). According to such a standard, $CO_2$ emissions related to imported goods would not be included statistically in a country's emissions, even though they are consumed in the country that imports them. In today's highly globalized world, this distinction should not be overlooked.

The idea of measuring emissions based on consumption is known as consumption-based $CO_2$ emissions. In developed countries, the share of the service sector generally increases as incomes rise, while the share of manufacturing declines and final and intermediate goods are imported from abroad, including from developing and emerging countries. This can lead to an increase in consumption-based $CO_2$ emissions but a decrease in production-based emissions, which are generally used as an indicator. For example, the UK's production-based $CO_2$ emissions declined by 5.6% from 1990 to 2004, according to UNFCCC standards, while consumption-based $CO_2$ emissions are estimated to have increased by 14% over this period (Druckman and Jackson 2008). Although consumption-based emissions are difficult to estimate because they are linked to production activities in other countries, data have been developed in recent years. For example, according to OECD statistics, consumption-based $CO_2$ emissions for OECD member countries as a whole are 13.8 gigatons ($GtCO_2$), while production-based $CO_2$ emissions are 12.3 $GtCO_2$ (both in 2018)—a difference of over 10%.[2]

The relationship between growth and $CO_2$ emissions is uncertain. Even if it were an inverted U-shaped, there are various problems in attribution, as described above. Some studies suggest that the relationship is actually N-shaped, which makes the problem even more difficult to solve. For example, Álvarez-Herránz et al. (2017) analyzed the period between 1990 and 2014 for 28 OECD countries and found that the relationship is N-shaped. Balsalobre-Lorente et al. (2018) found an N-shaped relationship for five European Union (EU) countries from 1985 to 2016. They explain that at a certain income level, the increasing effect of economic size begins to outweigh the decreasing effect of technology and economic structural change, and emissions begin to increase again. In the EU example, $CO_2$ emissions turn downward once per capita income reaches USD 29,647, but at USD 38,535, emissions start to increase again due to technological obsolescence (see Fig. 5.2). Other studies show a simple increasing relationship, such as those by Shafik and Bandyopadhyay (1992) and Andrée et al. (2019). If the impact of growth on GHG emissions is an N-shaped relationship or a simple increase, it will be very difficult to control emissions and maintain them within acceptable levels.

Previous empirical studies suggest that environmental pollution with direct impacts on human health and the living environment is more likely to be halted due to concern for life and health. Such pollution is often limited to a specific

[2] Based on OECD (2021). Accessed August 3, 2022.

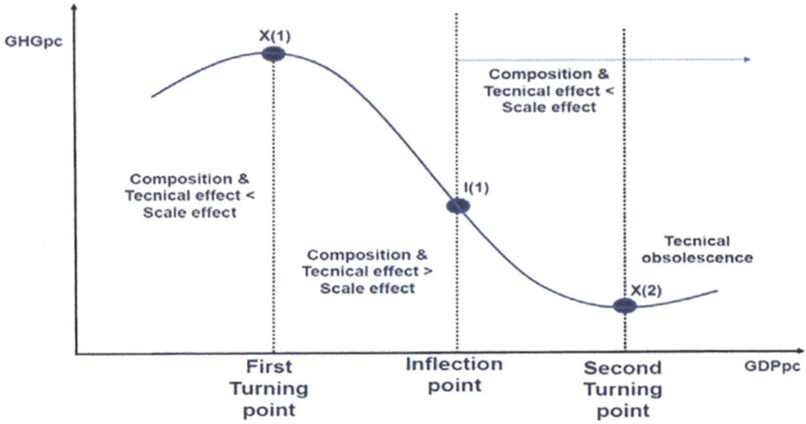


**Fig. 5.2** N-shaped relationship between economic growth and increase in GHGs (*Source* Balsalobre-Lorente et al. 2018)

geographical area and the causal relationship is clear. For this reason, governments have regulated pollution, and companies have borne the costs of dealing with it, while compensating the affected residents. Laws and regulations have been developed in many countries, and environmental impact assessments for large investments have become commonplace. Through this process, the price of the goods rises and demand falls, leading to socially optimal production levels. Consequently, economic activities that have a direct negative impact on the environment surrounding our society are gradually brought under control.

However, many forms of environmental degradation cannot be controlled in this way. For example, urban waste increases monotonically with growth. This is analogous to the fact that people do not feel any direct negative effects of waste as it is disposed of. Therefore, from a sustainability perspective, it is better to build societies and industries in which limited resources can be reused and recycled, thereby changing the trend of ever-increasing urban waste. It should be noted that if the cost of recycling is higher than the cost of new production, it will not be commercially viable, so technological developments or policy interventions will be needed to advance recycling and circulation.

The reason why the relationship between $CO_2$ emissions and growth does not show a clear trend is probably related to the fact that it does not immediately affect human health. Moreover, the impact of global warming on economic activity is also complex. The next section examines this relationship—i.e., how GHG emissions affect the economy—moving in the opposite direction from the environment to economic outcomes. Estimating the environmental changes, economic impacts and social costs of GHG emissions remains a major challenge. Furthermore, determining who will bear the costs and what global and political mechanisms need to be established will be essential. To advance these discussions, it is first necessary to consider what will happen if GHG emissions increase, the estimated economic losses and the costs of preventing them, and the extent to which it is desirable to limit emissions. These concerns need to be scientifically analyzed, based on very long-term forecasts, and shared widely.

### 5.2.2 Impact of GHG Emissions on the Economy

GHG emissions increase the concentration of $CO_2$ and other warming gases in the atmosphere, raising the average global temperature. Changes in the average global temperature cause a variety of phenomena, including melting ice sheets, rising sea levels, extreme weather events and disasters, ecosystem shifts, crop changes and the spread of infectious diseases. Increased acidification of the oceans will have further atmospheric changes. Two-thirds of GHG emissions come from the energy sector, including power, transport, industry and buildings, while the remaining one-third are emitted through agriculture and land use, which includes deforestation, peatland development and methane emissions from livestock and fertilizers (Stern 2006). GHG emissions cause long-term economic losses as global warming increases. As future generations will most likely be affected by current emissions, the current generation needs to bear the additional costs required to prevent environmental degradation due to economic activities. As these additional expenditures do not increase current output, they depress productivity, lowering the current growth rate in the short term (Cabinet Office 2011 and others). This is the fundamental tradeoff between the utility of future and current generations.

Achieving sustainable growth conceptually means that the current generation sacrifices some of its current growth to curb GHG emissions, thereby ensuring that the growth of future generations is not compromised. The international community agreed on such limits in the Paris Agreement on climate change in 2015. A common global long-term goal has been set to limit the increase in global average temperature since pre-industrial times to within 2 °C, and to make efforts to limit warming to 1.5 °C.[3] While there is uncertainty about what changes global warming will bring about, GHG emissions must be curbed to meet these targets. Since GHG emissions from the past up to the present have been estimated, it is possible to calculate how much can be emitted in the future to limit the temperature increase to 2° or 1.5 °C —a limit known as the "remaining carbon budget." Before the carbon budget is used up, carbon neutrality (zero GHG emissions) must be achieved. The IPCC reported that the remaining carbon budget from the beginning of 2020 is estimated at 1,350 $GtCO_2$ for the 2-degrees Celsius target (the 50% probability case) and 500 $GtCO_2$ for the 1.5-degrees Celsius target (IPCC 2021). Since annual $CO_2$ emissions are around 40 $GtCO_2$, if GHG emissions continue at the current rate, the remaining carbon budget for the 1.5-degrees Celsius target will likely be exhausted in a decade or so.

[3] At COP 26 (Glasgow Climate Pact) in 2021, a target of 1.5 °C was agreed.

In order to achieve sustainable growth, it is necessary to take this background into account and identify a scenario for GHG emissions that satisfies both current and future growth rates. The most common way of estimating this is through modeling projections. William Nordhaus, a Nobel Prize laureate in economics for his work modeling the relationship between the economy and climate change, states that the economic losses from global warming are estimated to be relatively small. Nordhaus (2013) cites a review of previous studies by Tol (2009),[4] which estimates damages to be at most 5% of global GDP, and around 1.5% in the case of a 2.5-degree Celsius rise. However, he points out that there is great uncertainty due to the fact that the amount of damage is on an increasing trend and that the idea of a critical point has not been incorporated. He argues that the real threat of global warming occurs in the areas furthest away from the market. Threats beyond human control include sea level rise, increased hurricane intensity, ocean acidification and biodiversity loss, simultaneously referring to the limitations of economic modeling in that the catastrophic damage caused by the latter two events, for example, cannot be captured (Nordhaus 2013). Despite this, economic modeling can demonstrate how GHG emissions impact the economy and remains one of the most important sources of information for policy discussions.

Such impacts can be obtained by estimating how GHG emissions from economic activities change the economy, with results depending on the magnitude and speed of warming. By changing GHG emissions under different scenarios, it is possible to estimate the magnitude of losses and discuss effective policies to curb GHG emissions. The key point is that the benefits (loss reduction) from GHG emission reductions made now will be obtained at a future point in time. Regarding the impact of GHG emission reductions on the current generation, we need to compare costs (investment for reduction) and benefits (loss reductions) using discounting to present value. The results will vary greatly depending on how the

[4] Tol (2009) surveys the major research and categorizes temperature changes and their impact on GDP according to regions with the greatest impacts and those with the smallest impacts. As a result, the range of temperature changes is estimated at 1 to 3 °C and the impact on GDP ranges from −4.8 to +0.9%. He then states that the conclusions generally agreed upon in previous research are as follows:

(a) The impact of a doubling of GHG concentrations is relatively small, with a decrease in GDP of around a few percentage points. However, this impact is permanent and therefore cannot be ignored.
(b) Although rising temperatures bring benefits in the early stages, they result in losses once a certain level is exceeded.
(c) Global warming has a relatively large negative impact on low-income countries.
(d) Estimates of the economic impact of GHGs have become less pessimistic as research has accumulated (for example, because earlier analyses did not take into account positive impacts).
(e) There is a great deal of uncertainty.

discount rate is set. While the discount rate sounds like a rather technical discussion, it is very important because it quantifies the tradeoff between future and current generations.

The impact of GHG emissions covers almost every area of the economy. For this reason, a typical approach is to capture the overall economic changes using a macroeconomic tool. Specifically, a model is constructed that includes variables such as GHG emissions, global temperature and key economic indicators. The model then estimates how the average global temperature will change due to GHG emissions and the resulting effects on the economy as a whole. A representative model for assessing the impact of global warming is the Dynamic Integrated Climate-Economy (DICE) model by Nordhaus, one of integrated assessment models (IAMs).

The simultaneous equations that make up the DICE model consist of an equation for the objective (utility maximization), several equations for economic relationships (production function, etc.) and equations representing the climate-emission-loss mechanism. The equations for the climate-emissions-damage mechanism, a core part of the model, include equations for determining GHG emissions, temperature, and losses due to temperature rise. GHG emissions are obtained by multiplying GDP by the carbon intensity (with GHGs other than $CO_2$ converted to $CO_2$). Carbon intensity is a technology parameter and is exogenously given, so it is assumed to improve according to historical trends. By changing the variable to represent its improvement, policy initiatives aimed at achieving an optimal level of emission reduction can be discussed. The concentration of $CO_2$ in the atmosphere, determined by the current level of its concentration and the amount of $CO_2$ to be emitted, influences the magnitude of the radiative forcing, which in turn changes the temperature of the Earth. Finally, the product of the temperature increases and the size of GDP is multiplied by a certain rate to ascertain the losses.

The cost of GHG emission reductions, on the other hand, is obtained by multiplying GDP by a specific coefficient at a macroeconomic level. From the derived losses and GHG emission reduction costs, the coefficients required for inclusion in the production function can be obtained (Nordhaus 1992). The DICE model has since been refined, but the basic structure has not changed (Nordhaus 2019). The development of the IPCC scenario also begins with this model. To date, a number of IAMs have been created, and according to Nordhaus (2013), the average results of the DICE model and 11 models under the aegis of the Energy Modelling Forum at Stanford University were more or less the same in terms of $CO_2$ emissions. He stated that the key takeaway from this comparison is that, for one thing, all models predict a continued increase in $CO_2$ emissions, and for another, there is no significant difference in predictions in the short term, while as time progresses, the difference in predictions between the models widens. Thus, the uncertainty of future $CO_2$ emissions and their impacts is so great that measures need to be taken at an early stage to avoid risks.

The aim of the DICE model is to maximize utility using economic and climate variables. The reduction of GHG emissions requires additional costs, which reduce future losses and damage to the economy. Such costs could rise sharply if the time required to implement measures is shortened. On the other hand, the later measures are taken, the greater the cost of achieving targets. Climate change impacts will occur in various sectors, but according to Nordhaus (2013), only 1% of the US economy is strongly affected by climate change, and moreover, the number of vulnerable sectors is decreasing. He goes on to state that under ideal circumstances, where all countries cooperate and reduce emissions efficiently, the annual cost of achieving a 2-degrees Celsius rise would only be around 1–2% of global GDP.

On the other hand, preventing a 2-degrees Celsius rise is not possible with the technology currently available, unless all countries cooperate soon. In the subsequent publication by Nordhaus (2019) that shows the results of a simulation on global average temperatures, the projections based on six scenarios are presented,[5] stating that it is no longer realistic to achieve the temperature increase within 1.5–2 °C. This is because, according to the simulation results, this would require negative $CO_2$ emissions (absorption). He also noted that in the cost–benefit optimum, the temperature increase in the year 2100 is at a level above 3 °C.[6]

In analyzing costs and benefits, particular attention should be paid to the discount rate mentioned above. Depending on the magnitude of the discount rate used, future benefits and costs will differ significantly. In general, there are two views on it: normative (or prescriptive) and descriptive. Nordhaus (2019) argues that since investments to limit global warming compete with other investments, a discount rate should reflect market opportunities—thus using a value of 4%. The normative view, on the other hand, is based on ethics and takes the view that discounting the welfare of future generations is morally wrong. A representative study that takes this view is Stern (2006). This study is one of the leading international studies that comprehensively analyzes the economic impact of global warming and uses a discount rate of 1%. A low discount rate does not make future benefits smaller. A low discount rate can be considered a concept that incorporates sustainable growth, since it takes future generations into account. Such differences as 1 and 4% may not seem very large, but if the future figure is calculated, for example, 100 years later, the difference will reach 18 times the original value.[7] On the other hand, if economic growth continues, even at a lower rate, then by the same logic applies for future generations: their incomes will be higher in the future, implying that it is unacceptable for the current generation to bear the costs for future generations who will be richer than them.

[5] The six scenarios are: (1) no measures, (2, 3) optimize costs and benefits (two scenarios), (4) limit temperature increase within 2 °C, (5) limit temperature increase within 2 °C over 100 years in average and (6) limit temperature increase to 2 °C over 200 years in average.

[6] Nordhaus (2019) adds a new scenario that not only considers the rise in peak temperatures but also the rise in average temperatures over a certain period of time. He states that the cost benefit optimum (3 °C temperature increase in 2100) is close to a scenario with a 200-year average temperature increase of 2 °C.

[7] If the nominal loss after 100 years is 100, the present value would be 37 when the discount rate is 1% and only 2 when the discount rate is 4%.

Stern (2006) uses three approaches to estimate the costs and benefits associated with climate change. The first relies on disaggregated techniques, which build up the individual elements, identifying the impacts on the economy, human life and the environment, and assessing the accumulated costs of countermeasures. The second utilizes economic models, including IAMs, to verify costs and effects. The third is a cost-comparison approach, which compares the marginal abatement costs of reducing emissions with the social costs of warming brought about by increased emissions.[8] In other words, if the social costs that express the magnitude of benefits exceed the marginal abatement costs, GHG reductions will benefit society. Stern (2006) uses USD 85 as an estimate of the social cost (price of carbon). These approaches lead to the conclusion that the costs of GHG emission reductions are all below the benefits that can be obtained from them, so early and resolute actions are desirable. He noted that the business-as-usual scenario would result in a loss of 5–20% of GDP, while the average cost of reducing GHG concentrations to the equivalent of 500–550 ppm (including non-$CO_2$ GHGs converted to $CO_2$) would be around 1% of GDP.

### 5.2.3 Policies Against Global Warming

A common global long-term goal for global warming was set out in the Paris Agreement in 2015. Policies in the direction of decarbonization have been adopted in many countries, albeit to varying degrees. However, there are still fundamental difficulties in steadily implementing policies in each country. The first is the issue of intergenerational equity. The optimal solution to the problem of how to balance the reduction of future losses with the reduction of current growth within a range such that global-level GHG concentrations do not exceed a critical point might be suggested by economic models, but these are not easy to implement because of the various interests involved. Based on the assumption that the current GHG reduction outlook makes it difficult to achieve the international target of 1.5 °C or remain under 2 °C, it will be necessary to accelerate emission reductions in a feasible way. This highlights the problem of externalities that always accompanies the issue of free riders. At the moment, national targets can be set on a voluntary basis, but to avoid this problem, the cooperation of all stakeholders is necessary. However, complete coordination seems difficult to achieve currently due to the different stances of different countries on, for example, the phase-out of coal-fired power generation, which was also observed at COP 26.

Second, countries and regions have different cost burdens and benefits from global action. This makes it difficult to promote global climate action. As GHGs have no national borders, it is necessary to promote discussions on the creation of common global mechanisms to accelerate emission reductions. For example,

[8] Studies based on the IAM have found that the most efficient policies are those in which the social cost of carbon and the carbon price are equal (Nordhaus 2019).

global consensus is needed in various areas, from frameworks such as emissions trading to discount rates, which are important for analyzing intergenerational tradeoffs.

Third, the social indicators themselves should, in my view, be reconsidered. If a balance between economic growth and GHG emission reductions must be contemplated, then instead of using GDP, an indicator integrating the two should become the goal of society. Currently, GDP serves as the basis for many international economic discussions. For example, UN contributions are based on the size of a country's GDP, and the lending criteria set by the World Bank also use GDP per capita. Thus, as long as GDP is the ubiquitous indicator used, policymakers will make increasing GDP the primary goal of the economy. This would make policy more inclined to focus on growth rather than GHG emission reductions. A direction may be sought to create an indicator that integrates both and applies it globally. This point is discussed again in Chap. 9.

Specific policies for global warming can be broadly divided into mitigation and adaptation. The former is related to the reduction of GHG emissions, while the latter refers to the response to the changing environment caused by global warming. With regard to mitigation, as GHG emissions are a global externality, the policies taken are based on economic theory and are typically direct regulation or the internalization of the externality into the market. The internalization can be further classified into two approaches, namely carbon taxes and emissions trading. A key aspect in this process is the setting of a carbon price. Adaptation is a response to disasters and environmental changes (e.g., increasing desertification) that are intensified by global warming. Policies to strengthen resilience in this context were discussed in the previous chapter.

As for policy options, there could be a variety of measures in the field of regulation, including those related to transport and building codes, encouraging people's daily consumption and behavior toward a carbon-free lifestyle. Nordhaus (2013), referring to previous studies, states that the internalization of $CO_2$ elements into the market—i.e., reductions of $CO_2$ through carbon taxes or emissions trading—would be the most effective and least expensive. Both carbon taxes and emissions trading have advantages and disadvantages. In theory, a carbon tax is a measure of the size of the social cost, but the size of the tax varies widely from country to country.[9] As a carbon tax is a tax on GHG emissions, governments can utilize a familiar policy tool—the tax system. While it is administratively easy to implement, how much emissions are reduced depends on the actions of companies. In other words, the reductions to be realized as a result of the carbon tax tool are uncertain.

[9] Nordhaus (2019) estimates that, according to the DICE model, the social cost under the optimal scenario is USD 36 per tonne $CO_2$ (2015), but USD 158 to 279 (2020) is required to realize the goal of keeping warming below 2 °C. This wide range reflects differences in policy objectives. The carbon tax rate varies considerably between countries that have introduced carbon taxes, such as France (2,540 yen) and Sweden (15,130 yen), compared to 289 yen in Japan (Ministry of the Environment, Japan 2018).

Emissions trading, on the other hand, allows the size of the reductions to be set as a cap on $CO_2$ emissions, but there are administrative difficulties in setting up a new market for trading. For companies, $CO_2$ trading functions like normal market trading, as the price of $CO_2$ is determined in the market, although policy predictability is a risk for them in this case. There is a need to accelerate policies that make the whole system of society an integrated part of the climate regime, so that carbon taxes or emissions trading can efficiently reduce GHGs. It is not possible here to discuss an exhaustive menu of potential policies in each economic sector. Instead, this section provides a list of possible policy measures in the energy sector, one of the main emission sources, as an example (see Table 5.3; World Bank 2010).

As there has already been a great deal of research carried out related to growth and climate change, I will concentrate on those issues that are relevant to the subject of this book. Finally, I will touch on the relationship to technological development. Currently, policies that promote technological innovation toward a decarbonized society are positioned as major drivers of economic growth. Such technological developments can be accelerated by the establishment of a carbon price. Social transformation will proceed and economic growth will accelerate as new innovations take place. Growth is promoted by the accelerated entry and exit of firms into and out of markets. The development of decarbonizing technologies used to take place outside the market, as market mechanisms did not internalize negative externalities related to climate change. If the market economy framework is modified to include elements of decarbonization, it will also be necessary to incorporate an internalization of decarbonization (externalities) into indicators to measure country's prosperity. This will make the idea of growth that does not burden future generations the mainstream.

### 5.2.4 Weak and Strong Sustainability

In addition to the environment and climate change, another important issue when discussing growth without passing the burden to future generations is the consumption of finite natural resources. Natural resources such as oil and mineral resources, once consumed, cannot be regenerated and therefore inevitably reduce the amount available to future generations. For example, Nauru—a Pacific island nation in the Oceania region—was once as rich as any oil-producing country thanks to its abundant phosphate exports. However, per capita income plummeted in the 1990s as resources approached depletion (mining from a secondary layer started from the mid-2000s). In a country that is heavily dependent on limited natural resources, effective management is essential to ensure that future incomes can continue to grow.

Natural resources are one of several types of capital required for production. The World Bank (2021) classifies capital as produced capital, non-renewable and renewable natural capital, and human capital. Capital is essential for growth as it generates production, which will be discussed in more detail in the next chapter.

**Table 5.3** Policy interventions for energy efficiency, renewable energy, and transport

| Policy area | Energy efficiency and demand-side management interventions | Renewable energy interventions | Barriers addressed |
|---|---|---|---|
| Economywide | Removal of fossil-fuel subsidies<br>Tax (fuel or carbon tax)<br>Quantitative limits (cap-and-trade) | | Environmental externalities not included in the price<br>Regressive or demand-augmenting distortions from subsidies for fossil fuels |
| Regulations | Economywide energy-efficiency targets<br>Energy-efficiency obligations<br>Appliance standards<br>Building codes<br>Industry energy-performance targets<br>Fuel economy standards | Mandatory purchase, open and fair grid access<br>Renewable portfolio standards<br>Low-carbon fuel standards<br>Technology standards<br>Interconnection regulations | Lack of legal framework for renewable independent power producers<br>Lack of transmission access by renewable energy<br>Lack of incentives and misplaced incentives to save<br>Supply-driven mentality<br>Unclear interconnection requirements |
| Financial incentives | Tax credits<br>Capital subsidies<br>Profits decoupled from sales<br>Consumer rebates<br>Time-of-use tariffs<br>Fuel taxes<br>Congestion tolls<br>Taxes based on engine size<br>Insurance or tax levies on vehicle miles traveled<br>Taxes on light trucks, SUVs | Feed-in tariff, net metering<br>Green certificates<br>Real-time pricing<br>Tax credits<br>Capital subsidies | High capital costs<br>Unfavorable pricing rules<br>Lack of incentives for utilities and consumers to save |

(continued)

**Table 5.3** (continued)

| Policy area | Energy efficiency and demand-side management interventions | Renewable energy interventions | Barriers addressed |
|---|---|---|---|
| Institutional arrangements | Utility<br>Dedicated energy-efficiency agencies<br>Independent corporation or authority<br>Energy service companies (ESCOs) | Utility<br>Independent power producers | Too many decentralized players |
| Financing mechanisms | Loan financing and partial loan guarantees<br>ESCOs<br>Utility energy-efficiency, demand-side management program, including system benefit fund | System benefit fund<br>Risk management and long-term financing<br>Concessional loans | High capital cost, and mismatch with short-term loans<br>ESCOs' lack of collateral and small deal size<br>Perceived high risks<br>High transaction costs<br>Lack of experience and knowledge |
| Promotion and education | Labeling<br>Installing meters<br>Consumer education | Education about renewable energy benefits | Lack of information and awareness<br>Loss of amenities |

*Note* SUV = Sport Utility Vehicle
*Source* World Bank (2010, 214)

Natural resources fall under the second category. As they are expended in the production process, the newly formed capital must increase by more than the amount of resources expended in order to avoid sacrificing the growth of future generations. The issue in this context is the substitutability between natural resources and other capital.

One of the leading principles regarding this tradeoff is known as the "Hartwick Rule." Under this rule, the current generation expends natural resources but can preserve intergenerational equity by investing the profits or rents from natural resources into renewable capital, such as machinery, that yields the same rate of return. If this condition is met, then the production of future generations will not decline, thereby preserving intergenerational equity (Hartwick 1977). Such a relationship has often been supported by neoclassical economics. Solow (1986), for example, uses an economic model to explain how the Hartwick rule ensures that intergenerational welfare, represented by consumption, is constant.[10] In cases

[10] Solow (1986) states that the Hartwick rule must satisfy the following conditions: (1) capital and labor are fully utilized; (2) the price of unused natural resources is equal to the current marginal

where this assumption of substitutability between production or human capital and natural capital holds, growth can be sustainable through increases in produced and human capital—i.e., total capital stock increases—even if natural capital declines. This concept is known as "weak sustainability."

In contrast, there is a recognition that natural capital is not fully substitutable for either productive or human capital. It is also argued that an increase in produced capital, such as machinery, can lead to a further expenditure of natural capital (e.g., an increase in the number of fishing boats leads to an increase in the amount of fish caught, thereby depleting natural capital). The view that discusses sustainability from this perspective is called "strong sustainability." From the weak sustainability perspective, it is sufficient to sustain growth as long as the total amount of future capital stock is not less than today's, regardless of the form of capital.

However, Pearce (1993), in his widely cited argument, points out that there is a type of natural capital—referred to as critical natural capital (CNC)—that is essential for human life and ecosystems. As CNC is not substitutable for productive or human capital, the amount used should not be determined by the results of market economic activity (Pearce and Warford 1993). This means that at least the part of natural capital that is essential for life and ecosystem functioning needs to be protected. Taking a strong sustainability perspective, Costanza and Daly (1992) state that population size should be within the Earth's carrying capacity, or remaining natural capital. They then present several implementation principles: specifically, the use of renewable natural capital should not exceed the rate at which it is regenerated, pollution emissions should not exceed the assimilative capacity of the environment, and mining of non-renewable natural capital should be carried out at the same rate as the rate at which renewable alternatives are produced.

Elkins (2003) states that essential natural capital refers to natural capital that maintains the critical functions of the environment and cannot be substituted by other forms of capital. These functions include serving as a source and sink, life support, and human health and welfare, and maintaining these functions requires limiting climate disruption, for example.[11] However, recent studies suggest that we have already exceeded the limits of what is considered safe in several areas. If these limits are exceeded, the Earth will no longer have the resilience to cope with change and could irreversibly shift to another state of equilibrium. Rockström et al. (2009) and Rockström and Klum (2015) note that of the nine Earth limits or planetary boundaries—climate change, biosphere integrity, land-system change,

productivity of productive capital (i.e., the Hotelling rule is established); and (3) investment in productive capital is made as the amount equal to the rent derived from the use of natural resources.

[11] Elkins (2003) states that it is necessary to limit the following: (1) climate disruption, (2) ozone depletion, (3) biodiversity reduction, (4) pollution affecting livelihoods, (5) use of non-renewable capital, (6) environmental risk; and (7) destruction of landscapes.

and biochemical flows (nitrogen and phosphorus pollution in freshwater)—several have already been exceeded and are now in a danger zone.[12]

Thus, there are two views of sustainability: "weak" and "strong." To summarize, the weak sustainability perspective is concerned with capital directly involved in production. Thus, non-renewable natural capital, such as mineral resources, and renewable natural capital, including forests, are at the forefront of the discussion. By contrast, the strong sustainability perspective focuses on maintaining CNC. Natural resources like oil and mineral resources are not considered CNC, as even if they were to be depleted, this would not fundamentally undermine the maintenance of ecosystems. The concern therefore becomes whether the resource rents are being invested in accordance with the Hartwick Rule. This is similarly noted by Costanza and Daly (1992), referring to the relationship between the rate of resource extraction and the rate of formation of renewable capital. If such principles were adopted in practice, it should be possible to sustain growth in natural resource-dependent countries while creating other types of capital.

However, GDP alone is insufficient to ascertain whether this process is underway or not. It is not easy to know how much the stock of natural resources has decreased and whether the increase in productive capital is sufficient to offset that decrease. Moreover, resource-rich countries face inherent difficulties in economic management, politics and governance. A number of studies exist on this point. For example, Ross (2012) discusses in detail the "oil curse," which is the reason why oil-producing countries have difficulty achieving economic growth compared to non-oil-producing countries—noting that oil accounts for 90% of the world's mineral trade. The next section will discuss this mechanism.

## 5.3 Natural Resources and Sustainable Growth

Developing countries often record very high economic growth rates—sometimes reaching double digits—when natural resources are discovered, mined, and exported. In some countries, the value added from natural resources exceeds non-resource GDP, and if all other factors remain equal, natural resources can be a blessing that multiplies wealth. In reality, however, abundant natural resources often prove to be an unreliable foundation for sustainable growth, especially in developing countries, where they can have negative impacts on governance and non-resource industries. Although analytical results vary due to methodological differences,[13] many economists have statistically demonstrated that countries with abundant natural resources are slower to develop economically. This section explores the relationship between natural resources and sustainable growth.

[12] The nine planetary boundaries are stratospheric ozone depletion, novel entities, ocean acidification, freshwater change, atmospheric aerosol loading, in addition to the four areas mentioned in the text.

[13] For example, Lederman and Maloney (2007) conclude from econometric and other analyses that there is no evidence that abundant natural resources have a negative impact on economic growth.

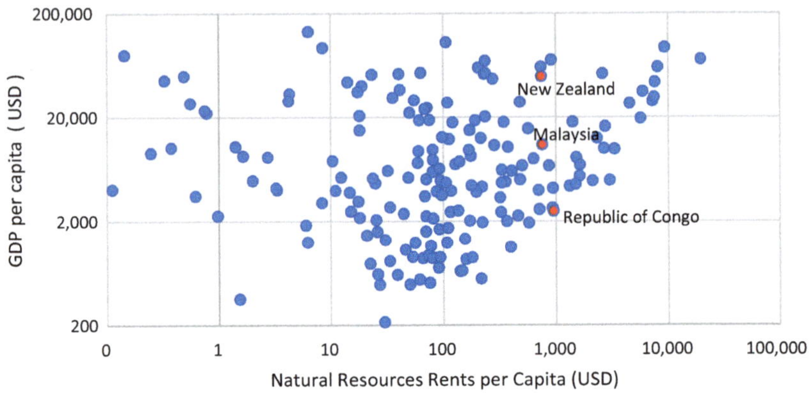


**Fig. 5.3** Natural resources and income levels (*Source* WDI, data obtained in January 2025)

The existence of natural resources such as crude oil and gold naturally brings wealth to a country through their production and export, but the paradox that these resource-rich countries have not necessarily become rich is well known and has been named the "resource curse" by Auty (1993). As shown in Fig. 5.3, countries with abundant natural resources tend to have higher income levels, but the variation is large. For example, New Zealand, Malaysia, and the Republic of Congo have similar per capita natural resource rents[14] ranging from USD 700 to USD 1,000, but their per capita GDPs vary widely: USD 50,000, USD 11,000, and USD 2,500 in 2021, respectively.

Many papers define resource-rich countries by the share of natural resources in GDP and exports, demonstrating that they are inversely related to economic growth or income level. However, this may not be sufficient to show a causal relationship, as countries with low economic growth have a high share of resources as a result of limited non-resource production and exports. In this paper, the World Development Indicator is processed to determine whether a country is rich in natural resources by using natural resource rent per capita.

Much research has also been conducted on the causes of the "resource curse," which can be broadly divided into three main categories. Namely, (1) resource price instability, (2) the crowding out effect on the manufacturing sector (Dutch disease), and (3) deteriorating governance (including dictatorship and disorder).

The first point, the instability of resource prices, has been reflected in the recent sharp fluctuations in crude oil prices, which have oscillated widely over the years. Since it takes time for supply and demand to adjust to price changes, external shocks such as weather events, shifts in global economic conditions, changes in

[14] WDI defines natural resource rents as the sum of the difference between revenues and extraction costs for oil, natural gas, coal, minerals, and forests. The USD amount per capita was calculated by multiplying both total natural resources rents (percent of GDP) and GDP per capita (current USD) in 2021.

industrial structure, evolving environmental regulations, and new developments are likely to result in wild price variability. Speculative trading in the market can also amplify these trends. Hausmann and Rigobon (2003) point out that in resource-dependent countries, the magnitude of fluctuations in resource revenues is directly related to fluctuations in real exchange rates. In financial markets, interest rates rise due to higher bankruptcy concerns, resulting in a vicious cycle that reduces investment in non-resource trade goods and further increases resource dependence.

Arezki et al. (2011) found that resource-rich countries tend to have procyclical policies that amplify business cycles more than non-resource-rich countries. When resource prices are high, the economy is booming and fiscal stimulus is unnecessary or should be tightened to avoid inflation. However, when resource prices are high, the economy is booming, and royalty or tax revenues are increasing, it is difficult for the government to resist political pressure to increase spending, which sometimes results in expenditure surges, such as inefficient public investment and increases in civil service wages. Under a procyclical fiscal policy, when resource prices fall and the economy slumps, there is little room for a stimulus spending increase, and rather, the government is forced to adopt austerity measures while facing a fiscal crisis.

Even when exports are increasing due to rising resource prices, an increase in government spending can lead to a larger increase in imports, resulting in a current account deficit and accumulation of external debt. In such countries, when resource prices fall, repayment becomes difficult due to a shortage of foreign currency, and the crisis is exacerbated by the increased burden of falling exchange rates and higher refinancing interest rates due to deteriorating credit risk.

The second problem was pointed out in a leading study of the resource curse by Sachs and Warner (2001). The resource curse is a phenomenon in which domestic resources are concentrated in the resource industries unless there is policy intervention, making it difficult for manufacturing industries to grow. It is also called the "Dutch disease" after the Netherlands, which faced this problem after the discovery of natural gas fields in the 1960s. A sharp increase in foreign currency inflows due to resource exports would, in the absence of offsetting outflows by other items in the balance of payments, lead to an appreciation of the nominal exchange rate under a floating exchange rate system, given the large surplus in the overall balance.

In fact, it is often the case that the appreciation and depreciation of exchange rates are linked to the rise and fall of resource prices. Even under a fixed exchange rate system, foreign currency inflows will be met with the foreign exchange intervention of purchasing foreign currency and selling domestic currency. Unless sufficient sterilization is achieved, the increase in the money supply will cause inflation, which will lead to an appreciation of the real exchange rate. In addition, the increase in money inflows will also raise the prices of nontradable goods such as real estate, resulting in fewer domestic resources being allocated to nonresource tradable goods (e.g., manufacturing), thereby weakening the country's international competitiveness (Fig. 5.4).

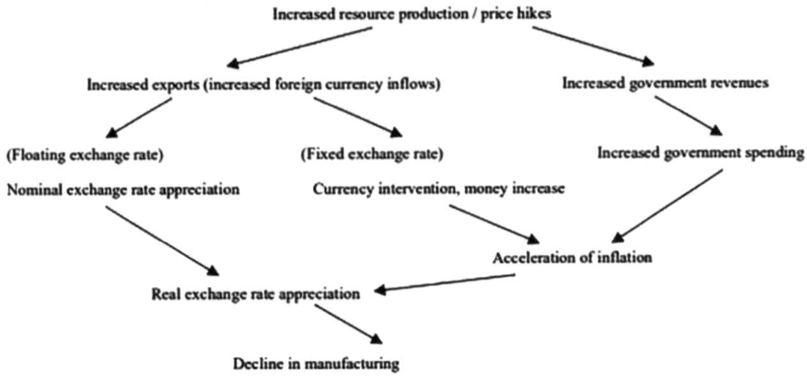


**Fig. 5.4** Structure of manufacturing crowding out (*Source* Prepared by Author)

According to classical economic theory, countries should specialize and trade in industries in which they have a comparative advantage, thereby contributing to mutual growth. From this perspective, it is natural for countries that can produce abundant natural resources at low cost to concentrate their resources in their resource industries. However, Asanuma and Obama (2013) argue that while manufacturing industries are expected to increase productivity through economies of scale and continual technological progress due to the learning effect, resource industries are capital-intensive and often operate in remote areas. This can lead to limited job creation and minimal spillover effect to the overall economy through technology transfer and human capital accumulation. Ross (2012) presents an analysis showing that in countries with high oil revenues, the distribution of subsidies and other payments from the government to households will increase, and employment in export-oriented factories, such as the sewing industry, which requires relatively less muscle power, will decrease, thereby reducing labor opportunities for women.

Even if resource prices fall again and return to their original levels, it is very costly to reverse the transformation of the industrial structure once it has occurred. And if prices do not fall to their original levels and the manufacturing industry declines as a result of specialization into the resource industry—as mentioned above—the possibility of developing a higher value-added industry over the medium to long term may be reduced.

Third, there is a governance problem unique to resource-rich countries. As the source of wealth is concentrated in resource revenues, this can easily lead to corruption, connection-based politics, dictatorship, or civil war over the distribution of wealth. Resources that are difficult to access, such as forests, are easily depleted through over-cutting and over-mining. Governments with high resource revenues have less need to collect taxes extensively from their citizens, and as a result, democracy is less likely to mature (Luciani 1987). In many cases, exclusive development rights for resources are granted to state-owned companies, but this can easily become a breeding ground for corruption and an obstacle to a healthy environment for private sector competition.

For example, in Indonesia, there have been cases where state-run companies that monopolized the development and sale of oil resources have subsequently expanded into unrelated sectors, such as manufacturing, agriculture, and other areas, and then failed. Even when private companies are granted development rights, there are cases of non-transparent transactions or excessive tax benefits. Zambia reportedly lost USD 8.8 billion over a 10-year period due to the "transfer pricing"[15] method of major foreign copper mining companies, which export copper to low-tax countries once at a low price on paper, thereby reducing tax payments in Zambia (Neate 2012).

Some analyses suggest that resource revenues can be widely used for the benefit of the public when there is already a good organizational structure in place at the time of resource discovery (e.g., Collier and Goderis 2007). However, there are many cases in developing countries where resource abundance has had a negative impact on governance and, as a result, hindered the sustainability of economic growth. As shown in Fig. 5.5, Norway and Australia have very high governance indicators[16] despite the abundance of natural resources, while other resource-rich countries such as the Republic of Congo, Iran, and Iraq have very low governance ratings. Although these countries have relatively high GDP per capita, backed by natural resources, they face political and social problems, such as autocratic regimes and large disparities between rich and poor.

The experience of a resource curse is not inevitable for resource-rich countries. For example, Australia, one of the world's leading resource-rich countries, recorded the world's longest absence of two consecutive quarters of negative growth—the definition of a recession—for 26 years in 2017. It is now one of the world's most developed countries, with a GDP per capita of approximately USD 60,000.

Both located on the African continent, Botswana, the world's second-largest producer of diamonds,[17] and the Democratic Republic of the Congo, the fifth-largest, had roughly similar income levels 40 years ago. While Botswana has generally sustained strong economic growth, the DRC has frequently experienced negative growth in the face of dictatorship and conflict, resulting in a more than tenfold difference in GDP per capita in 2021. While the differences in population, land area, history of conflict with neighboring countries, and other factors

---

[15] Transfer pricing arises from differences in tax systems and tax rates, and there is also an element of competition among countries to obtain tax revenue. The OECD published its Benefit Erosion and Profit Shifting (BEPS) Action Plan in 2013, and it has since become a framework involving more than 100 countries.

[16] The governance indicators used for the chart are the six items from the WGI: "Voice and accountability of the people," "Political stability and absence of violence," "Government effectiveness," "Regulatory quality," "Rule of law," and "Curbing corruption" (all in 2021 rank percentile, averaged).

[17] See 2023 Annual Summary Table from Kimberley Process Rough Diamond Statistics.

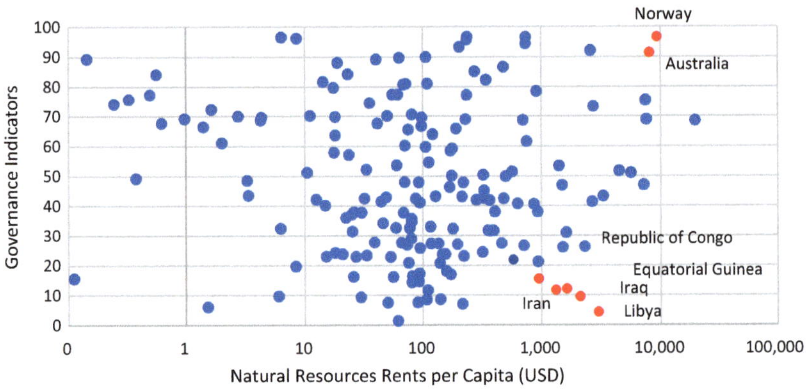


**Fig. 5.5** Natural resources and governance (*Source* WDI for resource rents; Worldwide Governance Indicators (WGI) for governance indicators, both in 2021, data obtained in January 2025)

that cannot be controlled by policy and should not be simply compared, sustained economic growth will create large disparities in income levels over the long term. Botswana, which is recognized for its success in maintaining good governance, including tribal coordination, is considered a successful example of an African country that avoided the "resource curse" (Acemoglu et al. 2001).

There are several policies that countries rich in natural resources have been working on to avoid the "resource curse" and achieve sustainable economic growth. Below are some representative policies, including actual efforts in individual countries.

The first is industrial diversification. A representative example is Malaysia, which has succeeded in industrial diversification without becoming overly dependent on its abundant natural resources and without falling victim to the "Dutch disease" through appropriate industrialization policies. Malaysia was the world's largest producer of natural rubber and tin until around the 1970s, and as of 1980, primary products still accounted for 77% of its exports. However, by 2015, the share had fallen to 19%. Policies such as tax incentives for export-oriented companies under the Investment Incentives Act of 1968 and the Free Trade Zone Act of 1971 attracted multinational companies and led to the gradual growth of manufacturing—especially in the labor-intensive electronics and textile industries—and later efforts to attract high-tech industries.

Although Malaysia's industrial policies followed in the footsteps of Singapore and South Korea, which had led the way in economic development, the experience of Malaysia, a country with abundant natural resources, is instructive in that it was able to maintain sustained high growth while gradually shifting the main industries that drove its economy. Asanuma and Obama (2013), who observed Malaysia's economic growth process, point out that there is no generic optimal strategy and that optimal policies differ depending on the stage of development and the situation of competing countries. They conclude that Malaysia succeeded because it had a political leader who was strongly committed to a growth and development strategy and talented technocrats to support him, and they appropriately shifted his development strategy according to the situation.

However, Malaysia's industrialization policy also provides an example of a failure. The national car manufacturer, Proton, received generous government protection, including protective tariffs. Over time, the company lost its domestic market share due to declining international competitiveness, and its factory utilization rate became extremely low. On the other hand, smaller resource-rich countries in the Persian Gulf, such as the UAE, have succeeded in establishing a degree of industrial diversification by establishing free zones, developing infrastructure, taking special measures for investment and taxation, and attracting foreign companies to develop their financial and tourism industries to a large extent.

Second is the establishment of a transparent sovereign wealth fund. Botswana established the Pula Fund in 1994, and a portion of the proceeds from diamond exports were invested by the fund in foreign currency-denominated securities and other long-term investments. The management of the fund was entrusted to experts who were independent from the government to avoid political interference, and Frankel (2012) evaluated it as a better model than the Norwegian Petroleum Fund, which is the world's largest sovereign wealth fund, in terms of eliminating political influence.

In addition to accumulating wealth for future generations before future natural resource depletion, sovereign wealth funds, if properly managed, have the desirable effect of preventing Dutch disease by investing the proceeds outside of countries when resource prices rise. When prices fall, budgetary resources are withdrawn from the fund, thereby supplying it for the general account to enable fiscal mobilization to support the economy. This is expected to have the desired counter-cyclical effect of reducing the swings in the economy.

According to the Sovereign Wealth Fund Institute (SWFI), which collects and analyzes information on sovereign wealth funds around the world, more than 40 sovereign wealth funds have been established since 2005. On the other hand, many sovereign wealth funds lack transparency and proper governance.[18]

A third policy is a fiscal rule that is counter-cyclical to changes in resource prices. In Chile, a structural fiscal balance rule was introduced in 2000, which allows a budget deficit when GDP falls below trend due to recession or when the price of copper, a key export resource, falls below trend. In theory, this policy looks reasonable and persuasive: when resource prices rise, Chile saves the increased revenue to avoid overheating of the economy coming from expanding government spending, and when prices plummet, it admits a deficit to prop up the economy. In practice, however, it is difficult to predict which stage of the business cycle a country is in and how export resource prices will move in the future. The forecasts

[18] Regarding Botswana's "Pula Fund," some have pointed out that the Ministry of Finance frequently withdraws funds without giving clear reasons and that the accumulation is insufficient ("Botswana repeatedly raids preservation fund," Mail and Guardian, 05 February 2016).

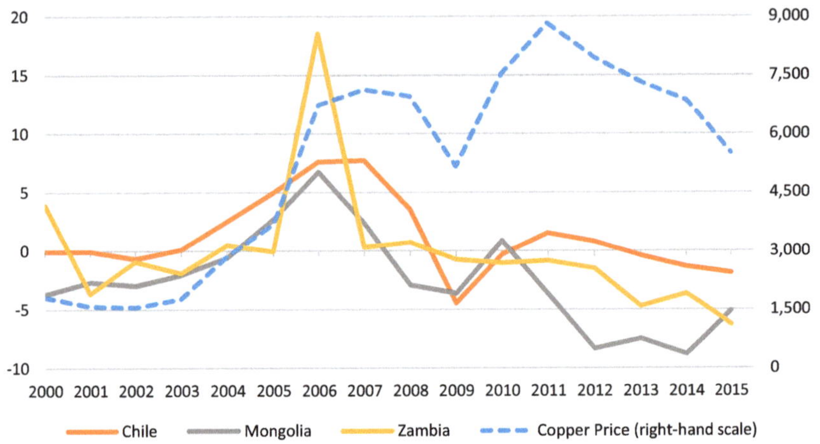


**Fig. 5.6** Copper producing countries' primary balance (percent of GDP) and international copper prices (USD/tonne) (*Source* Adapted from World Economic Outlook [WEO] 2016 Oct.)

themselves can be subject to bias in order to allow for spending expansion, which is politically popular. The ingenuity used in Chile was to have copper price trends forecasted by external experts who are independent from the political process, which has been credited with avoiding the mistake of making optimistic price forecasts (Frankel 2012).

Figure 5.6 compares the primary balance of Mongolia and Zambia, where, like Chile, copper is a major export commodity, with changes in copper prices.[19] The international copper price (per tonne) peaked at USD 7,000 in 2006–2008, then plunged to USD 5,000 in 2009 when the Global Financial Crisis (GFC) hit. This was followed by another surge to nearly USD 9,000 in 2011, and then a sharp decline to USD 5,500 in 2015. Revenues in all three countries tended to rise when copper prices rose and fall when prices fell. However, Chile was able to reduce its spending growth when revenues rose—unlike Mongolia and Zambia—and achieved a larger budget surplus. The country was also able to run a large budget surplus during the recession in 2009. It should be noted that Mongolia and Zambia ran larger fiscal deficits than Chile when copper prices declined after 2012, but this was accompanied by large-scale external borrowing, largely because surpluses had not accumulated before then. Toward 2016, when copper prices fell even further, the countries were not in a sustainable counter-cyclical fiscal management in that their balance of payments deteriorated, their exchange rates plummeted, and their public debt surged, leading to a fiscal crisis and stagnating economic growth, both of which required IMF support.

[19] Zambia's extremely large surplus in 2006 was due to the debt reduction of over 20% of GDP that took place in that year, which was recorded as a gift.

Fourth, financial derivatives can be used to mitigate the impact of international resource price fluctuations on their economies. The growing market for such instruments allows resource-rich countries to hedge against the risk of price volatility; according to the IMF (2016a), Mexico uses hedging instruments for oil, Ghana for cocoa, South Africa for gold, and Zambia for copper. In addition to transaction costs, there are political costs associated with the use of hedging instruments. If the government fixes prices through futures contracts and market prices later rise, it could be accused of failing to capitalize on the gains. Buying put options offers protection against a sharp drop in revenue when prices plummet while also enjoying the revenue increase from higher prices. However, if the price fluctuation is small, the option cost may draw attention and could still be politically harmful. Accumulating foreign currency reserves as a buffer against a possible future crisis can also be considered a cost, in that the funds are invested in low-yielding US T-bills, etc. However, hedging instruments may be more vulnerable to criticism. The IMF (2016b) assessed that Mexico's oil put option reduced the sovereign debt spread by 30 basis points compared to the unhedged situation, equivalent to a 0.4% constant increase in consumption.

Fifth, as mentioned above, the abundance of natural resources can easily lead to tyranny and corruption, making it difficult to deepen democracy and transparency. The Extractive Industries Transparency Initiative (EITI) aims to make the flow of funds from the extractive industries to the governments of resource-rich countries transparent by clarifying information from both sides. It also seeks to ensure that resource revenues do not promote corruption and conflict.

One example where transparency contributed to improving governance in resource-rich countries is the case of the Democratic Republic of Congo. In 2013, the Africa Progress Panel, a non-profit organization chaired by former UN Secretary-General Kofi Annan, noted that between 2010 and 2012, the country sold five mining assets to foreign companies with complex and secret ownership structures for an average of 1/6th of their estimated market value, resulting in losses totaling at least USD 1.36 billion. Corruption was implicated in the background, and the Democratic Republic of Congo, with the support of the EITI, subsequently adopted a new law proposing that the government ensure public access to information on the actual beneficial owners of mining concession holders.

The relationship between the above policies and the problems identified as the "resource curse" can be depicted as shown in Fig. 5.7.

While this perspective differs from the "resource curse," it is important to note that countries dependent on natural resources tend to have a concentration of export trading partners. For example, China accounts for about 50% of global consumption of copper, zinc, and nickel, all of which are consumed domestically (JOGMEC 2017). As a result, resource-rich countries tend to have a high share of their exports going to China. Mongolia, for example, exports more than 80% of its goods to China. If exports are excessively concentrated in China, the impact of a downturn in China's economy could be significant, making it more difficult to maintain sustainable economic growth through various policies.

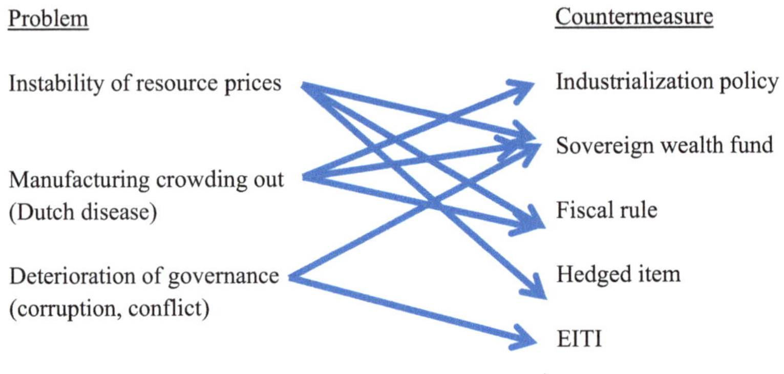


**Fig. 5.7** Resource curse problems and remedies (*Source* Prepared by Author)

China is also approaching resource-rich countries in the developing world in ways that differ from the traditional approach of Western countries (Collier 2010). For example, it offers loans at low interest rates that are repaid through the proceeds from resource exports, a process known as the "Angola model." There is also considerable support for direct infrastructure construction by Chinese workers, which may help prevent construction delays and the spread of procurement-related corruption. However, there are many concerns from the perspective of resource-rich countries related to the sustainability of economic growth. These kinds of infrastructure construction can limit some benefits of development, such as process transparency, which contributes to market confidence, improved governance, and enhanced skills through job creation and technology transfers.

## References

Acemoglu, Daron, Simon Johnson, and James Robinson. 2001. "An African Success Story: Botswana." MIT Department of Economics Working Paper 01-37. MIT.

Álvarez-Herránz, Agustín, Daniel Balsalobrem, José María Cantos, and Muhammad Shahbaz. 2017. "Energy Innovations-GHG Emissions Nexus: Fresh Empirical Evidence from OECD Countries." *Energy Policy* 101: 90–100.

Andrée, Bo Pieter, Johannes, Andres Chamorro, Phoebe Spencer, Eric Koomen, and Harun Dogo. 2019. "Revisiting the Relationship Between Economic Growth and the Environment: A Global Assessment of Deforestation, Pollution and Carbon Emission." *Renewable and Sustainable Energy Reviews* 114: 109221.

Arezki, Rabah, Kirk Hamilton, and Kazim Kazimov. 2011. "Resource Windfalls, Macroeconomic Stability and Growth: The Role of Political Institutions." IMF Working Paper WP/11/142. IMF.

Asanuma, Shinji, and Hirohisa Obama. 2013. *Tojyōkoku no tabi: Kaihatu seisaku no narratives* [Travels in Developing Countries: Narratives of Development Policy]. Keiso Shobo.

Auty, Richard. 1993. *Sustaining Development in Mineral Economies: The Resource Curse Thesis*. Oxford University Press.

Balsalobre-Lorente, Daniel, Muhammad Shahbaz, David Roubaud, and Sahbi Farhani. 2018. "How Economic Growth, Renewable Electricity and Natural Resources Contribute to $CO_2$ Emission?" *Energy Policy* 113: 356–367.

Bo, Sun. 2011. "A Literature Survey on Environmental Kuznets Curve." *Energy Procedia* 5: 1322–1325.

Cabinet Office, Japan. 2011. White Paper on the Economy and Public Finance, 2010 Edition.

Collier, Paul. 2010. *The Plundered Planet: How to Reconcile Prosperity with Nature.* Viking Adult.

Collier, Paul, and Benedikt Goderis. 2007. "Commodity Prices, Growth, and the Natural Resource Curse: Reconciling a Conundrum." CSAE WPS/2007–15. African Development Bank.

Costanza, Robert, and Herman E. Daly. 1992. "Natural Capital and Sustainable Development." *Conservation Biology* 6 (1): 37–46.

Dinda, Soumyananda. 2004. "Environmental Kuznets Curve Hypothesis: A Survey." *Ecological Economics* 49 (4): 431–455.

Druckman A., and T. Jackson. 2008. "The Surrey Environmental Lifestyle Mapping (SELMA) Framework: Development and Key Results to Date." RESOVE Working Paper 08-08. University of Surrey.

Elkins, Paul. 2003. "Identifying Critical Natural Capital: Conclusions About Critical Natural Capital." *Ecological Economics* 44: 277–292.

Frankel, Jeffrey A. 2012. "The Natural Resource Curse: A Survey of Diagnoses and Some Prescriptions." HKS Faculty Research. Working Paper Series RWP 12–014. John F. Kennedy School of Government, Harvard University.

Grossman, Gene M., and Krueger Alan B. 1991. "Environmental Impacts of a North American Free Trade Agreement." NBER Working Paper No. 3914. NBER.

Hartwick, John M. 1977. "Intergenerational Equity and the Investing of Rents from Exhaustible Resources." *Economic Review* 67 (5): 972–974.

Hausmann, Ricardo, and Roberto Rigobon. 2003. "An Alternative Interpretation of the 'Resource Curse': Theory and Policy Implications." NBER Working Paper 9424. NBER.

Intergovernmental Panel on Climate Change (IPCC). 2021. "Summary for Policymakers." In *Climate Change 2021: The Physical Science Bases. Contribution of Working Group 1 to the Sixth Assessment Report of the Intergovernmental Panel on Climate Change*, eds. Masson-Delmotte, V. P. Zhai, A. Pirani, S. L. Connors, C. Waterfield, O. Yelekçi, R. Yu and B. Zhou, https://www.ipcc.ch/report/ar6/wg1/chapter/summary-for-policymakers/. Accessed June 24, 2025.

International Monetary Fund (IMF). 2016a. "Adequacy of the Global Financial Safety Net." IMF Policy Paper. IMF.

International Monetary Fund (IMF). 2016b. "Mexico Selected Issues." IMF Country Report, 19–31.

Japan Organization for Metals and Energy Security (JOGMEC). 2017. "2017 Kinzoku shigen report (2017.7)" [Metals Resources Report (2017.7)].

Lederman, Daniel, and William F. Maloney. 2007. *Natural Resources: Neither Curse nor Destiny.* World Bank and Stanford University Press.

Luciani, Giacomo. 1987. "Allocation vs. Production States: A Theoretical Framework." In *The Rentier State*, ed. Giacomo Luciani, 63–82. Routledge.

Ministry of the Environment, Japan. 2018. "Shogaikoku ni okeru tansozei tō no dōnyū jyōkyō." [Introduction of Carbon Taxes and other Taxes in other Countries]. https://www.env.go.jp/content/900498772.pdf.

Narita, Daijyu. 2016. "Kankyō no jizokukanōsei to keizei seichō no kankei nituite" [Relationship Between Environmental Sustainability and Economic Growth]. Development Cooperation Literature Review No. 2. JICA Ogata Sadako Peace and Development Institute.

Neate, Rupert. 2012. "£5bn Illegally Taken Out of Zambia over Past Decade, Says Report." *The Guardian.* December 18, 2012. https://www.theguardian.com/world/2012/dec/17/5bn-illegally-taken-out-zambia-report.

Nordhaus, William D. 1992. "The 'Dice' Model: The Background and Structure of a Dynamic Integrated Climate-Economy Model of the Economics of Global Warming." Cowles Foundation Discussion Paper No. 1009. Cowles Foundation.

Nordhaus, William D. 2013. *The Climate* Casino*: Risk, Uncertainty, and Economics for a Warming World*. Yale University Press.

Nordhaus, William D. 2019. "Climate Change: The Ultimate Challenge for Economics." *American Economic Review* 109 (6): 1991–2014.

Organization for Economic Co-operation and Development (OECD). 2021. "Dataset: Carbon Dioxide Emissions Embodied in International Trade (2021 edition)." OECD Stat. https://data-explorer.oecd.org. Accessed August 3, 2022.

Panayotou, Theodore. 1993. "Empirical Tests and Policy Analysis of Environmental Degradation at Different Stages of Economic Development." World Employment Programme Research Working Paper, WEP 2-22/WP_238. International Labour Organization.

Pearce, David. 1993. *Blueprint 3: Measuring Sustainable Development.* Earthscan Publications.

Pearce, David, and Jeremy J. Warford. 1993. *World Without End*. Oxford University Press and World Bank.

Rockström, Johan, and Mattias Klum. 2015. *Big World Small Planet: Abundance within Planetary Boundaries.* Bokförlaget Max Ström.

Rockström, Johan, Kevin J. Noone, Will Steffen, and Åsa Persson. 2009. "Planetary Boundaries: Exploring the Safe Operating Space for Humanity." *Ecology and Society* 461/24 September 2009.

Ross, Michael, L. 2012. *The Oil Curse.* Princeton University Press.

Sachs, Jeffrey, and Andrew Warner. 2001. "The Curse of Natural Resources." *European Economic Review* 45: 827–838.

Shafik, Nemat, and Sushenjit Bandyopadhyay. 1992. "Economic Growth and Environmental Quality." Background Paper for World Development Report 1992, Policy Research Working Paper 904. World Bank.

Solow, Robert M. 1986. "On the Intergenerational Allocation of Natural Resources. "*The Scandinavian Journal of Economics* 88 (1): 141–149.

Stern, Nicholas. 2006. *Stern Review: The Economics of Climate Change.* Cambridge University Press.

Tol, Richard S. J. 2009. "The Economic Effects of Climate Change." *Journal of Economic Perspectives* 23 (2): 29–51.

Uchiyama, Katsuhisa. 2009. "Shou jizokukanō na hatten to kankyō Kuznets kyokusen" [Sustainable Development and the Environmental Kuznets Curve]. In *Chikyū ondanka to keizai hatten: Jizokukanō na seichō wo kangaeru* [Global Warming and Economic Development: Considering Sustainable Growth], eds. Hirofumi Uzawa and Yuko Hosoda, 159–184. University of Tokyo Press.

United Nations Development Programme (UNDP). 2017. *UNDP's Strategy for Inclusive and Sustainable Growth.* UNDP.

World Bank. 2010. *World Development Report 2010: Development and Climate Change.* World Bank. http://hdl.handle.net/10986/4387.

World Bank. 2021. *The Changing Wealth of Nations 2021: Managing Assets for the Future.* World Bank.

**Koki Hirota** earned his B.A. in Economics from the University of Tokyo and holds a Ph.D. in Economics from Saitama University in Japan. His professional career spans several prominent roles in international development finance and policy, including Chief Economist, Director General of Operation and Strategy Department, and Director General of Southeast Asia and Pacific Department at the Japan International Cooperation Agency (JICA), and Chief Representative in Jakarta for Japan Bank for International Cooperation and in Hanoi for the Overseas Economic Cooperation Fund. In academia, he was a Professor at the Graduate School of Humanities and Social Sciences at Saitama University and a Visiting Fellow at the JICA Ogata Sadako Research Institute for Peace and Development. His recent publications include *Challenges in Fiscal and Monetary Policies in Mongolia* (co-edited, Springer, 2023) and *Addressing Social Infrastructure Needs in Asia: Towards a Pandemic Resilient Society* (co-edited, JICA, August 2025).

**Keiichiro Yuasa** is a Senior Director of Public Governance and Financial Management Team of Japan International Cooperation Agency (JICA). He leads the team to implement development cooperation in the areas of Public Administration, Financial Sector Development, Public Financial Management, Trade Facilitation and Customs Modernization. In his overseas assignments, he has been stationed at JICA Offices in Thailand and Sri Lanka where he had played important roles to plan and implement various development cooperation projects in the fields of governance, transportation, agriculture, etc. He occasionally delivers lectures on macroeconomics or credit risk analysis at the University of Tokyo or training courses organized by International Monetary Fund (IMF). He earned his B.A. in Economics from the University of Tokyo and holds a Master in Public Administration from Harvard University.

# Innovation, Economic Transformation and Sustained Growth

6

Koki Hirota and Keiko Kubota

## 6.1 Background Theory for Sustained Growth

### 6.1.1 Introduction

In the previous chapter, I discussed two key aspects of growth sustainability. This chapter focuses on another issue: the mechanism by which growth is sustained over the medium to long term. The basic approach to this can be drawn from the growth theory of economics.

Economic growth is defined as an increase in the size of the economy (output) in terms of flows, as measured by GDP. While demand is a prerequisite for production, discussions of medium- to long-term growth typically focus on the supply side. Thus, the discussion in this chapter focuses primarily on how production can be continuously expanded. The factors that determine production are capital and productivity. The former comprises labor and physical capital, while productivity encompasses all other aspects related to production, referred to as total factor productivity (TFP), as mentioned earlier, including technology and the quality of labor, which are important factors. A society with sustained growth is one in which these factors are continuously increasing or improving. This chapter first briefly introduces the basic relationship between production, labor, capital, and productivity, followed by the factors that influence the accumulation of these factors and the paths of their improvement—specifically, innovation and economic transformation, as well as macroeconomic policies and institutions. In addition,

K. Hirota (✉)
Tokyo, Japan

K. Kubota
Department of Economics, Tohoku Gakuin University, Sendai, Miyagi, Japan



K. Hirota (ed.), *Introduction to Quality Growth*,
https://doi.org/10.1007/978-981-95-6220-6_6

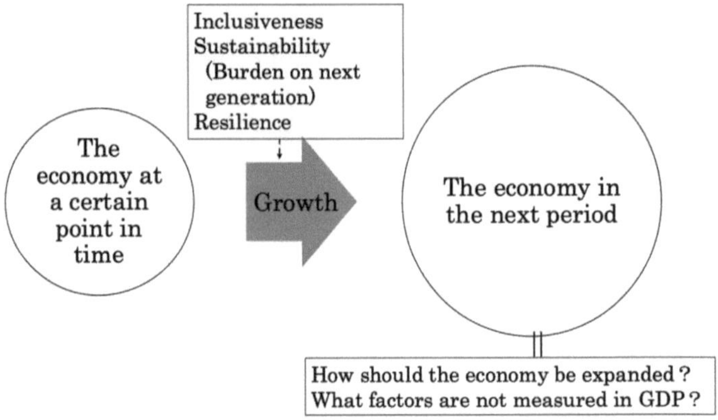


**Fig. 6.1** Rationale for sustained growth. *Source* Author

the chapter also introduces the idea that the goods and services produced contain values that cannot be captured by GDP.

When innovations occur, resources in a society are reallocated, thereby transforming the economy and society, including industrial structures and the portfolio of human skills. Growth can be sustained when such changes occur continuously. Based on this recognition, APEC has identified innovative growth as one element of quality growth, as introduced in Chap. 2. The question of how such transformation can occur on a continuous basis is therefore essential. While exploring this question, it is also important to consider that not all results of innovation can be measured by GDP indicators. This relationship is conceptually organized in Fig. 6.1. In this chapter, I will attempt to explain what kind of economic expansion leads to sustained growth, as expressed in the bottom right of Fig. 6.1.

### 6.1.2 Development of Growth Theory and Its Relevance to Quality Growth

Growth theory is one of the areas of macroeconomics that has accumulated a vast amount of research, so this chapter will refer to only some of this corpus where it is relevant to the subject of this book. When considering the mechanism of growth, it is common to decompose it into the three factors of production—i.e., capital, labor and productivity. Modern growth theory, beginning in the 1940s, considered capital as the source of growth. This was demonstrated at the time in the classic model by Harrod and Domar model, where the economic growth rate was considered to be proportional to the investment rate (with capital in this case not considered a substitute for labor). The idea that investment determines the magnitude of economic growth is particularly important in developing countries, where capital is highly constrained.

In Chap. 3, I introduced the argument that growth can be promoted in societies with large inequalities. The basis for this discussion is that a high savings rate leads to substantial investment, which in turn promotes a country's economic growth. I also introduced the relationship between growth and resilience, where the focus was on physical investment as a determinant of growth. This perspective is still important today when looking at a country's economy. For example, there is an indicator called the incremental capital-output ratio (ICOR) that looks at the relationship between investment and GDP. This indicator is simply obtained by comparing investment with incremental GDP to express the investment efficiency of a country. Countries require substantial investments with high efficiency in order to accelerate growth. For example, in recent years, there has been concern about deteriorating investment efficiency in China, with the large increase (i.e., deterioration) in ICOR used as evidence of this.[1] The argument then leads to the suggestion that these phenomena may be the result of continued over-investment, which has led to funds being allocated to investments/projects with low marginal rates of return.

The basis of current growth theory is the Solow model from the 1950s. Solow (2000) recalls that, as the three factors of production are independent, the possibility of constant growth under the balanced development of these factors becomes entirely unlikely. He then shows that, by allowing for elasticity in production technology, there is a pathway through which economic growth can be constantly materialized. The Solow model basically consists of two equations: the production equation and the capital accumulation equation. Output per capita is determined by technological development, per capita saving (investment) rate and population growth rate. The changes of the latter two affect the level of output per capita but are temporary until a new steady state is achieved. Ultimately, the growth rate of output per capita will be the growth rate of technology, and the rate of economic growth will depend on this technological progress.

Solow (1957) presents a method of decomposing output growth rates into several production factors—i.e., growth accounting. This method of analysis is still widely used today. Specifically, it decomposes the growth of output into the growth of the capital stock (K), labor (L) and other factors (A) in the production function equation: $Y = AK^{\alpha} L^{(1-\alpha)}$. The variable A is generally referred to as TFP, and Solow considered TFP to represent technological development. Here, the key point is that he assumed it to be exogenously given from outside the equation. This would mean that we would have to wait for technological progress to happen by chance. However, technological development does not occur randomly in the real world but is rather concentrated in certain countries and at certain times (e.g., in developed countries). The mechanisms by which this happens were clarified in the models that followed.

Another issue related to this model is that the quality of labor and capital is assumed to be uniform, which is highly relevant to the sustainability of growth.

[1] Wolf, Martin, "The Chinese Economy is rebalancing, at last." Financial Times. April 4, 2018.

Today, when conducting a growth accounting analysis, it is possible to isolate factors such as the quality of labor separately, allowing for a deeper analysis. A model that takes into account differences in the quality of labor and capital was presented by Jorgenson and Griliches (1967). Different technologies lead to differing input and cost structures across various sectors of the economy, as well as differing rates of change. For example, labor inputs vary according to age, sex, occupation, education and wages, while capital also varies according to differences in machinery, construction, and other assets. In the process of growth, these input structures of production change (i.e., the quality of labor and capital changes), and productivity increases as resources are reallocated.

Such analyses have since been carried out by industry, and differences in productivity growth have also been estimated by industry: Jorgenson and Griliches (1967) found that, excluding differences in the quality of labor and capital in the US, the growth rate of TFP over the period between 1945 and 1965 was only 0.1% (the overall growth rate of TFP over this period was 1.6%). The Japan Industrial Productivity Database shows that for the period from 1995 to 2020, the contribution of labor input to growth was negative due to population decline etc., while capital input and TFP contribute to growth positively (note that labor and capital quality are not included in TFP here), with a GDP growth rate of 0.58%. In comparison, the total contribution of labor and capital quality is 0.25%, indicating that these are substantial for economic growth.

Although there have been ups and downs in economic growth since the Industrial Revolution, the economy has expanded considerably over the long term, driven by technological progress. However, the theoretical framework, in which such progress is exogenously given, does not explain the factors that keep technology permanently progressing. In addition, according to the neoclassical theoretical framework, the accumulation of capital leads to diminishing returns, but the fact that the economy still grows means that technological progress is occurring at a rate that exceeds this law. The question is whether such high rates of technological progress have continued to occur by chance and on a continuous basis.

There may also be a problem with the assumption of diminishing marginal returns in the first place. In response to these questions, a theory has emerged that incorporates the mechanisms of technological progress into growth theory, elucidating why technology grows. This endogenous economic growth theory, presented by Romer, Lucas, and others, emerged in the late 1980s. The theory is based on the idea that the source of growth (technological development, according to Solow) is not given exogenously, but grows endogenously in the process of growth. In other words, the theory explains that there are factors and mechanisms within the economic system that promote sustained growth.

Solow (2000) states that there are, broadly speaking, three approaches to endogenous growth theory. The first attempts to study the endogenous accumulation of human capital, the second builds a theory of technological innovation, including R&D, while the third removes one or several of the standard assumptions of the neoclassical growth model. What is usually removed is the assumption of diminishing returns to capital, an idea that has become known as the AK model. The AK model can be considered in the following cases: (1) all factors of production are reproducible (all growing at the same rate), (2) the existence of externalities, and (3) production with increasing returns in a monopoly market and R&D activities (Saito 1999). The following is a brief introduction to models by Romer and Lucas, representing endogenous growth theories.

Romer (1986) found that historical growth data indicted that the Solow model could not explain long-term growth trends, and that knowledge was one of the factors of production, with marginal returns to knowledge increasing due to its positive externality. Romer (1990) formulates the relationship between "new design" and growth. The endogenous part of Romer's model is that the more researchers there are, the more ideas are generated, and the rate of idea discovery depends on the accumulation of ideas from the past. Romer explains that engineers today are better able to develop technologies based on the results of technological progress than engineers 100 years ago. In this way, new technologies and ideas will not only produce the new products in question but will also increase the productivity of subsequent research as a whole through an increase in the knowledge stock.

This view also appears to explain why so many ideas are generated in developed countries. Romer also points out that when open trade occurs, the number of researchers required for idea generation is not limited to a single country but extends to a global pool. In other words, open trade facilitates the generation of ideas in emerging and developing countries.

By contrast, Lucas (1988) focuses on human capital rather than the knowledge stock. He assumes that the level of human capital increases as workers make efforts to accumulate skills. In other words, the level of human capital at a given point in time is multiplied by the amount of time spent on skill accumulation. In this model, the rate of growth of human capital increases as the effort spent on human capital accumulation increases. Furthermore, the level of human capital can be raised by policies that increase the amount of time individuals spend acquiring skills. In other words, even in the absence of technological progress, effective learning-by-doing will improve workers' skills and growth will be sustained. In the endogenous growth concept, there is no upper limit to the growth of knowledge and human capital levels, which can continue to provide sustained growth within the framework of economic development.

As mentioned above, capital, technology and endogenous growth are all indispensable for achieving sustained growth. Therefore, it is desirable to have macroeconomic policies, trade policies, technology transfer and institutions that foster a society supportive of these factors. Next, I will briefly introduce some of the empirical analyses on growth and present a discussion of the relationship between what has been described so far and quality growth. This will be followed by a discussion of innovation in Sect. 6.2, macroeconomic and trade policies in Sect. 6.3, and institutions in Sect. 6.4.

### 6.1.3 Empirical Analyses of Factors Influencing Growth

Many empirical studies—e.g., growth regression analyses—have been conducted as endogenous growth theory emerged. The variables used in these studies to explain growth vary between researchers, encompassing not only economic indicators but also social and political indicators such as education, institutions, policies and political regimes. For example, Barro (1997), extending the scope to law and democracy, found that growth is enhanced by the rule of law, low inflation, life expectancy, male secondary and tertiary education levels, low fertility rates, terms of trade and greater political rights. Underpinning the view that institutions are important as drivers of economic growth is the school of new institutional economics (NIE). This school argues that politics and economic institutions determine economic performance, just as institutions and technology determine the magnitude of transaction costs (North 1994). While institutions are discussed in more detail in Sect. 6.4, Yeager (1999), using transition countries as examples, states that the key to success is an institutional framework that provides incentives for low transaction costs and technological progress.[2]

Empirical studies with a regional focus have also been conducted. A famous example is *The East Asian Miracle,* first published in 1993 (World Bank 1993). It found that eight East Asian countries (Japan, Hong Kong, South Korea, Singapore, Taiwan, Indonesia, Thailand, and Malaysia) were the only regions where high growth and narrowing inequality occurred simultaneously, noting some common features, such as a high share of private investment and accumulation of human capital. It found that two-thirds of the growth could be explained by the accumulation of physical and human capital, while the remaining one-third could be attributed to the increase in TFP. It then examined why TFP improved, particularly in the region.

The analysis highlights, firstly, the fact that the macroeconomic environment was stable. This environment gave investors the confidence to invest. Secondly, the governments of these countries ensured that companies had access to imports at international prices and to credit, which promoted exports. With regard to industrial policies, it states that, in general, they did not necessarily lead to growth. However, their openness to foreign technologies and ideas allowed companies to absorb new technologies. Other aspects mentioned include the benefits of institutional finance. Through these economic policies and institutional improvements,

[2] This institutional perspective, coupled with endogenous growth theory, appears to have had a significant impact on aid to developing countries. Based on the view that productivity improvements through institutional and policy improvements are necessary to sustain growth in developing countries, the World Bank and other international organizations have encouraged such reforms through conditionality under structural adjustment programs. Although the content of policy actions has shifted in emphasis—from the former Washington Consensus, which focused on removing trade barriers, deregulation and privatization—to improving governance, public expenditure management, and the investment climate, the basic emphasis on institutions has not changed. The continued provision of policy-supported loans by these institutions is evidence of this.

the accumulation of physical and human capital, as well as technological advances, was considered to have occurred, providing the driving forces of economic growth.[3]

*The East Asian Miracle* also discusses endogenous growth theory, but it is not always clear how the policies and institutional improvements observed to be effective have stimulated endogenous growth. Solow (2000) noted that cross-sectional studies in general do not sufficiently distinguish between differences in economic levels and differences in long-term growth rates. Some policy and institutional improvements have a level effect only for a time, while others have an effect over a certain period. For example, if new tax incentives are provided for foreign investors, new foreign investment may subsequently increase for several years, while improvements in the education system that encourage improvements in labor quality can lead to self-sustaining growth according to endogenous growth theory. Even so, as Krugman (1994) states, for example, it is unlikely that the majority of workers in Singapore will have PhDs 30 years from now. Solow (2000) argues that it is overly ambitious to try to find a theory that rigorously formulates growth rates or policies that will permanently increase them. The effects of policies and institutions that increase TFP and promote the accumulation of physical and human capital should often be considered to last only for a certain period.

### 6.1.4 Implications for Quality Growth

The following are considered essential from a quality growth perspective in relation to the growth theory reviewed so far. First, investment continues to be important for developing countries. An increase in the rate of investment has a transitory effect on output, but does not guarantee that growth will be endogenously sustained. However, it is, of course, still important, especially in developing countries where investment funds are usually scarce and there is often considerable scope for institutional improvements in business environments to increase investment. When developing policies and institutions, it is essential to maintain a long-term perspective to avoid becoming overly focused on short-sighted policies and institutions.[4]

[3] Krugman (1994) criticized East Asian growth as anything but a miracle. The underlying point was that resource mobilization was the biggest factor in the high growth of these newly industrialized Asian countries, and that there was little that could be explained by the increase of TFP. Furthermore, in response to the view that other Asian countries would develop in the same way, citing Japan's achievement of high growth, he noted that Japan experienced not only an increase in inputs but also a significant increase in economic efficiency. The growth rate has since slowed, and therefore he argued that there were not many similarities between Japan and the other countries.

[4] Regarding the long-term perspective, the relationship between institutions, policies and economic growth should be emphasized from both the NIE and endogenous growth theory perspectives—i.e., that knowledge and human capital accumulate through policies and institutions, and that growth continues endogenously. Both short-term outcomes and long-term directions need to be considered, and these should be measured in an integrated manner.

Second, in addition, balanced investment in physical and human capital is needed. The engine of economic growth is not necessarily the same at different stages of development. Growth is the result of a complex relationship between various factors, and the contribution of these factors to growth differs according to the stage of development. In poor countries, the constraints on capital needed to achieve growth are particularly high. Scarce capital is therefore typically drawn towards economic capital. However, this does not mean that investment in human capital (e.g., education)—an important element of long-term endogenous growth—should be disregarded. Conversely, if investment in human capital becomes excessively concentrated, there is a possibility that unemployment will lead to social unrest, as employment will not be commensurate with the investment in human capital. It is the role of development strategies to outline scenarios for medium- to long-term development and determine how to allocate domestic resources to achieve those goals. In the past, such medium- to long-term perspectives were set out in development plans such as five-year plans. Recently, with the exception of several countries such as China, such medium- to long-term plans have become less common, but it is still necessary to have provide fundamental guidance toward future growth.

Third, institutional measures are needed to promote productivity improvements that lead to endogenous growth. How production factors can be more effectively accumulated remains a key concern of growth strategy. How human capital development policies facilitate the accumulation of knowledge, or how societies and institutions are structured to make learning more likely, remains a real issue. In the next section of this chapter, I will touch on innovation and technology.

The fourth aspect is the relationship with the global economy, an area that Romer (1990) also touches upon. The integration into the global economy is particularly important for countries with economies that are not large or are geopolitically isolated. The endogenous growth theory suggests that countries with larger economies and populations have advantages in knowledge accumulation and human capital, which makes them more likely to grow than smaller countries. Indeed, many of the emerging economies that have increased their share of global GDP since the end of the twentieth century have been large countries. That is why the issue of small countries has always been a central concern in discussions of development in developing countries. In this case, the primary policy tool available to small countries is integration into the global economy.

In the global economy, there is effectively unlimited demand for the export-producing sectors of small countries. Technology transfer is another reason for open trade policies, and this is why many countries have, in practice, adopted policies such as encouraging foreign investment and improving access to international markets. Although questions remain as to whether comparative advantage sectors—in which greater resource allocations are directed through trade—are more likely to promote endogenous growth, there are examples of countries in East Asia with small domestic markets, such as Taiwan, Hong Kong and Singapore, that have achieved growth based on export-led manufacturing.

The above applies to growth strategies in general, but in order to achieve quality growth, it is necessary to explore the relationship between sustainability—in the sense of not being at the expense of future generations—growth theory and inclusiveness, and resilience. These elements are not usually considered part of growth theory, but the relationship between capital, productivity, and the elements of quality growth are a fundamental concern of this book. I have discussed this relationship in the previous chapters, so to avoid repetition, I will highlight the relationship between the disaggregated factors of production (quality of labor/capital and investment) and the three themes of quality growth. First, equality of opportunity, a particularly important aspect of inclusiveness, is indispensable for labor quality, promoting the endogenous nature of growth. Whether the savings rate or the reduction in consumption due to income inequality is more dominant depends on the economic and social structure at a given time.

Secondly, regarding sustainability—the relationship with future generations—the quality of labor and capital is not directly linked to the environment or climate change. Although climate change-oriented policies have led to increased investment, this is interpreted as a response to negative externalities due to policy objectives rather than productivity gains. Therefore, such investments will increase production costs in the short term. However, this will naturally help to mitigate the losses caused by global warming and support long-term growth. Finally, with regard to resilience, there are its short-term growth-suppressing effects, which come at the expense of production. On the other hand, accepting a certain level of risk through these measures encourages investment in innovation and prevents long-term "scars" in the event of shocks, thereby making it easier to bring about endogenous growth. In summary, while these three factors do not necessarily have a unidirectional relationship with endogenous growth, they are closely related in that they collectively lead to long-term productivity improvements.

## 6.2 Productivity, Innovation and Societal Transformation

As mentioned in the previous section, productivity is the key to sustained growth, as the potential to generate endogenous accumulation essentially lies in productivity. But what improves productivity? TFP includes everything except the amount of capital and labor. The quality of physical capital, the quality of labor and the efficiency of capital utilization are particularly important. I review the first two in this section, discussing technology for the quality of physical capital, education and skills for the quality of labor, and innovation to improve both. In an economic crisis, demand for goods and services declines, leading to a lower utilization of capital and a decrease in output. Every country's economy goes through these kinds of changes as it develops.

Productivity improvement means a greater output for a given amount of capital and labor input. As productivity increases, more productive companies enter the market and increase their sales, while less productive companies exit. The preconditions for such entry and exit into the market are a business environment that supports start-ups and allows new companies to enter the market and compete fairly. This entry-exit occurs not only between companies but also between industries, which means industrial sophistication and high value-adding. Japan, for example, has sustained growth by shifting from light industries such as textiles to manufacturing—mainly in the assembly industry—before moving on to higher-value-added industries. In Thailand, supporting industries have grown up through automobile assembly, with some sophisticated automobile parts now manufactured locally. In developing countries where similar developments have been successful, the economic structure has been transformed over time to achieve sustained growth. This path of development is more or less the pattern seen in all countries, but the degree of change varies widely.

### 6.2.1 Innovative Growth as Defined by APEC

As introduced in Chap. 2, APEC identifies Innovative Growth as one of the five components of quality growth (APEC 2010). APEC defines innovative growth as efforts to "create an economic environment that promotes innovation and emerging economic sectors," and it considers creating such an environment essential for future growth. It emphasizes that technological innovation—particularly in information and communications—is a driver of growth and that innovation can facilitate the tackling of key global issues such as the environment, energy, transport, agriculture, healthcare, logistics, emergency preparedness, administrative services and education. It then identifies seven elements of innovative growth, as shown in Table 6.1. APEC (2010) expresses the view that technological progress through innovation can be the source of future growth and that the ICT/digital field is a particularly important area in modern society, as described above. At the same time, it states that human resources and institutions such as intellectual property rights are essential elements in generating innovation. I discuss the definition of innovation and the mechanisms and policies that generate it in the following sections.

### 6.2.2 Global Productivity Trends

Looking at changes in global TFP growth rates since the mid-1990s, although there are significant differences by region, a common trend is that they declined significantly during the period of the Global Financial Crisis (GFC) and have remained stagnant in the 2010s compared to the pre-GFC period. Dieppe (2021), in the World Bank report, provides a comprehensive global perspective on the productivity changes and the impact of COVID-19.[5] It states that the decline in labor

[5] The analysis of productivity in Dieppe (2021) is based on labor productivity as an indicator. In other words, since output per worker is used as a measure of productivity, productivity here

**Table 6.1** APEC's innovative growth

| Item | Contents |
|---|---|
| ICT application | Promoting smart socioeconomic activities through enhanced use of ICT |
| Digital prosperity | ICT innovation policy; adoption of globally accepted standards; investment in next-generation high-speed broadband; building a competitive environment; ensuring privacy protection |
| Human resources development | Development, education and training of ICT personnel; nurturing energy efficiency experts for the green economy; facilitating the mobility of experts |
| Policy dialogue and information sharing | Sharing best practices for innovation policies, including human resources and entrepreneurship development, R&D investment, tax incentives, financial measures, public–private partnerships (PPPs) and international cooperation |
| Innovation through intellectual property system | Cooperation on the protection, enforcement and use of intellectual property rights and improvement of the commercialization environment, anti-counterfeiting and piracy measures and patent acquisition procedures |
| Cooperation on standards | Promotion more alignment of domestic standards with international standards and cooperation on the standardization of advanced technologies |
| Life science | Promotion of innovation in the medical and life sciences sectors, encouraging investment, supporting pharmaceutical development, harmonizing regulations on medicines and preventing trade in counterfeit medical products |

*Source* APEC (2010), summarized by Author

productivity since the GFC has been a generally observed phenomenon in both advanced and emerging economies, and this has been attributed to weak investment and sluggish TFP growth in equal measure (Fig. 6.2), indicating that it is not a temporary phenomenon due to the business cycle, but a structural change.

Falling TFP means that technological advancement and resource reallocation have stagnated compared to earlier periods. Dieppe (2021) first states that history has shown that labor productivity growth is driven by innovation, education and investment, and then points out that in emerging economies, with the exception of China, R&D expenditure has not increased, so the gap with developed countries in terms of number of patents is widening. Moreover, participation in global

includes not only TFP but also capital deepening through investment (increase in capital stock per capita).

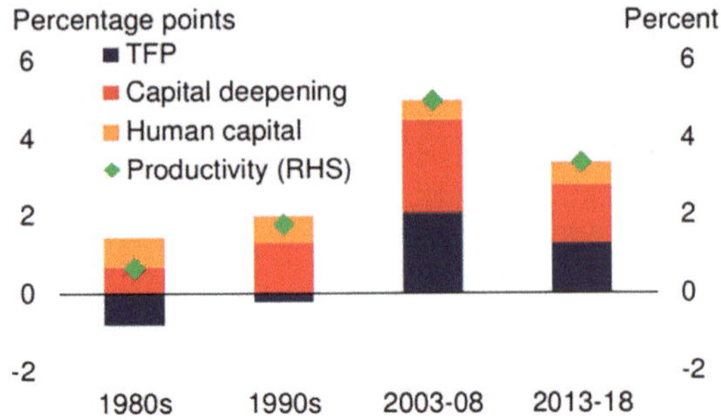


**Fig. 6.2** Drivers of productivity change in emerging economies. *Source* Dieppe (2021)

value chains (GVCs) has facilitated technology transfer, effectively reallocating resources. Yet, this process has become slower than before.

Furthermore, regarding the reallocation of resources, it is noted that urbanization and the concurrent shift from agriculture to manufacturing and services have become less evident. Other contributing factors include changes in the composition of the working population (the proportion of young people has fallen from its peak), the gap in higher education, differences in the diversification of economic structure, income inequality, gender inequality, financial development and institutional quality are also influencing this trend.

The decline in productivity growth has also been discussed in terms of long-term economic stagnation in advanced economies. Regarding the argument that these economies have entered a period of long-term stagnation since the GFC, there are two main views: one focuses on demand-side factors, while the other looks at supply-side factors. For the former, for example, Summers (2016) argues that the imbalances caused by the rising propensity to save and falling propensity to invest have led to a "secular stagnation." In terms of the latter, Gordon (2012) analyzes the factors behind the observed decline in productivity in the US in relation to technological innovation. He states that the period of rapid growth since 1750 can be divided into three historical phases, and the technological innovations representing each of these are steam engines and railways from 1750 to 1830; electricity and internal combustion engines in the period 1870 to 1900; computers, the Web and mobile phones from 1960 to today.

The in-between period of each is assumed to be a period of spin-offs, with inventions related to the previous period being created but with a slightly lower growth rate. With regard to technological innovation in the third period, since the end of the 1980s, a debate has arisen as to whether the diffusion of personal computers (PCs) has led to an increase in productivity (the so-called Solow paradox argument). Brynjolfsson (1993) summarizes the arguments from that time, and the factors cited as reasons include measurement problems, time lags, redistribution and mismanagement.[6] These explanations remain relevant to the quality growth

[6] The measurement problem is that the benefits of ICT technology development are not adequately reflected in the current GDP statistics. Time lag refers to the point that ICT investments take several

perspective, and of these, the measurement problems are presumed to be the most significant factor.

### 6.2.3 Digital Technology and Consumer Surplus

Gordon (2012) states that the rapid spread of the internet, web systems and e-commerce made a difference in the late 1990s, but not to a significant extent and that the impact on productivity disappeared around 2004. He states that the third phase of technological innovation as a whole offers new opportunities with regard to hobbies and consumption, rather than replacing human labor with machines, as has been the case with previous technological innovations. This point is particularly interesting when considered in conjunction with the growth strategy whereby APEC has placed digital as a core technological area for innovative growth. Additionally, technological innovations such as AI, automation and virtual reality are targeted toward developed countries such as Japan. How should the relationship between digital technology and growth be considered?

Figure 6.3 shows the changes in TFP in the US overlaid with the progress of digitalization in the economy. Overall, it is difficult to say that the evolution of digitalization and TFP are changing on the same basis. While the internet had already spread to around 70% of the US population before the GFC, it was not until after the GFC that Amazon saw a real increase in sales. This phenomenon also applies to the social networking business: it was only after the GFC that Facebook, which started operating in 2004, saw a real increase in the number of subscribers. These examples suggest that there is a time lag between when the internet became popular and widely used by the public and when new businesses began to grow rapidly. The figure clearly shows that, although digitalization as represented by these technologies has made significant progress in the twenty-first century, TFP, on the other hand, has not grown so rapidly. It is also unclear at the moment whether new business models based on new digital technologies will emerge one after the other, as they have in the recent past—i.e., whether these transformations will continue on a permanent basis or whether they will be a one-off impact, a phenomenon lasting only a few years.

There are several different views on the relationship between digital technology and growth. The Ministry of Internal Affairs and Communications, Japan, summarized them in its White Paper, as reproduced in Table 6.2. Technological pessimism reflects the same argument presented by Gordon (2012), while technological optimism advocates for the significant impact of digital technology—albeit with some

years to bear fruit. Considering the investment strategy and learning period for new technologies, a certain period of time is needed before they become profitable, with a survey of managers suggesting that around five years are needed. Redistribution is the view that while investment in ICTs brings profits, it does not necessarily increase overall productivity in the aggregate as a result of the redistribution of resources across society as a whole. The last point is that individual firms do not always make appropriate business decisions.

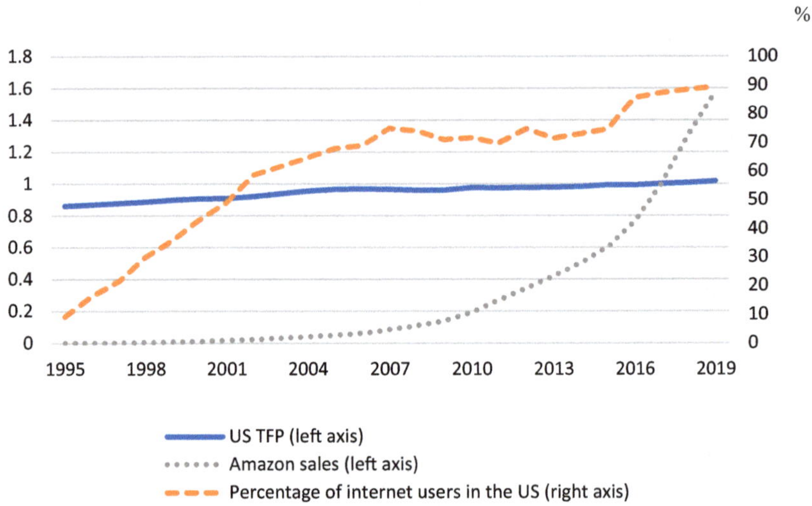


**Fig. 6.3** TFP and digital economy trends. *Source* Penn World Table 10.0 for TFP, Amazon sales from Amazon's annual report and number of internet users from World Bank Open Data. *Note* TFP and Amazon sales produced figures for each year with 2017 as the basis (one)

time lag. Between the two, some theorists state that there are wide differences in the use of technology among companies and that, on average, overall productivity growth is sluggish. Thus, at present, there is still no consensus on whether digital technology will be a significant driver of growth, whether it will be a one-off, or whether it will continue to drive growth on a sustained basis. In addition to this, another issue has been included as the second item in Table 6.2: whether all benefits of digitalization are reflected in the current GDP statistics.

Many of the services that have evolved as a result of ICT developments are now offered for free. Users commonly access many free apps on mobile phones and take photos for free. They rely on search services like Wikipedia and Google to find information and use free video, music streaming and maps. Some of these apps and sites are run on a voluntary basis, such as Wikipedia, while others, like Google and Facebook, derive their main source of revenue from advertising fees. However, these advertising revenues are not linked to the size of the users' utility, and it is estimated that the latter may be considerably larger (Collis 2020). Even for these, the use of free services through digital devices does not fully reflect the size of consumers' utility in GDP. There are also many paid-for services, such as streaming services for music and video. In the case of paid services, consumers are seen to perceive a greater benefit than the price set. In summary, the magnitude of consumer utility for many digital services is not properly reflected in GDP, while still increasing people's satisfaction. While this relationship between technology and growth is typical for digital, it is also possible in other service areas. The concept of consumer surplus can explain this situation.

**Table 6.2** Summary of the debate on the relationship between slow GDP/productivity growth and ICT

| | |
|---|---|
| Pessimism about technology | • Compared to the technological innovations of the Industrial Revolution, the impact of ICT on human life is limited<br>• ICT-driven innovation is limited to fields such as entertainment and information and communication<br>• Therefore, despite the development of ICT, productivity stagnation will continue in the future |
| Views that focus on the issues in measuring the digital economy | • ICT promotes the provision of free services and the sharing of existing goods<br>• There is a possibility that existing GDP statistics do not fully capture these effects, and discussions are needed on whether they should be captured or not |
| Optimism about technology | • ICT is an innovative technology that affects all areas of the social economy<br>• However, there is a time lag between the introduction and spread of ICT and its effect of improving productivity. The effect is not yet fully apparent at present |
| Compromising views between pessimism and optimism about technology | • Cutting-edge companies are greatly increasing their productivity through ICT<br>• On the other hand, other companies are not seeing such effects, and on average, overall productivity growth is stagnant |

*Source* Ministry of Internal Affairs and Communications (2019)

Consumer surplus is the difference between the value consumers gain by consuming and the price they actually pay to purchase it. Consumer surplus is a concept used to express consumer utility and is not captured by GDP. Brynjolfsson et al. (2019) include Fig. 6.4 in their Annex to explain consumer surplus with respect to a digital good. CASE 1 applies to common goods such as cars. When the supply curve is fixed, if the demand curve shifts to the right as consumption increases, consumer surplus A increases by the area of C and market sales B increase by the area of D. The latter is reflected in GDP. CASE 2 represents purely digital goods. Examples include search engines and e-mail, which consumers can use for free. If usage by consumers increases, consumer surplus A increases by the area of B. CASE 3 applies to transitional goods, examples of which are encyclopedias and digital photos. Due to the development of digital technology, many users of encyclopedias have now shifted to Wikipedia. This increases consumer surplus A by B + C and, conversely, the sales B of encyclopedia companies have declined, so GDP is reduced by that amount. CASE 3 is a redistribution argument by Brynjolfsson (1993) concerning ICT and productivity growth. Note that CASE 3 here assumes zero prices, but it does not necessarily have to be zero: if prices

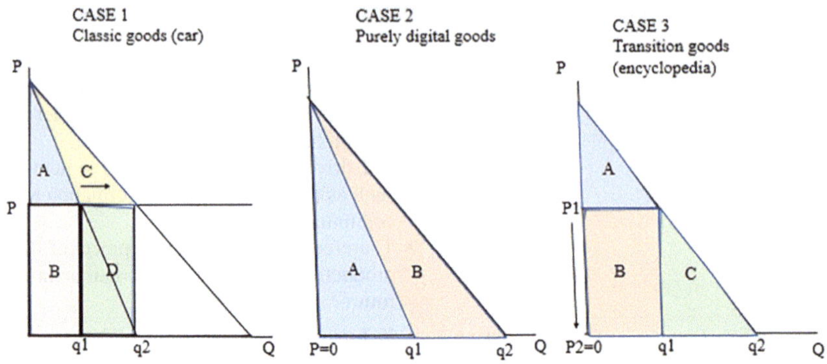


**Fig. 6.4** Digital goods and consumer surplus. *Source* Brynjolfsson et al. (2019)

fall due to the development of digital technology, consumer surplus will increase, while alternative real consumption will decline and GDP will decrease.

For example, in the music industry, streaming services are the current mainstream way of enjoying music. Streaming is a mixture of paid and free services, but in any case, the emergence of this new form of service will result in a significant decline in sales of compact discs and other content, which in turn will reduce GDP. On the other hand, consumer utility is increasing significantly. The same is true of the development of digital photography, for example, with most people now taking photos on their smartphones instead of using a camera and film. Meanwhile, sales of film and prints have declined significantly and photo shops have disappeared from street corners. The number of photos people take has increased dramatically, resulting in a substantial increase in consumer surplus.

As a further exercise, consider a scenario where the price remains the same due to technological development, while the quality of the product has improved. In this case, the utility gained by consumers is clearly greater, while the size of sales, and thus GDP, remains the same. To adjust for this, the GDP calculation employs the hedonic method to account for some goods, such as PCs, comparing them under the same technological level—i.e., taking into account improvements in quality within GDP. However, as Coyle (2014) states, the adjustment by the hedonic index is limited to some products. Moreover, she states that GDP was not intended to be a measure of people's wellbeing in the first place, nor do GDP measures capture the effects of innovation well.[7] Nordhaus (2004) states that most of the benefits of technological progress are gained by consumers, not producers.

[7] Coyle (2014) uses the example of lighting to explain why GDP does not capture the effect of innovation. The quality of lighting has increased immensely compared to the days of candlelight, but GDP data does not tell us how much we enjoy higher quality lighting at a lower price. In other words, the impact of technological advances, such as the change from candlelight to lighting, on people's utility has not been accurately reflected in GDP.

This means that technological progress is increasing consumer surplus, but is, to some extent, not reflected in GDP.

Monetizing consumer surplus is considered difficult, but several studies have attempted to do so: Brynjolfsson et al. (2019) used the concept of willingness to accept (WTA) to estimate the size of consumer surplus in relation to Facebook.[8] As a result, they estimated that the compensation for not being able to use Facebook for a month was around USD 40 to 50 (USD 48.49 in the 2016 survey and USD 37.76 in the 2017 survey). Another survey conducted online reveals the extent of WTA due to unavailability for a year across various digital platforms. Large WTAs are for search, e-mail and maps that are considered due to business necessity. With regard to video, they found that people felt a consumer surplus of five to ten times what they actually paid, while the cost of using YouTube and Netflix is around USD 10 to USD 20 per month. Other pioneering research has attempted to estimate the consumer surplus that consumers obtain from digital goods.[9] Developments in digital technology have benefited consumption in various sectors, not just digital platforms, such that e-commerce and streaming remove the physical constraint on shops, allowing consumers to choose from a larger assortment of goods. The sharing of goods through flea market apps enables second-hand goods to be put to good use. While these changes will increase consumer surplus, they have a negative impact on GDP when, for example, trade in second-hand goods is not recorded in GDP, while consumption of new goods is reduced.

Other arguments on the relationship between digital technological progress and quality growth are as follows. A common argument is that income inequality increases with the progress of digital technologies. Digital technology is characterized by a large network effect, as the marginal cost is close to zero. The more users there are, the more convenient it becomes for subscribers, so a one-sided win situation is likely to emerge, and consequently, the speed of business growth is rapid. These characteristics continue to create super-rich individuals in a short period of time. In addition, the high remuneration rates for highly skilled workers and, conversely, the wages for low-skilled workers are declining due to the spread of digital technology, the advance of globalization and the replacement of simple labor by machines. Digital technologies, on the other hand, also have the potential to contribute to the equalization of quality and opportunities in education and health. Access to high-quality education, health services, and employment anywhere in the world online could make it easier for individuals to fulfil their potential.

[8] WTA is the amount of compensation that is acceptable for the loss of a benefit. A similar concept is willingness to pay (WTP), which is the maximum amount that one is willing to pay for a given benefit. WTP is usually considered to be smaller than WTA.

[9] Collis (2020) introduces some studies estimating consumer surplus by electronic transactions (lower prices and search costs), time savings, replacement of television with the internet, savings in search costs (compared to libraries), and conversion from dial-up to broadband.

So far, I have focused on digital technologies, but the GDP constraints and the idea of consumer surplus are not limited to digital technologies. These principles are also more or less applicable to many other technological fields. Such technological developments may also be relevant to theories of innovation.

### 6.2.4 Innovation and Wellbeing in Relation to Quality Growth

In APEC's quality growth strategy, innovation is positioned as a driver of energy, transport and agricultural promotion and environmental improvement. Schumpeter's (1926) classic work on innovation distinguishes between economic cycles and development. Schumpeter states that what brings about development is a change in the combination of various materials and forces used to carry out production, referred to as "new combinations." This view subsequently became one of the fundamental concepts of economic development.[10] New combinations are discontinuous and include five typologies, such as (1) development of new products; (2) introduction of new production methods; (3) opening of new markets; (4) acquisition of new sources of raw materials or semi-manufactured products; and (5) the new organization of industry.

Type (1) refers to the creation of new products that have never existed before, such as cars and smartphones, and are generally conceived of as innovations. Type (2) refers to improvements related to production methods, such as the *Kanban* (just-in-time) system and *Kaizen* (continuous improvement) activities. It also includes streamlining production that utilizes digital technology and AI. Sudo (2018) broadly categorized these five types into the development of new products and markets and the improvement of existing processes related to production and distribution, with the former being product innovation and the latter being process innovation. He states that both have an impact on both producer and consumer surplus. However, product innovation has a greater impact on producer surplus, while process innovation has a greater impact on consumer surplus. He then notes that, in the case of Japan, producer surplus was the major focus during the high-growth period, whereas process innovation became the major focus during the period of stable growth.

Product innovation creates new products while adding value to existing ones. This creates new demand, thus boosting GDP. Process innovation, on the other hand, increases a company's profit margin by reducing costs rather than creating new products. Companies engage in process innovation to increase profits and

[10] In the endogenous economic growth theory introduced in the previous section, a model based on Schumpeter's theory was also established. Grossman and Helpman (1991) assume that goods in the market have a "quality ladder." Firms undertake R&D when they expect to make a profit from their investment, and as such, their motivation is the acquisition of profit in imperfect markets. When obsolete products disappear, the process of creative destruction occurs. The knowledge trait causes technology to spill over and growth to be endogenously sustained.

market share while avoiding price increases of goods and services sold in the market. In Japan, companies have been particularly committed to avoiding price rises due to the high price elasticity of demand. This leads to more efficient and automated production in the manufacturing sector against a backdrop of labor shortages. It also means that prices remain unchanged while the quality of goods improves.

At the same time, due to the increasing globalization of production, many manufacturing activities in Japan—excluding many service industries, which are situated in the non-trade sectors—have been transferred to developing countries through the shift to more cost-effective global optimization. Price levels in Japan remained remarkably stable from the 1980s until recently, while Japan has been the world's third-largest investor in R&D. In an economy where the quality of goods and services improves even as prices remain stable, partly due to such innovations, consumer utility expands without being fully reflected in an increase in GDP. As such, it appears that the benefits brought about through process innovation, such as *Kaizen* activities, were not fully captured by existing GDP indicators. Sudo (2018) identifies how process innovation on the distribution side increases consumer surplus and states that changes in business due to the digitization of the economy further reinforce this trend.

In general, economic growth rates in developed countries are lower than those in emerging and developing countries. In emerging economies, the growth rate tends to slow as technology catches up. It is the developed countries that undertake larger R&D spending, but despite such active R&D activities, they have lower growth rates than developing countries. As a country matures, people tend to focus not only on the quantitative expansion of consumption but also on the quality aspects that make their lives more convenient and affluent. However, not all the increases in utilities due to the improvement of the quality of consumption are fully reflected in GDP, as stated above. This structure might affect the trend that developed countries experience lower growth rates in the statistics.

In summary, some aspects of innovation in high-income countries may not be reflected in growth under the current definition of GDP, even if they increase the utility of consumers. Moreover, there are issues with the current definition of GDP—for example, when healthcare costs are high, as in the US, the GDP will be larger. On the other hand, if the healthcare system improves, as a result of process innovation, and people can be admitted to hospital as outpatients without being hospitalized, their individual utility will be larger, but GDP will be smaller. I will continue to discuss this point and its relation to quality growth in more detail.

Kanbur et al. (2019), introduced in Chap. 2, stated that transforming the results of growth into dimensions of wellbeing other than income should be considered one of the elements of quality growth. This suggests that we should take stock and focus on areas that improve people's wellbeing even if such areas are not reflected in GDP. Kanbur et al. (2019) provided the examples of education, health and security. In the same book, Fioramonti (2019) lists social wellbeing, such as education and health, along with unpaid domestic work and self-consumption, as items to be measured in quality growth. The reason why education and health are highlighted as non-income wellbeing is because they are major areas in which people can fulfil their potential. They also have positive externalities, providing people with happiness and utility that exceeds the size measured in the market. Unpaid services derived from domestic work are not included in GDP, but people also derive utility from them. If the quality of household services improves, the utility of the family also increases.

For example, the post-war Japanese livelihood improvement movement improved sanitation and increased people's wellbeing, but because they were unpaid services, the increased utility was not reflected in GDP, although the definition from the study referred to above does not have the quality of consumption in mind. In other words, it is a matter of consumer surplus. Together with the positive externalities, such as those from education and health, I propose that improvements in the quality of consumption, which are not reflected in income but improve wellbeing, should be included in the non-income component of quality growth. These points are discussed again in Chap. 9. In considering quality growth, it is desirable to capture these qualitative changes in society and the economy as one aspect of growth. I consider this essential in indicating the direction that a future vision might take after emerging economies have reached a certain level of high per capita income.

### 6.2.5 Sustaining Innovation, Economic Transformation and Growth in Developing Countries

I will now examine innovation in developing countries. Figure 6.5 summarizes the innovation function in developing countries, as presented by Cirera and Maloney (2017) of the World Bank. The inputs include technology and equipment, human capital and managerial capital. These inputs are the factors that have the potential to generate endogenous growth. Cirera and Maloney (2017) argue that companies in poor countries often innovate in minor areas rather than cutting-edge, modern technologies and products. They refer to this as a paradox, as such technology catch-up away from the technological frontier, despite potentially high rates of return, actually results in only small investments. Stiglitz and Greenwald (2015) note that standard analysis divides productivity gains from innovation into improvements that bring it closer to the production possibility frontier and improvements that shift the curve itself outward. It is self-evident that the former is important in the case of developing countries.

Cirera and Maloney (2017) cite market failures and innovation systems as the theoretical background for such low levels of innovation. The first of these, market failures, is a classical idea: due to the existence of positive externalities, the benefits gained by those who invest in innovation are smaller than the benefits that society as a whole gain from improvements in knowledge and technology. This leads to underinvestment in innovation. Policies that address this are innovation subsidies, tax incentives and greater utilization of public research institutions and universities to engage in innovation. The latter means that innovation requires a

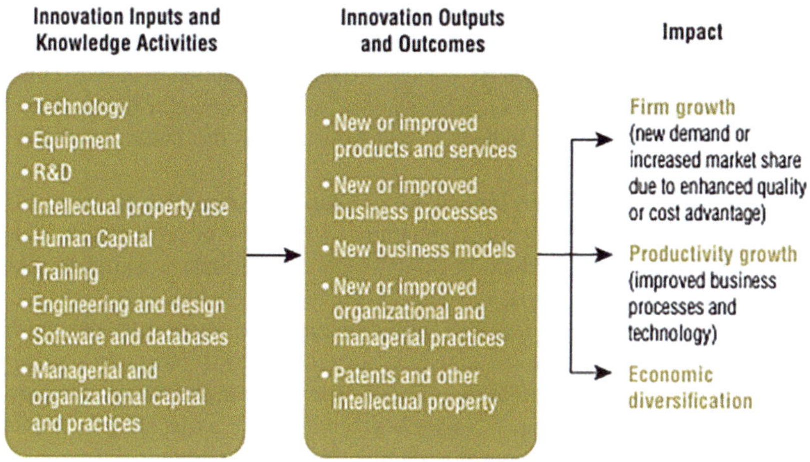


**Fig. 6.5** Innovation functions. *Source* Cirera and Maloney (2017)

dynamic system in which the actors involved in innovation, typically companies, governments and universities, interact with each other, and for this, the organizational capacity of companies and governments is crucial. In summary, Cirera and Maloney (2017) point to the following three reasons for the innovation paradox in developing countries: (1) the low capacity of enterprises, (2) the lack of complementarity in innovation, and (3) the lack of capacity to manage innovation policy.

The first category of company competencies includes basic management competencies such as bookkeeping and factory layout. It is possible to foster these through policy—for example, post-war Japan introduced a self-assessment system (blue return system), leading to the widespread dissemination of bookkeeping knowledge to small and medium companies. Cirera and Maloney (2017) state that the government should adopt policies that are in line with the current state of a company's capacity. This is because the effectiveness of innovation policies is limited if capacity strengthening does not take place.

On the second point, developing countries—especially poor countries—are far from the technological frontier, so the effects of catch-up are significant. However, without an educational system and business environment that complements the accumulation of knowledge within companies, the results of *new combinations* will be limited. The final point is that in developing countries, there is a dilemma in innovation policy: there are significant market failures that need to be addressed and a lack of complementarity, yet government capacity remains low.

In developing countries, innovations moving toward the technological frontier are particularly important. For such catch-ups to occur, the transfer of technology from developed countries is particularly crucial. Given the above basic constraints, how can innovation, social transformation and sustaining growth occur? ADB

(2013) refers to economic transformation in developing countries as (1) reallocation of factors of production; (2) diversification, upgrading and deepening of production and export baskets; (3) use of new production methods and processes and different inputs; (4) urbanization; and (5) social change. The first three are transformations of industrial structures, while the latter two are social transformations.

Hosono (2022) outlines the framework of economic transformation that fosters sustained growth, stating that the comparative advantage of an industry is determined by the factors of production (labor, land and capital) working in relation to the three endowments. These three endowments are learning, infrastructure and institutions. In other words, learning, infrastructure, and institutions are the basis for such transformation to be sustained, as sustained growth means that economic transformation occurs endogenously and industries with a continuous comparative advantage emerge. While Fig. 6.5 lists key inputs, such as technology for innovation, Hosono (2022) points out that endowments are important for these inputs to produce results and raise productivity. He also notes that there are four pathways (patterns) for the realization of transformation: catch-up type, participation in GVCs, innovation on its own, and inclusive business.[11]

Figure 6.6 summarizes this model, adapted by the author, where learning, infrastructure and institutions improve productivity, allow new industries to flourish and change the social and economic structure of developing countries. It will also change urbanization and the nature of society. The continuation of such a process is sustained growth, and an essential part of this is the improvement of endowments.[12] Next, I touch on learning, whereas for other endowments, institutions are discussed in Sect. 6.4 of this chapter and infrastructure is discussed in Chap. 7.

### 6.2.6 Learning and Technology Transfer

The quality of labor and the quality of capital are important for TFP, as stated at the beginning of this chapter. Learning corresponds to the former and technology transfer to the latter. Learning is a factor that can cause endogenous growth, with particular emphasis by Hosono (2022), who emphasizes, among other things, that

[11] The first type is the most common transformation and is referred to, for example, as the flying geese model. The second type is the automobile industry in Mexico. The third type is the large-scale agricultural development in the Cerrado region in Brazil, where unique innovations in breeding and cropping have been developed. The fourth is exemplified by poverty-oriented businesses.

[12] Hosono (2022) further discusses how growth can be compatible with work and inclusiveness, urbanization, environmental sustainability and disaster resilience, and provides a wealth of examples. As these cases present specific development approaches, the analysis is considered to be extremely meaningful in embodying quality growth.

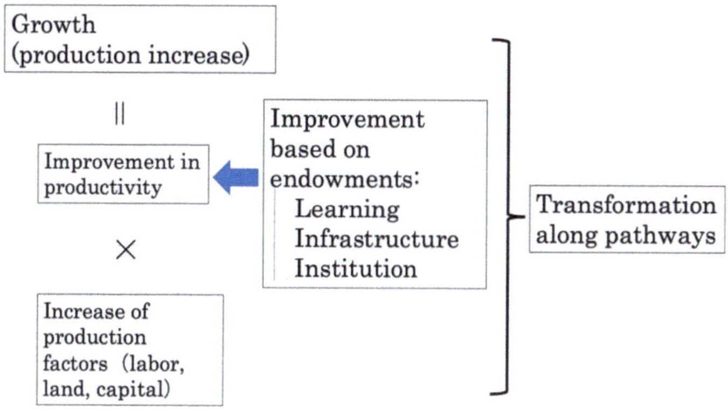


**Fig. 6.6** Productivity, endowment and social transformation. *Source* Author, adapted from Hosono (2022)

the ability to learn what to learn ("learning to learn") is an indispensable competence for achieving sustainable development through the process of finding and solving problems independently.

Stiglitz and Greenwald (2015) provide a comprehensive explanation of learning theory and policy. They distinguish between improvements in best practice and improvements in the productivity of companies to catch up, assuming that learning is about how to increase productivity. The latter, as discussed so far, is particularly important in developing countries. Arrow (1962), in a famous early study, notes that learning is the acquisition of knowledge, which is gained through experience that increases with the accumulation of investment. Stiglitz and Greenwald (2015) also state that most learning is gained through experience and that it is not limited to the field of production processes but includes organizational management and learning how to learn. They further argue that learning in a society is determined by six factors, including learning capabilities.[13]

Policies to enhance learning entail building educational and social institutions that strengthen these factors. If much of the learning is gained through experience, an accumulation of investment is needed to create the right conditions, and macroeconomic, investment and trade policies that encourage this are important. Stiglitz and Greenwald (2015) also argue that it is essential to go beyond mere investment accumulation and that developing countries should adopt innovation policies that are appropriate to their current circumstances (e.g., resource-saving or labor-saving) and implement industrial policies that allow country-specific learning to develop. Here, the aim of industrial policy is to enhance learning and spillover. Several examples of industrial policy are presented in Hosono (2022), such as the

[13] In addition to the learning capabilities, access to knowledge, catalysts for learning, the cognitive frame, contact with people who build the cognitive frame and act as catalysts for learning, and the context of learning were mentioned.

case of Kenya, where significant learning was generated for smallholders in the cultivation of horticultural crops, resulting in improved incomes.

Investment and trade are closely related to the transfer of technology as well as learning. For investment, the transfer of technology through foreign investment is particularly crucial, as catch-up is crucial in developing countries. For example, one of the factors behind the development of East Asia was its openness to introducing foreign technology (World Bank 1993). Much of the transfer of technology to developing countries occurs through foreign investment and trade. Todo (2008) provides a comprehensive review of theories and an empirical study on how trade and foreign investment affect technological progress and economic growth in developing countries (trade and growth are discussed in detail in the next section and are therefore not mentioned here). His overview of previous studies can be summarized as follows:

- Growth in developing countries is brought about by the introduction of technologies from developed countries, but the introduction is often fraught with difficulties.
- Trade and foreign direct investment (FDI) do not always involve technology transfer.
- Trade and FDI promote technology transfer only when developing countries have high absorptive capacity, such as education levels, imports of high-tech products and strong linkages of FDI to local companies.
- FDI, especially with R&D, is a channel for technology dissemination to local companies.
- Developing countries with low levels of technology depend on foreign companies for production and therefore remain at low incomes. Subsidies for R&D are ineffective.
- The scale of R&D by companies in developed countries depends on the size of the market in which they invest.

It then states that effective policies include preferential treatment for human capital development and R&D, including one conducted by foreign companies.

It is interesting to note that Todo (2008) states that imports of high-technology products have a significant effect on growth through technology diffusion. In developed countries, the digital-related sector has been the engine of growth, but in general, digitalization is also likely to have a transformative effect on growth in developing countries across four aspects. First, digital technology is a so-called leapfrog, meaning that new technologies spread in developing countries without a time lag. Second, digitalization has led to the emergence of fast-growing start-ups, even in developing countries. Third, it brings growth to countries that use global outsourcing and freelancing. And fourth, as in developed countries, the nature of digital technologies has led to forces that contribute to income inequality within the country.

Some developing countries have been able to develop their manufacturing industries through the growth of GVCs as a result of globalization. However, since the mid-2010s, trade growth has been lower than economic growth in many years (the so-called "slow trade"). It has been noted that tariff rates and non-tariff barriers that drive globalization are approaching a point where it is difficult to lower them any further. In addition, the increasing shift to domestic production of parts and components of manufacturing for assembly in China has impacted the industrialization of Asian countries, in particular (Hong et al. 2016). These trends appear to reduce the role of manufacturing and exports in developing countries.

Furthermore, we face emerging phenomena, such as the premature deindustrialization discussed previously. In the current international environment, the sectors that sustain growth are changing, shifting from manufacturing to digitally related industries. However, as noted, it remains unclear whether the development of digital technology can lead to sustained growth. The digitalization of the economy has also made inclusivity more challenging. The technological and business transitions brought about by digitalization may not only alter the path of sustained growth but also make it more difficult to reconcile growth with inclusiveness. Furthermore, changes in social systems and the widespread adoption of corporate strategies and business institutions are frequently observed in the US and may exacerbate inequalities. With the current development of new digital technologies, previous patterns of development may no longer necessarily apply. In order to cope with these circumstances, the ability to "learn to learn" will be required even more urgently. In the following sections, the remaining issues will be reviewed for sustained growth, covering macroeconomic and trade policy in Sect. 6.3 and institutions and sustaining growth in Sect. 6.4.

## 6.3 The Role of Macroeconomic and Trade Policies in Sustainable Growth

This chapter discusses the possible impact of policies on making growth sustained. What is meant by "sustained," as discussed in the previous chapter, is "continued with little or no interruption, over a period of time." One way of defining sustained growth is by counting how many years real growth (positive or above a certain percentage per annum) has continued. Another way is to focus on the overall results: a higher average growth rate implies that growth has been sustained, regardless of the trajectory in the intervening years. A large majority of the vast literature on growth and macroeconomic policies focuses on the average growth rate, and only a small strand focuses on the continuity of growth *per se.*

In fact, a large majority of the growth literature is not even about growth, strictly speaking. What is examined are changes in income levels or transitory effects, especially in empirical studies, although this is also sometimes the case in theoretical reflections. While endogenous growth theory provides a framework to analyze how government policy may affect long-term growth, in neoclassical growth theory, policies can only have a transitory effect. Hall and Jones (1997) argue that "[t]here is a great deal of empirical and theoretical work to suggest that the primary reason that countries grow at such different rates for decades at a time is *transition dynamics*" [italics in original]. Because transition dynamics can last for a long time,[14] it may be appropriate—over time spans relevant to policymakers—to treat transitory changes in income as growth, even though they are conceptually distinct from steady-state growth. The standard procedure in empirical studies of slicing up time series data on GDP per capita (or output per worker) into decade- or five-year increments of "growth" periods does not allow the analyst to distinguish between higher growth rates and transitional level changes.

## 6.3.1 What Makes Growth Episodes Sustained?

### 6.3.1.1 Analysis of Growth Spurts

The literature focusing on the length of growth episodes is relatively new. Easterly et al. (1993) initiated the discussion by observing that growth rates are highly unstable over time, whereas country characteristics tend to be stable. Furthermore, they found that much of the variation in growth rates is due to random shocks, rather than good policies or country characteristics. Pritchett (2000) further contrasts the experiences of advanced countries, whose growth trajectory tended to be a relatively smooth upward-sloping curve, with those of developing economies, which included a variety of patterns of steady growth, stagnation, rapid growth followed by decline or even catastrophic falls. The literature then branched naturally into roughly four areas of investigation: the determinants and mechanisms for takeoffs, end-of-growth spells, length of growth spells and switching between growth and other states.

Studies examining "takeoffs" have produced mixed results. Easterly (2006) employs a definition of a takeoff as going from about zero growth to permanently stable positive per capita growth (about 1.5%), but finds only nine takeoffs out of 127 countries studied. In contrast, Hausmann et al. (2005) found that growth episodes are ubiquitous: "the unconditional probability that a country will experience a growth acceleration episode sometime in a decade is around 25 percent." Like Easterly et al. (1993), however, they are unable to answer the questions most relevant to policymakers: what causes and sustains growth episodes. While "[s]tandard determinants"—such as positive terms of trade shocks, economic reforms, political regime changes (both towards autocracy and democracy) and financial liberalization—are statistically significantly correlated with the start of growth acceleration episodes, the relationship is not straightforward. The evidence shows that the vast majority of growth accelerations are unrelated to these standard determinants, and most instances of economic reform do not produce growth accelerations. Aizenman and Spiegel (2010) find that *de jure* trade openness is robustly associated with takeoff. *De jure* openness, however, is not associated

[14] In Rutherford and Tarr's (2002) simulation model, the transition effects of a decrease of uniform tariff rate by 10 percentage point lingered even after 50 years (albeit to a small degree).

**Table 6.3** Determinants of growth episodes reviewed

| Aspects studied | Studies |
|---|---|
| Growth patterns | Easterly et al. (1993), Pritchett (2000) |
| Accelerations | Easterly (2006), Hausmann et al. (2005), Aizenman and Spiegel (2010) |
| Decelerations/collapse | Ben-David and Papell (1998), Jones and Olken (2008) |
| Switching | Jerzmanowski (2006), Kerekes (2012) |
| Length of episodes | Berg and Ostry (2011), Cuberes and Jerzmanowski (2009), Berg et al. (2012) |
| Case studies | Johnson et al. (2007), IMF (2008) |

*Source* Author's compilation

significantly with sustained spells, but the share of commodity output (associated negatively) and the share of service output (associated positively) are.

Investigating the "end of growth spells," Ben-David and Papell (1998) demonstrate that most countries experienced slowdowns in the post-war period. They also find that developing countries—particularly Latin American countries—tend to experience much more severe slowdowns or "meltdowns." Jones and Olken (2008) observe that growth collapses typically feature reduced investment amidst increasing price instability, whereas growth takeoffs are primarily associated with large expansions in international trade. Their results show that rapid growth is possible, even for very poor countries, but sustaining it is difficult and may pose a different set of challenges from starting it (Table 6.3).

Looking into how countries switch between growth regimes, Jerzmanowski (2006) shows—using a Markov switching classification model—that the quality of institutions helps to determine the transition probabilities between four distinct growth regimes: stable growth, "miracle" catch-up, stagnation and crisis. He finds that better institutions improve long-run growth by making episodes of fast growth more persistent, and that low average growth rates in countries with weak institutions are a result of these countries spending more time in stagnation regimes rather than being incapable of fast growth altogether. Kerekes (2012) extends Jerzmanowski's (2006) framework with a clustering mechanism, in which countries are endogenously grouped together according to the growth patterns featuring similar transition probabilities. In contrast to Jerzmanowski (2006) and the institutional view of econometric growth (e.g., Acemoglu et al. 2001; Acemoglu and Robinson 2012; Rodrik et al. 2004), she notes that institutions are not significantly different between "moderately successful" and "failing" countries (although better in "successful" countries). What causes different growth patterns in the two categories of countries with poor institutions, she argues, is policies: moderately successful countries have invested more in infrastructure and human capital, opened up their economies earlier and conducted less volatile macroeconomic policy.

Research on the length of growth spells includes the work by Berg and Ostry (2011), who find that the indicator most associated with increasing the chances of a growth spell surviving was income equality (as measured by the Gini coefficient), followed by trade openness and political institutions. Cuberes and Jerzmanowski (2009) demonstrate that democracies are more likely to maintain a stable growth path, while undemocratic countries tend to experience stop–go cycles characterized by "growth-trend volatility." The underlying mechanism is economic diversification, which is promoted or hindered by the size of entry barriers that entrepreneurs face when investing in risky but high-potential sectors. The entry barriers are inversely correlated with the level of democracy in a country, resulting in entrepreneurs in less democratic countries investing in a smaller number of sectors, but a larger amount per sector.

The likelihood of having a successful sector is smaller for countries with fewer sectors in the economy, but the growth spurt is faster if a sector is successful, because there is more capital invested per sector. In this model, the rapid acceleration of growth can be interpreted as a symptom of the underlying weakness of the economy, which in turn foretells a sharp deceleration in the next period. Countries with extremely high barriers to entry are also stable, since no entrepreneur takes the risk of investing in high-growth potential sectors so the economy never experiences growth accelerations and stays in a low-growth steady state. Berg et al. (2012) find evidence that growth duration is positively related to equality of income distribution, democratic institutions, export orientation and macroeconomic stability.

#### 6.3.1.2 Data Issues

Early works found most of the variations in growth volatility to be unexplainable, while later studies found evidence that certain elements were decisive, although such results were often contradicted by other studies. Findings remain inconclusive, possibly because no single process governs all growth episodes, but also likely due to limitations in the data. As any practitioner knows, most macroeconomic data, including GDP and population, are measured with a great deal of imprecision, and qualitative indicators are even harder to measure. Researchers often rely on using similar sets of data, such as trade openness (Sachs and Warner 1995), the government antidiversion index (Hall and Jones 1999), the voice and accountability indicator from Worldwide Governance Indicators (WGI); produced by Kaufmann and Kraay[15]), the indicator for judicial independence (La Porta et al. 2004), the business environmental risk indicator (Knack and Keefer 1995), and ethnolinguistic fractionalization[16] (Mauro 1998). These are the best currently

[15] https://www.worldbank.org/en/publication/worldwide-governance-indicators.

[16] According to Mauro (1998), "The raw data from which the index of ethnolinguistic fractionalization is constructed refer to 1960 and come from the *Atlas Narodov Mira* [Department of Geodesy and Cartography of the State Geological Committee of the USSR (author's note; Union of Soviet Socialist Republics) 1964]. The latter is the result of a vast project whose goal was to provide an extremely accurate depiction of the ethnolinguistic composition of world population. The criteria for characterizing groups as ethnically separate related mainly to historical linguistic origin, and no economic or political variables were considered during the project."

available, but institutions and democracies are multifaceted, and their quality is difficult to measure objectively and consistently across different countries and over time.

#### 6.3.1.3 Case Studies

As a clear set of determinants of sustained growth has remained elusive, the notion that each growth episode is context-specific has gained weight, and this naturally led to the collection of case studies. The prospects for sustained growth in Africa, in particular, have been studied extensively.

Johnson et al. (2007) seek to benchmark constraints on sustained high growth for sub-Saharan African countries by comparing them to other economies that had weak institutions in 1960 but nevertheless subsequently experienced sustained high growth. They counted 12 economies that were initially poor with weak institutions but had managed to sustain rapid growth over the last 50 years: China, Indonesia, Malaysia, Singapore, South Korea, Taiwan, Thailand, Vietnam, Tunisia, the Dominican Republic, Egypt, and Chile. The good news is that many sub-Saharan African countries—those for which they have data—generally have stronger institutions and a lower likelihood of being in a civil war or violent conflict today than the 12 high-growth countries prior to their takeoff, meaning the quality of institutions in sub-Saharan Africa should not represent a binding constraint on sustained growth.

The corollary is, of course, that they have not identified the reasons why sustained growth in sub-Saharan Africa has remained elusive.[17] They do find, however, that the tendencies for exchange rate overvaluation and microeconomic constraints on doing business, specifically, the costs of entry, are much higher in sub-Saharan African countries than in the economies experiencing sustained growth since 1960. The Regional Economic Outlook for Sub-Saharan Africa (IMF 2008) broadly confirms the findings of Johnson et al. (2007) and acknowledges that growth constraints and challenges change over time and across countries. It suggests a set of necessary conditions for sustained takeoff: engaging the global economy at some level; avoiding macroeconomic instability, high inflation and indebtedness in particular; adopting some form of market economy; and lastly, avoiding civil war.

### 6.3.2 Can Macroeconomic or Trade Policies Enhance Growth?

Given the findings on the fluctuations in growth rates within a country discussed in the previous section, the results of investigations into the relationship between policies and growth rates discussed in this section must be interpreted with caution.

[17] Six years later, Martinez and Mlachila (2013) were in a position to examine the quality of the recent growth episode in sub-Saharan Africa and found that growth over the previous 15 years had been stronger, less volatile, accompanied by productivity improvements, more broad-based and more export-oriented compared to the preceding 15 years.

The literature on growth and policies has a longer history than the "episodes of growth" branch, and partly as a result, a significant portion of it overlooks the fact that almost all countries experience growth episodes, which in turn eventually come to an end. On the other hand, average growth rates over a reasonably long period are the manifestations of the degree to which growth has been sustained, and hence, it would be remiss to ignore this rich literature completely.

This literature is extensive and continues to grow, partly because the relationship between macroeconomic policy and growth—which seems obvious intuitively—remains ambiguous both theoretically and empirically. There is no lack of models and empirical findings showing a positive relationship between "good" policy and growth. The East Asian "miracles," so described in the World Bank (1993) publication for their rapid growth *and* declining inequality between 1965 and 1990, are the poster children for achieving high-quality growth by getting macroeconomic policies right.[18] The "Washington Consensus"[19] represented a collective belief by practitioners that good policies lead to good results.

However, there are just as many theories and empirical findings refuting the link between good macroeconomic policies and growth. Easterly (2005) is one of the skeptics, noting several caveats to the belief that a strong link exists between the two. First, despite extensive efforts, a stable link between growth and macroeconomic policies has yet to be found—even for taxes, the most obvious candidate for a policy that influences growth. Second, national policies are generally measured over the period after 1960, when countries had independent governments, but history did not begin in 1960. In other words, the economies evolved over the course of their long histories, extending back before they became independent countries. Thus, the post-independence period represents only a small part of the overall story. Moreover, the correlation between per capita income in 1960 and 1999 is 0.87: one can reasonably accurately predict a country's per capita income in 1999 without knowing anything about its macroeconomic policies simply based on its per capita income in 1960.

Third, developing countries generally had higher growth rates in 1960–79 than in 1980–2000, yet what can be considered "good policies" were only adopted after 1980. Fourth, there are many income differences within nations that cannot be explained by national economic policies. Gill et al. (2006) were more hopeful

[18] The debate in the 1990s was at least as much about whether the interventionist stance and industrial policies, including the import substitution strategy adopted by some of the "miracle" countries, were the secret of their successes as appropriate macroeconomic policies. The World Bank (1993) did not come to a strong conclusion on this matter. The publication also attributed their successes to strong institutions, defined as "a high-quality civil service with the capacity to monitor performance, and which is insulated from political interference." This definition differs from the *New Institutional Economics* definition, which emphasizes the protection of property rights, as discussed in the Institutions subchapter of this book.

[19] The term was originally coined by Williamson in 1989 to describe a list of policies widely believed to be desirable and advocated for developing countries in general by the international financial institutions (primarily the IMF and World Bank) and the US Treasury (Williamson 2004).

about the role of good policies in discussing the growth experience of the 1990s, but they were far from advocating for any particular policy. They note that what differentiates "successful countries (those that reduce their per capita GDP gap with industrial economies) from unsuccessful ones (those that do not)" is the ability to reduce the risk and frequency of financial crises, which is a reflection of "decisive responses to shocks and macroeconomic policies that reduced vulnerabilities, and hence, the costs of shocks." These caveats should be borne in mind in the following section.

### 6.3.3 Macroeconomic Policy

#### 6.3.3.1 Fiscal Policy

Broadly speaking, fiscal policy has three distinct objectives: to reduce volatility, provide public goods and redistribute wealth.[20] The redistributive role is discussed in Chap. 3, which examines inclusiveness. The provision of public goods—particularly through addressing externalities and improving efficiency or productivity—is the gist of the endogenous growth literature. Reducing volatility may be a topic that rightly belongs in the Resilience chapter, since lower volatility itself can be a policy objective, as it is almost certainly preferable to higher volatility for the same average growth rate. In addition, volatility is thought to influence the average growth rate, which makes it an appropriate discussion for this chapter. An extensive review can be found in "Fiscal Policy and Long-Term Growth," a report issued by the IMF (2015b).

Theories suggest both positive and negative relationships between volatility and growth. Those supporting a positive relationship include Black (1987), who argues that countries may choose between high-variance, high-expected-return technologies and low-variance, low-expected-return technologies. In such a world, countries with high average growth would also exhibit high variance. Mirman (1971) also supports a positive relationship, theorizing that if there is a precautionary motive for saving, then higher volatility should lead to a higher savings rate and, hence, a higher investment rate. Theories supporting a negative link between volatility and growth include those involving irreversible investments, where increased volatility leads to lower or suboptimal investment (e.g., Bernanke 1983; Pindyck 1991; Ramey and Ramey 1991; and Aizenman and Marion 1993).

Empirical evidence seems to support a negative association between fiscal volatility and *growth* (for example, Ramey and Ramey 1995[21]; Woo 2009), but the evidence is mixed on the relationship between fiscal policy and *output*. Part of

[20] Fiscal policy also plays a role in building popularity or capturing rent in less scrupulous regimes.

[21] Ramey and Ramey (1995), using a sample of 92 countries from 1960 to 1985, find that countries with higher volatility have lower growth. They do not find a role for the investment share in the relationship between volatility and growth, but they do find that government spending volatility is negatively correlated with the average growth rate.

the challenge in this endeavor is the difficulty of distinguishing between discretionary and automatic components of fiscal policy in the data. There is a consensus that *well-designed* automatic stabilizers, such as tax payments that move in sync with income and spending—as well as social transfers such as unemployment benefits—can reduce output volatility. The IMF (2015a) analyzes data for approximately 50 countries between 1970 and 2013, finding that automatic stabilizers do play an important role in mitigating the decline in demand during downturns in advanced economies. "Well-designed" is the operative word here, as the same study notes that automatic stabilizers work less well in developing economies. In fact, fiscal policy is found to be on average procyclical in countries other than advanced economies, as procyclical policies tend to magnify volatility. Approaching the question slightly differently, Fatás and Mihov (2013) find that what matters for long-term country performance is the volatility of policy (measured by the standard deviation of the residuals from country-specific regressions of government consumption on output) rather than the volatility of output.

There is less agreement on the effectiveness of using discretionary fiscal policy in helping economies exit recessions, because it depends on the timeliness of execution as well as the quality of the policymaking apparatus. Blanchard et al. (2010a, b) note that discretionary fiscal policies tend to come too late to combat a standard recession and are perceived as being distorted by political constraints, much more so than monetary policy. On the other hand, the use of discretionary fiscal policy may be warranted in developing countries to resist standard recessions, as they do not have adequate public resources to allocate to automatic stabilization. Woo (2009) argues that social polarization tends to make fiscal policy procyclical—and hence volatile—which in turn is related to lower growth rates. Fatás and Mihov (2003) present evidence, using data for 93 countries, that volatility in discretionary fiscal policy increases output volatility, and output volatility exerts a negative impact on growth. Afonso and Furceri (2010) report that the share and volatility of government revenue and spending are detrimental to growth for EU and OECD countries for the period covering 1970–2005. Afonso and Jalles (2012) conclude that large governments (which translate into higher automatic stabilization) can be detrimental to growth for developing countries.

Even if fiscal policy can reduce output volatility, certain costs potentially associated with large governments may offset the benefits. The IMF (2015a) notes that higher levels of total government spending are associated with lower growth volatility in advanced economies but with higher growth volatility in emerging and developing economies. This is partly because a larger government sector could magnify the impact of inefficient public interventions. As discussed in more detail in Sect. 6.4 on institutions, in practice, governments are far from being a social welfare-optimizing entity. Examples of government inefficiency include subsidies that benefit the wealthier segment of the population, such as energy subsidies and transfers to loss-making and inefficient state-owned enterprises; high marginal tax rates that create excess burdens while reducing overall revenue; red tape designed to allocate scarce resources in a discretionary manner, and inadequate regulations that create moral hazard or perverse incentives in diverse areas such as banking and health. Empirical investigations that treat all government expenditures alike are bound to find mixed signals, but gathering appropriate data for such large samples is understandably extremely challenging.

#### 6.3.3.2 Public Debt

The effects of public debt on growth are not direct but depend on how it is financed and how its proceeds are used. In a world without frictions, Ricardian equivalence[22] would hold, and the level of debt would have no impact on the real economy: higher public borrowing now means higher taxes later by the equivalent amount in real terms, and vice versa. The impact comes from the specific nature of the frictions and what is achieved through the fiscal policy financed by the debt. When the proceeds of debt are assumed to be dissipated, standard growth theory predicts that an increase in government debt leads to slower growth because fewer resources are available for productive investments—temporarily in neoclassical models and permanently in endogenous models. The channels through which public debt may affect growth include higher long-term interest rates affecting capital accumulation, higher future distortionary taxation, inflation, and greater uncertainty about prospects and policies. In principle, there is no particular reason to believe that inflation, uncertainties, and other related effects caused by public debt differ from similar phenomena arising from other causes. Nevertheless, at the risk of redundancy, the studies specifically related to public debt are surveyed in this subsection.

Empirically, the debt level relative to the size of the economy is considered to be at least weakly inversely related to growth. In extreme cases of debt crises, a banking or currency crisis can be triggered, which is clearly detrimental to growth. There is also a notion that a threshold level of the debt-to-GDP ratio exists, above which economies experience lower growth.

**Higher Interest Rates and Reduced Capital Accumulation**

The theory suggests that higher public debt tends to lead to higher long-term interest rates, all else being equal, but empirical evidence has been mixed. A comprehensive survey by Gale and Orszag (2002) on the impact of fiscal deficits on interest rates reports that about half of the studies show a positive and significant relationship, while the other half find mixed or insignificant effects. They argue that the second group of studies does not take into account the effects of future deficits, but that increases in expected future deficits raise long-term interest rates. Baldacci and Kumar (2010) also find empirical evidence that higher fiscal deficits and government debt lead to higher sovereign bond yields, using panel data for 31 advanced and emerging market economies during 1980–2008.

---

[22] Ricardian equivalence was developed by David Ricardo. The theory suggests that when a government tries to stimulate an economy by increasing debt-financed government spending, demand remains unchanged because consumers save the extra money to pay for expected future tax increases that will be used to pay off the debt.

Kumar and Woo (2010) conducted a growth accounting exercise using data from advanced and emerging economies. They found that an increase in the initial debt level is associated with slower capital accumulation, which in turn reduces labor productivity growth. Initial debt level has a weaker impact on subsequent TFP growth and a negligible effect on human capital accumulation.

**Distortionary Taxation**

Cuts in the distortionary tax rate on capital financed by increases in government debt are generally considered to lead to higher investment and output. Dotsey (1994) argues, however, that when government deficits are financed by future distortionary taxation instead of a non-distorting lump-sum tax—as is often assumed—lower tax rates and higher deficits may lead to reductions in investment and output.

**Inflation Caused by Public Debt**

Cochrane (2011) analyzes the potential inflationary consequences of the "Great Recession of 2008–2009," when the central banks of advanced economies flooded the market with money. He argues that what determines inflation in the new era of massive fiscal deficits and credit guarantees is not central bank monetary policies but fiscal constraints. There is a limit to how much tax a government can raise, and its willingness to levy distortionary taxes would typically run out before that point. He refutes the view that fiscal stimulus tends to come too late, because demand is not stimulated as public expenditure is executed, but when consumers form expectations that additional debt (deficit) will not be repaid via future surpluses but through inflation. The distinction between nominal and real debt is crucial. Ricardian equivalence presumes that the government issues *real* debt, when in fact, it issues *nominal* debt. Unless the real interest rate and personal discount rate coincide, there is no need for irrationality, market incompleteness or market failure for the equivalence to break down and for consumers to react to the fiscal stimulus. In other words, additional debt (extra fiscal spending) that does not cause higher inflation would have no real impact.

While not addressing growth directly, the very high levels of public debt after the Great Recession of 2007–2012 have prompted a strand of literature that asks whether inflation can be an effective tool for reducing real public debt. Such a discussion is relevant for governments that issue debt largely in their own currencies, and the empirical analyses focus mostly on the US. Rogoff (2008) postulates that increasing inflation by a few percentage points for a short time can reduce real debt significantly. Aizenman and Marion (2011) support this view, while Krause and Moyen (2016) find that only a persistent increase in inflation has significant effects on real public debt.

**Uncertainty About Prospects and Policies**

Mayer et al. (2013) argue that the effect of fiscal policy on macroeconomic variables such as inflation, consumer response and investments becomes erratic over time when the government is permanently indebted—that is, it has a positive level of debt in a steady state.

**Thresholds for Public Debt**

The existence of a critical threshold of debt levels was suggested by Reinhart and Rogoff (2010) and Reinhart et al. (2012). Adam and Bevan (2005) examine a panel of 45 developing countries, presenting evidence of a threshold effect at relatively low levels of deficit. Ilzetzki et al. (2013) analyze panel data covering 44 developed and developing countries and report that fiscal multipliers turn negative when the country's public debt-to-GDP ratio exceeds 60%. Kumar and Woo (2010) identify some evidence of nonlinearity with higher levels of initial debt having a proportionately larger negative effect on subsequent growth. They also observe an inverse relationship between initial debt and subsequent growth. The existence of a threshold has been contested by Herndon et al. (2013), among others, and there is no agreement among researchers on the matter. Cochrane (2011) argues that there is no particular common threshold under which debt is considered sustainable—what matters is public confidence in the future sustainability of debt. Pescatori et al. (2014) conclude that no critical threshold emerges in their examination of 34 advanced economies.

#### 6.3.3.3 Inflation

The effects of inflation on real economic performance have been analyzed by many. Fountas and Karanasos (2007) provide an excellent review of this vast literature. Inflation is fundamentally neutral, but frictions—such as information asymmetry, imperfect transmission mechanisms of monetary policy, changes in relative prices, and menu costs—can have an impact on real variables. The relationship remains theoretically and empirically ambiguous. Some theories suggest that higher inflation can lead to greater uncertainty in the presence of asymmetric information.[23] Friedman (1977) argues that while high inflation per se does not affect real variables in the long run, an increase in the variance of inflation can generate economic inefficiencies and affect long-term economic performance. Others argue the opposite: higher inflation leads to lower uncertainty because economic actors are induced to invest more resources in forecasting inflation. There is also a hypothesis that higher uncertainty leads to higher inflation[24] when asymmetric information and imperfect monetary policy transmission are combined. The literature is unanimous on at least one point: hyperinflation is detrimental to growth.

Empirical investigations are data-intensive, and most studies are conducted in the US, with some also focusing on other Group of Seven (G7) countries and only a few on developing countries. Even so, the results tend to be mixed or sensitive

[23] The "Friedman-Ball hypothesis" is named after Friedman (1977) and Ball (1992).

[24] The "Cukierman-Meltzer hypothesis" is named after Cukierman and Meltzer (1986), which develops a positive model of Federal Reserve Board's behavior.

to specifications. The empirical investigation by Fountas and Karanasos (2007), using G7 data, supports the hypothesis that inflation is a determinant of inflation uncertainty, but shows mixed results on the negative relationship between inflation uncertainty and welfare (output growth).

As empirical investigations have not established a clear relationship between inflation and growth or other real economic variables, some have suggested the possibility of nonlinearities—i.e., threshold effects—in the relationship between inflation and growth, although there is no particular theoretical basis to support this hypothesis. The paper by Fischer (1993) is one of the first studies. Using panel data for a set of developed and developing countries, Fischer finds a non-linear negative relationship between inflation and growth. Bruno and Easterly (1998) estimate the threshold rate to be around 40%, above which inflation becomes harmful to growth.

Ibarra and Trupkin (2016) also identify threshold levels of inflation and show that they are influenced by the quality of institutions in the case of developing countries. Judson and Orphanides (1999) use a large sample of up to 119 countries and quarterly inflation data, finding that the level of inflation is significantly negatively correlated with growth, but only for inflation levels higher than about 10% per year. In addition, they conclude that inflation volatility is also robustly negatively correlated with growth after controlling for the level of inflation. To summarize, studies have found that high inflation is bad for growth. This relationship is weak or nonexistent at "low" levels of inflation, but evidence that inflation is good for growth has not been found.

In his classic work, Cagan (1956) defines hyperinflation as beginning in the month when inflation first exceeds 50% (per month) and as ending in the month before the monthly inflation rate drops below 50% for at least a year. According to this definition, Hanke and Bostrom (2017) report that there have been 58 episodes of hyperinflation in history, of which 34 have occurred since 1990.[25]

Instances of hyperinflation, as defined by Cagan (1956), are rare. Fischer et al. (2002) use an alternative definition of inflation exceeding 100% per year in their study of "very high inflation." They find inflation remained under 25% per annum in most countries, most of the time—that is, the monthly inflation rate remained under 1.9% (corresponding to 25% per annum) in over 80% of the country-month observations in their sample. They observe that countries with low inflation (below 25%) tend to continue to have low inflation, and countries with higher inflation are more likely to experience rising inflation than those with low inflation. An extremely high inflation rate of above 200% was defined as "explosive," meaning that countries with such a rate were more likely to see inflation rise than fall in the following year. Transition economies were prone to higher inflation, with all of them experiencing at least one episode of inflation above 25% per annum.

[25] To operationalize the definition, Hanke also required that (1) 50% inflation had to persist for at least 30 consecutive days, and (2) the inflation episode had to be fully documented and inflation rate estimates had to be replicable.

**Determinants of Inflation**

There is also a large body of research on what determines the inflation rate, primarily based on the premise that low and stable inflation is optimal, and it explores why real economies deviate from this ideal. In their seminal paper, Kydland and Prescott (1977) demonstrate that the absence of pre-commitment in monetary policy can lead to inefficiently high inflation. Some researchers, for example, Barro and Gordon (1983), consider the mechanism of generating inflation identified by them to be applicable to actual monetary policies, but others, such as Taylor (1983), consider it to be an issue that can be overcome by appropriate institutional arrangements and hence, not directly applicable. Romer (1993) reports lower average inflation in smaller, more open economies because the benefits of unanticipated expansion are decreasing in the degree of openness. He notes that the link between openness and inflation holds across virtually all types of countries, with the exception of the most highly developed countries. Cukierman et al. (1992) conclude that inflation is higher in countries with politically polarized and unstable governments, because they tend to rely more on seigniorage and less on efficient tax collection compared to more stable and less polarized countries.

#### 6.3.3.4 Exchange Rate

Exchange rates did not feature in the early growth literature because the first-generation models assumed a closed economy, and hence, there were few international transactions. Even after the models were extended to account for the gap not explained by savings, investment or other observable factors, exchange rates were initially not treated as a prominent feature. The more recent literature on export-led growth has given an important role to the real exchange rate, and there is now a large body of literature on the relationship between the level or volatility of the real exchange rate and growth. Yet, there is still a lack of consensus, theoretical or empirical, on the role of the real exchange rate in influencing economic growth. Eichengreen (2008) conducts an exhaustive review of this vast literature and concludes that "the real exchange rate matters. Keeping it at competitive levels and avoiding excessive volatility are important for growth. That said, the statistical evidence is not overwhelming."

In the export-led growth literature, maintaining an undervalued currency is considered conducive to growth, as it helps shift resources to the export sector, which is more productive and/or subject to increasing returns than the nontradable or traditional sector. Rapid growth in East Asian countries is often cited as a successful application of this model, which contrasts with the experiences of countries that adopted overvalued currencies in Latin America and Africa. This view has been challenged for several reasons. First, it is a hypothesis extrapolated from a handful of cases, the underlying mechanisms of which are not explained convincingly. At a minimum, the Marshall-Lerner condition[26] would have to be satisfied for the economy's imports and exports to behave in the way that proponents of this hypothesis suggest. Second, there are costs as well as benefits to maintaining an artificially undervalued currency. Third, the real exchange rate is not a variable that can be controlled directly by policies in the long run, and even if it were, it is clearly not a policy that can be pursued successfully by all countries.

Those who find that undervaluation is good for growth include Gala (2007), who suggests that activities subject to increasing returns tend to be located in the tradable rather than the nontradable sector. Rodrik (2008), using a dataset covering a maximum of 188 countries and 11 five-year periods from 1950–2004, shows that the undervaluation of a currency is strongly associated with higher growth and that overvaluation hurts growth (see Fig. 6.7), but *only* in developing countries. He interprets this evidence to mean that the relative price of tradable and nontradable goods (that is, the real exchange rate) can be used as a mechanism to alleviate impediments to growth frequently found in developing countries, such as market failures and weak institutions. His list of market failures includes learning externalities (technological, marketing and other information spillovers), coordination externalities (efforts needed to get complex investments off the ground), credit market imperfections and wage premiums (skilled labor tends to be scarce).

Regarding low-quality institutions, Rodrik cites a lack of property rights, poor contract enforcement and corruption as examples. He argues—plausibly but without justifying his position formally—that international traders are disproportionately affected by such an environment because their products are more institution-intensive than those who produce nontradables, such as barbers. Undervaluation (increasing the relative price of tradables) acts as the second-best mechanism to alleviate such distortions; the first-best mechanism is, of course, to improve institutional quality and devise ways for correcting the market failures. Using panel data for 150 countries, Habib et al. (2017) confirm Rodrik's empirical findings that real depreciation significantly increases annual real GDP growth for developing countries. They claim to have obtained sharper results than Rodrik and others by using external instruments, such as global capital flows, a country's own financial openness, and official reserves, to address the possible reverse causality problem.

The Dutch disease is a specific manifestation of a real exchange rate appreciation harming the economy. The phenomenon is considered a problem for two broad reasons. First, the natural resources sector generally does not employ as many people as the export sectors it displaces. Second, the natural resources are likely to be exhausted at some point, by which time alternative industries may have been largely lost. Corden (1984) discusses various theoretical possibilities arising

[26] Marshall-Lerner condition states that for a real devaluation/depreciation of the currency to improve the current account balance in a country, the sum of the elasticities (in absolute values) of the demand for imports and exports with respect to the real exchange rate is greater than one. and if the current account is balanced. If there is a deficit, then the Marshall-Lerner condition is a necessary but not sufficient stability condition when measured in home currency.

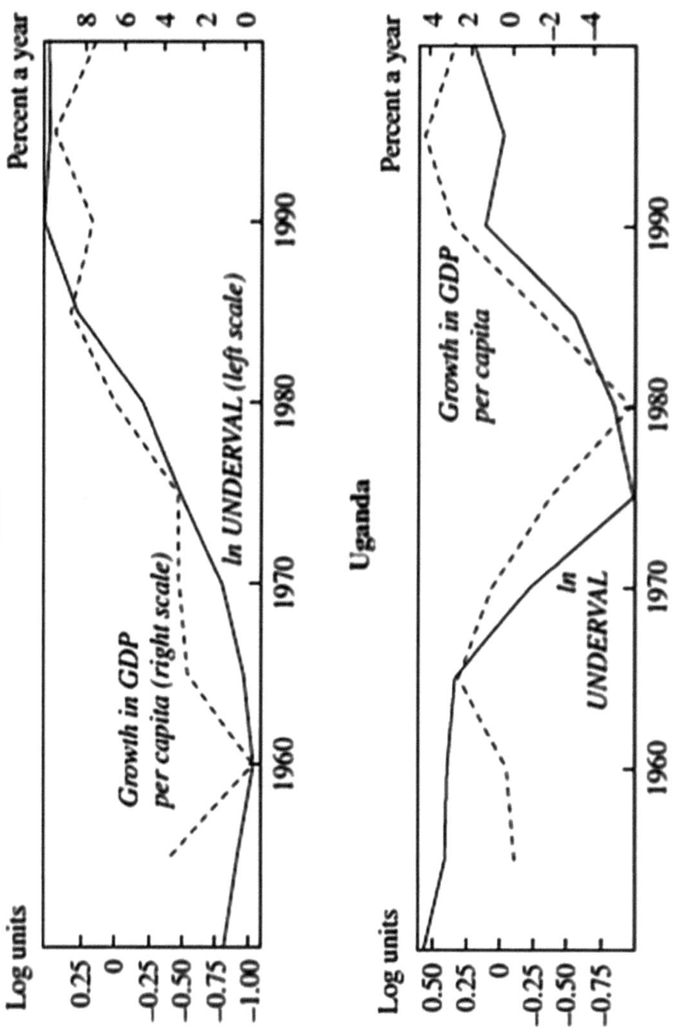


**Fig. 6.7** Undervaluation and economic growth in selected developing countries, 1950–2004. *Source* Rodrik (2008)

**Table 6.4** Impact of choice of exchange regimes (selected studies)

| | Pegs are better | Floats are better | Other |
|---|---|---|---|
| Growth | | | Gosh et al. (2002)[3]; Tsangarides (2012)[4] |
| Growth volatility | Levy-Yeyati and Sturzenegger (2003)[1] | Levy-Yeyati and Sturzenegger (2003)[2] | |
| Absorbing shocks | | Cespedes, Chang and Velasco (2004); Curdia (2007) Berkmen et al. (2009) | Hutchison, Noy, and Wang (2010)[4], Blanchard et al. (2010, b)[4] |
| Recovering from shocks | | Tsangarides (2012) | |

*Note* [1] For low income countries, [2] For emerging markets, [3] Intermediate regimes are better, [4] No effect
*Source* Author's compilation

from the Dutch disease. The Dutch disease can affect growth performance if the nature of growth is different between the industries that are resource-based and others (see the next section for international trade policy).

Another strand of literature focuses on the volatility of the real exchange rate, claiming that its variability is detrimental to growth as it discourages investment and trade. Currency crises are extreme cases of such volatility, which can obviously trigger large costs to the economy. The relationship between the real exchange rate volatility and growth, however, is ambiguous both theoretically and empirically. Aghion et al. (2009) demonstrate empirically that real exchange rate volatility significantly reduces productivity growth if the country's financial development is not sufficiently advanced, because financial market shocks are amplified in thin or underdeveloped capital markets.

Finally, there is a debate on fixed versus floating exchange rate regimes.[27] See *Fixed or flexible? Getting the exchange rate right in the 1990s* by Caramazza and Aziz (1998) for an excellent summary of the history and salient points of this debate. Which regime is right for a country may depend on factors such as economic size, exposure to shocks, openness and so forth. What is appropriate for the economy may also change over time. Moreover, the choice may depend on how "right" is defined. Do the authorities wish to maximize growth, minimize volatility, enhance resilience or fight inflation? Empirical evidence, as ever, is mixed on whether the choice of the exchange rate regime has any bearing on these policy objectives (Table 6.4 shows the findings from selected studies).

[27] The regime could also be neither completely fixed nor floating. In fact, a clean float is very rare. Pegging can be to a single currency or a basket, or involve the complete abandonment of one's own legal tender.

### 6.3.4 International Trade Policy

Openness to international trade has long been identified as a contributing factor to growth. Like the studies of the impact of other policy variables, what is being investigated often concerns the level of income more than growth itself. In the case of trade policies—unlike macroeconomic policies discussed in the previous section—the explanatory policy variable is specifically about trade only in some cases. More often, it refers to a broader set of policies and institutions that are generally considered liberal or market-determined, and terms such as "openness," "trade liberalization," and "outward orientation" are often used interchangeably by the authors.

This phenomenon is partly due to the measurement problems discussed further below, but also because the relationship between "openness to trade" and "growth" has not been established conclusively, theoretically or empirically, despite the vast literature. There are many variations to the theme and a few influential papers, some of which are rebutted vigorously[28] and a sample of the debate is presented below. The conclusion is that the relationship is indeed ambiguous and depends on the specific circumstances of the country, while avoiding obvious mistakes is always a good idea, as Easterly (2005) suggests about macroeconomic policies in general.

According to Rodríguez and Rodrik (2001), modern trade theory does not support an unambiguous negative relationship between trade barriers and growth rates. They argue that:

i. In static models with no market imperfections or other pre-existing distortions, the effect of a trade restriction is to reduce the level of real GDP at world prices. In the presence of market failures, such as externalities, trade restrictions may increase real GDP (although they are rarely the first-best instruments for doing so).
ii. In standard models with exogenous technological change and diminishing returns to reproducible factors of production (e.g., the neoclassical model of growth), a trade restriction has no effect on the long-run (steady-state) rate of growth of output. This is true regardless of the existence of market imperfections. However, there may be growth effects during the transition to the steady state (These transitional effects may be positive or negative, depending on how the long-run level of output is affected by the trade restriction).
iii. In models of endogenous growth generated by non-diminishing returns to reproducible factors of production or by learning-by-doing and other forms of endogenous technological change, the presumption is that lower trade restrictions boost output growth in the world economy as a whole. However, a subset of countries may experience diminished growth, depending on their initial factor endowments and levels of technological development.

[28] See Baldwin (2004) for an excellent review of the literature on this issue.

**Table 6.5** The effects of trade barriers on growth, various models

| Effects of trade barriers on: | Trade models | | Neoclassical growth | Endogenous growth | |
|---|---|---|---|---|---|
| | No distortions | Distortions | | Positive externalities in tradable sector | Comparative advantage in lower growth sector |
| GDP level | – | Possibly + | . | . | . |
| Growth | No impact | No impact | No impact (steady-state) | – | + |

*Source* Author's compilation from Rodríguez and Rodrik (2001)

In other words, only endogenous growth models predict a relationship between trade barriers and growth, with the direction of the relationship depending on the nature of the externalities. There is no presumption that liberalizing trade would unambiguously lead to a higher growth rate. These predictions are summarized in Table 6.5.

Reducing trade barriers leads to higher growth when there are positive externalities such as learn-by-doing, technology transfer or economies of scale (such cases would be classified in the second right-most cell in the bottom row of Table 6.5). The export-led growth literature, mentioned in the exchange rate section above, supports this view, and sometimes advocates industrial policy[29] to nudge the economy in the "right" direction (see World Bank 1993 for a review). Enthusiasm for industrial policy has waned since its heyday, but diversification of production or exports as a means of improving the resilience of an economy—a form of industrial policy—has retained some devotees among government authorities and development practitioners. The track record of this policy, however, is not the reason for its popularity, as the results are decidedly mixed.[30] The strategic trade literature (for example, Krugman 1987; Young 1991) maintains that comparative advantages can evolve over time, potentially justifying the protection of infant industries.[31]

[29] Industrial policy refers to any selective intervention or government policy that seeks to alter the structure of production toward a more desirable form (usually industrialization) than would occur in its absence.

[30] This is possibly because it has not been implemented correctly. See De Rosa et al. (2014) for an analysis of the Eurasian experience in diversification.

[31] The infant industry argument, first formulated by Alexander Hamilton, proposes that in the presence of positive externalities, it is justifiable to provide protection *temporarily* for an industry that has the potential to gain a comparative advantage dynamically. The problem in practice is that no one knows *ex-ante* which industry has this potential, and selecting the industry to be supported is fraught with discretion, and that the protected infant tends never to grow up. These problems are exacerbated when combined with governance issues. This argument served as the basis for the import-substitution strategy, which was adopted by many newly independent countries after World War II. Many were forced to abandon this strategy when it triggered the debt crisis in the 1980s.

Conversely, there may be cases where the export sector is associated with negative externalities—for example, having a comparative advantage in a lower productivity growth sector (Matsuyama 1992) or being prone to volatility or poor governance (Auty 2001). In such cases, increasing trade barriers may lead to higher growth (these cases would be positioned in the bottom right-hand corner cell of Table 6.5). The Dutch disease can have growth implications to the extent that the export industries that lose competitiveness are associated with positive externalities, or the resource-based sector has negative externalities.

The issues associated with possessing a comparative advantage in extractive industries have spawned the "resource curse" literature. The performance of resource-rich countries such as Bolivia, Democratic Republic of the Congo, Nigeria, Sierra Leone, and Venezuela—compared with that of resource-poor East Asian countries—provides a convincing, if anecdotal, backdrop. The resource curse is predominantly about governance. As Collier and Hoeffler (2005) explains, "heavy reliance on primary commodities is associated with a large share of location-specific 'rents,' in national income. In turn, rents are associated with large nontax income for the state or any other organization that can control the territory on which the rents are generated. Reliance is also associated with proneness to shocks.... which imply volatile growth rates, make economic management far more difficult, and are liable to confuse citizens' comprehension of government performance."

The empirical investigations on trade and growth share challenges with the efforts to identify the impact of macroeconomic policies on growth discussed earlier: high correlation among the explanatory policy variables, the endogeneity issue and problems of measurement. The last challenge is particularly acute for trade policies. Researchers have used either trade volume (exports plus imports as a share of GDP) or composite measures of openness, both of which are problematic. The first reflects many more factors than just the trade regime, such as the size of the economy, geographic location, whether the country is a part of a global value chain, and so on.

With the second type, whether it measures the trade policy stance is open to debate, and the selection of elements to be included in the composite index is subjective, leaving it open to criticism of cherry-picking. A third, less frequently used measure is ironically the most obvious: the average tariff rates and coverage of non-tariff barriers—although they are not free of biases either. For example, the impact of high tariff rates or non-tariff barriers tends to be underrepresented when a trade volume-weighted average rate is used and overrepresented when a simple average is used.[32] The probable reason for which they are rarely used, however, is not the potential bias, but rather that they tend not to yield the desired results.

[32] Using a trade-weighted average tariff rate assigns lower weights on tariff lines with higher rates because such imports are discouraged. An unweighted average can place undue importance on outlier lines with "prohibitive rates," even when such lines are exceptional.

The openness index proposed by Sachs and Warner (1995) is still one of the most frequently used in the literature. Their binary index classifies an economy as open if none of the following conditions apply and closed if any one of them does apply:

i. nontariff barriers covering 40% or more of trade,
ii. average tariff rates of 40% or more,
iii. a black market exchange rate that is depreciated by 20% or more relative to the official exchange rate, on average, during the 1970s or 1980s,
iv. a socialist economic system, and
v. a state monopoly on major exports.

The authors claim that these criteria are chosen to cover all the major types of trade restrictions. Using this index, they demonstrate that during the period 1970–1989, "open economies" outperformed "closed economies" in growth—a finding that is robust and statistically significant.

Rodríguez and Rodrik (2001) argue that the strength of Sachs and Warner's openness index primarily derives from the black market premium and the state monopoly variables. Nontariff barriers and average tariff rates, the two variables most directly related to trade, contribute very little: if they are dropped from the formulation, very little of the statistical power would be lost from the index. They maintain that the black market premium measures a much broader set of macroeconomic policies and institutional arrangements of an economy than just openness. They also contend that the state monopoly variable serves as a proxy for a regional dummy for sub-Saharan Africa, which again raises more complex issues than trade policies.

Another influential paper in the literature is Dollar's (1992) investigation of 95 developing countries for 1976–1985, which shows that outward-oriented developing economies grow more rapidly. He constructs two measures of outward orientation. The first measure is an international comparison of price levels for the same basket of consumption goods converted to USD using nominal exchange rates and corrected for factor endowments to account for the Balassa–Samuelson effect[33] in non-traded goods. The variation in price levels is taken as a measure of inward or outward orientation caused by trade policy. This measure yields some significant anomalies, prompting him to construct a second measure: real exchange rate variability. He finds that per capita GDP growth is significantly negatively related to the two measures of inward orientation, controlling for the investment rate. Rodríguez and Rodrik (2001) are skeptical of the validity of both measures. They argue that a significant part of the variation in the price levels is due not to trade policies but to monetary and exchange rate policies. The measure also assumes the law of one price holds continuously, which is generally found not

[33] The Balassa-Samuelson effect predicts that prices of non-traded goods will be higher in higher income countries (while prices of traded goods should converge internationally).

to be true. They contend that the real exchange rate variability index has little to do with inward or outward orientation but instead measures economic instability at large: the ten countries with the highest score of variability are those that experienced very high inflation rates and/or severe political disturbances during 1976–1985.

"Does trade cause growth?" by Frankel and Romer (1999) is a seminal paper in the literature and is explicitly about the effects of trade on *living standards*—and not on growth, despite the title. They use exogenous geographical data as an instrument for trade volume, finding that countries that trade more have higher income, although the effects are not estimated with great precision. An important caveat is that geography is not a policy variable, and the relationship identified in their paper is not directly applicable to the effects that trade policies may have on income.

Edwards (1998) employs a different tactic for analyzing the robustness of the relationship between openness and total factor productivity (TFP) growth using nine existing indices of trade policy on a sample of 93 countries. The indices examined are:

i. Sachs and Warner (1995): Openness Index;
ii. World Bank (1987): Outward Orientation Index
iii. Leamer (1988): Openness Index;
iv. Average Black Market Index;
v. Average Import Tariff on Manufacturing;
vi. Average Coverage of Non-Tariff Barriers (4–6 are United Nations Conference on Trade and Development (UNCTAD) data, reported in Barro and Lee 1994);
vii. The Heritage Foundation Index of Trade Policy;
viii. Collected Trade Tax Ratio (data from the IMF); and
ix. Wolf (1993): Index of Import Distortions.

Using weighted least squares estimation, Edwards finds that the openness indicators are associated with growth with the expected sign and statistically significant in the majority of the cases. Rodríguez and Rodrik (2001) take issue with the choice of the weighted least squares technique, arguing that its use is justified only if the error terms are heteroscedastic and their functional form is known. They argue that using White's heteroskedasticity-robust standard errors is more appropriate; however, when this approach is employed, most of the results become insignificant or switch to the "wrong" sign.

Hausmann et al. (2007), in "What you export matters," postulate that export specialization patterns predict subsequent economic growth. The mechanism they propose is a knowledge externality associated with discovering the costs of production for the first mover, which leads to a suboptimal number of entrepreneurs undertaking investments. More investments in cost discovery are expected to lead to higher productivity of the resulting set of activities. To provide empirical support for their hypothesis, they develop an indicator (called EXPY) that captures the income and productivity level associated with a country's export basket. Using data covering the period 1962–2003, they find that countries with higher EXPY scores tend to grow faster.

Their approach has been used by many subsequent studies and has also been subject to critique. Some have challenged whether the EXPY indicator accurately captures what the authors claim (for example, Wang et al. 2010), while others have noted that what countries export is not necessarily what they produce (Johnson 2014). Grancay et al. (2015) point out the problem of associating higher income levels with the sophistication of exports for commodity exporters, especially oil producers.

Although the growth-enhancing effects of a liberal trade stance have not been established to everyone's satisfaction, at least there is no evidence that trade restrictions are systematically good for growth. Taken together, the research suggests that openness or liberal trade regimes are effective when combined with other good policies. Some studies have shown that trade regimes affect growth by influencing other variables, such as investment—see, for example, Taylor (1998) and Wacziarg (2001)—and in the case of corruption, see Ades and Di Tella (1997), Wei (2000), and Gatti (2004). The size of the rent and the ease with which it can be extracted are considered to be related to the level of corruption. Applied to trade restrictions, this principle implies that low and uniform tariff rates limit the scope of discretion compared to high and dispersed rates and nontariff barriers. Less restrictive trade regimes would hence be more conducive to growth, to the extent that corruption is detrimental to growth. The corruption-related literature implies that the fundamental factor influencing growth is the quality of institutions.

Recent empirical studies tend to be more microeconomic and often country- or even industry-specific because the failure of broad-brush investigations such as those discussed above led to an acknowledgment that a more nuanced approach was necessary to gauge the impact of trade. After all, it is firms that export and import, not countries. Statistical inference is conducted with much greater precision when firm-specific data are used, partly because the number of observations is an order of magnitude larger and also because the types of questions being asked are much more specific. Such studies might find that export-oriented firms have higher productivity growth or tend to stay in business longer, but they make no claim that trade liberalization leads to higher economic growth, as that is not the question being investigated.

It is worth recalling that even in standard trade theory, opening up to trade increases the welfare of the economy *as a whole*, but there are winners and losers within the economy because the reallocation of productive factors is precisely the mechanism that increases welfare. Consumers in general are "winners," as they have more choices at lower prices than when international trade is restricted. Producers, however, can win or lose depending on the trading pattern resulting from liberalization. For example, low-skilled workers in advanced economies are often "losers" if the factory they worked for relocates to a lower-wage country as a result of trade liberalization, and they are unable to find comparable jobs or if their real wages fall. Even if the direct applicability of the Stolper–Samuelson theorem[34] to the real world is limited, some observed facts are consistent with its prediction. For example, between 1970 and 2017, the hourly inflation-adjusted wages received by nonsupervisory employees in the US grew by only 0.2% per year (Shambaugh et al. 2017), whereas the country's average per capita real GDP growth over the same period was roughly 1.7% (World Bank data) (Fig. 6.8).

Trade liberalization can accentuate inequalities in an environment where domestic policies do not function well to manage transitional costs and redistribute the gains. Because losses are concentrated while gains are widespread, liberalizing trade is difficult—see Fernandez and Rodrik (1991) for a theoretical explanation and Stiglitz (1998) for his experience in the White House. Protectionism can reassert itself when perceived inequality stemming from trade policies becomes acute. In discussing the implications of the slowdown in global trade growth since the Great Recession of 2007–2012, the IMF, World Bank and WTO (2017) jointly note that "Trade is leaving too many individuals and communities behind.... Adjustment to trade can bring a human and economic downside that is frequently concentrated, sometimes harsh, and has too often become prolonged."

On the other hand, "Trade openness, underpinned by the expansion of the multilateral system, has brought about higher productivity, greater competition, lower prices, and improved living standards." They stress that "the rule-based trading system remains a pillar and a key strength of the global economy" and advocate for transparent and well-enforced rules for both conventional trade measures and "behind-the-border" measures, coupled with complementary domestic policies to ensure that gains from trade are shared widely (IMF, World Bank, and WTO 2017).

## 6.4 Institutions and Growth

### 6.4.1 Introduction

The notion that institutions are important to economic outcomes has a long history. As Adam Smith (1776) noted:

> Commerce and manufactures can seldom flourish long in any state which does not enjoy a regular administration of justice, in which the people do not feel themselves secure in the possession of their property, in which the faith of contracts is not supported by law, and in which the authority of the state is not supposed to be regularly employed in enforcing the payment of debts from all those who are able to pay. Commerce and manufactures, in short, can seldom flourish in any state in which there is not a certain degree of confidence in the justice of government.

[34] Stolper–Samuelson theorem predicts that under certain conditions—associated with the Heckscher-Ohlin model of international trade—a decline in the relative price of a good is reflected proportionately more in the price of the factor that is used intensively in the production of that good.

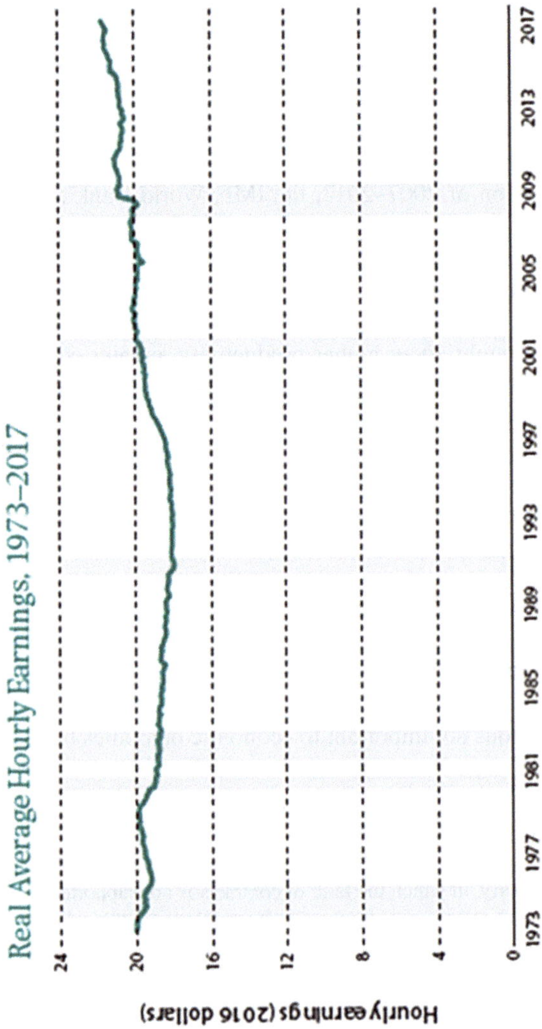


**Fig. 6.8** Real average hourly earnings, 1937–2017. *Source* Shambaugh et al. (2017)

There is a strand of literature called *New Institutional Economics* (NIE), which originated in Coase's seminal articles "The Nature of the Firm" (1937) and "The Problem of Social Cost" (1960). In the first article, he provides the key insight that firms exist because price-based market transactions are costly, which is a departure from the standard neoclassical assumption that a firm is a profit-maximizing black box, represented simply by a production function. In the second article, he proposes a fundamental rethinking of welfare economics, maintaining that Pigouvian solutions[35] to negative externalities are inappropriate when the operation of a pricing system is costly. He argues that:

> The government is, in a sense, a super-firm. The government is able, if it wishes, to avoid the market altogether, which a firm can never do. Just as the government can conscript or seize property, so it can decree that factors of production should only be used in such-and-such a way. Such authoritarian methods save a lot of trouble (for those doing the organising). Furthermore, the government has at its disposal the police and the other law enforcement agencies to make sure that its regulations are carried out. But the governmental administrative machine is not itself costless. Furthermore, there is no reason to suppose that the restrictive and zoning regulations, made by a fallible administration subject to political pressures and operating without any competitive check, will necessarily always be those which increase the efficiency with which the economic system operates. It is my belief that economists, and policy-makers generally, have tended to over-estimate the advantages which come from governmental regulation.

Along with Coase, Douglass North and Oliver Williamson are considered the founding figures of New Institutional Economics.[36] NIE differs from the old institutional economics in that it does not eschew the orthodox assumptions of neoclassical economic theory, such as scarcity and competition. It diverges from the standard neoclassical assumptions by rejecting the ideas that individuals have perfect information and unbounded rationality and that transactions are costless and instantaneous (Menard and Shirley 2005).

A slightly different strand of literature focuses more on the consequences (i.e., growth, volatility, etc.) of different institutions rather than the workings of the institutions themselves. Authors such as Hall and Jones (1999) and Acemoglu et al. (2001) played a key role in sparking the most recent revival of the literature on the role of institutions in economic outcomes.

While the notion that institutions are crucial is persuasive, a consensus on what causes growth has yet to be reached for several reasons. First, institutions mean various things to different people. Second, and more importantly, even if it could be agreed that institutions determine economic outcomes, the fundamental question of what causes countries to have different institutions remains unanswered. Third, empirical investigations of which attributes of institutions matter are, again,

[35] In an example of a firm contaminating a stream, harming the livelihood of fisher-people, a Pigouvian solution is to tax the negative externalities to reflect the social cost of the firm's activity.
[36] See Menard and Shirley (2012) for an excellent narrative of the history of New Institutional Economics.

fraught with problems of endogeneity, omitted variables, spurious relationships, measurement errors, and so forth.

Those who disagree with the supremacy of institutions propose geography, endowment, human capital accumulation and history—in addition to policies discussed in the previous chapter—as alternatives.

### 6.4.2 Institutions as the Determinant

North (1981, 1990, and 1994, among others) postulates that the decisions made by the political process are the critical element affecting the functioning of economies. He argues that "institutions are the rules of the game in a society or, more formally, are the humanly devised constraints that shape human interaction. In consequence, they structure incentives in human exchange, whether political, social, or economic." In contrast to economic behavior, which is almost always assumed to be rational, institutions are generally not considered to be constructed with efficiency as an objective. He notes that "[r]ulers devised property rights in their own interests and transaction costs resulted in typically inefficient property rights prevailing.... Institutions, together with the standard constraints of economic theory, determine the opportunities in a society. Organizations are created to take advantage of those opportunities." Efficient institutions promote productive activities, and one gets efficient institutions by a polity that has built-in incentives to create and enforce efficient property rights." He does not claim to have all the answers but maintains that macroeconomic theorists must do better to incorporate the institutions that affect economic outcomes if one hopes to understand what fosters economic growth.

Williamson pioneered the term "transaction cost economics,"[37] which he describes as "an effort to better understand complex economic organization by selectively joining law, economics, and organization theory" (Williamson 2010). Using a transaction as the unit of analysis, he postulates that a combination of various costs arising from human factors (such as bounded rationality), the incompleteness of contracts, the time it takes to complete a transaction and the burden of enforcement determines the optimal choice of production, with market (in its neoclassical form) and hierarchy (i.e., employing a large firm) being the two extreme choices.[38] He argues that "the practice among public policy analysts of assuming that transaction costs in the public sector are zero... is nonsense." Market failure occurs precisely because of positive transaction costs, which do not disappear when the action is transferred to the public sector.

---

[37] Transaction cost economics and New Institutional Economics are used virtually synonymously. See the website of the Society for Institutional & Organizational Economics. https://www.sioe.org/field/transaction-cost-economics.

[38] "Markets and hierarchies" is the title of Williamson's (1973) article in American Economic Review as well as his seminal 1975 work.

Hall and Jones (1999) argue that differences in institutions and government policies, which they refer to as "social infrastructure," drive variations in *output* per worker across countries, noting that physical capital and education attainment explain only a part of these variations. They focus explicitly on *levels*, rather than *rates of growth,* for two reasons. First, they believe that outputs are fundamentally a more appropriate measure of welfare. Second, growth rates observed in the data may merely reflect transitional effects, whereas the authors' aim is to explain the variation in long-run economic performance—for more on this aspect, see Hall and Jones (1997), cited in Sect. 6.3 of this chapter.

As for how institutions develop, Sokoloff and Engerman (2000) find strong evidence in their study of New World economies regarding the initial factor endowments that predispose them toward development paths. They classify the New World economies into three categories according to the degrees of inequality in wealth, human capital and political power. First, those specialized in high-value crops, such as sugar—associated with extensive use of slaves—had the highest per capita (including slaves) incomes in the New World. This category includes Barbados, Cuba, and Brazil. The second category is "Spanish America," whose economies were rich in mineral resources. The native populations survived contact with the European colonizers in large numbers but were placed under the rule of colonizers (elites) and suffered prolonged inequality. This category includes Peru and Mexico. The final category was in the part of North America that later became the US and Canada. Development in this area was based on laborers of European descent because the native population was not numerous enough to provide labor, and the soil and climate were not suited for crops associated with slave labor. This category had rather homogeneous populations and was amenable to equitable distributions of wealth. They postulate that these paths of institutional development in turn have affected growth.

While these insights into the idea that intuitions play a key role in determining economic performance have intuitive resonance, it has proven difficult to test them empirically. Various authors have employed measures such as the frequency of coups, revolutions and political assassinations, as well as political freedoms and civil liberties, to capture certain aspects of the quality of institutions. The contribution by Knack and Keefer (1995) was an early attempt to measure the extent of property rights protection directly. They use indicators such as expropriation risk, rule of law, repudiation of contracts by government, corruption in government and quality of bureaucracy from International Country Risk Guide[39] and contract enforceability, infrastructure quality, nationalization potential and bureaucratic delays from Business Environmental Risk Intelligence.[40] Using these measures, they find that institutions that protect property rights are crucial to both economic growth and investment.

[39] https://epub.prsgroup.com/products/international-country-risk-guide-icrg.
[40] http://www.beri.com/.

Other empirical studies seek to measure different aspects of institutional quality. For the level of social infrastructure, Hall and Jones (1999) utilize a combination of the Index of Government Anti-Diversion Policies from the International Country Risk Guide and the Openness Index from Sachs and Warner (1995). Mauro (1998) focuses on corruption, employing Business International[41] indicators on corruption, red tape, and the efficiency of the judicial system to test whether they affect investment and growth, finding some evidence supporting his hypothesis. Persson and Tabellini (2003, 2004) conclude that the forms of democracy have important implications for the size of government (although not necessarily for growth): presidential regimes[42] have smaller governments than parliamentary ones; majoritarian elections lead to smaller governments.

The groundbreaking work by Acemoglu et al. (2001) catapulted the literature on institutions and growth to the forefront of cutting-edge research. They test their claim that the institutions—particularly those that protect property rights and provide checks and balances against government power—are the principal determinants of growth. They make creative use of the mortality rates of colonizing Europeans as an instrument for measuring the quality of institutions more than 100 years later, claiming that colonizers settled and developed their home-country-like institutions if the mortality rate was low but established predatory (or extractive) regimes without a settler community where the risk of dying was high. They demonstrate that institutions, thus proxied, account for the differences in per capita incomes. In Acemoglu et al. (2003), they develop the theme further and argue that distortionary macroeconomic policies cause poor economic outcomes. However, such institutions cause poor macroeconomic policies, and they are therefore the underlying cause.

Easterly and Levine (2003) test the influence of endowments, policy views, and institutions on development using cross-country evidence and conclude that the first two affect development only through their effects on institutions. Rodrik et al. (2004) likewise identify institutional quality as the most important factor when they estimate the contributions of institutions, geography and trade in determining income levels. In particular, they observe that geography has mostly weak direct effects on incomes once the quality of institutions is controlled for, but it exerts a strong indirect effect through institutions.

In discussing the "impoverished little countries at the bottom of the world economy," home to the "bottom billion" people, Collier (2009) argues that state-building is a prerequisite for prosperity. He finds that violence-prone countries

[41] Business International is now incorporated into The Economist Intelligence Unit.

[42] For the purpose of their study, "presidential regime" means the chief executive is not accountable to the legislature through a vote of confidence in the sphere of economic policy. Therefore, France and Finland are classified as "parliamentary" despite their directly elected presidents, but Switzerland, which does not have a popularly elected president, is "presidential" because its permanent coalition executive cannot be brought down by the legislative assembly (Persson and Tabellini 2004).

are systematically among the slowest growing, and that slow growth is a significant risk factor for violent conflict, whereas prosperous countries are largely successful democracies that no longer experience violent conflict. He maintains that state-building is not fundamentally about institutions, which he dismisses as a "fashionable nostrum." In his view, newly independent states fail to transform into nations because their leaders have failed to forge a national identity to reduce the risks of ethnic fractionalization, they are too small to reap the economies of scale needed to provide effective security, and their governments lack accountability to the people—that is, they have not made the transition from a ruler to server. He concludes that visionary leadership is necessary for transforming a state into a nation, but that it has not been forthcoming in most of the societies of the bottom billion.

The views of Acemoglu and Robinson (2012) are similar to Collier's. The prevalence of extractive institutions is the reason why nations do not prosper—or indeed fail. They define extractive institutions as those "designed to extract incomes and wealth from one set of society to benefit a different subset." Inclusive institutions, the opposite of extractive institutions, are those that are sufficiently centralized and pluralistic with checks and balances, and they are the crucial determinants of economic development. They note sensibly, if unhelpfully, that a recipe for building such institutions does not exist, but suggest a few factors that may help the process along, including:

> some degree of centralized order so that social movements challenging existing regimes do not immediately descend into lawlessness; some preexisting political institutions that introduce a modicum of pluralism, so that coalitions can form and endure; the presence of civil society institutions that can coordinate the demands of the population so that opposition movements can neither be easily crushed by the current elites nor inevitably turn into a vehicle for another group to take control. The media can play a transformative role in the process of empowerment.

They argue that policy advice dispensed by international organizations, such as improving macroeconomic stability, reducing the size of the government, introducing flexible exchange rates, enhancing efficiency of public service provision, emphasizing better governance, is misguided, as it fails to recognize the political constraints under which the existing regime operates. North (2005) is more adamant in his views on this:

> I wish to emphasize the limits to our understanding because there is a certain amount of hubris evident in the annual surveys by the World Bank and in the writing of orthodox economists who think that now we have it right. But it is important that we understand that even if we did have it right for one economy it would not necessarily be right for another economy and even if we have it right today it would not necessarily be right tomorrow.

### 6.4.3 Alternatives to Institutions as the Key Determinant

Those who disagree with the supremacy of institutions propose geography, endowment, human capital accumulation and history as alternatives. Some consider these underlying fundamentals to be the critical determinants of growth, while others believe that institutions develop endogenously in conjunction with such factors. In most cases, these disagreements seem to arise because institutions have different meanings for different people, and empirical investigations to establish the role of institutions are often hindered by measurement problems. Some alternative views are reviewed below.

#### 6.4.3.1 Factor Accumulation

Glaeser et al. (2004) argue that human capital accumulation leads to improvements in the institutions, and as such, human capital, rather than the institutions, is the source of growth. Through their empirical analysis, they find that the initial level of education is a strong predictor of subsequent economic growth. They claim "the economic success of East Asia in the post-war era, and of China more recently, has been a consequence of good-for-growth dictators, not of institutions constraining them." They also question the indicators of institutional quality used by those who claim the supreme importance of institutions, the International Country Risk Guide, WGI and Polity IV. Whereas institutions should be "a set of rules, compliance procedures, and moral and ethical behavioral norms designed to *constrain* the behavior of individuals in the interest of maximizing the wealth or utility of principals," the indicators used are outcome measures and not underlying permanent characteristics. More specifically, these comprise the following:

- International Country Risk Guide
  The data include subjective assessments of risk for international investors along such dimensions as law and order, bureaucratic quality, corruption, risk of expropriation by the government and risk of government contract repudiation. These measures reflect what actually happened in a country rather than some permanent rules of the game.
- Worldwide Governance Indicators (WGI)
  The "government effectiveness" variable is a clear outcome measure. It is a combined measure of "perceptions of the quality of public service provision, the quality of the bureaucracy, the competence of civil servants, the independence of the civil service from political pressures, and the credibility of the government's commitment to policies." (Kaufmann et al. 2003). These are ex-post outcomes, highly correlated with the level of economic development, rather than political constraints per se.
- Polity IV
  "Constraints on the executive" refers to "the extent of institutionalized constraints on the decision-making powers of chief executives." A closer examination of how this variable is constructed reveals that it is an outcome measure

> reflecting what occurred in the most recent election. When countries have inconsistent electoral experiences, their scores fluctuate wildly. As rich countries are more likely to hold regular elections, "constraints on the executive" may well be a consequence of development rather than the other way round. The measure of "democracy" reflects the most recent experiences.

Easterly and Levine (2001) disagree with the view that factor accumulation drives growth because factor accumulation is persistent while growth is not, and the growth paths of countries exhibit large variation. They maintain that, rather than factor accumulation—whether physical or human—the "residual" (or TFP) accounts for most of the income and growth differences across countries. They believe, however, that empirical work does not yet distinguish among the different theoretical conceptions of TFP growth.

#### 6.4.3.2 Geography

Geography is presented as an additional factor of growth by some, while others claim that it is a fundamental determinant of the long-term growth trajectory. Even those who argue that geography matters to economic development—for example, Gallup et al. (1999)—do not claim that it explains everything, but that it should not be omitted from analysis of growth. Sachs (2003) refutes the findings of empirical studies showing that geography operates primarily or exclusively through institutions. In particular, he contends that the results presented in Acemoglu et al. (2001), Easterly and Levine (2003) and Rodrik et al. (2004) are not robust for methodological reasons, in particular, oversimplified specifications using only one variable (at a time) to represent geography. There are indeed several dimensions of geography that may influence the development paths of an economy, a few of which are discussed briefly below.

Landlocked countries and island economies that are far from major consumption centers, such as those in the US and Europe, face higher transportation costs and are disadvantaged in international trade. Landlocked countries, in particular, incur the physical cost of land transportation (with the exception of airfreight-based trade), as well as geopolitical costs arising from their relationship with their neighbors and the type of neighbors they have. It should be noted, however, that countries are landlocked not exclusively because of geography but also for historical and political reasons that led to the international borders being drawn where they are. Collier (2009) would argue that landlocked countries grow more slowly not because of their geographical properties but because they have not attained the attributes necessary to become a prosperous modern nation.

Tropical countries are said to face more diseases than those in temperate climates, and diseases, in turn, lead to lower productivity (Fig. 6.9). The soil is also believed to be less arable in the tropics and more prone to natural disasters. Empirical studies have shown that countries with a large portion of their territory in the tropics tend to have lower growth rates (for example, Sachs and Warner 1997). However, it is also true that such countries tend to be located in sub-Saharan Africa, and the tropics may be standing in for an unobserved variable. Diamond

(1997) develops a theory of a much longer time span than those usually treated in empirical studies, in which germs and crops affect the technological development of societies, not just in the tropics but everywhere in the world.

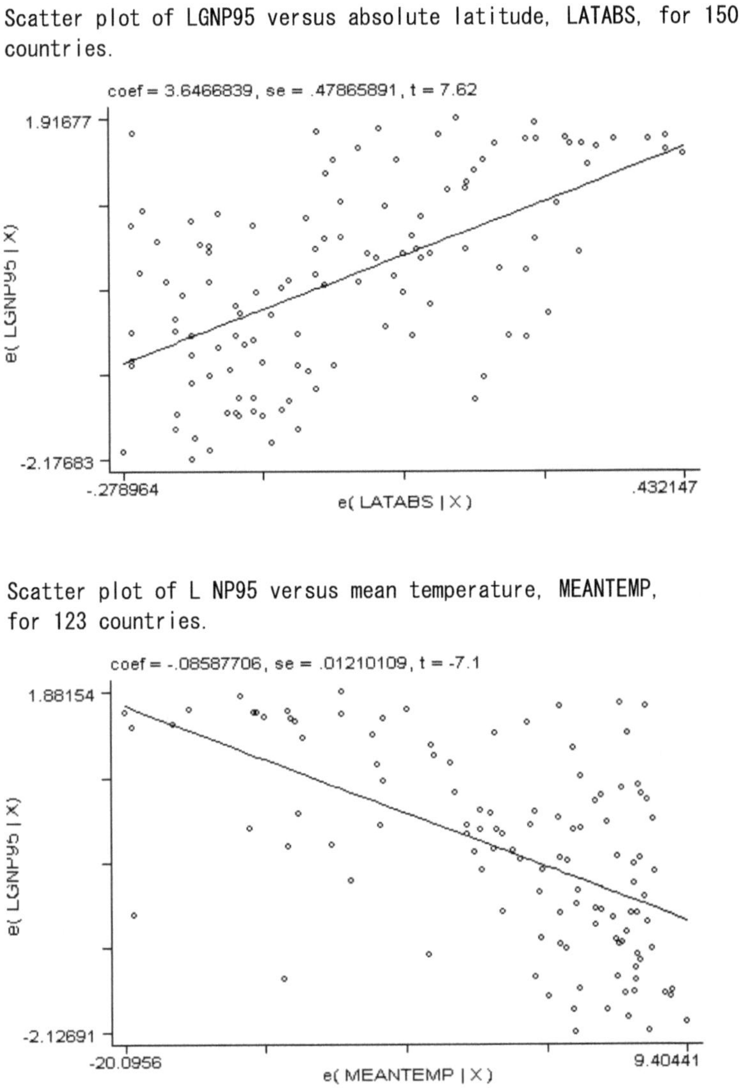


**Fig. 6.9** Relationship between Log GNP in 1995 and absolute latitude and mean temperature. *Source* McArthur and Sachs (2001). *Note* LGNP = natural log of real GNP per capita at PPP in 1995 USD, LATABS = absolute value of latitude, MEANTEMP = 1987 mean annual temperature in degrees Celsius

The geography branch of the literature at least does not suffer from endogeneity or measurement problems that plague others, although some of the very long-term hypotheses do suffer from a lack of data.

#### 6.4.3.3 History

There is also a school of thought that considers historical events to be important determinants of economic development.[43] The idea of path-dependence[44] in the presence of multiple equilibria distinguishes this branch, although there is a significant overlap with institutions, geography, endowments and capital accumulation branches of the literature. For example, Banerjee and Iyer (2005) find that historical differences in how property rights were allocated explain sustained variations in economic outcomes in Indian states and present their findings as supporting evidence for the primacy of institutions advocated by Acemoglu and others.

La Porta et al. (1999) look for empirical evidence on what brings about good governments, taking for granted that "good government"—a form of good institutions—contributes to economic development. Using various measures of government performance, such as public sector efficiency, public good provision, size of government and political freedom, they find historical factors are important determinants of government performance. Specifically, they demonstrate that "countries that are poor, close to the equator, ethnolinguistically heterogeneous, use French or socialist laws, or have high proportions of Catholics or Muslims exhibit inferior government performance."

Nunn (2007) proposes a game-theoretic model that links how a decision during the colonial era might lead to an economy converging to a low equilibrium (underdevelopment). The players in his model are the colonizer, productive entrepreneurs, and unproductive entrepreneurs who steal from their productive peers. The colonizer chooses how "extractive" it should be based on the likelihood that it will stay in power, the (endogenously determined) share of unproductive entrepreneurs in the colony, and the amount of resources that unproductive entrepreneurs can steal. His model complements that of Acemoglu et al. (2001) and provides a possible explanation for the persistence of the colonial legacy decades after independence.

---

[43] See Nunn (2009) for a survey of literature that emphasizes the importance of history in economic development.

[44] Path dependence is the idea that economic outcomes depend on the path of previous outcomes, rather than simply on current conditions and decisions—that is, history matters in current decision-making.

## References

Acemoglu, Daron, Simon Johnson, and James Robinson. 2001. "The Colonial Origins of Comparative Development: An Empirical Investigation." *American Economic Review* 91 (5): 1369–1401.

Acemoglu, Daron, Simon Johnson, James Robinson, and Yunyong Thaicharoen. 2003. "Institutional Causes, Macroeconomic Symptoms: Volatility, Crises and Growth." *Journal of Monetary Economics* 50 (1): 49–123.

Acemoglu, Daron, and James Robinson. 2012. *Why Nations Fail: The Origin of Power, Prosperity, and Poor.* Crown Publishers.

Adam, Christopher, and David Bevan. 2005. "Fiscal Deficits and Growth in Developing Countries." *Journal of Public Economics* 89 (4): 571–597.

Ades, Alberto, and Rafael Di Tella. 1997. "National Champions and Corruption: Some Unpleasant Interventionist Arithmetic." *Economic Journal* 107 (443): 1023–1042.

Afonso, António, and João Jalles. 2012. "Fiscal Volatility, Financial Crises and Growth." *Applied Economics Letters* 19 (18): 1821–1826.

Afonso, António, and Davide Furceri. 2010. "Government Size, Composition, Volatility and Economic Growth." *European Journal of Political Economy* 26 (4): 517–532.

Aghion, Philippe, Philippe Bacchetta, Romain Ranciere, and Kenneth Rogoff. 2009. "Exchange Rate Volatility and Productivity Growth: The Role of Financial Development." *Journal of Monetary Economics* 56 (4): 494–513.

Aizenman, Joshua, and Nancy Marion. 1993. "Policy Uncertainty, Persistence and Growth." *Review of International Economics* 56 (4): 494–513.

Aizenman, Joshua, and Nancy Marion. 2011. "Using Inflation to Erode the US Public Debt." *Journal of Macroeconomics* 33 (4): 524–541.

Aizenman, Joshua, and Mark Spiegel. 2010. "Takeoffs." *Review of Development Economics* 33 (4): 524–541.

Arrow, Kenneth J. 1962. "The Economic Implications of Learning by Doing." *Review of Economic Studies* 29 (3): 155–173.

Asia-Pacific Economic Cooperation (APEC). 2010. "The APEC Leaders' Growth Strategy." Yokohama, Japan, November 14, 2010. https://japan.kantei.go.jp/kan/topics/201011/aelmdeclaration2010_e04.pdf

Asian Development Bank (ADB). 2013. *Key Indicators for Asia and the Pacific 2013: Asia's Economic Transformation: Where to, How, and How Fast?* ADB.

Auty, Richard M. 2001. "The Political Economy of Resource-Driven Growth." *European Economic Review* 45 (4–6): 839–846.

Baldacci, Emanuele, and Manmohan Kumar. 2010. "Fiscal Deficits, Public Debt, and Sovereign Bond Yields." IMF Working Paper WP/10/184. IMF.

Baldwin, Robert. 2004. "Openness and Growth: What's the Empirical Relationship?" In *Challenges to Globalisation: Analysing the Economics*, eds. R. Baldwin and L. Winters, 499–525. University of Chicago Press.

Ball, Laurence. 1992. "Why Does High Inflation Raise Inflation Uncertainty?" *Journal of Monetary Economics* 29 (3): 371–388.

Banerjee, Abhijit, and Lakshmi Iyer. 2005. "History, Institutions and Economic Performance: The Legacy of Colonial Land Tenure Systems in India." *American Economic Review* 95 (4):1190–1213.

Barro, Robert J. 1997. *Determinants* of *Economic Growth: A Cross-Country Empirical Study.* MIT Press.

Barro, Robert J., and David B. Gordon. 1983. "A Positive Theory of Monetary Policy in a Natural Rate Model." *Journal of Political Economy* 91 (4): 589–610.

Barro, Robert J., and Jong-Wha Lee. 1994. "Sources of Economic Growth." *Carnegie-Rochester Conference Series on Public Policy* 40: 1–46.

Ben-David, Dan, and David H. Papell. 1998. "Slowdowns and Meltdowns: Postwar Growth Evidence from 74 Countries." *Review of Economics and Statistics* 80 (4): 561–571.
Berg, Andrew G., and Jonathan D. Ostry. 2011. "Inequality and Unsustainable Growth: Two Sides of the Same Coin?" IMF Staff Discussion Note. SDN/11/08. IMF.
Berg, Andrew, Jonathan D. Ostry, and Jeromin Zettlemeyer. 2012. "What Makes Growth Sustained?" *Journal of Development Economics* 98 (2): 149–166.
Berkmen, Pelin, Gaston Gelos, Robert Rennhack, and James Walsh. 2009. "The Global Financial Crisis: Explaining Cross-Country Differences in the Output Impact." IMF Working Paper No. 09/28. IMF.
Bernanke, Ben S. 1983. "Irreversibility, Uncertainty and Cyclical Investment." *Quarterly Journal of Economics* 98 (1): 85–106.
Black, Fischer. 1987. *Business Cycles and Equilibrium.* Basil Blackwell.
Blanchard, Olivier, Giovanni Dell'Ariccia, and Paolo Mauro 2010a. "Rethinking Macroeconomic Policy." IMF Staff Position Note. SPN/10/03. IMF.
Blanchard, Olivier, Hamid Faruquee, and Mitali Das. 2010b. "The Initial Impact of the Crisis on Emerging Market Countries." Papers on Economic Activity, Brookings.
Bruno, Michael, and William. Easterly. 1998. "Inflation Crises and Long-Run Growth." *Journal of Monetary Economics* 41 (1): 3–26.
Brynjolfsson, Erik. 1993. "The Productivity Paradox of Information Technology." *Communications of the ACM* 36 (12): 66–77.
Brynjolfsson, Erik, Avinash Collis, and Felix Eggers. 2019. "Using Massive Online Choice Experiments to Measure Changes in Well-Being." *PNAS.* 116 (15): 7250–7255.
Cagan, P. 1956. "The Monetary Dynamics of Hyperinflation." In *Studies in the Quantity Theory of Money,* ed. Milton Friedman, 25–117. University of Chicago Press.
Caramazza, Francesco, and Jahangir Aziz. 1998. "Fixed or Flexible? Getting the Exchange Rate Right in the 1990s." *International Monetary Fund Economic Issues.* https://doi.org/10.5089/9781455220038.051.
Cespedes, Luis Felipe, Roberto Chang, and Andrés Velasco. 2004. "Balance Sheets and Exchange Rate Policy." *American Economic Review* 94 (4): 1183–1193.
Cirera, Xavier, and William F. Maloney. 2017. *The Innovation Paradox.* World Bank.
Coase, Ronald H. 1937. "The Nature of the Firm." *Economica* 4 (16): 386–405.
Coase, Ronald H. 1960. "The Problem of Social Cost." *Journal of Law and Economics* 3: 1–44.
Cochrane, John H. 2011. "Understanding Policy in the Great Recession: Some Unpleasant Fiscal Arithmetic." *European Economic Review* 55 (1): 2–30.
Collier, Paul, and Anke Hoeffler. 2005. "Resource Rents, Governance, and Conflict." *Journal of Conflict Resolution* 49 (4): 625–633.
Collier, Paul. 2009. *Wars, Guns, and Votes: Democracy in Dangerous Places.* Harper Collins.
Collis, Avinash. 2020. "Consumer Welfare in the Digital Economy." The Global Antitrust Institute Report on the Digital Economy 14. https://doi.org/10.2139/ssrn.3733700
Corden, W. M. 1984. "Booming Sector and Dutch Disease Economics: Survey and Consolidation." Oxford Economic Papers 36 (3): 359–380.
Coyle, Diane. 2014. *GDP: A Brief but Affectionate History.* Princeton University Press.
Cuberes, David, and Michał Jerzmanowski. 2009. "Democracy, Diversification and Growth Reversals." *Economic Journal* 119 (540): 1270–1302.
Cukierman, Alex, Sebastian Edwards, and Guido Tabellini. 1992. "Seigniorage and Political Instability." *American Economic Review* 82 (3): 537–555.
Cukierman, Alex, and Allan H. Meltzer. 1986. "A Theory of Ambiguity, Credibility, and Inflation under Discretion and Asymmetric Information." *Econometrica* 54 (5): 1099–1128.
Curdia, Vasco. 2007. "Monetary Policy under Sudden Stops." Federal Reserve Bank of New York Staff Reports No. 278. https://www.newyorkfed.org/medialibrary/media/research/staff_reports/sr278.pdf
De Rosa, Donato, Indermit S. Gill, Ivailo Izvorski, and Willem van Eeghen. 2014. *Diversified Development: Making the Most of Natural Resources in Eurasia.* World Bank.
Diamond, Jared. 1997. *Guns, Germs and Steel: The Fates of Human Societies.* Norton & Co.

Dieppe, Alistair. 2021. *Global Productivity: Trends, Drivers, and Policies.* World Bank.
Dollar, David. 1992. "Outward-oriented Developing Economies Really Do Grow More Rapidly: Evidence from 95 LDCs 1976–1985." *Economic Development and Cultural Change* 40 (3): 523–44.
Dotsey, Michael. 1994. "Some Unpleasant Supply Side Arithmetic." *Journal of Monetary Economics* 33 (3): 507–524.
Easterly, William. 2005. "National Policies and Economic Growth: A Reappraisal." In *Handbook of Economic Growth,* eds. Aghion, P. and S. Durlauf, 1013–1059. Elsevier.
Easterly, William. 2006. "Reliving the 1950s: The Big Push, Poverty Traps, and Takeoffs in Economic Development." *Journal of Economic Growth* 11: 289–318.
Easterly, William, Michael Kremer, Lant Pritchett, and Lawrence H. Summers. 1993. "Good Policy or Good Luck? Country Growth Performance and Temporary Shocks." *Journal of Monetary Economics* 32 (3): 459–483.
Easterly, William, and Ross Levine. 2001. "It's Not Factor Accumulation: Stylized Facts and Growth Models." *World Bank Economic Review* 15 (2): 177–219.
Easterly, William, and Ross Levine. 2003. "Tropics, Germs, and Crops: How Endowments Influence Economic Development." *Journal of Monetary Economics* 50 (1): 3–39.
Edwards, Sebastian. 1998. "Openness, Productivity and Growth: What Do We Really Know?" *Economic Journal* 108 (447): 383–398.
Eichengreen, Barry. 2008. "The Real Exchange Rate and Economic Growth." Commission on Growth and Development Working Paper No. 4. http://hdl.handle.net/10986/28013
Fatás, Antonio, and Ilian Mihov. 2003. "The Case for Restricting Fiscal Policy Discretion." *Quarterly Journal of Economics* 118 (4): 1419–1447.
Fatás, Antonio, and Ilian Mihov. 2013. "Policy Volatility, Institutions, and Economic Growth." *Review of Economics and Statistics* 95 (2): 362–376.
Fernandez, Raquel, and Dani Rodrik. 1991. "Resistance to Reform: Status Quo Bias in the Presence of Individual-Specific Uncertainty." *American Economic Review* 81 (5): 1146–1155.
Fioramonti, Lorenzo. 2019. "Beyond Gross Domestic Product: Measuring the Quality of Growth in Africa." in *The Quality of Growth in Africa,* eds. Ravi Kanbur, Akbar Noman, and Joseph E. Stiglitz, 33–53. Columbia University Press.
Fischer, Stanley. 1993. "The Role of Macroeconomic Factors in Growth." *Journal of Monetary Economics* 32 (3): 485–512.
Fischer, Stanley, Ratna Sahay, and Carlos Végh. 2002. "Modern Hyper- and High Inflations." *Journal of Economic Literature* 40 (3): 837–880.
Fountas, Stilianos, and Menelaos Karanasos. 2007. "Inflation, Output Growth, and Nominal and Real Uncertainty: Empirical Evidence for the G7." *Journal of International Money and Finance* 26 (2): 229–250.
Frankel, Jeffrey. A., and David H. Romer. 1999. "Does Trade Cause Growth?" *American Economic Review* 89 (3): 379–399.
Friedman, Milton. 1977. "Nobel Memorial Lecture: Inflation and Unemployment." *Journal of Political Economy* 85 (3): 451–472.
Gala, Paulo. 2007. "Real Exchange Rate Levels and Economic Development: Theoretical Analysis and Economic Evidence." *Cambridge Journal of Economics* 32 (2): 273–288.
Gale, William G., and Peter R. Orszag. 2002. "The Economic Effects of Long-term Fiscal Discipline." Urban-Brookings Tax Policy Centre. Discussion Paper. The Brookings Institution.
Gallup, John L., Jeffrey D. Sachs, and Andrew D. Mellinger. 1999. "Geography and Economic Development." NBER Working Paper Series 6849. National Bureau of Economic Research. https://www.nber.org/system/files/working_papers/w6849/w6849.pdf
Gatti, Roberta. 2004. "Explaining Corruption: Are Open Countries Less Corrupt?" *Journal of International Development* 16 (6): 851–861.
Gill, Indermit, Gobind Nankani, and Roberto Zagha. 2006. "Rethinking Growth." *Finance and Development* 43 (1): 7–11.
Glaeser, Edward L., Rafael La Porta, and Florencio Lopez-de Silanes, and Andrei Shileifer. 2004. "Do Institutions Cause Growth?" *Journal of Economic Growth* 9 (3): 271–303.

Gordon, Robert, J. 2012. "Is U.S. Economic Growth Over? Faltering Innovation Confronts The Six Headwinds." NBER Working Paper 18315. National Bureau of Economic Research.
Gosh, Atish R., Anne-Marie Gulde, and Holger C. Wolf. 2002. *Exchange Rate Regimes: Choices and Consequences*. MIT Press.
Grancay, Martin, Nora Grancay, and Tomas Dudas. 2015. "What You Export Matters: Does it Really?" *Contemporary Economics* 9 (2): 233–244.
Grossman, Gene M., and Elhanan Helpman. 1991. *Innovation and Growth in the Global Economy*. MIT Press.
Habib, Maurizio M., Elitza Mileva, and Livio Stracca. 2017. "The Real Exchange Rate and Economic Growth: Revisiting the Case Using External Instruments." *Journal of International Money and Finance* 73: 386–398.
Hall, Robert E., and Charles I. Jones. 1997. "Levels of Economic Activity Across Countries." *American Economic Review* 87 (2): 173–177.
Hall, Robert E., and Charles I. Jones. 1999. "Why Do Some Countries Produce So Much More Output?" *Quarterly Journal of Economics* 114 (1): 83–116.
Hanke, Steve, and Erik Bostrom. 2017. "Zimbabwe Hyperinflates Again: The 58th Episode of Hyperinflation in History." *Studies in Applied Economics* 90. The Johns Hopkins Institute for Applied Economics, Global Health, and the study of Business Enterprise.
Hausmann, Ricardo, Jason Hwang, and Dani Rodrik. 2007. "What You Export Matters." *Journal of Economic Growth* 12 (1): 1–25.
Hausmann, Ricardo, Lant Pritchett, and Dani Rodrik. 2005. "Growth Accelerations." *Journal of Economic Growth* 10 (4): 303–329.
Herndon, Thomas, Michael Ash, and Robert Pollin. 2013. "Does High Public Debt Consistently Stifle Economic Growth? A Critique of Reinhart and Rogoff." *Cambridge Journal of Economics* 38 (2): 257–279.
Hong, Gee Hee, Jaewoo Lee, Wei Liao, and Dulani Seneviratne. 2016. "China and Asia in Global Trade Slowdown." IMF Working Paper 2016/105. IMF.
Hosono, Akio. 2022. *SDGs, Transformation, and Quality Growth: Insight from International Cooperation*. Springer.
Hutchison, Michael M., Ilan Noy, and Lidan Wang. 2010. "Fiscal and Monetary Policies and the Cost of Sudden Stops." *Journal of International Money and Finance* 29 (6): 973–987.
Ibarra, Raul, and Danilo R. Trupkin. 2016. "Reexamining the Relationship Between Inflation and Growth: Do Institutions Matter in Developing Countries?" *Economic Modelling* 52: 332–351.
Ilzetzki, Ethan, Enrique G. Mendoza, and Carlos A. Végh. 2013. "How Big (Small?) Are Fiscal Multipliers?" *Journal of Monetary Economics* 60 (2): 239–254.
International Monetary Fund (IMF). 2008. "The Great Sub-Saharan African Growth Takeoff: Lessons and Prospects." Economic Outlook, fall edition.
International Monetary Fund (IMF). 2015a. "Now Is the Time: Fiscal Policies for Sustainable Growth." Fiscal Monitor April 2015. IMF.
International Monetary Fund (IMF). 2015b. *Fiscal Policy and Long-Term Growth*. IMF.
International Monetary Fund (IMF), World Bank, and World Trade Organization (WTO). 2017. "Making Trade an Engine of Growth for All: The Case for Trade and Policies to Facilitate Adjustment." Discussion Paper for the Meeting of the G20 Sherpas.
Jerzmanowski, Michał. 2006. "Empirics of Hills, Plateaus, Mountains and Plains: A Markov-Switching Approach to Growth." *Journal of Development Economics* 81 (2): 357–385.
Johnson, Robert. C. 2014. "Five Facts about Value-Added Exports and Implications for Macroeconomics and Trade Research." *Journal of Economic Perspectives* 28 (2): 119–142.
Johnson, Simon, Jonathan D. Ostry, and Arvind Subramanian. 2007. "The Prospects of Sustained Growth in Africa: Benchmarking the Constraints." IMF Working Paper WP/07/52. International Monetary Fund.
Jones Benjamin F., and Benjamin A. Olken 2008. "The Anatomy of Start-Stop Growth." *Quarterly Journal of Economics* 90 (3): 582–587.
Jorgenson, Dale W., and Zvi Griliches. 1967. "The Explanation of Productivity Change." *Review of Economic Studies* 34 (3): 249–283.

Judson, Ruth, and Athanasios Orphanides. 1999. "Inflation, Volatility and Growth." *International Finance* 2 (1): 117–138.

Kanbur, Ravi, Akbar Noman, and Joseph E. Stiglitz (eds.). 2019. *The Quality of Growth in Africa.* Columbia University Press.

Kaufmann, Daniel, Aart Kraay and Massimo Mastruzzi.2003. "Governance Matters III: Governance Indicators for 1996–2002." Policy Research Working Paper 3106. World Bank.

Kerekes, Monika. 2012. "Growth Miracles and Failures in a Markov Switching Classification Model of Growth." *Journal of Development Economics* 98 (2): 167–177.

Knack, Stephan, and Phillip Keefer 1995. "Institutions and Economic Performance: Cross-Country Tests Using Alternative Institutional Measures." *Economics and Politics* 7 (3): 207–227.

Krause, Michael U., and Stéphane Moyen. 2016. "Public Debt and Changing Inflation Targets." *American Economic Journal: Macroeconomics* 8 (4): 142–176.

Krugman, Paul. 1987. "The Narrow Moving Band, the Dutch disease, and the Competitive Consequences of Mrs. Thatcher: Notes on Trade in the Presence of Dynamic Scale Economies." *Journal of Development Economics* 27 (1): 41–55.

Krugman, Paul. 1994. "The Myth of Asia's Miracle." *Foreign Affairs* 73 (6): 62–78.

Kumar, Manmohan S., and Jaejoon Woo. 2010. "Public Debt and Growth." IMF Working Paper WP/10/174. International Monetary Fund.

Kydland, Finn E., and Edward C. Prescott. 1977. "Rules Rather than Discretion: The Inconsistency of Optimal Plans." *Journal of Political Economy* 85 (3): 473–491.

La Porta, Rafael, Florencio Lopez-de-Silanes, Andrei Shleifer, and Robert Vishny. 1999. "The Quality of Government." *Journal of Law, Economics and Organization* 15 (1): 222–279.

La Porta, Rafael, Florencio Lopez-de-Silanes, Cristian Pop-Eleches, and Andrei Shleifer. 2004. "Judicial Checks and Balances." *Journal of Political Economy* 112 (2): 445–470.

Leamer, Edward E. 1988. "Measures of Openness." In *Trade Policy and Empirical Analysis,* ed. R. Baldwin, 145–204. University of Chicago Press.

Levy-Yeyati, Eduardo, and Federico Sturzenegger. 2003. "To Float or to Fix: Evidence on the Impact of Exchange Rate Regimes on Growth." *American Economic Review* 93 (4): 1173–1193.

Lucas, Robert E. Jr. 1988. "On the Mechanics of Economic Development." *Journal of Monetary Economics* 22 (1): 3–42.

Martinez, Marcelo, and Montfort Mlachila. 2013. "The Quality of the Recent High-Growth Episode in Sub-Saharan Africa." IMF Working Paper WP/13/53. International Monetary Fund.

Matsuyama, Kiminori. 1992. "Agricultural Productivity, Comparative Advantage, and Economic Growth." *Journal of Economic Theory* 58 (2): 317–334.

Mauro, Paolo. 1998. "Corruption and the Composition of Government Expenditure." *Journal of Public Economics* 69 (2): 263–279.

Mayer, Eric, Sebastian Rüth, and Johann Scharler. 2013. "Government Debt, Inflation Dynamics and the Transmission of Fiscal Policy Shocks." *Economic Modelling* 33: 762–771.

McArthur, John W., and Jeffrey D. Sachs. 2001. "Institutions and Geography: Comment on Acemoglu, Johnson and Robinson (2000)." Working Paper 81. National Bureau of Economic Research.

Menard, Claude, and Mary M. Shirley. 2005. "Introduction." In *Handbook of New Institutional Economics,* eds. Claude Menard and Mary M. Shirley, 1–20. Springer.

Menard, Claude, and Mary M. Shirley. 2012. "The Future of New Institutional Economics: From Early Intuitions to a New Paradigm?" *Journal of Institutional Economics* 10 (4): 541–565.

Ministry of Internal Affairs and Communications, Japan. 2019. *White Paper on Information and Communications 2019.*

Mirman, Leonard J. 1971. "Uncertainty and Optimal Consumption Decisions." *Econometrica* 39 (1): 179–185.

Nordhaus, William D. 2004. "Schumpeterian Profits in the American Economy: Theory and Measurement." NBER Working Paper 10433. National Bureau of Economic Research.

North, Douglass C. 1981. *Structure and Change in Economic History.* W.W. Norton & Company.

North, Douglass C. 1990. *Institutions, Institutional Change, and Economic Performance*. Cambridge University Press.
North, Douglass C. 1994. "Economic Performance through Time." *American Economic Review* 84 (3): 359–368.
North, Douglass C. 2005. "Institutions and the Performance of Economies over Time." In *Handbook of New Institutional Economics*, eds. Claude Ménard and Mary M. Shirley, 21–30. Springer.
Nunn, Nathan. 2007. "Historical Legacies: A Model Linking Africa's Past to its Current Underdevelopment." *Journal of Development Economics* 83 (1): 157–175.
Nunn, Nathan. 2009. "The Importance of History in Economic Development." *Annual Review of Economics* 1 (1): 65–92.
Persson, Torsten, and Guido Tabellini. 2003. *The Economic Effects of Constitutions: What Do the Data Say?* MIT Press.
Persson, Torsten, and Guido Tabellini. 2004. "Constitutional Rules and Fiscal Policy Outcomes." *American Economic Review* 94 (1): 25–45.
Pescatori, Andrea, Damiano Sandri, and John Simon. 2014. "Debt and Growth: Is There a Magic Threshold?" IMF Working Paper No. 14/34. International Monetary Fund.
Pindyck, Robert S. 1991. "Irreversibility, Uncertainty, and Investment." *Journal of Economic Literature* 29 (3): 1110–1148.
Pritchett, Lant. 2000. "Understanding Patterns of Economic Growth: Searching for Hills among Plateaus, Mountains, and Plains." *World Bank Economic Review* 14 (2): 221–250.
Ramey, Garey, and Valerie A. Ramey. 1991. "Technology Commitment and the Cost of Economic Fluctuations." NBER Working Paper No. 3755. National Bureau of Economic Research.
Ramey, Garey, and Valerie A. Ramey. 1995. "Cross-Country Evidence on the Link between Volatility and Growth." *American Economic Review* 85 (5): 1138–1151.
Reinhart, Carmen M., and Kenneth S. Rogoff. 2010. "Growth in a Time of Debt." *American Economic Review: Papers & Proceedings* 100 (2): 573–578.
Reinhart, Carmen M., Vincent R. Reinhart, and Kenneth S. Rogoff. 2012. "Public Debt Overhangs: Advanced-Economy Episodes Since 1800." *Journal of Economic Perspectives* 26 (3): 69–86.
Rodríguez, Francisco, and Dani Rodrik. 2001. "Trade Policy and Economic Growth: The Skeptic's Guide to the Cross-National Evidence." *University of Chicago Annual* 15: 261–338.
Rodrik, Dani. 2008. "The Real Exchange Rate and Economic Growth." *Brookings Papers on Economic Activity* 2008 (2): 365–412.
Rodrik, Dani, Arvind Subramanian, and Francesco Trebbi. 2004. "Institutions Rule: The Primacy of Institutions over Geography and Integration in Economic Development." *Journal of Economic Growth* 9 (2): 131–165.
Rogoff, Kenneth S. 2008. "Inflation is Now the Lesser Evil." Project Syndicate. December. http://www.project-syndicate.org/commentary/rogoff51/English
Romer, David. 1993. "Openness and Inflation: Theory and Evidence." *Quarterly Journal of Economics* 108 (4): 869–903.
Romer, Paul M. 1986. "Increasing Returns and Long-Run Growth." *Journal of Political Economy* 94 (5): 1002–1037.
Romer, Paul M. 1990. "Endogenous Technological Change." *Journal of Political Economy* 98 (5): S71–S102.
Rutherford, Thomas F., and David G. Tarr. 2002. "Trade Liberalization, Product Variety and Growth in a Small Open Economy: A Quantitative Assessment." *Journal of International Economics* 56 (2): 247–272.
Sachs, Jeffrey D. 2003. "Institutions Don't Rule: Direct Effects of Geography on Per Capita Income." NBER Working Paper 9490. National Bureau of Economic Research.
Sachs, Jeffrey D., and Andrew Warner. 1995. "Economic Reform and the Process of Global Integration." *Brookings Papers on Economics* 1995 (1): 1–118.
Sachs, Jeffrey D., and Andrew Warner. 1997. "Sources of Slow Growth in African Economies." *Journal of African Economies* 6 (3): 335–376.
Saito, Makoto. 1999. *Atarashii macro keizaigaku* [New Macroeconomics]. Yuhikaku.

Schumpeter, Joseph A. 1926. *Theorie der Wirtschaftlichen Entwicklung* [Theory of Economic Development]. Translated in Japanese by Yuichi Shionoya, Ichiro Nakayama, and Seiichi Higashihata, 1977. Iwanami Bunko.

Shambaugh, Jay, Ryan Nunn, Patrick Liu, and Greg Nantz. 2017. "Thirteen Facts about Wage Growth." The Hamilton Project. Brookings.

Smith, Adam. 1776 [1976]. *An Inquiry into the Nature and Causes of the Wealth of Nations*, ed. E. Canaan. University of Chicago Press.

Sokoloff, Kenneth L., and Stanley L. Engerman. 2000. "Institutions, Factor Endowments, and Paths of Development in the New World." *Journal of Economic Perspectives* 14 (3): 217–232.

Solow, Robert M. 1957. "Technical Change and the Aggregate Production Function." *Review of Economics and Statistics* 39: 312–320.

Solow, Robert M. 2000. *Growth* Theory*: An Exposition,* Second Edition. Oxford University Press.

Stiglitz, Joseph E.1998. "The Private Uses of Public Interest: Incentives and Institutions." *Journal of Economic Perspectives* 12 (2): 3–22.

Stiglitz, Joseph E., and Bruce C. Greenwald. 2015. *Creating A Learning* Society. Columbia University Press.

Sudo, Tokihito. 2018. "Innovation wa keizai wo seichō saserunoka" [Does Innovation Grow the Economy?]. *Securities Review* 58 (10): 94–113.

Summers, Lawrence H. 2016. "The Age of Secular Stagnation." *Foreign Affairs,* March/April 2016.

Taylor, Alan M. 1998. "On the Costs of Inward-Looking Development: Price Distortions, Growth and Divergence in Latin America." *Journal of Economic History* 58 (1): 1–28.

Taylor, John B. 1983. "Comments on 'Rules, Discretion and Reputation in a Model of Monetary Policy' by Robert J. Barro and David B. Gordon." *Journal of Monetary Economics* 12 (1): 123–125.

Todo, Yasuyuki. 2008. *Gijyutsu denpan to keizai seichō* [Technological Transmission and Economic Growth]. Keiso Shobo.

Tsangarides, Charalambos G. 2012. "Crisis and Recovery: Role of the Exchange Rate Regime in Emerging Market Economies." *Journal of Macroeconomics* 34 (2): 470–488.

Wacziarg, Romain. 2001. "Measuring the Dynamic Gains from Trade." *World Bank Economic Review* 15 (3): 393–429.

Wang, Zhi., Shang-Jin Wei, and Anna Wong. 2010. "Does a Leapfrogging Growth Strategy Raise the Growth Rate? Some International Evidence." ADB Working Paper Series on Regional Economic Integration No. 59. Asian Development Bank.

Wei, Shang-Jin. 2000. "Natural Openness and Good Government." NBER Working Paper 7765. National Bureau of Economic Research.

Williamson, J. 2004. "The Washington Consensus as a Policy Prescription for Development." Institute for International Economics. Unpublished manuscript.

Williamson, Oliver E. 1973. "Markets and Hierarchies: Some Elementary Considerations." *American Economic Review* 63 (2): 316–325.

Williamson, Oliver E. 2010. "Transaction Cost Economics: The Natural Progression." *American Economic Review* 100: 673–690.

Wolf, Holger, C. 1993. "Trade Orientation: Measurement and Consequences." *Estudios de Economía.* University of Chile, Department of Economics 20: 49–86.

Woo, J. 2009. "Why Do More Polarized Countries Run More Procyclical Fiscal Policies?" *Review of Economics and Statistics* 91 (4): 850–870.

World Bank. 1987. *World Development Report 1987*. Oxford University Press.

World Bank. 1993. *The East Asian* Miracle*: Economic Growth and Public Policy.* Oxford University Press.

Yeager, Timothy J. 1999. *Institutions, Transition Economies, and Economic Development*. Westview Press.

Young, Alwyn. 1991. "Learning by Doing and the Dynamic Effects of International Trade." *Quarterly Journal of Economics* 106 (2): 369–405.

**Koki Hirota** earned his B.A. in Economics from the University of Tokyo and holds a Ph.D. in Economics from Saitama University in Japan. His professional career spans several prominent roles in international development finance and policy, including Chief Economist, Director General of Operation and Strategy Department, and Director General of Southeast Asia and Pacific Department at the Japan International Cooperation Agency (JICA), and Chief Representative in Jakarta for Japan Bank for International Cooperation and in Hanoi for the Overseas Economic Cooperation Fund. In academia, he was a Professor at the Graduate School of Humanities and Social Sciences at Saitama University and a Visiting Fellow at the JICA Ogata Sadako Research Institute for Peace and Development. His recent publications include *Challenges in Fiscal and Monetary Policies in Mongolia* (co-edited, Springer, 2023) and *Addressing Social Infrastructure Needs in Asia: Towards a Pandemic Resilient Society* (co-edited, JICA, August 2025).

**Keiko Kubota** is a professor of Economics at Tohoku Gakuin University in Japan. Prior to the current post, she worked as an economist for the World Bank, with assignments in Madagascar, Vietnam, Indonesia, Cameroon as well as Washington, D.C. She also served as a Deputy Director for the G20 Presidency Secretariat in the Ministry of Finance, Japan and as an Economic Advisor for the Credit Risk Assessment Division of the Japan International Cooperation Agency. She has a Ph.D. in economics from Columbia University, New York. Her areas of research interest include international trade and climate change.

# 7 Quality Growth and Quality Infrastructure Investment

Koki Hirota

This chapter focuses on policies for infrastructure development, considered one of the "three endowments" for the transformation of the economy, as introduced in the previous chapter. Here, I not only show how infrastructure contributes to growth but also discuss how it can serve as an example of policies that help to realize quality growth. The Japanese government began using the term "quality infrastructure investment" (QII) more frequently in the mid-2010s, around the same time that the DCC was issued. While it uses the same term—quality—there are questions about whether the objective of QII is the same as that pursued by quality growth, an issue explored in detail in this chapter. Following a review of the relationship between infrastructure and growth in Sect. 7.1, I will touch on the definition of QII along with its background in Sect. 7.2, the productivity of infrastructure as an endowment to growth in Sect. 7.3 and discuss why QII is considered an example of policies to promote quality growth in Sect. 7.4.

## 7.1 Infrastructure Investment and Growth

Infrastructure is an investment in itself, so spending on infrastructure increases GDP. In addition, it contributes to growth by boosting the production activities of companies. Many infrastructure investments made by governments, such as national roads and river embankments, do not charge fees, and therefore, only the costs are recorded in GDP. However, there are significant social benefits from infrastructure, even though they are not included in the total GDP figures. Infrastructure not only increases production in the short term but also increases

K. Hirota (✉)
Tokyo, Japan


K. Hirota (ed.), *Introduction to Quality Growth*,
https://doi.org/10.1007/978-981-95-6220-6_7

productivity and facilitates innovation by encouraging the accumulation of investment, ideally leading to medium- to long-term growth. Infrastructure is generally considered a public good with positive externalities, and therefore, its promotion benefits society by compensating for market failures. However, the question of how much of the limited resources should be allocated to infrastructure is difficult. For example, fiscal spending for infrastructure investment may lower growth if it leads to tax increases, additional borrowing or crowding out of manufacturing investment later.[1] Furthermore, regarding the rate of return on infrastructure investment, accumulated investment includes opposing effects: the network effect (increasing yield) and diminishing marginal returns. The relative magnitude of each effect will depend on the country's circumstances at the time.

There are both micro and macro methods for identifying the contribution of infrastructure to the economy. The former calculates the benefits of individual projects to society and is generally undertaken using cost–benefit analysis (CBA). However, the results of these analyses do not usually incorporate their contribution to the growth of the country as a whole. In addition, CBA cannot capture social transformation over the medium- and long-term, including spillover effects of infrastructure on a country or region. Therefore, the contribution to growth is usually studied through macro analysis.

Before providing an overview of the macro approach, it should be noted that there are difficulties in discussing the contribution of infrastructure to growth in general terms, as geography, population size and density, and stage of development vary greatly from country to country. For example, there must be a considerable difference in the size of infrastructure investment to GDP considered appropriate between South Korea, with its relatively compact and easily connected landmass, and Indonesia, which comprises approximately 15,000 islands. Looking elsewhere, a country like Japan faces significantly higher disaster risks compared to countries in Europe, so infrastructure spending for disaster management will necessarily be higher. Despite such constraints, numerous studies have been conducted on the role of infrastructure in economic growth.

Estimation methods for measuring the relationship between infrastructure and growth are mostly based on econometric analysis. In these analyses, the variables used to estimate the relationship between the two are public investment (the amount of annual flows, capital stock expressed in monetary terms), physical stock of infrastructure and others (such as access to infrastructure) as representing infrastructure, and output, income, growth rate and employment as representing growth (Fig. 7.1).

[1] For example, Huntley (2021) estimates the impact of the Biden administration's USD 2 trillion infrastructure investment program on US economic growth. This investment will increase the public capital stock by 4.6% in 2040, thereby increasing the productivity of private capital. On the other hand, the government would have to increase borrowing by 5.1% to finance this major investment, resulting in crowding out and a 0.8% decrease in private capital. Due to these offsets, Huntley estimates that the overall effect of the USD 2 trillion investment on GDP in 2040 will be roughly zero.

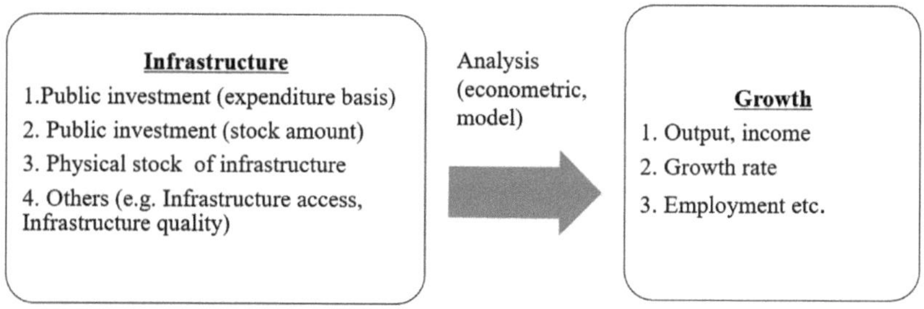


**Fig. 7.1** Indicators used in studies on the effect of infrastructure on growth. *Source* Author

The most direct and cross-sectoral indicator for infrastructure is the expenditure on infrastructure itself, but it can be difficult to capture the total amount in the current GDP system. For example, infrastructure spending is broken down into several items in GDP statistics, and maintenance expenditures that do not create additional value in the economy are not included in GDP. Due to these limitations, many studies use (1) public investment expenditures, (2) public investment stock in monetary terms, and (3) the physical stock of infrastructure (e.g., total road length or total electricity generation). Each of these has its own pros and cons.[2] Timilsina et al. (2020) note that other research employs infrastructure quality as a variable for infrastructure to estimate the relationship with growth. For example, the waiting time for telephone installation, transmission and distribution losses, and the pavement rate of roads can be used as variables.

Econometric analysis seeks to correlate infrastructure and growth based on historical data. Timilsina et al. (2020) note that early studies used public investment flows as explanatory variables. However, these studies faced problems of spurious correlation, endogeneity and reverse causality between the explanatory and

[2] First, the public investment expenditures have the advantage of capturing records for analysis. However, this approach contains several problems. Arslanalp et al. (2010) points out its endogeneity with growth, and impacts of budget constraints. Timilsina et al. (2020) note that public investment includes non-infrastructure, that there is no distinction between new and maintenance expenditure, that the appearance of investment results varies from sector to sector, and that quality and quantity cannot be distinguished. The second concern is public investment stock in monetary terms, which, in addition to containing the same problems as the first, is significantly affected by depreciation. For example, Arslanalp et al. (2010), stating that the larger the public capital stock, the greater its burden for the economy, notes that in non-OECD countries, where the ratio of public capital stock to GDP is less than 30 %, depreciation is 1% of GDP, whereas it is 2% of GDP in OECD countries where the stock amounts to 70% of GDP. Third, infrastructure stock is the quantity of facilities measured in physical terms. Canning (1999) analyses the relationship with growth using the number of telephone lines, electricity generation, and road and rail extensions. As production activities are based on infrastructure stocks rather than the flow of funds, this approach is more consistent and, in fact, many studies use infrastructure stocks for estimating future demand for infrastructure. However, there are some limitations, such as the pros and cons of using only one variable to proxy the stock or the difficulty of reflecting the quality of infrastructure in an analysis.

response variables. Spurious correlation is due to a common trend in infrastructure and public investment historical data over time. The reverse causality is the question of whether infrastructure development promotes growth or whether growth leads to infrastructure development. Therefore, to avoid these issues, analytical methods used for the estimate include panel data analysis and the instrumental variable method, and the vector autoregression model. Analyses using macroeconomic models such as computable general equilibrium models have also been conducted.

Empirical analysis of the relationship between infrastructure and growth does not necessarily lead to a consensus. However, a number of previous studies have shown that at least infrastructure stock is positively correlated with growth.[3] The following are some key insights from the comprehensive review conducted by Timilsina et al. (2020) on the relationship between infrastructure and growth:

- A study on North America conducted in the 1990s found a positive correlation. However, it included the problems of spurious correlation, endogeneity and reverse causality.
- The meta-analysis by Elburz et al. (2017) concludes that (1) there is no positive correlation between infrastructure and growth in the US, (2) the results of studies differ depending on the method, and (3) a negative correlation is found for public investment across regions.
- Several studies suggest that the stage of economic development influences whether infrastructure promotes growth or not. In developed countries, infrastructure is not a constraint on growth, while infrastructure and growth are more positively correlated in countries where infrastructure is currently insufficient. The results of studies on developing countries are mixed, showing both positive and non-positive correlations—i.e., negative, no relationship, and no long-term effects, among other findings.

According to Li (2010), who compiled previous related studies on Japan, the effect of infrastructure on productive capacity has generally been positive in Japan. However, she also noted that the effect differs from period to period, with a strong effect during the high-growth period and a declining trend since the 1970s. There are empirical studies showing that the relationship between infrastructure and growth is not necessarily stable elsewhere. For example, Shi et al. (2017) find that the correlation between infrastructure stock and growth in China varied across periods and regions, with the negative impact of road construction being particularly significant in lagging regions. They then point out that the results support the view that when infrastructure investment becomes too dominant, it can lead to the

[3] For example, a review by Romp and de Haan (2005) finds that there is more consensus than before that public investment stimulates growth. The review by Timilsina et al. (2020) reports that most studies on the physical stock of infrastructure and growth show a positive relationship, although studies on developed countries indicate that there is no consensus on the relationship between public investment and growth.

crowding out of private capital. It can also result in an inverse U-shaped relationship between infrastructure investment and growth—i.e., infrastructure investment initially stimulates growth, but once a threshold is crossed, the growth effect turns negative. Fernald (1999) observes that the impact of road investment on productivity growth in the US varies across industries. For example, in the 1950s and 1960s, road investment increased productivity, particularly in the automotive sector; however, this effect was a one-off, given the decline in productivity that occurred in the 1970s.

Research on the correlation between infrastructure quality and growth remains rather limited. For example, in a study on sub-Saharan Africa, Calderón and Servén (2010), based on panel data from 1960 to 2005 for 136 countries, found that both the quantity and quality of infrastructure—represented by the telecommunications, electricity, and road sectors—are positively correlated with long-term growth. Kodongo and Ojah (2016) argued that improvements in infrastructure quality in 45 sub-Saharan African countries—encompassing these three sectors plus water and sanitation—affect growth indirectly through the channels of export diversification and cross-border capital flows. Timilsina et al. (2020) summarized research in this field, noting that the results of previous studies have not reached clear conclusions. Furthermore, they point out that the quality indicators used in these studies, such as transmission and distribution losses, waiting times for installing telephone lines, and so on, are problematic, as they are not necessarily appropriate indicators to represent infrastructure quality. Regarding infrastructure quality and quantity—for example, roads—both total length (quantity) and road specifications, paving rates, and road surface conditions (quality) affect the time required for people's travel and the transport of goods. Therefore, when examining the correlation between infrastructure and growth, it is preferable to integrate both quality and quantity aspects. Similarly, in the estimation of future infrastructure demand, introduced in the next section, recent studies have begun incorporating quality elements alongside infrastructure stock, with infrastructure quality indicators derived from the Global Competitiveness Index (GCI). Going forward, as analytical methods that incorporate infrastructure quality and data related to infrastructure quality are developed, empirical analysis in this field is expected to advance further.

As mentioned above, while infrastructure is generally considered to contribute to growth, some studies have proposed different results. However, there are also differences between countries in terms of the profitability of infrastructure. I believe that, in addition to the differences in the initial conditions in each country—and the resulting balance with investment in direct productive activities—specific outcomes are also shaped by the effectiveness and efficiency of public investment. These include factors such as government capacity and the public investment system. While the discussion so far has looked at the relationship between infrastructure and growth as expressed in terms of GDP, it is also important to consider benefits that are not measured by GDP. I consider the policy proposal of QII to be an approach that must include these aspects.

## 7.2 What is Quality Infrastructure Investment?

QII, as advocated by the Government of Japan from the mid-2010s, cannot be defined in a few simple words, and the background and thinking behind it have not always been clearly defined. Consequently, some experts have developed their own perspectives—even in international discussions.

The Government of Japan released the case study of QII.[4] The report explains the concept of QII and its specific elements and presents individual case studies demonstrating its application. Subsequently, the G7 Ise-Shima Principles for Promoting Quality Infrastructure Investment were adopted at the G7 Summit in 2016, as shown in the BOX below and the Group of Twenty (G20) Osaka Summit in 2019 endorsed the G20 Principles for Quality Infrastructure Investment.[5]

**BOX 7A: G7 Ise-Shima Principles for Promoting Quality Infrastructure Investment**

Reaffirming the crucial importance for stakeholders to work coherently to bridge the existing global demand–supply gap of infrastructure investment by promoting quality infrastructure investment so as to promote strong, sustainable and balanced growth and to enhance resilience in our society, as well as to contribute to the global efforts for the SDGs, we strive to align our own infrastructure investment with the following principles. We further encourage the relevant stakeholders, namely governments, international organizations, including multilateral development banks (MDBs), and the private sector, such as in PPP projects to align their infrastructure investment and assistance with these principles, including the introduction and promotion of a transparent, competitive procurement process that takes full account of value for money and quality of infrastructure.

Principle 1: Ensuring effective governance, reliable operation and economic efficiency in view of life-cycle cost as well as safety and resilience against natural disaster, terrorism and cyber-attack risks

Quality infrastructure investment should ensure effective governance, economic efficiency, sustainability and reliable operation during the life span of a project as well as safety and resilience against natural disaster, terrorism and cyber-attack risks.

Principle 2: Ensuring job creation, capacity building and transfer of expertise and know-how for local communities

[4] Ministry of Foreign Affairs, International Cooperation Bureau (ed.). n.d."shitsu no takai infura toushi jirei shu" [Case Studies of Quality Infrastructure Investment] https://www.mofa.go.jp/mofaj/gaiko/oda/files/000083884.pdf. Accessed Oct. 28, 2025.

[5] The G20 documents comprise six principles, each of which is described in more detail than the G7 declaration: (1) Maximizing the positive impact of infrastructure to achieve sustainable growth and development; (2) Raising economic efficiency in view of life-cycle costs; (3) Integrating environmental considerations in infrastructure investments; (4) Building resilience against natural disasters and other risks; (5) Integrating social considerations in infrastructure investment; (6) Strengthening infrastructure governance. In comparison with the principles agreed by the G7, the basic content was retained but its organization is somewhat different and more comprehensive. It can be said to describe the role of infrastructure investment in a more comprehensive manner. For example, Principle (1) emphasizes that infrastructure investment is necessary for sustainable growth while also referring to the SDGs, thereby articulating more clearly that QII is a policy approach to realizing quality growth. In this paper, I refer to the G7 principles to introduce the background to the first appearance of the idea of QII with the basic elements, but it is the agreed principles of the G20 that are currently referred to for international discussions.

Quality infrastructure investment should seek to contribute to job creation for local work forces and to transfer of expertise and know-how to local communities.

Principle 3: Addressing social and environmental impacts

Quality infrastructure investment must consider the social and environmental impacts of infrastructure projects and duly address such impacts including by applying social and environmental safeguards that are in line with international best practices as reflected in the most relevant standards including those of existing MDBs.

Principle 4: Ensuring alignment with economic and development strategies including aspect of climate change and environment at the national and regional levels

Quality infrastructure investment should be aligned with economic and development strategies at the national and regional levels, through dialogues with stakeholders from the project preparation and prioritization phases. Relevant elements of economic and development strategies to be considered include the development of a global supply chain through enhanced connectivity; use of latest technology such as information and communication technology; promotion of private investment and attraction of new industries; medium and long-term plans based on a long-term and cross-sector demand forecast and other relevant information; and debt sustainability and fiscal outlook. Climate change resilience, energy security and sustainability, conservation of biodiversity, disaster risk reduction should be considered including through further promotion of ecosystem-based approaches and green infrastructure.

Principle 5: Enhancing effective resourcemobilization including through PPP

Quality infrastructure investment should effectively mobilize resources including from the private sector through PPP and other forms of innovative financing, including through MDBs. To this end, joint efforts among stakeholders including host country governments to strengthen the enabling investment environment at national and sub-national government levels, as well as to enhance due process and transparency are essential.

https://www.mofa.go.jp/mofaj/gaiko/oda/files/000160272.pdf

### 7.2.1 What Does the Term "Quality" Mean?

What does quality infrastructure actually mean? Most people would answer this question by saying that it refers to the physical condition of the facilities or the level of services available. For example, road surfaces are paved, smooth, and easy to drive on; potable water is readily available with no risk of supply outages; and trains run regularly, ensuring that people can travel comfortably and conveniently. In the studies on infrastructure and growth introduced in the previous section, the term "quality" was used in this sense. This perspective is, in fact, employed in an international context to determine how infrastructure quality can be evaluated. The WEF publishes an annual Global Competitiveness Report that compares the competitiveness of nations' economies, and infrastructure is one of the key components of its competitiveness indicators. Consequently, the composition of infrastructure indicators includes "quality" as a subcategory. For example, for roads, quality is assessed by average speed and straightness (for ease of driving), as well as by width and condition. These are, of course, important because they represent the

**Table 7.1** Two perspectives on infrastructure quality

| Category | Demand-side perspective | Supply-side perspective |
|---|---|---|
| Whose view of quality | User's | Supplier's/operator's |
| What qualities to target | Facilities and services | Investment |
| Assessment criteria | User satisfaction | Socioeconomic contribution |

*Source* Author

viewpoints of those who use the infrastructure. However, when looking at the elements of QII in the G7 and G20 declarations, most do not relate to the condition of the facilities or the level of services provided.

Discussions of infrastructure quality incorporate two perspectives: quality from the user's perspective and quality from the supplier's perspective. I propose that QII is primarily based on the context of the latter perspective, as it tends to refer to the quality of investment in infrastructure rather than to the infrastructure facilities themselves. This view is summarized in Table 7.1.

For example, the G7 declaration on QII states that investment in infrastructure should contribute to the creation of local jobs and the transfer of expertise and knowledge, and the G20 declaration more clearly states that it should further stimulate economic growth in the country concerned. These are not from the perspective of infrastructure users. QII is about investment activities and is primarily viewed as a principle for increasing the contribution of infrastructure to the national economy. In other words, the items listed as elements of QII are those that have an impact on the quality of investment. Being an investment, the most important criterion is, of course, profitability. High investment effectiveness means that, on the micro level, the project selected can achieve a higher rate of return, and on the macro level, it is a question of how the country as a whole can significantly contribute to growth through infrastructure development. This aspect of accelerating growth is consistent with sustaining high growth, which is one factor of quality growth discussed so far. At the same time, as infrastructure is a public good, it is also important to determine how much it improves people's lives and welfare.

### 7.2.2 Background to the Development of Quality Infrastructure Investment

For many years, infrastructure has been a key theme in economic development, which raises the question of why the concept of QII has only gained such prominence in recent years. The background to this lies in the changing international landscape. Two basic factors have caused infrastructure development to evolve and have given rise to the concept of QII: (1) the accelerating growth of emerging economies since 2000 has led to a global surge in demand for infrastructure funding, and (2) development issues have become more complex as economies have advanced.

#### 7.2.2.1 Growing Demand for Infrastructure Funding

As introduced in Chap. 1, since 2000, growth in emerging and developing countries has significantly outpaced that of developed countries. Needless to say, infrastructure development in emerging and developing countries has lagged behind developed countries, so the acceleration of economic growth in these countries has created greater demand for new infrastructure construction. In the face of these changes, current levels of infrastructure spending do not meet the growing demand. Estimates of global demand for infrastructure funding have only been made since around 2000, and the multiple regression model developed by Fay and Yepes (2003) remains the standard used in infrastructure demand estimation today. According to this model, rising income levels, as well as increasing industrialization and urbanization, will boost demand for infrastructure. Therefore, as economic development progresses in emerging and developing countries, with higher income levels and social transformation, infrastructure demand will grow at an accelerated rate.

Many of these forecasts have been made by international organizations and private think tanks. Estimates vary depending on the time period and the methodology used.[6] Regional demand estimates have also been made for Asia, Africa and Latin America. For example, ADB (2017) estimated demand at USD 1.5 trillion per year (USD 1.7 trillion if climate change responses are included) from 2016 to 2030. This is more than double the USD 750 billion per year forecast by the previous estimate from ADB and ADBI (2009).[7] Various estimates have been made, and the scale tends to expand with each passing year, even as actual infrastructure spending has not been able to match demand.[8]

Furthermore, we need to take into account that current estimates may underestimate future demand for three reasons. Firstly, many estimates cover four sectors of economic infrastructure—electricity, transport, communications and water—and

---

[6] Some examples of forecast estimates are as follows:

① Bhattacharya et al. (2012): USD 1.6 to 2.0 trillion per year or USD 1.8 to 2.3 trillion per year with climate change response in 2020 (2008 prices, excluding operations and maintenance).
② MGI (2013): USD 3.2 trillion per year (2013 to 2030 average, 2010 prices).
③ MGI (2016): USD 3.3 trillion per year (2016 to 2030 average, 2015 prices).
④ Oxford Economics (2017): USD 3.7 trillion (2016 to 2040 average, 2015 prices, excluding maintenance costs but including replacement costs).

[7] ADB and ADBI (2009) estimates are for 32 countries, while ADB (2017) covers 45 countries.

[8] ADB (2017) estimates that for 25 major Asian countries, assuming current spending levels, the infrastructure financing gap is 2.4% of GDP, or 5% when excluding China, which has a high proportion of infrastructure spending in GDP.

therefore do not include other infrastructure, although significant demand exists for infrastructure outside these four sectors. According to the Cabinet Office (2022), more than 40% of the net stock of public social capital is in areas other than the above four. For example, the capital stock of disaster prevention accounts for 14.3% of the total, while educational facilities, agriculture, forestry and fisheries also account for around 5 to 10%. Social infrastructure, such as education and health, is not usually included in global discussions on infrastructure estimates, but its size is significant.[9] As development accelerates in emerging and developing countries, the role of human capital in sustaining growth becomes increasingly important, which will drive further spending on social infrastructure.

Moreover, most of these demand estimates do not account for the condition of the facilities. For example, for roads, the condition of road surfaces and ancillary facilities generally differs significantly between developed and developing countries, but demand forecasts treat roads uniformly as stock and do not take differences in road quality into account. Therefore, if, in the process of growing, developing countries improve the quality of their infrastructure facilities to the level of developed countries, the demand for funds would be even greater. In recent years, demand estimates incorporating infrastructure quality have emerged. GIH and Oxford Economics (2017) estimate future demand by incorporating differences in infrastructure quality indicators based on the GCI. Hirota (2024) similarly uses infrastructure quality indicators from the GCI to argue that differences in infrastructure quality are reflected in construction unit costs, aiming to estimate the scale of demand more precisely.

Finally, the estimates usually do not include the costs of major rehabilitation or upgrades. Regarding costs beyond initial construction and routine maintenance, the replacement of infrastructure also requires substantial spending at the end of its lifetime. Ishizuka et al. (2019) state that social infrastructure demand for rehabilitation and replacement activities in Japan is estimated to average 2.67% of initial construction costs annually. The financial demand for existing infrastructure other than initial construction will be even greater if the costs of routine maintenance and management are factored into the estimates. This is important from two perspectives.

The first concerns the relationship between stock and the sustainability of infrastructure. The infrastructure stock generally continues to increase in a society as the economy develops. Therefore, public expenditures on regular rehabilitation and routine maintenance of infrastructure, as well as on the replacement at the end of its useful life, increase as these stocks accumulate, putting pressure on government finances. This is becoming a major social issue in developed countries such as Japan and the US. Even in developing countries, it will likely be a burden in the future—in other words, it will become a sustainability issue. A concept

[9] For example, Ishizuka et al. (2019) estimate that the demand for social infrastructure in Japan (from 2016 to 2030) will be around 0.57 to 0.68% of GDP for educational facilities and 0.86 to 1.20% for medical facilities. When added to government facilities and public housing, the total rises to between 1.80 and 2.36%.

that encapsulates this is "life cycle costs," which are considered one of the most important factors in QII. As a concept, life cycle costs encompass the overall costs incurred over the lifetime of a facility, addressing the essential issue of sustainability with regard to infrastructure. In other words, it requires us to look at short-term construction costs (efficient use of funds) and future burdens (sustainability) in an integrated way, which leads to the issue of the sacrifice of future generations, as discussed in the previous chapter.

The second is a statistical issue. Maintenance and rehabilitation of facilities are not recorded in Gross fixed capital formation (GFCF) in GDP statistics, as they relate to intermediate consumption—unless they extend the function or the service life of the facility. However, when infrastructure is maintained, it continues to provide additional benefits to society in the form of positive externalities and spillover effects, in addition to the specific benefits derived from its cost. Also, since infrastructure has a positive network effect, the additional benefits of infrastructure investment are even greater if the current infrastructure's functionality is maintained. For example, the effects generated by additional road construction will be greater if the current road network continues to function. Maintenance thus increases the utility to consumers. As a country develops and its stock of infrastructure accumulates, it will incur significant costs for maintenance and rehabilitation, some of which are not reflected in GDP and therefore may even have a statistically negative impact on growth. This may contribute to why growth rates in developed countries are generally lower than in developing countries.

#### 7.2.2.2 Challenges of a Changing Society

Another background factor is the social transformation associated with rapid economic growth in emerging economies. Infrastructure investment must respond to these social changes. Firstly, infrastructure investments that give proper consideration to the environment and climate change need to support development while maintaining a sustainable environment. Infrastructure is a particularly important area in tackling climate change, and renewable energy investments can limit the increase in GHG emissions. Secondly, with regard to disasters, as economic development advances and globalization progresses, the amount of damage caused by disasters increases, as mentioned in the previous chapter. Therefore, the rapid growth of emerging economies increases the need for investment in disaster management.

Thirdly, the relationship between infrastructure, inequality and inclusiveness has become increasingly important. Calderón and Servén (2014) state that, according to previous research on the relationship between infrastructure and inequality, increased availability of infrastructure has the effect of reducing inequalities. For example, services that previously could only be purchased by higher-income groups can now be substituted by the development of public infrastructure (e.g., from private cars to public transport).[10] There are two types of empirical studies on infrastructure and inequality: using the Gini coefficient to express inequality, and focusing on changes in the incomes of the poor in the targeted area through specific infrastructure projects. Calderón and Servén (2014) demonstrate that, for the Gini-related studies, inequality either improves with infrastructure development or that the two remain uncorrelated. The second group of studies utilizes empirical analysis, which includes assessments of the impact of development projects. The World Bank (2016) cites previous studies on the income-enhancing effects of several rural infrastructure projects, arguing that rural roads and electrification are key areas for reducing inequality and promoting gender equality. As the G20 declaration explicitly mentions the inclusiveness of infrastructure, increased emphasis is now being placed on the relationship between infrastructure development and inclusiveness.

## 7.3 Investment Efficiency and Productivity of Infrastructure

Because infrastructure development is an investment, it needs to be highly effective. In Sect. 7.1, it was noted that the investment effectiveness of infrastructure is measured by its contribution to economic growth, and that previous studies have estimated the effect of infrastructure on growth in various ways. This implies that the effect of infrastructure on growth varies from country to country. The factors that cause such differences can be broadly divided into two: those that are due to country-specific conditions, such as geography, climate and population, and those related to policies and institutions. With regard to country-specific conditions, for example, if a country has a large land area with a low population density, the cost of generating the same amount of electricity per capita will differ significantly. Regarding policies and institutions, there are issues such as policy choices on how infrastructure spending is allocated, and for institutions, on how to improve the efficiency of infrastructure spending.

The level of financial expenditure on infrastructure development depends to a large extent on the geography, climatic conditions and stage of development of each country. However, the development experiences of many countries to

[10] Additionally, Calderón and Servén (2014) focus on labor skills. Infrastructure development makes more intensive use of unskilled workers, meaning that capital shifts from skill-intensive to unskilled-labor-intensive sectors. Therefore, wages in the unskilled sector rise relative to the skilled sector and, as a result, inequalities narrow. Furthermore, there is the perspective of the impact of private participation in infrastructure. If the private sector operates infrastructure more efficiently and the scope of infrastructure supply is expanded, inequalities will narrow. However, the growth effect may be offset if private-sector activity causes job reductions. Changes to the infrastructure system may also alter prices and supply, reducing access and affordability for the poor. This is often the case when subsidies are reduced or prices increase as a result of privatization. However, Calderón and Servén also note that, in practice, privatization has, in many cases, improved access for the poor.

date suggest a certain benchmark. The Commission on Growth and Development (2008), established by a group of esteemed experts in the Growth Commission at the World Bank, identified a figure of 7% of GDP as the scale of infrastructure investment required for sustained high growth. For example, public investment in infrastructure in high-growth Asian countries was 5 to 7% of GDP. However, many countries did not reach this rate, with some investing less than 2%, which was linked to their low growth rates. Using these figures as a guide, each country needs to determine its infrastructure development strategy, taking into account its fiscal situation, the balance with other investment expenditures, political imperatives and other factors.

On the other hand, the efficiency of infrastructure spending can be improved regardless of differences in national conditions and endowments. As infrastructure is the result of investment—which is a flow—it is important to consider how efficiently public investment is converted into a stock of infrastructure, and then how effectively that stock delivers infrastructure services, thus contributing to economic growth. The conversion of flows into stocks and the productivity of the capital stock are likely to be influenced by the planning and implementation process of the investment. In other words, the public investment system affects the efficiency of infrastructure investment. This process can be organized as depicted in Fig. 7.2.[11]

If public investment is efficiently converted into public capital stocks and this stock generates greater benefits (production), growth will be accelerated. For example, if corruption occurs, some of the investment funds do not go into infrastructure building. Alternatively, the lack of competitive tendering can make contracts more expensive. If implementation capacity is low, projects are delayed and project costs increase. If the capacity to formulate and screen projects is limited, the most profitable projects may not be selected. Alternatively, the greatest benefits may not be achieved due to suboptimal technology selection or operational methods.

Some analyses have shown that the efficiency with which flows of public investment are converted into public capital stock, and how productive that capital stock is, depends to a large extent on the institutions and processes of planning and implementing public investment. Gupta et al. (2011) attempt to quantify this issue, stating that by adjusting for the efficiency of public investment, the scale of public capital stock is estimated to be only about half of what it would be without

[11] IMF (2015) measures this efficiency by assessing how far the actual infrastructure deviates from the minimum input and maximum output from the same input. Productivity in this case is measured by the relationship between capital stock and growth. Figure 7.2, on the other hand, considers the benefits (revenues) of infrastructure investment to be the effect of, for example, how much road congestion is alleviated or how much more electricity is generated with the same input. This is because, first of all, we want to assess the direct relationship between how much individual expenditure produces the originally envisaged value—i.e., its cost-effectiveness—at the micro level.

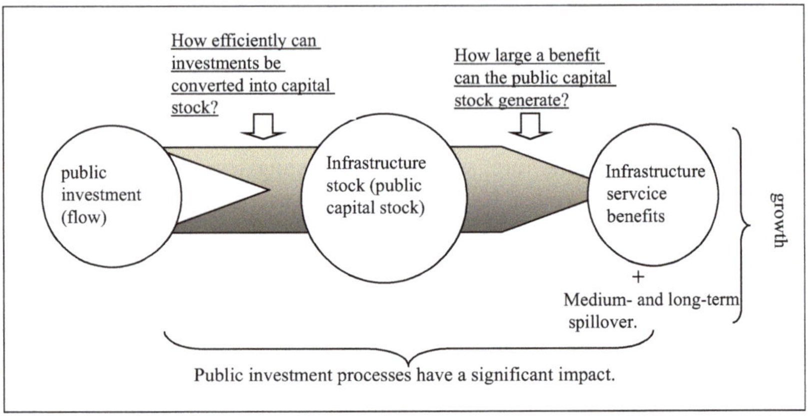


**Fig. 7.2** Investment, stocks and production *Source* Hirota (2017)

efficiency considerations—i.e., a nominal figure. How public investment is converted into public capital stock will depend on, for example, public investment procedures such as competitive tendering and the process of selecting projects. The difficulty lies in determining which indicators to use in evaluating the quality of the institutions and processes of public investment.

In addressing this difficulty, Gupta et al. (2011) use the index developed by Dabla-Norris et al. (2011) to evaluate the public investment process. This index seeks to assess the qualitative aspects of public investment management using a framework comprising 17 components, classified into four phases of the project management cycle, and it was the first time such an index was formulated.[12] Specifically, for each of the four phases—strategy guidance and appraisal, project selection, project implementation, and project evaluation and audit—the index establishes checkpoints, including whether screening criteria are published, whether CBA is conducted, and other relevant indicators. Gupta et al. (2011) found that when this framework was applied, the greatest impact on efficiency occurred at the project implementation stage. On this basis, a high-quality public investment process leads to the efficient conversion of investment into productive public capital stock, which in turn enhances a country's overall public capital stock, thereby driving economic growth.

QII contains many of these elements of public financial management. These include: consistency with national development strategies and master plans to be checked at the planning stage; economic viability over the entire life of the project, along with fiscal and debt sustainability, to be checked at the appraisal stage; dialogue with the public at the implementation stage; and proper governance,

[12] In its 2015 staff report on public investment management assessment, IMF (2015) proposed a new Public Investment Management Assessment (PIMA) framework to assess the process of planning, investment allocation and implementation stages.

including increased transparency and accountability as cross-cutting concern. The proper formulation of development strategies and master plans ensures clarity in project preparation and prioritization while also enhancing efficiency. With QII, upstream planning becomes even more important, as the rapid economic development of emerging and developing countries requires careful and consistent investment that goes beyond the simple calculation of an individual project's economic return.

Life cycle costs in terms of economic efficiency throughout a project are one of the key areas of discussion in QII. Life cycle costs refer to the expenses incurred throughout a project period, from planning and design to the end of operations. A development strategy that focuses solely on the lowest possible initial cost may shorten the lifespan of the infrastructure assets or lead to higher maintenance and operating costs. In developing countries with harsh climatic conditions, infrastructure facilities are likely to deteriorate more quickly, so proper maintenance will become even more important. In terms of QII, this is considered a major risk. Bhattacharyay (2010) estimated that infrastructure demand in Asia consists of roughly 68% for the costs of new construction and 32% for maintenance and operating costs. Furthermore, as Asian countries continue to grow and their infrastructure stock expands, the share of maintenance costs is expected to rise. The life of infrastructure has a significant impact not only on project profitability but also from a macro financial perspective. In other words, the life of an infrastructure asset is closely linked to the depreciation of the asset: the longer the life, the lower the annual rate of depreciation. The emphasis on life cycle costs in QII is based on the prior experience of Japan and other developed countries.

Improving these aspects by strengthening public financial management can enhance the efficiency of fund utilization. Moreover, it is also necessary to mobilize private funds as new sources of financing in developing countries, where funding is often insufficient. Public–private partnerships (PPPs) for infrastructure began in the 1990s—especially in the electric power and telecommunications sectors—and have since expanded to emerging and developing countries. PPPs for infrastructure development have been promoted for their positive benefits, such as better management efficiency and a lower financial burden due to participation by the private sector. Most emerging and developing countries now aim to use the PPP model for infrastructure development, but contrary to government expectations, in many cases, significant progress has not been realized. Some of the factors cited for this are the risk-sharing arrangements between the public and private sectors, with the private sector in particular often viewing the government as not bearing enough of the risk, and the lack of progress in forming bankable projects. These are also the issues that relate to public financial management, particularly at the upstream stage of development, such as strategy formulation and project identification and preparation.

QII also emphasizes local job creation and the transfer of technology and know-how. These are both important elements in promoting the endogenous growth discussed in the previous chapter. One of the factors contributing to the focus on employment is likely that at the time the QII was being developed, the number

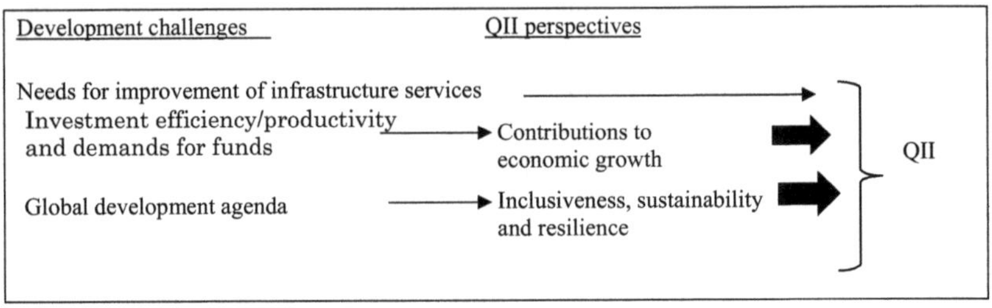


**Fig. 7.3** Origins of QII. *Source* Hirota (2017), partially modified

of Chinese workers dispatched by Chinese companies to undertake construction in Africa and Asia had increased rapidly since the late 2000s. Negative commentary on this phenomenon may have been behind the cautionary warning about the creation of local employment during the construction of infrastructure projects.[13] Growth is more likely to be sustained over the long term if the economy is stimulated by the creation of local jobs and the development of human resources. Notably, technological enhancements are a driver of long-term economic growth. Globally, the issue of the "middle-income country trap" in countries such as Latin America has been widely discussed. The solution to the middle-income country trap is generally considered to involve high-value additions to the economy. QII takes this into account and emphasizes the importance of technology transfer in infrastructure projects as well. In other words, it suggests that when foreign companies participate in infrastructure projects, it is essential that they contribute to raising the technological capabilities of emerging and developing countries through the transfer of skills, technology and know-how.

Based on what I have discussed so far, the relationship between QII and the development challenges faced by emerging and developing countries can be depicted as shown in Fig. 7.3.

[13] According to Zhang (2014), most of the Chinese workers dispatched under overseas construction contracts were destined for Asia and Africa. A regression analysis using labor migration from China to various countries as the explanatory variable shows that as the size of the population (i.e., labor market) increases, the number of workers dispatched also tends to increase. An additional finding is that labor migration is greater in regions with smaller migrant stocks but is not correlated with distance, which may reflect the fact that a lot of labor migration has been directed to Africa. Zhang (2014) states that the increased labor force deployment may be driven by the availability of energy resources and the export of infrastructure systems to African countries.

## 7.4 Quality Infrastructure Investment as a Policy Argument for Quality Growth

The declarations at the G7 and G20 demonstrate that QII is a concept that has emerged in response to the current challenges in global development and the strong demand for infrastructure funding. For example, G7 Ise-Shima Principles for Promoting Quality Infrastructure Investment, as introduced, state at the outset that it is "crucial importance for stakeholders to work coherently to bridge the existing global demand–supply gap of infrastructure investment by promoting QII so as to promote strong, sustainable and balanced growth and to enhance resilience in our society, as well as to contribute to the global efforts for the SDGs." The idea of pursuing economic growth while taking into account the challenges of global society is the essence of quality growth, which is not merely about increasing quantitative growth but also increasing non-income welfare. In a nutshell, the goal of QII can be described as contributing to the realization of quality growth. As illustrated in Fig. 7.4, the fundamental framework articulates the relationship between QII and quality growth. Table 7.2 organizes the specific elements of QII principles that have achieved international consensus, based on their contributions to growth, inclusiveness, sustainability and resilience.

The QII principles agreed upon at the G7 and G20 provide guidance on achieving quality growth through infrastructure investment and outline priority items to be considered. These principles must be incorporated into real policies. In practice, infrastructure investment involves first making macroeconomic decisions on how much to allocate, followed by selecting specific projects to receive funding and determining the key considerations that should guide the process.

Finally, I propose a desirable cross-sectoral basic policy framework to realize QII as follows. The first is to give greater priority in the allocation of actual

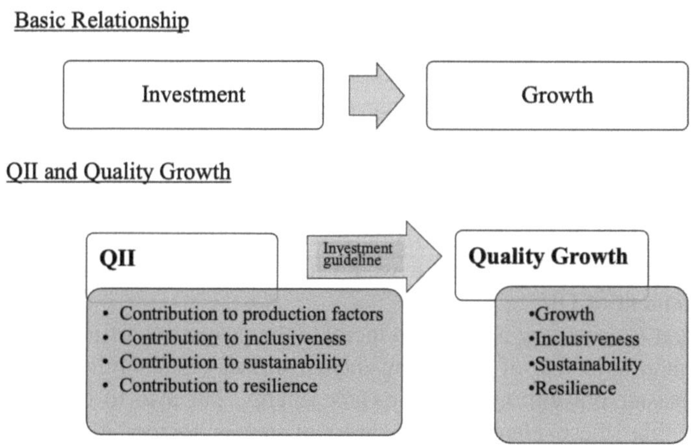


**Fig. 7.4** Basic relationship between QII and quality growth. *Source* Author

**Table 7.2** Development issues and QII elements in a quality growth framework

| Objective | Issues in emerging and developing countries | QII as an answer to issues |
|---|---|---|
| *Economic growth*<br>To address the factors of production (capital accumulation, employment) | 1. Increased demand, inefficiency of capital<br>• Positive impact of investment<br>• Efficient use of fund<br>• Mobilization of new funds<br>2. Lack of employment opportunities<br>3. Technological advancement | Improved governance<br>Development strategies & master plans<br>Greater focus on life cycle costs<br>Effective mobilization such as PPP<br>Creation of local employment<br>Technology transfer, Human resources development |
| *Inclusiveness* | Urbanization, Regional inequalities<br>Vulnerable groups | Equal access to markets & public services<br>Social support for vulnerable groups |
| *Sustainability* | Rapid increase in GHG emissions<br>Degradation of the natural environment | Reduction of GHG emissions<br>Environmentally friendly development |
| *Resilience* | Vulnerability to natural disasters | Resilient to disasters |

*Source* Hirota (2017), partially modified

funds to projects that include elements that enhance inclusiveness, sustainability and resilience—or to create a framework for incorporating such elements within individual projects. Available funds are, of course, limited, particularly in developing countries, so it is not possible to take on all desirable projects that include these elements. Thus, funding needs to be allocated realistically. However, the internationally agreed implications of the approach of QII (or quality growth) can be seen as a response to the inadequate allocation of funds to inclusiveness, sustainability, and resilience in many countries to date. QII has emerged because it was necessary to explicitly emphasize it, although it has not been possible to test this point quantitatively. There are several ways to enable such priority allocation—for example, by setting numerical targets and action plans (e.g., investing YY amount in renewable energy over XX years), or by implementing model projects and drawing up guidelines for project formation. It would then be necessary to monitor progress on each element of QII.

Second, it is necessary not only to increase the proportion of individual projects with the main objective of enhancing inclusiveness, sustainability and resilience, such as disaster prevention and renewable energy, but also to create investment criteria to take these elements into account across sectors. Once such investment criteria are in place and evaluation methods are established, this will lead to an overall shift of resource allocation to include more elements of inclusiveness, sustainability and resilience from the project formation stage. Currently, the most commonly used investment criterion is CBA. In this context, including new investment criteria in the CBA will allow calculations of how many of the poor will benefit from a project and the extent of those gains. Weighting the benefits to the poor by a certain coefficient, depending on the degree of emphasis on poverty reduction, would encourage the design and selection of projects that reduce inequality. In fact, while such an idea is not theoretically new, it appears to have been rarely implemented in practice.

The idea of carbon neutrality in terms of sustainability appears to be gaining ground, although it will be necessary to mainstream it further. This should not only be a criterion for project design and project selection but also for evaluating contractors and suppliers at each procurement. The same applies to life cycle costs. With regard to resilience, for example, aspects of disaster preparedness could be mainstreamed (e.g., designing roads to act as dikes in case of floods, or enabling schools and government buildings to serve as shelters in the event of disasters or pandemics).

Third, governance—particularly public investment management—should be improved. Although it is often overlooked in discussions on QII, as discussed in Sect. 7.2, capacity building for this purpose—along with the prevention of corruption and promotion of transparency—is indispensable. These improvements should be indexed and monitored, so that, through statistical visualization, society as a whole will be able to assess the progress of its efforts for the first time. Fourthly, a national framework should be established that allows sufficient budgetary resources to be allocated to maintenance and rehabilitation, based on earlier discussion of their importance in maintaining infrastructure. To this end, it is necessary to forecast future demand for infrastructure, analyze funding gaps in a more sophisticated manner, and clearly indicate the financial burden in the medium and long term. Of course, it would also be desirable to strengthen the life cycle costs perspective from the project formation stage.

This chapter is based on Hirota (2017) with some modifications.

## References

Arslanalp, Serkan, Fabian Bornhorst, Sanjeev Gupta, and Elsa Sze. 2010. "Public Capital and Growth." IMF Working Paper WP/10 /175. International Monetary Fund.

Asian Development Bank (ADB). 2017. *Meeting Asia's Infrastructure Needs.* Asian Development Bank.

Asian Development Bank and Asian Development Bank Institute (ADBI). 2009. *Infrastructure for a Seamless Asia.* Asian Development Bank Institute.

Bhattacharyay, Biswa Nath. 2010. "Estimating Demand for Infrastructure in Energy, Transport, Telecommunications, Water and Sanitation in Asia and the Pacific: 2010–2020." ADBI Working Paper No. 248. Asian Development Bank Institute.

Bhattacharya, Amar, Mattia Romani, and Nicholas Stern. 2012. "Infrastructure for Development: Meeting the Challenge." Policy Paper. Center for Climate Change Economics and Policy; Grantham Research Institute on Climate Change and the Environment; Intergovernmental

Group of Twenty-Four on International Monetary Affairs and Development. https://www.lse.ac.uk/GranthamInstitute/wp-content/uploads/2014/02/PP-infrastructure-for-development-meeting-the-challenge.pdf

Cabinet Office, Director-General for Policy Coordination (Economic and Social Systems), Japan. 2022. *Nihon no shakai shihon 2022* [Japan's Social Capital 2022]. Cabinet Office. https://www5.cao.go.jp/keizai2/ioj/docs/pdf/ioj2022.pdf

Calderón, César, and Luis Servén. 2010. "Infrastructure and Economic Development in Sub-Saharan Africa." *Journal of African Economies* 19 (AERC Supplement 1): i13-i87.

Calderón, César, and Luis Servén. 2014. "Infrastructure, Growth, and Inequality: An Overview." Policy Research Working Paper WPS7034. World Bank.

Canning, David. 1999. "Infrastructure's Contribution to Aggregate Output." Policy Research Working Paper WPS 2246. World Bank.

Commission on Growth and Development. 2008. *The Growth Report: Strategies for Sustained Growth and Inclusive Development.* World Bank.

Dabla-Norris, Era, Jim Brumby, Annette Kyobe, Zac Mills, and Chris Papageorgiou. 2011. "Investing in Public Investment: An Index of Public Investment Efficiency." IMF Working Paper WP/11/37. IMF.

Elburz, Zeynep, Peter Nijkamp, and Eric Pels. 2017. "Public Infrastructure and Regional Growth: Lessons from Meta-analysis." *Journal of Transport Geography* 58: 1–8.

Fay, Marianne, and Tito Yepes. 2003. "Investing in Infrastructure." Policy Research Working Paper 3102. World Bank.

Fernald, John, G. 1999. "Roads to Prosperity? Assessing the Link Between Public Capital and Productivity." *American Economic Review* 89 (3): 619–638.

Global Infrastructure Hub (GIH), and Oxford Economics. 2017. *Global Infrastructure Outlook*, Global Infrastructure Hub.

Gupta, Sanjeev, Alvar Kangur, Chris Papageorgiou, and Abdoul Wane. 2011. "Efficiency-Adjusted Public Capital and Growth." IMF Working Paper WP/11/217. IMF.

Hirota, Koki. 2017. "Shitsu no takai infrastructure tōsi to shitsu no takai seichō ni kansuru yobiteki k osatsu" [Preliminary Considerations on "Quality Infrastructure Investment" and "Quality Growth"]. *Development Cooperation Literature Review* 12. JICA Sadako Ogata Peace and Development Institute.

Hirota, Koki. 2024. "Gurōbaru na infura jyuyō suikei saikō" [Revisiting Global Infrastructure Demand Estimation Analysis]. *Shakaikagaku Ronshu* [The Social Science Review] 171: 5–20. The Economics Society of Saitama University.

Huntley, Jon. 2021. "Explainer: Economic Effects of Infrastructure Investment." June 15, 2021. Penn Wharton, University of Pennsylvania. https://budgetmodel.wharton.upenn.edu/issues/2021/6/15/economic-effects-of-infrastructure-investment

International Monetary Fund (IMF). 2015. *Making Public Investment More Efficient.* IMF.

Ishizuka, Fumiaki, Tsuyoshi Hara, Yu Namba, and Koki Hirota. 2019. "Estimating Social Infrastructure Demand: The Case of Japan." JICA RI Working Paper No. 191. JICA Ogata Research Institute.

Kodongo, Odongo, and Kalu Ojah. 2016. "Does Infrastructure Really Explain Economic Growth in Sub-Sahara Africa?" *Review of Development Finance* 6: 105–125.

Li, Hongmei. 2010. "Nihon ni okeru shakai shihon no seisanryoku kōka ni kansuru bunken kenkyū." [Literature Study on Productivity Effect of Public Capital in Japan]. *Gendai Shakai Bunka Kenkyu* [Journal of the Study of Modern Society and Culture] 48: 87–104. Niigata University.

McKinsey Global Institute (MGI). 2013. *Infrastructure Productivity: How to Save $1 Trillion a Year.* McKinsey Global Institute.

McKinsey Global Institute (MGI). 2016. *Bridging Global Infrastructure Gaps.* McKinsey Global Institute.

Oxford Economics. 2017. "Global Infrastructure Outlook." Global Infrastructure Hub: A G20 Initiative.

Romp, Ward E., and Jacob de Haan. 2005. "Public Capital and Economic Growth: A Critical Survey." EIB Papers. European Investment Bank.

Shi, Yingying, Shen Guo, and Puyang Sun. 2017. "The Role of Infrastructure in China's Regional Economic Growth." *Journal of Asian Economics* 49: 26–41.

Timilsina, Govinda R., Gal Hochman, and Ze Song. 2020. "Infrastructure, Economic Growth, and Poverty: A Review." Policy Research Working Paper 9258. World Bank.

World Bank. 2016. *Poverty and Shared Prosperity 2016: Taking on Inequality.* World Bank.

Zhang, Hongyong. 2014. "Kakudai suru Chūgokujin roudousha no kokusai idō" [Expanding International Migration of Chinese Workers]. REITI Column, July 1, 2014. Research Institute of Economy, Trade and Industry. http://www.rieti.go.jp/jp/columns/a01_0401.html.

**Koki Hirota** earned his B.A. in Economics from the University of Tokyo and holds a Ph.D. in Economics from Saitama University in Japan. His professional career spans several prominent roles in international development finance and policy, including Chief Economist, Director General of Operation and Strategy Department, and Director General of Southeast Asia and Pacific Department at the Japan International Cooperation Agency (JICA), and Chief Representative in Jakarta for Japan Bank for International Cooperation and in Hanoi for the Overseas Economic Cooperation Fund. In academia, he was a Professor at the Graduate School of Humanities and Social Sciences at Saitama University and a Visiting Fellow at the JICA Ogata Sadako Research Institute for Peace and Development. His recent publications include *Challenges in Fiscal and Monetary Policies in Mongolia* (co-edited, Springer, 2023) and *Addressing Social Infrastructure Needs in Asia: Towards a Pandemic Resilient Society* (co-edited, JICA, August 2025).

# Measuring Quality Growth

# 8

Koki Hirota

In previous chapters, I have occasionally referred to the importance of using indices to measure quality growth. There are two important implications to consider when discussing how they apply. First, growth is currently measured primarily by using GDP, which does not necessarily represent the wellbeing of people and does not capture the key elements of quality growth, such as changes in inequality or progress toward addressing the problems of climate change. Therefore, a new index that takes these factors into account will be needed for the purpose of achieving and measuring quality growth.

Second, I have argued that the relationship between growth and inclusiveness, sustainability, and resilience is complex. Some forces operate in complementary directions, moving between each of these elements, while others are trade-offs. In addition, the direction of such forces may change depending on the time period, i.e., short-term versus long-term. In practice, these relationships are not easily quantified, particularly as they differ greatly depending on the country and its economic and social environments. Therefore, it is essential to assess the overall progress of quality growth by measuring changes occurring as a result of policies that have been implemented. In this way, we will be able to assess whether long-term progress is occurring. This chapter aims to examine how indices can be used to support quality growth while exploring some of the issues related to their use. For this purpose, first, the limitations of GDP and the current debates on its revision are introduced, followed by a review of the debate on new indices that attempt to measure factors beyond GDP in Sects. 8.2 and 8.3.

K. Hirota (✉)
Tokyo, Japan



K. Hirota (ed.), *Introduction to Quality Growth*,
https://doi.org/10.1007/978-981-95-6220-6_8

## 8.1 GDP: Its Nature, Limitations and the Need for Improvements

When measuring growth, GDP has become the globally accepted standard measure. In regard to growth, GDP refers to the sum of value added produced over a period of time and is measured according to the System of National Accounts (SNA) provided by the UN. The sum of production equals the sum of expenditure or income. The formal basis for national income statistics emerged after the Great Depression of the 1930s, and GDP is now generally recognized as the primary means to express the prosperity of a country. However, as we have seen, while income is the basic element that represents the fruits of growth, prosperity is more than just that.

In the early days of the debate on its formulation of GDP, Kuznets, who was at the center of the discussions, believed that GDP should represent private income because income provides a guide to wellbeing. Therefore, it should not include government spending or other spending that would be considered a necessary evil, such as those to remove inconvenience and military spending. However, at that time, as the economy was moving from the Great Depression into a wartime economy, the US government found it difficult to accept a definition of GDP in which any increases in government spending did not make the economy larger. Against this background, the GDP was designed to include government spending (Coyle 2014; Masood 2021). As such, it is clear that GDP was not developed to provide an indicator of people's wellbeing in the first place.

The definition of GDP has remained under continuous review at the UN Platform. The ongoing debates include not only ways of refining the measurement but also the fundamental issues of how to treat items that cannot be easily measured in monetary terms, such as the environment and wellbeing. For example, with regard to the environment, the creation of a satellite account was advocated in the 1993 SNA adopted by the UN. The SNA is regularly reviewed by the UN Statistical Commission and the UN Statistics Division. The current version of the SNA is the 2008 SNA, and at the time of writing, discussions are underway to revise it for the next edition in 2025.

One of the research areas that is particularly relevant to the themes in this book concerns wellbeing and sustainability.[1] The first priority in the terms of reference of the review task team is to produce one or more guidance notes on "unpaid household work; distribution of household income, consumption; environmental-economic accounting; and defining a broader framework for capturing economic activities, well-being and sustainability."[2] The other key research areas in this category—which have already been discussed as elements closely related to quality growth—are "education and human capital, labor and productivity, health and

[1] https://unstats.un.org/unsd/nationalaccount/Update_Issues.asp. Accessed April 18, 2025.

[2] https://unstats.un.org/unsd/nationalaccount/snaupdate/TOR_WSTT.pdf. Accessed April 18, 2025.

social condition." Furthermore, there are additional research items in other categories related to quality growth, such as "digitization," which includes both the household production and consumption of digital products.

The results of these ongoing debates and subsequent modifications to SNA in the future will significantly affect the extent to which the concept of quality growth will be reflected in actual policy. However, despite these discussions, the basic objective of GDP—to measure the flow of production (expenditure or income) in a specific period of time—is likely to remain unchanged. For example, if a conceptually different type of stock is to be incorporated into GDP, the likely response would be to develop satellite accounts to capture this information while preserving the core GDP concept and its statistical processes. Furthermore, as GDP is based on monetary transactions in the market, it is likely to face limitations in incorporating the element of happiness through imputed calculations in monetary terms. Given the importance of GDP to policymakers, it is especially desirable to make changes that enable external factors—those currently identified as central to quality growth—to be reflected within the overall GDP indicator.

## 8.2 Discussion of a New Index

The search for an index that can provide an alternative to GDP in measuring wellbeing and growth has been particularly active since the 2000s. There are several categories of discussions, each with its own central focus on (1) human development, (2) happiness, (3) environment, (4) stock rather than flows, or (5) creation of a new composite index (Table 8.1).

Before introducing an overview of each of these indices, I would like to touch on some general issues related to indices. First, they usually consisted of several indicators, with the number of components varying between indices. For example, the Human Development Index (HDI) and Happy Planet Index have only three components each, while the Social Progress Index has 54 components (Easterlin 2021). The way of displaying several components of an index in a format that allows a list of figures for each component is referred to as a dashboard. In

**Table 8.1** Types of new indices related to wellbeing and growth

| Main focus | Representative example |
|---|---|
| Human resources development | Human development index; Human capital index |
| (Subjective) happiness | Gross national happiness |
| Environment | Ecological footprint |
| Capital stock | World Bank wealth of the nation |
| New composite index | Genuine progress indicator; Better life index |

*Source* Author

**Table 8.2** Types of indices related to wellbeing

| | Composite score available | No composite score |
|---|---|---|
| Score within a range | Gross national happiness<br>Global peace index<br>Happy planet index (HPI)<br>HDI<br>Legatum prosperity index<br>Multidimensional poverty index<br>Social progress index | Many indicators of better life index (e.g. housing, expressed as a percentage) |
| No upper limit to score | Genuine progress indicator<br>Index of sustainable economic welfare<br>(GDP) | Some indicators of better life index (e.g. income and household wealth) |

*Note* The indicators listed here are based on those presented as dashboard indicators for wellbeing provided by Easterlin (2021)
*Source* Author

this section, I will attempt to organize the indices related to growth and wellbeing to determine whether or not there is a composite score for these components (Table 8.2).

I will also distinguish between those indicators without an upper limit (e.g., GDP will continue to increase forever as long as income grows) and those that are expressed as a number within a range, such as 0 to 1 (or 1 to 100). The former are absolute values, while the latter are relative values. As these indices were developed for different purposes, at first glance, it may seem that there are many indices that provide a composite score and are expressed as relative values. This is likely due to the fact that a composite score makes the results easier to understand intuitively. However, to obtain a composite score, there is the question of what weighting to use to integrate the different units of indicators. On the other hand, the absolute value has the advantage that the degree of change can be visualized clearly over time. In the next section, I discuss the characteristics of each of the major indices and their relationship to quality growth.

### 8.2.1 Human Resources Development

Even though there is a common starting point between these indices—that wellbeing and growth cannot be assessed by income alone—there are several alternative approaches on how it can be measured. The HDI focuses on human resources development, an approach that derives from the capability approach by Sen, who argues that wellbeing and development depend on whether people are able to fully realize their potential. For individuals to reach their potential fully, they need more than just income, but they also to live safely, be healthy, and acquire sufficient knowledge. Since people experience greater happiness from their respective actions than from their income, as explained later, being in a situation that allows individuals to fully realize their potential determines the magnitude of their wellbeing.

HDI, the leading index focusing on human resource development, was first proposed by UNDP in 1990 and, since then, scores for each country have been published annually up to the present. Mahbub ul Haq, who took the initiative in reconstructing Pakistan's economy after independence and later played a central role in developing the HDI, argued that economic development should not be promoted based on the GDP indicator alone. Drawing from his experiences working at the World Bank, ul Haq created the HDI, which has health and education indicators as its core. It also includes income as one of its components—based on Sen's recommendation in the team—that it was better not to diverge too greatly from mainstream economics and the thinking of policymakers (Masood 2021).

According to the UNDP Human Development Reports, HDI is specifically comprised of the following three indicators:

- Health: life expectancy at birth,
- Education: adult literacy rate (changed to expected years of schooling in 2010), school enrollment rate (changed to mean years of schooling), and
- Income: GDP per capita (USD, PPP), changed to gross national income (GNI) per capita in 2010.

Since each of the above indicators has a different unit of measurement, they are integrated by converting their values to a scale between 0 and 1 and summing them to reach a total score. This makes it somewhat difficult to intuitively grasp what the HDI indicates, and it is also challenging to assess the extent of development that has been achieved simply by tracking changes in the HDI. In general, when examining the HDI rankings in 2022, it can be observed that the lower the HDI score, the poorer the country. However, the degree of divergence varies from country to country, particularly for resource-rich countries. For example, Guyana ranked 54 places higher in GNI per capita (41st) than in HDI (95th), making it the country with the largest difference between HDI and GNI (UNDP n.d.). In other words, compared to the size of its income, its performance in education and health is significantly worse.

A new indicator focusing on human resources development is the Human Capital Index (HCI), released by the World Bank in 2018. It stems from the idea of emphasizing the role of human resources in production, with scores ranging from zero to one.[3] This score reflects the extent to which human capital deviates from the ideal state—i.e., the lower the score, the lower the labor productivity. Human

[3] The assessment is composed of *Survival* (under-5 mortality rate), *School* (expected years of school and harmonized test score), and *Health* (adult survival rate, proportion not stunted) and does not include income. HCI scores are somewhat different from the HDI. For example, the top countries of HCI in 2018 are (1) Singapore (0.88), (2) South Korea (0.84), and (3) Japan (0.84) (World Bank 2018), which differ from the top three of HDI (Norway, Iceland, Switzerland).

capital is the key to sustainable growth, as already discussed, and therefore it can be said that the HCI approach takes that dimension and indexes it specifically.

It has been over 30 years since the HDI was first introduced, and its use has since become widespread. It is often employed in research because it enables long-term comparisons. However, its usage has remained somewhat limited, and it is not always used by policymakers to inform the achievement of national objectives. HDI includes an income component and, to some extent, reflects the performance of economic growth. Moreover, since education and health are at the core of equality of opportunity, the HDI can incorporate elements of inclusiveness. It reflects some elements of sustainability, since human resource development is one of the major factors that bring about sustained growth.

On the other hand, HDI does not provide information on factors other than human resources necessary to improve productivity, nor does it capture the perspective of the future burden of sustainability or the status of resilience. One point to note here is that while income is the outcome of past economic activities, the status of human resources development is both the result of previous efforts and an indicator of the possibility or potential for future growth. This suggests that high human resources development facilitates the creation of future growth through innovation, not just present prosperity—an essential perspective for any quality growth index. Therefore, education and health are considered to be two important pillars in the development of an index for quality growth.

### 8.2.2 Happiness

If income alone cannot measure wellbeing, then an alternative approach is to ask people about it directly. Coyle (2014) identifies two ways to measure wellbeing. The first approach is subjective indexation, which involves asking people questions from various angles and surveying their subjective perceptions of happiness. The representative of this would be Gross National Happiness (GNH). The second approach is to explore happiness based on objective data, such as economic data. In terms of assessing happiness, GNH is the best-known of the indices. King Jigme Singye Wangchuck of Bhutan, who was crowned in 1971, has made maximizing happiness a policy goal of his country. The index itself was developed by Dasho Karma Ura, based on the responses from the people of Bhutan to questions about happiness.

The four pillars in the index are good governance, sustainable socio-economic development, preservation and promotion of culture, and environmental conservation, with the questions covering nine domains, such as psychological wellbeing, cultural resilience and promotion, time use, good governance, community, living standards, education, health, and the environment. The percentage of people who answer that they are satisfied with each question indicates the magnitude of their wellbeing—i.e., it is a relative index. In Bhutan, GNH is also expressly stated in the constitution, which defines its pursuit as a "multidimensional development approach seeking to achieve a harmonious balance between material well-being and the spiritual, emotional, and cultural needs of society."[4] GNH has been criticized by some as being anti-consumption, based on Buddhist ideology, but according to Masood (2021), Dasho Karma Ura has denied this. GNH is characterized, first, by its recognition of the importance of factors other than income for people's happiness; second, by its measurement based on subjectivity; and third, by its linking of policies with the index, making the improvement of wellbeing the primary goal of the country.

The idea of using surveys to capture wellbeing has been adopted globally. The approach has been conducted in many countries, and the OECD has published guidelines on how subjective happiness should be collected and measured. The UN Sustainable Development Solutions Network (SDSN) has published an overall happiness index via the World Happiness Report since 2012. This is based on a Gallup poll, in which the magnitude of happiness (scores of 0–10) for each country is indicated using a subjective rating. Such values obtained were analyzed using six explanatory variables: GDP per capita (log), social support (support from family and friends in times of need), healthy life expectancy at birth, freedom to make life choices, generosity, and perception of corruption—with these variables explaining more than three-quarters of the magnitude of happiness (Helliwell et al. 2022). These explanatory variables include both subjective perceptions and objective values, such as income.

Two points about subjectivity and objectivity in wellbeing measurement warrant closer examination. The first concerns whether objective data, especially income, is unable to satisfactorily measure the magnitude of wellbeing and how this relationship is theoretically organized. The other relates to the question of what makes people happy in the first place if not income. This is a question of the theoretical background that underpins the GNH and World Happiness Report, which brings these approaches into the realm of psychology. Regarding the first point—the relationship between income and happiness—people generally feel happier when they have larger incomes. When applied to countries, people living in rich countries feel happier than those living in poor countries.

However, Easterlin (2021) observes that while real income in the US has tripled over the past 70 years, the long-term trend in happiness has remained constant or even declined, indicating that there is no positive correlation between happiness and income change in the long run. Figure 8.1 presents a conceptual diagram illustrating this relationship, showing that income increases and decreases are correlated with happiness in the short run, but not in the long run. In general, in most countries, income tends to trend upward in the long term, with short-term fluctuations also occurring. In the short run, happiness and income move in the same direction: people feel happier when their incomes increase and feel unhappy when their incomes decrease. In the long run, however, while income is rising steadily, the magnitude of happiness remains approximately the same. This relationship between happiness and income is called the "Easterlin Paradox," and it provides

[4] GNH Center Bhutan https://www.gnhcentrebhutan.org/ (Accessed January 3, 2023).

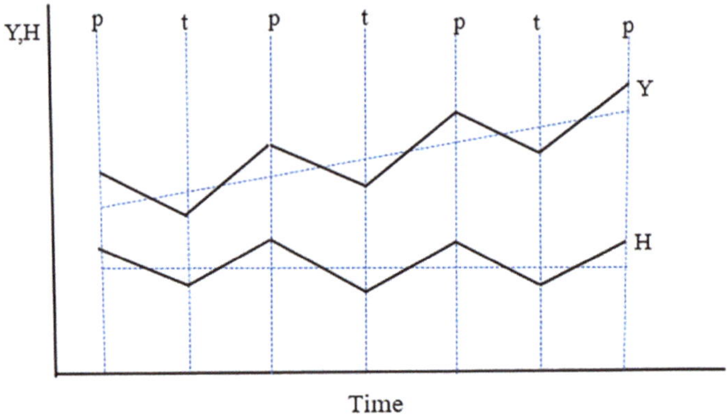


**Fig. 8.1** Short-term fluctuations and long-term trends in happiness and income. *Source* Easterlin (2021)

one interpretation of why an increase in GDP does not simply increase people's wellbeing in the long run.

Easterlin (2021) cites social comparison as a reason for this paradox. This perspective aligns with behavioral economics theory, which suggests that people benchmark against a reference point, typically the income of others. For example, if other people's incomes remain constant, they feel happier when their own income increases. However, they are not as happy if their income changes at the same rate as that of others. This point is also important in relation to quality growth: that increasing income inequality lowers people's overall sense of wellbeing, i.e., their perception of happiness. Thus, I believe that the element of inequality is indispensable in measuring wellbeing.

Easterlin (2021) also discusses the relationship to happiness more broadly, including not only income but also health and family relationships. As noted above, the question of when people feel happy is also related to psychological research. Lyubomirsky et al. (2005) identify three determinant areas of happiness. The first is the set-point, which is genetically determined and unchanging over the long term. This means that the degree of happiness felt by individuals differs depending on their personality traits, such as temperament and extroversion. The second is related to circumstances, which include culture, geography, family environment, income, and health. The third comprises intentional activity. The individual's independent decision-making and actions are one factor in determining happiness. In their study, the ratio of these three factors to determine happiness is "set-point: circumstances: intentional activity = 50:10:40." Regarding the fact that the circumstances had only a 10% impact, the authors stated that they were surprised by this result, as they initially thought that income and health had a great deal to do with happiness. Much debate and criticism of the study subsequently ensued, and the later review by Sheldon and Lyubomirsky (2021) acknowledged that people's

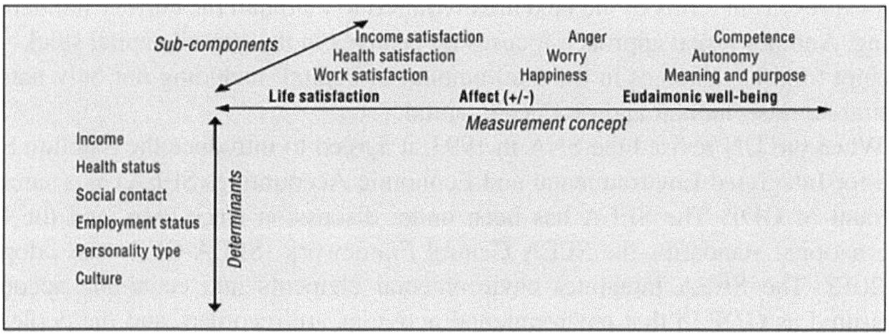


**Fig. 8.2** A simple model of subjective wellbeing. *Source* OECD (2013, Fig. 1.1)

wellbeing can still be enhanced over time through proactive actions, noting that the effect may be smaller than 40%.

The notion that proactive behavior is important in considering wellbeing has two major implications for quality growth. The first is that changes in income (i.e., growth) may not be a decisive factor in considering people's subjective wellbeing. People tend to become accustomed to the environment in which they find themselves and take it for granted, particularly in the case of the wealthy. Lyubomirsky (2013) presents a study showing that two-thirds of the wellbeing benefits of an increase in income disappear after only one year. However, income is still an important factor that enables people to choose their actions based on what is at their disposal. This viewpoint on a major source of wellbeing is relevant to the capability approach and human security. Therefore, an income that enables adequate education and healthcare should never be underestimated.

If we try to measure quality growth, we need to include elements that enable proactive action. In taking this approach, there is some difficulty in determining how to reconcile subjective scores (relative value) with objective indicators. To address this concern, the starting point would be to first clarify what happiness and wellbeing are comprised of. In Fig. 8.2, OECD (2013) shows that the indicators being measured are those expressed as standardized proportions, while the determinants are a mix of absolute value, such as income and standardized proportions (relative value). How these should be reflected in the index of quality growth will be discussed in the remaining part of this chapter and the next chapter.

### 8.2.3 Environment and Capital Stock

The focus on the environment reflects the growing emphasis on sustainability. The idea that economic growth should be assessed alongside the cost of the Earth's finite resources and environment is now commonplace. Such discussions are not new and have been raised by the UN in the context of revisions to SNA. One index relevant to this perspective is the idea of an ecological footprint, which measures the extent to which economic activities are accompanied by resource consumption.

It is expressed in terms of the land area required to maintain the current standard of living. Another broad approach focuses on changes in the overall capital stock—an attempt to grasp changes in the total amount of capital, including not only natural capital but also human and produced capital.

When the UN revised the SNA in 1993, it agreed to introduce the Satellite System for Integrated Environmental and Economic Accounting (SEEA) as a satellite account of GDP. The SEEA has been under discussion since then, and the first international standard—the SEEA Central Framework (SEEA-CF)—was adopted in 2012. The SEEA integrates environmental elements into economic accounts measured as GDP in that environmental activities are recorded, and the depletion of natural resources is deducted from GDP.

Amidst this trend, the Japanese government conducted initial estimates based on SEEA 93 in 1998 and presented the trend of Japan's environmentally adjusted GDP from 1970 to 1995, showing (1) the difference between GDP and environmentally adjusted GDP is relatively small, at around 1%, and (2) the magnitude of environmental imputed costs as a percentage of GDP has decreased with economic development, from 3.1% in 1970 to 1.0% in 1995 (EPA-Economic Research Institute 1998).[5] While the former suggests that the cost of environmental maintenance need not be large, the latter may provide evidence for the Environmental Kuznets Curve (EKC) hypothesis. SEEA-CF provides such useful information, but it retains satellite account status. Masood (2021) gives three reasons for this. First, data quality remains a problem. Second, it has proven difficult to attract international support for such a change. For example, even those with a strong interest in the environment have remained negative about the possibility of the greater use of such indicators, as it could reduce the impact of environmental policies. Third, he states that this is because large countries, such as the US and China, have little interest in changing the method of calculating GDP, which would lead to a decrease in their own countries' GDP.

Ecological footprint, on the other hand, is an index that expresses a sustainability perspective in terms of land area. The Global Footprint Network, an international non-governmental organization, publishes an index for each country every year. This index represents the amount of land considered necessary for people to maintain their current standard of living in each country. It then compares the demand with how much land would be needed to meet the supply (i.e., the biological capacity of the Earth) to provide information on whether current living is sustainable or which countries are "consuming" more than their land capacity and which countries are compensating for such shortfalls. For the demand, an overall national footprint account is calculated using coefficients for each of the six landforms (cropland, grazing land, fishing grounds, forests, built-up land, and carbon footprint). The overall global ecological footprint continues to grow at a pace that

[5] The imputed costs of excess $CO_2$ emissions are deemed unmeasurable and are not included in the estimate. Moreover, SEEA was subsequently revised in 2003 and 2012, and the SEEA-CF adopted in 2012 excludes environmental degradation from its general scope (Cabinet Office–Economic and Social Research Institute 2016).

exceeds the growth of the Earth's biological capacity, exceeding one Earth around 1970, then increasing to about 1.7 Earths based on the 2014 estimates. The largest share of the total ecological footprint is the carbon footprint, which has increased from a level of only 1% of the total 150 years ago to 44% today (Borucke et al. 2013; Lin et al. 2018).

The basic perspective of the ecological footprint is that of strong sustainability (Ohashi 2006). For example, the carbon footprint is based on the estimated forest area required to absorb $CO_2$ emissions. In this framework, the perspective of substituting natural capital for other capital to sustain growth is not considered. In contrast, sustaining growth based on can be measured by changes in capital. The World Bank is working to develop this form of measurement. Since the publication of a World Bank (2006) report that estimated the total amount of capital in 120 countries, the organization has continued to publish new edition of the report every three or four years, refining its methodology each time.

The latest version of the report documents changes in wealth from 1995 to 2018 for 146 countries (World Bank 2021). It measures the economic value of capital by dividing it into renewable natural capital (forests, mangroves, fisheries, agricultural land and protected areas), non-renewable natural capital (fossil fuels, minerals), human capital (employed and self-employed), produced capital (machinery, structures, urban land), and net foreign assets. The amount of capital is obtained by converting stock into a monetary value. In the case of human capital, this is expressed in terms of the present value of lifetime income (with a discount rate of 4%). Table 8.3 compares the ratio of these forms of capital by income category. As might be expected, the share of natural capital is higher in low-income countries, while the shares of produced capital and human capital are higher in higher-income OECD countries.

Since the amount of human capital is calculated based on the present value of lifetime wages, its size increases as the economy develops and per capita income increases. Produced capital also primarily increases through investment and therefore increases steadily as the economy develops. Neither has an upper limit. On the other hand, the total amount of natural capital is capped by the global environment, although its price fluctuates according to market conditions. Growth sustainability

**Table 8.3** Distribution of wealth by income category, 2018 (percent of total)

| | Natural capital | Produced capital | Human capital | Non-renewable natural capital |
|---|---|---|---|---|
| Low-income | 25.6 | 27.7 | 50.0 | 2.4 |
| Lower-middle-income | 13.5 | 27.2 | 62.1 | 3.3 |
| Upper-middle-income | 7.9 | 25.8 | 66.2 | 3.6 |
| High-income: non-OECD | 30.8 | 23.2 | 33.6 | 29.9 |
| High-income: OECD | 2.1 | 35.0 | 63.8 | 0.6 |
| World | 5.6 | 31.2 | 63.6 | 2.5 |

*Source* World Bank (2021), extracted partly from Table 9.1 (p. 197)

can be confirmed by checking the degree of changes in the capital of society as a whole, particularly the trends in the substitution of natural capital with human and produced capital. For example, the World Bank (2021) compares resource-rich and non-resource-rich countries, finding that the average level of human capital per capita in the former is lower than in the latter group. In other words, this suggests that the abundance of non-renewable resources prevents the accumulation of human capital through Dutch disease and other factors.

These indicators suggest a degree of sustainability that cannot be derived from GDP, which is a measurement of the results of economic activity up to that point. GDP does not tell us whether such growth has been achieved by consuming the "heritage" of natural resources and environment, or whether those resources have been successfully replaced by other means of production, or even the extent to which carbon is a threat to sustainability. For this reason, information on the environment and the quantity of capital is considered essential when considering indices of quality growth.

### 8.2.4 Composite Indices to Encompass Multiple Elements (1): The Genuine Progress Indicator

So far, I have presented the main trends in revisions to GDP and indices that focus on human resource development and happiness, as well as environmental and capital stock, which represent a component of quality growth. If so, perhaps integrating them will provide comprehensive information on the amount of quality growth. There are two further approaches related to the creation of a new, more composite index. One is the Genuine Progress Indicator (GPI), which evolved from the Index of Sustainable Economic Welfare (ISEW) proposed by Cobb and Daly in 1989. The other is the Better Life Initiative, which evolved from discussions at the Commission on the Measurement of Economic and Performance and Social Progress (Sarkozy Commission) in 2008 and 2009 and was ultimately finalized by the OECD. The former is presented as a composite index while the latter is a dashboard.

The GPI is a development of the ISEW. To correct for the deficiencies in GDP, ISEW deducts defensive expenditures and loss of resources from GDP, while adding unpaid domestic work etc., as well as adjusting for income inequality. Refining Progress, a US-based nonprofit organization, inherited the ISEW methodology and revised it to include additional items that had not been substantially accounted for before, such as volunteer work and the cost of crime in government consumption (Ujikawa 2011). As such, GPI was established as a means of expressing wellbeing not fully captured in GDP. Since then, its methodology has improved in response to the criticisms described later. Currently, GPI has been published for more than 30 countries (Berik 2020). Local governments are also working to calculate the GPI. In Japan, for example, Shiga and Hyogo prefectures made estimates in the mid-2000s. Since GPI is an index that integrates economic, environmental, and social factors, recent studies on GPI have increasingly referred to the SDGs, such as those by Cook and Davíðsdóttir (2021) and Cook et al. (2022). This implies that GPI indicators have a high affinity with the SDGs and quality growth.

The Redefining Progress explains the concept of GPI as follows (Talberth et al. 2006). First, summarizing previous studies, they argue that any approach that improves the deficiencies of GDP will need to include (1) welfare equivalent income, (2) sustainable income, and (3) net social profit. The first welfare equivalent income includes not only goods produced in a given period, but all services from goods produced in the past. It also deducts the harmful aspects of consumption rather than adding only positive benefits. Sustainable income refers to the maximum value of consumption in the current period that would allow the same amount of consumption in the next period. This requires the deduction of expenditures, such as depreciation of human-built and natural capital stocks and security. The net social benefit can be obtained through CBA. The GPI calculation begins with per capita consumption, then adjusts this figure according to the level of income inequality, and adds items not reflected in the market (such as volunteer work, unpaid housework and parenting, and services from the capital of the household and government). Defensive expenditures are then subtracted—such as those for environmental pollution, automobile accidents, other undesirable expenditures, and the cost of deterioration and loss of natural capital, as shown in Table 8.4.

GPI has significant relevance to quality growth. Private consumption is adjusted to account for the degree of inequality. This may be due to the fact that the utility derived from the same amount of consumption is greater for the poor than for the rich, and thus, the overall utility of a society with large income inequality is

**Table 8.4** Items included in GPI

| Area | Contributions to GPI | Item |
|---|---|---|
| Economy | + | Personal consumption, consumer durables (net), services of highway and street |
| | ± | Adjusted personal consumption based on income distribution (±), net capital investment (±), net foreign borrowing (±) |
| Environment | + | |
| | − | Cost of household pollution abatement, cost of water pollution, cost of air pollution, cost of noise pollution, loss of wetlands, loss of farmland, loss of primary forests and damage from logging roads, depletion of non-renewable energy resources, carbon dioxide emissions damage, cost of ozone depletion |
| Society and people | + | Housework and parenting, higher education, volunteering |
| | − | Cost of crime, loss of leisure time, cost of unemployment, cost of commuting, cost of automobile accidents |

*Source* Items from Talberth et al. (2006), Table 1, Area by Author expected to be smaller than that of a society without inequality. For this reason, the amount of personal consumption in the calculation of GPI is adjusted based on the ratio of the benchmark value of the Gini coefficient to the actual value (Berik 2020).[6] Next, for produced capital, net investment—which takes depreciation into account—is used rather than gross investment. Gross fixed capital formation (GFCF) in GDP accounted for 26% of the total on average worldwide in 2021, making it a major component of GDP.

In contrast, countries with large capital accumulation, such as developed countries, require large expenditures to maintain their current capital stock. Since maintenance expenditures have to be deducted when using the GPI, this increases the gap between GDP and GPI as the economy develops. In Japan, for example, net fixed capital formation can be even negative in some years while GFCF remains consistently and strongly positive. On the other hand, since the stock of capital provides benefits to the public, services derived from the stock are included in the GPI. In Table 8.4, while only road services are accounted for in GPI calculations—because in the US, roads and highways are free—government spending on public infrastructure is generally counted (e.g., Cook and Davíðsdóttir 2021).

In addition, some other government expenditures, such as education, are counted, while most government spending is considered to be for the maintenance of society and is therefore not included (Makino 2008). Cost items related to the environment are recorded negatively. Items related to society are included after imputed costs and opportunity costs are estimated. Empirical analysis shows that the gap between GPI and GDP per capita has increased with development in both the US and Japan (Talberth et al. 2006; Makino 2008). A breakdown of this difference suggests what is negative for the growth of the GPI. For example, in both Japan and the US, the major negative factors are widening income inequality and increasing $CO_2$ emissions, and the GPI has the significant advantage of capturing these changes related to inclusiveness and sustainability that are not represented by GDP.

There have also been criticisms of the GPI. Talberth et al. (2006) note major critiques as follows. The first is that it is unreasonable to link current wellbeing to sustainability indicators. For example, the loss of natural capital, which is important for future generations, has little to do with the wellbeing of the current generation. Another criticism concerns the use of a weak sustainability approach in its calculations, despite the fact that the applied principles of GPI reflect strong sustainability. This is because the GPI may be boosted by produced and human capital, even if natural capital is lost. The most serious criticism is that the elements of GPI are selected arbitrarily, in that "the GPI corrects for income inequality but does not include corrections for the degree of political freedom or degree of equality between the sexes" (Talberth et al. 2006). With regard to the calculation

[6] In some cases, the Atkinson Index is used instead of the Gini coefficient when adjusting for income inequality. This is because the Gini coefficient makes it difficult to determine the base year, whereas the Atkinson index expresses the deviation from the equal distribution as an index, thus avoiding the debate on the choice of base year (Nakano and Yoshikawa 2006).

method, there are also criticisms regarding the valuation of natural capital loss, the cumulative damage caused by environmental destruction, and the method of adjusting for income inequality.

Responding to these criticisms, Berik (2020) argued that a consensus is emerging among researchers on the need for revisions to the GPI. Several directions are being pursued, such as the use of the Atkinson index rather than the Gini coefficient to adjust for income inequality. Among the criticisms, the arbitrariness in the choice of index and its relationship to happiness is considered closely related to the weakness of its theoretical foundations, as pointed out by Berik (2020).

Berik (2020), in her summary, compares potential alternatives to GDP from several perspectives (Table 8.5). The GPI improves the deficiencies of GDP by incorporating elements of inclusiveness (inequality), sustainability (environmental and climate change, natural resources), and sustained growth (human resource development, including education). In many ways, it aligns with the idea of quality growth. However, some important differences remain. The first is about the treatment of investment. This is because GPI takes individual consumption as its starting point and focuses primarily on wellbeing. For produced capital, GPI uses the net figure of investment, deducting depreciation, rather than the gross amount—or it totally excludes all investment amounts from the aggregate calculation. Instead, it includes the utility derived from infrastructure and durable consumer goods.

However, since quality growth is essentially a sort of growth theory, the investment component cannot be excluded from consideration, as discussed in Chap. 6. The allocation of limited resources for total investment, including replacement investment, is examined, and the relationship between growth and investment is based on this. In order to measure the level of national income, taking into account social welfare aspects, analysis needs to be conducted using gross investment as a factor of quality growth.

Second, GPI essentially does not take resilience into account. From the perspective of GPI, government spending on disaster management is defensive in nature in that it maintains the current status. However, disaster prevention also enhances people's sense of security, which in turn can lead to accumulated investment in the region and enhance economic sustainability. Finally, because GPI does not employ any subjective measures of happiness, the theoretical rationale for linking the chosen items and happiness remains somewhat unclear.

### 8.2.5 Composite Indices to Encompass Multifaceted Elements (2): The Better Life Initiative and Discussions at the OECD

Finally, I would like to introduce the "Beyond GDP" discussion at the OECD and the Better Life Initiative. Discussions on developing an alternative index began in 2008, when then-French President Nicolas Sarkozy invited three prominent economists such as Joseph Stiglitz (President of the Commission), Amartya Sen

**Table 8.5** Strengths and shortcomings of the main beyond-GDP indicators

| | | GPI (1989) 2006 version | HDI (1990) 2010 version | HPI (2006) 2016 version | Cantril's Ladder[a] (2012) 2019 version | OECD BLI (2011) |
|---|---|---|---|---|---|---|
| Approach | | Monetary | Composite index | Composite index | Subjective evaluation | Dashboard |
| Relation to GDP | | Adjusts | Includes | No | No | No |
| Incorpo-rates: | Inequality | Yes | No | Yes | No | No |
| | Environment | Yes | No | Yes | No | Yes |
| | Non-market activities | Yes | No | No | No | Yes |
| | Dynamics of paid work | Yes | No | No | No | Yes |
| Enables: | Cross-country comparability | No | Yes 189 in 2018 | Yes 140 in 2016 | Yes 156 in 2019 | Yes 35 in 2017 |
| | Assessment of change over time for each country (%) | Yes | No | No | No | No |

[a]Cantril's Ladder is a survey question that asks respondents to rate their level of happiness on a scale from 0 to 10. It was proposed by social psychologist Hadley Cantril in the 1960s. By inviting respondents to identify the best and worst aspects of their lives and then asking them to rate their happiness on a scale, it is possible to identify the areas that most influence happiness (Easterlin 2021)
*Source* Berik (2020)

(Advisor) and Jean Paul Fitoussi (Coordinator) to lead the study. A committee of 24 experts was formed to discuss the proposal. The Stiglitz Commission's 12 recommendations incorporate the following pillars. First, material wealth is a useful starting point for measuring living standards and wellbeing, but the focus should be more on consumption and income rather than production, and it should account for the distribution of income and non-market activities.

Second, wellbeing encompasses multiple dimensions, including people's capabilities and their freedom to make choices. Subjective measures of happiness should also be considered. Third, sustainability should be measured using a well-defined dashboard, as composite indices rely on arbitrary means of assigning weights to various components. In this case, the monetary aspect of sustainability—which occupies a specific role in this category—is measurable, so it is necessary to look at changes in it. The monetary component includes produced capital, human capital, and natural resources traded on the market, and the World Bank has established a methodology for evaluating this component. If the rate of change is positive, then it means the growth will be sustainable (Stiglitz et al.2010). This is where it connects to the World Bank's wealth assessment mentioned earlier.

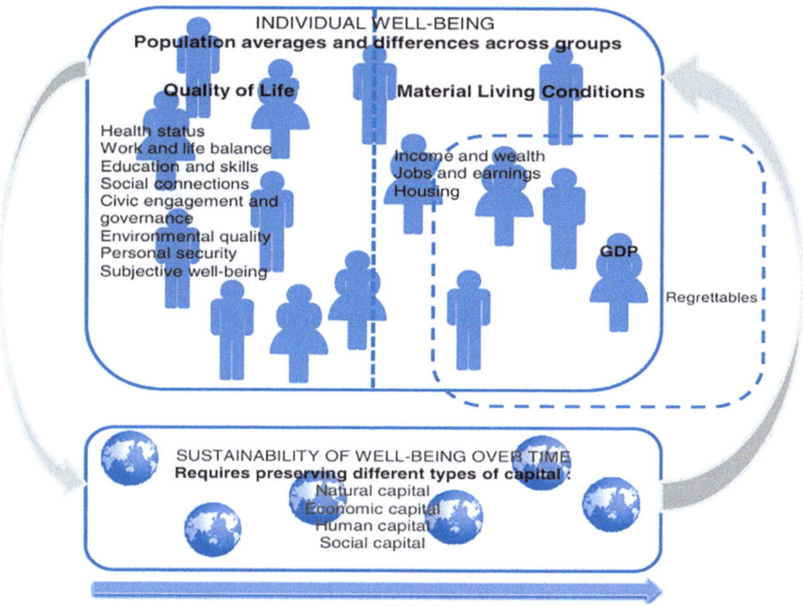


**Fig. 8.3** The "How's Life?" framework for measuring wellbeing and progress. *Source* OECD (2011, Fig. 1.2)

The OECD then took over from the Stiglitz commission, presenting two outcomes under the Better Life Initiative. The first approach was disseminated in a report titled "How's Life," which presented a basic framework for measuring people's wellbeing, proposing 11 items related to material living conditions and quality of life to measure. It also stated that the various forms of capital—natural, human, economic, and social capital—would determine future wellbeing. The overall conceptual diagram is shown in Fig. 8.3 (OECD 2011, 2020).

"How's Life?" is published every two years and reports on the current status of OECD countries on 11 items. Country reports are also published, which include the situation of resources. Another product is the Better Life Index (BLI), which includes one to three indicators for each of the 11 categories. While the differences between the BLI and How's Life? index are somewhat unclear, they share many common features.

It is important to note that the How's Life? framework employs the four types of capital as indicators for future wellbeing, in accordance with the sustainability recommendations of the Stiglitz committee. The specific indicators are shown in Table 8.6. This basic framework—i.e., the perspective of looking at current and future wellbeing using different indicators—has not been previously proposed. Such a distinction is important for the conceptual organization of quality growth as well as its indicators. Compared to this arrangement, the GPI is oriented toward a single index that includes resources, but its integration of items related to current and future wellbeing seems problematic.

**Table 8.6** Headline Indicators of resources for future wellbeing

| Dimension | Label |
|---|---|
| Economic capital | Produced fixed assets, Financial net worth of general government, Household debt |
| Natural capital | GHG emissions, Material foodprint, Red list index of threatened species |
| Human capital | Education attainment among young adult, Labor underutilization, Premature mortality |
| Social capital | Trust in others, Trust in government, Gender parity in politics |

*Source* OECD (2020), Annex Table 1.A.3 (This is an adaptation of an original work by the OECD, where Dimension and Label are extracted from the original table)

Alongside BLI, OECD hosted the High-Level Group on the Measurement of Economic Performance and Social Progress in 2013. There, prominent academics discussed how to measure economic outcomes and social progress until its end in 2018. Fifteen experts, chaired by Stiglitz, Fitoussi, and Durand, summarized the discussions in the main report and in a book that provides substantial academic detail (Stiglitz et al. 2018a, b). These works likely represent the most comprehensive synthesis of findings to date. Notably, the report also addresses resilience—an area rarely covered in many previous discussions of "Beyond GDP"—by presenting a method for measuring economic insecurity.

Economic insecurity, needless to say, has a significant impact on people's wellbeing, a concern that has increased following the GFC. The Stiglitz committee recommended that this should ideally be measured in terms of both the frequency of risk and the consequences of that risk (Stiglitz et al. 2010).[7] These discussions have not yet resulted in the development of a global indicator and are expected to continue in the future.

[7] There are two ways to measure economic instability: one is to ask subjective questions through household surveys or similar instruments, while the other is based on objective data. Hacker (2018) notes that with regard to the objective data, there are four categories: (1) measures of household and individual buffers; (2) estimates of the probabilities of economic shocks; (3) indexes of observed security; and (4) various measures of over-time economic (in)stability. An example of an index of observed security is an approach that combines elements of shocks, losses, and buffers against named risks, such as unemployment, illness, widowhood, disability and old age. As for economic stability, economic fluctuations mean changes in income and consumption. However, he argues that economic security and economic volatility are not synonymous, and he instead focuses solely on declines for indexing economic insecurity. He devised an index based on the percentage of people whose disposable income, including public benefits, has decreased significantly (by 25%). In this case, the important point in terms of resilience is the extent to which policies can avoid income declines due to external shocks. This indicator assumes that by providing figures for both the substantial decline in income and the substantial decline in disposable income after government transfers, it becomes clear how much loss has been avoided and how much decline in wellbeing has been averted. In other words, it helps to assess the extent of the government's contribution to the safety net through unemployment insurance, workers' compensation coverage, and pensions.

At the beginning of this book, I noted that quality growth is moving in the same direction as the international debate on indices beyond GDP. Moreover, the discussion at the OECD is consistent with the quality growth perspective described in this book—not only in its attention to factors other than income but also in its distinction between present and future implications, a division previously omitted from discussions on indices, as well as its incorporation of resilience. I will follow on from these findings in my discussion of a quality growth index, an approach that will be presented in the next chapter. In doing so, however, I believe that a composite index is still needed for the purpose of promoting quality growth, for example, among political leaders. This is because some of the elements that constitute quality growth involve trade-offs. As long as we are discussing it as a theory of growth, information on overall changes over time will be necessary for policy formulation and evaluation. Since this approach involves looking at wellbeing at two points in time—the present and the future—it will require two composite indices. In this regard, I can draw significantly from the GPI approach for insights on how to integrate the constituent elements.

## 8.3 Discussion on Indices Under the Name "Quality Growth"

To conclude this chapter, I will review whether an index has ever been developed under the name "quality growth." First, it was APEC and Japan who initially advocated for quality growth, but so far, they have not provided a quality growth index. However, APEC released an assessment of quality growth in 2020 based on commonly used statistics to assess progress in each of the five growth components of quality growth, as mentioned. For example, for balanced growth, these include the current account balance, the savings and investment ratio to GDP, and the debt to GDP (APEC 2020).

Stiglitz and Kanbur, who were members of the committee, comprehensively discussed quality growth in "The Quality of Growth in Africa" (Kanbur et al. 2019). In the first chapter of this book, Fioramonti (2019) explored ways of measuring quality growth. Beyond GDP, quality growth and the SDGs are all considered to share the same starting point, and indeed, what Fioramonti presented in "The Quality of Growth in Africa" was introduced earlier when discussing the sustainable wellbeing index in his co-authored essay (Costanza et al. 2016).

Fioramonti (2019) argues that in order to achieve a better quality of sustainable and inclusive growth in Africa, it is necessary to measure economic development using a different set of indicators. For this purpose, he suggests that a dashboard format is desirable and should have three pillars: social wellbeing, real economy and natural welfare. Under social wellbeing, he proposes that formal employment and income inequality should be included, as these factors have already been shown to significantly affect wellbeing. The real economy should include non-marketable and unpaid services in the statistics. Natural wellbeing is the suggestion that the consumption of natural resources to generate growth should be

**Table 8.7** Dashboard for quality growth based on the three pillars

| Category | Contents |
|---|---|
| Social wellbeing | Education, health, work-life balance, decent work |
| Real economy | Paid and unpaid work, social cohesion, household production/consumption, integrated reporting for public and private enterprises |
| Natural welfare | Natural resource use, biodiversity, ecological/carbon footprint, ecosystem preservation |

*Source* Fioramonti (2019)

taken into account. To measure the quality of growth, it is necessary to look at these three elements in an integrated manner through a dashboard (Table 8.7).

Fioramonti (2019) also proposes a composite index that integrates the dashboard components. He notes that the reason for the proposal is that there are trade-offs among indicators, so it is necessary to integrate them to see the overall picture, and policymakers need indices that are easy to use. Specifically, the Quality of Growth Index (QGI) is a function of the above three items, QGI = f (R, S, N), where R is the real economy contribution, S is the social wellbeing contribution, and N is the natural welfare contribution. He argues that the quality of growth perspective involves optimizing the balance between these three factors. The resulting equation is expressed as follows:

$$QGI = L_{max} \times (R/(k_r + R)) \times (S/(k_s + S)) \times (N/(k_n + N))$$

where: $L_{max}$ = the maximum achievable QGI when all factors are simultaneously at their maximum,

$k_r$ = the half saturation constant of R, that is, the value of R where the result of this term achieves half its maximum value[8],

$k_s$ = the half-saturation constant of S, and

$k_n$ = the half-saturation constant of N.

Here, the simplest representation of $L_{max}$ would be a scale from 0 to 10 or 100. When all three terms following $L_{max}$ approach one, QGI will approach its maximum value. If R, S or N are very large, the value of that term will approach one. Conversely, if the value of a term is small, that element becomes a variable that constrains the size of the overall $L_{max}$ (Constanza et al. 2016; Fioramonti et al. 2022). Maximizing $L_{max}$ in this equation means that balanced growth is achieved, which will be the desirable policy option. As discussed in previous chapters, since there are trade-offs or uncertain relationships among the elements of quality growth, this approach is useful for representing them.

[8] For example, if $k_r$ = 10, the value of $R/(k_r + R)$ approaches 0.5 when R is 10, or 0.67 when R = 20, or 0.83 when R = 50.

Thus far, there have been very few studies that have attempted to capture wellbeing under the name of a "quality growth index" by taking a comprehensive view of the limitations of GDP and the consumption of resources. In one study, Mlachila et al. (2014) propose an index of growth quality for developing countries. The authors argue that high growth rates alone are insufficient and that good quality growth is needed. Good quality growth is "strong, stable, and sustainable, increases productivity and leads to socially desirable outcomes, like improved standards of living, especially in the reduction of poverty." Mlachila et al. therefore propose the following Quality of Growth Index (QOGI):

(1) The QOGI shall be a composite index that integrates two components: a sub-index representing the nature of growth (growth fundamentals) and a sub-index representing desired social outputs from growth.
(2) Growth fundamentals consist of its (a) strength, (b) stability, (c) diversification of sources, and (d) outward-orientation, for a given period of growth episode.
(3) Social outputs consist of health (infant mortality and life expectancy at birth) and education (completion of primary education).
(4) QOGI first standardizes these variables and then sub-indexes them without weights. The two sub-indexes are then added together without weights to form an index. A geometric mean is also computed at the same time to see the robustness of the index.

The QOGI calculated this way confirms that for the majority of countries, the quality of growth has improved from 1990 to 2011, but at the same time, there are large differences by income and region.[9] Mlachila et al. (2014) then explore the relationship between such elements as political stability, institutions, macroeconomics and growth quality, noting that the advantage of the QOGI is that it is a relatively simple index of quality growth. On the other hand, it does not take into account issues such as the discussion of the limits of GDP, wellbeing, and the consumption of natural resources, as previously discussed.

The above is an international discussion on how to measure quality growth, starting from a review of GDP and progressing to the latest debates on the development of an index under the name of quality growth. The proposition of measuring quality growth is thus moving in the same direction as the broader international debates on the limits of GDP and measuring wellbeing. Discussions of HDI, happiness, environment and capital stock are all very much related to the fundamental aspects of measuring quality growth. The GPI and the OECD Dashboard, which themselves include most elements of quality growth, provide us with a basic framework for indexing quality growth. Based on these indices and the previously

[9] The conclusions are that (1) the quality of growth has improved in most countries over the past 20 years, (2) the rate of convergence among countries is slow, (3) there is wide variation across regions and income levels, and (4) the quality of growth is strongly positively related to external factors such as political stability, pro-poor fiscal spending, macroeconomic stability, financial development, institutional quality, and FDI.

proposed "quality growth index," in Chap. 9, I will present what a quality growth index should look like in the context of the definition and concept of quality growth that is developed in this book.

## References


Asia-Pacific Economic Cooperation (APEC), Policy Support Unit. 2020. APEC Strategy for Strengthening Quality Growth: Final Assessment Report. APEC.

Berik, Günseli. 2020. "Measuring What Matters and Guiding Policy: An Evaluation of the Genuine Progress Indicator." *International Labour Review* 159 (1): 71–94.

Borucke, Michael, David Moore, Gemma Cranston, Kyle Gracey, Katsunori Iha, Joy Larson, Elias Lazarus, Juan Carlos Morales, Mathis Wackernagel, and Alessandro Galli. 2013. "Accounting for Demand and Supply of the Biosphere's Regenerative Capacity: The National Footprint Accounts' Underlying Methodology and Framework." *Ecological Indicators* 24: 513–533.

Cabinet Office, Economic and Social Research Institute, Japan. 2016. "Kankyō keizai kanjyō sentoraru fureimuwāku ni kansuru kentōsagyō SEEA-CF gaisetsusho" [Study Work on the Central Framework for Environmental and Economic Accounts SEEA-CF Summary]. https://www.esri.cao.go.jp/jp/sna/sonota/satellite/kankyou/contents/1219519_6014.html.

Cook, Davíd, and Brynhildur Davíðsdóttir. 2021. "An Estimate of the Genuine Progress Indicator for Iceland, 2000–2019." *Ecological Economics* 189: 107154.

Cook, David, Brynhidur Davíðsdóttir, and Ingunn Gunnarsdóttir. 2022. "A Conceptual Exploration of How the Pursuit of Sustainable Energy Development Is Implicit in the Genuine Progress Indicator." *Energies* 15 (6): 2129.

Costanza, Robert, Lew Daly, Lorenzo Fioramonti, Enrico Giovannini, Ida Kubiszewski, Lars Fogh Mortensen, Kate E. Pickett, Kristin Vala Ragnarsdottir, Roberto De Vogli, and Richard Wilkinson. 2016. "Modelling and Measuring Sustainable Wellbeing in Connection with the UN Sustainable Development Goals." *Ecological Economics* 130: 350–355.

Coyle, Diane. 2014. *GDP: A Brief but Affectionate History*. Princeton University Press.

Easterlin, Richard A. 2021. *An Economist's Lessons on Happiness: Farewell Dismal Science*. Springer.

Economic Planning Agency (EPA), Economic Research Institute, Japan.1998. "Kankyō keizai tōgō kanjyō no shisan ni tsuite" [Estimates for the Integrated Environment and Economy Account]. https://www.esri.cao.go.jp/jp/sna/sonota/satellite/kankyou/contents/g_eco1.html.

Fioramonti, Lorenzo. 2019. "Beyond Gross Domestic Product: Measuring the Quality of Growth in Africa." In *The Quality of Growth in Africa*, eds. Ravi Kanbur, Akbar Noman, and Joseph E. Stiglitz, 33–53. Columbia University Press.

Fioramonti, Lorenzo, Luca Coscieme, Robert Costanza, Ida Kubiszewski, Katherine Trebeck, Stewart Wallis, Debra Roberts, Lars F. Mortensen, Kate E. Pickett, Richard Wilkinson, Kristín Vala Ragnarsdottír, Jacqueline McGlade, Hunter Lovins, and Roberto De Vogli. 2022. "Wellbeing Economy: An Effective Paradigm to Mainstream Post-Growth Policies?" *Ecological Economics* 192: 107261.

Hacker, Jacob S. 2018. "Economic Security." In *For Good Measure: Advancing Research on Well-being Metrics Beyond GDP*, eds. Joseph E. Stiglitz, Jean-Paul Fitoussi, and Martine Durand, 203–240. OECD Publishing.

Helliwell, John F., Richard Layard, Jeffrey D. Sachs, Jan-Emmanuel De Neve, Lara B. Aknin, and Shun Wang (eds.). 2022. *World Happiness Report*. Sustainable Development Solutions Network.

Kanbur, Ravi, Akbar Noman, and Joseph E. Stiglitz (eds.). 2019. *The Quality of Growth in Africa*. Columbia University Press.

Lin, David, Laurel Hanscom, Adeline Murthy, Alessandro Galli, Mikel Evans, Evan Neill, Maria Serena Mancini, Jon Martindill, Fatime-Zahra Medouar, Shiyu Huang, and Mathis Wackernagel. 2018. "Ecological Footprint Accounting for Countries: Updates and Results of the National Footprint Accounts, 2012–2018." *Resources* 7: 58.

Lyubomirsky, Sonja. 2013. *The Myth of Happiness: What Should Make You Happy, but Doesn't, What Shouldn't Make You Happy, but Does.* Inkwell Management LLC.

Lyubomirsky, Sonja, Kennon M. Sheldon, and David Schkade. 2005. "Pursuing Happiness: The Architecture of Sustainable Change." *Review of General Psychology* 9 (2): 111–131.

Makino, Matsuyo. 2008. "Genuine progress indicator no keisoku: 1970–2003 nen data ni motozuku kaitei ban" [Measuring the Genuine Progress Indicator: 1970 to 2003: Revised Version based on 2003 data]. Economic and Business Administration Research Institute, Kenkyuu Shiryo. No. 223. University of Hyogo.

Masood, Ehsan. 2021. *GDP: The World's Most Powerful Formula and Why it Must Now Change.* Icon Books.

Mlachila, Montfort, René Tapsoba, and Sampawende J. A. Tapsoba. 2014. "A Quality of Growth Index for Developing Countries: A Proposal." IMF Working Paper WP/14/172. IMF.

Nakano, Katsura, and Eiji Yoshikawa. 2006, "Genuine progress indicator to sono kanōsei" [Genuine Progress Indicator and its Potential]. *Hikone Ronso* 357: 175–193. EBRISK, Shiga University.

Ohashi, Michio. 2006. "Ecological footprint ni tsuite no hihanteki ichi kōsatsu" [A Critical Consideration on Ecological Footprints]. *Wakayama Economic Review* 329: 43–65. Wakayama University.

Organization for Economic Co-operation and Development (OECD). 2011. How's Life? Measuring Well-being. OECD. https://www.oecd.org/content/dam/oecd/en/publications/reports/2011/10/how-s-life_g1g14dc9/9789264121164-en.pdf.

Organization for Economic Co-operation and Development (OECD). 2013. OECD Guidelines on Measuring Subjective Well-Being. OECD. https://www.oecd.org/en/publications/oecd-guidelines-on-measuring-subjective-well-being_9789264191655-en.html.

Organization for Economic Co-operation and Development (OECD). 2020. How's Life? Measuring Well-being. OECD. https://www.oecd.org/content/dam/oecd/en/publications/reports/2020/03/how-s-life-2020_b547d82c/9870c393-en.pdf.

Sheldon, Kennon M., and Sonya Lyubomirsky. 2021. "Revisiting the Sustainable Happiness Model and Pie Chart: Can Happiness Be Successfully Pursued?" *Journal of Positive Psychology* 16 (2): 145–154.

Stiglitz, Joseph E., Jean-Paul Fitoussi, and Martine Durand. 2018a. *Beyond GDP: Measuring What Counts for Economic and Social Performance.* OECD.

Stiglitz, Joseph E, Jean-Paul Fitoussi, and Martine Durand (eds.). 2018b. *For Good Measure: Advancing Research on Well-being Metrics Beyond GDP.* OECD.

Stiglitz, Joseph E., Amartya Sen, and Jean-Paul Fitoussi. 2010. *Mismeasuring Our Lives: Why GDP Doesn't Add Up*, Preface. The New Press.

Talberth, John, Clifford Cobb, and Noah Slattery. 2006. "The Genuine Progress Indicator 2006: A Tool for Sustainable Development." Redefining Progress.

Ujikawa, Keiji. 2011. "Jizoku kanō shihyō ni okeru shūyakuteki na keizai shihyō deno kankyō hyōka no hikakubunseki" [Comparative Analysis of Environmental Valuation in Aggregate Economic Indicators in Sustainability Indicators]. *Yokohama Journal of Social Science* 16 (3): 13–27 AYISSS. Yokohama National University.

United Nations Development Programme (UNDP). n.d. *Human Development Index (HDI) dataset.* Accessed March 10. 2025, https://hdr.undp.org/data-center/human-development-index#/indicies/HDI

World Bank. 2006. *Where is the Wealth of Nations? Measuring Capital for the 21st Century.* World Bank.

World Bank. 2018. *The Human Capital Project.* World Bank.

World Bank. 2021. *The Changing Wealth of Nations 2021: Managing Assets for the Future.* World Bank. http://hdl.handle.net/10986/36400.

**Koki Hirota** earned his B.A. in Economics from the University of Tokyo and holds a Ph.D. in Economics from Saitama University in Japan. His professional career spans several prominent roles in international development finance and policy, including Chief Economist, Director General of Operation and Strategy Department, and Director General of Southeast Asia and Pacific Department at the Japan International Cooperation Agency (JICA), and Chief Representative in Jakarta for Japan Bank for International Cooperation and in Hanoi for the Overseas Economic Cooperation Fund. In academia, he was a Professor at the Graduate School of Humanities and Social Sciences at Saitama University and a Visiting Fellow at the JICA Ogata Sadako Research Institute for Peace and Development. His recent publications include *Challenges in Fiscal and Monetary Policies in Mongolia* (co-edited, Springer, 2023) and *Addressing Social Infrastructure Needs in Asia: Towards a Pandemic Resilient Society* (co-edited, JICA, August 2025).

# Achieving Quality Growth

# 9

Koki Hirota

This chapter summarizes the previous discussions and presents policies to realize quality growth. In the first section of this chapter, I briefly discuss how quality growth complements the SDGs. As stated at the beginning of this book, quality growth shares the same background as the SDGs and, therefore, can be considered an approach to their realization. In Sect. 9.2 of this chapter, I present an overall framework for the quality growth concept, summarizing the earlier discussions. Quality growth, as noted earlier in this part, encompasses several elements: some are complementary while others involve trade-offs, spanning different time frames, and covering both current and future generations. Here, these elements are reorganized as a whole to meet two main objectives—enhancing present wellbeing in ways not captured by income alone, and achieving growth that will continue into the future. This is followed by a proposal on what indicators could be used to measure both.

Finally, in Sect. 9.3, I present a common, cross-cutting framework for society as a whole to achieve quality growth. In the previous chapters, policies and growth strategies to enhance inclusiveness, resilience, and sustainability were presented. Readers seeking knowledge of country-specific good practices for quality growth may also appreciate the companion book by Hosono (2022), as noted in the Foreword. Therefore, in Sect. 9.3 of this chapter, I focus on how an overarching policy framework can be established to integrate various policies and development strategies in an integrated manner. Then, in the Appendix of this chapter, I attempt to index quality growth for nine countries. At this stage, this constitutes only a preliminary and incomplete proposal, primarily due to a lack of empirical evidence and data. However, I believe that this proposed index will help to establish a more

K. Hirota (✉)
Tokyo, Japan


K. Hirota (ed.), *Introduction to Quality Growth*,
https://doi.org/10.1007/978-981-95-6220-6_9

concrete idea for readers of how quality growth can be expressed, highlighting the characteristics of each country's development of quality growth.

## 9.1 Quality Growth and the SDGs

### 9.1.1 Background to the SDGs

The SDGs are international goals for building a better world by 2030. They consist of 17 goals and 169 targets, including poverty eradication, education, health, inequality, and climate change, and were adopted unanimously by all countries at the 2015 UN summit. The targets are designed not only for developing countries—as the MDGs had been—but also apply to developed countries. One of the key concepts underpinning the SDGs is the development of human resources in developing countries. Prior to the introduction of the SDGs, the MDGs were the international development goals for the period from 2000 to 2015. The MDGs targeted developing countries, following international discussions on poverty reduction at the end of the last century. As the successor to the MDGs, the SDGs address the same development challenges as the MDGs, as clearly stated in the UN document, "Transforming our World: The 2030 Agenda for Sustainable Development," formally adopted by the UN in September 2015 (SDGs Outcome Document).

Another underlying principle of the SDGs is related to the outcomes of major UN conferences, which are referred to as the foundation of the SDGs in the Outcome Document. Among these, the Rio Declaration on Environment and Development—adopted at the UN Conference on Sustainable Development (Rio +20) in 2012—is considered particularly important (Hirota 2019). This followed an intergovernmental negotiation process that agreed to incorporate the Rio + 20 discussions into the MDGs and to develop international targets for the post-2015 agenda. Rio +20 marked the 20th anniversary of the 1992 United Nations Conference on Environment and Development (also known as the Earth Summit), which aimed to integrate environmental and developmental considerations to achieve sustainable development.

Paragraph 12 of the Outcome Document states: "We reaffirm all the principles of the Rio Declaration on Environment and Development, including, inter alia, the principle of common but differentiated responsibilities…" The term "common but differentiated responsibilities" refers to the idea that while humanity shares responsibility for global warming, as developed countries have emitted the majority of GHGs to date and have created today's problematic situation, they should bear a greater share of the responsibility for financial and technological contributions to address it. As a result of this perspective, the SDGs have become a development goal not only for developing countries, as was the case with the MDGs, but also for developed countries. Although the discussions at Rio +20 largely focused on the environment and climate change, they were comprehensive and encompassed many other areas. "The Future We Want," the outcome document of Rio +20, outlines several themes and cross-cutting issues that form a framework for action, incorporating agriculture, energy, tourism, transportation, and other economic sectors, as well as health, education, gender, and other areas of human development.

International discussions to establish a post-2015 agenda following Rio +20 in 2012 took place across several platforms. The open working group based on Rio +20; the UN interagency task team, involving all UN development agencies; the High Level Panel of eminent persons on the post-2015 development agenda comprising 27 members to advice to the UN Secretary-General; and the Sustainable Development Solutions Network (SDSN), an independent network established by the UN Secretary-General, each gathered opinions and provided recommendations. Looking at the process that led to the SDGs, it is clear that the 17 goals were formulated through wide-ranging international discussions. Hirota (2019) states that this process of formulation differs significantly from the process of formulating the MDGs, which was primarily donor-led and compiled, and that these differences have shaped the SDGs into what they are today. In other words, the MDGs reflected the aid priorities of donors, whereas the SDG formulation process was the result of open discussions and the proactive participation of developing countries—the parties to development—in the discussions. Thus, the SDGs incorporate economic sectors in addition to human resources development and environmental and climate change issues.

### 9.1.2 Content and Structure of the SDGs

The Outcome Document for the SDGs consists of the Preamble, Declaration, Sustainable Development Goals and Targets, Means of Implementation and the Global Partnership, and Follow-up and Review. The Preamble states that eradicating poverty remains the greatest global challenge, and that the SDGs "are integrated and indivisible and balance the three dimensions of sustainable development: the economic, social and environmental." The Preamble also presents five domains for the SDGs: People, Planet, Prosperity, Peace, and Partnership (5Ps), along with objectives for actions on each. Therefore, each goal and target of the SDGs relates to one of the three dimensions or 5Ps.

Next, it refers to the "interlinkages and integrated nature" of the SDGs, which overlaps strongly with the quality growth approach. The 17 goals and 169 targets in the outcome document are listed without indicating which of the three aspects or 5Ps each corresponds to. This is likely because, while some of the MDG-derived goals can be completed exclusively within a single dimension or domain (for example, Goals 3, 4, and 5 fall only within the social dimension), there are many areas where simple categorization is difficult. For example, Goal 1 includes targets for society (e.g., protection of the poor) and the economy (e.g., per capita income, access to finance for the poor), and Goal 2 includes targets for multiple aspects, including society (e.g., hunger), economy (e.g., agricultural production), and environment (e.g., genetic resources). This is because, as noted in the SDGs, development in many areas requires integrated efforts in economic, social, and environmental aspects.

Although the relationship between the goals and targets of the SDGs and their structure is not explicitly shown, it is stated that they are considered integrated and indivisible, with direct and indirect causal relationships among them. For example, take Target 1.1 "By 2030, eradicate extreme poverty for all people everywhere, currently measured as people living on less than $1.25 a day." Raising per capita income requires both economic growth and reducing income inequality, and achieving the former requires Industrial development and infrastructure (Goal 9) and Agricultural development (Goal 2), while the latter requires income redistribution (Goal 10) and equal opportunities for all in many fields (Goals 3, 4, 5, etc.). How one perceives these relationships, and thus the structure of the SDGs, may depend on the position and awareness of the party to consider. For example, JICA states that the SDGs ultimately aim to eradicate poverty, achieve gender equality, correct inequality, and achieve peace, and that Goals 3 (Health) and 4 (Education) are considered fundamental requirements and prerequisites to be addressed in order to achieve the various goals (JICA 2016). This is indicative of their characteristics, whose primary mission is to develop human resources in developing countries.

To contrast the SDGs with quality growth, it may be better to base the overall picture on the three aspects of social, economic, and environmental, or the five Ps, rather than focusing on each of the goals from 1 to 17. Hirota (2019) simplifies the structure of the SDGs as shown in Fig. 9.1. Here, the economy is placed at the center, as increasing per capita income through economic growth is essential to achieve the ultimate goal of poverty eradication. Economy refers to activities directly related to production and includes targets, such as infrastructure, energy, and agriculture. Surrounding it is society, the place where production activities occur, and the people who engage in economic activities. What is important to people is not only income, but also human resource development, including education and health, which are indispensable in meeting their basic needs. At the same time, as we saw in Chap. 6, human resources are a source of endogenous growth, and productivity growth is a result of human resources development. As such, economy and society are interconnected. Finally, the global environment surrounding society is affected by people's activities and production, enabling people to live prosperously and facilitating the enhancement of economic activities. This structure is similar to the structure of quality growth as organized in Chap. 2.

### 9.1.3 Quality Growth as an Approach that Complements and Realizes the SDGs

In this section, I divide each of the goals and targets of the SDGs into three dimensions and consider which element of quality growth each objective falls under. This method of organization allows for an overview of how quality growth is integrated into the SDGs (Table 9.1). Taking the example of the economic dimension,

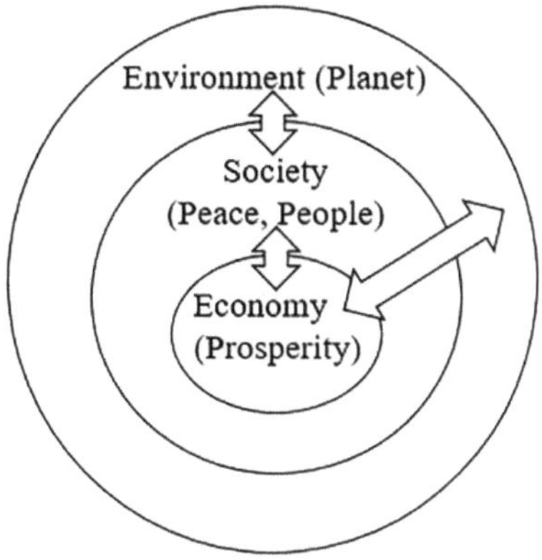


**Fig. 9.1** Three aspects of the SDGs with the economy at the center. *Source* Hirota (2019)

improving energy efficiency (Target 7.3: Double the global rate of improvement in energy efficiency) primarily promotes sustained growth, while pro-poor ownership and access to finance (Target 1.4) primarily promote inclusiveness. Such categorizations may be less than straightforward in some cases, as a single target may include multiple elements of quality growth. Moreover, there may be disagreements about how the categorization has been applied. Nevertheless, by organizing them in this way, it becomes possible to contrast quality growth and the SDGs, and to ascertain what the SDGs address in terms of the social, economic, and environmental dimensions in order to realize quality growth.

Below, I review how the elements of quality growth correspond to the SDGs. First, growth is directly addressed in Goal 8, "Promote sustained, inclusive and sustainable economic growth," where the word "sustained" is used to indicate that growth will be uninterrupted, as previously noted. The term "growth" appears only here among the 17 goals, but targets that refer to productive activities and their continuation can be found in Goals 7, 8, and 9. However, the number of targets directly related to growth in the SDGs is somewhat limited. Regarding inclusiveness, the term "inclusive" is used in the titles of Goals 4, 8, 9, 11, and 16. Moreover, some goals are aimed at increasing inclusiveness across both the economic and social dimensions. The economic dimension includes targets related to per capita income for the poor, finance, energy and transportation access, etc. The social dimension has the largest number of targets among the SDGs, incorporating MDG-derived targets (Goals 3, 4, 5, etc.), as well as those related to reducing inequality and improving human settlements (see Chap. 3 for more on inequality). It has been noted that these targets have a causal relationship with the economy, in that they enable people to live a life of dignity and fulfill their potential, while also contributing to economic growth and poverty reduction in the long run as a result.

The term "sustainability" is used repeatedly throughout the goals and targets. Most of the targets in Goals 13, 14, and 15 focus on sustainability, where they fall under the environmental dimension. Goal 12 is concerned with the economic aspects of production and consumption, but its objective is global environmental

**Table 9.1** SDGs and quality growth

| Three dimensions | Objective (elements of quality growth) | SDG targets* |
|---|---|---|
| Economy | Sustained growth | 7.3, 8.2–3, 8.9, 9.2–3, 9.5 |
| | Inclusiveness | 1.1, 1.4, 2.3, 7.1, 8.1, 8.10, 9.1, 10.1, 10.4–6, 11.2 |
| | Sustainability | 7.2, 8.4, 9.4, 12.1–7, 14.6–7 |
| | Resilinece | 2.4 |
| Society | Sustained growth | – |
| | Inclusiveness | 1.2–3, 2.1–2, 3.1–8, 4.1–6, 5.1–6, 6.1–2, 8.5–8, 10.2–3, 10.7, 11.1, 11.3–4, 11.7, 16.1–10 |
| | Sustainability | 4.7, 12.8 |
| | Relience | 1.5, 11.5 |
| Environment | Sustained growth | – |
| | Inclusiveness | 3.9, 6.4 |
| | Sustainability | 2.5, 6.3, 6.5–6, 11.6, 13.2–3, 14.1–5, 15.1–9 |
| | Resilience | 13.1 |

*Note* This table omits the targets under Goal 17, as they relate to the means of implementation, as well as the implementation targets within each of the 17 goals (i.e., target numbers ending in an alphabetical letter)
*Source* Author

sustainability. Some of the targets in Goal 11 also relate to sustainability, particularly across the social dimensions of cities. Finally, with regard to "resilience," this term is used in the titles of Goal 9 and 11 and targets under Goals 1, 2, 13, and 14. However, many of these are not primarily about resilience alone, for example, "Inclusive, safe, resilient, and sustainable cities…" (Goal 11). Therefore, although only a few of the targets in Table 9.1 appear to fall under the category of resilience, such as a target related to climate resilience, it should be noted that some of them, although not shown in this table, aim to achieve resilience while simultaneously addressing other elements. Notably, the viewpoint of resilience to economic crises does not appear in the SDGs.

By contrasting quality growth and the SDGs as described above, I argue that there are two major implications. First, there are many similarities in the basic perspectives and core elements between the two. That is, both income and other aspects are important for people to be prosperous, and a holistic approach to the three dimensions of the economy, society, and the environment is necessary. Second, due to their origin, the SDGs face a number of limitations.[1] For example, there is little recognition that growth is a major driver of poverty reduction, and,

[1] In addition to the issues raised in the text, some of the limitations of the SDGs appear to stem from their roots in the MDGs (which focused on human resource development) and the Earth Summit (which focused on environment and climate change). The main limitations, in the author's view, are as follows:

therefore, the goals are limited to those that directly refer to growth. There is also no mention of resilience with respect to the economy, and the goals do not always specifically address what activities are expected of the private sector to enable growth.[2] Despite these limitations, the discussion of quality growth, although not perfect, covers these issues in its scope. For example, APEC's strategy places digital development at the center of innovation. In conclusion, quality growth is an approach that aligns with the realization of the SDGs, while also emphasizing poverty reduction through growth, a goal not fully articulated in the SDGs.

## 9.2 Summarizing the Concept and Background Theory of Quality Growth

### 9.2.1 Purpose

Quality growth is a proposal for how growth should be. The argument that "quality" of growth is important has been made in various forms, most directly and notably in the report of the World Bank Institute, which uses the term "quality" in its discussion, as described in Chap. 2. The concept of quality growth is an approach to growth that integrates several key elements of growth quality that have been discussed to date, and I noted in Chap. 8 that this direction is consistent with the international discussions on "Beyond GDP," where people's wellbeing or

a. Underestimating the significant role of economic growth;
b. Lack of an overarching structure, clear relationships, and prioritization between the goals; absence of a theoretical framework to guide the SDGs;
c. Minimal attention paid to economic aspects, including economic management, fiscal and monetary policy, debt and crisis management;
d. Failure to address the flaws in current market mechanisms, such as socially responsible investment, predatory capitalism, and excessive marketization;
e. Insufficient attention to the specific challenges of developed countries, including declining birthrates and aging populations;
f. Neglect of capital accumulation and its maintenance, such as degradation of public capital, depletion of natural resources; and,
g. Absence of an integrated framework for measuring outcomes.

[2] In Japan, the SDG Promotion Headquarters was established in May 2016, and the Implementation Guiding Principles were formulated in December of the same year. Regarding these principles, in relation to private sector activities, areas such as the environment and climate change and digital innovation are emphasized as drivers of future growth in the context of promoting the SDGs, and expectations for business and finance are clearly stated. Although I mentioned that the SDGs do not specifically articulate the activities of the private sector, in Japan's case, the government has specifically indicated the role the private sector should play, such as using digital technology and big data to address social problems. In other words, what was lacking in the SDGs is compensated for in the national implementation principles in Japan. The 2023 version of the principles refers to digital transformation and green transformation.

overall welfare of society cannot be measured solely by growth in monetary measures, and other factors, such as inequality, must be improved. Quality growth is a form of growth that continuously improves the integrated outcomes of various factors' progress. In essence, quality growth aims to realize the following two major objectives:

1. As society's overall welfare cannot be measured by GDP alone, it should be viewed as encompassing factors other than income and should aim to improve all of them.
2. It should aim to ensure that overall social welfare continues to improve in the future.

Areas such as inclusiveness, resilience, sustainability, and innovation are elements that must be given special consideration in order to achieve these two objectives. To achieve quality growth, it is necessary not only to sustain growth but also to change the way in which the very nature of current growth itself is perceived. While the two are interrelated, the measures required to achieve each are different. As discussed in Chap. 5, while GHG emissions have limited effects on the current generations, they may compromise the wellbeing of future generations. The components of quality growth presented by APEC and Japan are not categorized into current and future objectives. To make this point clearer, I consider it appropriate to define the central aims of quality growth as the pursuit of these two objectives.

The elements of quality growth—such as inclusiveness and others that APEC and Japan advocate—can be thought of as representing the main areas of focus for achieving these two objectives. For example, by adding elements of inclusiveness, the first objective, the overall welfare of society, becomes more comprehensive. Suppose that a country's policy objective is solely the pursuit of sustainability; if implemented in an extreme way, GHG emissions can be reduced by curbing economic activity. But this is, of course, inappropriate as a policy argument at the national level. Taking quality infrastructure investment (QII), discussed in Chap. 7 as an example, investments in infrastructure for disaster prevention will of course increase a country's resilience. However, it is insufficient to pursue this kind of investment alone, and it is necessary to allocate limited resources to other purposes in a way that benefits society most effectively as a whole. Instead, a more optimal approach would comprise a combination that maximizes results as measured by a quality growth index. In reality, policy management in any country—not limited to infrastructure—is conducted while considering the balance between growth, inequality, environment, disaster prevention, and so on. In other words, even if not explicitly stated, such balanced policy management has been taken to a greater or lesser extent. Quality growth is a discussion that seeks to pursue a society in which people can lead more affluent lives by clarifying the theoretical underpinnings of such growth, emphasizing the elements that constitute it such as inclusiveness, clarifying the relationship between these elements and growth, and then measuring changes in it as a result of policy efforts.

### 9.2.2 Relationships Among the Components of Quality Growth

Under this objective, Table 9.2 briefly summarizes the elements, purposes, targets, and means of implementation that comprise quality growth.

For the items presented in Table 9.2, the main objectives of sustained growth—the ability to generate future growth and the expansion of welfare, including non-monetary, for society as a whole—are fundamentally different. While there are many complementary relationships between the two, some elements conflict with one another. These relationships are summarized in Table 9.3. It should be noted that I focus here only on income. This is because the monetary component constitutes a major part of welfare, so it is appropriate to first examine the impact on income. The results can then be used to extend the analysis to non-monetary factors that are not represented in the market but contribute to wellbeing. In the discussion in the Appendix of this chapter, I estimate the measurement of quality growth in this way. There, I use the magnitude of consumption as the base and reduce the loss of welfare due to inequality or add the consumer surplus, among other adjustments.

Table 9.3 summarizes much of what has already been discussed, but it is worth revisiting the key elements to offer some additional clarification. The extent to which inclusiveness is associated with monetary growth is unclear in the short term. Partly because of this, inequality has not been discussed so far in relation

**Table 9.2** Keywords constituting quality growth (summary)

| Elements | Purpose | Target | Means |
|---|---|---|---|
| Inclusiveness | Overall social welfare<br>Sustained growth | Improving situations of vulnerable groups<br>Correcting income inequalities that have arisen | Equality of opportunities<br>Redistribution by government |
| Resilience | Overall social welfare<br>Sustained growth | Resistance and recovery to external shocks | Preparedness and response to external shocks |
| Sustainability | Sustained growth | Equity between the current and future generations | Reduction of GHG emissions<br>Maintaining critical natural capital (CNC) |
| Growth mechanisms | Sustained growth | Continuous expansion of economy | Productivity increase<br>Capital increase |
| Welfare beyond measurable in the market | Overall social welfare | Increased wellbeing beyond income | Development of digital technologies and others to increase consumer surplus |

*Source* Author

**Table 9.3** Interrelationships among elements that form quality growth

| Quality growth elements (A) | Elements affected (B) | Impact of A on B |
|---|---|---|
| Inclusiveness | Sustained growth | + (Human capital enhanced by equal opportunity) |
| | National income | ? (No consensus, although many recent studies have shown that reducing inequality increases national income) |
| Resilience | Sustained growth | + (Investment accumulation is more likely to occur) |
| | National income | ? (Avoiding economic downturns, but increased risk preparedness can reduce allocation of investments that expand production) |
| Environmental sustainability | Sustained growth | + (Enabling global environment to be maintained, through which economic activities will be promoted, providing long-term benefits) |
| | National income | – (In the short term, cost increases as social costs are added to production) |
| Sustained growth | Inclusiveness | ? (No consensus, while the inverted-U shaped curve is now generally considered not to apply) |
| | Resilience | ? (Long-term accumulation of investments in disaster prevention, but loss and damage may also increase as a result of asset growth) |
| | Environmental sustainability | ? (Carbon intensity improves as economy develops, but no consensus on whether the environmental Kuznets U curve applies to GHG emissions) |
| National income | Inclusiveness | ? (Relationship between the scale of GDP and inequality is uncertain) |
| | Resilience | + (Reserves for external shocks can easily be prepared, but this depends on resource management) |
| | Environmental sustainability | – (Large per capita GHG emissions in high-income, developed countries) |
| Inclusiveness | Resilience | + (Mitigating economic shocks by increasing the savings of the poor and improved social safety net) |
| | Environmental sustainability | ? (Unknown impact of inequality on GHG emissions) |
| Resilience | Inclusiveness | + (The poor who are more vulnerable to external shocks benefit greatly) |
| | Environmental Sustainability | ? (Unknown impact of resilience on GHG emissions) |
| Environmental sustainability | Inclusiveness | + (Vulnerable groups more severely affected by global warming benefit significantly) |
| | Resilience | + (Mitigating vulnerability if the intensity of the disaster is reduced) |

*Source* Author

to economic policies that target growth. Even in developed countries, the widening of inequality has been tolerated, at least to some extent. Today, as inequality continues to widen and become increasingly detrimental, many argue that it has a negative impact on growth. The Japanese government, for example, has made a virtuous cycle of distribution and growth its main policy goal. The view that the demand-creation effect generated by improving inequality is greater than the savings-expansion effect of inequality seems to fit Japan's current situation. However, as already noted, there are two sides to the argument as to which effect is greater, and I believe the answer depends on the country's situation at the time. Rather than attempting to establish a one-way relationship between the two, it is more important to frame this relationship as a universal policy principle: reducing inequality increases the welfare of society as a whole, including income resulting from growth,[3] and promotes future growth by increasing the equality of opportunities for the poor.

With regard to sustainability, climate change mitigation efforts have a negative impact on short-term growth. They may also lay the foundations for long-term growth and contribute to building a safer society by reducing disaster risks for vulnerable groups who may be disproportionately affected, although these efforts may lead to a smaller allocation of resources to productive activities, restraining growth in the short term. The impacts of enhanced resilience on growth are uncertain in the short run, but by increasing preparedness to respond to incidents of external shocks, safer societies will be constructed, contributing to an increase in overall social welfare. In the long run, increased resilience will encourage investment and have a greater effect on protecting vulnerable groups.

### 9.2.3 Identifying the Overall Welfare of Society Beyond Income (Horizontal Expansion)

The relationships among the elements of quality growth are thus intricate. One of the characteristics of "wicked" public problems is their complexity, whereby a policy in one area relates to other areas. Policies related to growth are no exception to this characteristic. In this case, the feature relates to the fact that there are two objectives of quality growth, which involve a trade-off between short-term (current income and welfare) and long-term (future growth potential) objectives.

I will delve first into the short-term objective of overall societal welfare. For this, it is necessary to consider factors beyond income, since individual wellbeing cannot be measured by income alone. Here, I primarily discuss expenditures, one of the three dimensions of GDP, because consumption is an essential component of wellbeing. As for the size of the economy, as previously mentioned, volunteer

[3] As previously noted, the GPI index adjusts the size of income for inequality. By indexing it in this way, it is possible to quantify the impact of reducing inequality on the economy. Such an adjustment can be quantitatively transformed based on certain assumptions. The concept of making this assumption, i.e., how much weight to give to it, is most likely a policy decision.

and unpaid housework have been overlooked in GDP statistics and have therefore long been considered a significant shortcoming of GDP. Fioramonti (2019) also presents the idea of the real economy to include these when measuring quality growth, as introduced in Chap. 8. Including unpaid housework under the umbrella of social welfare has implications beyond simply revealing the true state of the economy from the standpoint of quality growth. This is because, by doing so, a more dynamic picture of social transformation and productivity growth can be visualized. When attempting to impute unpaid housework, it is assumed that a certain wage can be accrued to cover it. Once the size of the housework sector is estimated, the labor productivity of this sector can also be visualized. This will be one of the key pieces of information for understanding changes in a country's productivity.

In general, there are two paths for labor productivity growth: a shift from low-productivity to high-productivity sectors, and evolution within the same sector due to technological development, among other factors. Since housework is unpaid and not included in GDP, when the labor participation rate of women increases, labor productivity is calculated as if a new labor force were added. It is generally recognized that employment in formal occupations increases labor productivity more than before; thus, this would be an indication of societal progress. However, this may not necessarily be an accurate reflection of social change. For example, an individual who has been performing unpaid housework may sometimes engage in a job that is less productive than the imputed housework (intersectoral shift). Alternatively, the quality of household services may improve as a result of years of engagement in housework, increasing the utility of the individual within a family receiving the service (intra-sectoral evolution). A good example of the latter is the postwar Japanese livelihood improvement movement, described by Hosono (2022). Women in rural villages identified areas they wanted to improve through their own efforts and achieved these improvements in their kitchens and other living conditions, as well as nutrition and sanitation. This greatly enhanced the utility of family members who received their services. It is desirable to situate such social transformation in the theory of growth as well. The current imputation may not be able to fully capture the degree of improvement in utility as a result of the improvement in the quality of housework. However, incorporating these factors into our understanding of social welfare would be a first step toward making such transformations visible.

The primary importance of consumption in terms of wellbeing was emphasized by Stiglitz et al. (2010). Based on this, it becomes possible to expand our scope to include factors not shown in the GDP figures, thereby better capturing an individual's utility. One significant issue is that of income inequality, where inequality reduces the total utility that individuals derive from consumption. This is because the marginal utility that people perceive differs depending on the size of their income, even if the amount of consumption is the same. Therefore, the size of consumption must be adjusted for the utility impaired by inequality. This is the approach adopted by the Genuine Progress Indicator (GPI) as shown in Chap. 8.

Of the two aspects of inclusiveness, the correction of "inequality of outcomes" is considered here. In addition, the following three aspects should be considered.

First, any surplus that is not reflected in the market should be added to consumption. Consumer surplus, which by definition refers to the benefits that exceed what consumers are willing to pay, should be included first. One item that has become particularly important in recent years is related to the development of digital services, as discussed in the previous chapter. Consumers are receiving a large additional surplus from free digital services, which improves our utility, although the methodology to estimate its magnitude is not yet well established. Related to this, there may be a general increase in the surplus of other goods and services due to technological progress and improvements in service quality. As already mentioned, most of the benefits of technological progress ultimately accrue to the consumer, who receives more than just price benefits from it. In the service sector, the quality of service provision improves year by year due to the expanded knowledge and skills, as well as the evolving use of digital technology. As discussed in Chap. 6—on process innovation and consumer surplus—improvements in the healthcare system and the use of digital and other technologies may, for example, reduce the time required for healthcare services while prices remain unchanged. Alternatively, if tests that once required hospitalization can be carried out on a day trip, expenditure can be reduced. If a wider range of quality factors can be taken into account, this can reflect the magnitude of improvements in consumer surplus that are not fully captured by price. As services are non-tradable goods, their quality is expected to vary widely from country to country. Quality growth should take into account not only the quantitative expansion of consumption but also the qualitative changes that occur as a result of economic development and capture associated surpluses.

This perspective may be related to the general trend toward lower growth rates in developed countries. Their growth rates are generally lower than those of emerging countries, but it is assumed that their overall wellbeing will continue to increase, as some innovations are improving the quality of goods and services while maintaining prices. Quality growth offers an approach that looks at the transformation from quantity expansion to quality improvement as one of its growth paths. Otherwise, once emerging economies reach high income levels, their growth rate will inevitably slow down, and consequently enter a world where wellbeing is hardly improved, when in fact it is not. Quality growth can be thought of as revealing a new form of growth—transformation through improved quality—even at the stage when quantitative expansion slows down. To do this, it is necessary to measure the magnitude of utility beyond income.

The second relates to public goods and externalities. Externalities, by definition, are benefits or costs that are received by the public, including third parties, and not incorporated into the market mechanism; they are therefore not considered a part of income. Education and healthcare, which are typical examples of positive externalities, benefit individuals through a larger lifetime income and benefit society as a whole by increasing innovation, facilitating communication, reducing the spread of infectious diseases, among other benefits. Since public goods cannot be adequately provided by the market alone, the government intervenes to provide support. For this reason, much of government spending is regarded as a positive externality. On the other hand, services provided by the government are deemed not to generate profit in GDP calculations and are instead represented by input costs. However, in reality, individuals benefit from these expenditures. Moreover, third parties benefit from positive externalities. Therefore, as noted by Mazzucato (2018), government expenditure should have a value greater than its input value—i.e., a social benefit, which should be reflected in the quality growth index.

Regarding education and healthcare externalities, the question arises as to whether the entities affected are current or future generations. The impacts are not always short-lived. For example, through human resource development, they contribute to the overall productivity of the economy and sustain growth in the long run. This aspect is particularly strong in the case of education, which plays a significant role in promoting future growth. For the current generation, education and healthcare are among the key factors in improving the wellbeing of individuals. This is because free choice of action is considered a major source of happiness, and can be achieved through education and healthcare. Infrastructure is another important area in producing positive externalities. It contributes to future growth by, for example, enabling the clustering of firms and expanding employment opportunities for individuals. Disaster prevention similarly encourages firms to invest and has the effect of preserving future human capital by protecting individual lives from disasters. Thus, as with education and healthcare, government spending on infrastructure should be considered to have social benefits, with value exceeding input costs.

Negative externalities are also not built into the market mechanism and are likewise related to current wellbeing and future growth. For example, noise, pollutant emissions from factories, and deterioration of the landscape depress the wellbeing of the current generation. As behavioral economics points out, we are more sensitive to loss than to gain. Consequently, efforts to prevent negative externalities related to the living environment are, to a significant extent, managed by governments. At least for environmental pollution other than global warming, governments in all countries are regulating and, where necessary, spending money to address and remedy these effects. Such spending is called defensive spending, and the GPI deducts such spending in its calculation. On the other hand, GHG emissions are mostly related to future growth, as they cause long-term warming and do not affect the wellbeing of the current generation in the short term.

I am still concerned that there is a methodological difficulty in bringing together factors with different time periods into a single indicator, such as the GPI. Since quality growth has two objectives, it is not necessary to compile the two into a single indicator. However, it is better to separate the amount of wellbeing of the current generation from its impact on the sustainability of future growth. Environmental pollution caused by production activities is generally controlled by government regulations, yet despite such government action, a certain level of environmental degradation continues to be observed. In response to this situation, governments spend public funds on purifying water and improving road intersections for preventing noise and air pollution. Ideally, such spending should also be incorporated into the market mechanism as a social cost, but market failures have prevented this from happening. Therefore, government spending in these areas should be deducted when measuring quality growth as defensive spending in order to estimate the magnitude of welfare-adjusted national income.

For example, if there are two countries with the same level of environmental pollution and there is a difference in public spending on environmental measures, the amount deducted would be larger for the country with higher spending, even though residents in that country may enjoy a better environment than the lower spending country. This would result in a larger national welfare after adjustment in the country with the poorer environment. To avoid such an incongruous situation, the size of the deduction should be adjusted in accordance with the current level of environmental pollution. On the other hand, the impact of climate change due to GHGs is exclusively related to the wellbeing of future generations. For this reason, these impacts should be considered as items aimed at sustaining growth, rather than as components of current social welfare.

The same argument can be applied to public safety and crime prevention with regard to the treatment of defensive expenditures. Police activities may prevent some crimes or arrest criminals to prevent future crimes. Such defensive expenditures should also be deducted, adjusting for the security situation and crime rate. By treating them in this way, it is possible to incorporate the factors of the short-term environment of sustainability and "secure growth" defined by the APEC into the elements of quality growth.

The perspective of preventing negative impacts is related to resilience. Two responses to external shocks are necessary: preparedness in advance and quick recovery after the event. With regard to the former, the negative impact of a shock can be mitigated by strengthening infrastructure against disasters or ensuring the soundness of financial institutions in the face of financial crises. Well-developed infrastructure and sufficient fiscal space facilitate quick recovery after a crisis. For the current generation, it is desirable to at least include the social benefits generated from the investments in disaster prevention. While preparation for such shocks may detract from short-term growth, as stated before, from a longer-term perspective, the accumulation of physical and human capital is more likely to occur as a result of strengthened resilience. By not leaving "scars: of a shock in the economy from a long-term perspective, it will function to help sustain growth, and therefore, it is necessary to include this as one element that contributes to sustaining growth.

The last point concerns how to incorporate subjective happiness. The method is either survey-based or involves identifying and including the elements that constitute happiness. The survey-based approach is preferable in the sense that it is more direct, but it is limited by its practical availability. There is also the limitation that surveys produce results in a yes–no or 0–1 range, making it challenging to capture long-term development. For this reason, it is better to focus on changes in factors that constitute happiness. In terms of what builds happiness, the OECD lists income, health, social contact, employment, personality, and culture (see Fig. 8.2).

From the perspective of psychology, happiness is considered a function of circumstances and intentional activity, with the latter playing a particularly crucial role. In addition to health, education, and safety and security, which have already been discussed, good governance and institutions form the basis for individual action, and freedom of behavioral choice is very important as a source of people's happiness. Society and culture also influence wellbeing; however, since it is difficult to design standards and assign value in estimating improvement or deterioration, only the impact of institutions and governance on the economy is included here.

These are the elements that appear necessary when considering welfare-adjusted national income. This can be captured by extending the magnitude of national income horizontally—that is, across a wider range of factors at the present time. What is captured here are elements that would constitute quality growth. This "horizontal spread" is summarized in a conceptual diagram in Fig. 9.2. Quality growth requires first increasing overall social welfare, which includes not only income at the center but also the broader components of welfare at its outermost edges. Another objective is to simultaneously achieve the potential for future growth, i.e., the "vertical" direction.

Tier I: Maximization of national income remains a traditional and important policy goal. Adjustments are made to the amount of expenditure representing national income—particularly consumption expenditure—according to the size of income inequality.

Tier II: Unpaid housework and consumer surplus are included. Key drivers to increase consumer surplus, such as technological development, improved quality of services, and digital diffusion, are pursued.

Tier III: Social benefits of public spending are estimated and included, while defensive spending is deducted. Note that long-term positive and negative externalities will be considered as a factor of sustained growth.

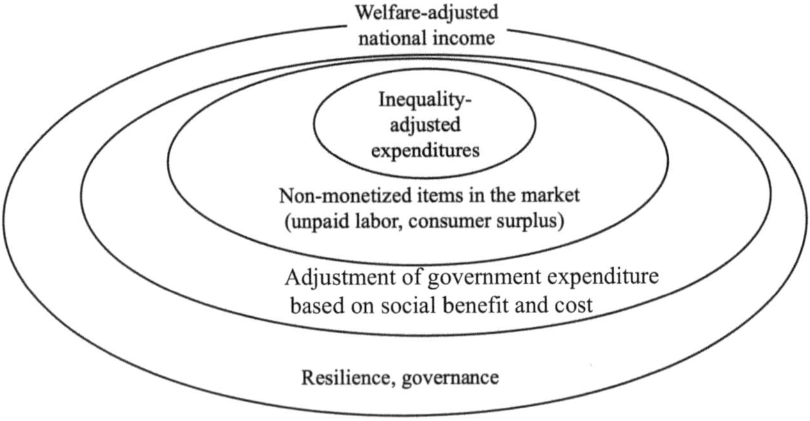


**Fig. 9.2** Welfare-adjusted national income from the quality growth perspective. *Source* Author

Tier IV: Resilience to external shocks is related to both short-term wellbeing and sustained growth. The impacts of governance and improved institutions are also considered.

### 9.2.4 Ensuring that Growth Continues into the Future (Vertical Linkages)

Another goal of quality growth is to ensure that the overall welfare of society continues to improve over time. Several elements are required, the first of which is capital—an essential factor for economic growth. Capital constraints remain significant, especially in developing countries. The perspective of quality growth stands on weak sustainability, as discussed in Chap. 5, where the increase in the aggregated amount of different forms of capital is important. This can be measured by changes in all three types of capital, while crucially, natural capital must also be maintained. The second is to address negative externalities that would impose the expense on future generations. GHG emissions that increase beyond the Earth's capacity to absorb them must be avoided. Third, productivity must improve in the future. This is a matter of improving the quality of human resources, technology, and capital. Productivity is the key to growth, and its continuous improvement is made possible by technological progress through innovation and the accumulation of knowledge and skills via learning, which occurs through education, healthcare, and other forms of human resources development. The accumulation of investment creates agglomeration effects and enhances production, so it is necessary to have institutions that enable such a cycle. In developing countries, where the gap with the technological frontier is substantial, it is essential to utilize technology from abroad, which requires human resource development and institutions as a precondition for transfer. Finally, it is also necessary to add the element of resilience. These components are illustrated in the following diagram (Fig. 9.3).

### 9.2.5 Measuring the Two Objectives of Quality Growth

Suppose quality growth has two objectives, and they are conceptually distinct. In that case, measurement would also be based on two composite indices. Such a distinction is essentially the same in the Better Life Index (BLI), discussed in the previous chapter: the two indices represent overall social welfare beyond income, which captures the total welfare of the current generation, as well as future growth potential. Since quality growth is an approach to growth that encompasses a wider scope of elements, it is my view that the preferred approach for overall social welfare beyond income is to use GDP as a base and then add the necessary elements to incorporate a social welfare perspective. Although it may be desirable to rationally integrate the two into a single index, there are valid questions about the feasibility of combining measures that differ in character and the time frame of interest. Therefore, I consider it more appropriate to measure current welfare and

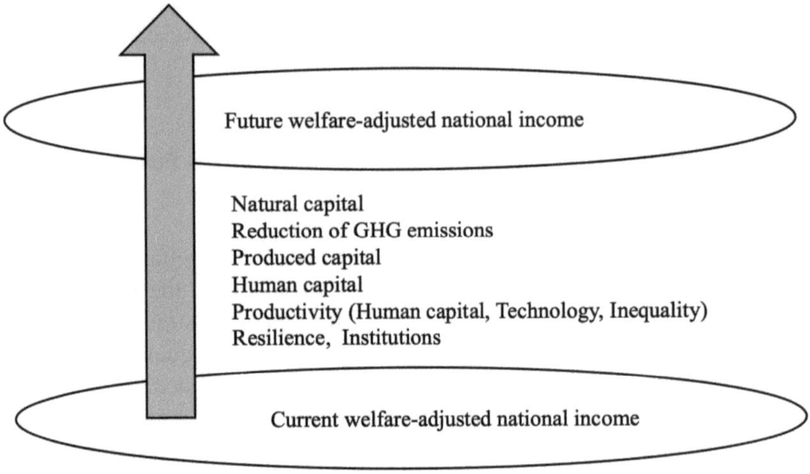


**Fig. 9.3** Sustaining growth from a quality growth perspective. *Source* Author

future growth potential using two indices, so that each situation can be captured separately.

#### 9.2.5.1 Size of Overall Social Welfare, Including Non-income Components

A key task is finding a way to measure the size of social welfare of society beyond income, as shown conceptually in Fig. 9.2. There are detailed definitions and technical discussions contained in national accounts and new indicators, and I have attempted to select and integrate approaches from them that are appropriate to the quality growth perspective described in this book. What I will outline here is only the basic framework; however, in order to avoid merely presenting concepts, I have included a preliminary proposal at the end of this chapter as the Appendix on how quality growth might actually be expressed in numbers. I hope that such supplemental discussion will offer a concrete image of what we are discussing in this book.

The starting point, as noted above, is GDP, which is the result of economic activities expressed in terms of flows and does not include stock items. There is ongoing discussion over whether GDP accurately represents the real picture of the national economy, and one item that has been identified as missing is unpaid housework and volunteer work. The first index of quality growth includes these. The other components that contribute to overall social welfare, such as inclusiveness and sustainability, will also be adjusted. Specifically, the following equation is proposed to measure the size of welfare-adjusted national income.

$$\text{QG-1} = \left(\text{C}_{\text{adj}} + \text{G}_{\text{adj}} + \text{I}_{\text{adj}}\right) \times \text{Inst} + \text{NetTrade} \tag{9.1}$$

where: QG-1 (Quality Growth-1): Size of welfare adjusted national income
$C_{adj}$: Adjusted consumption expenditure.[4]
$G_{adj}$: Adjusted government spending
$I_{adj}$: Adjusted investment
Inst: Institutions and governance coefficient
NetTrade: Net export (export–import)

Consumption is a major pillar of wellbeing. As mentioned above, I first adjust for the negative impact of income inequality based on inclusiveness, using the calculation in the GPI as a reference. I then adjust for the ratio between the reference value of inequality and the actual level of inequality in the year of interest, using the Gini coefficient or other indicators. In a country with high levels of inequality, the adjusted consumption expenditure will be smaller than the nominal amount in GDP. The reason for this adjustment is that, as noted earlier, inequality reduces the utility of society as a whole. In addition, adjustment is made for consumer surplus, including those related to the benefits of free digital services, technological progress and improvements in the quality of services, as well as the utility from unpaid housework. In terms of improvements in the quality of goods due to technological progress, the value of these goods is primarily reflected in their prices. However, as discussed in Chap. 6, when process innovation improves the efficiency of production, goods can be produced more cheaply. Part of the surplus generated in this process will be retained by the producer, but consumers will receive a larger surplus. In the case of goods, the effects of innovation spread globally through trade in the modern era.

On the other hand, improvements in the quality of nontraded goods and services may lead to international differences in quality, even if prices are the same. In this regard, since many services are essentially non-tradable, even if they are provided at the same price level, they may differ from country to country in terms of service quality, operating hours, customer friendliness, cleanliness, and other aspects. Consumers receive greater utility for the same price if the quality of service is higher. However, in GDP, such differences do not always appear, so it is worthwhile to consider adjusting for them. Although the concept of hedonic adjustment exists, international comparisons are required to reveal these national differences. One such empirical study demonstrated that there are differences in the quality of services between Japan and the US, even after international price adjustments (JPC

[4] Adjusted consumption includes unpaid housework. People obtain utility from unpaid housework despite it not being represented in GDP. Unpaid housework is for the household's self-consumption (strictly speaking, the members of the household other than the individual performing such work receive these services). The magnitude of utility gained from such services can be considered equal to the value of the labor input, although it is difficult to measure because they are free of charge. The value of unpaid housework is presented in satellite accounts of GDP in Japan and European countries. Its calculation is derived by multiplying hours worked by the opportunity cost or imputed cost of the service provider (the wage of the person engaged in the occupation) by the population (UNECE 2017).

2017; Fukao et al. 2018). The methodology used for this analysis involved conducting a survey of consumers who have used services in both Japan and the US, asking them whether the differences between services in the two countries could be converted into a monetary value. The results showed that while Japanese labor productivity in the service sector is about 50% of that of the US, when the quality factor is taken into account, the difference narrowed, raising Japanese labor productivity by 10–20%. The conclusion is that while Japan needs to close the labor productivity gap with the US—for example, by improving inefficient staffing and promoting more systemic operations—it should at the same time aim to reflect such differences in quality in prices (e.g., Yamada 2015).

These arguments are from the supply-side perspective. However, low labor productivity of services may include the aspect that consumers are purchasing quality services at a lower price. In other words, consumers are gaining a larger consumer surplus by purchasing quality services at a discount (Takizawa 2020). These discussions have primarily focused on elucidating the causes of low productivity in Japan's service sector, with the aim of improving Japan's productivity. If, according to the concept of quality growth, improving the quality of services while keeping prices low constitutes a part of growth, then our perspective may change entirely. To put this argument into concrete figures, one can either take the supply-side perspective—adjusting the output of GDP by adding a quality factor to labor productivity—or add the surplus generated from this factor as an increase in wellbeing. This book employs the latter perspective.

The government, as a public service provider, delivers education, healthcare, and infrastructure either for free or at low prices. Governments do not earn profits from these activities, and therefore, their input costs become the figure of expenditure in GDP statistics. However, individuals benefit from such public services. For example, education enables people to obtain better jobs, leading to higher lifetime salaries and an increase in vocational choice. Generally, when projects related to public services are implemented, an internal rate of return—a measure of benefit versus cost generated for the country as a whole—is calculated, which is the same concept as profit in a private corporation. Therefore, for public expenditures, the social rate of return should also be included in GDP statistics rather than only recording input costs.[5] Indeed, in recent years, some countries have adopted an approach to the education and health sectors that does not simply use input

[5] For example, there is no difference in benefit for people receiving education from either private or public schools. But if the private sector operates a school, gross profit is included in GDP. The same applies to infrastructure, where the private sector operators of infrastructure also generate positive externalities. In Japan, the four public utilities—electricity, gas, railroads, and telecommunications—are largely operated by the private sector. Such infrastructure businesses also have positive externalities because of their agglomeration effects and so on, and, therefore, are granted tax incentives and additional privileges to ensure that their management remains institutionally stable. In my calculation, these privileges are assumed as a reflection of positive externalities, so no special adjustments are considered.

costs in GDP, but rather takes into account a quality factor to determine the magnitude of output (Bean 2016). Government spending also includes expenditures required to respond to situations resulting from the negative externalities of economic activities, such as the costs of maintaining the current environment. Such public expenditures are deducted as a cost of running society, with adjustments based on their outcomes (for example, in the case of the environment, the amount of pollution being controlled). For example, if environment-related expenditures are inadequate and people suffer from pollution, wellbeing should be adjusted accordingly.

Investment increases the total amount of capital stock, so as the capital stock grows, the public expenditures for its rehabilitation and replacement at the end of its useful life must also increase. When the rehabilitation and maintenance improve a part of the function or prolong the usable life of infrastructure, such expenditures constitute GFCF in the GDP statistics. In developed countries, this portion increases year by year. Since I focus on the infrastructure stock as one indicator of sustained growth, I do not use net investment, which deducts depreciation. No special adjustment is made for net exports—that is, exports minus imports.

Finally, there is the factor of how efficiently consumption, government spending, and investment are conducted. For example, as discussed in Chap. 7, government spending on infrastructure is greatly undermined by corruption and other government inefficiencies. In countries where corruption is widespread, people are disadvantaged because competition does not function effectively, making the economy inefficient and increasing costs. In such contexts, government spending tends to be higher and individual utility from the same amount of spending will be lower than in less corrupt countries. Thus, face value alone does not represent a true comparison. This applies not only to corruption but also to governance in general, such as law and order and government efficiency. Its impact extends to all areas: government spending, investment and consumption. For this reason, I consider it necessary to adjust all expenditures according to the degree of institutional quality and governance.

Based on the above discussion, Table 9.4 summarizes the basic framework for measuring overall social welfare beyond income.

#### 9.2.5.2 Continued Growth for Future Generations

Simply looking at the growth rate of welfare-adjusted national income does not tell us whether it will be sustained in the future. Knowing this is the purpose of the second index of quality growth. As stated, the necessary elements for this are the amount of capital, GHG emissions, and changes in the foundations for productivity and resilience. For example, growth obtained by expending natural resources will eventually come to a standstill unless it is converted into other forms of capital. Indicators other than QG-1, as discussed, are required to determine whether there are constraints on the current growth of social welfare.

Whether capital will continue to increase or productivity will continue to improve should be examined from a supply perspective. Produced capital is a source of today's expansion of production, but to assess sustained growth from a

**Table 9.4** Measuring Quality Growth-1; magnitude of welfare-adjusted national income

| | Consumption | Unpaid services | Government expenditures | Investment |
|---|---|---|---|---|
| Basic items in GDP | Consumer spending | Not included | Government consumption; Public investment, including inventory | Investment for housing; capital goods, inventory |
| Adjustment | Income inequality; Consumer surplus; Quality of services/ technology; Surplus from unpaid services | Unpaid services (domestic work, volunteering etc.) | Adding social profits or deductions of expenditures: Education; Health; Employment protection; Environment; Security and police; Infrastructure and disaster prevention | – |
| | Impact of institutions and governance | | | |

*Source* Author

long-term perspective, it is instead necessary to look at the total amount of capital—including natural and human capital—in a comprehensive manner. Then, as mentioned above, the control of $CO_2$ concentration as CNC should also be considered. With regard to productivity, the drivers of technological development and learning in the long term should be considered. The second index of quality growth confirms the direction of sustainability of growth expressed in Eq. (9.2) as follows:

$$\text{QG-2} = \dot{K}_{adj} + \dot{A} - G\dot{H}G + R\dot{E}S \tag{9.2}$$

where QG-2 (Quality Growth-2): Change of foundation for growth to continue into the future

$\dot{K}_{adj}$: Rate of change in aggregated capital stock
$\dot{A}$: Progress in creating conditions that improve productivity
$G\dot{H}G$: Change in GHG emissions
$R\dot{E}S$: Change in resilience

The first two terms are based on the growth accounting approach and represent the growth rates of the basic factors of production: capital (including human capital) and the foundations for nurturing productivity. However, the capital in this context encompasses all types of capital in the broadest sense, while the foundation of productivity includes various factors that could potentially affect a country's overall productivity over the long term. Then, changes in GHG emissions and resilience are added. These items should ideally be summed, if possible, after applying theoretical and empirical coefficients (weighting), but this has not yet been attempted at this point in time. The following section provides some additional information on each item.

The idea that changes in the capital stock represent the factors of sustained growth follows the World Bank's reports on wealth (World Bank 2021 and others). As mentioned above, the World Bank classifies capital into natural capital, produced capital, and human capital, and estimates the stock of each. These estimates are carefully compiled, providing useful basic data for confirming sustained growth.

The next item is GHG emissions. Among the negative externalities, pollution related to the residential environment is included in the QG-1 index. However, the impact of GHG emissions will primarily affect future generations. The World Bank (2021) assumes that $CO_2$ alters the value of natural and produced capital. Because natural capital has a carbon retention function that adds to its value, any change in the quantity of natural capital will also affect its value. For example, if deforestation occurs, the value of carbon retention decreases. The value of non-renewable resources, especially fossil fuel assets, also varies with changes in the price of $CO_2$. In countries undergoing a slow transition to a low-carbon society, these assets become risk assets. $CO_2$ emissions are included in the calculation in the sense that they change the value of these assets in this way. On the other hand, GHG emissions have a variety of impacts, such as sea level rise, more severe disasters, declining agricultural production, and the spread of infectious diseases, but the impact of negative externalities on the international community due to increases in GHG emissions is a separate issue from the increase or decrease in the valuation of capital. If the atmosphere of the entire planet is viewed as a public good, changes in emissions should also be considered from the perspective of sustaining a country's growth.

Improvements in the quality of capital and labor are important for long-term productivity change. The quality of capital results from technological development and innovation. Innovation is encouraged by the accumulation of research and ideas, the accumulation of investment via infrastructure development and other factors, and improvements in governance and institutions. Expanding human capital development through education, healthcare, and reducing inequality improves the quality of labor and facilitates innovation over the long term. How these elements evolve will determine whether they facilitate sustained growth over the long term. Public spending on education and healthcare increases an individual's lifetime wage, and since the size of human capital is calculated in terms of lifetime wages, the benefits to individuals are already included, which also increases the amount of human capital among the three types of capital mentioned above. However, there are additional positive effects on society as a whole through learning and innovation (as positive externalities), which must be considered separately. These factors are illustrated in Fig. 9.4. Items in this figure are considered as elements of productivity change in the second index of quality growth.

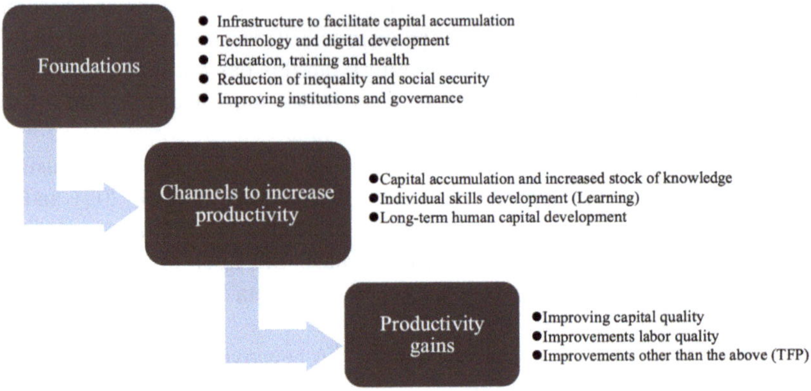


**Fig. 9.4** Key factors leading to productivity gains. *Source* Author

The final term is the element of resilience. Resilience enhances sustained growth by reducing losses and enabling quicker recovery from external shocks. With regard to public finance, while fiscal spending can help stabilize the economy in response to financial crises and major disasters, these functions are often overlooked during normal times. Having fiscal space allows for a response to external shocks, though it may not positively affect economic growth in the short term. In this index, in view of the function of resilience to external shocks, the positive effects of fiscal soundness—such as fiscal balance as a percentage of GDP—are considered elements of the second index of quality growth. Similarly, for finance, it is necessary to take into account changes in financial soundness in order to assess resilience to shocks. Taken together, these considerations offer insight into whether overall social welfare is on a long-term growth path.

## 9.3 Achieving Quality Growth

In closing, I would like to touch on policy discussions regarding how to achieve quality growth. Each component of quality growth—i.e., GDP growth, social welfare improvement beyond income, reducing inequality, strengthening resilience to external shocks such as disasters and financial crisis, and combating global warming—has already been widely considered. Many discussions have taken place, and various responses have been pursued by outstanding leaders in many countries. As I have mentioned from time to time in this book, a menu of policies for achieving quality growth is, in fact, already in place and will continue to be improved in various ways in the future, regardless of the discussions of quality growth. The argument that the goal of improving overall social welfare is essential is not new: the SDGs are fundamentally based on this perspective. Arguments for the importance of non-economic aspects are often linked to calls for prioritizing education and healthcare, which have been repeatedly discussed in this book.

However, education and healthcare are not a panacea, and expansion of total social welfare cannot be achieved by these alone. An optimal balance of various factors is necessary to achieve quality growth.

A quality growth approach would shift the focus of current policy objectives in several crucial ways. In short, the primary goal of policy should not be merely to increase income, i.e., GDP. Even if GDP growth is somewhat constricted, other factors—such as narrowing inequality, human resource development, and non-income surpluses and wellbeing—may improve. Thus, if overall social welfare is increased, then such a policy mix should be preferred. To date, the increase in social welfare has not been measured in an integrated manner in most countries, suggesting that it has not been treated as an ultimate policy goal. Developing a new composite index for quality growth, such as those presented in the previous section, would help promote these new policy directions. In fact, as we saw in the case of Japan's efforts to combine equality with growth, it seems that we are beginning to see the seeds of a shift toward such a recognition: that growth is not limited to the quantitative, but includes qualitative aspects, and the pursuit of policies that will make this possible. Adopting such a direction will also determine the path that emerging economies should follow once they transition to being high-income countries.

In addition to being integrative and encompassing social welfare, including non-market factors, another policy pillar for achieving quality growth is the continuous transformation of society and the economy. In this book, continued productivity improvement is presented as a means of achieving sustained growth for future generations. Productivity growth can occur within the same sector, but in developing countries, it more commonly takes the form of a shift to new industries as they develop. The traditional two-sector model of development economics—modern and traditional sectors—offers a simplified representation of this. We know from the experience of Japan and other Asian countries that have followed such paths, shifting from agriculture to light industry, from assembly to component manufacturing, and then to higher value-added sectors, that growth will be sustained over the long term as these transformations continue. How these transformations have occurred, and what specific strategies have been put in place to encourage them, are important policy issues. As this book does not explore this point in depth, Hosono (2022) provides a very detailed description of examples of social transformation and the development strategies that have brought them about.

As the final discussion in Part I of this book, I examine the overarching policy framework and direction that underpin individual strategies to achieve the key elements of quality growth. First, the framework for the evaluation of individual policies and projects should be aligned with the framework of quality growth. The discussion of quality infrastructure investment (QII) in Chap. 8 provides an example that broadens the perspective from which infrastructure projects are evaluated, shifting from a cost–benefit analysis (CBA) to looking at their contributions to a broader perspective of growth. This includes evaluating the degree of contribution to reducing income inequality, combating global warming, and strengthening resilience in all development activities. For example, although equity is one of the major principles in the evaluation of public policies, it has not been the subject of CBA in the case of infrastructure development. More attention should be paid than in the past to the effects of reducing income inequality and the proportion of benefits gained by the poor among the beneficiaries, and these should be quantified to the extent possible. This applies not only to infrastructure but also to policies in other areas. In this way, inclusiveness will be better promoted by mainstreaming key elements of quality growth into government activities—and even into national income indicators.

Mainstreaming the global warming perspective into policy is already underway in many countries, with some countries beginning to tie carbon neutrality to the implementation of all policies aimed at achieving it. With regard to resilience, much of the expenditure in the areas of environment and disaster prevention was typically only made after risks had materialized. The statistics show that spending on disaster reduction increases sharply in the year following a major disaster. It is essential not to underestimate risks that are not normally distributed, and preparedness for shocks should be viewed as a component of growth. This does not mean that the amount of reserve capacity for preparedness, such as fiscal space, should be excessively large. With regard to disasters, the preferred approach is to gradually reduce the risk of disasters through pre-emptive investment in disaster prevention. It will be important to build a social consensus on how resources should be allocated and to set a national goal for resilience.

Second, in addition to conventional growth strategies aimed at increasing GDP, policies should be strengthened to enhance the consumer surplus that does not appear in the market and the factors that sustain growth for future generations. In the previous section, I introduced studies demonstrating that digital development and service quality improvement will increase the overall welfare of society. The role of government is also essential in this regard. For example, governments have many public research labs that develop technologies, including in basic areas. As discussed by Mazzucato (2018), the role of basic research conducted by governments is often essential. For example, the technology for the Internet originally came from the US Department of Defense. Therefore, government R&D spending should not be evaluated solely on the basis of input costs but by the magnitude of social benefits equivalent to its contribution to society. If social value is correctly positioned, spending levels could be raised.

It is also necessary to rethink the positioning of unpaid housework. As exemplified by the postwar life improvement movement in Japan, improvements in the quality of housework services will not only increase the utility of family members but also contribute to the long-term growth of society through human resources development. The government should focus on the positive aspects of housework and explore ways to develop them further. For example, with the development of ICT, even small improvements in the home can spread quickly through YouTube and other media. This is an issue relevant to the new era of government extension services, including the dissemination of accurate information and preventing the spread of harmful and fake information.

There is also room for the government to enhance its role with regard to improving the quality of services. For example, my hometown in Japan once prospered as a coal-producing area, but with the closure of the coal mines, the local population plummeted. The wealth generated by coal was not replaced by other forms of capital, and growth was not sustainable. On the other hand, an interesting example in recent years is a high school in this city that was once closed due to population decline but later reopened as a municipal high school specializing in cooking. While such cases tend to be reported by the media only as isolated or unusual events, from a broader perspective, they may have underlying significance in terms of social change and responsive policy direction. In a society where the global economy is becoming increasingly service-oriented, there may be new opportunities for the public sector to strengthen educational programs to improve the quality of services, just as the government has taken the initiative in the past to teach the basics of manufacturing technology through technical colleges and vocational training. In fact, the government is already strengthening ICT education in Japan and other countries.

This direction should also be considered in other service sectors. Earlier in Chap. 8, I introduced how people derive much of their happiness through their intentional acts rather than the environment. Therefore, one major source of happiness lies in having a decent job. In order to realize happiness through work, education that enhances one's capacities is required. This is also related to changes in business circles and institutions. In the past, in Japan, skills training and business education were provided in the workplace through the lifetime employment system, and, in my view, this was largely linked to the long-term happiness gained from work. Today, however, it is evident that the importance of education in companies has been declining in Japan as the working patterns have changed and non-regular employment has become more common worldwide. To compensate for this, one of the new policy directions for governments, including local governments, could be to support such education, particularly in the service sector. The majority of positive externalities of education, healthcare, and infrastructure can be obtained for future generations rather than the wellbeing of the current generation. This may be a global issue of concern: assessing how, in the contemporary world, governments should intervene to promote education and strengthen the service sector. In fact, such a trend is already evident in digital technology. The soft domain is becoming increasingly important. To achieve quality growth, it is indispensable to promote digital education in tandem with the increasing adoption of digital technology, ensuring that there are no disparities in digital literacy based on income. In doing so, as Azhar (2021) argues, governments should ask platform businesses to assume their social responsibility given their handling of personal data, and to make data protection a corporate responsibility. Enhanced risk management and security may lower the profits of platform businesses, but it will increase their overall utility to society.

Thirdly, as challenges that cannot be resolved by the market—such as income inequality and climate change—become more serious, it is important to strengthen policy interventions in areas that involve public goods and linked to quality growth. This does not necessarily mean advocating for "big government." However, for example, with regard to infrastructure, it is important that the objective of privatization and public–private partnerships (PPPs) is not simply to reduce the government's burden. Even if the government contributes to expanding the supply—thereby helping to compensate for market shortages—then such policies are worth pursuing. As noted in Chap. 8, the costs associated with maintaining facilities, which are not necessarily reflected in GDP, and life cycle costs must be recognized as fundamental issues related to sustained growth and addressed accordingly. To address these fundamental challenges related to sustainable growth, it is necessary to consider the entire national system, encompassing both supply and demand—or production and consumption. For example, even though the majority of hospitals in Japan are privately operated, the increase in hospital beds to an internationally top-ranked level has been underpinned by demand for healthcare through national health insurance. This is a major reason why the government subsidizes the national health insurance deficit. Responding to climate change requires building a similarly comprehensive nationwide system. We have entered an era in which the capabilities of governments will be tested more than ever before. The appropriate scale of government interventions is a complex question and solutions will vary from country to country, as well as within the same country at different times. In general, however, there needs to be a greater focus on externalities, which ought to be reflected in the welfare-adjusted national income in the statistics. To support this, theoretical research should be conducted to guide decisions about the government's burden sharing from the perspective of its contribution to sustaining medium- and long-term growth.

Fourth, as discussed in detail in this chapter, it is necessary to establish an index to measure quality growth. Further efforts are required to improve GDP statistics and to explore new indicators that could replace them at an international level. It is expected that such results will be used to inform policy and implementation. Although this aspect has already been extensively discussed, I have included a draft quality growth index at the end of the chapter. Although still insufficient in many respects, I hope that it will serve as a useful reference for future research in this area. The overarching policy framework and direction that I have proposed are depicted in Table 9.5.

These are the key elements in the overarching policy framework for achieving quality growth that I propose. They require further detailed study, and while the policy prescriptions naturally vary considerably from country to country and cannot follow a one-size-fits-all approach, the basic directions appear to be widely shared. In this book, apart from some examples presented in the previous chapters, I have not touched on specific strategies for economic growth, inequality reduction, resilience, and sustainability, many of which have been developed in various countries. For a more in-depth discussion of these, please refer to the country case studies in Part II. In the case studies, experts in each country have identified the strategies that have been adopted and assessed their performance with respect to inclusiveness, resilience, and sustainability, as well as growth. I hope that they will

**Table 9.5** Directions for a cross-cutting policy framework to achieve quality growth (example)

| Category | Policy framework |
|---|---|
| Mainstreaming | Mainstream growth (productivity) and reduce inequality; integrate GHG emissions reductions and resilience into policy and program/project evaluation criteria; For resilience, shift from ex-post to ex-ante actions and establish national resilience targets |
| Utility and consumer surplus not appearing in the market figures | Expand government R&D (with appropriate evaluation of value added); larger government role and public spending to improve the quality of services, including unpaid housework; greater digital diffusion with clarification of responsibilities for platform businesses |
| Public goods, Externalities | Enlarge the effects to sustain growth in education, healthcare, and infrastructure (appropriate public–private burdens, maintenance etc.)<br>Build a national system, including both supply and demand sides, that addresses issues affecting sustainable growth |
| Measurement | Create new index to measure progress in achieving quality growth |

*Source* Author

serve as a useful reference in further considering policies and specific strategies to achieve quality growth.

## Appendix: Preliminary Proposal for Measuring Quality Growth

This Appendix to this chapter examines how quality growth can be measured and presents my ideas on possible indexation. As described earlier in this chapter, the proposed index comprises two components: (1) welfare-adjusted national income, as the first index of quality growth, and (2) changes in the foundation for sustained growth over future generations, as the second index of quality growth. Indicators for these two components have been calculated for the group of case study countries in Part II: Indonesia, Vietnam, Peru, Costa Rica, and Madagascar. In addition, I also calculate indicators for Japan as an example of an advanced country, China as an example of an emerging country, and El Salvador and Burkina Faso as points of comparison with the case countries. The data used were mostly drawn from global databases to ensure data consistency. This also provides a basis from which anyone would be able to discuss these indicators.

The approach and ideas proposed here are still preliminary, and there may be some objections and doubts. Many items—such as the magnitude of consumer surplus and service quality—are not currently available in the statistical data. To address this, I used estimates from previous studies, where available. Where there were no such studies, I employed variables considered to be proxies. As a result, some of the items lack theoretical confirmation of causal relationships based on empirical studies. In addition, data is imperfect, and while I applied linear interpolation for the years in which data was missing, the accuracy of the data remains a constraint. Due to these limitations, the index presented here should not be interpreted as statistics in the strict sense, but rather as a rough indication of what quality growth might look like when indexed from the perspective discussed in this book.

## Size of Welfare-Adjusted National Income

### Adjustment for Inequality

As discussed in this chapter, GDP figures (on an expenditure basis) are used in indexing overall social welfare beyond income. Among these, consumption is at the center of people's wellbeing. Several adjustments need to be made to consumption from the viewpoint of quality growth. The first is to reflect income inequality against the size of household consumption. The approach used in the GPI is used as a reference for the calculation. That is, household consumption is adjusted by using the difference between the base year—the year with the smallest income inequality—and each year of the target period as a coefficient. For example, if the Gini coefficient for a given year is 30% larger than the base year, the adjusted amount is calculated by dividing the household consumption by 1.3. In addition, I not only take into account the time series comparison but also make international comparisons using the Gini coefficient. If only the time-series comparison is considered, two countries with different absolute levels of Gini coefficients would be treated equally if their rates of change were the same. However, the country with the larger Gini coefficient would have a greater degree of relative poverty, and thus the country's overall utility from consumption would be smaller by that amount at that point in time.

To reflect this, I set reference values for both cross-sectional and time-series comparisons and established composite adjustment coefficients. For the former, the Gini coefficient with the lowest international value in the year in question is used as the reference point, and for the latter, the Gini coefficient with the lowest observed value since 2000 is used. While inequality affects the magnitude of social welfare in the short run through differences in utility, in the long run, it is related to productivity (i.e., sustained growth) through its impact on human resource development. Therefore, it is also considered a factor in the second index of quality growth. Next, I make adjustments to incorporate non-monetized factors related to household consumption. Specifically, adjustments are made for consumer surplus not reflected in market transactions and for differences in the quality of services not captured in prices, as well as for unpaid housework.

## Consumer Surplus

For consumer surplus, I add the estimated surplus over actual consumption, adjusting it to reflect technological progress over time. The general definition of consumer surplus is the amount that consumers are willing to pay minus the amount actually transacted in the market. To estimate the size of the consumer surplus, a survey of consumers is typically conducted, in which consumers are asked the amount they are willing to pay for the goods and services in question, allowing data on the difference between actual prices and the stated amounts to be obtained. In recent years, this approach has been used in studies on the benefits of digital technology (e.g., NiCT 2016). However, it is not practically feasible to obtain exhaustive data for each country on consumer surplus using this method.

In this Appendix, I use the results of previous studies to make rough estimates, based on the aim of presenting a general framework of an index of quality growth using a simple method. Specifically, I use the estimates of consumer surplus presented by Manyika et al. (2021), who analyze value flows from firms to households for large firms with annual revenues of more than USD 1 billion for 37 OECD countries. They estimate that the share of the consumer surplus (2016–2018 average) was USD 0.40 for every USD 1 of a firm's income, and that this has increased by 4% over the 25 years from the period of 1994 and 1996 to that of 2016 and 2018.[6] Although there are differences in this ratio depending on the industrial structure of the countries, I use this ratio for all countries in this Appendix. In doing so, the size of the consumer surplus generated by non-large firms—not analyzed in Manyika et al. (2021)—is assumed to be 55% that of large firms, based on differences in productivity with non-large firms.[7] I also use the ratio of the market share between large and non-large firms, based on the OECD average. While there may be questions about applying the OECD average to developing countries, consumer surplus is universally generated in market economies. At least with respect to goods, the benefits of technological progress have reached developing countries

[6] Manyika et al. (2021) estimate consumer surplus using a two-step approach. First, based on the assumption that value is equally distributed between firms and households in the long run. Therefore, the magnitude of a company's profit above the average opportunity cost of capital is regarded as equal to the consumer surplus. Then they identify the relationship between this surplus and price changes. As one might easily imagine, when prices fall, consumer surplus increases. In addition, if consumption increases due to lower prices, the surplus will be added to that amount. The difficult part in this process is to extract the relationship between the price change and the improvement of goods/services quality. They state that the hedonic index is used here. After obtaining company-level data in this way, these are summed to estimate the change in consumer surplus of large companies for the country as a whole. For time-series changes, after calculating how much surplus is generated in each of the major sectors, they estimate how the overall surplus changes with changes in the composition of the sector.

[7] On the OECD average, the level of labor productivity of small companies is 55% of that of large companies (Ministry of Health, Labor and Welfare 2008). Assuming that differences in productivity lead to differences in markup rates, I simply use this ratio to calculate the consumer surplus figure generated by non-large (small and medium-sized) companies.

through international trade, thereby increasing the consumer surplus for their citizens. Needless to say, more precise data would be desirable, but I use this as a preliminary estimate for the consumer surplus in this Appendix.

## Quality of Service

Next, I consider possible differences in the quality of services between countries. As discussed before, not all differences in service quality between countries are reflected in prices. As innovation progresses, the utility to consumers obtained at the same price will increase. In the case of goods, price and quality are expected to converge internationally through trade, but as services are basically domestic industries and are non-tradable, the benefits of innovation in this sector will be exclusively enjoyed by domestic consumers. Such progress could lead to differences in the quality of services provided, even if the international price adjustments are made through purchasing power parity (PPP).[8] We have learned from our experiences that the services provided differ in terms of technique, customer service, cleanliness, service menu options, and so on. For example, convenience stores in Japan provide home delivery, public bill payments, and are equipped with clean toilets and freely accessible ATMs, but this is not always the case in other countries, and these local differences may have an impact on the size of the utility.

In a previous study focusing on service quality based on the PPP by sector, Fukao et al. (2018) compared the productivity of the service sector in Japan and the US. They found that consumers in both countries evaluate the quality of services relative to price as higher in Japan than in the US in all sectors except education. However, such data are not generally available, and to the best of my knowledge, there are no previous studies that link differences in service quality to differences in utility. For this reason, I have selected several indicators that serve as proxies for the factors that constitute service quality, taken from Parasuraman et al. (1988). Based on the five components of service quality presented there, I construct a time series index (see Table 9.6).[9] Then, I multiply the magnitude of consumer surplus

[8] PPP adjusts for both currency and price level. The latter, for example, according to the World Bank (2020), is 140.9 for Japan, 92.8 for China, and 52.6 for Indonesia in 2017.

[9] Comparing service quality is extremely challenging. For example, in relation to productivity—which I introduced above—Japan's productivity is estimated to be about half that of the US, and this difference includes both efficiency and service quality differences. In terms of efficiency, this may be attributable to differences in business practices in Japan, such as slow decision-making, inefficient organizational forms, and lagging ICT investment. With regard to service quality differences, lower productivity in Japan means that more personnel are engaged in services, which might increase the utility of consumers. Fukao et al. (2018) demonstrate that consumers evaluate the quality of service as being 10 to 20% higher in Japan.

Regarding the five factors cited by Parasuraman et al. (1988) as contributing to differences in the quality of services, items related to facilities and education are easy to compare, but those related to firms have data limitations or make simple comparisons difficult. For example, Japanese companies invest relatively little in human resources within their companies compared to other

**Table 9.6** Constructs of an index of service quality

| Dimensions | Definitions | Proxy example |
|---|---|---|
| Tangibles | Physical facilities, equipment, and appearance of personnel | Capital accumulation (capital stock per capita etc.) |
| Reliability | Ability to perform the promised services dependably and accurately | Level of expertise and skills (level of education and years of service etc.) |
| Responsiveness | Willingness to help customers and provide prompt service | Communication skills and understanding (basic competencies etc.); commitment to work |
| Assurance | Knowledge and courtesy of employees and their ability to inspire trust and confidence | Knowledge level (enrollment ratio in higher education etc.); in-company education |
| Empathy | Caring, individualized attention the firm provides its customers | Empathy; hospitality (presumably rooted in culture and values) |

*Source* "Dimensions" and "Definitions" are terms derived from Parasuraman et al. (1988). "Proxy example" has been added by Author

derived from service expenditures by this index as an adjustment for differences in utility by quality. This approach is based on the assumption that process innovation increases the utility of consumers and that people derive utility above price in countries with higher service quality. However, this approach is not supported by empirical research, including the choice of indicators.

Nevertheless, I believe it is worthwhile to present this kind of indexation, albeit prematurely, because it suggests the importance of increasing welfare by improving the quality of service, even if these results are not reflected in GDP, rather than pursuing quantitative growth indefinitely. This can provide insights into ways of measuring the improvements in people's wellbeing in emerging economies, where

developed countries. However, this may be correlated with the large role of on-the-job training under the lifetime employment system, and it is unclear whether this alone is sufficient to make a simple judgment. As for empathy, it is thought to be rooted in culture and values, and while it is thought to have a certain intuitive impact on comparisons between Japan and the US, for example, it was not possible to account for these differences. Due to the above-mentioned differences in business and employment practices, cultural differences, and data limitations, only three indicators are selected for indexing service quality: capital stock per capita, educational attainment (Programme for International Student Assessment [PISA] score), and education level, and each was normalized and then simply averaged.

I then adjust the size of consumer surplus in the service sector (the size of the consumer surplus increases or decreases according to the degree of deviation from the average). This approach to indexation tends to increase the consumer surplus in developed countries, although it is consistent with the discussion that process innovation would further enhance consumer surplus. Moreover, I am unable to capture the indication from the empirical result showing differences between Japan and the US. Although the estimation here may suggest the magnitude of the differences in the broad framework of developing and developed countries, future empirical studies that go into factors such as empathy and *omotenashi* [hospitality] are needed.

economies are increasingly becoming more service-oriented as they develop. Many of the components that constitute service quality are considered to be related to human resources, such as the service provider's customer service, knowledge, trust, and empathy. In other words, the quality adjustment suggests that it may be possible to visualize the potential benefits of improved human capital. By incorporating this aspect into the quality growth indicator, the importance of promoting human capital development as a policy measure becomes more evident.

## Free/Unpaid Services

The final adjustment related to consumption is the provisions of free or unpaid services. First, there is the treatment of the utility given by free services. Among others, in recent years, the development of ICT has led to a particular enrichment of digital services provided free of charge. Brynjolfsson and Oh (2012) note that in the US, individuals spend 8.4 h per week on the Internet at home, which accounts for 12% of their time, excluding sleep. Furthermore, more than two-thirds of their time spent online is on free sites. Since people spend so much time online, they must be earning a substantial benefit from it—even if it is free. In other words, differences in a country's digital penetration situation are likely to make a big difference in the overall utility gained by the public.

There are two types of utility obtained from free digital services: money-based and time-based. The former is based on Internet usage fees, while the latter relates to the opportunity cost of time. Since the former is conceptually considered to be included in the consumer surplus already estimated, the latter is the issue here. As an estimate of consumer surplus using the time approach, Varian (2009), for example, estimates that the largest value of a Google search is the time savings, equivalent to USD 500 per person per year. Brynjolfsson and Oh (2012) estimate that most of the consumer surplus from the Internet is due to the time factor and that the consumer surplus in the US generated from the use of free sites (Facebook, YouTube, Twitter, Google, etc.) within the Internet is equivalent to 0.74% of GDP (based on a 2007–2011 average). This estimate serves as a benchmark for estimating the size of consumer surplus from free digital use, based on internet penetration and time spent using the internet in each country. The number of digital platforms available for free use has been increasing over the years, and this trend is reflected in an increase in the time spent using them. It is noted that digital development is considered one of the factors that drive innovation, as APEC also emphasizes. For this reason, it is also considered a factor in the second index of quality growth.

The second issue is unpaid housework. These services, if performed by a housekeeper, would be compensated in the market. However, when housework is performed within the home and self-consumed, it is not reflected in the GDP. This creates a now well-established contradiction: cleaning, meal preparation, and nursing care—when outsourced—lead to an increase in GDP even though the size of services consumed remains the same.[10] Since it is difficult to measure the magnitude of self-consumed household services, the estimation here is based on the assumption that the magnitude of self-consumed household services is the same as the magnitude of unpaid household labor hours. In fact, unpaid housework is calculated as such in a satellite account of GDP.

The United Nations Economic Commission for Europe (UNECE) has issued guidance for such calculations, with Western countries and Japan publishing the results. The basic idea is to estimate the magnitude of unpaid housework for an entire country by multiplying the time used for self-consumption by the unit cost per hour and the size of the population. The unit cost per hour can be estimated in two ways: the income lost by performing such services (the opportunity cost concept) or the wage of the provider of such services (UNECE 2017; ESRI 2018). The value of unpaid housework is estimated here using the following simplified method, including developing countries for which data are not available. For hours of housework, I use World Bank data, and for countries for which no data exist, it is estimated using a regression where labor participation rates and per capita income are explanatory variables (for men and women, respectively).[11] For the unit labor cost per hour, I employ the average wage of the service provider. There are two approaches to unit labor costs: the specialist approach (wages for specialists in housekeeping and nursing care) and the generalist approach (wages for domestic helpers). Here, I adopt the latter and use the minimum wage as unit labor cost in each country, based on ILO statistics. These two variables are multiplied by the working-age population (by sex) to estimate the value of unpaid housework. I then also adjust the magnitude of the utility of this service due to inequality. These are the adjustments made to the category of consumption. However, it is likely that the size of the utility in this expenditure will differ depending on differences in institutions and governance. The adjustments for institutions and governance are discussed collectively at the end of this section.

## Government Spending—Public Goods and Positive Externalities

The size of government spending in each country over the past 30 years has averaged in the low twenties as a percentage of GDP (although it increased to over 30% in 2020–2021 due to the COVID-19 response). Capital formation by the government, especially in infrastructure, is important; in Japan, for example, about

[10] Volunteer work, like unpaid housework, does not require compensation for services. Although this should be also included, it is not included in the calculations here due to data limitations.

[11] It is assumed that as the female labor participation rate increases, the number of hours of unpaid housework is expected to decrease. Here, it is assumed that as per capita income increases, the number of hours of unpaid household work simply decreases. In the regression, these variables were statistically significant, but the coefficient of determination was not very large, only showing that there was a weak relationship, therefore further elaboration of this approach is desirable in the future.

20% of GFCF comes from the government. Among responses to several market failures, one that is particularly relevant to government spending concerns investment in public goods, which include infrastructure and basic research, as well as those addressing externalities. Infrastructure can be supplied directly by the government, as in the construction of public roads and river improvements, or through public enterprises and public–private partnerships (PPPs).

For example, when roads are built, users benefit from shorter travel times and lower travel costs. However, in GDP, only the input costs are recorded as government expenditures. The gross profit (as would be recorded in the case of private investment) that infrastructure brings is not included. On the other hand, when making infrastructure investment decisions, CBA is usually conducted, which calculates the benefits that citizens gain from the savings in road travel time and travel expenses. Therefore, it is theoretically possible to estimate how much social benefit users derive from public investment by accumulating individual project evaluations. However, since such aggregated data are not available in practice, I use the internationally recognized discount rate in cost–benefit calculations of public investment to represent the standard rate of return—usually between 4 and 9%, depending on income status—and multiply this by the relevant government expenditures to obtain the social benefit. I also add the consumer surplus generated from it, as with general consumption. Finally, an additional adjustment is made to assess how efficiently the government uses fiscal resources (see the next section for details on how it is adjusted according to government efficiency).

On the other hand, positive externalities—such as innovation through agglomeration and knowledge enhancement—are not included in the scope of the CBA for infrastructure projects. In the case of roads, agglomeration of investment occurs as transportation becomes more convenient, and human resource development is enhanced as people are able to travel to distant schools and workplaces. In the medium to long term, this leads to increased productivity through the accumulation of knowledge. Research on the "wider economic benefit" to capture these benefits is ongoing; yet, it will be some time before practical estimation methods are fully developed. The benefits of infrastructure are not limited to the individuals who use it. Infrastructure contributes to productivity growth over the medium term through investment accumulation and human resource development and is therefore also considered a factor in the second index.

Basic research is a pure public good that satisfies non-competition and non-exclusion with respect to the scope of knowledge use, but the rate of return on basic research is unknown. It is assumed that the results of basic research funded by governments will be used in applied research with a certain time lag, leading to widespread social innovation. So, like infrastructure, future generations will benefit. Accordingly, I include government spending on basic research in the same way as infrastructure—i.e., by adding social profit and surplus. The benefits of education and healthcare services extend beyond individuals to benefit society as a whole by increasing a country's overall productivity over the medium to long term through human resource development. Because of these positive externalities, governments, either directly or indirectly, invest in and subsidize education and healthcare. In this indexation, I include public education and healthcare services in the same manner as infrastructure, adding a rate of return of 4–9% of expenditures and consumer surplus, as well as the elements of the second index. Finally, social protection spending is related to the size of inequality. In this exercise, I did not make adjustments to government spending related to this because the adjustment of GDP due to inequality is already considered, as stated. However, social protection and safety nets, like education and healthcare, are related to sustained growth, so they are considered elements of the second index.

## Government Spending—Negative Externalities and Defensive Spending

Government spending includes expenditures in response to negative externalities. Typical items are those related to the environment and climate change. As previously noted, in the GPI, spending on environmental conservation is deducted from GDP, providing a more accurate representation of the economy as defensive spending aimed at maintaining the current situation. The magnitude of the negative externality is theoretically a social cost that lies outside the market mechanism. The current generation is directly impacted by environmental degradation caused by business activities, leading to calls for government regulation. However, governmental regulations alone are sometimes insufficient.

In this Appendix, government spending on the environment is considered as the sum of costs of improving environmental degradation that could not be fully prevented by regulation and is deducted from GDP as defensive spending. In this calculation, for example, for two countries with the same pollution levels, this expenditure is subtracted after adjusting for the current level of environmental degradation to avoid discrepancies where the country without environmental protection measures (i.e., with a smaller deducted amount) has a larger social welfare indicator than the country with environmental protection measures.

And here, I use the air pollution indicator as a proxy variable for environmental pollution in general—specifically, the rate of deaths from air pollution per unit of population is used as an indicator. Higher death rates are interpreted as insufficient government expenditure on the environment and a larger amount is deducted than the actual expenditure. This adjustment is indicative only, as there is no empirical support for proxying overall environmental pollution with air pollution mortality, nor for calculating the magnitude of the negative externalities to be converted. However, I consider it necessary for some adjustments to be made, as current government spending on the environment is clearly inadequate in countries with severe air pollution in their capitals, such as China and India. In such cases, residents may be severely negatively affected, and it is obviously inappropriate to deduct only a nominal amount of environmental spending as defensive spending while ignoring this broader impact. On the other hand, future generations will be disproportionately affected by climate change; therefore, GHG emissions are included in the second index as a factor expected to worsen future social welfare.

Government spending on public safety and crime is another type of defensive spending. As with the environment, social security is maintained by government spending for this purpose, so it is deducted from GDP. However, as in the case of the environment, there can be situations in which a country with poor public security (smaller spending for safety) has a higher level of social welfare simply because of its smaller deduction from government spending for public safety purposes. For this reason, adjustments are made based on the security level, specifically utilizing the homicide rate per head of population. This is similar to the environment in that these adjustments are only indicative, as they are not necessarily supported by empirical evidence.

## Elements of Resilience

Resilience is being addressed to a greater or lesser extent in every country to mitigate or quickly recover from external shocks such as natural disasters, economic crises, infectious diseases, terrorism, and cyberattacks. There are significant differences in vulnerability and resilience between countries, and several institutions and experts have attempted to index resilience. Many of these are related to specific events, such as disasters or economic crises, or to specific countries, but there are also attempts to assess resilience across sectors.[12] However, no attempt has been made to integrate such indicators into overall social welfare or GDP. In this Appendix, I organized this point as follows: resilience affects both social welfare and sustained growth, and how this is incorporated into the index of quality growth will depend on the specific resilience-enhancing activities (inputs) and their outcomes (outputs). These are shown in Table 9.7.

As shown here, government capacity and governance are considered important in responding to any type of external shock. Strengthening these will lead to better prevention, a rapid response and more effective recovery from external shocks, thereby improving people's lives. As it is difficult to extract specific elements of governments' capacity related to resilience, I use the "government effectiveness" indicator in the Worldwide Governance Indicators (WGI), published by the World Bank. This is included in the overall governance adjustment described in the next section.

Expenditures related to disaster reduction are a part of infrastructure, as discussed before, and this means that the social benefits from disaster reduction have already been included in our index. Government stockpiles for disaster preparedness and infectious diseases, if they exist, are also recorded in the GDP figures

[12] The Fund for Peace, a non-profit organization in the US, has published a comprehensive State Resilience Index (Fund for Peace 2022). The index calculates an overall score by assigning 40 items in seven components of resilience: social inclusion, social cohesion, national capacity, individual capacity, environment and ecology, economy (including infrastructure), and civic space (civic dialogue, social contract, etc.) The highest scores in the 2022 index are Norway (8.4), which is three times higher than South Sudan (2.9), the lowest score.

**Table 9.7** Factors that enhance resilience (examples)

| Event | Ex-ante response | Immediate and ex-post response |
|---|---|---|
| Natural disasters | Investment in disaster prevention infrastructure;<br>Social system building (government capacity, social cohesion, etc.);<br>Preparation of individuals, such as savings, etc. | Government capacity;<br>Social cohesion;<br>Fiscal space, enabling emergency government expenditures |
| Economic crises | Systematic prevention such as introduction of swaps etc.;<br>Banking sector soundness;<br>Economic diversification;<br>Fiscal soundness;<br>Improvement of economic system, such as social security, safety nets;<br>Personal savings | Government capacity;<br>Fiscal space underpinning the economy in times of recession |
| Infectious diseases | Invest in medical infrastructure;<br>Social system building for infectious disease, including testing and hospitalization;<br>Prevention by individuals | Government capacity;<br>Social cohesion;<br>Fiscal space, enabling necessary compensation in times of pandemics |

*Source* Author

as inventory investment and government consumption. It should be noted that it is not possible to determine whether such investments and stockpiles are at an appropriate level or not.

Finally, there is the question of how to assess the impact of such spending on overall social welfare, because spending on resilience is made at the expense of short-term productive use. In this regard, from the perspective of the opportunity cost of capital and arbitrage, government investment in disaster reduction is undertaken because it is a project with a higher (social) return than investments for alternative purposes to which the funds were not redirected. Consequently, the benefits of spending on resilience can be visualized by multiplying the rate of return on disaster reduction infrastructure. Furthermore, as disaster reduction progresses, regional investment is promoted, creating agglomeration effects. For this reason, this aspect is emphasized in the second index, discussed in detail later.

How should we think about financial soundness and fiscal surpluses? For example, if financial institutions increase their lending without adhering to capital adequacy regulations, production may increase in the short run. This can be viewed as production exceeding the normal capacity of the factors of production, and in some cases, exceeding even the potential growth rate of GDP. With regard to public finances, for example, if the government borrows above a threshold level and increases spending, the economy is stimulated at that point in time, which may then lead to overproduction beyond normal capacity. If such choices are made, the result will be reflected in GDP, and the magnitude of social welfare will increase in the short run. Because the current GDP statistics reflect these choices, no adjustment to the size of social welfare in the first index is made here. On the other hand, these choices will affect future growth. Fiscal and financial soundness are largely an indicator of growth mechanisms that promote sustained future growth. If, through prudent economic and fiscal management and adequate safety nets, a major downturn during an economic crisis can be prevented, it will be possible to avoid the long-term damage that undermines future growth. For this reason, these items are included as elements of the second index.

## Governance—Government Capacity and Effectiveness

As mentioned in the previous section, there is a need to adjust overall expenditures in accordance with the level of institutional capacity and governance. The WGI lists governance items as (1) voice and accountability, (2) political stability and absence of violence/terrorism, (3) government effectiveness, (4) control of corruption, (5) rule of law, and (6) regulatory quality. All of these items have direct or indirect impacts on people's lives. Of these, government effectiveness, control of corruption, and rule of law and regulatory quality are the most frequently discussed items when assessing their economic impacts.

Public capital, accumulated through government spending, is as much an engine of economic growth as private capital. However, with government investment, arbitrage and competition through markets do not operate. At the same time, it is widely acknowledged that there are significant differences in government capacity and effectiveness. This makes it necessary to take into account differences in the effectiveness of investments. If we look at one of the governance items of the WGI, the government effectiveness score (expressed with a range of −2.5 to 2.5), the difference between Singapore (2.29), the highest, and South Sudan (−2.38), the lowest in 2021, is extremely large.

As discussed in Chap. 7, for example, with regard to public investment, project costs tend to be higher when competitive bidding and project evaluation procedures are not in place, or when the most optimal project is not selected due to limited project selection capacity. Therefore, I draw on the results of Gupta et al. (2011) by adopting the idea of a public investment quality index to reflect differences in government effectiveness. The index developed by Dabla-Norris et al. (2011), which was used by Gupta et al. (2011), is a simple average of the four aspects, such as strategic guidance and project appraisal; project selection; project management and implementation; and project evaluation and audit, during 2007–2010 for 71 countries. The scores are expressed on a scale with a maximum of 4 and a minimum of 0. Gupta et al. (2011) assumed that this indicator is invariant over time, as improving the quality of public investment takes time to achieve. In the discussion of this Appendix, I use a similar measurement (0–1), but due to the relatively long time period covered, I also take into account the possibility of improvement over time. In other words, I use the government effectiveness indicator in the WGI as a proxy variable for the quality of public investment.[13] Other government expenditures than infrastructure—such as education and healthcare—are also adjusted using this effectiveness indicator. Since government effectiveness influences future productivity through infrastructure, education and healthcare spending, it also sits within the second index.

## Governance—Corruption

Corruption affects the economy through a variety of channels. In a society where corruption is pervasive, not just the direct exchange of money, such as bribes, the allocation of public funds and private investment are distorted, lowering economic efficiency, and tax revenues fall below the point where they should be. This affects overall expenditures in GDP, including investment, government spending, and consumption, and the losses from these are considered to far exceed the total amount of bribes paid (Fisman and Golden 2017). The World Happiness Report also considers corruption perceptions as one of the explanatory variables of happiness, in which the well-being of individuals is reduced by corruption (Helliwell et al. 2022). There is a certain amount of research on the extent to which corruption affects the economy, which can be divided into two main types: those that estimate the magnitude of corruption, such as bribes, and those that attempt to determine how corruption correlates with economic growth and the like.

With regard to corruption estimations, Kaufman (2005), for example, estimated that the amount of bribery worldwide was about USD 1 trillion by integrating several enterprise and household surveys of the World Bank and others. However, it is difficult to capture the magnitude of corrupt money transfers, since they are essentially hidden acts.

In contrast, the estimates of the effects on growth are undertaken using a growth regression analysis that includes corruption as an explanatory variable to identify its correlation (e.g., Mo 2001; Pellegrini and Gerlagh 2004; Dreher and Herzfeld 2005; Ugur and Dasgupta 2011). With a few exceptions, the conclusion is commonly drawn that corruption has a negative impact on economic growth (e.g., IMF 2016). These studies are related to this current index, as regression analysis estimates the extent to which corruption negatively affects economic growth, both directly and indirectly. Following the approach of Mo (2001), I use the Perceived

[13] Dabla-Norris et al. (2011) confirm that this indicator is highly correlated with relevant items of the World Bank's Country Policy and Institutional Assessment (CPIA). Specifically, the indicator correlates well with the average of the following CPIA items: debt, public finance, budget and financial management, administrative management and transparency, and accountability and corruption. However, due to the limited number of countries with CPIA and the fact that corruption, whose impact is considered separately in this report, is included among the CPIA items, I do not adopt the CPIA as a proxy for government capacity for public investment, but instead adopt the government effectiveness indicator from the WGI, which has also been confirmed to have a positive correlation, although the correlation is weaker than that of the CPIA.

Corruption Index by Transparency International (expressed in the range of 0–10) to express the corruption situation and estimate the impact of corruption on GDP growth by country, using the benchmark rate as a 0.55 decline of growth per unit of corruption. The adjustment due to corruption is added to the figure obtained as a result of the adjustments made so far to the various items of GDP (excluding net exports and error omissions).

## Governance—Rule of Law and Regulation

The view that institutions determine long-term economic growth was introduced in detail in Chap. 6. Acemoglu and Robinson (2012), in their historical analysis, conclude that economic growth is closely linked to inclusive institutions that enable many citizens to participate in economic activity. Institutions generally include not only the rule of law and regulation but also political regimes such as democracy and authoritarianism. The growth regression analysis introduced in Chap. 6 also included institutions as explanatory variables when analyzing the impact on growth of various factors. One frequently cited example is the establishment of intellectual property rights, which is believed to make innovation more likely. In general, as the rule of law advances and the quality of regulation improves, investment is encouraged, leading to economic growth. Laws and regulations provide the framework on which economic activity depends and generally address market failures, such as the failure of competition, incomplete markets, and information failures. The results of these laws and regulations are reflected in GDP and the consumer surplus discussed in the previous section as well.

In the case of public investment by governments, the amount of spending is adjusted by the social rate of return and the effectiveness of each government. However, this adjustment is not applied to the rate of return on private economic activity. This is because, first, laws and regulations are a response to market failures, and second, the results of laws and regulations are already reflected in the economic activity in the market. However, through the expansion of investment, as in the case of intellectual property rights and ensuring competition, they affect the accumulation of investment, which is one of the engines of future growth. For this reason, I include law and regulation as a component of the second index.

## Results of the Indexation of Quality Growth Taking into Account Welfare (First Indicator)

Based on the above, I estimate the size of welfare-adjusted national income for nine countries. Their income status is shown below, according to the World Bank classifications in 2023:

- High-income countries: Japan

- Upper-middle-income countries: Peru, Costa Rica, China, Indonesia, El Salvador (Indonesia and El Salvador moved from lower middle to upper middle-income countries in 2022)
- Lower-middle-income countries: Vietnam
- Low-income countries: Madagascar, Burkina Faso

For each of these nine countries, Fig. 9.5 shows the trend in GDP and estimated social welfare since 2000. In order to analyze the sources of differences between countries, a cross-sectional comparison of GDP and its quality growth components was also conducted. For this comparison, I primarily use 2019 data to avoid the impact of COVID-19. Household consumption and government spending, with adjustments, are identified as particularly important. Finally, for consumption—which accounts for the largest share and causes the largest differences from the GDP statistics—I compare how the percentage of GDP allocated to each item in each country's consumption breakdown has changed over time.

The key findings from the analysis are as follows. First, I look at the major characteristics by income group. For this purpose, to facilitate comparison, I have plotted the degree of difference between real GDP and the first indicator of quality growth since 2000 (Fig. 9.6). The highest-performing country is Japan—an example of an advanced country. Japan's quality growth index is on average more than 10% larger than its GDP, which makes it significantly different from others. The only other countries with positive averages for the entire period are Peru and Vietnam, while Burkina Faso is almost zero, and all others show negative values. This suggests that although developed countries, represented by Japan, have smaller GDP growth rates than developing countries, their elemets of social welfare that do not appear in GDP is likely higher than in developing countries. Simply put, there is a shift from quantitative to qualitative growth, and in the case of Japan, this trend has been increasing over time. In other words, the qualitative part of growth is accelerating. On the other hand, for developing countries, no common trend characteristics by income group are observed. There are large differences by country. For example, even among the same lower-middle-income countries, the trends are quite contrasting: Indonesia has stagnated, while Vietnam has experienced a steady increase. Such differences in patterns suggest the possibility that differences may be caused by policies and other factors.

Where does this difference originate? The analysis reveals a difference between Japan and the rest of the world in adjusting for the surplus from free services and the quality of services in household consumption. In Japan, the sum of these two adjustments accounts for about 8% of the country's GDP. For free services, the differences in digital penetration rates are directly reflected. For quality of services, most developing countries are below average, and thus the surplus from quality of services is negative (for example, it is –3.6% for Burkina Faso, the largest negative value among the nine countries). Thus, this indexation provides one indication of the extent of the shift from quantity to quality in consumption.

Regarding household consumption, following the approach used by the GPI, the magnitude of household consumption in GDP is adjusted according to the level of

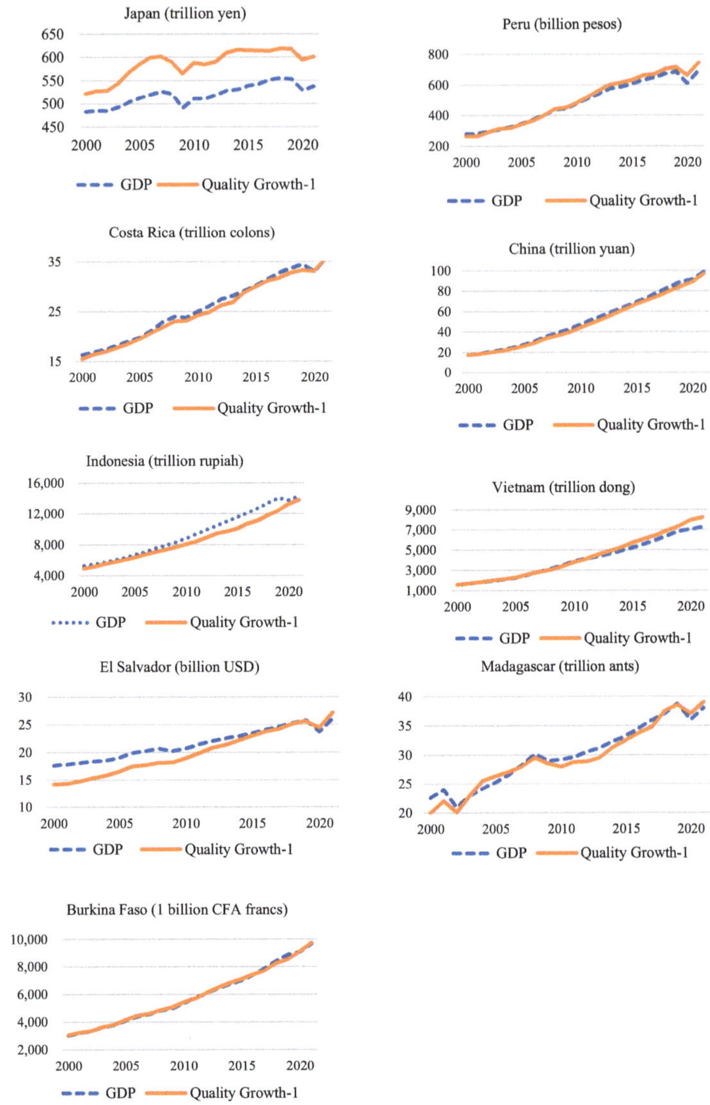


**Fig. 9.5** Trends in GDP and Quality Growth-1. *Source* Author's estimates for Quality Growth-1, GDP by UN National Accounts (see Table 9.13)

inequality. As a result, there is a considerable gap between household consumption and GDP across the nine countries after adjusting for inequalities. Table 9.8 compares the countries in 2019. There is a nearly 30% difference between Japan, the smallest adjustment, and Indonesia, the largest. As discussed, the size of inequality has a largely inconsistent relationship with income level, so it should be considered separately from the issue of stage of development. As noted in the table,

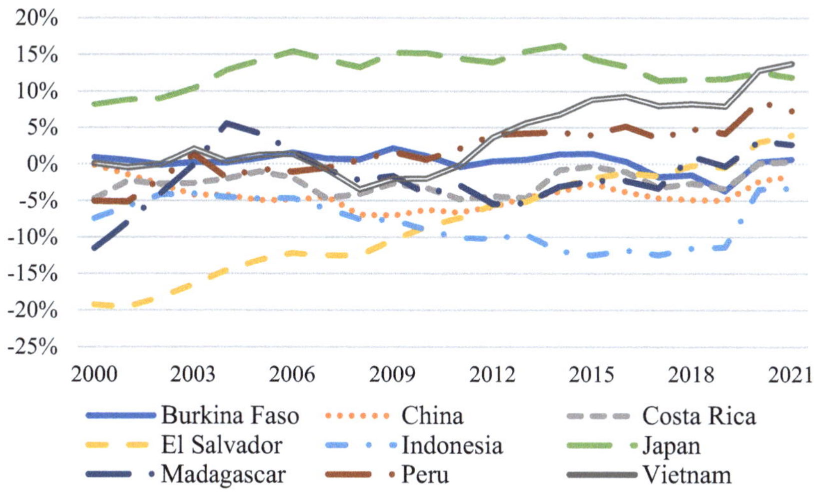


**Fig. 9.6** Differences between GDP and Quality Growth-1. *Source* Author's estimates

the after-tax Gini coefficient has remained almost constant in Japan, while it has worsened significantly in Indonesia over this period. In general, after-tax inequality adjustments tend to be applied more aggressively in developed countries. Through this method of analysis, it is evident that inequality adjustment is vital for overall social welfare and promotes quality growth. By presenting it in this way in the index, the importance of inclusiveness can be visualized.

The inequality adjustment took into account both cross-sectional comparison and changes over time. The countries that have made progress in reducing income inequality since 2000 have experienced a positive change in the rate of adjustment in this first index of quality growth, even if the absolute level of inequality remains relatively high. Specifically, in Peru and El Salvador, the improvement in inequality is the main factor behind the upward trend in welfare-adjusted consumption. Vietnam's social welfare is also larger than its GDP, as its absolute inequality is comparatively low compared to others, and it has been reducing the level of inequality over time.[14] Conversely, for countries where inequality shows a worsening trend, such as Indonesia, adjusted household income does not show the same upward trend as in Peru and Vietnam.

Another notable difference between Japan and other countries is the magnitude of adjustments in government spending. Coordination with respect to institutions could only be captured to a limited extent in this estimate. However, as discussed

[14] In addition, the amount of unpaid housework also tends to be larger in Vietnam. One hypothesis is that Vietnam follows a U-shaped relationship between economic development and female labor participation: as low-income countries become richer and household income increases, female labor participation declines, but as educational attainment further increases, it begins to increase again (World Bank 2012).

**Table 9.8** Differences of household consumption between GDP and Quality Growth-1 (2019)

| | GDP household consumption | Adjusted household consumption | Adjustment ratio | Change in Gini coefficient |
|---|---|---|---|---|
| Japan | 100 | 79.1 | 1.26 | Stable at around 30 (relatively low), with a slight upward trend |
| Peru | 100 | 67.7 | 1.48 | Improved from 51.1 in 2000 to 44.2 in 2019 |
| Costa Rica | 100 | 64.4 | 1.55 | 45–47, stably high |
| China | 100 | 68.7 | 1.46 | Trending upward from 38.6 in 2000 to 41.5 in 2019 |
| Indonesia | 100 | 61.7 | 1.62 | Worsened from 41.4 in 2000 to 47.4 in 2019 |
| Vietnam | 100 | 77.3 | 1.29 | At the mid-30s, with a slight improvement trend |
| El Salvador | 100 | 75.5 | 1.33 | Improved from 47.6 in 2000 to 37.3 in 2019 |
| Madagascar | 100 | 68.7 | 1.46 | 43% in early 2000s, not sufficient data |
| Burkina Faso | 100 | 72.8 | 1.37 | Improved from 45.8 in 2000 to 39.1 in 2019 |

*Source* Author's estimates, Gini index from WIID as shown in Table 9.13. Accessed March 3, 2023

above, government effectiveness influences the efficiency of government investment in education, health, and infrastructure, as well as its resilience to disasters. Table 9.9 summarizes the comparison of government effectiveness and subsequent adjustment to government consumption in the nine countries in 2019. There is a threefold difference between Japan (0.82) and Madagascar (0.27), resulting in a significant disparity in adjusted government spending. On the other hand, additions based on an assumed rate of return and deductions due to defensive spending within government spending vary across countries. Note that the assumed rate of return for Japan is the lowest because an internationally recognized discount rate for high-income countries is used, resulting in a lower rate compared to other income categories. For deductions, high levels of security spending and potentially poor security, especially in Latin American countries, have negative impacts on overall welfare. This indexation, therefore, allows us to visualize the security of societies, which APEC considers to be a key component of quality growth. For example, El Salvador is the only country where the result of the adjustment is negative. Moreover, government effectiveness is low, reducing overall social welfare to the extent that it cancels out the effects of reducing inequality.

Finally, the corruption situation also varies widely from country to country. Corruption is considered to affect the overall social welfare because it inefficiently distorts resource allocation. It is observed that corruption indices are generally lower in developed countries than in developing countries. Among the countries covered by this Appendix, the highest-rated country is Japan (7.2 in 2019), and the worst-performing is Madagascar (2.4), showing a difference by a factor of three. Therefore, while in Japan, adjustment is equivalent to about 1.5% of deductions

**Table 9.9** Adjustment of government consumption and government effectiveness (2019)

| | Government consumption | Addition | Deduction | Government effectiveness | Notes |
|---|---|---|---|---|---|
| Japan | 100 | 12.7 | –6.4 | 0.816 | High security, small deductions |
| Peru | 100 | 19.0 | –17.8 | 0.481 | Environmental indicator is poor and related spending is small; Large crime-related spending |
| Costa Rica | 100 | 26.9 | –19.2 | 0.574 | Environmental indicator is good; Large crime-related expenditures |
| China | 100 | 17.9 | –8.7 | 0.613 | Poor environmental indicator, suggesting potentials of large related spending |
| Indonesia | 100 | 18.2 | –8.4 | 0.535 | Stable security; Moderate environment indicator |
| Vietnam | 100 | 15.4 | –8.4 | 0.509 | High security; Moderate environment indicator |
| El Salvador | 100 | 15.0 | –21.5 | 0.397 | Large spending on public safety, but indicators are the worst and potential spending is large |
| Madagascar | 100 | 16.2 | –7.4 | 0.265 | Environmental spending is particularly small |
| Burkina Faso | 100 | 29.4 | –5.6 | 0.349 | Environmental spending is particularly small |

*Source* Author's estimates

due to corruption from social welfare, in Madagascar, the deduction reaches 4.1%. Figure 9.5 presents a total figure that does not indicate the source of the differences by country. However, these breakdowns provide insights into how the elements of quality growth are interrelated and how the positive and negative impacts are balanced to create an integrated picture.

## Sustained Growth

The annual rate of change in the size of welfare-adjusted national income in the previous section comprises the growth rate of "quality growth." However, this figure does not necessarily reflect the extent of growth that can be sustained beyond the current generation, as discussed in Chap. 6 regarding the mechanism of growth. Whether current growth is likely to continue in the future across generations is a matter of whether the foundations to support future growth are being established—thus constituting the second index of quality growth. Below, I present a proposal for an example of indexation that would represent changes in foundations that affect future growth over generations. The four elements to be incorporated are capital accumulation in the broader sense, negative externalities that impose sacrifices on future generations, fundamental elements that bring about productivity growth over the medium term, and resilience.

First, broadly defined, capital accumulation comprises the sum of produced capital, human capital, natural capital, and net foreign assets. Data were extracted from the World Bank's "Wealth of Nations" database. I use the country figures rather than capital per capita, because other indicators—such as negative externalities and productivity—are also measured at the national level. Next, I include changes in GHG emissions for each country as a negative externality related to the future burden on the next generations. Negative externalities related to the residential environment, as mentioned earlier, are not included here because they are assumed to be addressed primarily within the same generation.

With respect to productivity, and based on the theoretical background discussed in Chap. 6, I synthesize the changes in the factors presented in Fig. 9.4 that will affect long-term productivity. The items incorporated are education, health, infrastructure, technology and digital development, innovation, and inequality, as well as institutions and governance. There are two approaches to selecting indicators. One is the magnitude of inputs for each element, such as the amount spend on education. The other is the output result from the inputs, such as changes in the quality of education and healthcare, and technological development. In both cases, these are not direct indicators of productivity itself, such as TFP, but rather indicate the establishment of a foundation for long-term productivity growth.

As the first index of quality growth is primarily based on expenditure, using GDP as its foundation, an input indicator is used to estimate the first index. In contrast, I use outcome indicators for the second index to assess the changes to medium- and long-term productivity in response to the outcomes resulting from such expenditures. This approach is both consistent and coherent, since capital accumulation is the result of investment, and GHG emissions are also the outcome of accumulated past economic activities. The main indicator used is a survey by the Global Competitiveness Report.[15] The Global Competitiveness Index (GCI) incorporates items from many areas, including institutions, macroeconomics, the social sector, and businesses, and its purpose is to index and compare elements of long-term economic growth internationally (see Table 9.13). This objective aligns with the primary goals of this study.

Many of the indicators in the GCI are based on opinion surveys of business leaders, but they also include hard indicators such as GDP figures, trade data, public finance, and other financial metrics. While there are difficulties to assess, for example, the quality of education and healthcare or the ability of companies to use digital technology, subjective judgments by business leaders—viewed through a growth perspective lens at any given time—are desirable indicators because they are more comprehensive and include judgments in light of the standards of the time.

The following GCI overall scores are used to represent each foundational factor: Regarding education, the overall score for the major category "higher education and training" in the GCI is used, which includes the education system, the tertiary education enrollment rate, and items related to education quality. Regarding health, the overall score for "health and primary education" is used, which includes the business impact of several infectious diseases and infant mortality. Regarding infrastructure, the overall score for "infrastructure" is used, which includes business leaders' assessment of the quality of infrastructure. Regarding technology in general and digital development, the overall score for "technological readiness" is used, including hard data such as Internet users, in addition to assessments of technology transfer through foreign direct investment (FDI), firm-level technology absorption, and availability of the latest technology. Regarding innovation, the overall score for "innovation and sophistication factors" is used, which includes the quality of research institutes and capacity for innovation. Regarding institutions, the overall score for "institutions" is used, which includes items such as intellectual property protection as well as corporate ethics and accountability. The advantage of using an overall score for each of the above items is that it encompasses several elements, thus representing a more comprehensive set of basic conditions. Additionally, because it is standardized, it provides a score on the same scale. I

[15] The Global Competitiveness Index is a synthesis of the Growth Competitiveness Index (developed by Sachs and McArthur) and the Business Competitiveness Index (developed by Michael Porter) and was published annually by the WEF from 2004 until 2019. Its purpose is to index the factors that determine long-term economic growth, based on the idea that production factors (such as institutions and infrastructure, macroeconomic and human resources), efficiency (including technology and market efficiency), and innovation are the keys to growth. The number of items included has increased over the years. For example, the classification of major items increased from the previous 10 to 12 in 2007; in 2018, the score indicator was changed to the range of 0 to 100 from the previous 1 to 7. Therefore, when looking at item scores, it should be noted that the number of sub-items that comprise them is not necessarily the same.

also include the factor of inequality change, but since inequality is not included in the GCI, I use the change in the Gini coefficient and simply look at changes in income inequality within a country, because the impact of changes in inequality of opportunity on human resource development depends exclusively on the level of inequality within the country. Each of these items is chosen based on the theoretical background on the relationship with productivity. Note that when no weighting is used to integrate these factors, a simple average of these rates of change is used.[16]

The last item is resilience. As discussed, external shocks encompass various risks in terms of both scope and path of impact. Since it is not known in advance when and in what magnitude these shocks will occur, it is inherently difficult to construct a resilience index. For example, since the timing and magnitude of disasters vary, it is unclear how much resilience enhancement contributes to reducing the number of fatalities. One indicator is the change in related expenditures—like productivity—which should contribute to resilience. Another is changes in subjective measures, such as people's perception of safety with respect to disasters and terrorism, and their general assessment of safety. The factors that should receive attention are listed in Table 9.7. What is common across different types of risk is the establishment of systems to minimize the impact of shocks and the social response required to enable the desired post-event response. These can be strengthened by government capacity and social cohesion, among other things.

The indexing of resilience is primarily based on Legatum Prosperity Index (LPI). For government capacity, I use the "government effectiveness" indicator, and for social cohesion, I refer to changes in the "social capital" indicator, which includes social networks, interpersonal trust, personal and family relationships, and social tolerance. Second, in the case of any shock, public funds are essential for the post-event response. This capacity depends on fiscal surpluses and the ability to spend through borrowing. For this reason, I use "government budget balance" and "country credit rating" as indicators. Next, with regard to sector-specific resilience, strengthening disaster prevention through infrastructure improvement is particularly important. However, the LPI does not include indicators to capture the degree of improvement in disaster prevention infrastructure. Instead, I use the "overall infrastructure quality" from the GCI as a proxy for resilience in disaster prevention infrastructure, together with data from records on the extent of disasters (number of fatalities), and the results are adjusted for scale.[17] For economic

[16] The GCI also includes other items such as macroeconomic and market, financial, and labor efficiency. Macroeconomic includes hard indicators such as inflation and foreign exchange. Some of these were used as elements of resilience in this Appendix. Most items related to market, financial, and labor efficiency were excluded from this analysis, as they are considered to have short-term implications for the current generation, mainly in terms of growth through more efficient resource allocation, while among financial items, bank soundness was included as an element of resilience.

[17] The WEF (2006) conducted a survey on the impact of natural disasters on the operations and decisions of companies and considered the results as a score of resilience in this regard. However, such a survey was not conducted in any other years. Therefore, I conducted a simple cross-sectional

crises, there are several indicators for the soundness of the financial sector, but here I use the indicator of "soundness of banks." For infectious diseases and terrorism, I employ scores on health and security in LPI. For health, I use the average score for "preventive interventions" and "care systems" among several components. Although not limited to infectious diseases, it is generally assumed that preparedness is a proxy against infectious diseases. For safety, I use the "safety and security" indicator, which includes war and civil conflict, terrorism, and violent crime—for example, the extent to which people perceive the threat of terrorism.

## Results for the Second Index of Quality Growth

The results of the estimation are presented below. First, the relationship between capital growth, changes in GHG emissions, and the quality growth rate of the first indicator—as estimated in the previous section—is reviewed (Fig. 9.7). As a general trend, countries such as Peru, Costa Rica, China, and other upper-middle-income countries show similar patterns of changes in capital growth and the first indicator of quality growth.

This trend is to be expected to some extent, as capital accumulation primarily leads to GDP growth. Produced capital is the result of economic growth and investment accumulation, while the amount of human capital, by definition, increases as per capita income rises. On the other hand, as the World Bank (2021) points out, forest and fishery resources tend to decline with development. Since capital accumulation in aggregate is important from the perspective of weak sustainability, I confirm this by comparing the size of aggregate capital accumulation with the first indicator of quality growth over the period covered by the estimation (Table 9.10). As a result, it was confirmed that Costa Rica is the only country among the nine where the pace of capital accumulation exceeds that of the first indicator. They are internationally renowned in the field of environmental protection, which may reflect the results of such efforts. In six of the other countries, the growth rate of the first index slightly exceeds that of capital accumulation. The share of capital accumulated shifts from produced capital to human capital as incomes rise. For this reason, a simple comparison of these six countries in terms of total capital volume, such as Japan and Burkina Faso, cannot be used to discuss general trends. Further in-depth analysis is needed.

---

regression analysis for the 2006 results and used the results to estimate scores for other years. Specifically, the score for the evaluation of disasters by business leaders was used as the independent variable, and the score for the overall quality of infrastructure in the same year and the number of deaths due to disasters in the previous year were analyzed as explanatory variables. The reason for this was that resilience scores tend to be lower in countries with large disaster losses. As a result, a positive coefficient was obtained for the quality of infrastructure and a negative coefficient for the disaster experiences, both of which are statistically significant. Assuming that this relationship holds for other years as well, a multiple regression analysis is conducted using the overall quality

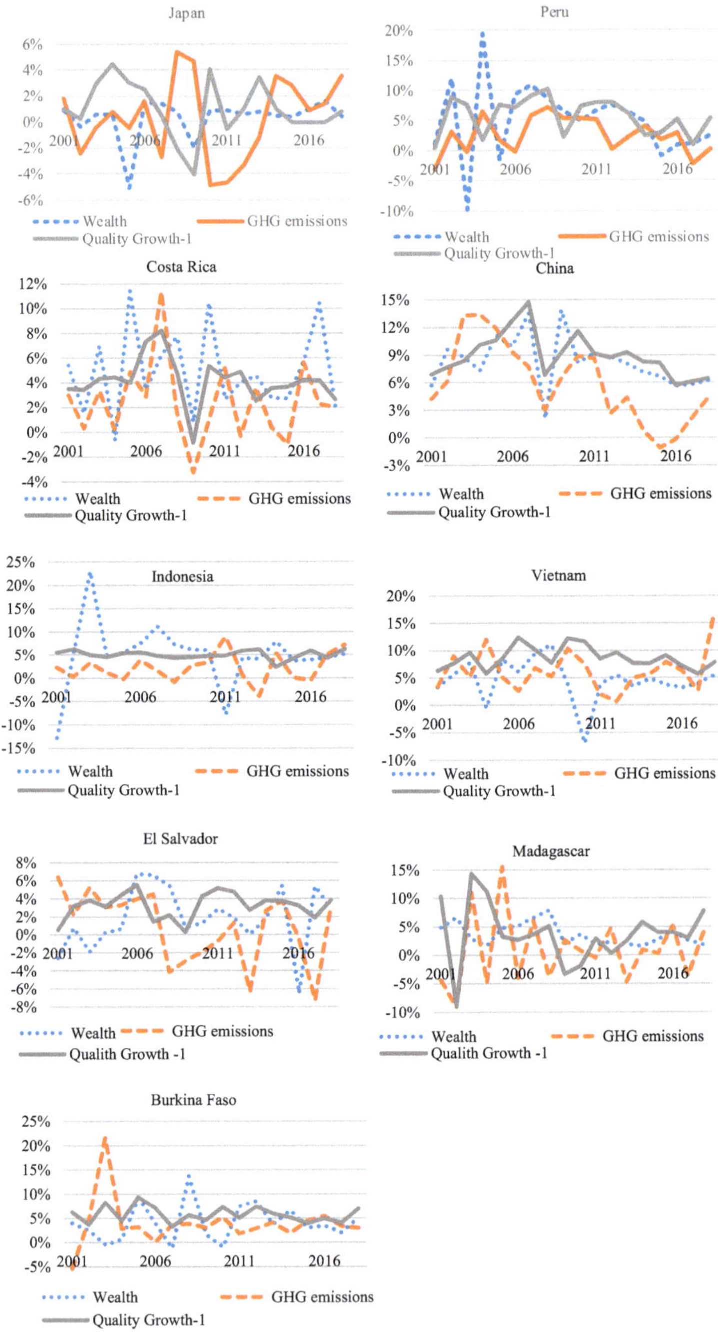


**Fig. 9.7** Quality Growth-1, wealth (capital) growth, and GHG emissions. *Source* Wealth (capital) from the World Bank database (for the Changing Wealth of Nations). Accessed August 1, 2023; GHG emissions from WDI. Accessed July 25, 2023; Quality Growth-1 from Author's estimates

**Table 9.10** Capital accumulation and Quality Growth-1 (2001–2018 in average)

| Relationship | Country |
|---|---|
| Capital accumulation > high quality growth rate | Costa Rica (4.9:4.1) |
| Capital accumulation = high quality growth rate | Indonesia (4.9:5.0), Madagascar (3.6:3.7) |
| Capital accumulation < quality growth rate | Japan (0.3:1.0), Peru (5.0:5.6), China (8.2:8.9), Vietnam (4.4:8.6), El Salvador (2.0:2.8), Burkina Faso (4.0:5.7) |

*Note* Figures in the parentheses show the average annual growth rates between 2001 and 2018—the first value is the average rate of capital accumulation, while the second value represents the average rate of quality growth
*Source* Author's estimates

The next relationship examined is between GHG emissions and the first index, showing that, on average, GHG emissions are below the latter in all nine countries. This indicates that the elasticity of GHG emissions with respect to the first index is less than one. However, the goal of reducing global GHG emissions requires a substantial reduction in carbon intensity relative to growth. The absolute amount of emissions must be reduced, not merely curbed. For Japan, for example, GHG emissions have continued to increase since 2014, resulting in a slight increase for the period as a whole. Even considering the shift in energy sources following the Great East Japan Earthquake, further efforts are still required. In China, GHG emissions have declined significantly in recent years, likely due to changes in the country's economic structure and national initiatives. Nevertheless, overall GHG emissions increased by 5.9% during the period, giving it the highest growth among all countries, along with Vietnam. China is already the world's largest emitter, and therefore, future reduction efforts are of global significance (Table 9.11).

The historical trend of foundations is expected to bring about an increase in productivity, as shown in Fig. 9.8. This figure indicates the potential for medium- to long-term growth, including non-income factors such as the quality of services. As an overall trend, the potential for productivity growth is generally proportional

**Table 9.11** GHG emissions growth (2001–2019 average, %)

| Country | Japan | Peru | Costa Rica | China | Indonesia | Vietnam | El Salvador | Madagascar | Burkina Faso |
|---|---|---|---|---|---|---|---|---|---|
| Growth rate | 0.3 | 2.5 | 2.4 | 5.9 | 2.2 | 6.2 | 0.1 | 0.8 | 3.8 |

*Source* Author's calculations from WDI

of infrastructure and the number of disaster fatalities as explanatory variables to generate a score for infrastructure resilience to disasters.

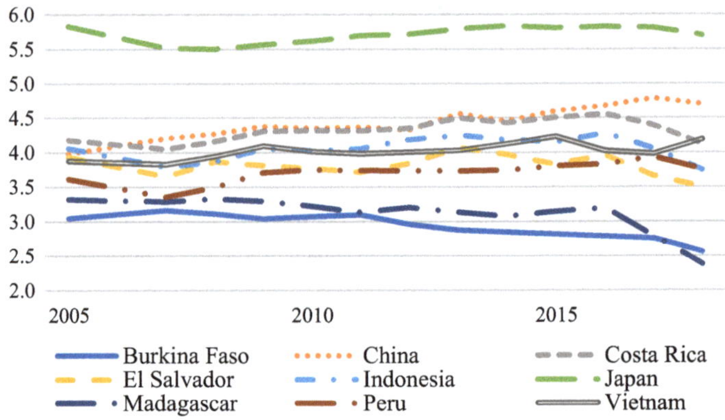


**Fig. 9.8** Trends in foundations for productivity. *Source* Author's estimates

to the level of per capita income. Japan, a high-income country, and Madagascar and Burkina Faso—both low-income countries—clearly differ from the other six countries in the magnitude of foundations for productivity growth. Among the other countries, recent improvement has been notable in China, while Costa Rica—which had previously shown almost the same trend as China—has, in contrast, stagnated in terms of growth in recent years. Among low- and middle-income countries, Vietnam has made progress in improving the foundations of productivity.

Figure 9.9, which uses 2005 figures as a base year—set at 100—shows changes in the foundations for productivity growth. China demonstrates particularly strong growth, followed by Vietnam and Peru. These countries are accelerating the development of the foundations for medium- and long-term productivity improvement. In China's case, this growth is largely driven by improvements in education, infrastructure, and innovation. In Vietnam, infrastructure and technology, including ICT, are the main drivers, and in Peru, education and infrastructure scores are driving improvement. Among the countries in decline, Madagascar has seen a significant drop in its technology and innovation scores. In particular, the GCI scoring system was revised in 2017 and scores have dropped significantly since then. This suggests that there are significant structural issues in the country, as it had fallen stagnant even before that time. Note that the three countries whose overall scores dropped in 2017 (Costa Rica, Indonesia, and El Salvador) all saw significant declines in their innovation scores. This may be due to the change in the scoring system, as many countries saw lower innovation scores for the same item in that year (although some countries, such as China, saw an increase in innovation scores in that year).

Finally, for resilience, the results are shown in Fig. 9.10. The overall trend is that resilience, like foundations for productivity, is generally proportional to the

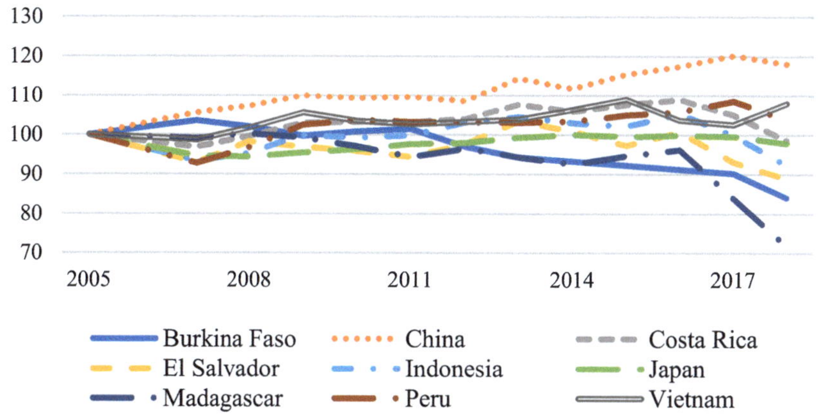


**Fig. 9.9** Changes in the foundations of productivity (% change). *Source* Author's estimates

amount of per capita income. The score of Japan is clearly different from that of Madagascar and Burkina Faso. Low-income countries are generally considered to be relatively more vulnerable to the impact of external shocks, and this tendency is evident in this indicator. Among the other six countries, China and Costa Rica are the most resilient, followed by Peru and Indonesia. These results are roughly proportional to per capita income. However, a different picture emerges when looking at the rate of change.

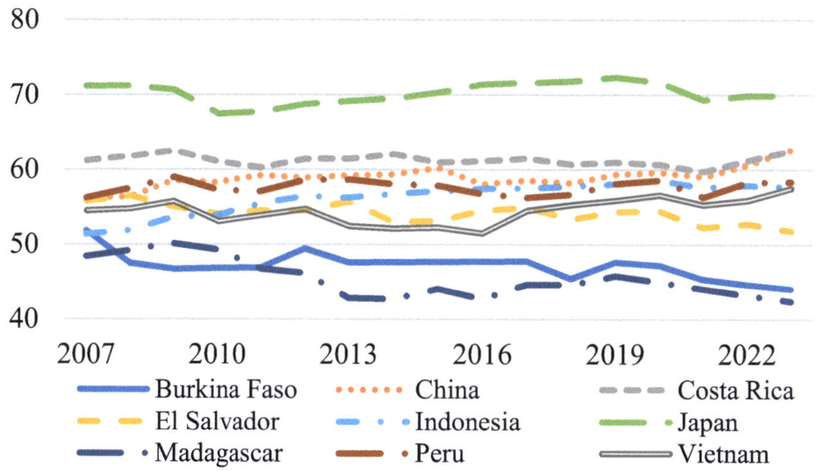


**Fig. 9.10** Trends in resilience. *Source* Author's estimates

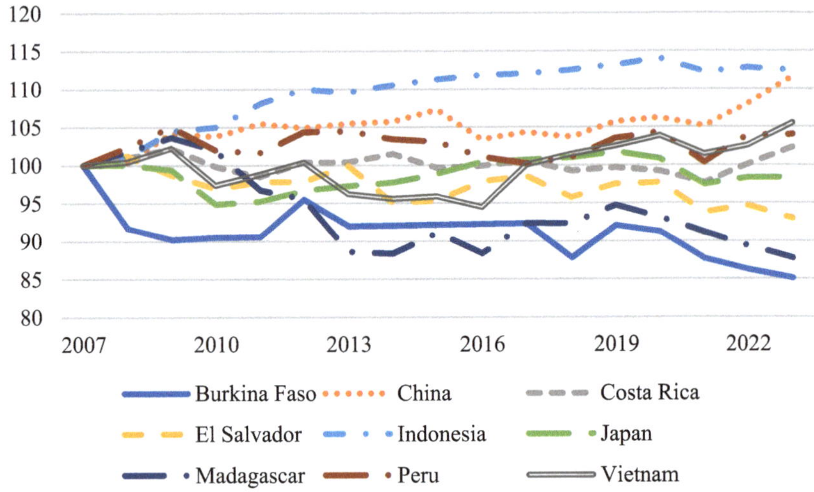


**Fig. 9.11** Changes in resilience (%). *Source* Author's estimates

Figure 9.11 examines changes since 2007, taking that year as the starting point (set at 100) to assess the foundations of productivity. What is particularly striking is the significant improvement in Indonesia's resilience. This includes progress in government effectiveness, social capital (e.g., social networks), disaster prevention, health, and terrorism. As will be discussed in the country case studies in Part II, Indonesia has experienced a series of shocks, including the Asian Financial Crisis (AFC) in the late 1990s, natural disasters such as the 2004 Indian Ocean earthquake and tsunami, and terrorism by Islamic extremists in the 2000s. In response, the government prioritized fiscal consolidation, counterterrorism measures, and disaster prevention as key policy objectives. These policy priorities may be reflected in the growth rate of this indicator. In China, factors contributing to the recent increase in scores include government effectiveness and improvements in social capital. On the other hand, for Madagascar, the decline in government effectiveness, and for Burkina Faso, a fall in the terrorism score, has led to lower resilience scores. Madagascar has been experiencing a humanitarian crisis since 2015, with conflicts with Islamic extremists resulting in significant internal displacement of people. This situation is likely to be reflected in the country's declining score.

Taken together, the trends in the second index of quality growth are illustrated in Fig. 9.12. Although the time period is limited due to the data constraints, what can be observed from this figure is the lack of an overall trend. The up-and-down fluctuation is also quite large, with a range of +16.5 to −21.2%. The main reason for this is the large variation of GHG emissions from year to year. For example, El Salvador's growth was 16.5% in 2008, the largest throughout the entire period for all countries, with its GHG emissions improving by 4.2%, a lower rate of increase than the previous year. Vietnam, on the other hand, experienced a decline of −21.2% in 2010, reaching the lowest point throughout the period, when its GHG emissions in that year were 7.5% higher than in the previous year. This, together with the large negative growth of wealth in that particular year, lowered the composite score of the second index. The average percentage change for each country over the entire period is shown in Table 9.12.

These results suggest that, regardless of the differences in income group, it seems possible to establish a foundation for sustained growth for future generations through policy. While detailed comparisons of the breakdown cannot be made here, the indexation provides hints on policy areas that will be prioritized in the future. For example, in Southeast Asia, it is striking that Indonesia's rate of change exceeded that of Vietnam. In addition to its GHG emissions score, its resilience score showed that Indonesia improved by an average of 1.08% annually over the period, while Vietnam's improvement was only 0.17%. The GDP growth is higher in Vietnam, but strengthening responses to external shocks may be a priority issue that needs to be addressed. GHG emissions in Vietnam also had the highest rate of increase among the nine countries, and it is hoped that visualizing the invisible element of GHG emissions and integrating it with other growth-related indicators will lead to more effective reductions of GHG emissions through policy. The simple process of summing the four items in this way, of course, requires further

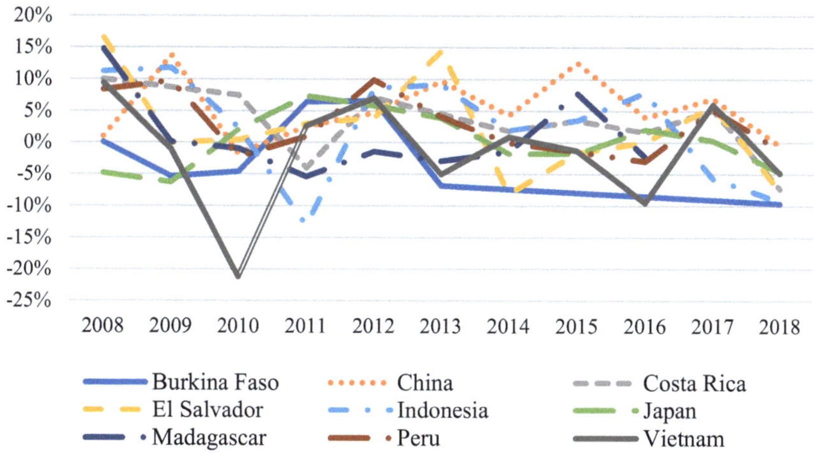


**Fig. 9.12** Quality Growth-2 (%, change). *Source* Author's estimates

**Table 9.12** Percentage change in Quality Growth-2 (2008–2018 average, %)

| Country | Japan | Peru | Costa Rica | China | Indonesia | Vietnam | El Salvador | Madagascar | Burkina Faso |
|---|---|---|---|---|---|---|---|---|---|
| Growth rate | 0.2 | 2.7 | 3.5 | 5.2 | 2.6 | −1.6 | 2.4 | 0.9 | −1.9 |

*Source* Author's estimates

consideration, and weighting based on policy may also be considered necessary. I hope that further discussions on this kind of indexing will be held in order to develop insights into the current status of foundations for productivity that will promote future growth, and ways that priority areas should be considered in the future.

In this Appendix, I have presented a preliminary proposal to address the issue of how to measure quality growth. Even though the purpose here is to present a broad picture, as readers will notice, there are many limitations in the methodology, empirical evidence, and data constraints. Below, I would like to present some final points regarding the limitations of this preliminary proposal in the discussion of the Appendix. First, how economic and social transformation is converted into differences in productivity is one of the major pillars of quality growth, but it was not explicitly incorporated here. Related to this, the informal economy was also not treated well. For government activities, a more sophisticated method of adjustment using common rates of return and of measuring government effectiveness would be desirable. The surplus is a distinctive focus of this proposal, but the accumulation of evidence on which to base estimates of differences in service quality, for example, is limited, and future research underpinned by evidence is strongly required. This issue is also indispensable when considering the future growth of high-income countries, particularly for Japan. I could not examine the question of how the balance between the two indices of quality growth should be considered and pursued. Despite the deficiencies presented here, I believe that showing this kind of broad picture, even though it is premature, is certainly a valuable first step. The next task is, of course, to elaborate on this way of approaching growth and to consider its application to actual policy concerns, such as how to derive an optimal policy mix and how to form a consensus in society. I plan to continue working on these issues in the future.

For reference, the following sources of data used in the Appendix are presented below (Table 9.13).

**Table 9.13** List of data used for quality growth indicators

| Item | Data | Source | Countries |
|---|---|---|---|
| GDP | GDP Breakdown by Expenditure | UN National Accounts (https://unstats.un.org/unsd/snaama) | |
| Income inequality | Gini coefficient (after tax) | The Standardized World Income Inequality Database, Versions 8–9 (https://doi.org/https://doi.org/10.7910/DVN/LM4OWF) | |
| Quality of service | Per capita capital stock | World Bank Open Data (https://data.worldbank.org/indicator) | |

(continued)

**Table 9.13** (continued)

| Item | Data | Source | Countries |
|---|---|---|---|
| Quality of service | Academic performance (reading) | OECD Programme for International Student Assessment (PISA), PISA Data Explorer. (https://pisadataexplorer.oecd.org/ide/idepisa/) | |
| Quality of service | Average years of schooling | UNESCO Institute for Statistics (http://data.uis.unesco.org/) | |
| Free digital | Internet penetration rate | World Bank Open Data | |
| Free digital | Internet usage time | Our world in data (https:ourworldindata.org/internet) | |
| Unpaid domestic work | Ratio of hours of household work (female, male) | World Bank Open Data | |
| Unpaid domestic work | Labor participation rate (female, male) | World Bank Open Data | |
| Unpaid domestic work | Minimum wage | International Labour Organization ILOSTAT (https://ilostat.ilo.org/data/) | |
| Unpaid domestic work | Working-age population (female, male) | ILOSTAT | |
| Unpaid domestic work | GDP deflator | World Bank Open Data | |
| Government expenditure | Government expenditure breakdown | IMF Government Finance Statistics (https://data.imf.org/?sk=a0867067-d23c-4ebc-ad23-d3b015045405) | Japan, China. El Salvador, Indonesia, Madagascar |
| Government expenditure | Government expenditure breakdown | UN Data, Table 3.1 Government final consumption expenditure by function (http://data.un.org/Data.aspx?d=SNA&f=group_code%3A301) | Costa Rica and Burkina Faso, not available in IMF data |
| Government expenditure | Government expenditure breakdown | World Bank (2012) Public Expenditure Review for Peru; Vietnam National Institute of Statistics HP, State budget expenditure by indicators (https://www.nso.gov.vn/en/banking-insurance-and-state-budget/) | Peru Vietnam |
| Government expenditure | Negative externalities | Air Pollution Mortality: Our World in Data (https://ourworldindata.org/grapher/share-deaths-air-pollution) | |

(continued)

**Table 9.13** (continued)

| Item | Data | Source | Countries |
|---|---|---|---|
| Security | Crime | Homicide Incidence, World Bank Open Data | |
| Governance | Government effectiveness | Worldwide Governance Indicators (https://www.worldbank.org/en/publication/worldwide-governance-indicators) | |
| Governance | Corruption | Corruption Perception Index (https://www.transparency.org/en/cpi/2022) | |
| Capital | Capital by type | World Bank's Changing Wealth of Nations Database (https://www.worldbank.org/en/publication/changing-wealth-of-nations/data) | |
| GHG | GHG emissions | World Development Indicators (https://databank.worldbank.org/source/world-development-indicators) | |
| Productivity | Education, health, infrastructure, technology, innovation, institutions | Global Competitiveness Report by World Economic Forum for each year (2006–2019) | |
| Resilience | Social cohesion, government effectiveness, fiscal balance, credit rating, bank health, health, terrorism | Legatum Prosperity Index (https://www.prosperity.com/) | |
| Resilience | Number of disaster fatalities | Our world in Data (https://ourworldindata.org/natural-disasters) | |

## References


Acemoglu, Daron, and James Robinson. 2012. *Why Nations Fail: The Origin of Power, Prosperity, and Poor.* Crown Publishers.

Azhar, Azeem. 2021. *Exponential: How Accelerating Technology Is Leaving Us Behind and What to Do About It.* Random House Business.

Bean, Charles. 2016. *Independent Review of UK Economic Statistics.* Statistics Office, Ministry of Internal Affairs and Communications. https://assets.publishing.service.gov.uk/media/5a7f603440f0b62305b86c45/2904936_Bean_Review_Web_Accessible.pdf.

Brynjolfsson, Erik, and Joo Hee Oh. 2012. "The Attention Economy: Measuring the Value of Free Digital Services on the Internet." ICIS 2012 Proceedings 9. https://aisel.aisnet.org/icis2012/proceedings/EconomicsValue/9.

Dabla-Norris, Era, Jim Brumby, Annete Kyobe, Zac Mills, and Chris Papageorgiou. 2011. "Investing in Public Investment: An Index of Public Investment Efficiency." IMF Working Paper WP/11/37. IMF.

Dreher, Axel, and Thomas Herzfeld. 2005. "The Economic Costs of Corruption: A Survey and New Evidence." SSRN. https://papers.ssrn.com/sol3/papers.cfm?abstract_id=734184.

Economic and Social Research Institute (ESRI), Cabinet Office, Japan. 2018. "Mushō rōdō no kaheihyōka (Reiwa gannen 6gatu 17nichi shūsei)" [Monetary Valuation of Free Labor (Revised June 17, 2048)]. https://www.esri.cao.go.jp/jp/sna/sonota/satellite/roudou/contents/pdf/190617_kajikatsudoutou1.pdf.

Fioramonti, Lorenzo. 2019. "Beyond Gross Domestic Product- Measuring the Quality of Growth in Africa." in *The Quality of Growth in Africa,* eds. Ravi Kanbur, Akbar Noman, and Joseph E. Stiglitz, 33–53. Columbia University Press.

Fisman, Ray and Miriam A. Golden. 2017. *Corruption: What Everyone Needs to Know.* Oxford University Press.

Fukao, Kyoji, Kenta Ikeuchi, and Miho Takizawa. 2018. "Shitsu wo chōsei shita nichibei service sangyō no rōdō seisansei suijyun hikaku" [Comparison of Labor Productivity Levels in Japanese and U.S. Service Industries Adjusted for Quality]. Productivity Report Vol. 6. Japan Productivity Center.

Fund for Peace. 2022. *State Resilience Index Annual Report 2022.* Washington, DC.

Gupta, Sanjeev, Alvar Kangur, Chris Papageorgiou, and Abdoul Wane. 2011. "Efficiency-Adjusted Public Capital and Growth." IMF Working Paper WP/11/217. IMF.

Helliwell, John F., Richard Layard, Jeffrey D. Sachs, Jan-Emmanuel De Neve, Lara B. Aknin, and Shun Wang (eds.). 2022. *World Happiness Report.* Sustainable Development Solutions Network.

Hirota, Koki. 2019. "Jizokukanō na kaihatsumokuhyō (SDGs) to korekarano chūshō kigyō keiei" [Sustainable Development Goals (SDGs) and Future SMEs Management]. Bugin Report, December 2019, Bugin Economic Research Institute.

Hosono, Akio. 2022. *SDGs, Transformation and Quality Growth: Insight from International Cooperation.* Springer.

International Monetary Fund (IMF). 2016. "Corruption: Costs and Mitigating Strategies." IMF Staff Discussion Note SDN/16/05. IMF.

Japan International Cooperation Agency (JICA). 2016. "SDGs heno kōken ni mukete: JICA no torikumi" [Towards Contributing to the Achievement of the SDGs: JICA's Efforts].https://www.jica.go.jp/Resource/aboutoda/sdgs/ku57pq00002e2b2a-att/JICA_torikumi.pdf.

Japan Productivity Center (JPC). 2017. "Service hinshitu no nichibei hikaku" [Japan-US Comparison of Service Quality].

Kaufman, Daniel. 2005. "Myths and Realities of Governance and Corruption." SSRN. https://papers.ssrn.com/sol3/papers.cfm?abstract_id=829244.

Manyika, James, Sven Smit, Lola Woetzel, Michael Birshan, Kevin Russell, and Lindsay Purcell. 2021. "Companies in the 21st century: A New Look at How Corporations Impact the Economy and Households." Discussion Paper. McKinsey Global Institute.

Mazzucato, Mariana. 2018. *The Value of Everything.* Penguin Random House.

Ministry of Health, Labor and Welfare, Japan. 2018. Heisei 30 nenban rōdō keizai no bunseki [Analysis of the Labor Economy, 2018]. https://www.mhlw.go.jp/wp/hakusyo/roudou/18/18-1.html.

Mo, Pak Hung. 2001. "Corruption and Economic Growth." *Journal of Comparative Economics* 29: 66–79.

National Institute of Information and Communications Technology (NiCT). 2016. "GDP ni arawarenai ICT no shakaiteki kōsei heno kōken ni kansuru chōsa hōkokusho" [Research Report on the Contribution of ICT to Social Welfare that Does Not Appear in GDP].

Parasuraman, A. Parsu, Valarie A. Zeithaml, and Leonard L. Berry. 1988. "SERVQUAL: A Multiple-Item Scale for Measuring Consumer Perceptions of Service Quality." *Journal of Retailing* 64 (1): 12–40.

Pellegrini, Lorenzo, and Reyer Gerlach. 2004. "Corruption's Effect on Growth and its Transmission Channels." *Kyklos* 57 (3): 429–456.

Stiglitz, Joseph E., Amartya Sen, and Jean-Paul Fitoussi. 2010. "Preface." in *Mismeasuring Our Lives: Why GDP Doesn't Add Up*, xvii–xxxiv. The New Press.

Takizawa, Miho. 2020. "Keizaigaku kara mita seisansei keisoku no kadai to service shakai" [Challenges of Productivity Measurement and Service Society from Economics Perspective]. *Serviceology* 6 (4): 4–7.
Ugur, Mehmet, and Nandini Dasgupta. 2011. "Evidence on the Economic Growth Impacts of Corruption in Low-Income Countries and Beyond: A Systematic Review." EPPI-Centre, Social Science Research Unit, Institute of Education, University of London.
United Nations Economic Commission for Europa (UNECE). 2017. *Guide on Valuing Unpaid Household Service Work.* UNECE.
Varian, Hal. 2009. "Economic Value of Google." http://cdn.oreillystatic.com/en/assets/1/event/57/The%20Economic%20Impact%20of%20Google%20Presentation.pdf.
World Bank. 2012. *World Development Report 2012: Gender Equality and Development.* World Bank.
World Bank. 2020. "Purchasing Power Parities and the Size of World Economies." World Bank.
World Bank. 2021. *The Changing Wealth of Nations 2021: Managing Assets for the Future.* World Bank.
World Economic Forum (WEF). 2006. *The Global Competitiveness Report 2006–2007.*WEF.
Yamada, Hisashi. 2015. "Nihon no service sangyō no seisansei ha hontou ni hikuinoka" [Is the Productivity of Japan's Service Industries Really Low?]. Research Focus No. 2015-020. Japan Research Institute.

**Koki Hirota** earned his B.A. in Economics from the University of Tokyo and holds a Ph.D. in Economics from Saitama University in Japan. His professional career spans several prominent roles in international development finance and policy, including Chief Economist, Director General of Operation and Strategy Department, and Director General of Southeast Asia and Pacific Department at the Japan International Cooperation Agency (JICA), and Chief Representative in Jakarta for Japan Bank for International Cooperation and in Hanoi for the Overseas Economic Cooperation Fund. In academia, he was a Professor at the Graduate School of Humanities and Social Sciences at Saitama University and a Visiting Fellow at the JICA Ogata Sadako Research Institute for Peace and Development. His recent publications include *Challenges in Fiscal and Monetary Policies in Mongolia* (co-edited, Springer, 2023) and *Addressing Social Infrastructure Needs in Asia: Towards a Pandemic Resilient Society* (co-edited, JICA, August 2025).

# Part II
# Country Case Studies

## About the Country Case Analysis

Part II provides a case study analysis of five countries from a quality growth perspective. Part I provided a conceptual framework, in which I argued that establishing a quality growth approach requires a theoretical foundation, a set of policies, and the measurement of results. In Part II, to understand how this translates into actual policies, country experts review the growth trajectories of target countries and discuss how inclusiveness, sustainability, and resilience have evolved over time, including the policies that were implemented and the outcomes. Through these case studies, we can see how country developments were evaluated from the perspective of quality growth, what was effective, and where problems arose. Further insights may be gained by looking at the case studies in conjunction with the indicators presented in the Appendix of Chap. 9.

The five countries analyzed are Indonesia, Vietnam, Peru, Costa Rica, and Madagascar. They were selected for their balance of regions and income levels. The analysis was conducted by experts in each country. The key findings can be summarized in a few words: in Indonesia, growth has been sustained, and the Asian Financial Crisis (AFC) has made strengthening economic resilience a priority. However, the widening inequality in this century raises concerns about the sustainability of growth. In Vietnam, high growth has been sustained, while inclusiveness and resilience have been maintained, resulting in a significant degree of quality growth. Peru's growth is robust and its resilience is increasing, but improvement in its traditionally large inequality is still desirable. Costa Rica has made good progress in its overall economic transformation, albeit with twists and turns. However, the widening inequality in recent years needs to be viewed with caution. Madagascar is facing serious problems in achieving growth.

In preparing the book, the conceptual chapter and the case study analysis were started simultaneously. Apart from Vietnam, the case analyses were first undertaken in 2018–2019, providing insights into establishing the concept of quality growth. These have now been updated, except for Costa Rica, to take advantage of the opportunity presented by the publication of this English version of the book. Given this background, please be aware of two limitations of the analysis in the case studies. First, the "growth" analyzed in Part II is primarily based on the GDP indicator. Therefore, growth does not explicitly include factors other than income, such as consumer surplus and externalities, as discussed in Part I. The second concern relates to the two perspectives of sustainability, and the discussion in the case studies primarily focuses on "sustained growth," a mechanism for achieving growth. Since GHG emissions are a global issue, it is difficult to discuss the direct relationship between GHG emissions in individual countries and the resulting impact on growth, and thus, this aspect is not discussed in depth. Please bear this in mind when reading Part II.

# Indonesia

# 10

Koki Hirota

Indonesia is a multi-ethnic archipelago nation, with the fourth-largest population in the world. While development-oriented autocratic rule during the late 1960s and later decades promoted national unification, the establishment of an inclusive political system had to wait until the political shift that followed the AFC. The country's abundant natural resources provide an economic advantage, but they also pose challenges that hinder economic transformation and evolution. Macroeconomic management has traditionally been carried out by experts from academia, with the goal of striking a balance between political and business considerations. Since the resignation of the Suharto on May 21, 1998, there have been sporadic terrorist attacks by Islamic extremists, and regional conflicts have continued until recently. The country is also susceptible to natural disasters, as exemplified by the 2004 Indian Ocean Earthquake and Tsunami. When looking at Indonesia from a quality growth perspective, these characteristics affect the inclusiveness, resilience, and sustainability of growth. Section 10.1 provides an overview of Indonesia's economic development and presents the issues from the perspective of quality growth. Sections 10.2 to 10.4 examine the trajectory of Indonesia's development from the perspectives of inclusiveness, resilience, and sustainability. Finally, the relationship between all of these factors is examined.

K. Hirota (✉)
Tokyo, Japan


K. Hirota (ed.), *Introduction to Quality Growth*,
https://doi.org/10.1007/978-981-95-6220-6_10

## 10.1 Economic Development Overview

After gaining independence following World War II, Indonesia's economy remained stagnant until the late 1960s. While the nationalist *Pribumi* policy was promoted, there was no steady growth of private capital, and the economy remained primarily under the direction of the government. Many state-owned enterprises (SOEs) were established, some of which were requisitioned from foreign companies. Also of note during this period was Indonesia's external relationship with the Soviet Union, which suggests some influence from the communist bloc states, where SOEs played a major economic role. The roots of the country's economic structure—in which SOEs still play a major role today—can be traced back to this history. In macroeconomic terms, Indonesia faced a series of challenges after gaining independence, such as hyperinflation caused by fiscal deficits and government borrowing from the central bank.

All of this changed after the anti-communist purge that began in September 1965. Suharto came to power and built a system in which economists were put in charge of economic management. This system essentially remains in place to this day. As they emphasized the stability of economic policy, Indonesia was once again able to benefit from external funds from international organizations and Western countries. From the late 1960s, Indonesia enjoyed continuous economic growth over a prolonged period. Figure 10.1 shows that the Indonesian economy has maintained high rates of growth to the present, except for three sharp falls: the period of falling oil prices after the sharp spike in the 1980s, the AFC at the end of the 1990s, and the COVID-19 pandemic in 2020. Per capita GDP growth averaged in excess of 5% in the 1970s and the 1990s until the AFC, and it has remained at around 4% for the most part since the mid-2000s up to 2019. Currently, it has returned to the growth rate trends it was experiencing prior to the COVID-19 outbreak. The first two external economic shocks caused fundamental changes in Indonesia's economic structure.

The Reverse Oil Shock in the 1980s prompted a shift to an economic structure that was less reliant on natural resources. The AFC prompted a shift in the economic management system toward a more resilient structure that could withstand external shocks. As a result, the Indonesian economy came through the 2008 Global Financial Crisis (GFC) largely unscathed. As described in detail in the following section, fluctuations in natural resource prices and the financial shock were both triggers that significantly impacted the country's economic structure and management, leading to an improvement in sustainability and resilience.

The structure of the Indonesian economy has followed a pattern similar to that of many developing countries. The composition ratio of agriculture in GDP dropped from 40% of GDP in the early 1960s to about 20% in 1990 and 15% by 2005. However, this ratio stopped falling due to a rise in palm oil and rubber prices, among other agricultural outputs. The ratio of the manufacturing sector was in the single digits in the 1960s, but began to increase in the late 1980s, reaching 22% in 1997. However, it began to slow in the 2000s and declined after peaking in the early 2000s. It currently comprises 20% of GDP in 2023. The ratio of the

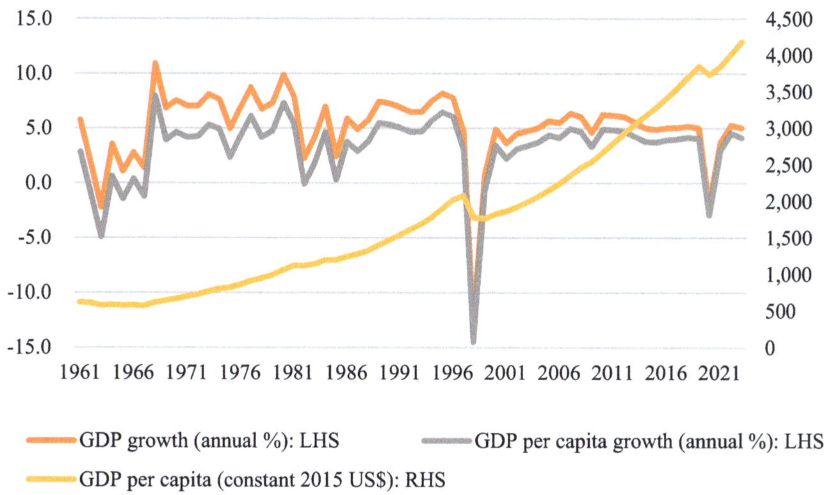


**Fig. 10.1** Trends in economic growth in Indonesia (%, USD). *Source* WDI. Accessed January 14, 2025

services sector has been growing almost consistently, except during the AFC, and currently stands at 46% in 2023 (based on WDI data). The ratio of the mining sector, based on the data from the ADB, was 20.8% in 1983, before the Reverse Oil Shock, and dropped to 9.6% in 1993 and 8.3% in 2003, before recovering to 11.0% in 2013. It dropped again to single digits due to the decline in natural resource prices, but has recovered to 12.2% in 2022 (ADB Key Indicators data 2000 and 2024).

Changes in economic structure may be more evident if we examine changes in exports. The following three trends can be seen: (1) Oil and gas exports began to account for the majority of exports following the oil shock, exceeding 80% of the total in 1982, but declined sharply in the latter half of 1980s due to the rapid fall in oil prices in the late 1980s, accounting for about 20% in 1998; (2). The ratio of manufacturing exports surged from the late 1980s, accounting for 3.6% of total exports in 1982, but over the subsequent ten years, reached over 50% in 1993; (3). From the mid-2000s to the early 2010s, the ratio of oil and gas exports recovered slightly, although at a lower level than in 1980, and mineral products, which previously accounted for 4 to 6%, reached more than 10% in 2007. Conversely, the share of manufacturing exports declined, falling below 50% in 2005 and shrinking to one-third of the total in 2011. It then returned to the 40% level, but has not yet reached 50%. Generally, economic development is accompanied by a shift from primary to secondary and tertiary industries, with exports becoming increasingly diversified and sophisticated. However, since 2000, Indonesia has not necessarily followed such a transition.

Poverty has declined significantly along with economic growth. The change in the poverty rate in terms of GDP per capita of USD 2.15 (2017 prices) shows a continuous improvement. About three-quarters of the total population was below this level in 1984, but the poverty rate dropped to about 50% before the AFC. It briefly increased to 68% in 1998, during the crisis, but dropped to 40% by 2001, falling below 10% by 2014 and to 1.8% by 2023. The poverty rate, as defined in Indonesia, decreased from 40% in 1970 to 11% in 1996, and the number of people in poverty declined from 54 million to 22.5 million. The ratio of those in poverty rose by about 50% due to the AFC (JBIC 2001), but declined thereafter as the economy began to grow once again. This indicates that external shocks hit those closest to poverty particularly hard. On the other hand, the Gini coefficient improved during this period. This is because the wealthy saw their incomes fall more sharply as a result of these external shocks. However, this improvement was only temporary, and inequality continued to widen, counter to the trend of reducing absolute poverty, with the Gini coefficient rising from 0.30 in 2000 to 0.39 in 2013, the worst level since 1970 (WDI). The deterioration in the Gini coefficient halted following President Joko Widodo's election in 2014.[1] This rise was much more pronounced than in neighboring countries. Indonesia's Gini coefficient had been low since the 1970s, indicating that the current deterioration is a more recent trend.

## 10.2 Growth and Inclusiveness

Poverty in Indonesia has consistently declined, with short periods of exception during the AFC and COVID-19. In addition to the improvements in income, the Human Development Index (HDI) in Indonesia has also improved faster than the global average.[2] To assess how Indonesia's economic growth is inclusive, this section reviews changes in inequality over time and considers the causes of change, drawing from previous studies on this issue.

Of the studies on inequality in Indonesia, van Leeuwen and Földvári (2016) cover the longest time period, examining the period from 1932 to 2008 and estimating inequality in Indonesia based on statistical data on household expenditures and demographics. They compared their results with those of other studies and found that the trends in changes in inequality were generally similar. Figure 10.2 illustrates trends in the Gini coefficient observed in several studies in relation to GDP per capita. Inequality was at its highest in the 1930s, before Indonesia's independence. During this period, agriculture, the leading industry, shifted to exports through the use of plantations. This led to income inequality between the landowning class and the farmers, which peaked during the Great Depression. Indonesia's income inequality subsequently narrowed due to the effects of World War II. This effect was accelerated by the fact that Dutch business owners (i.e., the wealthiest in Indonesia) returned to their native country, resulting in an increased share

[1] Besides WDI, the Standardized World Income Inequality Database (Versions 8–9) shows that the Gini coefficient of disposal income has been at 0.474 or 0.475 from 2014 to 2022.

[2] The average annual improvement in HDI from 1990 to 2023 was 0.64% worldwide, compared to 0.93% in Indonesia.

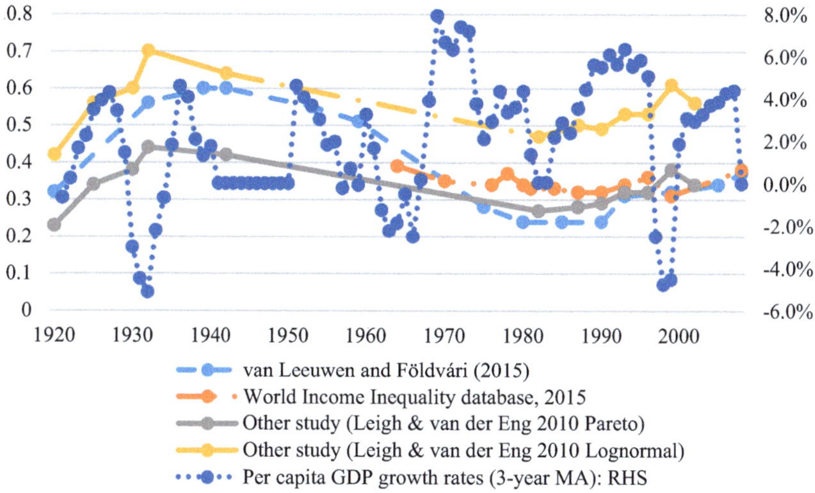


**Fig. 10.2** Trend of Gini coefficients and growth rates in Indonesia (LHS: Gini coefficients, RHS: growth rate). *Source* Created based on the figures from Table 5 of van Leeuwen and Földvári (2016), with per capita GDP growth from WDI also included.

of income for small farmers. Inequality began to narrow with the advent of the Suharto regime, and this remained a consistent trend until the mid-1980s.[3] Inequality remained broadly stable between 1980 and 1996 and then narrowed during the AFC, as it had a larger negative impact on the wealthy who had more assets (Nakamura and Hondai 2016). However, this trend was short-lived, and inequality then continued to expand gradually until relatively recently.

Looking at the relationship between inequality and growth, the growth rates were volatile before independence, when inequality was high, and the average growth rate was also lower than in subsequent periods. During the Suharto regime, per capita income rose significantly; however, the Gini coefficient remained in the low 0.3 range, having improved considerably. If this period is divided into two (i.e., pre- and post-Reverse Oil Shock), inequality declined considerably in the first half and remained relatively unchanged in the second half. The sustained growth period after 2000 exhibited slightly lower growth compared with the preceding period, accompanied by higher inequality. In the second half of the 2010s, this downward trend came to a halt. This is a broad overview of trends in inequality and growth rates in Indonesia. It is worth considering what factors underlie these trends.

[3] Timmer (2004) finds that for the period 1967 to 2002, the growth rate of real per capita income for the bottom 20% was the same as the overall average real per capita income growth rate. According to van der Eng (2009), in the period from 1960 to 1997, the Gini coefficient was slightly larger in the 1970s. This is attributed to the import-substitution policy adopted at the time, which led to a sharp increase in the wages of skilled workers.

According to van Leeuwen and Földvári (2016) and van der Eng (2009), from the latter half of the 1960s onwards, inequality narrowed significantly due to an increase in rice production (the so-called "Green Revolution"), and agricultural subsidies and infrastructure investment funded by the government.[4] Until around 1967, when rice was in short supply in Indonesia, more than one million tons of rice were imported annually; however, the country achieved self-sufficiency in rice in 1984. Between 1967 and 1984, annual growth in rice production averaged 5.7%, largely following the introduction of high-yielding crops during the Green Revolution (Akashi 2016). According to JICA and JBIC (2008), the combination of supply-side support measures (e.g., the introduction of high-yielding crops, chemical fertilizer subsidies, irrigation development, and agricultural financing) and demand-side policies (e.g., producer price support) played an important role. Regarding rice prices, the National Food Logistics Agency was established in 1967 and minimum purchase price policies were introduced. At the same time, consumer protection measures were adopted, and rice reserves were released when market prices rose above a predetermined ceiling, thus stabilizing the market (Nishimura 2009). In terms of both demand and supply, agricultural policies were generous to the poor.

Timmer (2004), citing previous studies, notes that Suharto instituted a policy to allocate the fruits of growth to the poor and promoted investments in infrastructure development and education.[5] The sharp rise in oil prices benefited Indonesia's growth through foreign exchange earnings, but discussion has been limited as to whether the growth of the natural resource sector had a direct effect on inequality, making the long-term impacts unclear. However, it is evident that the reallocation of increased wealth in the natural resources sector through agricultural subsidies and infrastructure spending helped increase development spending aimed at narrowing inequality, at least in the short term.[6]

[4] Indonesia is an archipelago nation. The increase in infrastructure spending in the 1970s and 1980s was seen as a positive factor in reducing inequality by promoting development on the outer islands. The eastern part of Indonesia is generally perceived to be underdeveloped; however, for example, in 1983, per capita income (excluding oil and gas) in the easternmost province of Irian Jaya (at that time) was ranked 8th, and Maluku was ranked 14th among all 27 provinces (at that time) (according to van der Eng 2009). Wicaksono et al. (2017) argue that location in the East only comprises about 1% or so of the total reasons for the inequality. At the same time, the provinces on Java island, excluding Jakarta, are not necessarily rich, with Central Java and Yogyakarta ranked 22nd and 21st, respectively. Against this backdrop, Indonesia is well known for its policy of large-scale migration from the densely populated island of Java to the land-rich outer islands. Farmers on the outer islands own 1.7 ha of land, which is more than twice as large as the 0.7 ha of land that farmers in Java own. However, to the best of my knowledge, there are no studies examining inequality in relation to these migration policies.

[5] As far as can be ascertained, there have been no studies on how much income was reallocated by means of taxation and how this affected changes in inequality.

[6] JICA and JBIC (2008) argue that the policy to allocate much of the crude oil revenues to infrastructure, social services, agriculture and manufacturing—particularly the enhancement of the agricultural and manufacturing production base—helped the country to avoid Dutch disease. However,

Following this period, the fall in crude oil prices in the 1980s led to sharp growth in export-oriented manufacturing, such as clothes, shoes, lumber and electronic components. Non-oil and gas exports began to surpass oil and gas exports. One explanation for the Kuznets hypothesis is the view that a shift in labor from agriculture to manufacturing initially widens inequality. Such a shift would be brought on by manufacturing development, and once the rural potential unemployed move from rural areas to manufacturing, agricultural productivity would increase and farm incomes would likely rise. However, as noted in Chap. 3, the Kuznets hypothesis is not necessarily supported in modern times, and there was little sign of a change in inequality in Indonesia during that period, despite an increase in the proportion of manufacturing. According to van der Eng (2009), this was because manufacturing employment increased primarily in labor-intensive, low-wage sectors, which curbed the wage gap between the manufacturing and non-manufacturing sectors. As such, inequality improved significantly under the Suharto regime, and this was conducive to high economic growth. Although not politically inclusive, the Suharto regime implemented economic measures to utilize revenues from natural resources to increase development spending and promote regional development, which contributed to keeping inequality at low levels.

Inequality narrowed temporarily following the AFC. Subsequently, however, income inequality in Indonesia has widened remarkably compared with neighboring countries, up to the period of the Joko Widodo administration. The Gini coefficient worsened from 0.30 in 2000 to 0.41 in 2012. The World Bank (2016) raised the following four factors:

a. Differences in health, nutrition, and education due to environmental factors at birth are a cause of future income inequality. The widening of inequality leads to disparities in education, which affects future career choices, further widening income inequality.[7]
b. The wage gap between skilled and unskilled workers is growing.
c. The significant concentration of wealth among the wealthy is exacerbating income inequality (Indonesia ranks third highest among 38 countries in terms of wealth concentration).

---

it should be noted that during this period, import substitution policies were promoted through SOEs, which led to higher wages for skilled laborers and thus widened inequality (van der Eng 2009).

[7] Educational opportunities for the poor may have been relatively equal for a long period of time, as low income inequality was maintained for years up to the AFC. However, it should be noted that Indonesia is considered to have low educational standards. For example, its score on the OECD's Programme for International Student Assessment (PISA) is fifth from the bottom among the 85 countries surveyed. The relatively low level of inequality over a long period of time seems not to have contributed to the quality of education, which is a completely separate issue. If income inequality translates into differences in educational levels, the wage level of laborers with low educational backgrounds would be lower than otherwise (e.g., less likely to acquire skills training, less likely to acquire adult education, etc.).

d. Low-income groups are less able to save and are therefore more likely to be susceptible to poverty when external shocks occur.

Based on Indonesia Family Life Survey data from 2000, 2007, and 2014, Wicaksono et al. (2017) analyze factors behind inequality using different methodological approaches, with findings similar to those of the World Bank (2016). An analysis of the factors behind inequality from 2000 onward shows that educational differences accounted for 21%, wealth differences for 19%, age differences (experience translates into income differences) for 15%, being a wage earner or not for 8%, and regional differences for 6%.

However, as of 2007, being a wage earner (wage-based labor) accounted for 21%, the highest of all the factors. This relates to education. The disparity in educational opportunities has forced some workers into the informal sector, contributing to income inequality. In addition, after the AFC, labor union activities increased due to a growing awareness of democracy, with the minimum wage rising significantly in the formal work sectors. In this regard, Grabowski (2017) argues that manufacturing employment slowed due to the steep rise in natural resource prices after 2000, particularly in labor-intensive sectors. This impeded growth in manufacturing employment and led to increased employment in informal sectors, which resulted in the widening of inequality. Wage labor remained the largest factor behind inequality in 2014, at 20%. Next to wage-based labor, education, wealth and age carry substantial weightings. Regional differences declined slightly as a factor from 6% in 2007 to 4% in 2014, which can be attributed to the decentralization of government control after 2000.

The factors behind inequality proposed by these studies are generally the same as those argued in the global discussion on inequality, as noted by Wicaksono et al. (2017). In other words, the factors that are considered to bring about inequality are not unique to Indonesia, but the magnitude of these factors determines the level of inequality. For example, the concentration of wealth is extreme, with the wealthiest 0.02% holding 25% of the nation's wealth, and the richest 40 individuals accounting for 10% of GDP (Tabar 2015). Such inequality in wealth and the education gap are likely to continue to widen in the absence of government intervention. To reduce inequality substantially, there needs to be social and economic change. Achieving this will not be easy, but several Indonesian government policies in the 2010s can be seen as moving in this direction. For example, the program to achieve universal health insurance by 2019 started in 2014, and the number of people covered by health insurance increased from 130 million (48% of the population) in 2015 to 175 million (65%) in 2021 (World Bank 2023). The tax amnesty was implemented in 2016 to target the undeclared income of high earners. These are examples of bold policies implemented by the Indonesian government to correct inequality.

Finally, it is worth considering how changes in inequality have contributed to poverty reduction. Miranti (2010) estimated the elasticity of economic growth and the Gini coefficient for poverty reduction for the period from 1984 to 2002. As a result, the elasticity of economic growth to poverty reduction remained almost

**Table 10.1** Contributions of growth and inequality to changes in poverty in Indonesia

| | | | Contribution to Poverty Change | | |
|---|---|---|---|---|---|
| Growth episodes | Year | Inequality change (Δ GINI) | Growth (%) | Inequality change (%) | Total change (%) |
| First liberalization period | 1984–1990 | −0.01 | −4.75 | −0.61 | −5.36 |
| Second liberalization period | 1990–1996 | 0.03 | −4.62 | 2.71 | −1.92 |
| Recovery period | 1999–2002 | 0.02 | −6.05 | 2.12 | −3.93 |
| Entire period | 1984–2002 | 0 | −9.74 | −0.08 | −9.83 |

*Source* Miranti (2010), excerpt from Table 7 (years added by Author)

unchanged at around −2.4. In contrast, the elasticity of inequality to poverty reduction varied somewhat from 0.78 to 1.30, depending on the time period. Miranti (2010) breaks down poverty reduction over this period by factors of growth and inequality change (see Table 10.1). When decomposing the contribution to poverty reduction as measured by national criteria, for the period from 1984 to 1990, the Gini coefficient improved, resulting in greater progress in poverty reduction. On the other hand, the inequality factor has slowed poverty reduction since the 1990s, albeit slightly.

To sum up the above, the conclusion is that inequality did not widen in the period of high growth before the AFC, because policies to promote farming villages in addition to the Green Revolution (i.e., technical factors) and develop infrastructure in local regions, adopted under the Suharto administration, helped to increase inclusiveness. On the other hand, the potential impact of inequality on growth rates in the period of high growth following the AFC remains unclear; however, the slowing of growth in the labor-intensive manufacturing sector may have led to a widening of inequality during that period.

## 10.3 Growth and Resilience

As shown in Fig. 10.1, the Indonesian economy has experienced three periods of economic downturn. These falls were caused by, such as the drop in oil prices in the 1980s, the AFC, which occurred in 1997, and the COVID-19 pandemic, which was different in character from the first two. Globally, there were other subsequent shocks, such as the 2008 GFC and the sharp fall in natural resource prices in the 2010s, but the Indonesian economy managed to avert a major economic slowdown on both of these occasions. The analysis here focuses on what Indonesia experienced after the first two shocks and what changed that made the Indonesian economy resilient to similar shocks.

Looking at Indonesia's exports, oil, gas, and coal exports accounted for 70 to 80% of the total from the mid-1970s to the early 1980s. It was a typical resource-dependent economic structure in which foreign currency earnings from resource exports were used for domestic development. However, oil prices fell by half in nominal terms during the Reverse Oil Shock. To overcome this, the Indonesian government launched a policy to promote the non-oil sector in 1983. International organizations also supported this move. The World Bank provided Indonesia with a structural adjustment loan for the first time, conditional on trade liberalization and deregulation. As a result of these efforts, non-oil exports doubled over three years from FY1985 to FY1988, reaching the level covering 85% of non-oil imports (Weaving 1990).

This marked a turning point in Indonesian exports, after which manufacturing exports rose sharply to surpass exports of natural resources. As shown in Fig. 10.3, the share of oil, gas and coal exports fell to about 30% of total exports in the first half of the 1990s. The decline in the share of oil and gas exports was attributed to the slow pace of oilfield development, which resulted in a decline in oil output and increased domestic consumption of oil and gas. In the 2000s, domestic oil consumption surpassed production, and Indonesia became a net importer of oil. In the meantime, palm oil and coal became the largest and second-largest shares, respectively, of Indonesia's exports. With the tailwind of soaring prices, natural resources once again became important export items in Indonesia. There are several reasons why the sharp fall in natural resource prices in the 2010s did not lead to a slump in the Indonesian economy. First, after the Reverse Oil Shock in the 1980s, the country had shifted to an economic structure that was not dependent on oil. At the same time, prudent policy management helped to preserve the soundness of the macroeconomy. The prudent macroeconomic policy management of today has its roots in the country's experience of the harsh economic damage wrought by the AFC.

Indonesia was, in fact, the country most severely damaged by the AFC, starting with the suspension of the business licences of 16 banks under the IMF program. The currency continued to depreciate and the rise in fuel prices led to riots, forcing President Suharto to resign. Exploring the reasons for the deepening of the crisis, Asanuma (2003) points out structural factors, such as the financial sector's vulnerability, lack of corporate governance, corruption and collusion. Although macroeconomic policies and indicators showed few signs of major problems prior to the crisis, the current account deficit deteriorated and private-sector debt, including short-term debt, increased sharply (Komatsu 2003). In order to inject public capital into banks to solve non-performing loan (NPL) issues, the government

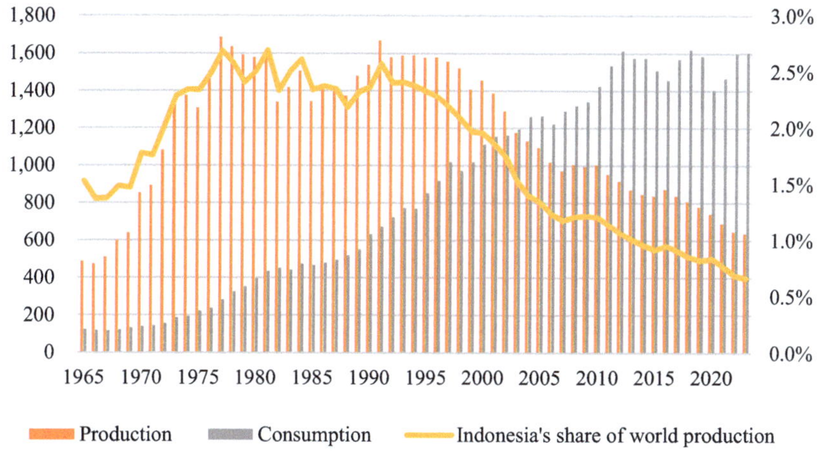


**Fig. 10.3** Trend of oil production and consumption of Indonesia (thousand barrels daily). *Source* Based on the data from the 2024 Statistical Review of World Energy https://www.energyinst.org/statistical-review. Accessed May 28, 2025

issued bonds with a maturity of around five years.[8] The outstanding balance of these bonds amounted to 133% of GDP. Thus, after the crisis, promoting fiscal consolidation against the huge government debt became a critical issue for Indonesian public finances in the 2000s. To sum up, structural issues (i.e., political and corporate governance problems) in a financial environment where large-scale global capital movements were common, and the vulnerability of the financial sector, were triggered all at once due to external shocks, leading to a grave economic crisis. Reform of these structural factors and the post-crisis process of fiscal consolidation and debt reduction were subsequently pursued in order to increase resilience to similar external shocks.

The next key question concerns how the 2008 GFC affected Indonesia and what its response was. According to Papanek et al. (2010), the impact of the GFC on Indonesia was relatively limited because of (1) its small dependence on trade, (2) its sound macroeconomic management, (3) its sound banking system, and (4) the appropriate government response to the crisis. Basri (2013) argues that there were four key differences between the GFC and the AFC. First, while Indonesia's domestic financial system had structural problems in 1997, these had been resolved by the time of the GFC. This enabled Indonesia to respond to the GFC as a purely external issue. Second, its foreign exchange policy had changed. Since 1997, as Indonesia shifted to a full floating exchange rate system, its currency fluctuated on a daily basis, with economic entities learning to hedge the risk of fluctuations.

[8] Indonesia had not issued government bonds until that time, but bond issuance became customary thereafter. Bonds issued for public capital injection to banks became marketable one year from issuance.

Third, the policy responses were appropriate. When the AFC broke out, monetary policy was tightened and fiscal spending was reduced, but these measures exacerbated the economic situation. In contrast, interest rates were reduced in response to the 2008 GFC, with efforts made to restore confidence to the financial sector. Also, in contrast with 1997, aggressive stimulus measures (tax cuts, increased fiscal spending) were adopted. As of 2008, Indonesia's external debt was reduced to 32.1% of GNI, compared with 95.6% in 2000. Foreign exchange reserves had also been built up. These improved fundamentals made the above economic policies possible. Lastly, political democratization had progressed, and then-President Yudhoyono promoted anti-corruption and eliminated crony capitalism.

As such, two external economic shocks brought about fundamental changes in Indonesia's economic structure. The fall in natural resource prices in the 1980s led to rapid manufacturing growth; the AFC prompted improvements in macroeconomic policies, particularly fiscal policy, and led to a wider scope of reforms, including governance. At the same time, several key points are worth noting. As pointed out in Papanek et al. (2010), the Indonesian economy's limited reliance on foreign trade means that the impact of an external shock can be relatively limited as long as domestic macroeconomic policy is managed prudently. Considering the scale of the domestic market, backed by the country's large population, domestic demand is likely to generate a certain level of economic growth. However, at the same time, this means external demand is not being viewed as an opportunity for growth. In particular, the slow growth of the manufacturing sector appears to be a significant issue that must be addressed to achieve sustained high growth.

Moreover, the pursuit of sound fiscal management has resulted in somewhat more restrained fiscal spending. While fiscal deficit indicators have improved significantly, infrastructure investment, for example, does not appear to have been sufficient.[9] Similarly, while the banks' financial indicators look healthy, financial deepening has not progressed, making Indonesia's credit size the smallest of the major economies in the Association of Southeast Asian Nations (ASEAN). It is not easy to strike a balance between the pursuit of resilience and the achievement of high economic growth. At least until now, Indonesia's policy priority seems to have been the pursuit of resilience, and such policies have produced some results. However, if Indonesia is to achieve 7% growth in the future, it will be necessary to address structural issues, including those discussed in the next section.

Note that growth resilience is a concept that includes resilience to natural disasters. Generally speaking, the 2004 Indian Ocean Earthquake and Tsunami made a strong impression on Indonesia as a disaster-prone country. Volcanic activity continues and the risk of earthquakes is ever-present. However, the country's overall disaster risk is considered to be moderate due to its weather conditions, which are not affected by typhoons. Thus, for example, investment in disaster reduction is about 0.03 to 0.07% of GDP, about one-tenth that of the Philippines (Hirota and

[9] For example, according to Global Competitiveness Report 2019 by the WEF, Indonesia is ranked 50 among 141 countries in its total score, but ranked lower at 72 in infrastructure.

Ishiwatari 2017). Needless to say, while appropriate investment needs to be made in disaster prevention, this issue is not considered further here.

## 10.4 Growth and Sustainability

### 10.4.1 Overview

Indonesia boasts one of the most consistently sustained economic growth rates in the world. Since 1968, there have only been three episodes of annual real GDP per capita growth falling below 2%. These were from 1982 to 85 (average growth rate of 1.7% during this period), from 1998 to 99 (−6.9%), and 2020 (−2.9%). This corresponds to a continuous growth period of 14 years (1968 to 1981), 12 years (1986 to 1997), and 20 years (2000 to 2019), respectively. Growth since 2000 has continued, including the period of the GFC, a longer uninterrupted period than previously experienced. Moreover, since 2022, the recovery has also been rapid, with a record growth of 4.5% in 2022. This can be seen as the result of building a strong economic structure in response to the negative impact of external shocks. Looking at per capita growth, the average growth rate for the entire period from 1968 to 2023 was 3.7%. For each of the three growth periods, the rates were 5.4%, 4.8%, and 4.0%, respectively. The growth cycle since 2000 is longer than previously, but the average annual growth rate has been lower.

Indonesia's economic structure used to be vulnerable to external shocks, as reviewed. Can we now say that there is no longer vulnerability in the Indonesian economy and its growth will continue at high rates in the future? How should we interpret the average rate of growth since 2000, given that it is lower than the previous two growth episodes? According to Basri and Hills (2010), Indonesia has changed in two respects since the AFC. First, its growth rates have declined since then, even though they have remained moderately high, and secondly, the engines of growth have changed. The growth drivers of the Indonesian economy are considered below.

First, in the components of GDP expenditure, consumption has accounted for around 60% since the 1980s. Gross fixed capital formation (GFCF) generally exceeded 30% in the 1990s, but fell to 20% for several years after the AFC (so to speak, an investment shock). However, in the 2010s, it recovered to over 30%. Although falling short of China, Indonesia's GFCF remains fairly high, suggesting growth acceleration over the medium to long term. The characteristics of the investment are worth noting. The recent expansion of investment is characterized by the domestic demand backed by strong consumption driven by the growth of the middle class. Examples include automobiles and the service sector, such as shopping malls, transportation, and telecommunications. With the world's fourth-largest population, domestic demand is Indonesia's greatest strength. The other key aspect is infrastructure development. Since government finances remain somewhat low, infrastructure development is heavily reliant on public–private partnerships (PPPs) and SOEs. Given this, the slow development of PPPs has led to a severe infrastructure gap, which has become a social issue. This has led the government to look for the SOEs to play a larger role (Muto and Hirota 2015), including the recent movement to provide additional capital contributions to them.

In the 2000s, the ratio of exports to GDP was in the 20 to 30% range, except during the period of the AFC, but in the 2010s, this ratio has been slightly lower. The export mix has also changed over time. The oil sector was once the primary driver of exports until the latter half of the 1980s, but its importance declined in the 2000s. Exports of other primary commodities once increased, but their share has declined again in years of lower resource prices. To sum up, domestic demand has played a significant role in driving economic growth in recent years. While the role of exports was declining, the resources sector, which benefits from soaring prices, has contributed to the trade balance (e.g., Henstridge et al. 2013).

Sectoral economic growth has changed over time. Basri and Hills (2010) compared the two periods of 1990 to 1996 and 2000 to 2008, pointing out that manufacturing, mining, construction and utilities were high-growth sectors during the former period, while the latter period comprised agriculture, transportation and communications. With regard to agriculture, self-sufficiency in rice production was viewed as the most important policy goal for a long period since independence. In the 2000s, however, the production of commodity crops such as palm oil and rubber expanded against the backdrop of soaring resource prices. This led to improved productivity in farming villages and increased farming income, contributing to higher economic growth. Basri and Hills (2010) note that the manufacturing sector, by comparison, is struggling. They argue that the strong exchange rate, high logistics costs due to slow infrastructure development, and a sharp increase in labor costs have had a negative impact on manufacturing growth.

In terms of production factors, van der Eng (2010) estimated that for the period from 1880 to 2008, the contribution to growth was 44–62% for capital, 31–41% for labor, and 6–12% for total factor productivity (TFP).[10] The contribution of TFP was high from 1933 to 1941, from 1951 to 1961, from 1967 to 1974, and from 2000 to 2008, as shown in Table 10.2. This is attributable to the fact that productivity had fallen substantially before each of these periods, and the high TFP figures reflect the recovery process. In the period from 1967 to 1997, known as the "East Asian Miracle," TFP accounted for 10–11% of the contribution to growth (including −15% between 1975 and 1997). van der Eng (2010) suggests this might be due to the "Solow Paradox."[11] The slowing of productivity growth is not a positive factor, but the fact that such a sharp expansion of investment was possible may be considered as a positive. In other words, it can be said that the economic environment was favorable, allowing investment to expand on a scale

[10] The range of contribution rates for each factor of production is due to the assumption of two different distribution rates (50% and 70%) for labor prior to 1974, for which no data exist.

[11] The Solow Paradox refers to a situation where productivity growth did not materialize despite the increase in ICT investment since the 1980s. Whether the rapid growth of investment by the end of the 1990s led to productivity growth with a time lag is difficult to verify because of the disconnect in the economic environment caused by the AFC.

**Table 10.2** Decomposition of growth in Indonesia (%)

| Year | Capital | Labor | TFP | Annual growth rate of output |
|---|---|---|---|---|
| 1881–1899 | 50 | 30 | 20 | 1.8 |
| 1900–1929 | 102 | 22 | −24 | 2.6 |
| 1933–1941 | 21 | 21 | 58 | 3.8 |
| 1951–1961 | 18 | 22 | 59 | 4.2 |
| 1967–1974 | 19 | 19 | 62 | 8.5 |
| 1975–1997 | 84 | 32 | −15 | 6.0 |
| 2000–2008 | 37 | 31 | 32 | 5.1 |
| Total period | 62 | 31 | 6 | 3.6 |

*Note* This table is based on the assumption that the labor income share is 50% in 1880–1974. "Labor" is education-adjustment employment and includes a proxy for improvement in human capital
*Source* van der Eng (2010), excerpt from Table 2

that productivity growth could not keep up with (but could easily lead to overinvestment). In any case, the growth during this period was exclusively due to the expansion of investment.

Analytically, the use of Indonesian statistical data in estimates is characteristic of van der Eng (2010). Looking at changes in TFP with 2017 at "1" using an international database, Indonesia's figures are 0.9 in 1970, 1.12 in 1980, 0.98 in 1990, 0.82 in 2000, and 0.90 in 2010, which indicates that the role of TFP improvement in growth was not that significant (Penn World Table 10.1). By contrast, the same figures for Thailand are 0.65, 0.67, 0.73, 0.77, and 0.86, respectively. It should be noted that TFP contributed to growth for the period from the late 1980s to before the AFC, while TFP from 1975 to 1997 was negative, as shown in Table 10.2. The former coincides with the period when manufacturing exports surged and their share of exports increased dramatically. Based on these changes, I will discuss the three key aspects related to the sustainability of Indonesia's growth: natural resources, manufacturing, and institutions.

### 10.4.2 Natural Resources

Indonesia's oil and gas sectors were nationalized in 1960 and became the exclusive domain of Pertamina, a SOE established in 1968. Pertamina also financed domestic development outside of the government and invested in areas other than oil and gas. This model came to a halt in the mid-1970s. This led to a reduction in Pertamina's authority and it came under government supervision like other SOEs. Governance over resource rents is one of the core elements of the resource curse. By overcoming the situation of the Pertamina management crisis, Indonesia, in retrospect, was fortunate to have resolved the issue of governance at an early stage.

Another negative aspect of the resource curse is that a stronger exchange rate makes it difficult for non-resource sectors to grow. In this regard, the Reverse Oil Shock in the 1980s compelled Indonesia to diversify into other industries, as previously discussed. Particularly dramatic changes occurred in manufacturing, where labor-intensive industries grew at an annual rate of 40% from 1986 to 1992. Tabar (2015) states that Indonesia was a world leader in labor-intensive industries during this period. Unfortunately, this trend did not last long. This is because of the rise of China and other low-income economies, and also because of domestic constraints that started to cause difficulties.

The stagnant oil and gas production on one hand, and the increase in the domestic consumption of these resources on the other, led to a decline in their share of exports. However, the country was also rich in other natural resources, and benefited greatly from the soaring resource prices in the 2000s. Major commodities include coal (the world's second-largest exporter), palm oil (the world's largest producer and exporter), rubber, and metals such as nickel, the prices of which jumped threefold in the decade beginning in 2000. In addition to the price effect, the production of coal and palm oil increased.

Without doubt, the surge in natural resource prices in the 2000s benefited Indonesia, at least in the near term. This helped to boost private consumption, which led to considerable growth in the services sector. Resource-related investment also grew, and fiscal revenue also increased. However, the increase in fiscal revenue from higher resource prices was offset by increased spending on fuel subsidies. Also in 2012, exports of unprocessed minerals were banned. The goal was to add value to the resources by processing them domestically and to foster related industries, but at least in the short term, this hindered investment from overseas. Whether such a policy brings about the desired results depends on the competitiveness of resource-related industries in international markets.

Lastly, the boom in the resource market led to a strong exchange rate, which had a negative impact on manufacturing, especially for exports (see Basri and Hills 2010; World Bank 2015). This point is particularly important from the perspective of the resource curse theory. In this regard, the IMF (2010) and Henstridge et al. (2013) stop short of concluding that the resource price spike changed the economic structure. IMF (2010) states that it is unclear whether the exchange rate was overvalued and that manufacturing exports were actually growing from 2003 to 2008. Henstridge et al. (2013) also argue that it is not possible to conclude whether the manufacturing sector was affected by currency appreciation or not. They note that while manufacturing as a whole grew, the fact that the number of exporters decreased and productivity improved suggests that the exchange rate appreciation caused firms with low productivity to exit the market. That is, Dutch disease did have an impact, albeit a slight one. Looking at the ratio of manufacturing exports to the total, Indonesia's low ratio stands out compared to other ASEAN countries and China, and is further characterized by the fact that it peaked around 2000 and has remained stagnant. Apart from the strong currency valuation, the fundamental reason why manufacturing exports slowed is the low competitiveness of the manufacturing sector, characterized by its high logistics and labor costs.

### 10.4.3 Manufacturing Industry

The World Bank (2012) states that manufacturing causes structural transformation in the economy through higher growth rates than other sectors, greater productivity gains, innovation, and growth in R&D through the integration into international markets. In Indonesia, however, the share of manufacturing in GDP has been in continuous decline since the mid-2000s, and Palma (2014) argues that premature deindustrialization is caused partly by natural resources and Dutch disease. Trần (2016), regarding the pattern of development in developing countries, states that the early stage of development is factor input-based. Consequently, the role of TFP becomes important as the marginal productivity of capital declines in earnest, and sustained growth depends on upgrading comparative advantage industries from low-skilled to high-skilled sectors. Trần and Karikomi (2015), comparing the international competitiveness of manufacturing industries in emerging Asian economies, find that Indonesia's competitiveness across the high-, medium-, and low-skilled sectors has declined since 2000. They attribute this to a lack of thorough opening up to foreign companies, a lack of productivity growth commensurate with wage increases, sluggish development of infrastructure, and the rapid emergence of China.

Following independence, Indonesia aimed at industrialization of the "full set" of light industries, natural resource processing industries and heavy industries. However, heavy industry, such as aircraft, shipbuilding and petrochemicals, did not progress as expected (Sato 2011). As mentioned, Indonesia's labor-intensive industries began to boom from the late 1980s. However, this did not last long and they were subsequently overtaken by China and others. Manufacturing employment elasticity has declined from 0.7 in the 1990s to 0.3 in the 2000s (World Bank 2012). In addition, Indonesia is less integrated into global value chains (GVCs) than neighboring countries: the share of manufacturing employment integrated into GVCs is 24.5%, the lowest among Asian emerging economies. Moreover, it has declined from 28.6% in 2000 (de Vries et al. 2016).[12] As stated by the World Bank (2012), parts and component industries are sensitive to transaction costs and are affected by levels of human resource development. As Indonesia lags in infrastructure development, logistics costs account for approximately 14% of production costs, compared with 5% in Japan. Low educational levels have translated into a skills gap, and minimum wage has continued to rise, all of which serve as constraints (Tabar 2015).

Despite this, foreign investment into Indonesia has continued to increase. Manufacturing has made progress in business areas that utilize Indonesia's rich natural resources and take advantage of its large domestic market. As noted by the IMF (2010), growth in Indonesia's capital-intensive industries, such as automobiles and

[12] Of the eight emerging economies, Bangladesh, India, the Philippines, China, and Vietnam saw their GVC integration ratio rise in the period from 2000 to 2011. This ratio declined in Thailand and Malaysia, but has remained at 30% or higher. In Indonesia, the GVC integration ratio is the lowest among the eight countries and is also declining.

machinery, is relatively high, while natural resources-related industries, including food, fertilizers and synthetic rubber, have experienced moderate growth. According to Sjöhlom (2016), over the period from 2005 to 2014, foreign investment flows increased by 170%, and the share of foreign investment in manufacturing expanded from 20% in 1990 to 40% in 2012. With foreign companies attracted into the Indonesian market by domestic demand, the lag in infrastructure development may not be a decisive factor for them. Due to this inflow of foreign investment, the government may not see an urgent need to accelerate infrastructure development.

This aside, in Indonesia, the labor productivity of average foreign firms is six times higher than that of domestic firms. Foreign investment, bringing sophisticated technology and higher productivity, has the potential to bring about major structural changes in the Indonesian economy (Sjöhlom 2016). In spite of low integration with GVCs, if foreign investment inflows into the manufacturing sector continue in search of domestic demand, structural reform will occur. It is also expected that the competitiveness of the manufacturing sector will improve. However, even if Indonesia were to improve its competitiveness, there would be a clear need to close the gaps in infrastructure and skills and improve its business environment.

### 10.4.4 Institutions

Regarding institutions, governance reform is important, although it remains a work in progress. Since the presidency of Yudhoyono, in particular, transparency has been strengthened and anti-corruption measures have been taken. While these efforts may require more time and procedures in some aspects of public administration, they are essential for long-term sustainable development. The current policy priority is the improvement of business-related legal systems, as mentioned earlier.

One theme that is particularly relevant to the efficient allocation of domestic resources is the role of the SOEs. The significant role of these companies is one of the key characteristics of the Indonesian economy. Although aggregated statistics are not published, some estimates suggest that even in recent years, they have accounted for about 40% of GDP in Indonesia.[13]

The origin of the structure in which SOEs played a major role dates back to the Sukarno era, before the Suharto regime. Indonesia was no exception among

[13] The IMF (2006) stated that the number of SOEs was 158, accounting for about 40% of GDP, and the WTO (2013) found the number of SOEs as of 2011 to be 139, accounting for about 40% of GDP. Looking back to the 1980s, Matsui (1992) estimated the share of SOEs over the period from 1979 to 1983 between 12.2 and 14.6% (the numbers estimated at between 213 and 222). Sungkar (2008), citing a World Bank report of the time, puts the 1991 share at 15%. As the basis for each figure is unknown, a simple comparison is not valid. Compared with the 1980s and 1990s, the number of SOEs has declined, but as the banking, communications and petroleum/gas sectors are still state-owned, their share is likely to have remained high.

countries that gained independence after World War II, where SOEs played an important role in economic development up until the development of domestic capital. Later, in the 1980s, when oil prices fell, calls for their privatization increased (Matsui 1992). The number of SOEs in Indonesia, which had exceeded 200 in the 1980s, fell to about 150 in the mid-2000s and 118 in 2016. However, based on the ratio to GDP, it is unlikely that their share of the industry has shifted entirely to the private sector. If state-run enterprises demonstrate high productivity and do not crowd out the private sector, this may be considered a viable approach to development. Regarding productivity, SOEs are generally considered inefficient, but there have been no studies of this topic with respect to Indonesia. However, looking at the current situation in which, for example, the four state-owned banks all rank high in terms of the total bank assets of the country, and SOEs also occupy dominant positions in some manufacturing industries such as steel and cement. In the construction sector, this indicates that private companies are likely to have been crowded out by the SOEs.

Two strategic moves can be seen in the direction of SOEs. The first seeks to strengthen them through more efficient operations, while promoting further consolidation through shareholdings and clustering.[14] Second, a larger role is anticipated for the SOEs in infrastructure development. To this end, in 2015, the government increased the provision of capital to SOEs in the infrastructure sector. As PPPs did not progress as expected in infrastructure development, the government looked to strengthen the financial base of SOEs so that the developments could proceed in a way that reduces the overall financial burden. After a policy of scaling down the SOEs implemented under the previous administration, the capital of these companies is now once again being strengthened. State-owned construction companies have also received capital injections, which may not lead to a fair and competitive environment. It is unclear if this will support the development of the private sector and/or sustained economic growth.

Regarding the environment and climate change, another important aspect of growth sustainability, Indonesia is one of the world's largest emitters of GHGs when emissions from land use change are included.[15] Although not discussed in this paper, the Indonesian government is aware of global warming countermeasures, as evidenced by its adoption of the world's first official development assistance (ODA)-supported policy program, in collaboration with Japan and others to combat climate change. For example, the Indonesian government has focused on promoting geothermal power generation and is interested in developing

[14] As of 2023, the number of SOEs is 65 and the number of participating subsidiaries is 298. Excluding the 23 holding companies, the cluster with the largest number of SOEs is infrastructure with nine companies, followed by insurance (five companies) and banking (four companies) (Ministry of State-owned Enterprises 2024).

[15] Indonesia's annual $CO_2$ emissions (in 2023), including land use change, are the sixth largest in the world, after China, the US, India, Russia, and Brazil (Our World in Data).

technologies to capture and store $CO_2$ through a science and technology cooperation program with Japan. By promoting these interventions, measures against global warming will likely provide new growth opportunities.

## 10.5 Conclusion

The economic development of Indonesia from the perspective of quality growth—i.e., high growth rates, inclusiveness, resilience and sustainability—can be summarized in three points. First, Indonesia has achieved fairly high growth on a sustained basis. In the process, the relationship with inclusiveness has not always been unidirectional. Second, two external economic shocks triggered a shift in the economic structure and increased structural resilience. This enhanced the sustainability of subsequent growth. Third, growth after 2000 was not necessarily inclusive, which may constrain the sustainability of future growth.

Regarding the first point, Indonesia's sustained high growth reflects sound macroeconomic management, a stable political system, and rich natural resources. In the 1970s and 1980s, the growth engines that enabled long-term growth were oil and agriculture, with self-sufficiency in rice production being achieved. In this process, inequality narrowed and inclusiveness increased. This enabled a shift of potential unemployed workers from farming villages to manufacturing sectors, and the economy diversified as manufacturing exports increased sharply for a period following the latter half of the 1980s. Even though external factors were significant, in a sense, such a development process can be said to have been in line with Hartwick's law, as introduced in Chap. 5. After the AFC, natural resource prices soared, leading to a sharp increase in commodity exports. From the late 2000s, the service sector and manufacturing for domestic demand grew based on the expanded domestic market. The changes in growth drivers have transformed the country's economic structure, making sustainable high growth possible. However, this has not been accompanied by productivity improvement, and there are concerns that a decline in the share of manufacturing and premature deindustrialization, for example, may impede future growth sustainability. In response to these concerns, many commentators have emphasized the importance of infrastructure development and the need to improve the business environment.

Second, two external economic shocks triggered structural transformations. The external shocks significantly reduced the growth rate of the Indonesian economy due to the vulnerability of its economic structure at that time. However, the external shocks triggered major reforms in economic diversification and fiscal and monetary management, which allowed the economy to avoid a major decline during the GFC and the sharp decline in resource prices in the 2010s. This is a typical example of increased resilience, ensuring the sustainability of growth.

Third, growth since 2000 has not necessarily been inclusive, and there are concerns that widening inequality will have a negative impact on future sustained growth. The factor specific to Indonesia is the slow growth of employment (wage labor), particularly in manufacturing. Stagnation of labor-intensive manufacturing sectors and growth in capital-intensive manufacturing sectors led by large companies are factors that have contributed to a widening of inequality. Slow growth in the manufacturing industry, which tends to drive technological development and productivity, leads to concerns about the rate of growth and growth sustainability. There is concern that widening income inequality will constrain education spending by low-income groups, which will hamper improvements in human capital and, ultimately, sustainable growth. In addition, the relatively poor quality of education is also problematic, impacting Indonesia's future quality growth in terms of both inclusiveness and sustainability.

## References

Akashi, Koichiro. 2016. "Indonesia: Shuyō nōsanbutsu no jyukyū to nōgyō seisaku" [Supply and Demand of Major Agricultural Products and Agricultural Policy]. in *Heisei 27 nendo country report: Soukatu hen* [FY 2015 Country Report Summary]. Research Material 9: 137–146. Policy Research Institute, Ministry of Agriculture, Forestry and Fisheries, Japan.

Asanuma, Shinji. 2003. "Dai 3 shō: Indonesia keizai no kadai" [Challenges for the Indonesian Economy]. in Japan Center for International Finance. *Indonesia no kōzō kaikaku to Nihon no enjyo seisaku* [Structural Reforms in Indonesia and Japan's Aid Policy], 27–40. Japan Center for International Finance.

Basri, Muhammad Chatib, and Hal Hills. 2010. "Indonesian Growth Dynamics." Working Paper No. 2010/10, Arndt-Corden Department of Economics, Crawford School of Economics and Government, ANU College of Asia and the Pacific, Australian National University.

Basri, Muhammad Chatib. 2013. "A Tale of Two Crises: Indonesia's Political Economy." JICA-RI Working Paper No. 57. JICA Ogata Research Institute.

de Vries, Gaaitzen, Quanrun Chen, Rana Hasan, and Zhigang Li. 2016. "Skills and Activity Upgrading in Global Value Chains: Trends and Drivers for Asia." ADB Economics Working Paper No. 496. Asian Development Bank.

Grabowski, Richard. 2017. "Premature Deindustrialization and Inequality." *International Journal of Social Economics* 44 (2): 154–168.

Henstridge, Mark, Gaber Burnik, Mateo Cabello, Federica Chiappe, Les Crawfurd, Sourovi De, Maham Farhat, and Maja Jakobsen. 2013. "Growth in Indonesia: Is It Sustainable? An Overview." Oxford Policy Management. https://www.opml.co.uk/files/Publications/8057-analysis-growth-indonesia/growth-in-indonesia-an-overview.pdf.

Hirota, Koki, and Mikio Ishiwatari. 2017. "Estimating Demand for Flood Control Infrastructure." Presentation Materials at 10th Meeting of the High-level Experts and Leaders Panel on Water and Disaster (HELP), September 21, 2017, Gyeongju, Republic of Korea. http://www.wateranddisaster.org/cms310261/wp-content/uploads/2017/09/01_02_Dr.-Koki-Hirota.pdf.

International Monetary Fund (IMF). 2006. "Indonesia: Selected Issues." IMF Country Report No. 06/318. IMF.

International Monetary Fund (IMF). 2010. "Indonesia: Selected Issues." IMF Country Report No. 10/285. IMF.

Japan Bank for International Cooperation (JBIC). 2001. "Hinkon profile youyaku: Indonesia kyōwakoku" [Poverty Profile Summary: Republic of Indonesia]. JICA.

Japan International Cooperation Agency (JICA), and Japan Bank for International Cooperation (JBIC). 2008. "'Africa kaihatsu to Asia no keizaiseichō' kentōkai hōkokusho" ['African Development and Asian Economic Growth' Study Group Report]. JICA.

Komatsu, Masaaki. 2003. "Dai 2 shō: Keizai kiki to kinyūzaisei bumon no kadai" [Chapter 2: Economic Crisis and Challenges for the Monetary and Fiscal Sector]. in *Indonesia no kōzō kaikaku to Nihon no enjyo seisaku* [Structural Reforms in Indonesia and Japan's Aid Policy]. Japan Center for International Finance.

Matsui, Kazuhisa. 1992. "Dai 3 shō: Indonesia kokuei kigyō no minneika mondai" [Chapter 3: The Problem of 'Privatization' of Indonesian State-Owned Enterprises]. in *Ajia shokoku niokeru minkatsu seisaku no tenkai* [Formulation and Implementation of Privatisation Policy in Asian Countries], ed. Michio Kimura, 73–98. Institute of Developing Economies.

Ministry of State-owned Enterprises, Indonesia. 2024. "State-Owned Enterprises Portfolio." http://www.bumn.go.id/storage/kontenlaporan/files/files_1726317559.pdf. Accessed April 12, 2025.

Miranti, Riyana. 2010. "Poverty in Indonesia 1984–2002: The Impact of Growth and Changes in Inequality." *Bulletin of Indonesian Economic Studies* 46 (1): 79–97.

Muto, Megumi, and Koki Hirota. 2015. "Dai 2 shō: Tōnan Asia ni okeru Nihon no ODA no hensen to kadai" [Chapter 2: Transition and Challenges of Japanese ODA in Southeast Asia]. In *Korekara no Nihon no kokusai kyōryoku* [Japan's International Cooperation in the Future], eds. Takashi Kurosaki and Keijiro Otsuka, 35–60. Nihon Hyouronsha.

Nakamura, Kazutoshi, and Susumu Hondai. 2016. "Indonesia ni okeru shotoku bunpu no kōzō: 1980–2009 nen" [The Evolution of Income Distribution in Indonesia]. *Faculty of Economics Journal, University of Nagasaki* 49 (4): 25–52.

Nishimura, Yoshihiko. 2009. "Indonesia no nōgyō seisaku: Kome seisaku wo chūsin ni shokuryō kakuho ni muketa torikumi, kadai, kongonotenbou ni tsuite no chōsa" [Agricultural Policy in Indonesia: A Survey on Efforts, Challenges and Future Prospects for Securing Rice Production]. in Food Marketing Research and Information Center. *2008 Report on Asia Region of Overseas Agricultural Information Survey and Analysis Project*, 125–149. Food Marketing Research and Information Center.

Palma, José Gabriel. 2014. "De-Industrialization, 'Premature' De-Industrialization and the Dutch Disease." *Revista NECAT* 3 (5): 7–23.

Papanek, Gustav F., M. Chatib Basri, and Daniel M. Schydlowsky. 2010. "Section I: The Impact of the World Recession on Indonesia and an Appropriate Policy Response: Some Lessons for Asia." in *Poverty and Sustainable Development in Asia,* eds. Armin Bauer and Myo Thant, 13–51. Asian Development Bank.

Sato, Yuri. 2011. *Keizai taikoku Indonesia* [Indonesia, A Major Economic Power]. Chuko Shinsho 2143, Chuokoron-sha.

Sjöhlom, Fredrik. 2016. "Foreign Direct Investment and Value Added in Indonesia." Working Paper 2016:31. Department of Economics, School of Economics and Management, Lund University.

Sungkar, Yasmin. 2008. "Indonesia's State Enterprises: From State Leadership to International Consensus." *Journal of Indonesian Social Sciences and Humanities* 1: 95–120.

Tabar, Steven R. 2015. "Constraints to Indonesia's Economic Growth." ADB Papers on Indonesia No. 10. ADB.

Timmer, C. Peter. 2004. "The Road to Pro-poor Growth: The Indonesian Experience in Regional Perspective." *Bulletin of Indonesian Economic Studies* 40 (2): 177–207.

Trần, Văn Thọ. 2016. "Asia shinkokoku to chūshotokukoku no wana" [Emerging Economies and the Middle Income Trap in Asian Perspective]. *International Economics* 67: 69–103.

Trần, Văn Thọ, and Shunji Karikomi. 2015. "Asia no gankōgata hatten to bōeki kōzō no henka" [Asia's Flying Geese Pattern of Development and Changes in Trade Structure]. *International Trade and Investment Quarterly* 102: 60–74. Institute for International Trade and Investment.

van der Eng, Pierre. 2009. "Growth and Inequality: The Case of Indonesia, 1960–1997." MPRA Paper No. 12725. Australian National University.

van der Eng, Pierre. 2010. "The Sources of Long-term Economic Growth in Indonesia, 1880–2008." *Explorations in Economic History* 47: 294–309.

van Leeuwen, Bas, and Péter Földvári. 2016. "The Development of Inequality and Poverty in Indonesia, 1932–2008." *Bulletin of Indonesian Economic Studies* 52 (3): 379–402.

Weaving, Rachel. 1990. *Trade Policy Adjustment in Indonesia.* OED Precis; No. 1. World Bank. http://documents.worldbank.org/curated/en/330021468752742392/Trade-policy-adjustment-in-Indonesia.

Wicaksono, Eno, Hidayat Amir, and Anda Nugroho. 2017. "The Source of Income Inequality in Indonesia: A Regression-based Inequality Decomposition." ADBI Working Paper Series No. 667. Asian Development Bank Institute.

World Bank. 2012. *Why the Manufacturing Sector Still Matters for Growth and Development in Indonesia,* Policy Note 1. World Bank Jakarta Office.

World Bank. 2015. *Indonesia Systematic Country Diagnostic: Connecting the Bottom 40 Percent to the Prosperity Generation.* Report No. 94066-ID. World Bank.

World Bank. 2016. *Indonesia's Rising Divide.* World Bank.

World Bank. 2023. *Indonesia Poverty Assessment: Pathway Towards Economic Security.* World Bank.

World Trade Organization (WTO). 2013. *Trade Policy Review, Indonesia, Revision,* WT/TPR/S/278/Rev.1.

**Koki Hirota** earned his B.A. in Economics from the University of Tokyo and holds a Ph.D. in Economics from Saitama University in Japan. His professional career spans several prominent roles in international development finance and policy, including Chief Economist, Director General of Operation and Strategy Department, and Director General of Southeast Asia and Pacific Department at the Japan International Cooperation Agency (JICA), and Chief Representative in Jakarta for Japan Bank for International Cooperation and in Hanoi for the Overseas Economic Cooperation Fund. In academia, he was a Professor at the Graduate School of Humanities and Social Sciences at Saitama University and a Visiting Fellow at the JICA Ogata Sadako Research Institute for Peace and Development. His recent publications include Challenges in Fiscal and Monetary Policies in Mongolia (co-edited, Springer, 2023) and *Addressing Social Infrastructure Needs in Asia: Towards a Pandemic Resilient Society* (co-edited, JICA, August 2025).

# 11 Vietnam

Yasuo Fujita

Vietnam is one of the few countries in the world that has sustained high economic growth rates over the long term. Until the mid-1980s, Vietnam was characterized by inefficient economic management, low economic growth, and an equally poor society under the socialist regime. In 1986, the country initiated *Doi Moi* (renovation), which led to the development of a market economy and the opening of the economy to the outside world. Since then, the country has achieved remarkable poverty reduction through more than 35 years of long-term economic growth.

Vietnam's strategy for transitioning to a market economy was, like that of China, one of gradualism. It has achieved rapid economic development since the 1990s without the major political and economic disruptions that occurred in the former Soviet Union and Eastern European countries. However, gradualism also preserved inefficiencies and vested interests in the public sector, especially since 2010, when the postponement of reforms through "Vietnam-style gradualism" caused problems (Tran and Karikomi 2019, 229). Gradualism is also thought to affect the quality of economic growth—namely, its inclusiveness, resilience, and sustainability.

This chapter is organized as follows: Sect. 11.1 provides an overview of Vietnam's economic development and raises issues from the perspective of quality growth. Sections 11.2, 11.3, 11.4 examine the trajectory of Vietnam's economic

In preparing this chapter, the author would like to thank Mr. Eiichi Murashima, Credit Guarantee and Investment Facility (a former JICA Vietnam Officer), for assisting me in reviewing one of the main references, World Bank (2016).

Y. Fujita (✉)
Tokyo, Japan


K. Hirota (ed.), *Introduction to Quality Growth*,
https://doi.org/10.1007/978-981-95-6220-6_11

development from the perspectives of inclusiveness, resilience, and sustainability. Finally, Sect. 11.5 provides a discussion of these relationships.[1]

## 11.1 Economic Development Overview

Vietnam gained independence as a result of the Indochina War that followed World War II. In the early stages of the Cold War, the country was divided into North and South Vietnam. After the Vietnam War with the US came to an end in 1976, North and South Vietnam were once again unified to form the current Socialist Republic of Vietnam.

However, it took Vietnam even longer to put its economy on a growth trajectory, and it lagged far behind other Asian countries for the following reasons. First, it had adopted a socialist economic system. The inefficient centrally planned socialist economic system implemented in the North after 1954 was broadened nationwide after the North-South unification. Second, it took a long time to achieve peace and the country was internationally isolated. The war with the US, the conflict with China, and military involvement in the Cambodian conflict continued until about 1986. The Vietnam War also destroyed the country's socioeconomic infrastructure. Moreover, the country's involvement in the Cambodian conflict led to the suspension of development assistance from much of the international community. The collapse of the Soviet Union in 1989 also led to a cessation of aid from the former communist bloc. Consequently, the Vietnamese economy deteriorated (Tran 2010, 287–288; Furuta 2017, 155–171).

Stalled in its economic management, the government initiated the *Doi Moi* policy in 1986, beginning a process of progressively adopting free-market policies. Following the initial success of the experiment in rural areas, *Doi Moi* began with the liberalization of the agricultural sector and then expanded to many other areas, including the development of private sector institutions, the opening of the economy to the outside world, state enterprise reform, and various deregulation measures.[2] The Cambodian conflict ended in 1991, and development assistance from countries around the world resumed in 1992. In 1995, Vietnam normalized diplomatic relations with the US and became an official member of ASEAN, improving relations with neighboring countries. Integration into the global economy also progressed, with accession to the World Trade Organization (WTO) in 2007 and the conclusion of numerous free trade agreements, including the Trans-Pacific Partnership Agreement in 2016. In parallel, infrastructure development (electricity, transportation, etc.) to support economic activities, as well as human

[1] The period analyzed in this article begins with the start of *Doi Moi* in 1986, with a particular focus on its implementation through the 1990s. This focus is due to the period of low economic growth in the late 1980s due to the turmoil caused by institutional changes introduced during *Doi Moi*, as well as limitations in the available data.

[2] World Bank and MPI (2016), Tran (2010), and Furuta (2017) provide an overview of the history of *Doi Moi*.

resource development and basic social services for the people, also improved, supported by development assistance agencies, including those from Japan (Yamada 2021, 117–133).

As a result of these developments, Vietnam's economy has seen remarkable growth. Vietnam was one of the poorest countries in Asia from 1970 until 1990, with a GDP per capita of USD 383 (2010 prices) in 1985—a level similar to that of Laos, Cambodia, Nepal, and Myanmar. Immediately prior to the start of *Doi Moi,* economic growth was declining and inflation exceeded 400% per year (World Bank and MPI 2016, 80). Due to the turmoil caused by its introduction and the high inflation that began in 1986, economic growth was unstable and sluggish until 1990. After 1990, high growth continued, largely as a result of *Doi Moi,* and economic growth in 1990–2019 averaged 6.8% per year. In particular, the period from 1992 to 1997 saw a high growth rate of 8–9%. In 1999, the annual growth rate fell to 4.8% due to the AFC, but it remained above 6% per year until just before the GFC in 2007. From 2012 to 2014, the annual growth rate was below 6%, but it picked up again after 2015 and recovered to 7% per year in 2019 (Fig. 11.1).

GDP per capita has also risen steadily, with Vietnam becoming a lower-middle-income country by World Bank standards in 2010, with GDP per capita (2010 prices) reaching USD 2082 in 2019, a 5.4-fold increase in the 35 years since 1985 (Fig. 11.1). These high growth rates of the economy over a long period of time were second only to China. However, due to the decline in economic growth rates around 2008–2014, there are risks of the middle-income trap and limitations of the current growth model (World Bank and MPI 2016, 109–111; Tran and Karikomi 2019, 229–252).

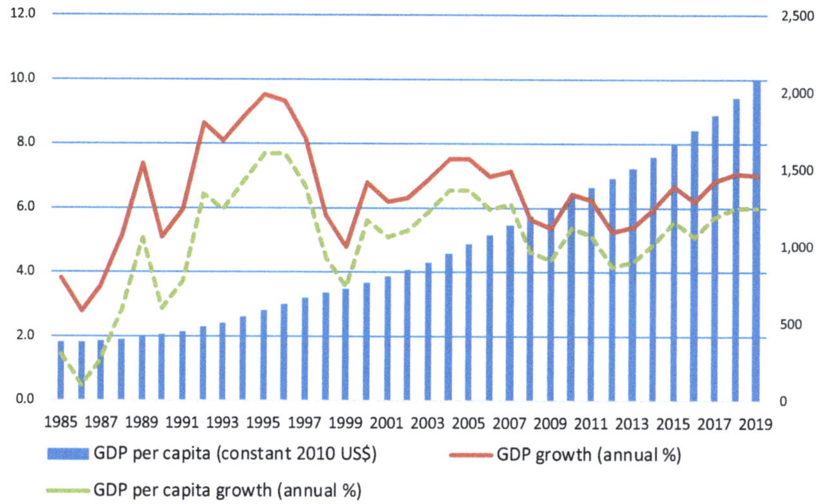


**Fig. 11.1** Economic growth of Vietnam (*Source* Author's compilation from World Bank 2021a data)

Vietnam's economic growth, like that of other developing countries, occurred in the context of an economic structural shift from an agriculture-led economy to one led by manufacturing and service industries. Vietnam's industrial structure was such that in 1985, primary industry accounted for 40% of GDP, but by 2019, the share of primary industry had declined to 14%, with tertiary and secondary industries accounting for 41.6% and 34.5% of GDP, respectively (World Bank 2021a).

Following the opening of the economy to the outside world, foreign direct investment (FDI) and trade have rapidly increased, resulting in export-led economic growth induced by FDI. Export amounts as a percentage of GDP were only 6.6% in 1986 but reached 106.8% in 2019. Export items have changed dramatically from 44% for industrial products, 33% for agriculture and food products, and 18% for crude oil in 1997 to 85% for industrial products, 11% for agriculture and food products, and 1.4% for crude oil in 2019 (World Bank 2021a).

Export goods have also become more technologically advanced, with the share of medium-tech and high-tech products in exported industrial products going from 16.4% in 1997 to 54.6% in 2018 (World Bank 2021a). The structural change is even more evident when looking at specific commodities. According to JETRO (2010, 123) and JETRO (2020), the industrial goods produced in 2009 were low-wage, low-tech, and labor-intensive sewn products accounting for 15.9% and footwear for 7.1%, while most others were commodities (crude oil, commodity crops, food). By 2019, however, telephones and computers accounted for 33% of the total, while machinery and transportation equipment also rose high on the list. Sewing goods and footwear, both labor-intensive light industrial goods, remain important exports with a combined share of 19.3%.

The fruits of such rapid economic growth were widely distributed among the population, contributing significantly to poverty reduction. The poverty headcount ratio (defined as living below the international poverty income line of USD 1.90 per day, based on 2011 PPP [purchasing power parity]) declined from 52.3% in 1992 to 1.8% in 2018 in Vietnam, although there were periods of slight increases between 1997 and 2002 (Fig. 11.2). The pace of poverty reduction was similar to that in China or Indonesia. The Gini coefficient, which indicates inequality in income distribution, has not changed significantly at almost 35–36, although it increased slightly from 2008 to 2010. Compared to ASEAN countries and China, the Gini coefficient is relatively low and tends to remain stable (World Bank 2021a).

## 11.2 Growth and Inclusiveness

As shown in the previous section, Vietnam's poverty rate has declined significantly, and the Gini coefficient, which indicates income inequality, has remained essentially unchanged, suggesting that economic growth has been inclusive. This section examines this trend in more detail.

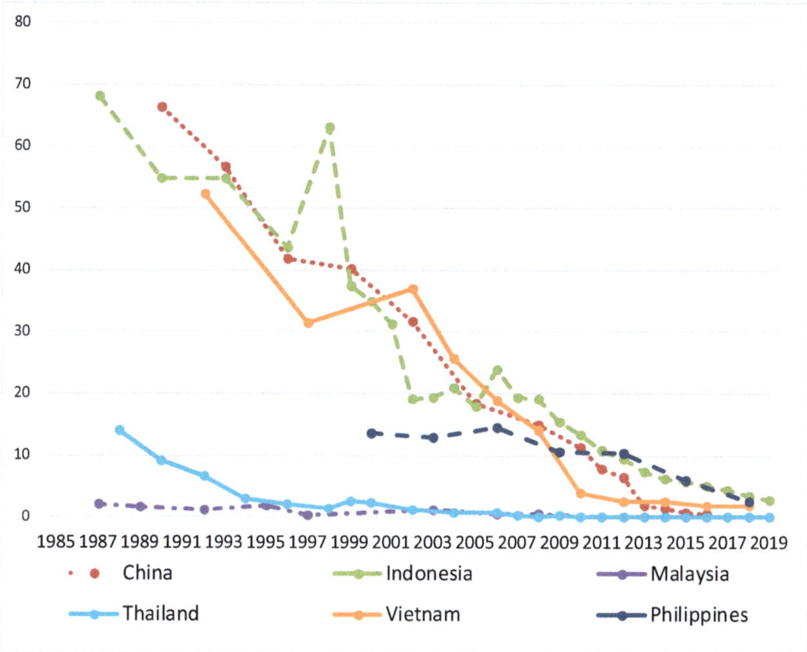


**Fig. 11.2** Poverty headcount ratio (% of population) (Poverty income line at $1.90 a day, 2011 PPP) (*Source* Author's compilation from World Bank 2021a data)

The factors contributing to the achievement of poverty reduction in Vietnam are as follows. First, economic growth has created a large number of employment opportunities (World Bank 2016, 29). Employment opportunities increased from 34.1 million in 1992 to 55.3 million in 2020, creating more than 20 million job opportunities (ILO 2021). The "demographic bonus" from steady population growth met labor demand from the supply side. Employment opportunities were created in the industrial and service sectors, where income levels are higher, and the share of workers in both sectors rose from about 30% in 1991 to over 60% in 2020. In addition, the share of wage workers as a form of employment increased from about 18% in 1991 to 42% in 2020 (World Bank 2021a). That is to say, along with changes in economic structure, there has been a shift from informal employment, mainly in agriculture, to formal employment in the higher-wage industrial and service sectors.

Second, public investment, supported by economic growth, has improved basic social services (education, health care, water, electricity, etc.) (Baum 2019; World Bank 2016, 45–48). Public investment was also used for large-scale infrastructure and other areas that promoted economic growth, but this was directed toward improving inclusiveness, as discussed below. The situation in education, health, and basic social services has further improved in many ways since 2000 (World Bank 2021a; WEF 2020).

Vietnam has placed significant emphasis on human resources development, and the country has been recognized for its success (e.g., Parandekar and Sedmik 2016),[3] with rapid increases in enrollment rates. In 2017/18, net enrollment in primary education reached 98%, gross enrollment in secondary education was 92.5%, and gross enrollment in higher education was 28.6% in 2019. The country's improved health services have reduced the infant mortality rate to 15.9 (per thousand live births), and life expectancy at birth has increased to 75.4 years. Basic infrastructure (electricity, sanitation facilities, drinking water, and telephones) is also being developed throughout the country, and although the penetration rate in rural areas is lower than in urban areas, development in rural areas is also rapidly progressing. Vietnam's growth has been highly inclusive, with many people participating in productive activities and playing a role in economic growth, while at the same time receiving the benefits of this growth in the form of income and public services.

Regarding the HDI, Vietnam has also shown significant improvement in the HDI value, rising from 0.483 in 1990 (with an average of 0.517 for developing countries) to 0.704 in 2019 (against the average of 0.689). The country has thus achieved above-average human development for developing countries over the last 30 years. Additionally, the Inequality-adjusted Human Development Index (IHDI),[4] which adjusts for domestic inequality, shows that Vietnam's IHDI value in 2019 was 0.588 (compared to the average of 0.535), and the loss due to domestic inequality was 16.5% (against the average of 22.4%). This indicates that the relatively small domestic inequality levels in Vietnam when compared internationally contributes to human development in a positive way (UNDP 2020, 347–354).

Since 2010, inclusive growth and development have gained increasing prominence, and there has been a movement to create synthetic indices to evaluate and compare countries. One contributor to this movement is Mlachila, Tapsoba, and Tapsoba (2014), whose Quality of Growth Index ranked Vietnam highly, along with China, among developing economies. The World Economic Forum (WEF) also published the Inclusive Development Index (IDI) in 2017 and 2018 for more countries, including developed countries. Comparing China and Vietnam based on WEF (2017), Vietnam is seen as more inclusive. China's Inclusion Score, one of the components of the IDI, ranks 53rd out of 79 developing countries, while Vietnam ranks 27th. According to the Net Income Gini coefficient and Wealth Gini coefficient—both elements of the Inclusion Score—China has slightly greater income and asset inequality than Vietnam. This is also consistent with Vietnam's

[3] Parandekar and Sedmik (2016) attribute Vietnam's good performance in the 2012 Programme for International School Assessment (PISA) to student diligence, parental expectations for education, teacher work environment, and higher investment in education infrastructure than other countries at the same income level.

[4] The IHDI is an indicator that takes into account not only average country-level achievement in human development in the three dimensions of health, education, and income but also gaps in achievement within a country (https://www.undp.org/sites/g/files/zskgke326/files/migration/tr/faq_ihdi.pdf).

lower Gini coefficient compared to that of China, as mentioned in Sect. 11.1. Even in global comparisons, it appears that Vietnam is fundamentally more inclusive.

Vietnam's economic growth can be described as inclusive in terms of aggregate data at the national level. However, significant challenges remain. The World Bank (2021b) conducted a micro-analysis of poverty and inequality based on the Vietnam Household Living Standards Survey, a series of five household surveys conducted from 2010 to 2018. According to this analysis, Vietnam has made progress in reducing absolute poverty and increasing the number of middle-income earners, but poverty persists, especially among ethnic minorities living in rural areas, and absolute inequality has continued to grow (8–19).

While the overall progress in reducing poverty and narrowing inequality has been a great success, the contrast between the rapid development of large cities and the socioeconomic situation in the North Central region, where many ethnic minorities live, indicates that inequality is not decreasing for all. Addressing the ethnic minorities left behind, as well as the emergence of new forms of absolute inequality in the context of rapid economic development, remains a challenge for further inclusive growth.

## 11.3 Growth and Resilience

From 1988, after the start of *Doi Moi,* up until 2019, Vietnam's economic growth rate exceeded 5%, with the only exception being 4.8% in 1999. While some countries, such as Indonesia, experienced negative economic growth due to the AFC in 1998, Vietnam is, to some extent, resilient to domestic and international economic shocks.

Looking at Vietnam's economic fluctuations since 1986, there were three periods of significant declines in economic growth. The first occurred in 1990, falling from 7.4% in 1989 to 5.1% in 1990. The key factor was that while the liberalization of the agricultural sector immediately after the start of *Doi Moi* led to a rapid increase in agricultural production, the disruptions caused by *Doi Moi* also negatively affected economic growth. The second occurrence was when the economic growth rate fell from 8.2% in 1997 to 5.8% in 1998 and then to 4.8% in 1999. This decline was due to the impact of the international economic turmoil brought about by the AFC and the slowdown of the *Doi Moi* reforms (World Bank and MPI 2016, 80).

The third occurrence extended from 2008 to 2012 and saw a period of macroeconomic instability due to the GFC, with economic growth rates of 5.4% in 2009 and 5.2% in 2012. Immediately prior to the crisis, Vietnam was in the midst of an economic boom, with an inflow of foreign capital, a rapid expansion of credit, and a real estate bubble. After the crisis emerged, it faced shrinking international demand triggered by the GFC. The government changed its macroeconomic policy stance to contain high inflation and tightened economic policy, including raising interest rates (World Bank and MPI 2016, 83), which further exacerbated the recession. Learning from this experience, Vietnam's fiscal authorities and the Central Bank began to pay more attention to macroeconomic stability.

However, the fact that the economic growth rate did not fall into negative territory in any of these three periods and recovered within a short time is thought to indicate a certain degree of resilience in the economy. One reason for this may be that, in terms of production, a wide range of industries have contributed to economic growth since 1990. APO (2019, 134) breaks down economic growth rates by industry, demonstrating that when economic growth rates fell during the AFC, agriculture, mining, and manufacturing together accounted for more than half of the economic growth rate. When the manufacturing sector temporarily declined in the 2008–2012 period, it recovered in the short term, and on the demand side, private consumption (around 65% of GDP) and investment (around 35% of GDP) underpinned economic growth (169). Nevertheless, during the AFC, the Vietnamese financial sector was underdeveloped and closed, which reduced external shocks.

Vietnam has achieved economic growth through economic liberalization and globalization. By contrast, the economy has rapidly become more dependent on external factors, making it more susceptible to external economic shocks. The second and third economic recessions mentioned above were both triggered by external shocks. Figure 11.3 shows the trade (exports plus imports) to GDP ratio. Vietnam's trade-to-GDP ratio continued to rise from 23% in 1986 to 210% in 2019. This is high compared to ASEAN and China and is almost double the 110–120% achieved by Malaysia and Thailand (2019). The index of financial openness (Chinn-Ito Index) of Vietnam also improved from minus 1.920 in 1990 to minus 0.148 in 2018, which is higher than those of China and Thailand, and the same as those of Indonesia and Malaysia.[5]

In addition to these factors, there are other areas of increasing vulnerability behind economic growth. One is the persistent budget deficit and the resulting increase in public debt. Another is the fragility of the financial sector, which is still reeling from the effects of the GFC.

Government fiscal spending increased due to the support of economic growth, fiscal policies to combat recession, and a lack of fiscal discipline. As a result, government budget deficits have become chronic. Data since 1998 show that the only year without a budget deficit was 1996 (a 0.2% of GDP surplus), with budget deficits in all other years. In particular, the fiscal deficit in 2012–2015 recorded 5–6% of GDP, and the fiscal deficit to GDP ratio in this period was larger than those of the four ASEAN countries and China, although the fiscal balance has been improving since 2016 (IMF 2021a). Accordingly, public debt has been increasing: the general government's total debt (as a percentage of GDP) has been on an increasing trend since 2000, and especially since 2011, the pace of increase accelerated, reaching 47.6% of GDP in 2016. Since 2017, the debt control policy of reducing the public debt-to-GDP ratio to 63% or less, in accordance with a parliamentary resolution, has led to a slight decline to 43.4% of GDP in 2019 (IMF 2021a). The Vietnamese government has been working on fiscal consolidation and public debt reduction, with advice from the IMF and the World Bank.

[5] The indicators were developed by Chinn and Ito (2006). Indicators through 2018 published on July 13, 2020 are referred to in this section.

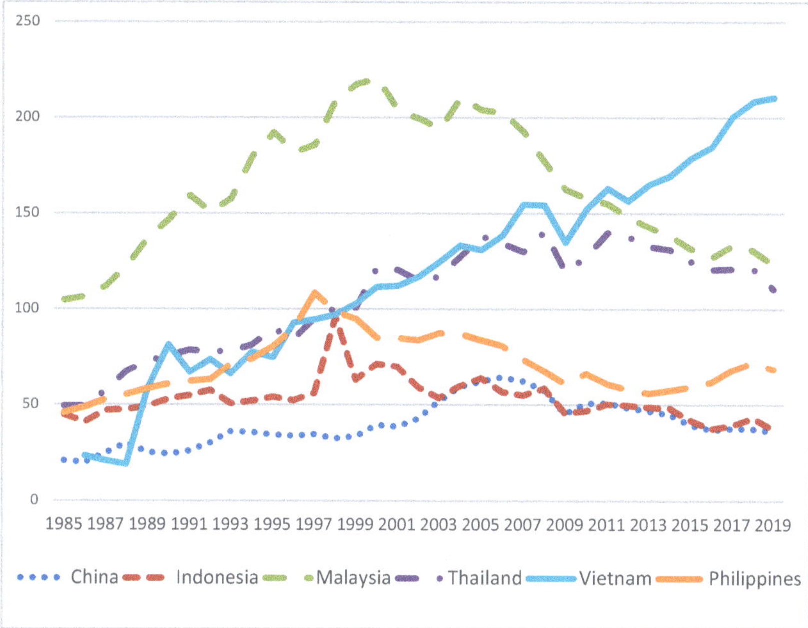


**Fig. 11.3** Degree of dependence on foreign trade (% of GDP) (*Source* Author's compilation from World Bank 2021a data)

In addition, the external buffer (foreign exchange reserves) to prepare for external shocks was at a level sufficient by IMF standards in 2007–2008, but since then, it has been rapidly declining, falling below the level considered sufficient. In particular, around 2011, it fell to about 50% of the level considered adequate. Since then, the country has recovered through trade, tourism, and FDI, reaching a level considered sufficient, at 88.9 billion USD in September 2020 (IMF 2021b, 52), and external vulnerability has been alleviated to some extent.

Another issue is the vulnerability of the financial sector. In Vietnam, financial sector vulnerabilities became apparent during the GFC and subsequent macroeconomic instability. The World Bank and MPI (2016, 142–145) provide the following overview of Vietnam's financial sector vulnerabilities:

- With economic growth, Vietnam's financial sector expanded rapidly beginning in the early 1990s. The dominant player in the financial sector was the banking sector, especially the state-owned commercial banks, which mostly provided loans to SOEs and connected private companies.
- During the period of macroeconomic instability in 2008–2011, the fragility of the banking sector became apparent. Returns on assets in the banking sector declined and NPLs increased. These NPLs and loans with relaxed terms and conditions were related to SOEs. In order to solve the banking sector's problems and reduce

> the risk of crisis, the Vietnamese government has implemented a number of measures, including stricter risk classification of loans and financial assets, strengthening banking sector regulations and supervision, capacity building of government agencies, stricter financial reporting and capital adequacy regulations, and the establishment of the Vietnam Asset Management Company.

Regarding the vulnerabilities in the financial sector, the IMF's 2020 Article IV Consultation continued to point to problems. Specifically, while the profitability of the banking sector has improved, it remains low compared to other ASEAN countries. The capital adequacy ratio of the banking sector has been declining, and the capital adequacy ratio of state-owned commercial banks is relatively low—among the lowest in the ASEAN region. The NPL ratio is gradually declining, but there are concerns that NPLs may rise again due to increased borrowing by the household sector (IMF 2021b, 11–12, 29).

In summary, Vietnam has regained macroeconomic stability in recent years, but vulnerabilities resulting from the GFC and the bursting of the real estate bubble (2008–2011) persist, although they are improving. The NPL problem in the financial sector—especially in the banking sector—has been a constraint on economic stability and the supply of funds by banks. Moreover, the government's fiscal space is limited by fiscal deficits and public debt, which hamper fiscal policy in the face of external shocks (World Bank 2016, 34).

Natural disasters and climate change are two interlinked vulnerabilities for the Vietnamese economy. There are two major risks. First, economic damage, mainly from storms and floods, landslides, drought, and saltwater intrusion, is likely to affect the agricultural sector. There will also be an impact on the poor who are engaged in agriculture, with negative effects on inclusiveness, including poverty and inequality. Second, disasters may impact production activities in Ho Chi Minh City and economic clusters in the south, the center of economic activity. During the rainy season, the region is frequently flooded following torrential rains, and although flood control measures have been taken, there remains a risk to the logistics of industrial clusters around Ho Chi Minh City, which could affect investment and economic growth. Vulnerability to natural disasters and climate change must be addressed, including public investment, even within the constraints of limited fiscal capacity.

## 11.4 Growth and Sustainability

Vietnam's economic growth to date has been sustained. As noted above, negative growth occurred in 1980 before the start of *Doi Moi,* and since then, Vietnam has experienced consistent positive economic growth for more than 35 years. However, this does not necessarily mean that the Vietnamese economy will continue to be sustainable in the future.

Tran and Karikomi (2019, 234–238), while evaluating the achievements from 1986 to the late 2000s, argue that economic fundamentals were weakened and economic growth became inefficient in the late 2000s and early 2010s when the growth rate slowed to 5–6% per year. They attribute this to: (1) the shelving of SOE reforms under Vietnam's gradualist transition strategy; (2) the lack of fiscal and financial discipline and delays in strengthening the international competitiveness of industry; and (3) the delay in political and administrative reforms, and the uncertainty and inefficiency of economic management under the one-party dictatorship. This section discusses the factors that contributed to sustained economic growth in the past and identifies key issues that need to be addressed to realize a sustainable future.

### 11.4.1 Structural Changes in GDP and Growth Factors

Looking at GDP from the demand side, its composition in 2019 was 68.2% household consumption, 24.2% investment, 6.5% general government consumption, and 3.2% net exports. Household consumption exceeded 80% around 1990 but has gradually declined, stabilizing between 65% and 70% since 2000. The large and stable share of household consumption has been a factor supporting the rate of economic growth. General government consumption has also been stable at between 5% and just over 6% since 2000. By comparison, the share of investment in GDP has fluctuated. It rose from 24.3% in 1994 and peaked at 35.1% in 2007, following the investment boom. It then began to decline after the GFC, falling to between 20% and 25%, where it has remained in recent years. Net exports were negative until 2011 but have remained positive since 2012 (World Bank 2021a).

The changes in the economic structure of GDP were outlined in Sect. 11.1. Looking at the contribution of each industry to the economic growth rate, immediately after the start of *Doi Moi* in 1986, there was a period of 2–3% growth in the agricultural sector due to agricultural liberalization but this has gradually declined to less than 1% in recent years. The growth rate of the manufacturing sector was 1% in the early 1990s, but this has steadily increased and is currently around 2%, except during periods of external economic shocks. It now accounts for 20% to 30% of total economic growth. The service sector accounts for about 50% of total economic growth, with a growth rate of over 4% when the country's overall economic growth rate is high and 2% even when it is low (excluding 1998) (APO 2019, 134–135). In addition to the structural shift from agricultural to nonagricultural sectors, the service sector, along with manufacturing, has contributed to economic growth. Taking these points into account, some have pointed out that Vietnam is experiencing premature deindustrialization and are concerned that Vietnam's economic growth may be sluggish in the future.

Figure 11.4 is a disaggregation of growth factors using growth accounting from APO (2020, 137).[6] This shows that the contribution of capital input to growth is consistently large. Especially when *Doi Moi* began to take effect, the growth rate

[6] The economic growth rates in Fig. 11.4 are from APO (2020) and differ from those of World Bank (2021a). The same figure distinguishes between ICT and non-ICT capital inputs, and labor inputs into labor quality and labor hours, but these are combined into capital input and labor input, respectively, to simplify the discussion for this chapter.

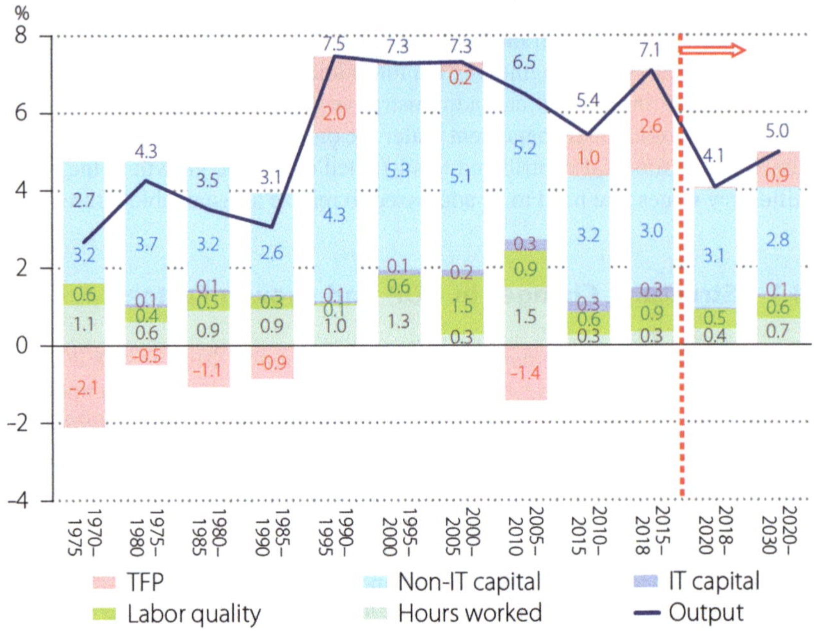


**Fig. 11.4** Disaggregation of economic growth rate using growth accounting (%) (*Source* Reprinted from APO 2020, 137. https://doi.org/10.61145/DJQX5383)

due to capital input was 4.4% between 1990 and 1995, and it exceeded 5% for the 15 years from 1995 to 2010. After 2010, however, the contribution from capital input declined to over 3%. In other words, strong capital input drove growth, especially until around 2010. This is also consistent with the changes in GDP on the demand side mentioned earlier.

Economic growth from labor input gradually increased from 1.1% in the 1990–1995 period to 2.4% in 2005–2010 but has remained around 1% since 2010. Until around 2010, the input from cheap labor was also considered a contributing factor to growth, supported by a demographic dividend.

Total factor productivity (TFP) fluctuates widely from period to period. From 1990 to 1995, it was 2.0%, which can be attributed to the *Doi Moi* reforms. From 1995 to 2010, TFP contracted, and from 2005 to 2010—a period of macroeconomic instability—it turned negative. Since 2010, it has reverted to positive and has become the second largest contributor to growth after capital input. The development of the ICT industry (e.g., smartphones) and machinery manufacturing are thought to have contributed to the increase in TFP. Although improving TFP has been an issue for Vietnam, it has been relatively high compared to other

ASEAN countries since 2010 (APO 2020, 177–179) and is expected to contribute to economic growth.[7]

### 11.4.2 Labor Productivity in Vietnam

One issue that has been identified as a challenge for future sustainable growth in Vietnam is its slow growth in labor productivity. While Vietnam's labor productivity has indeed been rising, the problem lies in the fact that its growth rate is insufficient for transitioning from a middle-income country to a high-income country. Over the long term, Vietnam's labor productivity level has remained among the lowest in Asia—despite high economic growth, the country's productivity gains have been limited. In 2018, labor productivity was USD 12.7 thousand per Vietnamese worker, or USD 5.9 per hour (2017 PPP price; same below). Labor productivity per hour in other countries was USD 10.8 in China, USD 12.1 in Indonesia, USD 25.6 in Malaysia, USD 9.1 in the Philippines, and USD 14.2 in Thailand, indicating that Vietnam falls well below its regional peers (the same trend applies to labor productivity per worker). However, Vietnam's labor productivity growth rate has been higher than that of any other Asian country since 2010–2015 at 4.9% and 2015–2018 at 6.4%, respectively (APO 2020, 46–51, 172–174), which is a positive sign for future development.

VEPR and GRIPS (2020, v-viii) provide a comprehensive analysis of Vietnam's productivity based on data from 1990–2015. The study finds that Vietnam's labor productivity growth has been moderate and unstable, not reaching the rapid growth experienced by countries that seem to have achieved economic take-off. It sets out the main reasons as follows: (1) labor productivity of public enterprises (state sector) and private enterprises (non-state sector) has risen steadily, but labor productivity of FDI enterprises has declined significantly since the early 2000s, and many foreign manufacturers have positioned Vietnam as a place for low-skilled and labor-intensive production; and (2) much of the labor force remains in the agricultural sector due to barriers to labor mobility, and the effect of shifting labor between sectors is insufficient, indicating room for improvement.

### 11.4.3 Efficiency of Capital Investment and Use of Natural Resources

Another important question concerns whether capital and other factors of production (natural resources, land, etc.) have been used efficiently. As the growth accounting analysis shows, Vietnam's economic growth has been supported by a massive capital input, but this capital input has not been used efficiently. Vietnam's capital productivity has been declining almost consistently, falling from

[7] In general, the analysis of growth factors using growth accounting has limitations and should be interpreted with caution.

the capital productivity index value of 1.0 in 2000 to about 70% of this level in 2018 (APO 2020, 35). While the diminishing return to scale due to capital stock increase may be one factor, investments in inefficient state enterprises and domestic private enterprises—as well as redundant investments caused by a lack of coordination between central and local governments—are thought to have reduced capital productivity (World Bank 2016, 37–39). Note that among the countries being compared, capital productivity has increased since 2000 in the Philippines, Malaysia, and Thailand, while Indonesia has declined slightly since 2000, but not as much as Vietnam (APO 2020, 108–133).

For Vietnam, the abundance of mineral resources (oil, natural gas, coal, etc.) and natural resources (land, water, forests, marine resources, etc.) in the country has been an asset for economic development. Crude oil production, natural gas, and inexpensive hydroelectric and coal power generation eliminated the need to rely on imports of these resources. Furthermore, crude oil and coal have been exported, contributing to foreign currency earnings and economic growth. Other natural resources became factors of production in agriculture, forestry, and fisheries. Agriculture still accounts for 36.2% of total employment, although its share of the economy and its contribution to growth have declined.[8]

While these resources have contributed to sustained economic growth, it must be noted that they have been over-exploited. From 2000 to 2010, natural resources declined by an annual average of about 5% of GNI (World Bank 2021a). In recent years, natural resource loss has decreased after peaking in 2011, but this is likely because resources have already been overused and few remain. Several issues have arisen, such as intensive use of land for agriculture (three cropping seasons and excessive use of fertilizers), inefficient use of water resources, deforestation and soil erosion due to commodity crops, and depletion of fishery resources due to overfishing (World Bank 2016, 63). Environmental destruction is also worsening. Air pollution is particularly serious, as is water pollution (due to wastewater, pesticides, and aquaculture), noise, and forest and mangrove loss.

### 11.4.4 Manufacturing

Export-oriented manufacturing has driven Vietnam's economic growth. In 2010, industrial exports were mainly light industrial goods such as sewing products and footwear (23.0% of export value), but by 2019, telephones and computers, as well as mechanical and transportation equipment, accounted for a total of 43.1% of export value, while light industrial goods continue to account for 19.3% of export value (JETRO 2010, 123; JETRO 2020). As VEPR and GRIPS (2020, vi) point out, though industrial exports are dominated by high-technology and high-priced

[8] Vietnam is among the world's top five exporters of rice, shrimp, coffee, cashew nuts, pepper, and rubber (FAO 2021).

goods, value-added remains low, as low-wage and labor-intensive processing and assembly continue to be conducted within Vietnam.

This is due to the formation of a dual economic structure, in which export-oriented FDI enterprises and domestic private enterprises are fragmented. Most domestic private enterprises are small or micro in scale, oriented toward the domestic market with low technological capacity and productivity. Among these, there are few large and superior technology enterprises engaged in manufacturing and high value-added services that lead to exports and global value chains (GVCs). Spillover effects from FDI enterprises to domestic private industry—such as the production and procurement of raw materials and components, new technologies and management know-how transfers—remain limited (World Bank 2016, 41–44).

High-tech products such as telephones, computers, mechanical equipment and transportation equipment—which currently drive Vietnam's export industry—are even more technology-intensive, so the spillover effect on domestic private enterprises is even more limited. According to JETRO (2020), the top 10 major imports in 2019 were computer electronic products and parts (20.3% share of total imports), machinery equipment and parts (14.5% share), and telephone equipment and parts (5.5% share). The trend is evident in the fact that FDI enterprises import parts, undertake labor-intensive processing and assembly in industrial parks in Vietnam, and export the finished products. Since the top 10 major imports also include woven fabrics and textiles (5.2% share) and fiber and leather materials (2.3% share), for sewn products and footwear, the pattern of importing the main raw materials, processing them, and exporting finished products appears likely to continue.

In order to increase the spillover effect of FDI enterprises on domestic private enterprises and for Vietnam's domestic private enterprises to participate in the high value-added sector of GVC, there is an urgent need to develop the country's small and medium enterprises (SMEs) and human resources.[9] Without this, Vietnam's manufacturing will stagnate as a provider of low value-added processing and assembly for GVCs, and it will not be able to play its central role as an engine of economic growth. Moreover, if the manufacturing sector fails to expand, the service sector will be the recipient of labor from the agricultural sector, leading to a premature deindustrialization of the country.

### 11.4.5 Governance and Institutions

Two main issues related to governance and institutions are discussed in this subsection. The first is to reduce government involvement in economic activities and

[9] Japan has been supporting improvements in the management of SMEs, development of supporting industries, and fostering of engineers through ODA. Between 2016 and 2018, when the author was stationed in Vietnam, several FDI companies (including smartphone manufacturing companies) were evaluating whether the quality of parts and technical capabilities of local Vietnamese companies was sufficient to explore the possibility of local procurement of parts.

markets, limiting it to essential areas only. The second is broader governance improvements. While improvements are being made in both areas, further efforts are needed to ensure future growth.

Regarding the first, Vietnam has progressively reformed its centrally planned economic system without experiencing major economic disruptions. However, the country has postponed more difficult reforms, particularly in SOEs. Vietnam still advocates a socialist-oriented market economy. Amid the *Doi Moi* reforms, the government has undertaken efforts to reform SOEs, selling off companies and introducing private capital. As the private sector has expanded, the share of SOEs in the economy has steadily declined, and in 2017, the GDP share of SOEs was 28.6% (Tran and Karikomi 2019, 233). However, in certain sectors—utilities, banking, resource development, and construction—SOEs continue to occupy dominant positions. While the productivity of SOEs has been picking up, it has been lower than that of private and FDI enterprises over the long term, dragging down the country's overall growth rate and productivity.

In addition, SOEs and enterprises with connections to the government have received favorable access to key factors of production, such as land and capital, which are under government oversight. These realities have undermined the fairness of business between state and private enterprises, undermined regulatory independence, and impeded the efficient allocation of resources. For further economic growth, substantial reforms are needed to ensure the efficient use of factors of production (World Bank 2016, 92–98; Tran and Karikomi 2019, 244).

The second area relates to broader governance improvements, which are needed to implement the reforms described in the previous point and to further improve inclusiveness. According to the World Bank's WGI 2020, Vietnam's "Government Effectiveness" (53.8 percentile rank,[10] improved over time), "Political Stability and Absence of Violence/Terrorism" (53.8, slightly worsened over time), and "Rule of Law" (53.4, improved over time) are in the middle of all the countries covered in 2019. "Control of Corruption" is in the bottom 30% (34.1, almost unchanged over time), and "Regulatory Quality" is in the bottom 40% (41.8, improved over time). "Voice and Accountability" is low, in the bottom 10% (11.8), and has made little improvement over time (World Bank 2021c). In particular, "Control of Corruption," "Regulatory Quality," and "Voice and Accountability" are related to the issues of favorable access to resources by SOEs and enterprises with connections to the government noted above and require further improvement.

## 11.5 Conclusion

This chapter has provided an overview of Vietnam from the perspective of quality growth. The country has achieved rapid economic development since 1986 by transitioning to a market economy and opening its economy to the outside world.

[10] In this percentile rank, 0 is the worst rated and 100 is the highest rated.

The analysis highlights three main points: (1) Vietnam has achieved high economic growth for more than 35 years to date; (2) it has secured highly inclusive economic growth; and (3) the country has realized robust growth supported by broad sources of economic growth and experienced the benefits of opening up to the outside world; however, the economy is becoming increasingly vulnerable. Each of these points can be further articulated as follows.

First, Vietnam has sustained high economic growth because of its gradual market transition strategy and its policy of opening up its economy to the outside world. As a result, since the start of *Doi Moi* in 1986, there has been no major political, economic, or social turmoil—even when the economic growth rate declined to a low point of 4.8% in 1999—and Vietnam has maintained stable long-term economic growth since 1990. At the beginning of *Doi Moi,* the economy developed through the growth of the agricultural sector, which was the main industry at that time, and achieved export-led economic growth through FDI as the opening up to the outside world progressed. Export industries were initially led by the low-wage and labor-intensive textile industry, but in recent years have diversified, shifting to higher value-added sectors such as smartphones and machinery equipment. However, while the gradualist transition strategy has not created turmoil, it has postponed difficult reforms and now acts as a constraint on growth—specifically, reforms of SOEs and factor markets. Looking ahead, sustainable development will require accelerated labor productivity growth, more efficient use of capital and natural resources, a reduction in the dual economic structure of FDI enterprises and domestic private enterprises, and stronger efforts to address environmental pollution and climate change.

Second, Vietnam's economic growth has been highly inclusive. Looking at the country as a whole, the poverty rate declined substantially with economic growth, and inequality, as measured by the Gini coefficient, did not increase. Economic growth and structural changes increased employment opportunities, and people participated in productive activities through work and received the fruits of economic growth as income. Furthermore, basic services were improved, and people enjoyed human resource development, health care, and infrastructure services—and human development progressed. In particular, human resource development has been a success, creating a virtuous cycle that expands opportunities for people to participate in productive activities through employment. However, from a micro perspective, it has been pointed out that there are still many poor people among ethnic minorities in rural areas and that absolute inequality is increasing, requiring further policy measures.

Third, while the country has realized robust growth supported by broad sources of economic growth and the benefits of opening up to the outside world, it remains vulnerable to global financial crises, such as the one that occurred in 2007 and the subsequent macroeconomic instability that ensued. While integration into the global economy, one of the drivers of economic development, has been rapid, it has also made the country more vulnerable to external shocks. Recently, government policies have led to improvements in fiscal deficits, public debt, and foreign exchange reserves compared to earlier periods. Some progress, though not complete, has also been made in addressing the NPL problem. The government will need to pay more attention to these vulnerabilities, as they may pose a threat to the sustainability of economic development.

## References


Asian Productivity Organization (APO). 2019. *APO Productivity Databook 2019*. APO.

Asian Productivity Organization (APO). 2020. *APO Productivity Databook 2020*. APO.

Baum, Anja. 2019. Vietnam's Development Success Story and the Unfinished SDG Agenda. *IMF Staff Working Paper WP/20/31*. IMF.

Chinn, Menzie D., and Hiro Ito. 2006. "What Matters for Financial Development? Capital Controls, Institutions, and Interactions." *Journal of Development Economics* 81 (1): 163–192. https://web.pdx.edu/~ito/w11370.pdf.

Food and Agricultural Organization of the United Nations (FAO). 2021. FAOSTAT. FAO. Accessed July 2, 2021.

Furuta, Motoo. 2017. *Vietnam no kiso chisiki* [Basic Knowledge of Vietnam]. Mekong.

International Labour Organization (ILO). 2021. *ILOSTAT*. ILO. Accessed June 23, 2021.

International Monetary Fund (IMF). 2021a. World Economic Outlook Database. IMF. Accessed June 25, 2021.

International Monetary Fund (IMF). 2021b. *Report on Article IV Consultation Vietnam*. IMF.

Japan External Trade Organization (JETRO). 2010. *Sekai bōeki tōsi dōkō hōkokusyo 2010* [Global Trade and Investment Report 2010]. JETRO.

Japan External Trade Organization (JETRO). 2020. *Sekai bōeki tōsi dōkō sirīzu (Vietnam)* [Global Trade and Investment Report Series (Vietnam)]. JETRO.

Mlachila, Montfort, René Tapsoba, and Sampawende J. A. Tapsoba. 2014. "A Quality of Growth Index for Developing Countries: A Proposal." IMF Working Paper WP/14/172. IMF.

Parandekar, Suhas D., and Elisabeth K. Sedmik. 2016. "Unraveling a Secret: Vietnam's Outstanding Performance on the PISA Test." World Bank Group. Policy Research Working Paper 7630. World Bank.

Tran, Van Tho. 2010. *Vietnam keizai hatten ron: Tyū syotoku koku no wana to aratana Doi Moi* [Development and Transition in the Vietnamese Economy]. Keiso Shobo.

Tran, Van Tho, and Shunji Karikomi. 2019. *Tyū syotoku koku no wana to Tyūgoku/ASEAN* [The Middle Income Trap from a China and ASEAN Perspective]. Keiso Shobo.

United Nations Development Program (UNDP). 2020. *Human Development Report 2020: The Next Frontier Human Development and the Anthropocene*. UNDP.

Vietnam Institute for Economic and Policy Research (VEPR), and National Graduate Institute for Policy Studies (GRIPS). 2020. *Vietnam Productivity Report. Preliminary Final Edition.*

World Bank. 2016. *Vietnam Systematic Country Diagnostics 2016*. World Bank.

World Bank. 2021a. World Development Indicators Database. World Bank. Accessed June 25, 2021.

World Bank. 2021b. *Shared Gains: How High Growth and Anti-Poverty Programs Reduced Poverty in Vietnam. Vietnam Poverty and Shared Prosperity Update Report*. World Bank.

World Bank. 2021c. Worldwide Governance Indicators 2020. World Bank. Accessed June 28, 2021.

World Bank, and Ministry of Planning and Investment (MPI) of Vietnam. 2016. *Vietnam 2035: Towards Prosperity, Creativity, Equity, and Democracy*. World Bank.

World Economic Forum (WEF). 2017. *The Inclusive Growth and Development Report 2017*. WEF.

World Economic Forum (WEF). 2020. *Global Competitiveness Report Dataset*. https://jp.knoema.com/atlas/sources/WEF. Accessed June 29, 2021. (Dataset available at https://data360.worldbank.org/en/dataset/WEF_GCIHH)

Yamada, Junichi. 2021. *Inhura kyōryoku no ayumi: Zizyo dyoryoku sien toiu messēzi* [Progress of Infrastructure Cooperation: A Message of Self-Help Support]. University of Tokyo Press.

**Yasuo Fujita** is former Director General, JICA Research Institute (present JICA Ogata Sadako Research Institute for Peace and Development), Japan International Cooperation Agency (JICA). In JICA, he held key positions including Director General of Credit Risk Analysis and Environmental Review Department, and Chief Representative of JICA Vietnam Office as well. He also worked for private companies, and United Nations High Commissioner for Refugees (UNHCR). His main interest is in economic growth, poverty reduction, infrastructure development, project financing, private sector development, and management of small and medium enterprises. He has some publications such as "Does a Rural Road Improvement Project Contribute to Inclusive Growth?—A Case Study from Bangladesh." JICA-RI Working Paper No. 138. (JICA Research Institute, 2017). He holds a Master of Economics from University of Tsukuba, Japan.

# Peru

# 12

Masayuki Eguchi

## 12.1 Economic Development Overview

Peru is a diverse resource-rich country with 3000 km of coastline, abundant fishery resources, its own Amazon region comprising the second largest tropical rainforest after Brazil, and mountainous regions with rich mineral deposits. On the other hand, the country's considerable size, complex and steep mountainous terrain, and the cultural and ethnic duality between Spanish and other settlers and Indigenous peoples have slowed social development.

In the 1970s, the military government adopted an anti-American policy of economic independence from the US and implemented socialist policies such as the nationalization of foreign capital. After the bloodless coup d'état in 1975, efforts were made to restore relations with international organizations and the US. The Belaunde administration, which came to power in 1980 after the transition to civilian rule, continued to pursue market liberalization under international cooperation. However, import liberalization led to a large current account deficit and an increase in external debt. The debt crisis of 1982 coincided with the El Niño phenomenon, and the government implemented austerity measures based on an agreement with the IMF. However, real GDP growth in 1983 was minus 9.3% and in 1984, the country effectively defaulted on its debt.

President Garcia was elected in 1985 on a platform of criticizing economic liberalization and correcting inequality. While adopting protectionist policies and promoting import-substitution industrialization, he declared at the UN General Assembly that he would limit foreign debt payments to 10% of exports or less. Consequently, the IMF declared Peru ineligible for investment, and relations with the international financial community deteriorated. The populist economic policy

M. Eguchi (✉)
Tokyo, Japan


K. Hirota (ed.), *Introduction to Quality Growth*,
https://doi.org/10.1007/978-981-95-6220-6_12

stimulated domestic consumption through price controls and fixed exchange rates, and the GDP growth rate reached 10% in 1986. However, the country faced a shortage of foreign currency due to increased issuance of government bonds and increased imports that lacked fiscal support, a decline in exports due to a prolonged strike in the mining sector, and the suspension of capital inflows from international financial institutions and developed countries. Inflation averaged over 2000% in 1988 and 1989 (reaching more than 7600% in 1990), real GDP growth was −10% for two consecutive years, and the Peruvian economy was in a state of collapse due to the failure of the currency and hyperinflation. In addition, along with the heavy debt crisis since the 1980s, armed conflicts between two rebel guerrilla groups against the backdrop of poverty and discrimination in rural areas resulted in the deaths of approximately 30,000 people, while bombings and power outages in the metropolitan area became a common occurrence.

President Fujimori, who took office in 1990, decisively liberalized and privatized key sectors to stabilize the economy and reintegrate the country with the international financial community. The Peruvian economy achieved economic growth driven by infrastructure development, resource development through foreign loans, and the inflow of foreign investments by privatization. In addition, although the military was mobilized to suspend the functions of the National Assembly and other coercive measures were taken, in terms of security, military offensives either destroyed or weakened guerrilla organizations.

Even after the ouster of President Fujimori, the Peruvian government continued to promote free trade policies and maintained high growth within Latin America, supported by the predominant market environment for mineral resources, with an average economic growth rate of 4.77% from 2000 to 2019, when the COVID-19 pandemic hit.

However, regionally and socially, disparities and poverty still remain in Peru, and recent growth has been supported by a favorable environment for commodity prices. Geographically, the country is also prone to earthquakes and other natural disasters. This report analyzes Peru's current situation and examines the challenges it faces in terms of inclusiveness, resilience, and sustainability in order to break out of the "middle-power trap" and achieve and maintain "high-quality growth" as the country has aimed to join the OECD on the occasion of its 200th anniversary (in 2021).

## 12.2 Growth and Inclusiveness

Poverty in Peru has continued to decline since the 1990s after worsening during the fiscal crisis of the 1980s. This chapter provides a factor analysis of inclusiveness in Peru's economic growth over time.

During the Fujimori administration, which began in 1990 and lasted until 1995, the economy was rebuilt by curbing inflation and eliminating the budget deficit in order to address the economic crisis that had persisted until the previous administration. As a result, per capita GDP began to recover, and the HDI continued

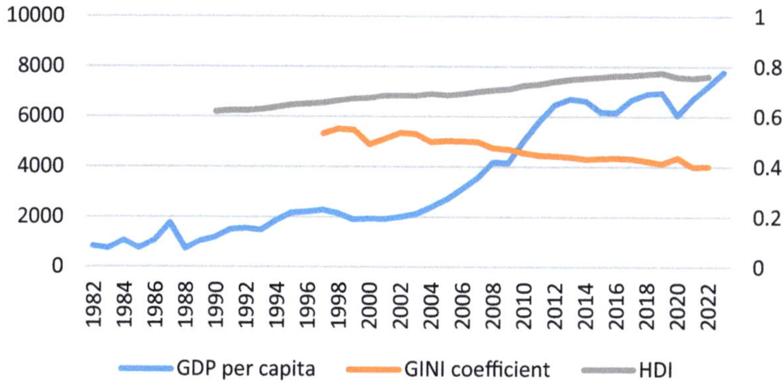


**Fig. 12.1** GDP per capita, Gini coefficient, and HDI. *Source* compiled by Author based on WDI [GDP, Gini coefficient), UNDP HDI

to slowly improve (see Fig. 12.1). The Fujimori administration also focused on poverty alleviation. For example, in 1991, the National Fund for Compensation and Social Development (FONCODES) was established under the direct control of the President, giving priority to the development of economic and social infrastructure in deprived areas.[1] As one of the measures to combat poverty, during the first Fujimori administration, investment in education increased by 94%, with an emphasis on building schools in deprived areas (Benavides et al. 2007).

On the other hand, the end of the Fujimori administration was marked by economic stagnation due to the AFC, and the poverty rate increased from 1997 to 2000 throughout the country. Osonoi (1995) also points out that although new jobs were created because of privatization and deregulation promoted by the Fujimori administration, most new jobs were for highly educated people with expertise in ICT and other technologies. As a result, there were few new jobs for low-income groups, and the Gini coefficient remained high—in the 50% range—for the decade beginning in the late 1990s.

Successive Peruvian administrations implemented poverty reduction and social inclusion as priority policies,[2] and while poverty declined for some time, it

[1] In Peru, it is important to consider poverty from the perspective of Indigenous peoples. Fujita (2009) states that after the suppression of the Tupac Amaru movement in 1780, Indigenous peoples were deprived of the right to read and write and were relegated to the rural poor. Regarding the extreme-left armed group Sendero Luminoso, which rose to power in the 1980s, Figueroa and Barron (2005) state that although not an ethnic conflict because the leaders were not indigenous, the movement can be considered a result of the poverty of rural Indigenous people. Since the 1990s, there has been an emphasis on poverty alleviation through the development of social infrastructure in rural areas, such as FONCODES and the National Project for the Management of Watershed Basins and Soil Conservation.

[2] The FONCODES was established by the Fujimori administration. JUNTOS is a cash transfer program aimed at supporting health and education for the poor and is directly overseen by the Prime Minister's Office. Both programs continue to be implemented to this day.

increased again following the stagnation of economic and social activities due to the COVID-19 pandemic in 2020 (see Fig. 12.2). In particular, the COVID-19 crisis led to a sharp increase in poverty in the relatively industrialized metropolitan areas and southern coastal areas. Peru's land area can be divided into the desert coastal area (Costa), the mountainous Andean area (Sierra), and the forested area (Selva) along the Amazon River basin. These disparities between regions also comprise a major issue (see Fig. 12.3).

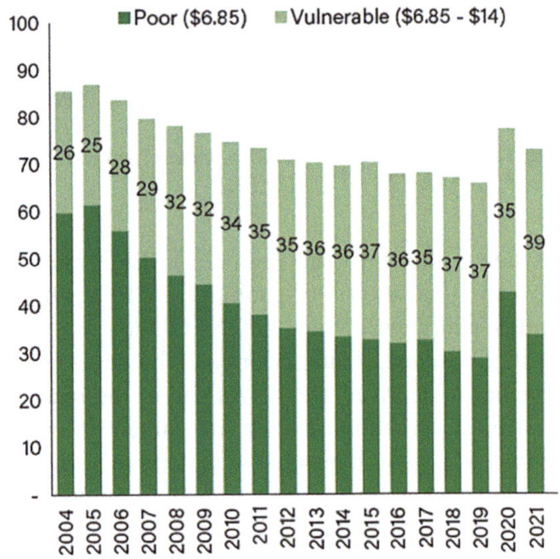


**Fig. 12.2** Percentage of the poor and vulnerable nationwide. *Source* World Bank (2023a)

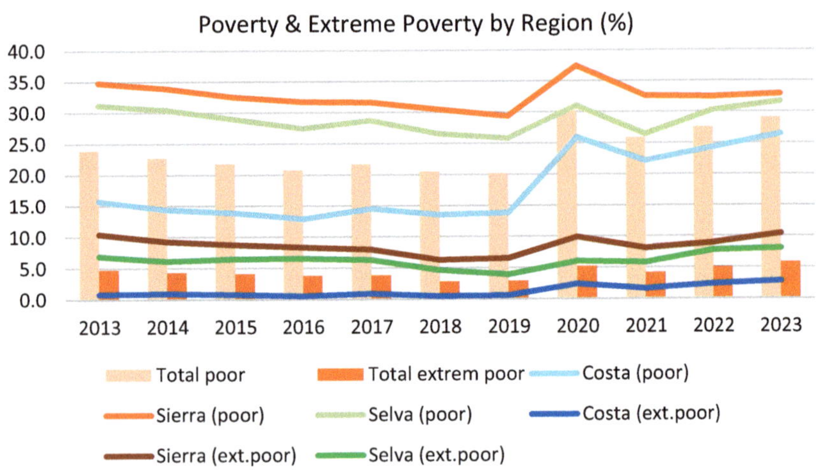


**Fig. 12.3** Poverty rates by region. *Source* Compiled by Author based on National Institute of Statistics and Informatics [INEI] Información estadística

Despite progress in poverty reduction associated with economic growth, several major challenges remain. The World Bank (2023b) points out that (1) there is inequality in access to public goods and quality of services, (2) a high proportion of the workforce is in the informal sector and has low productivity,[3] (3) income distribution functions are inadequate, with most tax revenues coming from indirect taxes, and (4) poor and vulnerable groups are disproportionately exposed to natural disasters and climate change impacts.

## 12.3 Growth and Resilience

In the 1980s and 1990s, Peru experienced resilience problems and faced an economic crisis with currency collapse and hyperinflation. However, since the beginning of 2000, the country has gradually gained fiscal and financial resilience, benefiting from an external environment of soaring resource prices.

Peru's resilience in the face of the global economic crisis of 2008–2009 can be seen in its public debt-to-GDP ratio, which peaked at 48% in 2003, declined significantly, and then stabilized at around 20% in recent years (see Fig. 12.4). This rapid decline in the ratio can be attributed to the Fiscal Responsibility and Transparency Law (FRTL) enacted in 2001, as well as the Fiscal Stabilization Fund, established in 1999. The fund mandated the accumulation of 10% of the national treasury surplus and concession fees, 10% of privatization revenues, and the use of any excess over the 4% of GDP cap for debt repayment. The sustained high prices of primary commodities during this period also contributed to a significant reduction in the public debt ratio.

Although the above policies were aimed at reducing the public debt ratio, they also included a countercyclical element by capping fiscal spending during periods of economic upswing, and it can be said that these policies contributed to the resilience of the Peruvian economy. The parameters of fiscal policy under the FRTL have changed frequently, and the application of discipline was temporarily suspended from 2009 to 2010—against the backdrop of the GFC—and resumed in 2011. In 2013, based on IMF (2013) recommendations, fiscal discipline based on

[3] Osonoi (1995) demonstrates that basic government services such as education, health, and social security declined during the economic collapse of the 1980s, leading to the formation of the informal sector as a recipient of employment during the economic crisis. Fukui (1999) attributes the formation of the informal sector mainly to illegal settlers, whose low incomes caused by the poor environment, low productivity, and small and micro agriculture in mountainous rural areas created poverty. There was an influx of these poor people into urban areas—especially to the capital, Lima—in search of employment opportunities (Fukui 1999). The World Bank (2016) also points out that between 2004 and 2014, wage growth in the informal sector was about twice as high as in the formal sector (56%). Since the early 2000s, the informal sector has expanded while the income gap between the formal sector and the informal sector has narrowed—resulting in a decline in poverty. In this regard, the World Bank (2017) attributes the increase in informal sector wages from 2001 to 2013 to the migration of many agricultural workers to the informal service sector in urban areas.

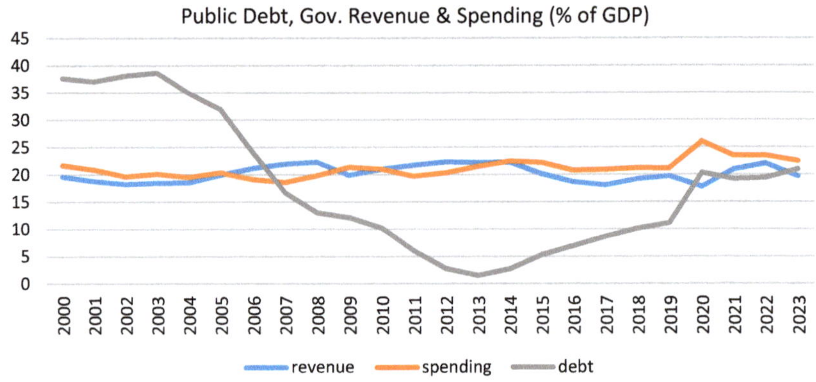


**Fig. 12.4** Public debt and governmental revenue and spending (% of GDP). *Source* Author's compilation from WEO database, November 2024

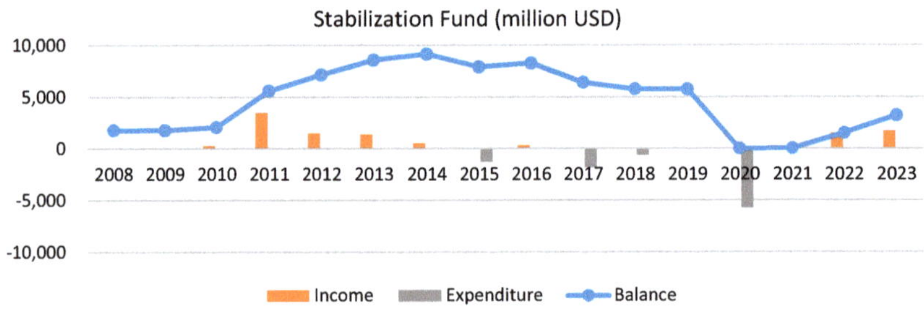


**Fig. 12.5** Peru fiscal stabilization fund balance. *Source* Author's compilation from Ministry of Economy of Peru website. 5330803-informe_iv_trimestre_2023_fef.pdf

structural fiscal balance was introduced, and in 2015, advanced fiscal policy was adopted, including the establishment of a fiscal council to monitor fiscal discipline.

Under such a firm fiscal policy, Peru's Fiscal Stabilization Fund has strict conditions set for its use as a fiscal stimulus and is, in effect, more of a sovereign wealth fund. However, the ample Fiscal Stabilization Fund also serves as a buffer against large external shocks,[4] including providing support during the COVID-19 crisis. The fund also served as a backstop to the resilience of the Peruvian economy during the COVID-19 crisis (see Fig. 12.5).

In response to the deteriorating external environment of lower resource prices, adjustments were made to both fiscal and monetary policies.

[4] In January 2009, a large fiscal stimulus package amounting to 3.5% of GDP on average for 2009–2010 was implemented, with spending mainly on infrastructure but some also being used to provide social security.

In terms of fiscal policy, on the expenditure side, Peru continued to increase government spending from 2011 to 2013 on the back of the fiscal space created by previous surpluses, and real GDP growth returned to a recovery trend in 2015. The IMF (2015) simulated economic outputs for six South American countries (Brazil, Chile, Colombia, Mexico, Peru, and Uruguay), finding that without the fiscal stimulus, the gross output of these six countries would have been 1.5–2% lower.

In terms of monetary policy, the deterioration in the current account balance associated with the rapid worsening of terms of trade led to adjustments through exchange rate depreciation in South America's resource-rich countries. In the case of Peru, the central bank's intervention in foreign currency markets helped keep the exchange rate depreciation at a moderate 6%, and the current account deficit expanded moderately from 2% in 2011 to 4.4% in 2015. In Peru, there was little change in imports and exports, with the exception of mineral resources. While inflationary pressures from exchange rate depreciation would have limited the scope for countercyclical monetary policy, the moderate exchange rate depreciation and the Central Bank's timely introduction of policy rates in line with its inflation-targeting policy have succeeded in controlling inflation (Fig. 12.6).

Regarding Peru's monetary policy in recent years, the de-dollarization of the financial system deserves attention. The dollarization of Peru's financial system began in the late 1970s against a backdrop of high inflation. In 1985, the government adopted a de-dollarization policy of forcibly converting foreign currency deposits into domestic currency, which resulted in a flight of capital. After the removal of restrictions on foreign currency deposits, about 80% of Peru's domestic credit was denominated in dollars by early 2000.

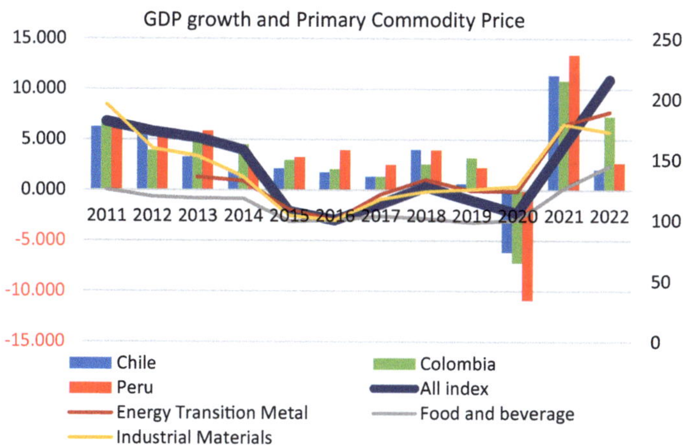


**Fig. 12.6** Real GDP growth rate and primary product prices (by type). *Source* Author's compilation from IMF WEO database, November 2024, compiled by IMF primary commodity prices

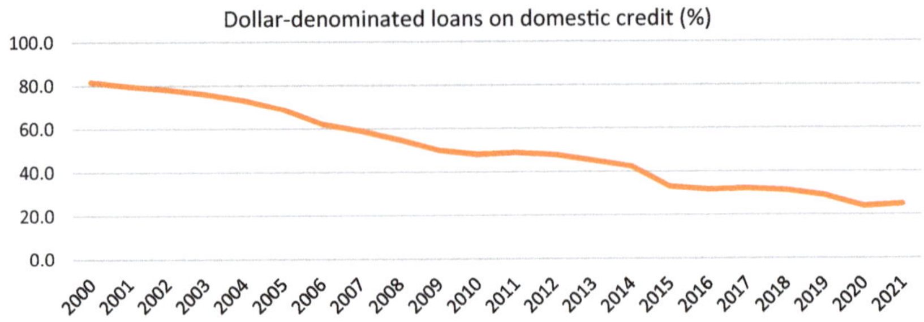


**Fig. 12.7** Percentage of Peru's domestic credit denominated in USD (%). *Source* Author's compilation from BCRP data

When financial systems become dollarized in this way, the Central Bank begins to lose its function as the lender of last resort, increasing liquidity risk in the banking sector. Moreover, when the local currency depreciates against the USD, the outstanding dollar-denominated debt, measured in the local currency, rises significantly. This increases the risk of bankruptcy, especially for borrowers who have no USD income and creates instability in the financial system.

Since the 2000s, Peru's Central Bank, in coordination with the Banking and Insurance Supervisory Agency and the Ministry of Economy, has worked to reduce the dollarization ratio through various policies, such as the risk management policy introduced in 2013, which aimed to reduce the risks posed by the financial system.[5] As a result, the dollarization ratio of Peru's domestic credit and deposits decreased significantly to 24.8% and 22.5%, respectively, at the end of 2021 (see Fig. 12.7).

Undertaking a resilience analysis must involve an assessment of the natural disaster risks that Peru faces. Peru has experienced flooding damage due to the El Niño phenomenon on numerous occasions, resulting in significant economic losses.[6] Peru has an extreme concentration of infrastructure, people, and housing in the Lima metropolitan area, and much of the infrastructure and housing

[5] In 2011–2012 especially—when quantitative easing measures in the US kept dollar-denominated interest rates low—local currency soles appreciated and dollar-denominated credit was again on an expansionary trend, slowing the pace of de-dollarization. In light of this, the Central Bank introduced a more ambitious policy of de-dollarization of domestic credit in 2013 under the risk management policy. Specifically, it began by setting limits on banks' dollar-denominated lending for housing and auto loans and additional reserves in the event that these limits were exceeded, and in September 2013, limits were also set for the total amount of dollar-denominated credit, excluding trade-related credit. Then, in December 2014, new limits were set to require reductions equivalent to 10% for housing and auto loans and 15% for total credit by December 2015, compared to 2013 levels. Those standards were then further tightened, requiring reductions of 30% and 20% from 2013 levels by 2016, respectively.

[6] The Andean Development Corporation estimates that economic losses (including direct losses in housing and other assets, and indirect losses in agricultural and fishery production) were about USD 3.2 billion for the 1982–83 El Niño event (11.6% of 1983 GDP) and about USD 3.5 billion for the 1997–98 El Niño event (6.2% of 1998 GDP) (CAF 2000).

is vulnerable to earthquakes. In the event of an earthquake, economic losses are expected on a scale unparalleled compared to previous natural disasters.[7] To cope with such emergency situations, it is important to raise necessary funds through the Fiscal Stabilization Fund and borrow from donors, in addition to government savings, and to promote policies for disaster prevention and disaster mitigation.

## 12.4 Growth and Sustainability

According to the World Bank (2015a), only thirteen of the 101 countries that were middle-income in 1960 had reached high income by 2008. Many Latin American countries did not graduate from middle-income status for 30 years; Chile took 15 years to graduate. In addition, one characteristic of Asian countries such as South Korea and Taiwan, which moved from middle-income to high-income countries in less than 10 years, is growth through productivity gains rather than investment. Under a free labor market and open economy, they developed infrastructure and networks and invested in human resource development, R&D, and other areas that promote innovation while defending intellectual property. In Peru's case, although economic growth was moderate and some downturns occurred up until the 1990s, the country has achieved high economic growth within the region since 2000. This chapter next analyzes Peru's growth drives to date in terms of economic structure and productivity and identifies issues that need to be addressed to achieve sustainable growth in the future.

Regarding Peru's economic structure, the secular change in nominal GDP composition by industry shows that the tertiary sector has accounted for a slightly larger share since 2005, mostly due to growth in the telecommunications and financial sectors, but the economic structure itself did change significantly between 1980 and 2022 (see Fig. 12.8). Mining of copper, gold, silver, and zinc accounts for the bulk of primary industry.

Looking at the growth rate of real GDP from the demand side, 2006–2012 saw significant contributions from private investment, although these declined due to the financial crisis of 2009 (see Fig. 12.9). Private investment made a negative contribution in the three years after 2014, as mining investment weakened due to the falling prices of primary commodities. The share of mineral resources among exports has remained high, and traditional exports, which include fisheries products, agricultural products, and petroleum and petroleum products, have remained around 70% for 30 years (before that, the country relied more heavily on traditional exports). However, the overall diversification of export commodities has not been realized.

On the other hand, Peru produces a large variety of commodities that are not highly correlated with prices. This has made the country more resilient to changes

[7] In a ranking of cities at risk by the University of Cambridge, Lima ranks first in economic loss of GDP (output) due to earthquakes over the 10-year period from 2015, estimated at USD 35.5 billion.

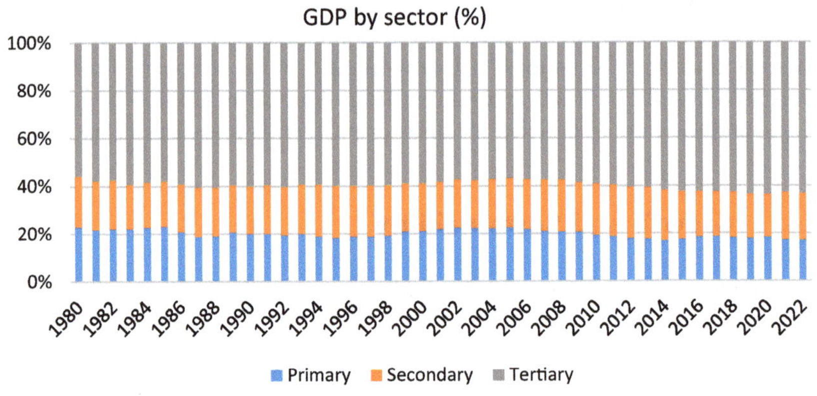


**Fig. 12.8** Breakdown of GDP by sector. *Source* Author's compilation from INEI Product bruto interno por sectores económicos, 1950–2023

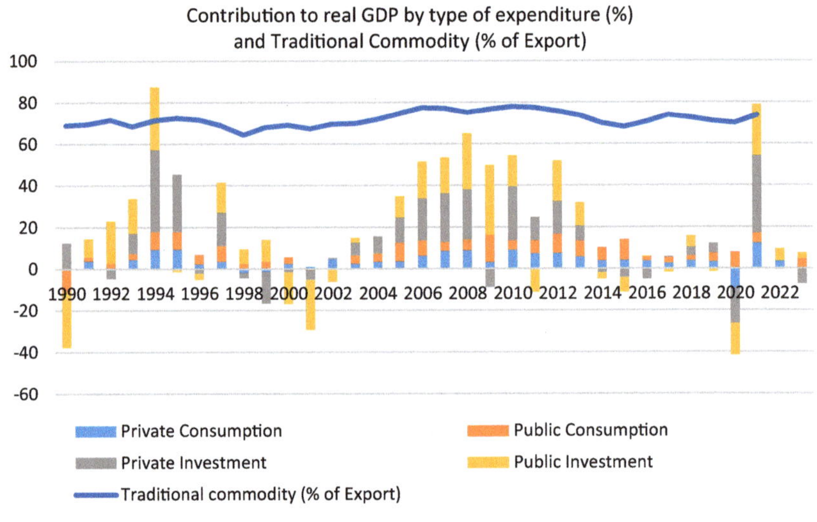


**Fig. 12.9** Contribution to real GDP (%) by type of expenditure. *Source* Author's compilation from Central Bank of Peru. https://estadisticas.bcrp.gob.pe/estadisticas/series/

in commodity prices than other resource-rich countries such as Chile, Ecuador, and Bolivia, where a single commodity accounts for most exports. In addition, Peru's minerals are of high quality, and its low utility and labor costs for development make it internationally competitive. With the exception of the terrorist and political turmoil of the 1980s–1990s, there has been a correlation between Peru's real GDP growth rate and changes in commodity prices, especially since 2000, when Peru's economic growth began to be driven by more diverse and competitive commodities.

Next, we look at the challenges of Peru's sustainable economic growth in terms of productivity. First, if we separate the drivers of growth in each decade into capital, labor, and total factor productivity (TFP), capital input has contributed to growth since the late 1990s. The World Bank (2015b) attributed this mainly to the increase in private investment, which had been restrained since the terrorist and political turmoil of the 1980s and 1990s, and to the mining industry, which was the driving force of Peru's economy during the 2004–2013 period due to the higher prices of primary commodities. Regarding TFP, structural reforms and robust macroeconomic policies since the 1990s have promoted efficient labor distribution, while urbanization has led to a shift of labor from agriculture, the least productive sector, to services, construction, and other sectors.[8] On the other hand, the IMF (2017) projects that if structural reforms continue at their current pace, the contribution of TFP to growth will decline, and continued productivity growth will be critical for Peru to achieve sustainable growth in the future.

The first of these productivity challenges in Peru is the lack of infrastructure.[9] The gap is particularly large in the transportation sector (see Fig. 12.10). According to the JICA (2014), logistics costs are around 10% of the price of production in developed countries and 15% in neighboring Chile, while in Peru, they are 34%, mainly due to the time required for transportation due to a poorly developed road and inland water transportation network. Inadequate infrastructure in the transportation sector makes the movement of people and goods, regional connectivity, and trade inefficient and prevents manufacturers in the logistics-oriented component export industry from attracting investment, which is a drag on productivity growth.

Since the 1990s, the Peruvian government has developed a legal system to promote infrastructure development that leverages private investment, such as establishing the Law for the Promotion of Private Investment and the Law for the Promotion of Public-Private Partnerships (PPPs). However, as shown by the WEF (2017), which ranks Peru 106th out of 138 countries in terms of the capacity of its administrative institutions, inefficient administrative procedures and other obstacles have hindered sufficient infrastructure investment.[10]

Another challenge to improving productivity is labor misallocation. As noted above, with the influx of population into the cities since 1990, labor has moved

[8] The contribution of TFP to real GDP growth in 2000–2010 was 2.6%, up from 0.8% in 1990–2000 (Central Bank of Peru 2017).

[9] According to the WEF (2017), Peru ranks 115th out of 135 countries in terms of its infrastructure development environment. The Peruvian government estimates that USD 31.5 billion and USD 98 billion are needed for short-term (5-year) and long-term (20-year) infrastructure gap investments in high-priority sectors, respectively.

[10] The Kuczynski administration promoted infrastructure investment by reforming the Investment Promotion Agency under the Ministry of Economy and Finance, which is responsible for the public investment management system and the procedures for forming and procuring PPP projects while speeding up administrative procedures. In 2015–2016, as a result of increased domestic infrastructure investment combined with the decline in commodity prices, infrastructure investment in private investment temporarily exceeded mining investment. However, the Odebrecht corruption

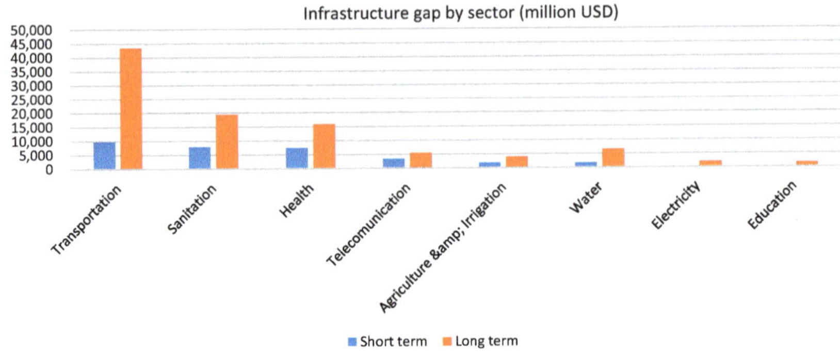


**Fig. 12.10** Infrastructure gap by sector: short-term (5 years), long-term (20 years) (USD million). *Source* Author's compilation from MEF [Ministry of Economy and Finance] (2022)

from agriculture, the least productive sector, primarily to the service sector. The service sector accounts for about 60% of GDP and generates the largest share of employment in the country, but except for the telecommunications and financial services sectors, there is a high informal employment rate and low productivity. According to the World Bank (2015b), service providers are not highly internationalized, so competition is not effective, and productivity is not improving.

Furthermore, the low productivity of the service sector has also led to a decline in the quality and productivity of the primary and secondary industries, which, in terms of their business model, involve service industries such as transportation, land, and administrative processing agents, etc. According to the World Bank (2015b), the low quality of the service sector forces companies to internalize the service and operate outside their core competence. The World Bank (2017) also finds that Peru's services sector adds only 8% of value to manufacturing exports, lower than Colombia (12%), Chile (15%), Thailand (17%), Malaysia (20%), South Africa (27%), which may be partly due to the lack of division of labor, as services need to be produced in-house, as noted above.

The reasons for the lack of growth in Peru's manufacturing sector include, as mentioned above, high logistics costs due to lack of infrastructure and, as discussed below, the delay in human resource development. This has limited investment in sectors such as the broad-based export-oriented parts industry. In addition, this paper cites the so-called "Dutch disease" of soaring resource prices, appreciation of the real exchange rate of resource-rich countries and decline of the manufacturing industry as one of the problems of the "resource curse" and the mechanism of "crowding out of the manufacturing industry." However, according to Alarco (2011) and Whittembury (2015), although an appreciation of the real exchange

scandal uncovered in December 2016 delayed progress on several infrastructure projects, including the suspension of the southern gas pipeline development project and other projects for which the company had received orders.

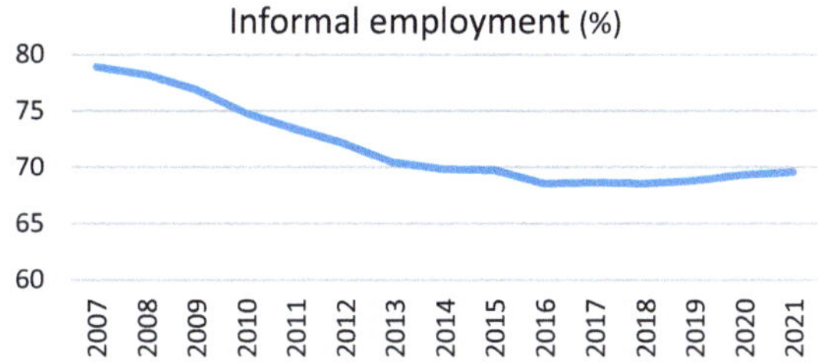


**Fig. 12.11** Informal employment (% of total labor). *Source* Author's compilation from INEI (2022)

rate due to soaring resource prices was observed in Peru, there was no correlation with Dutch disease, which typically leads to a decline in manufacturing and non-traditional product exports. In Chile, another Latin American resource-rich country that joined the OECD, the share of manufacturing employment fell from 18% in 1990 (Central Bank of Chile n.d.) to 12% in 2011 (INEI 2011). This indicates that while an increase in manufacturing employment is not always the primary driver of growth, there are cases where productivity growth makes it important to increase employment in the relatively high-productivity manufacturing sector.

Peru's high informality also poses a challenge to productivity growth. As noted earlier, migration to cities has increased since the 1990s, but most migrants are employed in the informal service sector. The share of informal employment in total employment is about 70% (see Fig. 12.11), a high percentage compared to neighboring countries, and the share of the informal sector in GDP has remained close to 20%, with little improvement. According to the World Bank (2017), informal sector workers are paid about one-third of the wage and have about one-sixth of the productivity compared to formal sector workers. The informal sector lacks opportunities to access credit, enter into value chains, and establish linkages with international firms, making it difficult to increase productivity. One of the causes of informal employment in Peru is a rigid employment system—for example, if an employee is to be dismissed for economic reasons, permission must be obtained from the Ministry of Labor. Such rigid labor regulations may be the cause of high informality (World Bank 2017). It is important that efforts to lower the cost of business formalization improve productivity through the benefits of formalization, such as better access to credit and the promotion of entry into domestic and international value chains.[11]

Finally, it is important to point out that investment in R&D and human resource development remains low. According to UNESCO (2024), R&D investment as a percentage of Peru's GDP is just over 0.1%, a low figure compared to the Latin American regional average of just under 0.6% (see Fig. 12.12).

[11] In 2016, a decree was enacted to simplify various procedures imposed on citizens and companies when dealing with government agencies. This simplified the procedures for formalization, mainly for SMEs, by eliminating the need to submit duplicate documents and permitting the electronic submission of documents. In addition, in 2017, corporate tax reforms were implemented to reduce the tax burden on formalized SMEs, including the introduction of a progressive corporate tax based on the size of net income.

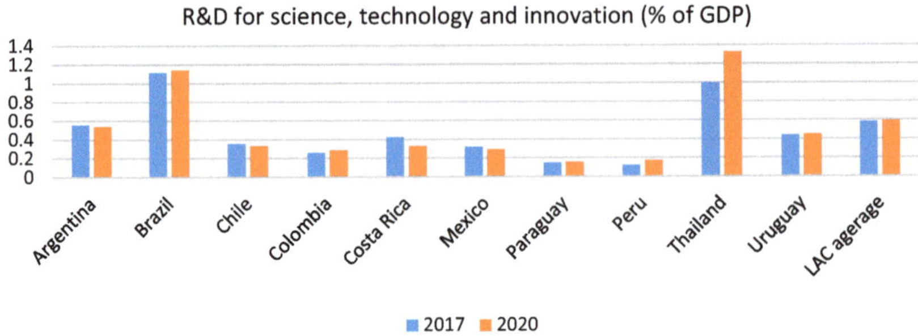


**Fig. 12.12** R&D investment (% of GDP). *Source* Author's compilation from UNESCO (2024)

Peru's economic growth has been driven by investment and exports from the mining industry, which is relatively resilient to changes in commodity prices and is internationally competitive. Business trends in the mining sector will continue to be a major factor in the country's economic growth, as the recent recovery in commodity prices has led to plans for investment in major mining projects. The country's real GDP growth rate has correlated with changes in commodity prices, apart from the 1980s–1990s.

To address the issue of resource price instability, which is discussed as the first problem of the resource curse in this chapter, the Peruvian government has undertaken several measures, including the management and use of a rich fiscal stabilization fund and the establishment of anti-recessionary fiscal rules. Regarding the second problem of the resource curse, crowding out of the manufacturing sector, the Dutch disease—the decline of the manufacturing sector due to real exchange rate appreciation—has not been confirmed. However, high logistics costs due to lack of infrastructure and slow human resource development have slowed the growth of the manufacturing sector. In response, the Peruvian government is promoting investment and attracting industry by investing in infrastructure and R&D and developing free trade zones and industrial parks. The third resource curse problem—deteriorating governance—has manifested itself in the form of corruption, such as the Odebrecht scandal, while Peru, as an implementing country of the Extractive Industries Transparency Initiative (EITI), received a "Meaningful Progress" rating in 2016, which means that the broad goals of the requirements are being met.

In order for the country to achieve sustainable growth without over-reliance on the volatile mining industry, it is important to further increase productivity in the manufacturing and service sectors, while promoting measures against the resource curse. In particular, it is important to promote investment in infrastructure development, formalization of the informal sector, and R&D and human resource development to encourage technological innovation.

## 12.5 Conclusion

A review of Peru's development from the perspective of quality growth—i.e., high growth rate, inclusiveness, resilience, and sustainability—can be summarized into the following points. First, Peru has continued its economic growth in recent years, partly due to the external environment of high resource prices, and the country has become more inclusive by reducing poverty inequality. However, the poverty situation in areas where mines and oil wells in key economic sectors are located is generally high, which is a destabilizing factor for resource development. From the perspective of sustaining economic growth, the challenge is to promote economic and social development in these areas while increasing their inclusiveness.

Second, the structural reforms implemented since the 1990s have provided the country with the resilience to cope with external macroeconomic shocks. However, while the country is prone to natural disasters, its economy is concentrated in metropolitan areas, and its resilience to natural disasters is not high. It is important to promote the development of regional economies to disperse shocks and ensure sustainability in the event of natural disasters. A third challenge is to improve the high informal sector and increase the productivity of secondary and tertiary industries. To this end, the development of the local economy and the improvement of the quality of education remain challenging.

Regarding the first point, poverty alleviation has been a priority for successive administrations in recent years. However, the urban-rural gap in education and health remains large and inclusiveness in the social development sector remains an issue. In particular, social conflicts in areas with oil and mineral resources have attracted attention as an issue of concern for resource development in recent years. Conflicts with Indigenous people against oil development in the Amazon region and with local residents against mining development in mountainous areas have resulted in deaths due to clashes with police and military forces. An understanding of local residents is essential to promote and maintain resource development, as it will continue to be a major industry in Peru, and the challenge from the perspective of sustainability is to ensure that the fruits of economic growth are returned to local residents, i.e., to increase the inclusiveness of rural areas.

The second point is that Peru's economy is less vulnerable to international market conditions and exchange rate fluctuations due to its traditional dependence on primary commodities and its dollar economy. The country has the capacity to undertake a large-scale fiscal mobilization in the event of an exogenous shock, such as GFC, and appropriate fiscal and monetary policies have been implemented. Even in the face of worsening terms of trade of mineral resources—as the major export product—economic growth has been maintained by skillful use of fiscal and monetary policies, including fiscal mobilization backed by sound financial conditions during recessions and the timely introduction of inflation targeting. In the early 2000s, when the dollarization of the economy was underway, 80% of domestic credit was denominated in USD, but in the last 15 years, the ratio of domestic dollar-denominated credit has been reduced to the 20% level to reduce foreign exchange risks, indicating that the government is implementing sound risk management in economic and financial terms. On the other hand, Peru is a country prone to natural disasters and remains exposed to natural disaster risks such as earthquakes, tsunamis, and floods. Heavy rains and floods caused by the El Niño phenomenon have so far accounted for about 10% of GDP. In particular, enhancing the disaster prevention function of metropolitan areas, where one-third of the population is concentrated, and promoting regional economic development to disperse the negative impact on the economy will enhance sustainability, as well as correct regional disparities and increase inclusiveness.

Regarding the third point, Peru's recent economic growth has been driven by competitive mineral resources, and the view remains that mineral resources will continue to be a key sector. On the other hand, the informal sector accounts for a high proportion of the economy, as urbanization has led to a significant shift of labor to the service sector in recent years. The existence of the informal sector has become a bottleneck for productivity improvement, including technological progress and efficiency through R&D investment and human resource development. Reform of the informal sector continues to be a challenge. Rural areas with lower levels of education and the poor have fewer employment opportunities, which is a factor in the formation of the informal sector and an obstacle to higher productivity and sustainable growth. Increasing the inclusiveness of rural areas will also enhance sustainability through productivity growth.

## References


Alarco, German. 2011. "Exports, Foreign Exchange, and Dutch Disease: The Peruvian Case." *Investigación Económica* 70 (275): 115–143.

Banco de Desarrollo de América Latina (CAF). 2000. "Las lecciones de El Niño. Perú."

Benavides, Martin, Martin Carnoy, Santiago Cueto, and Amber Gove. 2007. "Evaluation of the World Bank's Assistance to Primary Education in Peru." Working Paper No. 39152. World Bank.

Central Bank of Chile. "Indicadores Económicos y Sociales de Chile 1960–2000" [Economic and Social Indicators of Chile 1960–2000]. Central Bank of Chile.

Central Bank of Peru. 2017. "Categorías" [Categories]. https://estadisticas.bcrp.gob.pe/estadisticas/series/. Accessed December 14, 2024.

Figueroa, Adolfo, and Manuel Barron. 2005. "Inequality, Ethnicity and Social Disorder in Peru." CRISE Working Paper No. 8. Centre for Research on Inequality, Human Security and Ethnicity. University of Oxford. https://assets.publishing.service.gov.uk/media/57a08c68ed915d622c00131f/wp8.pdf.

Fukui, Chizuru. 1999. "Urbanization and Poverty in Peru: A Study of the Current Situation and Improvement Measures in the Lima Metropolitan Area."

Fujita, Mamoru. 2009. "Current Perceptions on Arable Indigenous Peoples." In *Cooperation with Indigenous Peoples of the Andean Highlands, JICA*, Ch. 1.

International Monetary Fund (IMF). 2013. "Peru Selected Issues." IMF Country Report No. 16/235. https://www.imf.org/external/pubs/ft/scr/2016/cr16235.pdf.

International Monetary Fund (IMF). 2015. "Fiscal Policy in Latin America: Lessons and Legacies of the Global Financial Crisis."

International Monetary Fund (IMF). 2017. "Peru: Staff Report for the 2017 Article IV Consultation."

Instituto Nacional de Estadística e Informática (INEI). 2011. "Encuesta Nacional de Empleo 2011."

Instituto Nacional de Estadística e Informática (INEI). 2022. "Producción y Empleo Informal en el Perú Cuenta Satélite de la Economía Informal 2007–2021" [Production and Informal Employment in Peru: Satellite Account of the Informal Economy 2007–2021].
Japan International Cooperation Agency (JICA). 2014. "Colombia, Peru Logistics Infrastructure Information Collection and Verification Survey."
Ministerio de Economia y Finanzas (MEF). 2022. "Plan Nacional de Infraestructura Sostenible para la Competitividad 2022–2025."
Osonoi, Shigeo. 1995. "Shittsui suru minsyu Seiken" [The Falling Democratic Regime]. In *Gendai Peru to Fujimori seiken* [Contemporary Peru and the Fujimori Regime]. Institute of Developing Economies, 65–102. https://ir.ide.go.jp/records/27886.
United Nations Educational, Scientific and Cultural Organization (UNESCO). 2024. "How Much Does your Country Invest in R&D?" http://uis.unesco.org/apps/visualisations/research-and-development-spending/. Accessed December 14, 2024.
Whittembury, Ana María. 2015. *Is the Peruvian Economy Suffering from Dutch Disease?* Superintendencia de Banca, Seguros y AFP (SBS).
World Bank. 2015a. "Larning Against the Wind: Fiscal Policy in Latin America and the Caribbean in the Historical Perspective."
World Bank. 2015b. "Peru Building on Success: Boosting Productivity for Faster Growth."
World Bank. 2016. "Peru: A Comprehensive Strategy for Financial Protection Against Natural Disasters." Working Paper, Report No. 108665. World Bank.
World Bank. 2017. "Perú Systematic Country Diagnostic." Report No: 112694-PE. World Bank.
World Bank. 2023a. "Informal Economy Database 2023." https://www.worldbank.org/en/research/brief/informal-economy-database. Accessed December 14, 2023.
World Bank. 2023b. "Rising Strong: Peru Poverty and Equity Assessment." World Bank.
World Economic Forum (WEF). 2017. *The Global Competitiveness Report 2016–2017*. WEF.

**Masayuki Eguchi** earned his B.A. in Economics from the University of Waseda and holds a master's degree in public economics from Chuo University in Japan. His professional career spans several prominent roles in international development finance and policy, including Deputy Director General of Evaluation Department, Director of Planning Division for Loan Operation of Operation and Strategy Department, Chief Representative in Brazil, Chief Representative in Peru at the Japan International Cooperation Agency (JICA).

# 13 Costa Rica

Stace Nicholson

## 13.1 Economic Development Overview

Among the poorest and most isolated of imperial Spain's colonies in the so-called New World—and possessing neither ample deposits of mineral resources nor a bountiful supply of exploitable indigenous labor—Costa Rica has since emerged as one of the wealthiest, globally integrated countries in Central America. It has come to epitomize for the region and beyond the development dividends to be accrued from a confluence of enduring democratic traditions, the rule of law, openness to global trade and investment, as well as far-sighted social and environmental policies.

After experiencing a deep and protracted economic crisis in the 1980s like many of its regional peers, which led to a cumulative 20% decline in per-capita income, Costa Rica subsequently upheld moderate—and for brief intervals high—GDP growth (Cornick and Trejos 2009). GDP growth stayed positive in both nominal and real terms over the quarter century before the GFC of 2007–08 and was second only to that of Chile between the early 1980s and 2007 on an average annualized basis (Cornick and Trejos 2009). Per-capita GDP more than doubled from 1986 to 2016, a renowned feat within Central America (Fig. 13.1) (OECD 2016b).

Costa Rica's laudable growth experience has involved considerable export diversification and labor migration from agriculture to the manufacturing and service sectors—albeit much more so toward the latter (Fig. 13.2). Trade and FDI have been indispensable enablers of this transition. Following the tumult of the 1980s, during a period of 'structural adjustment,' the Costa Rican state

S. Nicholson (✉)
USA Office, Japan International Cooperation Agency, Washington, DC, USA


K. Hirota (ed.), *Introduction to Quality Growth*,
https://doi.org/10.1007/978-981-95-6220-6_13

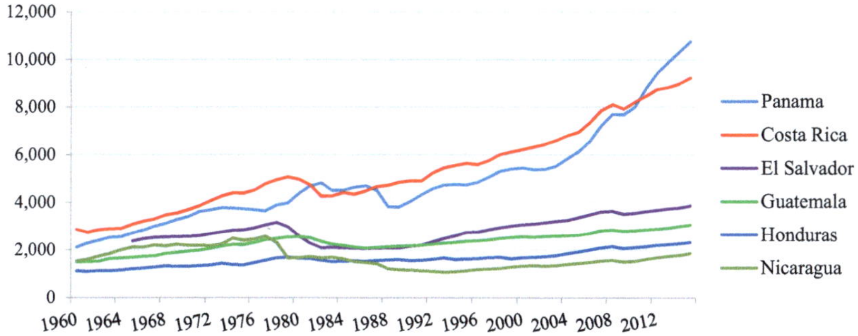


**Fig. 13.1** Per-capita GDP of Central American countries (Constant 2010 USD). *Source* Author's compilation from WDI (2017a, b)

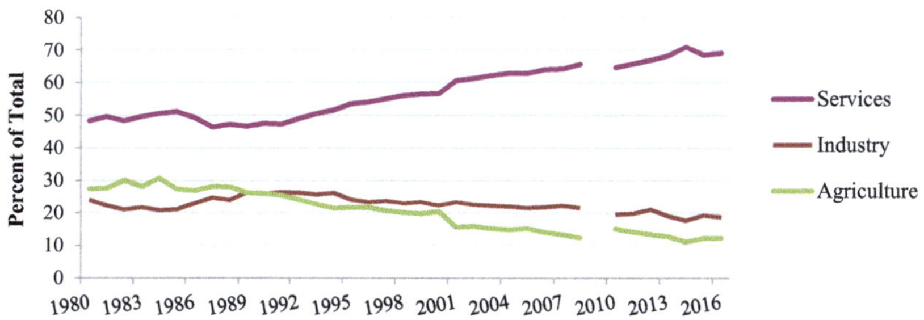


**Fig. 13.2** Composition of the Costa Rican labor force. *Source* Author's compilation from WDI (2017a, b)

scrapped import substitution industrialization (ISI) as the cornerstone of its economic development strategy and strove to tap new export markets via several trade agreements. It simultaneously sought to attract much-needed FDI by introducing a free trade zone regime in 1981 and establishing an autonomous investment promotion agency—the Costa Rican Coalition of Development Initiatives (CINDE).[1] This historic shift in economic policy has had a salutary effect: trade now makes up over half of Costa Rica's GDP, even as Costa Rica has become one of the most FDI-intensive economies in the world (Fig. 13.3) (Oviedo et al. 2015).

[1] The following is a partial list of countries with which Costa Rica has concluded trade agreements: Iceland, Liechtenstein, Norway, and Switzerland (2013); Colombia (2013); the EU (2012); Mexico (2011); Peru (2011); China (2010); Singapore (2010); and the US (DR-CAFTA 2004). However, the US remains the country's principal export market, accounting for 25% of its intermediate goods exports in 2015—up from 20.7% in 2008—and 46.47% of its manufactures exports—up from 39.15% in 2008 (World Integrated Trade Solution: WITS Database. Accessed August 17, 2017).

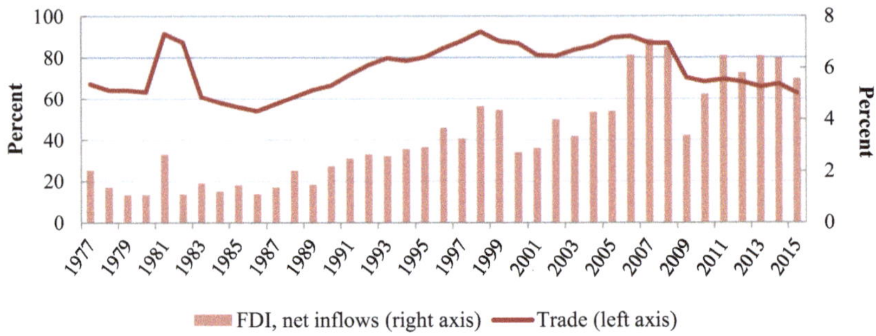


**Fig. 13.3** Trade & FDI as a share of Costa Rican GDP. *Source* Author's compilation from WDI (2017a, b)

A notable feature of Costa Rica's economic development is how rapidly the export sector has come to encompass more advanced manufacturing. In the context of ISI, manufacturing exports to fellow members of the Central American Common Market increased to the extent that Costa Rica's industrial production had already begun to branch out into higher value-added chemicals/chemical products and fabricated metals (Paus 2014). Exports of textiles and clothing, mainly to the US, also expanded appreciably and propped up the country's total exports after the demise of the captive Central American Common Market in the 1970s. In conjunction with the government—expressly, the administration of President José María Figueres (1994–98)—CINDE reacted adroitly to the ensuing decline of textile maquiladoras by shifting focus to FDI that could kick-start advanced non-traditional exports.[2] Costa Rica's propitious location, decent levels of human capital, alluring incentives for businesses (at least for foreign firms), and peaceful/stable political environment have been indelible selling points in this regard.

A seminal moment in Cost Rica's modernization drive came in 1996 when Intel—after coaxing from President Figueres' administration and CINDE—selected Costa Rica as the site for a microchip assembly and testing plant. That decision, as one retelling puts it, heralded the largest ever private project in Costa Rica (USD 770 million as of 2005) and catalyzed "realignment of the country's competitive platform as an investment location" (MIGA 2006). To underscore this point, manufacturing exports in total merchandise exports jumped from 25.4% in 1996 to 68% in 1999 (World Bank Development Indicators 2017a, b; Mosley 2011). Intel's entry into Costa Rica is also credited with putting the country "on the map" of fabricators of mid- to high-technology goods.

Nowadays, Costa Rica boasts several—mostly foreign—firms specializing in electronics and electric components (including integrated circuits/wires and low

[2] Dr. Roy C. Nelson provides an exhaustive overview of early efforts to obtain FDI in the book, *Harnessing Globalization: The Promotion of Nontraditional Foreign Direct Investment in Latin America* (University Park: Pennsylvania State University Press, 2009).

voltage protection equipment); office machine parts; film/broadcasting equipment; medical devices and orthopedic appliances; aerospace/aeronautics; automotive parts (namely, internal combustion piston engines); and life sciences products (Freund and Moran 2017; The Observatory on Economic Complexity). By 2015, exports of high-tech manufactured products had grown to 16.8% of total exports—a four-fold increase from 4% in 1996 (WDI 2017a, b).[3]

Services are also a major part of Costa Rica's exports and ongoing structural transformation, making up 43% of total gross exports in 2017 (WITS, World Bank). A variety of offshore shared/back-office business processes—including call centers, accounting, payroll, and engineering/design services—plus software development, other research/development activities, and ICT have grown markedly. As an illustration, services-related FDI inflows increased from 0.7% of GDP as of 1997–1999 to 34.6% of GDP in 2012–2014 (OECD 2016b).

At the same time, Costa Rica's tourism/hospitality sector continues to thrive owing to the country's commendable efforts in parlaying its ecological grandeur—as one of the most bio-diverse nations in the world—and farsighted environmental stewardship into an internationally recognizable brand of eco-tourism. After steadily growing from the mid-2000s to mid-2010s, tourism directly comprised 5–6% of GDP in 2016—although its total economic contribution was conceivably much bigger given a large multiplier effect—and the sector garners more foreign exchange than coffee, bananas, and pineapples (World Travel and Tourism Council 2017; OECD 2016b). Crucially, the generally conscientious and grassroots development of tourism/hospitality has allowed local communities to be more fully incorporated into—and hence benefit from—the sector (Miller 2012).

Agricultural production—long dominated by coffee and bananas,[4] followed by beef and sugar—has also become more varied to include tropical fruits, palm oil, ornamental plants, and processed agro-foods. Bolstered by the removal of import restrictions and expanded access to overseas markets, Costa Rica's agro-food exports have grown steadily, and its agricultural sector now ranks among the largest in the world on a per-capita export basis (OECD 2017a; Trejos 2013). In terms of productivity, the output gap between agricultural laborers and workers in other sectors had diminished by approximately 35% points by 2013 (Trejos 2013). Even so, the OECD (2017a) points out that value-added per agricultural laborer hardly changed from 1990–2012 as a more abundant, less-endowed subset of rural residents were harvesting traditional crops in lieu of higher-value alternatives that have imparted the bulk of productivity growth in the agricultural sector.

[3] High-tech exports declined after Intel shuttered its microchip assembly operations in Costa Rica in 2014. Also, the composition of FDI inflows tilted toward services after the 2007–08 GFC.

[4] In the 1960s, for example, coffee and bananas accounted for almost 90% of the total value of Costa Rican exports (Ferreira and Harrison 2012).

## 13.2 Growth and Inclusiveness

Costa Rica compares favorably with many other Latin American countries with regard to headline poverty, inequality, and living standards. Based on the internationally determined poverty line of USD 1.90 per day at the time, extreme poverty afflicted 1.6% of Costa Rican households in 2014—one of the lowest incidence rates in Latin America—after declining by the second fastest rate in the region during the mid- to late- 2000s (Trejos 2013).[5] Inequality also has been at the lower end of the regional spectrum.

Costa Rica's success in creating a middle-class society is also a significant achievement and represents a stark contrast vis-à-vis other Central American countries save for Panama. Dayton-Johnson (2015) estimates that growth of the Costa Rican middle class, as a percentage of the population, was one of the highest rates in the region from 2003 to 2008 (approximately 15%), and slightly more people entered the Costa Rican middle class between 2000 and 2010 than the country's per capita GDP growth would have implied (Perry 2014). Altogether, the middle class pocketed 53% of national income in 2009, the highest share in the Latin America region (Birdsall 2012). Viewed from a longer time horizon, Costa Rica had the fourth highest rate of intra-generational mobility in Latin America between 1989 and 2009, although the lion's share came from people exiting poverty but not earning enough to be considered part of the middle class—which entails a risk of lapsing back into poverty (Ferreira et al. 2013).

Costa Rica's steadfast attention to social welfare is habitually referenced as central to the comparatively high living standards of its citizens and the country's impressive economic inroads. Social spending as a percentage of GDP—20.9% in 2013, of which education expenditures alone were 5.5% of GDP[6]—is among the highest in Central America and on par with many member-countries of the OECD (World Bank Educational Global Practice 2015). Consequently, Costa Rica boasts stellar health outcomes—in some instances exceeding the regional average (including on child and maternal mortality) while rivaling high-income countries in others (especially on life expectancy). By 2004, Costa Rica stood out among Central American countries for having the lowest percentage of people without any formal education; conversely, literacy is nearly universal in the country, while its gender gap in academic attainment has essentially closed (Rennhack and Offerdal 2004). In line with these accomplishments, Costa Rica's HDI trended upward throughout the 2010s, reaching 0.766—66th place globally—in 2014 (UNDP 2015).

The extent to which Costa Ricans of lesser means have benefitted from the country's economic gains has varied widely and demonstrated sensitivity to the

[5] The extreme poverty incidence rate was 6.7% in 2014 per Costa Rica's nationally determined poverty threshold. Chile had the lowest extreme poverty rate (0.92%) in Latin America as of 2013 and experienced the fastest proportional decline in extreme poverty based on the USD 1.90 per day threshold over the time period under review.

[6] Education expenditures later increased to nearly 8% of GDP and 40% of total government expenditures.

prevailing rate and sources of GDP growth, price adjustments, and social transfers from the government. The country made substantial strides in reducing poverty immediately after structural reforms were first adopted in the 1980s: relative poverty declined from 32% in 1989 to 23% in 1994, and extreme poverty dropped from 9.9% to 6.6% over the same period (World Bank 2006). Throughout the following decade, amid rather buoyant but volatile GDP growth, poverty reduction stalled and inequality increased—with the Gini coefficient settling at 48.92 in 2004 (from 46.75 in 1994). With regard to income distribution, the poorest 40% of Costa Ricans saw their per-capita incomes grow by an average of 1.9% per year from 1988 to 2007, while annual income growth averaged 3.3% for the entire population and 3.6% for the richest 40% (Cornick and Trejos 2009).

An opportune external economic environment coincided with an uptick in income growth of poor Costa Rican households in the early 2000s. The income growth of the bottom 40% averaged 6% from 2003–07, among the best performances in Latin America and well above the average rate of income growth (3.9%) for the country as a whole. Even Costa Rica's poorest regions experienced relatively strong income growth from 2003–07, with that of the poorest 40% in some of the poorest areas reaching as high as 10% (Oviedo et al. 2015). In sum, the 3.8% point reduction in poverty that occurred from 2001–07 was mostly driven by economic growth and supplemented by declining inequality (the Gini coefficient fell from 51.1 in 2001 to 49.49 in 2007). On the other hand, rising food prices and poverty line price adjustments detracted from poverty reduction during this time period (Oviedo et al. 2015).

Whereas growth favored the less well-off prior to the GFC of 2007–08, higher-earning households experienced more income growth between 2010 and 2014 (Fig. 13.4). Incomes of the richest grew noticeably faster then than before the crisis (Oviedo et al. 2015). When homing in on the lowest and highest ends of the national income distribution, per-capita income disparities did not budge from 2000–12: the poorest 10% of households took in little more than 1.5% of national income during their peak years of 2007 and 2008, while the top 10% of households amassed no less than 35% of national income. Per-capita consumption growth of the poor was marginally better in 2013–2014 but still fell behind that of middle- and upper-middle-income households (Oviedo et al. 2015).

Perhaps unsurprisingly, both relative and extreme poverty increased in Costa Rica after the 2009 recession—from 21.3% to 22.4% and 5.8% to 6.7%, respectively (Oviedo et al. 2015). In fact, Costa Rica was one of only four Latin American countries in which poverty reduction stagnated from 2010–14 (Mexico, Honduras, and Venezuela were the others) and one of just two countries in the region to experience rising inequality from the early to late 2000s (inequality also increased in Honduras before falling swiftly after 2013) (Fig. 13.5) (Williams 2016).

From a geographical standpoint, poverty is a decidedly rural phenomenon in Costa Rica. In 2014, due to higher inflation and an ensuing loss of purchasing

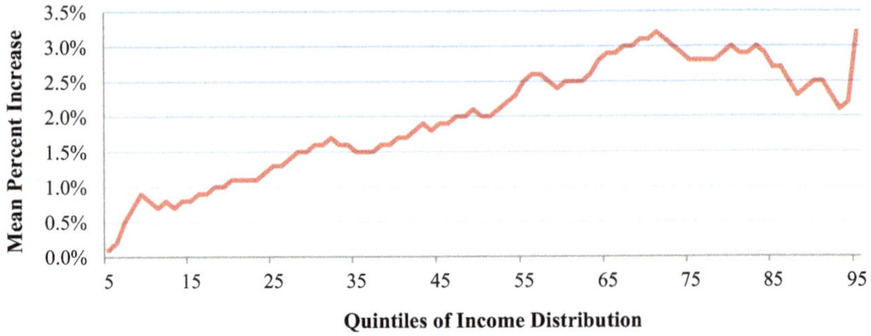


**Fig. 13.4** Growth incidence curve for Costa Rica, 2010–14*. *Source* Author's compilation from World Bank LAC Equity Lab tabulations of Socioeconomic Database for Latin America and the Caribbean [Center for Distributive, Labor and Social Studies]. *Growth incidence curves depict the annualized growth in mean per-capita income at different points/percentiles along the national income distribution, in this case expressed as quintiles. Lower quintiles on the horizontal axis denote successively less affluent income groupings

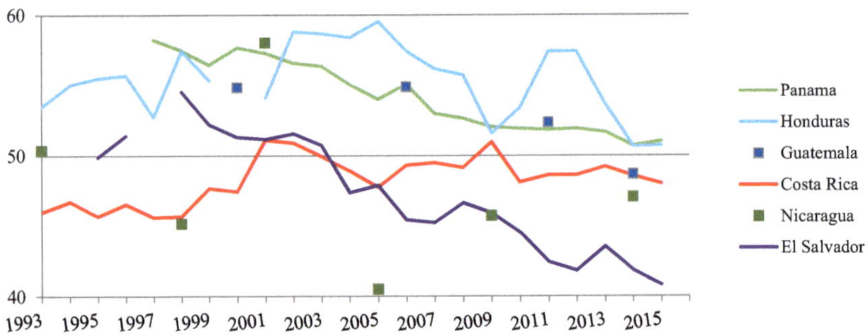


**Fig. 13.5** Gini coefficients of Central American countries *Source* Author's compilation from WDI (2017a, b)

power,[7] the poverty headcount in the countryside hit a post-crisis peak of 30.3%—a 2.5% increase from 2013—compared to 19.5% in urban areas (an increase of only 1.3% from 2013), and extreme poverty in rural areas (10.6%) was more than double that of cities (5.2%). By 2016, as rural income growth narrowly outpaced urban income growth (3.6% and 2.4%, respectively) because of lower inflation and government subsidies, roughly a quarter of rural households (25.7%) fell below the nationally determined poverty line versus 18.6% of urban households. Important variations exist within aggregated rural poverty data, however, as regions at the northern and southern extremities of the country are among its poorest and most

[7] Inflation exceeded 5% at end-2014 before dropping precipitously in 2015 due to declining oil prices.

unequal. For instance, the southernmost region of Brunca had the highest poverty rate (31.2%) in 2016 while Huetar Norte, in the far north, had the highest percentage of households living in extreme poverty (11.2%) (INEC 2014; INEC 2016). Historically, rural areas are also home to a larger share of the 'chronically' poor—i.e., those born into and remaining in poverty. In absolute terms, though, this group was roughly equal in size to the analogous urban cohort as of 2014–16—implying a widespread paucity of jobs for low-skilled workers (Vakis et al. 2015).

The livelihoods of vast swathes of Costa Rican smallholder farmers and other rural workers remain wedded to traditional agricultural goods sold domestically, including low-grade varieties of coffee, fruits, corn, rice, sorghum, and beans. Low productivity and limited connectivity with outside markets; scant knowledge of, or ability to meet, rigorous export product standards; high costs for fuel, fertilizer, and irrigation; as well as constrained access to credit prevent many smallholder farmers from diversifying their incomes. Meanwhile, feeble rural road networks inflict onerous transport costs, and too few warehouses/distribution centers or cold chain facilities keep them from their switching to more profitable but perishable export products. The public extension services and technical assistance that smallholder farmers do receive afford incomplete coverage, both geographically and in relation to their subject matter, while weak coordination among involved institutions further undercuts their effectiveness (OECD 2017a).

Government tariff and price-support policies, through which a large share of agricultural funding is channeled, tend to reinforce rather than assuage the sector's stratified structure. For example, whereas price controls and import levies for rice are intended to safeguard food security by incentivizing rice production, they end up disproportionately benefiting large-scale domestic rice producers and erode the purchasing power of both the rural and urban poor. Similarly, a state-mandated preference system and regulatory regime for sugar favor large-scale domestic sugar growers to the detriment of their smallholder counterparts (OECD 2017a).

It should be noted that indigenous smallholder farmers face added challenges heightening their vulnerability to falling into (or remaining in) poverty. Case in point: Bribri farmers in Talamanca, along the southern Atlantic coast, have experienced recurrent threats of forcible eviction from their ancestral lands, which prompted the United Nations Committee on Economic, Social, and Cultural Rights to issue a formal rebuke in 2016 while also calling for stronger protections of indigenous land rights (Anders 2016).

The plight of undocumented Nicaraguan migrants is also integral to poverty dynamics in Costa Rica. Initially sparked by a devastating earthquake that struck Managua in 1972, the southward trek of thousands of Nicaraguans to Costa Rica was sustained over later decades by political repression/upheaval and poor economic conditions in their home country. Nicaraguans living in Costa Rica have steadily numbered around 300,000—or roughly 7.8% of Costa Rica's total population—since 2005, meaning they comprise nearly 75% of all foreign residents (Sandoval-García 2015). Nicaraguan migrants have customarily worked for relatively low wages in agriculture and construction, as well as domestic servants. They tend to possess less schooling than native-born Costa Ricans, and their children are usually enrolled in primary and secondary school at lower rates—79% and 45%, respectively, as of 2006—which reduces their chances of entering better-paying occupations (OECD 2017b). Predictably, poverty typically is more prevalent among Nicaraguan migrant families than the native-born population. One reliable, albeit dated, estimate holds that approximately 30% of all Nicaraguan immigrants lived in poverty in 2006—with 9% living in extreme poverty (Marquette 2006). Proportionally, most impoverished Nicaraguan migrants reside in the Central/San José region but large concentrations also live in the northern regions of Huetar Atlántica, Huetar Norte, and Chorotega.

Restricted access to social services contributes to the insecurity of Nicaraguan migrants, with one-third of them lacking the required legal status to claim public benefits. Per Law 8764 on Migration, approved by the Legislative Assembly in 2010 and in effect since 2012, the Costa Rican Social Security Fund is obliged to restrict the provision of healthcare services to those who are in the country legally (Bravo 2016). Under this statute, unauthorized migrants can regularize their status and gain access to public services by obtaining employment-based temporary residency permits; however, cumbersome rules (especially for hiring domestic workers), complications in gathering required documentation, high application costs (mainly for migrants), and the lack of compliance incentives for businesses (as fees for hiring unauthorized foreigners have little enforceability), mean undocumented migrants can encounter de jure barriers to accessing social services. Nicaraguan migrants who can lawfully access social services may also face difficulties in doing so because of, inter alia, the transient nature of agricultural work and sheer demand overload—which can mean they are left to pay out of pocket for healthcare (Sandoval-García 2015). Indigenous communities' irregular access to public health and education services likewise reveals the limits of Costa Rica's supposedly universal social security system.

Gender, alongside changes in household structure and evolving labor market dynamics, also influences who experiences poverty in Costa Rica. As the country's transition to more advanced manufacturing and services was picking up steam in the late 1990s, a growing prevalence of female-headed single-parent households led to a multitude of women looking for jobs but "unable to find or unwilling to accept full-time work in the higher-paying formal sector"—with their 'unwillingness' naturally linked to child-rearing duties. For the most part, these women ended up unemployed or laboring as part-time and/or self-employed workers, which are categories highly correlated with poverty (Gindling and Oviedo 2008). Notably, even though women collectively have more education than men, their participation in the labor force has only averaged about 45% (Monge-González 2016). This not only makes Cost Rica a regional laggard with respect to female participation in the labor force, but it also means female-headed households disproportionately bear the brunt of (extreme) poverty.

Differences in academic achievement also underpin a divergence of personal fortunes in Costa Rica's changing economy. A sizable fraction of young people—8.4% as of 2016—leaves secondary school prematurely, many times compelled by personal circumstances to eke out a living. Adolescents who do not finish their studies are typically males from socioeconomically-underprivileged households—e.g., households with a woman head and/or five or more members—and whose parents did not complete school themselves. By the end of the elementary years, 30% of students had already dropped out of school (OECD 2017b). By 2013, 56% of the Costa Rican workforce did not have a high school diploma, and an even larger percentage (71%) had not obtained any post-secondary education (Williams 2016).

Costa Rica's secondary school dropouts tend to either work at smaller, less productive locally-owned firms or set up their own, often informal, enterprises out of necessity—causing a yawning wage gap between them and their better-educated compatriots who can find formal employment in the burgeoning export sector or with public/government agencies.[8] Average wages at firms operating within the free trade zone regime were found to be nearly double what other private sector workers earned in 2015, having increased by 7% from the year before (although real wage growth in 2015 was lower due to inflation) (CINDE 2016).

Rising informality in Costa Rica is conspicuously out of sync with the rest of Latin America, where school enrollment swelled ever since the 1990s. Although less pervasive than in many other Latin American countries, informality in Costa Rica had surged and drew in 1.5 million people—or 46% of total employment—as of 2016. Domestic services and agriculture are the main outlets for informal labor in the country (OECD 2017c). Like in other countries, the problems posed by informality go beyond the perpetuation of personal insecurity to depriving state coffers of essential funds for furnishing public goods[9] and deterring skills development, productivity growth, and job creation.

Unfortunately, public transfers have not been particularly effective in ameliorating inequality or helping the poor cope with shocks.[10] Lustig (2017) finds that fiscal interventions—inclusive of all taxes, transfers, public education, and health services—lowered the market income-based Gini coefficient by 10% points in 2010. However, the OECD (2016c) posits that taxes and cash transfers only reduced the Gini coefficient by 4% in 2013. Oviedo et al. (2015) similarly construe that social assistance had little impact on inequality before 2012 and became

[8] Avenues exist for secondary school dropouts to re-enter the public education system, but the burden of work and other responsibilities along with course repetition cause high attrition rates for programs targeting these individuals.

[9] Informal workers do not pay income taxes or contribute to the social insurance system, which is mainly funded through payroll taxes; additionally, the burden that social security taxes represent for employers (25% of employees' salaries/wages) is a deterrent to informal enterprises transitioning into formal ones.

[10] The growth of the middle class in Costa Rica is not disconnected from domestic political trends or how the government spends money. Dr. John Booth relates that middle class interests acquired "unprecedented political clout" in the decades after the 1948 civil war, in part through the expansion of the state as this opened up administrative positions in the public sector that allowed for a middle-class standard of living. This observation provides a useful political-economy insight into the Costa Rican government's difficulties in directing social spending to the poor. See page 98 of Booth, John A., *Costa Rica: Quest for Democracy* (Boulder: Westview Press, 1998).

regressive thereafter—mainly due to defective targeting and leakage of social program benefits resulting from poor institutional coordination.

Clearly, Costa Rica's ongoing transition toward more skills-intensive manufacturing and services has not taken place without ramifications in how income derived from these growing sectors is distributed. Consecutive generations of Costa Ricans—e.g., smallholder farmers, other rural laborers, women foregoing steady work because of household obligations, or secondary school dropouts with inadequate education/skills—have encountered difficulties entering into the formal labor force. Likewise, local businesses have fared less well overall than Costa Rica's export data might suggest (as will be discussed later).

It stands to reason that openness to trade/FDI is not enough to power broad-based economic growth. For this, public policy ought to uplift those individuals with the weakest chances of finding gainful employment in emerging industries. Social assistance measures, together with government spending writ large, do not uniformly abet inclusivity; as a matter of fact, increases in public sector salaries after the 2009 recession drove much of the observed growth in inequality from 2010–14 (OECD 2016c). Encouragingly, the Costa Rican government has occasionally delivered services and support to poor households and at-risk youth in a coordinated fashion.[11] This useful approach should be supplemented by other changes—such as better means testing, a more progressive tax rate structure, easier access to affordable daycare, and education reform—to make more readily available resources and incentives for empowering individuals to join the formal labor force. The suboptimal alternative would be too many Costa Ricans remaining locked out of, and unable to contribute to, a veritable engine of the economy.

## 13.3 Growth and Resilience

As a small, open economy, Costa Rica is vulnerable to exogenous shocks and depends on sound macroeconomic management to mitigate their impact; however, it has at times fallen short in this regard.

The country experienced a severe recession in the 1970s, precipitated by falling export revenues, surging oil prices, and the demise of the Central American Common Market on which ISI depended. The government acquired an unsustainable amount of external debt to try to counteract that recession, precipitating the 1980s balance of payments crisis and recession after international interest rates rose and

[11] The Ministry of Public Education launched a campaign in 2015, known as Yo Me Apunto Con La Educación/I'm in With Education, with support from the United Nations Children's Fund through which resources from a variety of government ministries and public agencies are channeled to at-risk youth and low-performing 166 educational centers in 75 priority high poverty districts, covering 112,170 beneficiaries (OECD 2017b). The program's funding base is small relative to total public education expenditures and so would need to expand into other, untargeted areas of the country to reduce the dropout rate further—ideally after a cost–benefit analysis (CBA) determining whether it would be the best use of funds.

the country's terms of trade weakened once again. Per-capita output was on an upward path by the mid-1980s—in line with macroeconomic stabilization and public sector attempts to widen the productive base—but heightened economic volatility buffeted Costa Rica once again during the 1990s. Empirically, Costa Rica's growth volatility was nearly twice the regional average during the 1990s and rose from 1996 to 2001 pursuant turbulence in international coffee and electronics markets[12] plus increasing domestic interest rates aimed at quelling high inflation (World Bank 2006; IMF 2003).[13]

Except for sharply higher oil prices in 2007–08, the early 2000s afforded Costa Rica a respite to grow and further diversify its economy. Specifically, strong global trade and a favorable business cycle in the US—Costa Rica counts among the Central American economies most sensitive to fluctuations in the latter (Roache 2008)—translated into high external demand, robust FDI inflows, and rising private consumption (IMF 2006). The number of Costa Rica's FDI source countries grew in tandem, as did the number of electronics industry investors (with 56 *electronics* firms setting up operations in the country by 2007) (Nelson 2009). The Costa Rican government leveraged these auspicious global economic tailwinds by courting trading partners throughout East Asia, Europe, and within Latin America.[14] Around the same time, circa 2006, Costa Rica leapt into the highest per-capita income grouping of Latin American countries (OECD et al. 2017d).

The 2007–08 global financial collapse jettisoned the general calm that had characterized the international economic landscape at the start of the 2000s. For the first time since 1982, Costa Rican real GDP contracted in 2009 (−1.0%). Unemployment reached a 20-year high that year (7.8%) and poverty escalated in kind.[15] Encountering a drop in FDI and loss of business and consumer confidence, the Costa Rican government entered into a Stand-by Arrangement with the IMF to mitigate any balance of payments shocks (IMF 2009). However, it lapsed since the Costa Rican government did not draw upon the underlying loan.

A nascent economic recovery took shape as early as the second quarter of 2009, with real GDP declines moderating in the second quarter of that year. By 2010, Costa Rica had mustered real GDP growth of 5% and absolute per-capita GDP was again ascendant (these figures are based on IFS statistics for 2017). Fiscal stimulus was enacted to reinforce this recovery but ended up becoming quasi-permanent and pushed the central government's fiscal deficit to −5.3% of GDP by 2016.[16] Public debt, mostly denominated in local currency and of fairly long maturities, duly rose from 39.4% of GDP in 2008 to nearly 60% of GDP

[12] A supply glut resulted in heightened coffee price volatility from 1989 to 1997, with coffee prices bottoming out in 1996 (page 70 of Miller (2012) and IFS Database).

[13] Year-on-year inflation reached 22.5% in 1995.

[14] Please refer to footnote #1.

[15] To put the 2009 recession into perspective, the recession of the 1970s–80s was more severe in both depth and duration as depicted in Fig. 13.8.

[16] In contrast, fiscal surpluses of 0.6% and 0.2% of GDP were posted in 2007 and 2008, respectively.

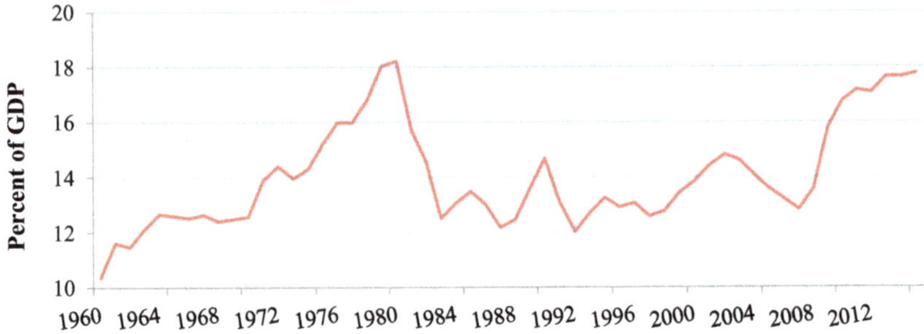


**Fig. 13.6** General government final consumption in Costa Rica's GDP. *Source* Author's compilation from WDI (2017a, b)

in 2016 (including pension-related debt). Accordingly, government's final consumption in the economy neared where it was in the late 1970s (Fig. 13.6). On the revenue side, tax policy constrained government revenues to just 22.3% of GDP in 2015—a relatively low figure for an upper-middle-income country—due to generous exemptions and inadequate taxation of services (Oviedo et al. 2015).

As a further indication of Costa Rica's impaired public finances at around this time, the country had one of the highest debt-service burdens in the world as of 2016—with loan repayments eating up approximately 19% of central government revenues that year.[17] Alas, the three main credit rating agencies repeatedly downgraded Costa Rican sovereign debt after 2013, causing the country's credit default swap spreads to spike.

Persistent fiscal profligacy and deficient tax revenues have together impaired the Costa Rican government's capacity to counteract economic headwinds, while also forestalling sensible course corrections in other policy areas that could help boost resilience—including a gradual transition away from dollarization and adoption of a fully flexible exchange rate regime. Tellingly, what modest fiscal restraint the Costa Rican government has managed to exercise often has come at the expense of capital expenditures, constituting a steep opportunity cost in view of foregone productivity growth and forsaken competitiveness (please see the next section for more information).

As alluded to previously, FDI inflows have been an unequivocal bright spot in Costa Rica's national accounts and show little sensitivity to the government's deteriorated fiscal position. After regressing in 2009 to 2003 levels, they recovered quickly but later plateaued as trade in GDP declined—consistent with slowing global trade growth (Fig. 13.3). Crucially, though, FDI inflows remained buoyant after Intel shuttered local microchip assembly operations in 2014. By then, the country had moved into other specialized manufactured products—chiefly medical devices—and offshore services investments had been growing since 2010

[17] Accommodative/loose monetary policy also led to a mini-boom in consumer credit—with credit card debt expanding by 20% (year-on-year) in October 2016.

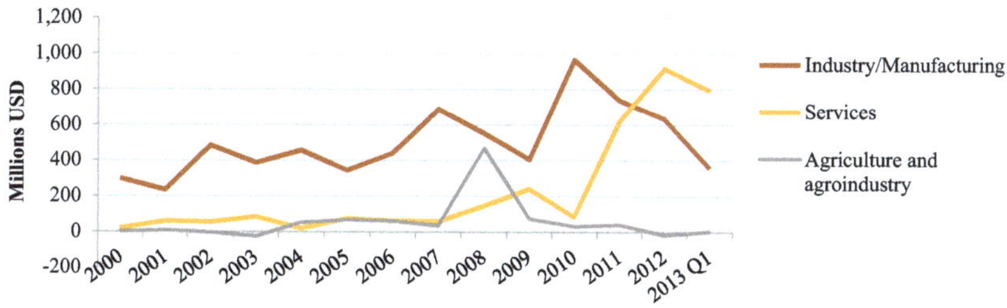


**Fig. 13.7** Composition of Costa Rica's FDI inflows, 2000—1st Quarter of 2013. *Source* Website of COMEX [Costa Rican Ministry of Foreign Trade]. *Please note that not all sectors that received FDI are shown in this graph

(Fig. 13.7). Clearly, FDI inflows and robust tourism receipts have made covering the chronic current account deficit (4% of GDP in 2015) less dependent on the vagaries of agricultural commodity markets—providing a welcome cushion for the balance of payments that was absent in the 1970s and 1980s.

In retrospect, Costa Rica bounced back rather quickly though not definitively from the recession that the 2007–08 GFC precipitated by undertaking fiscal stimulus and retaining sizable inflows of FDI. Nonetheless, much delayed fiscal consolidation—made difficult on political-economy grounds by how the stimulus was enacted—put future economic resiliency at risk and arguably forestalled stronger, more balanced GDP growth. As it did in the late 1970s and early 1980s, public policy took 'a turn towards a larger state'—albeit in favor of consumption instead of public investment/enterprise (World Bank 2006). It also bears mentioning here that copious inflows of foreign investment are not preordained and could quickly subside in the wake of external shocks.

## 13.4 Growth and Sustainability

Costa Rica has experienced approximately 47 years of positive per-capita GDP growth dating back to the early 1960s, as well as a minimum of six 'growth spurts' since then.[18] The longest growth spurt lasted for 13 years (from 1961 to 1973) while another lasted for 12 years (from 1997 to 2008). Yet per-capita GDP growth was only slightly higher than the regional average of 2.25% from 1999 to 2012 (Fig. 13.8). In short, Costa Rica has sustained a moderate pace of economic growth but has not undergone a structural growth lift-off capable of inducing rapid income convergence with developed economies—a striking divergence from the experiences of other middle-income countries, predominantly from East Asia, that have enmeshed themselves into sophisticated global value chains (GVCs).

[18] Growth spurts are defined as consecutive periods of positive annual GDP growth.

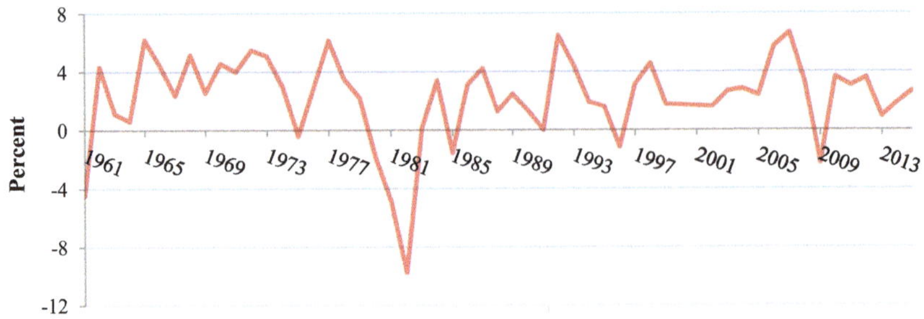


**Fig. 13.8** Costa Rica's per-capita GDP growth. *Source* Author's compilation from WDI (2017a, b) (Annual Percent Change)

Subdued total factor productivity (TFP) growth is key to understanding Costa Rica's record of oscillating per-capita income growth. Productivity levels suffered an abrupt drop-off in the mid-1970s and early 1980s, a repercussion of the economic doldrums of that period, and later turned positive—but not inexorably so—due to structural reforms and, to a lesser extent, improvements in education (World Bank 2006). By the late 1990s, after Intel made its inaugural investment in the country, Costa Rica posted higher TFP growth—more than 4% in 1999—only to see it nudge downward thereafter (Penn World Tables). Productivity picked up once again in the mid-2000s, surpassing the regional average by 40% in 2005. Yet TFP decelerated sharply following the 2007–08 GFC and even contracted in 2008–09, 2011–12, and 2014 (Fig. 13.9).

By international comparison, Costa Rica's TFP growth has recurrently fallen behind that of Chile, Colombia, Mexico, and Peru (Daude and Fernández-Arias 2010). In addition, the country has experienced a drawn-out productivity gap vis-à-vis the US that accounts for about a fifth of the difference in per-capita incomes between the two countries (Daude and Fernández-Arias 2010).

Against a backdrop of lackluster TFP growth, absolute increases in capital and labor were responsible for no less than 75% of Costa Rica's real GDP growth over nearly five decades through the mid-2010s (Monge-González 2016). Of those two inputs, capital accumulation has contributed more to Costa Rica's real GDP growth historically (Penn World Tables).

On a sectoral basis, manufacturing and services have performed asymmetrically when it comes to. Ureña and Quesada (2015) posit that whereas manufacturing productivity has been converging unconditionally with that of the US, service sector productivity declined from the early 1970s to the 2000s and only turned positive in the 2010s. Araujo et al. (2016) attribute this turnaround to the presence of foreign firms in certain types of services, such as retail and wholesale trade.[19]

[19] Araujo et al. (2016) look at labor productivity rather than TFP, and their analysis does not consider the growth of offshore business services in Costa Rica over the last several years.

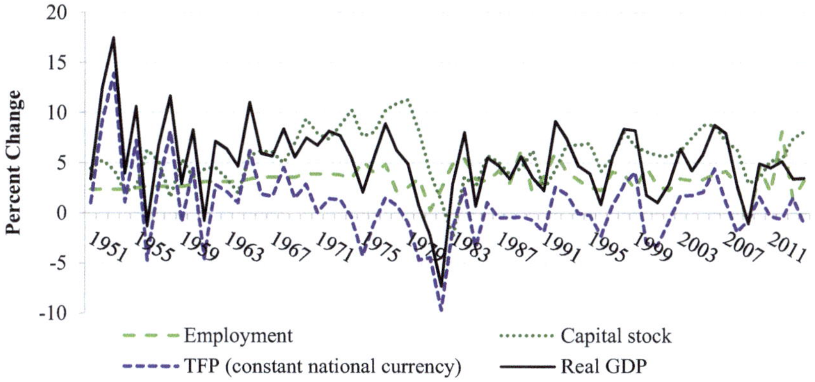


**Fig. 13.9** Capital, labor & TFP in Costa Rica's real GDP growth. *Source* Author's compilation from Penn World Tables

Costa Rica's predicament of having to contend with a growing but fairly inefficient services sector is not all that different from other Latin American countries. Nearly all economies from the region faced declining TFP growth from 1990 to the mid-2000s, as labor and capital moved from industry/manufacturing into services. Costa Rica managed to sustain positive productivity growth over the same period—notwithstanding contractions in 1994–96 and 2000–02—by dint of efficiencies realized in retail and wholesale trade (Araujo et al. 2016).

Costa Rica's meager rates of productivity growth over the years have been the consequence, at least in part, of limited labor mobility. Scarcely a third of Costa Rica's labor productivity growth from 1990 to 2005 resulted from labor shifts between sectors (Araujo et al. 2016). One reason why labor has not been very mobile is that an outsized number of Costa Ricans lack the credentials relevant to gaining employment in the export sector or undertaking other, more remunerative formal work. Costa Ricans had just 8.4 years of formal education overall as of 2013, fully two to four years less than their counterparts in 'technologically oriented' countries—e.g., Finland, Japan, the US, Ireland, South Korea, and Singapore (Monge-González 2016)—which presages a prolonged inability to foster the productivity improvements imperative for structural transformation.

Besides the aforementioned secondary school dropout scourge, the middling performance of students who opt to stay in school also weighs on Costa Rica's productivity performance. Despite placing third within Latin America in the 2015 iteration of the OECD's Programme for International Student Assessment (PISA), the country registered across-the-board declines in its average scores for reading (−14 points), mathematics (−7 points), and science (−9 points) compared to 2012—the first year PISA was administered in Costa Rica. Just as problematic, half of assessed students did not have basic proficiency in reading and science, and Costa Rican pupils scored far lower in each subject area than students from OECD member-states in the aggregate. As with secondary school enrollment, socioeconomic status proved pivotal in how well students did on the 2015 PISA round:

juveniles in the bottom socioeconomic quintile scored about 2.5 years of schooling below their peers in the top quintile (World Bank 2016). The shortcomings of the public education system in Costa Rica include scarce incentives for teachers to improve their performance and too little funding for pedagogical materials. Clearly, its capability to nurture socio-economic mobility and develop the human capital necessary for sustained and accelerated GDP growth, along with income convergence with advanced economies is showing signs of strain.

Limited knowledge and technology spillovers from foreign firms are also distinguishing features of Costa Rica's immersion into global commerce. Barriers to entry are often insurmountable for domestic firms that, on the whole, do not embody the size, quality, or reliability foreign companies seek in prospective suppliers. In response to this void, manufacturers of electrical equipment, electronics, and medical devices—to name but a few notable examples—source most inputs from abroad apart from local purchases of low valued-added products and services—explicitly, packaging and printing materials, office supplies, security, cleaning, and food (OECD 2016b). Succinctly stated, assorted varieties of advanced manufacturing have not grown enough to offset a decline in Costa Rica's traditional merchandise exports, prompting the country's share of global trade to fall relative to the early 2000s (IMF 2013; The Observatory on Economic Complexity).

With export-oriented manufacturing centered mostly on assembly, tradable services account for most of the value-addition occurring within the Costa Rican economy. The domestic value-added content of business services in total gross industry exports reached 90.7% in 2011, much higher than the 55% for computer and electronics exports—while the domestic services content of gross exports had been growing gradually through that year (International Trade Organization 2011). In spite of this, there are signs that Costa Rica has not irreversibly broken into higher value-added segments of the burgeoning offshore/business service sector—one of which is the continued predominance of multinational corporations and foreign-based outsourcing firms. Human capital limitations—such as circumscribed contingents of English language speakers, business school graduates, and ICT engineers—are a principal reason for this (Fernandez-Stark et al. 2013).

One can surmise that Costa Rica has not crafted a coherent strategy for supporting domestic firms' export prowess, including by inserting themselves into GVCs. The inability to compel a critical mass of domestic firms to become more productive is a longstanding weakness of Costa Rica's economic development aspirations dating back to the ISI period. During that earlier era, and unlike Costa Rica's faster-growing East Asian contemporaries, the government protected local firms from competition but did not force them to cultivate international competitiveness (Paus and Gallagher 2008). It also extended many carrots—in the form of subsidized credit and tax exemptions—to a few privileged homegrown firms but did not enforce 'disciplining mechanisms' to ensure they used these incentives as anticipated (Paus 2014). By evolving in a way that the beneficiaries of state largesse simply switched nationalities, Costa Rica's subsidization of production has not appreciably amplified the productivity of domestic firms or encouraged technological/knowledge spillovers to the degree necessary to jumpstart higher value-added production among a preponderance of local firms.

Nor has Costa Rica been able to convincingly exploit incipient breakthroughs in learning and innovation to move forward expeditiously in global product and service markets. Two noteworthy efforts to augment domestic firms' participation in international commerce commenced shortly after Costa Rica dispensed with ISI: the Program for Strengthening the Innovation and Technological Development of SMEs (PROPYME), established in 2002, and the Supplier Development Project for High-Technology Multinational Companies (Costa Rica [CR] Provee), launched in 1999 but housed within the Foreign Trade Corporation of Costa Rica (PROCOMER) since 2003. Both PROPYME and CR Provee try to rectify market failures so that targeted firms can export outright or sell goods and services in-country to foreign companies. Whereas PROPYME subsidizes investments in R&D to increase SMEs' technical competence, CR Provee directly facilitates linkages with foreign businesses. Monge-González and Rodríguez-Álvarez (2013) find that PROPYME and CR Provee have had positive but modest effects on beneficiary firms' labor demand, average wages, and export propensity (66); however, they also cite weaknesses in the design or implementation of each and maintain that the small size and disjointed implementation of each undercuts their utility. Moreover, bureaucratic inefficiencies have impeded smooth disbursement of public grants meant to help SMEs acquire costly certifications—though not necessarily under PROPYME.

Public universities also sponsor R&D for innovation purposes, with the University of Costa Rica's Office of Management and Knowledge Transfer for Innovation, well known for facilitating the transfer of intellectual property in various scientific sub-disciplines and engineering that is generated from across that university's specialized research units. However, here too limited interaction with the private sector curtails spillovers on the latter's aptitude to internalize new manufacturing processes (OECD 2017c). Disagreements over copyright ownership and licensing also have held back dual-track research projects. Relatedly, bottlenecks in higher education restrict the ranks of individuals with the experience and education sought by foreign firms. Anecdotal evidence indicates that public universities are reluctant to cater to increasingly stringent labor market demands—nor are they required to do so as autonomous institutions—while private universities are limited in how quickly or by how much they can adapt their curriculums. Adding to this stasis is a lack of university staff with the mandatory expertise in critical fields—another sign that the looming scarcity of skills within the Costa Rican labor force will persist for some time.

Rectifying these pitfalls calls for a 'whole-of-government' approach. For starters, reducing the regulatory burden on locally owned firms would be appropriate, as would offering them easier access to benefits under the free trade zone regime. In the same vein, Costa Rican authorities should reconsider regulations that inhibit true competition in services like logistics/transport, banking, insurance, and telecommunications—for they limit productivity growth and opportunities for firm-level linkages. Such regulations also restrain the scope and speed with which the country can exploit cutting-edge overlaps between manufacturing and services (OECD 2016a).

More systematic identification of, and responsiveness to, knowledge gaps as well as other impediments within the private sector is a necessary complement to regulatory reforms. Interventions to this effect could take the form of well-honed grant and technical cooperation programs for business development, R&D projects, worker training, and guarantee/trade finance schemes conducive to unlocking financing for medium-sized firms—which have difficulties accessing commercial loans. Where feasible, promising though under-utilized information-sharing platforms and matchmaking services that help multinational corporations incorporate local enterprises into their supplier networks also merit scaling up.

A redoubling of efforts to acquire the core competencies central to higher value-added activities, accompanied by attempts to discern how ICT/software and ancillary services meld with manufacturing, would also be worthwhile. Comprehensive and well-sequenced initiatives along these lines may even help export-oriented manufacturing transcend its dependence on a small basket of products and compensate for extant obstacles to its growth—including a dearth of regional production networks, high electricity/logistics costs, and the small size of the domestic market/labor pool.

Remedying inadequacies and logjams in the education system should also figure prominently in an invigorated national 'upgrading' agenda. Costa Rica's reliance on the talents of its people to achieve high-income status is not overtly apparent in the skills profile of the country's labor force. Steps to secure better outcomes for primary and secondary education expenditures are essential, and tertiary curriculums ought to be reoriented toward strategic growth sectors. The forging of deeper linkages between universities and the private sector—including on upstream research/development—could also go a long way in relieving constraints to higher value-added production and greater quality employment (Engel and Taglioni 2017).

## 13.5 Conclusion

Costa Rica has sustained economic growth for the better part of the last fifty years, permitting a preponderance of its people to escape poverty and enjoy middle-class living standards by avoiding kinds of self-inflicted setbacks that have bedeviled many neighboring countries. Political and macroeconomic stability combined with astute investments in public goods—other hallmarks of good governance—have made this exemplary progress possible, as has an emphatic embrace of foreign markets and investment.

However, Costa Rica's progress to date has fallen short along each of the dimensions of quality growth. Having demurred in crafting a cohesive plan for elevating economy-wide productivity, Costa Rica likewise has not proactively dealt with the skewed income distribution that arose from its participation in manufacturing and service-based GVCs. In this manner, public policy and the institutions charged with its execution have not kept pace with the multi-faceted exigencies instigated by structural transformation. Nor has enough attention been dedicated to linking smallholder farmers with non-traditional agricultural product markets. The development of off-farm activities, like small-scale processing and eco-tourism enticing vacationers to visit lesser-known rural areas of the country, is also negligible (OECD 2017a).

Tackling the acute needs of other marginalized groups—primarily indigenous communities and Nicaraguan immigrants—is also important, and a practicable way to do so is via a package of coordinated interventions similar to that of the 'Yo me Apunto Con La Educaci6n' campaign.[20] As for the latter group, since the informal status of many Nicaraguan immigrants makes reaching them more difficult, improvements to the legal/institutional framework for immigration—including by incentivizing legal residency in a way that better addresses private sector hiring needs, reducing the cost of adjusting one's immigration status, and working with the Nicaraguan government to expedite the conveyance of documentation needed to complete this regularization process—are also warranted.

Costa Rica can forge more inclusive, resilient, and sustained growth by improving domestic capabilities on multiple fronts. The country has a bifurcated labor market that is split between a comparatively small cadre of well-educated, highly paid professionals and a much larger faction of less educated/skilled workers with more precarious livelihoods. It is worth emphasizing that aside from dampening inclusiveness, the subdued secondary school completion rate for impoverished and vulnerable Costa Ricans suppresses human capital formation and productivity growth—with the potential of becoming a binding constraint to (per-capita) GDP growth by limiting the country's wherewithal to absorb innovation.[21]

Equally vexing, flaws in Costa Rica's fiscal framework culminated in hefty deficits and the attendant accumulation of public debt after 2009 that, inter alia, preclude the public investments necessary for enhancing competitiveness. Indeed, the displacement of public (infrastructure) investment can dilute the growth-enhancing effect of foreign capital by preventing it from becoming more tightly interwoven into domestic production frameworks.

Furthermore, the rather fragmented nature of Costa Rica's public sector undercuts its effectiveness at supporting domestic firms' upskilling to the degree necessary for the fields in which the country has established a foothold—with negative implications for the inclusivity and sustainability of economic growth. Closer alignment between parts of the public sector focused on FDI/export promotion and those with a more domestic mandate is needed, so that both the country's vibrant export sector may be more evenly balanced between the contributions of foreign

[20] Please refer to footnote #11.

[21] Nearly half of formal firms surveyed in 2015 reported difficulties in finding well-qualified staff for their job openings. See page 34 of OECD, Inter-American Development Bank, and Global Forum on Productivity, "Boosting Productivity and Inclusive Growth in Latin America" (2017).

and local firms and GDP growth can regain momentum.[22] Regardless of their precise contours, proactively coordinated policies/programs depicting a clear division of responsibilities among public institutions and provisions to hold them accountable can no longer be the exception if Costa Rica is to strengthen its position in the international economy.

Coordinated efforts to enhance local productive and innovation capacities, implement sound fiscal policy, improve the quality of education, and deliver more effective social assistance are both urgent and essential for Costa Rica to meet the challenges of structural transformation and enable its citizens to seize the opportunities it presents. This path will inevitably involve difficult trade-offs, requiring a degree of political consensus grounded in a shared national purpose and a clear understanding that postponing difficult decisions may ultimately demand more painful concessions. In a society where democracy is deeply rooted, meaningful progress depends on elevating deliberative dialogue above narrow interests and ideological divides. Drawing once again on the social cohesion and pragmatism that the Costa Rican people have demonstrated at other pivotal moments in their history will be vital to overcoming remaining barriers to indelible quality growth.

## References

Anders, Wendy. 2016. "UN Group Urges Costa Rica to Improve Health, Poverty, Native Rights." *The Costa Rica Star*. https://news.co.cr/un-group-urges-costa-rica-improve-health-poverty-native-rights/52376/. Accessed March 2, 2018.

Araujo, Jorge Thompson, Ekaterina Vostroknutova, Konstantin M. Wacker, and Mateo Clavijo (eds.). 2016 *Understanding the Income and Efficiency Gap in Latin America and the Caribbean*. World Bank.

Birdsall, Nancy. 2012. "A Note on the Middle Class in Latin America." Center for Global Development Working Paper 303.

Bravo, Josué. 2016. "Tres de cada diez nicas carecen de seguro social en Costa Rica." *La Prensa*. https://www.laprensa.com/2016/11/11/nacionales/2133614-tres-de-cada-diez-nicas-carecen-de-seguro-social-en-costa-rica. Accessed February 28, 2018.

Cornick, Jorge, and Alberto Trejos. 2009. "Political and Institutional Obstacles to Reform in Costa Rica." In *Growing Pains in Latin America: An Economic Growth Framework as Applied to Brazil, Colombia, Costa Rica, Mexico, and Peru*, ed. Liliana Rojas-Suarez, 153–191. Center for Global Development.

[22] Except for the establishment in 2010 of the Presidential Council for Competitiveness and Innovation—a high-level advisory body—concrete examples of high-level bureaucratic coordination in this realm are rare. For instance, Costa Rica's Policy for Productive Development 2017–2050 appears to not include among its main stakeholders PROCOMER, CINDE (responsible for attracting FDI to the country), or the Ministry of Public Education. Nelson (2009) rightly remarks that technocratic independence is a contributing factor to the success of investment promotion agencies by insulating them from political pressures; however, in this instance, CINDE's autonomy also obviates a systematic means by which it can pass on its knowledge to other government stakeholders besides PROCOMER and COMEX, stifling broad-based competitiveness and the 'endogenization' of advanced manufacturing processes.

Costa Rican Coalition of Development Initiatives (CINDE). 2016. "Multinational Companies Developing Successfully Under Free Trade Zone Regime in Costa Rica." http://www.prnewswire.com/news-releases/multinational-companies-developing-successfully-under-free-trade-zone-regime-in-costa-rica-300316510.html. Accessed May 12, 2017.

Daude, Christian, and Eduardo Fernández-Arias. 2010. "On the Role of Productivity and Factor Accumulation in Economic Development in Latin America and the Caribbean." Inter-American Development Bank Working Paper 155.

Dayton-Johnson, Jeff. 2015. *Latin America's Emerging Middle Classes: Economic Perspectives*. Palgrave Macmillan.

Engel, Jakob, and Daria Taglioni. 2017. "The Middle-Income Trap and Upgrading Along Global Value Chains." In *Global Value Chain Development Report 2017: Measuring and Analyzing the Impact of GVCs on Economic Development*. Organization for Economic Co-operation and Development, World Trade Organization, World Bank, Institute of Developing Economies-Japan External Trade Organization, and University of International Business and Economics.

Fernandez-Stark, Karina, Penny Bamber, and Gary Gereffi. 2013. "Costa Rica in the Offshore Services Global Value Chain: Opportunities for Upgrading." Duke University Center on Globalization, Governance, and Competitiveness.

Ferreira, Francisco H.G., Julian Messina, Jamele Rigolini, Luis Felipe López-Calva, Maria Ana Lugo, and Reno Vakis. 2013. *Economic Mobility and the Rise of the Latin American Middle Class*. World Bank.

Ferreira, Gustavo F.C., and R. Wes Harrison. 2012. "From Coffee Beans to Microchips: Export Diversification and Economic Growth in Costa Rica." *Journal of Agricultural and Applied Economics* 44 (4): 1–15.

Freund, Caroline, and Theodore H. Moran. 2017. "Multinational Investors as Export Superstars: How Emerging-Market Governments Can Reshape Comparative Advantage." Peterson Institute for International Economics Working Paper 17–1.

Gindling, T.H., and Luis Oviedo. 2008. "Female-Headed Single-Parent Households and Poverty in Costa Rica." *CEPAL Review* No. 94. Economic Commission for Latin America and the Caribbean.

Instituto Nacional de Estadistica y Censos (National Institute of Statistics and Census: INEC). 2014. "Encuesta Nacional de Hogares 2014." https://inec.cr/noticias/encuesta-nacional-hogares-2014. Accessed August 24, 2017.

Instituto Nacional de Estadistica y Censos (National Institute of Statistics and Census: INEC). 2016. "Encuesta Nacional de Hogares 2016: Pobreza Disminuyó Más de un Punto Porcentual." https://inec.cr/noticias/pobreza-disminuyo-mas-un-punto-porcentual. Accessed August 24, 2017.

International Monetary Fund (IMF). 2003. "Costa Rica: Staff Report for the 2002 Article IV Consultation." IMF Staff Country Report No. 03/82.

International Monetary Fund (IMF). 2006. "Costa Rica: Staff Report for the 2006 Article IV Consultation." IMF Staff Country Report No. 06/416.

International Monetary Fund (IMF). 2009. "Press Release: IMF Executive Board Approves US$735 Million Precautionary Stand-By Arrangement for Costa Rica." http://www.imf.org/en/News/Articles/2015/09/14/01/49/pr09124. Accessed August 18, 2017.

International Monetary Fund (IMF). 2013. "Costa Rica: 2012 Article IV Consultation." Country Report No. 13/79.

International Monetary Fund (IMF). 2017. International Financial Statistics Database. http://data.imf.org/?sk=5DABAFF2-C5AD-4D27-A175-1253419C02D1. Accessed August 18, 2017.

International Trade Organization. 2011. "Costa Rica: Trade in Value Added and Global Value Chains Statistical Profile." https://www.wto.org/english/res_e/statis_e/miwi_e/countryprofiles_e.htm. Accessed June 6, 2017.

Lustig, Nora. 2017. "Fiscal Policy, Income Redistribution, and Poverty Reduction in Low and Middle Income Countries." Center for Global Development Working Paper 448.

Marquette, Catherine M. 2006. "Nicaraguan Migrants in Costa Rica." *Población y Salud en Mesoamérica* 4 (1). https://doi.org/10.15517/psm.v4i1.4561.

Miller, Andrew P. 2012. *Ecotourism Development in Costa Rica: The Search for Oro Verde.* Lanham, Lexington Books.
Ministry of Foreign Trade (COMEX). "Inversión extranjera por sectores de destino económico 2000–2013." http://datosabiertos.comex.go.cr/datastreams/89097/inversion-extranjera-por-sectores-de-destino-economico/. Accessed September 1, 2017.
Monge-González, Ricardo. 2016. "Innovation, Productivity, and Growth in Costa Rica: Challenges and Opportunities." Inter-American Development Bank Technical Note 920.
Monge-González, Ricardo, and Juan Antonio Rodríguez-Álvarez. 2013. "Impact Evaluation of Innovation and Linkage Development Programs in Costa Rica: The Cases of PROPYME and CR Provee." Inter-American Development Bank Working Paper 461.
Mosley, Layna. 2011. *Labor Rights and Multinational Production.* Cambridge University Press.
Multilateral Investment Guarantee Agency (MIGA). 2006. *The Impact of Intel in Costa Rica: Nine Years After the Decision to Invest.* World Bank.
Nelson, Roy C. 2009. *Harnessing Globalization: The Promotion of Nontraditional Foreign Direct Investment in Latin America.* Penn State University Press.
Organization for Economic Co-operation and Development (OECD). 2016a. "Costa Rica Policy Brief: Trade." OECD Publishing.
Organization for Economic Co-operation and Development (OECD). 2016b. "OECD Economic Surveys: Costa Rica 2016." OECD Publishing.
Organization for Economic Co-operation and Development (OECD). 2016c. "Costa Rica Policy Brief: Inequality." OECD Publishing.
Organization for Economic Co-operation and Development (OECD). 2017a. "Agricultural Policies in Costa Rica." OECD Publishing.
Organization for Economic Co-operation and Development (OECD). 2017b. "Education in Costa Rica."
Organization for Economic Co-operation and Development (OECD). 2017c. "OECD Reviews of Innovation Policy: Costa Rica 2017." OECD Publishing.
Organization for Economic Co-operation and Development (OECD), Inter-American Development Bank (IDB), and Global Forum on Productivity. 2017d. *Boosting Productivity and Inclusive Growth in Latin America.* OECD Publishing.
Oviedo, Ana Maria, Susana M. Sanchez, Kathy A. Lindert, and J. Humberto Lopez. 2015. *Costa Rica's Development, From Good to Better*. World Bank.
Paus, Eva. 2014. "Industrial Development Strategies in Costa Rica: When Structural Change and Domestic Capability Diverge." 2014. In *Transforming Economies: Making Industrial Policy Work for Growth, Jobs, and Development*, eds. José M. Salazar-Xirinachs, Irmgard Nübler, and Richard Kozul-Wright, 181–211. International Labor Organization.
Paus, Eva A., and Kevin P. Gallagher. 2008. "Missing Links: Foreign Investment and Industrial Development in Costa Rica and Mexico." *Studies in Comparative International Development* 43: 53–80.
Perry, Guillermo. 2014. "Middle Classes, Mobility, Economic Growth, and Democracy in Latin America." Presentation at Second CAF-Oxford University Conference.
Rennhack, Robert, and Erik Offerdal (eds.). 2004. *The Macroeconomy of Central America.* Palgrave Macmillan.
Roache, Shaun K. 2008. "Central America's Regional Trends and U.S. Cycles." International Monetary Fund Working Paper 08/50.
Sandoval-García, Carlos. 2015. "Nicaraguan Immigration to Costa Rica: Tendencies, Policies, and Politics." Latin American Studies Association (LASA) Forum. https://lasa.international.pitt.edu/forum/files/vol46-issue4/Debates3.pdf. Accessed March 5, 2018.
The Observatory on Economic Complexity. "Costa Rica." http://atlas.media.mit.edu/en/profile/country/cri/. Accessed August 29, 2017.
Trejos, Alberto. 2013. *Economic Growth and Restructuring through Trade and FDI: Costa Rican Experiences of Interest to Cuba.* Brookings Institution.
United Nations Development Program (UNDP). 2015. "Human Development Report 2015: Country Briefing Note for Costa Rica."

Ureña, Alonso Alfaro, and Alberto Vindas Quesada. 2015. "Transformación structural y productividad sectorial en Costa Rica." Central Bank of Costa Rica. https://www.scielo.sa.cr/scielo.php?script=sci_arttext&pid=S2215-34032019000100048.
Vakis, Renos, Jamele Rigolini, and Leonardo Lucchetti. 2015. *Left Behind: Chronic Poverty in Latin America and the Caribbean.* World Bank.
Williams, Timothy. 2016. "Special Report: Costa Rica's Frustratingly Stagnant Poverty Rate." *The Costa Rica Star.* http://news.co.cr/special-report-costa-ricas-frustratingly-stagnant-poverty-rate/46042/.
World Bank. 2006. "Costa Rica Country Economic Memorandum: The Challenges for Sustained Growth." Report No. 36180-CR.
World Bank. 2016. "Costa Rica: PISA 2015 Takeaways."
World Bank Development Indicators. 2017a. "High-Technology Exports (current US$)." http://data.worldbank.org/indicator/TX.VAL.TECH.CD?locations=CR. Accessed June 30, 2017.
World Bank Development Indicators. 2017b. "High-Technology Exports (% of manufactured exports)." Available from http://data.worldbank.org/indicator/TX.VAL.MANF.ZS.UN?locations=CR. Accessed June 30, 2017.
World Bank Educational Global Practice. 2015. "Central America Social Expenditures and Institutional Review."
World Travel and Tourism Council. 2017. "Travel and Tourism Economic Impact 2017: Costa Rica."

**Stace Nicholson** earned his B.A. in Political Science from Manchester College in North Manchester, Indiana, and holds a M.A. in Global Finance, Trade, and Economic Integration from the University of Denver's Josef Korbel School for International Studies. As a senior program officer at the U.S.A. office of the Japan International Cooperation Agency (JICA), he facilitates JICA's multi-faceted engagement with the World Bank Group and International Monetary Fund, conducts research on a variety of international economic and development finance issues, as well as oversees consultancy services commissioned on behalf of headquarters departments for the purpose of advancing operational planning and credit risk due diligence—especially in relation to concessional loan projects. He also contributed to the World Bank's inaugural *Poverty and Shared Prosperity* report while working as a short-term consultant in its Poverty Global Practice and previously served as a microfinance client assessment fellow for FINCA International in Uganda.

# Madagascar

14

Keiko Kubota

## 14.1 Economic Development Overview

Madagascar is a large island nation with the land area a little under 600 thousand square kilometers (about 1.6 times the size of Japan) and approximately 30 million people in 2023. It is richly endowed with unique flora and fauna, minerals including oil, as well as arable land and marine resources. It is also one of the poorest countries in the world. Per capita income in 2023 was only USD 460.8 (constant 2015 USD), and 80.7% of the population lived under USD 2.15 (PPP) per day in 2012 (this is the year that the last census was conducted).

Madagascar's poverty headcount, in addition to being extremely elevated, has increased between 2001 (71% under USD 2.15 PPP constant 2017 threshold) and 2012 (80.7%),[1] and estimated to have increased slightly in the decade since (World Bank 2024). In other words, there are estimated 12.6 million more poor Malagasy people in 2022 than in 2001. This performance contrasts with Burkina Faso's, whose poverty headcount has declined from 79.9 in 1998 to 52.6 in 2009, and to 25.3 in 2021. Burkina Faso was chosen as the comparator country in this study because it is also a poor francophone country in sub-Saharan Africa with similar population size (Fig. 14.1).[2]

Madagascar's overwhelming poverty is caused by economic growth falling short of the rapid population increase, rather than an unequal distribution of the growth

[1] The last census in Madagascar was held in 2012.

[2] When this book project started in 2017, Burkina Faso was considered stable and reasonably well-governed, although a coup d'etat ousting President Compaoré had taken place in 2014. We decided against changing the comparator country despite the country's violent and unstable history in the intervening years because the economic analyses have stood up surprisingly well.

K. Kubota (✉)
Department of Economics, Tohoku Gakuin University, Sendai, Miyagi, Japan





K. Hirota (ed.), *Introduction to Quality Growth*,
https://doi.org/10.1007/978-981-95-6220-6_14

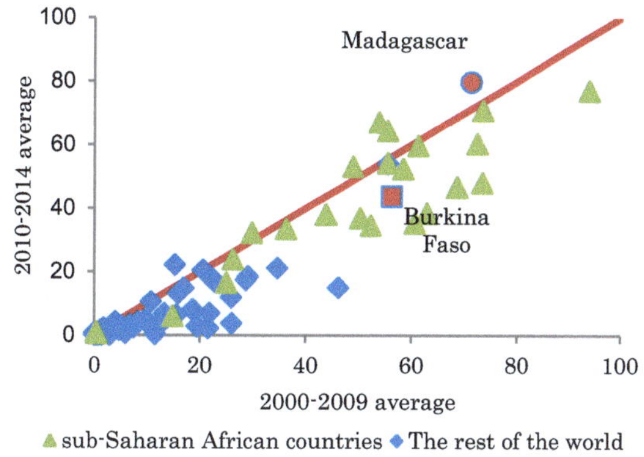


**Fig. 14.1** Poverty headcount, cross country-comparison, five-year averages. *Source* Author's compilation from WDI

dividends. The average real GDP growth rate since independence in 1960 and 2023 was 2.4%, while per capita income declined from USD 818 to USD 461 over the same period. This trajectory contrasts with Burkina Faso's, who was much poorer in 1960 (per capita GDP was USD 244), but achieved per capita GDP of USD 739 in 2023 (Fig. 14.2, left panel). This result was partly due to the speed of population growth: between 1960 and 2023, Burkina Faso's population quintupled from 4.8 million to 23.3, while Madagascar's sextupled from 5.1 million to 30.3 million. There was also a difference in the steadiness of growth of the overall economy. Burkina Faso's growth was almost always positive during the period, while Madagascar's experienced large negative spikes (Fig. 14.2, right panel).

In addition to the *speed* of growth, are there issues with the *quality* of growth that one might learn from Madagascar's experience?

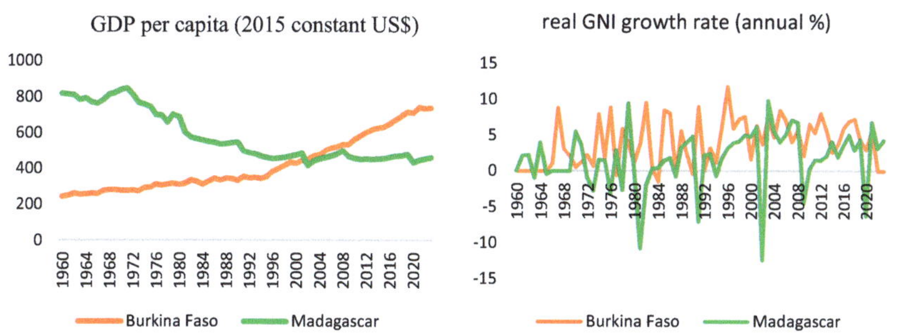


**Fig. 14.2** Per capita real GDP (left panel) and real GDP growth (right panel). *Source* Author's calculation based on WDI

## 14.2 Growth and Inclusiveness

Between 2001 and 2012, Madagascar's growth was arguably pro-poor, based on the incidence of increase in consumption; it was positive for the poorer segment of the population while negative for the richer. While poverty had increased over this period, both in terms of headcount and as a share of the population, the severity of poverty had declined and inequality declined somewhat, measured by Gini coefficient and by poverty gap (the distance of the poor to the poverty threshold). This seeming paradox stems from the fact that those around the poverty threshold are among the relatively well off in Madagascar. Those at the higher spectrum of expenditure distribution experienced a reduction in consumption, which led to an increase in poverty headcount, while those who were well below the threshold experienced some improvements. The urban population, especially around Antananarivo, the capital city, tended to be at a higher end of the income spectrum, and it was these people who had lost most from the political turbulence in the 2000s. In contrast, the rural population is largely disconnected from political events and experienced gradual improvements on its own, with no particular interventions from the State. This improvement took place probably more slowly than if the political events did not cause losses of formal sector jobs and a consequent increase in the share of the population engaged in agriculture. This share increased in the first half of 2000s, making agriculture the primary activity for close to 80% of the population. The shift occurred even though the sector has lower productivity than other sectors in the economy (World Bank 2014a).

The decade since 2012 saw stagnation in rural poverty and a dramatic increase in urban poverty. The COVID-19 pandemic and repeated cyclones did lead to job losses, but a more fundamental cause was persistent underinvestment in the economy attributable to poor governance. The last decade witnessed a decline in inequality, not because of welfare gains by the rural poor but because of the losses by the urban residents (World Bank 2024), thus continuing the pattern from the previous decade.

In a non-pecuniary dimension, however, Madagascar's poor may be better off than their counterparts in Burkina Faso. According to the 2022 HDI, compiled periodically by the United Nations Development Program, both countries are classified as "low human development," but Madagascar has scored consistently higher than Burkina Faso, who ranked among the "worst 10" in 2022 (Fig. 14.3).

Available evidence suggests that a lack of inclusiveness is not the most important problem with Madagascar's quality of growth, even if there are egregious examples of wealth concentration at the very top of the income distribution. The falling per capita GDP is an indication that other factors are critical in Madagascar's state of affairs.

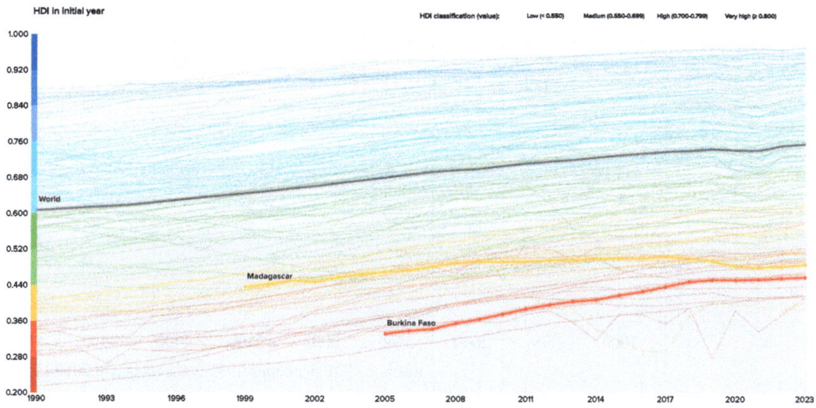


**Fig. 14.3** Human Development Index. *Source* UNDP. https://hdr.undp.org/data-center/human-development-index#/indicies/HDI

## 14.3 Growth and Resilience

Two types of shocks have interfered with Madagascar's development throughout its history, weather-related and political.[3] This section will discuss the first type of shocks, while the second is discussed in the following section.

According to the Global Climate Risk Index 2021 (Eckstein et al. 2021), Madagascar is among the top twenty countries (2000–2019 average) that are affected by extreme weather events. It experiences an average of three cyclones per year.[4] Agriculture and fisheries are very important to Madagascar, as a large majority of the Malagasy population derives livelihood from them. Indeed, many more people are employed in the agriculture sector in Madagascar than expected based on the income level (Fig. 14.4, showing countries with average per capita income of less than USD 5,000 in 1991–2022), suggesting that the economy is insufficiently diversified. A lack of diversification of the economic structure would reduce resilience to shocks, other things being equal. Burkina Faso is similar in this dimension: only Burundi employs a larger share of the population in agriculture.

Moreover, most of those engaged in the primary sector in Madagascar are subsistence farmers and fishermen, who are not protected against severe weather events and suffer devastating effects from them. On average, close to half a million people in Madagascar were affected by severe natural hazards between 1980 and 2020, and well over a million people in the last three of the five years in the data (Fig. 14.5).

[3] Madagascar is also subject to commodity price shocks. It started exporting nickel in 2015. In 2022, unwrought nickel represented a quarter of its export value (Source: World Integrated Trade Solution).

[4] For further details, refer to the following link: https://climateknowledgeportal.worldbank.org/country/madagascar.

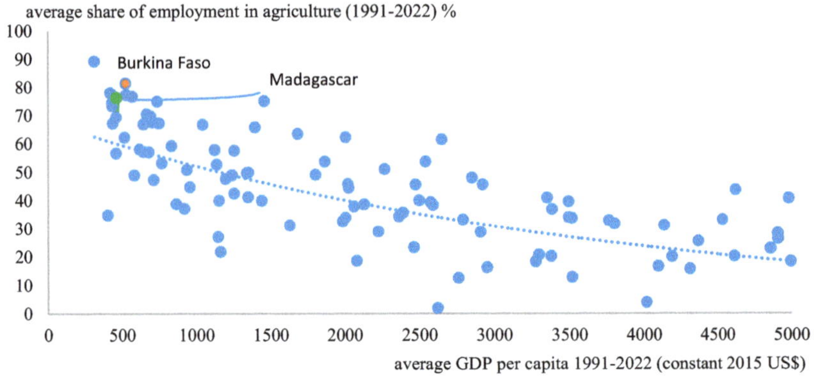


**Fig. 14.4** Madagascar's employment is concentrated in agriculture. *Source* Author's calculation based on WDI

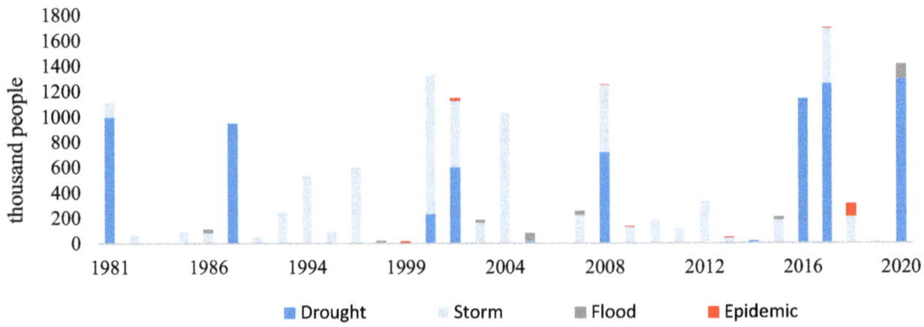


**Fig. 14.5** Number of people affected by the main natural hazards. *Source* https://climateknowledgeportal.worldbank.org/country/madagascar/vulnerability

Evidence for the heavy burden of weather-related shocks on households is also found in the surveys conducted by the national statistics institute. In what might be considered a silver lining, the primary sector has been the least affected by political shocks, partly because of the dualistic nature of the economy where much of the rural area remains disconnected from events in the capital and urban area. In the survey conducted in 2010 (Table 14.1), a year after the last coup d'ét,[5] political crisis was not among the top ten negative shocks mentioned by the households. Political crises do affect the sector negatively, however, as those who lost jobs due to the turmoil tended to shift into agriculture, depressing the already low productivity.

[5] At the time of writing. There has been another coup in 2025.

**Table 14.1** Top 10 negative shocks reported by households in 2010

| 2010 | |
|---|---|
| Shocks | % |
| Drought | 14.60 |
| Flooding | 10.50 |
| Cyclone | 9.70 |
| Crop diseases | 6.80 |
| Late rains | 6.40 |
| Illness or loss of livestock | 6.30 |
| General rise in consumer prices | 4.50 |
| Illness of an adult household number | 3.80 |
| Increase in input prices | 3.70 |
| Other climatic or environmental shocks | 3.60 |

*Source* Author's compilation based on World Bank (2015)

According to the Resilience Index,[6] Madagascar is the fourth least resilient country after Afghanistan, Yemen and Chad out of 142 countries surveyed. In contrast, Burkina Faso ranks more than 30 places ahead of Madagascar, despite the turbulent period it had traversed in recent years. Clearly, the Malagasy population is experiencing difficulties in overcoming shocks. Higher temperatures will intensify this challenge, as extreme events, such as cyclones, floods and droughts, are likely to become more frequent in a warmer world. National Policy to Combat Climate Change, developed in 2010 and updated in 2021, is the strategy document to face this challenge (MEDD 2021). Its implementation so far is assessed as inadequate (IMF 2022) due to financial and capacity constraints.

## 14.4 Growth and Sustainability

Madagascar has not been able to sustain growth needed to bring its population out of poverty. Between 1960 and 2023, Madagascar had six "growth spurts," defined as events where per capita GDP grew for more than two years consecutively, while Burkina Faso had ten. Not only did Burkina Faso have more spurts but theirs also tended to last longer. Perhaps more emblematic of Madagascar's problem is the frequency and length of its negative spurts, that is, negative growth of per capita GDP for two consecutive years or more. Whereas Burkina Faso had three such episodes, which lasted only for two years, Madagascar had six, one of which lasted for almost a decade (Table 14.2).

[6] "The index quantifies people's capacity for resilience and ability to deal with adversity, based on their personal circumstances and perceptions. [...] The index is a composite score based on four underlying dimensions: individual, household, community and societal resilience (Lloyd's Register Foundation 2024).

**Table 14.2** Growth spurt statistics

| | Spurt episodes | Maximum years of spurts | Negative growth spurt episodes | Maximum years of negative spurts | No. of years with positive growth |
|---|---|---|---|---|---|
| Madagascar | 6 | 6 | 6 | 8 | 31 |
| Burkina Faso | 8 | 10 | 3 | 2 | 44 |

*Source* WDI (GDP data) and Author's compilation

**Fig. 14.6** Repeating pattern of growth episodes and political crises. *Source* WDI (GNI data) and Author's compilation

Political crises are often identified as the culprit preventing Madagascar to sustain growth (Fig. 14.6). Throughout its independent history, growth episodes were interrupted by political crises, and the post-crisis decline in GDP per capita has more than offset the preceding growth gains,[7] resulting in a gradual decline of the per capita income since the peak reached in 1971.

The pattern of growth and political crises is so regular that some analysts claim growth is causing the political crises. The theory runs as follows: Madagascar's political system is a fragrant case of elite capture, where competing groups of elites jockey for the control of power; the distinction between political and economic power is blurred, and it makes for a predatory government that seeks to maximize personal gain while in power; economic growth is desirable for those in power, as their take will grow with it, but the temptation for those out of power to topple the incumbent increases as the size of the prize grows, culminating in a political crisis, involving an unconstitutional change of power. Until the first peaceful handover of power through the 2018 Presidential elections, every president since independence has assumed or has been removed from power through undemocratic means, sometimes both.

[7] The crisis in 2001–2002 was an exception where the economy picked up right after the crisis.

In contrast, Burkina Faso has managed to sustain growth despite its share of political crises: President Blaise Compaore had ruled without interruption between 1987 and 2014, but he had come to power and was removed from it in coups. There had been coups before, and there have unfortunately been many since 2014. The country's recent history has been turbulent with violent and frequent terrorist attacks. Yet, Burkina Faso's economy manages to grow. It is a largely agrarian economy dependent on cotton, with natural endowments less spectacular than Madagascar's, it has managed to increase per capita income three-fold between 1960 and 2023, while Madagascar decreased it by over 40%. Kaminski (2011) describe the model implemented in Burkinabe cotton sector as unique in sub-Saharan Africa in that it addresses government failures and local realities within the current institutional framework in adopting reforms, using a cautious, piece-meal approach. Kaminski (2011) describes Burkina Faso as a case of virtuous circle where a larger profit share for farmers reinforced production incentives, and infrastructure is funded by cotton revenues through private and public investments. Since the 1980s, investments in the cotton sector have also fostered technology adoption, thanks to high quality research, cooperation between foreign and local researchers and farmer organizations.

Political crises also seem to have caused the development community to be less generous with Madagascar than otherwise. As a very poor country with significant development challenges, Madagascar would be reliant on official aid, but it receives so little aid that OECD (2014) calls it an "aid orphan." Madagascar received less aid disbursement per capita than Burkina Faso since 1973, except for three years when Madagascar experienced spikes and when Burkina Faso a dip (Fig. 14.7 left panel). In 2022, Madagascar's aid receipt per capita was among the lowest in sub-Saharan Africa (Fig. 14.7 right panel), a little over half of what Burkina Faso received.

In addition to receiving "insufficient" amounts, what Madagascar did receive tended to be procyclical, declining when the country went through political crises (1991, 2001 and 2008–2009) and subsequent economic downturns, and picking up when the political crisis is resolved and the economy tended to be on the

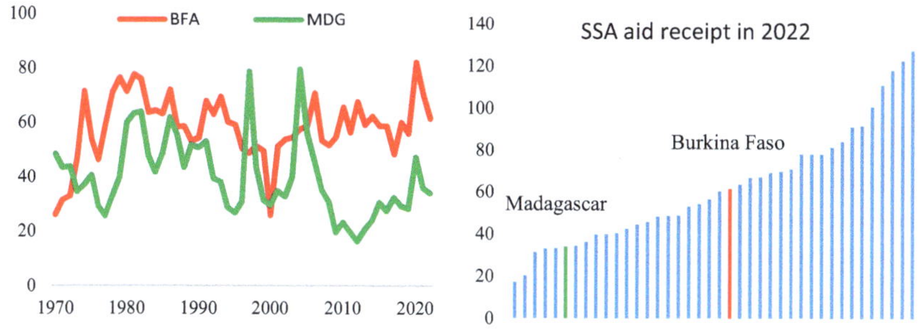


**Fig. 14.7** Per capita receipt of aid (constant $). *Source* Author's compilation from OECD and WDI

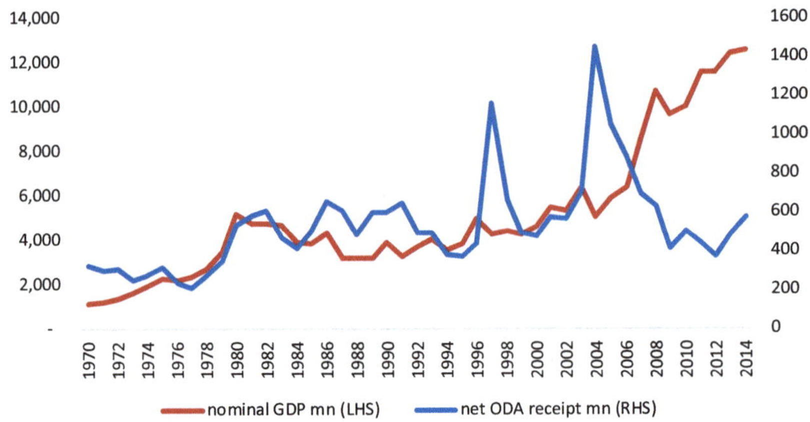


**Fig. 14.8** GDP and net ODA moved in tandem (million USD). *Source* Author's compilation from WDI and OECD DAC

upswing. Between 1960 and 2014, the correlation between Madagascar's GDP and the amount of ODA received (both measured in current USD) was 0.64 (source: Author's compilation using WDI and OECD DAC, Fig. 14.8). Procyclicality was even more pronounced until the most recent crisis starting in 2009 (0.76 between 1960 and 2009). There are explanations for this aid pattern, for example, legal or procedural restrictions do not allow many bilateral donors to provide economic aid to governments that have taken power unconstitutionally.[8] It is possible to argue, without necessarily making moral judgments, that official aid has not been effective in attenuating the volatile nature of Madagascar's growth. The volatility and procyclicality of aid is not a phenomenon limited to Madagascar; Bulír and Hamann (2008) argue that the "high volatility of inflows make the macroeconomy hard to manage" especially in very poor countries, and that "donors need to be able to respond more speedily and effectively to large adverse shocks, and their conditionalities need to become more flexible."

Another cause identified by observers (for example, Razafindrakoto et al. 2013) as Madagascar's volatile growth is poor governance. The theory advanced by North (1981), Acemoglu and Robinson (2012) and others would support such a hypothesis. Available information is not decisive, but by and large, Madagascar does not fare very well, and perhaps even more worryingly, appears to be worsening its performance over the years. In the World Bank's WGI, Madagascar scored higher than Burkina Faso in 1996 in four out of six indicators (Fig. 14.9). In 2023, the situation had reversed, and Burkina Faso scores higher than Madagascar in four out of six indicators. Madagascar's scores worsened between the two observations in

[8] World Bank, for example, has an operational policy that makes it difficult to disburse loans to *de facto* governments.

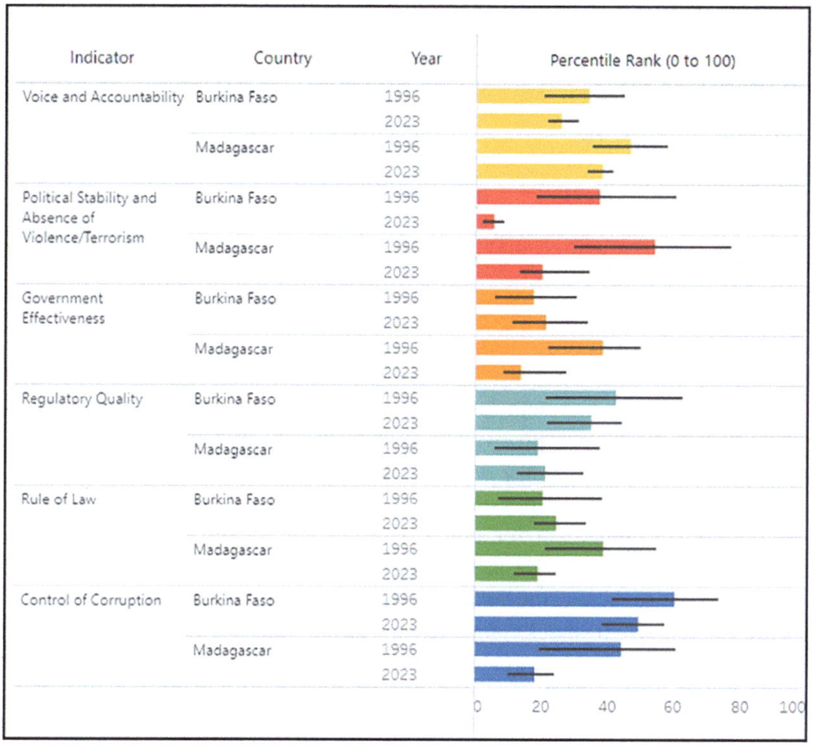


**Fig. 14.9** Governance indicators (higher = better) *Source* WGI

five out of six indicators, and the slight improvement of the last indicator, the regulatory quality, is not statistically significant. Burkina Faso had performed slightly better with two indicators improving, although not very significantly.

Madagascar's poor performance is echoed in Transparency International's perception of corruption indicator (Fig. 14.10). Perceptions has been consistently worse in Madagascar than in Burkina Faso in all years where observations are available. Here again, Madagascar's performance is deteriorating whereas Burkina Faso's has improved somewhat between the earlier observations and the later ones.

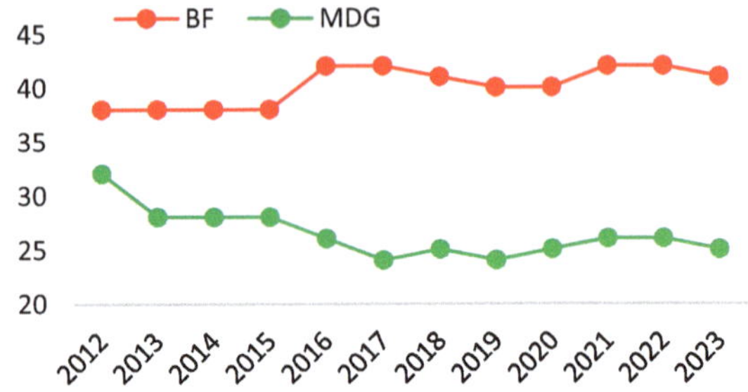


**Fig. 14.10** Corruption Perceptions Index Score (higher = better). *Source* Author's compilation from Transparency International. https://www.transparency.org/en/cpi/2023

## 14.5 Conclusion

Madagascar's quality of growth is found lacking as it has failed to lift its population out of poverty. Its growth over time has been insufficient because it has not been sustained, and the country was unable to sustain growth because it has not been resilient to shocks, or possibly because growth is inherently unsustainable due to the tacit arrangement for power sharing among the elites. It is also said that the shocks, especially the last political crisis, which was severe in duration and depth, have weakened the institutions, making the country less able to cope with shocks. Recurrent shocks deplete any buffer that the poor households may have had, rendering them poorer and less likely to escape poverty. Prevention of such shocks, when they are man-made, and mitigation and adaptation if they are weather-related, is crucial to better quality of growth for Madagascar. The government has maintained prudent macroeconomic and debt policy in the last decade (World Bank 2014b), which provides a basis upon which such growth might be built.

## References

Acemoglu, Daron, and James A. Robinson. 2012. *Why Nations Fail: The Origins of Power, Prosperity, and Poverty*. Crown Publishers.

Bulír, Aleš, and A. Javier Hamann. 2008. "Volatility of Development Aid: From the Frying Pan Into the Fire?" *World Development* 36 (10): 2048–2066.

Eckstein, David, Vera Künzel, and Laura Shäfer. 2021. "Global Climate Risk Index 2021: Who Suffers Most from Extreme Weather Events? Weather-Related Loss Events in 2019 and 2000 to 2019." Germanwatch e.V, Berlin. https://www.germanwatch.org/en/node/19777.

International Monetary Fund (IMF). 2022. Technical Assistance Report: Climate Macroeconomic Assessment Program.

Kaminski, Jonathan. 2011. "Cotton Dependence in Burkina Faso: Constraints and Opportunities for Balanced Growth." In *Yes Africa Can: Success Stories from a Dynamic Continent*, eds. Punam Chuhan-Pole and Manka Angwafo, 107–124. World Bank.

Lloyd's Register Foundation. 2024. World Risk Poll 2024 Report: Resilience in a Changing World. https://wrp.lrfoundation.org.uk/sites/default/files/2024-06/World%20Risk%20Poll%20Report%202024%20Resilience%20in%20a%20Changing%20World_1.pdf.

Ministère de l'Environnement et du Développement Durable (Ministry of Environment and Sustainable Development: MEDD). 2021. Plan National d'Adaptation au Changement Climatique

(PNA) Madagascar. Antananarivo, Madagascar. https://unfccc.int/sites/default/files/resource/PNA-Madagascar.pdf.
North, Douglass C. 1981. *Structure and Change in Economic History*. W.W. Norton & Company.
Organization for Economic Co-operation and Development (OECD). 2014. OECD-DAC Development Brief: Where Do We Stand on the Aid Orphans?
Razafindrakoto, Mireille, François Roubaud, and Jean-Michel Wachsberger. 2013. Institutions, Gouvernance et Croissance de Long Terme à Madagascar; L'enigme et le Paradoxe. https://dial.ird.fr/wp-content/uploads/2021/10/2013-13-Institutions-gouvernance-et-croissance-de-long-terme-a-Madagascar-lenigme-et-le-paradoxe.pdf.
Transparency International. Corruption Perceptions Index. https://www.transparency.org.
United Nations Development Program (UNDP). 2023. Human Development Index.
World Bank. 2014a. "Faces of Poverty in Madagascar: Poverty, Gender and Inequality Assessment." World Bank Report No. 78131-MG. World Bank. https://documents1.worldbank.org/curated/en/538821468271809604/pdf/781310priority0english0apr900may012.pdf.
World Bank. 2014b. *Opportunités et Défis pour une Croissance Inclusive et Resiliente: Recueil de Notes de Politique pour Madagascar* [Opportunities and Challenges for Inclusive and Resilient Growth: Compendium of Policy Notes for Madagascar]. World Bank. http://documents.worldbank.org/curated/en/130911468086644653.
World Bank. 2015. Systematic Country Diagnostic. https://hdl.handle.net/10986/23099.
World Bank. 2024. *Navigating Two Decades of High Poverty and Charting a Course for Change in Madagascar: Poverty and Equity Assessment*. World Bank. https://documents1.worldbank.org/curated/en/099021424172020915/pdf/P17796818b70320641878f166fa034723ca.pdf.
World Bank. Country Summary: Madagascar. https://climateknowledgeportal.worldbank.org/country/madagascar.
World Bank. World Bank Open Data. https://data.worldbank.org.
World Bank. Worldwide Governance Indicators. https://www.worldbank.org/en/publication/worldwide-governance-indicators.
World Development Indicators (WDI) https://databank.worldbank.org/source/world-development-indicators.
World Integrated Trade Solution (WITS). https://wits.worldbank.org.
Worldwide Governance Indicators, 2024 Update, World Bank. www.govindicators.org. Accessed October 30, 2024.

**Keiko Kubota** is a professor of Economics at Tohoku Gakuin University in Japan. Prior to the current post, she worked as an economist for the World Bank, with assignments in Madagascar, Vietnam, Indonesia, Cameroon as well as Washington, D.C. She also served as a Deputy Director for the G20 Presidency Secretariat in the Ministry of Finance, Japan and as an Economic Advisor for the Credit Risk Assessment Division of the Japan International Cooperation Agency. She has a Ph.D. in economics from Columbia University, New York. Her areas of research interest include international trade and climate change.

# Index




K. Hirota (ed.), *Introduction to Quality Growth*,
https://doi.org/10.1007/978-981-95-6220-6